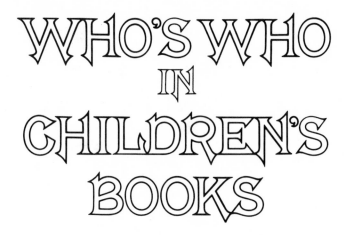

# WHO'S WHO
## IN
# CHILDREN'S
# BOOKS

# WHO'S WHO IN CHILDREN'S BOOKS

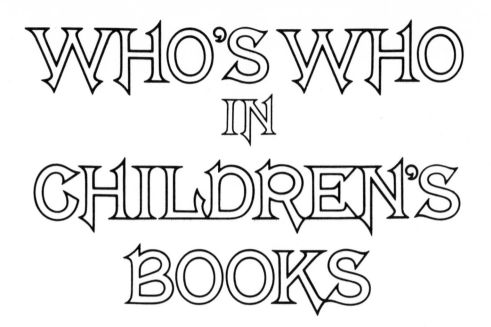

## A TREASURY OF THE FAMILIAR CHARACTERS OF CHILDHOOD

## MARGERY FISHER

ONCE·UPON·A·TIME

HOLT, RINEHART and WINSTON
NEW YORK

To my grandchildren:
Anthea and James Fisher
Rachel, Lucy, Katy and Sophie Charlton
Emily Fisher
Natalia Fisher
 who are busy meeting many of the characters in this book.

Library of Congress Cataloging in Publication Data

Fisher, Margery Turner, date
 Who's who in children's books.

 Includes indexes.
  1. Children's stories—Dictionaries. 2. Characters
and characteristics in literature—Dictionaries.
I. Title.
PN1009.A1F575     809'.89282          75–5463
ISBN 0-03-015091-4

Printed in Great Britain by
Butler & Tanner Ltd, Frome and London

Art director: Behram Kapadia
Designer: Sheila Sherwen
First Edition

# CONTENTS

# AUTHOR'S PREFACE

Character-drawing in a story is like a tremendous, complicated conjuring-trick. Appealing to imagination and goodwill, diverting attention by the sheer power of technique, the writer persuades us (for the period of reading and sometimes for long afterwards) to accept the identity of certain people who exist only between the covers of his book. With the devices of dialogue, description and narrative he will make words alone (and this is the conjuring trick) substitute for the actual physical sense-impressions and mutual responses which operate when we meet someone in real life.

The technique of character-drawing in books for the young is in some ways simpler, less allusive and more direct than it is in adult novels; this applies even to the borderland of teenage fiction. An ambiguous, gradual effect like that of Virginia Woolf or Iris Murdoch is hardly suited to books of limited length for readers who are still, as it were, in training for the reading of fiction. This is not to say that literature for children differs in quality from adult writing. Nobody would suggest that William Mayne or Beatrix Potter, for example, were any less skilful because their prestidigitation was adapted to young readers. Simply, they select and use the details in their illusion in a special way.

These two writers conveniently exemplify the two main types of character I am concerned with here. Mayne's characters are, almost always, what we are pleased to call 'real' people – that is, people whom the young could meet in the contemporary world. They are half recognizable, therefore, in the sense that children will already have terms of reference in their minds for, say, a little girl in present-day Yorkshire, boys on a school bus in Somerset, a schoolmaster, a grandmother. As a result Mayne is free to explore individual personality (in his case, mainly through dialogue), to encourage his characters to grow within the story after making firm general statements about their settings and circumstances. Beatrix Potter's case is somewhat different. The imagined characters of fantasy, whether they are humanized animals, fairies or extra-human figures of one kind or another, are drawn firmly first of all from the outside. We know what they look like and to a great extent what they are: Grey Rabbit leading the life of an old-style housewife, C. S. Lewis's White Witch casting her spell, a Zacathan looking for a lost civilization. It is not often that a character like Eeyore breaks mysteriously out of the confines of the fantasy description. By the same token, the characters in myth, folk-tale and nursery rhyme as a rule illustrate one strand of human behaviour and are recognized for this rather than for the indefinable amalgam which we call personality.

The distinction between 'real' and fantastic characters is also indicated by the degree of importance which we attach to physical appearance. In the stories about Paddington Bear, Babar the Elephant or Noddy, illustration has taken over a good deal of the duty of words. Through appearance we are directed to less tangible indications of character, and it is noticeable that those fantastic beings who are conceived in a way that is closer to the complex treatment of human nature – the Hobbit and Gollum, for instance, or Ursula Le Guin's Ged – are not readily illustratable.

It is not of first importance that we know what Mayne's schoolboys or Alan Garner's Gwyn or John Rowe Townsend's Arnold Haithwaite look like. Such people are realized far more effectively in the words they use, and children who read responsively are apt to be wary of any visualizing of, for example, the Marches or the Bastables, whom they feel they know personally. Eavesdropping on their conversations, they have realized what they are like in a subliminal way and can dispense with pictures.

The author, then, hears the voices of his characters, and we hear them through him. But we hear, too, the voice of the author himself. Sometimes it comes through the medium of the child in the centre of the story, who speaks for the author as the child he once was (as Kay Harker does, for example, in *The Midnight Folk* and *The Box of Delights*); sometimes a character reflects the author's relationship with a particular child (as Alice did for Lewis Carroll). Just as often he stands at a distance from his characters and manipulates them so that they become a mouthpiece for a theory, an attitude or a belief. One way or another, he makes it possible for us to identify with one or more of the characters. Young readers, who surrender more thoroughly to books than most adults do, are particularly inclined to recognize a fellow feeling with certain characters and their situation – with responsible Kevin, perhaps, in *Gumble's Yard*, or with Antonia Forest's Nicola Marlow and her problems or with Arnold Haithwaite and his fight for identity. Conversely, children can enjoy imagining themselves in desirable situations that differ from their own; the popularity of tales about horse-riding or football proves this easily enough.

Whatever 'identification' involves for each and every reader, it means that character in a story is a two-way affair. In conceiving and drawing his characters the author has used both will and emotion, memory and invention. A particular person may serve as a model (Noel Streatfeild has described her chance meeting with a girl who suggested the character of Margaret Thursday); a story may begin with a single proposition about a character seen only in outline (as *A Dog So Small* began with the idea of a boy desperately wanting a dog of his own); or it may be built round family toys (as *Poor Cecco* was) or family animals (like *Ginger Pye*). However they began, characters will be developed with innumerable details, conscious or unconscious, contrived or remembered. To this complex organism the reader brings his own ideas, experience and memories. He can never 'know' a character as the author knows it, nor can the author ever know, or expect to control, the way a reader interprets that character. Every story is different for every reader. This must be my excuse for the interpretation I have put on the characters in this *Who's Who*. I have lived with some of them for the whole of my reading life; others I have only met recently, as a visitor in the world of childhood. Some I like; others I dislike or fear or disapprove of; all of them I find absorbing. What I have said about them comes from my own reaction to them.

*Who's Who in Children's Books* is not intended primarily as a reference book. It could have been a check-list, with a great many more entries, each of them perhaps forty or fifty words long, merely locating certain characters in certain books. My aim is somewhat different. I have included as many as possible of the characters who have now become household names, together with others less familiar who interest me particularly; I have tried to place them in their setting and circumstances but also to discuss their identity as it seems to me and to make such comment as space would allow on the technique or the approach of the author to them. I have excluded nursery-rhyme characters and most mythological and fairy-tale figures, which are familiar to all readers and to a great extent fixed and static in their ambience. I have not included historical personages except when they appear in relation to fictional characters (as Richard II does in relation to Isabella in *The Gentle Falcon*) or when they are on the border-line of invention (like Robin Hood and Hereward the Wake).

For reasons of space it was clearly impossible to deal with all the characters in any one book; in any case, they will differ in their importance in the story. I have chosen for the most part those characters that are truly central and have included in the entries a certain amount of comment on other people in the same story. In a few cases I have chosen minor characters (Starr in *Member for the Marsh*, for example) because they help to create the effect which Robert Bridges called 'populousness', the impression that life is going on, in and around and after the action – a special way of achieving reality for fictional characters. In the case of family novels I have tried to describe not only individuals but also their relationships and alignments within the family, since their particular identity for the reader will depend to a great extent on these.

Fiction seeks to describe and investigate the mystery of personality. I hope that those who take up this book will find in it some at least of the characters who have always interested them and will perhaps be reminded of others they have forgotten; and I hope that those who work with children will be encouraged to introduce them to the diversity of creatures in the worlds which writers have known, learned about or imagined for them to inhabit.

M.F.

# A

**ABNER BROWN** *see* SYLVIA DAISY POUNCER, KAY HARKER

**ACHREN,** the wicked enchantress of Spiral Castle, has a name that suggests the attributes of the mythical spider-figure Arachne – namely, deceit and cruelty. Taran (q.v.) in his first encounter with her learns almost at once that her smooth words are false and that she secretly supports Arawn, the King of Evil, whose cauldron-born servants have captured the lad at the outset of his first mission. His hostility towards Achren deepens when he is visited in the dungeon by the sprightly orphan Eilonwy (q.v.), who has been sent to the castle to learn sorcery but who freely admits that her supposed aunt Achren is 'a mean, spiteful person' and not to be trusted.

After she has escaped from the destruction of Spiral Castle the enchantress helps to further the cause of evil by kidnapping the young Princess (in *The Castle of Llyr*) as part of her plan to gain total power in the kingdom of Prydain. Defeated by beneficent magic and reduced to an aged wreck, she becomes a servant to Dallben, Taran's old master and a high enchanter himself. Achren is now apparently submissive and reformed. But though she promises help to the comrades in their last struggle (in *The High King*) against Arawn and his cohorts, her intentions are put in doubt until the very moment of her death. Her last words, 'Have I not kept my pact, Gwydion?' do not altogether wipe out the first impression of a sinister, devious, dangerous woman.

In the Prydain chronicles Good and Evil are exemplified in different ways through different characters, some of them conceived in contemporary terms and others (like Achren) more markedly traditional. Lloyd Alexander's use of different kinds of characters lightens the difficulty that faces any writer of chivalric fantasy, of expressing moral truths dramatically. Achren conveys through her deeds and words the actuality of wickedness which is less directly described in the almost wholly unseen character of Arawn, the very fount and symbol of Evil. [Lloyd Alexander: *The Book of Three*, New York 1964; *The Castle of Llyr*, 1966; *Taran Wanderer*, 1967; *The High King*, 1968]

**ADAM CODLING** meets David Moss for the first time with an outburst of wrath. His canoe breaks away and drifts downstream, coming to rest against the landing-stage at the bottom of the Moss's garden. David, paddling up-river to try to find the owner of the craft, comes abreast of the garden of Codlings while Adam is standing there. Adam takes the boy for a thief but Adam's Aunt Dinah quickly gets to the bottom of the matter.

Adam has the quick temper that is usually associated with red hair. He is obstinate, hasty, changeable – and unhappy, as David soon discovers. The Codling family, established for centuries in Great Barley, have declined in substance and importance. When old Mr Codling dies it seems inevitable that Codlings must be sold and Aunt Dinah and Adam must go to live with relations in Birmingham. The only hope is the family treasure, buried by Jonathan Codling in the year of the Armada. In spite of Aunt Dinah's discouragement (for she knows how much unhappiness has been associated with earlier searches for the lost jewels and silver), Adam infects David with his furious determination, and the two boys set themselves to interpret the curious rhyme left by Jonathan and to explore the river banks, the old mill, the disused bridge, with the canoe 'Minnow' to convey them and the spirit of adventure to inspire them.

The treasure – hidden, then found, then hidden again – the ebb and flow of the boys' hopes, their successes and failures, give the story an onward movement which is matched by the movement of the river, the dominant entity of the story. With all its twists and surprises, it is not ultimately the treasure hunt that holds the attention longest, but the interaction of character. Everyone who plays a part in the story stands out clearly and emphatically – the miller Mark Tey and his disagreeable wife; the nervous old man Squeak Wilson, whose agency in the affair is so secret and unexpected; the persistent, unlikable Mr Smith.

The firm, unobtrusive arrangement of a background to which the characters really belong is most important when we come to the two boys, so dissimilar and so effective as allies. David's home background, with his firm, sensible bus-driver father and his comfortable, affectionate mother, accounts for his equable nature and his good sense just as Adam's sense of belonging to an old family, the feeling of obligation that has been instilled in him by his aunt and his grandfather, account for a good deal of his arrogance and wilfulness and for

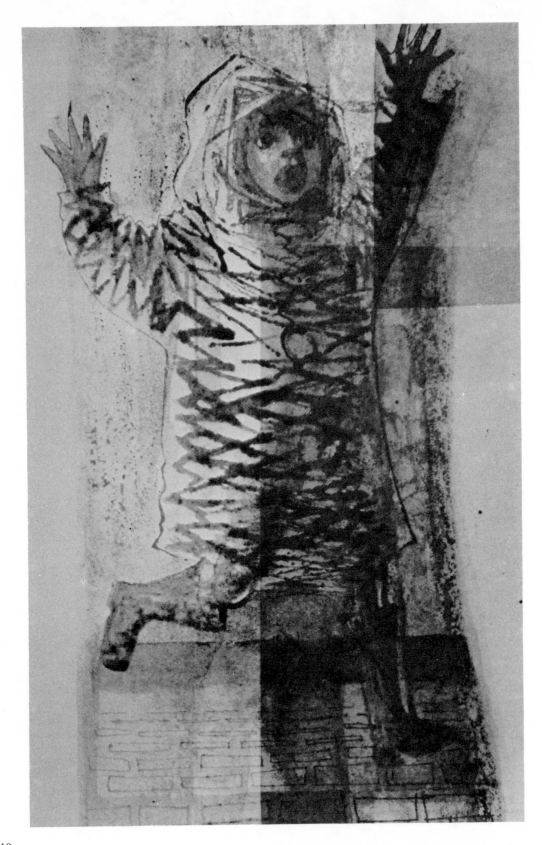

the generosity of his occasional apologies. While so many writers strive to redress an illusory literary balance between social classes, Philippa Pearce has shown, unobtrusively and firmly, how far character depends on environment and how far communication between two human beings depends on a community of interests. [A. Philippa Pearce: *Minnow on the Say*, London 1955]

**ALAN HOBBS** *see* JOHN WALTERS

**ALEKO,** who is fourteen, has lived with his grandmother in a shabby two-roomed shed since his parents were killed in a bombing raid. He finds a real purpose in life when his goat Lesbia uncovers on the hillside a bronze figure of a shepherd boy. Captivated by the beauty of the statuette, Aleko determines to find out more about it. He soon discovers that nobody else sees it simply for what it is. To his grandmother, always anxious about the future, it is a useless piece of metal; his restless friend Stelio hopes it is valuable so that they can both escape from the island to a wider world; the lawyer's wife covets it as an ornament for her salon; the schoolmaster is excited by its antiquity. Only a fat visitor, nicknamed Mr Fivechairs from his habit of idling in the café, advises Aleko not to let anyone persuade him to give up his treasure. His advice in fact goes deeper. 'Don't let anyone else tell you what you want. You find out for yourself.'

Through weeks of wandering with a painter who calls himself, significantly, Eleftheros, the free man, Aleko decides that if the figure goes to a museum he will still possess it, in a sense, while the money will help him to a training in archaeology; the shepherd boy represents, for him, the island which he now realizes is essential to his happiness in the future. Aleko epitomizes the lasting virtues of a certain way of life in a book which Edward Fenton has called his 'love affair with Greece'. [Edward Fenton: *Aleko's Island*, New York 1948]

**ALEXANDER** *see* GINGER AND PICKLES

**ALFIE** is a Cockney boy, living not far from the Thames in London. Shut in by high walls, in a drab part of the city, Alfie is stirred by the reminiscences of an old man who pushes an ancient gramophone about the streets on a pram and earns a few pence with his music. When the old man disappears and a newspaper seller says he has probably gone to 'the other side of the world', Alfie believes him. Wandering and dreaming, the boy drifts through a sudden fog down to the river, boards a ferry and soon finds himself in what is for him a strange world, a 'wonderland of sound and colour'. Before he has time to be alarmed he sees old Bunty's dog Stoker and follows him, to find his old friend busking outside a theatre whose sign flashes the words 'The Other Side of the World'. As the old man takes him

One of Charles Keeping's innovative illustrations for *Alfie and the Ferry Boat*.

home he explains where Alfie's journey has really taken him, across the river from the East End to the West End of London.

In this picture-book, which heralded an exciting experiment in illustration, Charles Keeping sets out to convey by visual means not personality but emotion. In scenes where shapes and figures are sometimes represented and sometimes suggested in the midst of a blaze of seemingly shifting colour, he conveys Alfie's reactions to a journey that takes him from dingy, fog-bound streets to the stirring, crowded night-life of the city. Keeping has been criticized for his use of symbol and abstraction in this and other books but children, less hidebound than their elders, are usually ready to let the point of the story enter them through their eyes so that they, in their turn, may enter into Alfie's imaginative experience. [Charles Keeping: *Alfie and the Ferry Boat*, London 1968]

**ALFRED, KING OF THE ENGLISH,** with his love of learning and his stand against invasion, can be made to seem relevant to our time, but history is dangerously subject to hindsight, and an oblique presentation of an historical character is often safer than a direct one. In his two stories of Alfred, *The Namesake* and *The Marsh King*, C. Walter Hodges has used the device of the fictional narrator to good effect. In the first book a lame boy escapes from the monastery of Thornham when it is sacked by the Danes and, on his wanderings, finds in a stable a set of harness, decorated with both Christian and Roman symbols; his crutch tells Alfred Daneleg in a dream that he is to take it to the King. The harness, a monk tells him, symbolizes the way 'a noble spirit in a weak body can control the strong but unskilled brute', and it may also suggest Alfred's belief in the continuity of history and the validity of the Christian faith. The lad realizes the truth of the monk's words when he becomes secretary to the King. He sees him in his strength, when he is planning his campaign against the invading Danes under their leader Guthorm; he listens to him as he explains why learning is more important to him than power and tells the boy 'Every man is a part of the bridge between the past and the future, and must feel how it stretches out both ways before and behind him'; and he sees how Alfred endures and overcomes his recurring fevers.

Alfred Daneleg knows the King in his youth, as a plainly dressed man of twenty-one, whose courage is a matter of intelligence and will rather than of physical strength. The second view of Alfred, as warrior and statesman in his later years, is given by a soldier, son of a Saxon mother and a Danish father, who adds to his own knowledge of the King various details which he has obtained from the old man known as Pegleg. Here is the King in the last stages of his struggle with Guthorm, hiding in the marshes of Athelney and planning to make England a unified, Christian country. The baptism of Guthorm after his defeat at Ethandune

Alfred Daneleg, the lame Saxon boy whose life is intertwined with that of King Alfred in *The Namesake*, written and illustrated by C. Walter Hodges.

King Alfred himself in the sequel, *The Marsh King*.

concludes a story which, unlike the reflective narrative of Alfred Daneleg, is fully active and preoccupied with the idea of the King as a ruler and statesman.

Geoffrey Trease, writing for readers younger and less well equipped with historical knowledge than those addressed by Walter Hodges, uses in *Mist over Athelney* his frequent device of placing children on the fringes of historical action. His central characters, Edward and Judith, the children of a thegn of Mercia, are hostages in Guthorm's camp, while their friend Elfwyn, an orphan whose artistic talent has been encouraged in the monastery where he grew up, is used as a slave after being captured in a raid. When the children overhear the Danish leader and his ally Hubba planning to break the truce with the King they resolve to warn Alfred. While Edward is forced to go with Hubba's army into Cornwall, Elfwyn and the dauntless Judith journey on foot from Gloucester to Chippenham and remain under the King's protection when he retreats to Athelney. Judith sees the King as a compassionate father-figure,

while Elfwyn, who has saved one precious illuminated manuscript from the sacked monastery, is drawn to him because of their mutual love of beauty and learning. The King's courage, his determination to promote civilization and the Christian faith, his strength as a war leader, are all shown in a suitably simple way in this adventure-story. [C. Walter Hodges: *The Namesake*, London 1964; *The Marsh King*, 1967. Geoffrey Trease: *Mist over Athelney*, London 1958]

**ALICE** and **THOMAS** and **JANE** are aged respectively five, eight and seven, but the youngest of the family is by far the most forceful character, perhaps because she is kept busy insisting on her right to join enterprises which the other two consider unsuitable for her. Certainly in spite of her terror of 'big worms' and her volatile temperament, Alice plays her part valiantly; most little girls would have shrunk from being towed in the dark behind a dinghy or hauled up the cliff in a basket – but not Alice. These enterprises depend, often, on momentary freedom from the careful eye of mother, father or governess; but, surprisingly, adventure often becomes possible even in a staid middle-class household in Rottingdean more than forty years ago.

On one occasion, the children dress up and perform as pavement artists in Brighton, until a policeman sends them home. On another, they watch at night as a ship lands a pet dog against quarantine regulations. Jane's conscience troubles her this time, in spite of Thomas's assurance that Alice 'could be a baby of less than five when she liked, but when you pushed her a bit she could be quite seven'.

However, it is Thomas who goes furthest. Bored by inactivity while in quarantine for whooping cough, he stows away on the Newhaven–Dieppe ferry. In the course of one evening in France he makes several useful discoveries – among them, that stewed snails do not agree with his digestion and that tortoises make an awkward package when you are trying to escape from inquisitive grown-ups.

*Alice and Thomas and Jane* exploits the age-old theme of children breaking bounds, with characters as typical of their period as the social details and circumstances that surround them. [Enid Bagnold: *Alice and Thomas and Jane*, London 1930]

**ALICE**'s adventures in Wonderland and through the Looking Glass began in a casual enough manner, in a story told to three little girls 'hungry for fairyland'. Dodgson recalled many years after the river-picnic of 1862 'how in a desperate attempt to strike out some new line of fairy-lore, I sent my heroine straight down a rabbit hole to begin with, without the least idea of what was to happen afterwards'. But even that first impromptu story had a unity in the idea of change, especially of changing size, while its sequel, which had no such accidental origin, is based on the pattern of a chess-game and also, again, on the idea of change – that is, growing up. So in both stories the inconsequent, sequential air of a dream is controlled by a basic shape and idea. A further control is imposed on the story by Alice herself.

She seldom thinks that she may be dreaming and when she does, she hopes it is her own dream and not the Red King's that she is involved in, and comments with typical briskness 'I don't like belonging to another person's dream...I've a great mind to go and wake him, and see what happens.' She is always herself, always aware of her reactions to the strange scenes she engages in and the strange creatures she meets; she is usually aware of who she is, and if she is visited by occasional doubts, she immediately sets herself to find her identity. In the wood where there are no names she works out ways of advertising to find hers, and this helps her to move forward with determination till she emerges from the trees and memory returns.

Alice is a child who has accepted for the whole of her seven and a half years the existence of rules – nursery rules of proper behaviour, the unchangeable laws of

Lewis Carroll at the age of sixty-six.

words and numbers, the immutable progression of Time. She controls her dreams – that is, she remains consciously herself – because she tries all the time to find the rules governing a particular set of circumstances. When she can see an obvious order and logic in absurdity she accepts politely and with interest the part allotted to her. Playing croquet with the Queen, in Wonderland, she is puzzled by the way her flamingo mallet behaves but is willing to play because the game clearly has rules, strange though they are. Her well-mannered, polite acceptance of nonsense is far from passive, however. She has always been a child who talked to herself, and as she argues, discusses, reflects and speculates, she keeps a remote control on events by constantly re-affirming her own identity. She only loses her temper when she is forced into a situation which has no rules at all. She brings the dream of Wonderland to an end herself through her indignation at the lack of order (rather than the injustice) of the trial of the Knave of Hearts.

Although she preserves her equanimity more easily in Looking Glass Land because she can perceive that it has a peculiar back-to-front order, the disorder and noise (and the lack of food) at the banquet finally exasperate her, and once more she brings herself out of the dream by pulling the cloth off the table and spilling all the guests.

Alice seen through the eyes of five different illustrators. *Above:* Lewis Carroll's original drawing from *Alice's Adventures Under Ground*.

The Mad Hatter's tea party, drawn by John Tenniel for the 1896 edition of *Alice in Wonderland*.

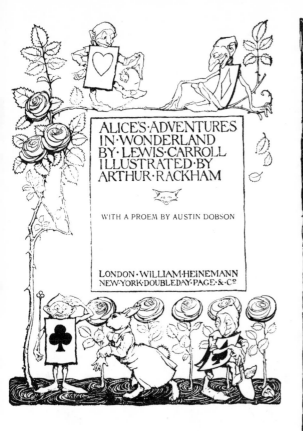

ALICE'S·ADVENTURES
IN·WONDERLAND
BY·LEWIS·CARROLL
ILLUSTRATED·BY
ARTHUR·RACKHAM

WITH A PROEM BY AUSTIN DOBSON

LONDON·WILLIAM·HEINEMANN
NEW·YORK·DOUBLEDAY·PAGE·&·Cº

*Above.* The title page and an illustration from the edition of 1907, illustrated by Arthur Rackham.

*Left.* The Duchess and the Baby, drawn by Ralph Steadman.

15

Anne-Marie Mallik as Alice in Jonathan Miller's television production of the story in 1966.

Lewis Carroll provided some authentication for the brilliant nonsense of the two dreams. Into the first one are woven the sounds of summer (wind and water, sheep bells and the distant 'confused clamour of the busy farm-yard') as Alice sleeps on the bank beside her sister, her last conscious sight being that of a rabbit running by. Her game with the kitten, the chess men on the floor, are a natural part of the dream in which she does get into the world she has looked at with such curiosity through the Looking Glass. Then, too, the every-day life of a well-brought-up middle-class child of the mid-Victorian era is visible in her behaviour. The personality of the dreamer is not as a rule important in a dream, but Alice's personality is shown clearly, in her rambling soliloquies with their fragments of past lessons and adult injunctions, her careful selection of a suitable mode of address for a Queen, a nursery-rhyme character, a sobbing Mock Turtle. The whimsical simplification called *The Nursery Alice* has almost no conversation; as a result, it reads like a blue-print for Alice's first dream and she becomes a mere mechanical pretext for it.

Jonathan Miller's remarkable interpretation of *Alice in Wonderland* in a television treatment showed Alice as a Victorian child bewildered, bullied and over-shadowed by a world of eccentric, inexplicable adults. The interpretation gave more weight to Carroll's fantasy and inverted logic than to his evident love and respect for the courage, directness and honesty of children. While it offered acceptable portraits of characters like the Caterpillar, the Mock Turtle and the Queen, it played down Alice's command of herself. Children who read the books when they are too young are often frightened by them, especially by the nightmarish changes of size and the persecution of Bill the Lizard; they are not ready to appreciate the core of self-command in Alice herself. They respond to the safer parts of the humour in the stories, while leaving to adults the pleasure of identifying parodies, playing the chess game, enjoying Carroll's erudition and logic and, sometimes, guessing at his secret longings and aberrations. *Alice in Wonderland* and *Through the Looking Glass* were the first celebrations of nonsense in children's literature; they have become a shibboleth of the English-speaking intellectual world and a favourite playground for super-erudite research. In the view of many they are not in fact suitable books for children: at least they are unmistakably stories of a child's world. [Lewis Carroll: *Alice's Adventures in Wonderland*, London 1865 (dated 1866); *Through the Looking Glass and what Alice found there*, 1871 (dated 1872)]

**ALISON** is spending three weeks of summer in a house in a Welsh valley left to her by her father; her widowed mother has recently married Clive Bradley, a divorced man with a son Roger, who like Alison is in his middle teens. Goodwill and determination cannot entirely hide the tension caused by differences in background and outlook, and the atmosphere of the house is uneasy also because Nancy, who has come back to her native valley to cook and clean for the Bradleys, is difficult and touchy, and the gardener known as Huw Halfbacon seems either stupid or half-crazy.

Alison and Roger have already formed a reasonably easy relationship with Nancy's son Gwyn and to these three young people comes a deeper disturbance than the evanescent, shifting, sexual undertones of their friendship. The valley hides a power released in an ancient conflict, when the wizard Gwydion made a wife out of flowers for a local princeling and the wayward impulses of Blodeuwedd turned her from flowers to destructive owl, and brought death to her husband and her lover. Century after century the conflict has been re-enacted. Gwyn's mother, the strangely impressive Huw, and Bertram, the cousin from whom the house was inherited, have been the last people to suffer until the summer that brings Alison, Roger and Gwyn together. Swept by a destructive spirit which manifests itself in various images of owls and flowers, Alison destroys Gwyn's precarious self-confidence and comes near to destroying the new family pattern which her mother and step-father are trying to create, until Roger, suddenly understanding the duality of her nature, frees her from emotional bondage.

Alan Garner has taken the Celtic legend of Blodeuwedd as the driving force for an intricately plaited narrative in which the ancient tragedy changes each time it is played out. In Alison, Roger and Gwyn it canalizes the unstable, indefinable stresses of adolescence as well as the intangible effects of class difference. The legend is no mere decorative parallel; the mystery of Blodeuwedd and the aura of ancient sorrow deepen the emotional problems that rise from a simple family holiday. The complex material of the book is contained almost wholly in dialogue, the best and most difficult tool any novelist has for revealing character. Spare, short sentences are exchanged between the three young people and their parents; Alison's mother, Margaret, who never speaks or appears, is revealed vividly in the comments or reported speech of the others. Dialogue in *The Owl Service* has to imply action, to sustain atmosphere, to reveal nuances of character, to build tension and to suggest the endless repetitiveness of human passion, and still sound unforced and natural. The power and the passion of the story justify the method Alan Garner has chosen. [Alan Garner: *The Owl Service*, London 1967]

**ALMANZO WILDER** *see* LAURA INGALLS

**AMANDA** has reacted badly to the divorce in her family and when her artist mother marries a man with four children she has no intention of adapting herself to a new family unit. David Stanley's premonition of trouble is confirmed when he sees Amanda, with elaborately plaited hair and long black dress, sequin glinting on her forehead and an enigmatic look on her face. In the confidence of her necromantic attire and her extensive, if immature, acquaintance with the occult, Amanda begins at once to try her power on eleven-year-old David, tough little Janie and the young twins Esther and Blair. At first the children agree to serve as her apprentices; but soon David notices that the tests Amanda imposes (to eat for a whole day without touching any metal, for instance, or to bring certain amphibians into her house) are sure to trouble or hurt her mother.

The younger children are inconveniently observant too. Janie keeps a sharp eye on the personal treasures which Amanda demands as a sacrifice to an invisible power, and Blair, whom Amanda mistakenly thinks is mentally backward, has a disconcerting way of exposing her petty deceits. Finally Amanda, enraged because the Stanley children so obviously like the mother she loves to hate, plays her best card. Overhearing tales of a poltergeist that once plagued the old house, she arranges a series of increasingly unpleasant and mystifying happenings which disrupt the household and frighten everybody – everybody, that is, except Blair, for he not only catches Amanda in action but he also shows, when he finds the carved head missing from the stairs, that he has something of the power which Amanda so ingeniously pretends to possess.

Amanda's frantic manipulation of the truth is all the

more significant because it is not presented to the reader in an obvious sequence of cause and effect. It is almost entirely through the chatter of the children, through Blair's few, devastating utterances and David's blundering comments and guesses, that we realize that Amanda is hiding from herself, in a complicated campaign against her mother, the fact that her father does not want to have her to live with him. The author's constant use of dramatic irony intensifies her portrait of a child who is reacting in her own aggressive way to a difficult situation. [Zilpha Keatley Snyder: *The Headless Cupid*, New York 1971]

**AMELIA–BEDELIA** dresses correctly for her life as a servant but interprets her duties in a manner entirely her own. When her new employer, Mrs Rogers, leaves written instructions for her, the conscientious girl obeys them to the letter – dusting the furniture with talcum powder, changing the towels by cutting fancy patterns in them, and performing other absurdities; all is forgiven, however, for the sake of the superb lemon meringue pie which she finds time to bake. Great Aunt Myra's visit to the house and a party for a prospective bride inspire her to fresh idiocies, which Fritz Siebel puts into amusingly descriptive line. [Peggy Parish: *Amelia-Bedelia*, New York 1963; *Thank You, Amelia-Bedelia*, 1964; *Amelia-Bedelia and the Surprise Shower*, 1966]

**AMELIARANNE STIGGINS** is the eldest of six children, and very much an eldest child too; she is loving and careful with the younger ones, especially Wee William, and her hard-working mother, who takes in washing, relies on her a great deal and is often heard to remark: 'When things go wrong she can generally find a way out'. Certainly things seem to have a way of turning out well for Ameliaranne, even if she sometimes startles Mrs Stiggins with her 'Ideas' (for example, when she organizes a concert to raise money for the village hall and borrows a circus elephant to take the tickets at the door).

The various exploits of this resourceful child fit into an environment as remote from our own times as her neat felt hat, white gloves and sturdy lace-ups. But there is nothing in these entertaining little tales to affront or perplex children accustomed to contemporary social alignments. Ameliaranne knows her place but she also has the courage of her convictions. She may be embarrassed when the cakes smuggled in her umbrella from the Squire's teatable fall to the ground in front of her as she is saying a polite goodbye, but she accepts with perfect calm the generous basketful of good things which the housekeeper packs up for her to take home to her brothers and sister. What more natural, when she digs up a pot in the garden, than to take it straight off

Title page of one of the many Ameliaranne stories.

19

to the Squire; what could be more natural than that he should order the butler to show her in to his study, for 'Ameliaranne's a sensible child', as he says, and a very real personality. [Constance Heward, ill. Susan Beatrice Pearce: *Ameliaranne and the Green Umbrella*, London 1920; several other titles, some by other authors, including *Ameliaranne Keeps Shop*, 1928; *Ameliaranne, Cinema Star*, 1929; *Ameliaranne at the Farm*, 1937; *Ameliaranne Gives a Christmas Party*, 1938; *Ameliaranne Camps Out*, 1939; *Ameliaranne Keeps School*, 1940]

**AMY** and Clarissa develop the stories that Amy's mother tells them about an old witch into a drawing game which lasts from a Hallowe'en to a Hallowe'en and which reflects their characters and home backgrounds. Both little girls have blue eyes and long, straight fair hair, but Amy's is 'the colour of moonlight' and Clarissa's 'the colour of sunlight' and this fits their natures, for Amy is as dreamy and imaginative as Clarissa is matter-of-fact. Clarissa is brave enough to go to the library alone and she has a certain sophistication (with French blood and custom in the family) that shows itself in a love of long words. It is Amy who initiates the events in the game, Amy who 'enjoyed being sad sometimes, especially when she had been the one to think up the sadness'.

The game begins with the banquishment (Amy's word) of Old Witch to a bare home on a bleak glass hill because of her villainy in causing hurly-burlies and eating Easter rabbits. As the game develops (the little girls solemnly drawing each scene and discussing it together) their characters grow for the reader. Amy has promised Old Witch a day's freedom to be wicked next Hallowe'en if she behaves well till then. The old hag's lapses from grace clearly give Amy the chance to escape from the orderly progress of her home life. Because the children come to fear Old Witch a little they invent Malachi, a bee whom a magic spell has enabled – to spell! This beautifully logical idea preserves the balance of mischief and obedience essential to the children, while Malachi's solemn buzzing pronouncements seem to reflect Clarissa's sturdy and amusing affectation of adult behaviour.

As the days pass other characters are invented – the Little Witch Girl Hannah and the baby sister she longed for, a whole school of malicious little witch girls, a mermaid in a glass cavern with a baby sister of her own, the Easter rabbits and their painted eggs; each one stands for some wish or vagary, some remembered fear or joy – for instance, I am sure Clarissa sees herself in Brave Jack the rabbit guard. Amy emerges as a child dependent on affection, her own and that of other people. Her letters to Old Witch always end in her special way: 'I love you and you love me.' After a last mock-scarifying dream adventure on the night of Hallowe'en when she experiments with Hannah's broomstick and is carried up to Old Witch's house, she decides to allow the wicked old woman some grass and flowers for comfort, since she appears to have reformed. But not entirely – for as Amy says, and as Clarissa agrees, 'What is the good of Old Witch if she is good all the time. Oblique character drawing has seldom been as shrewd or as comical as it is in this American family tale [Eleanor Estes: *The Witch Family*, New York 1960]

**ANATOLE** lives in 'a small mouse village near Paris with his wife and children. Dressed Parisian style in smock, red neckerchief and black beret, he bicycles

FONDLY, FOR MY SON RICK

NOT SO GOOD needs more ... Anatole

The French mouse Anatole, illustrated by Paul Galdone in *Anatole and the Toyshop*.

briskly through the streets or fossicks through houses for food, but one day, overhearing a housewife inveighing against the dirt and damage caused by mice, he determines to vindicate the honour of his race.

Creeping into Duval's factory, he pins pertinent comments on each of the stacked cheeses. His exquisite taste brings prosperity to the factory and makes him so famous that, in subsequent books, he is consulted again and again – about the notorious Cheese Robbery organized by Baptist the Baker, Blanchard the Barber and Bernard the Bookseller and about the dastardly trick played by the Borgia Brothers in Rome on their rivals. He bells the cat in Duval's factory, fishes Madame Duvaletti's pearls out of the piano just in time for her concert and performs many other exploits in which resource and Gallic insouciance are comically and mousily evident. [Eve Titus, ill. Paul Galdone: *Anatole*, New York 1956; *Anatole and the Cat*, 1957; *Anatole and the Robot*, 1960; *Anatole over Paris*, 1961; *Anatole and the Poodle*, 1965; *Anatole and the Piano*, 1966; *Anatole and the Thirty Thieves*, 1969; *Anatole and the Toyshop*, 1970; *Anatole in Italy*, 1974]

**ANDREI ALEXANDROVITCH HAMILTON** owes his names to a mixed parentage. A Jacobite ancestor of his father's had taken service with the Russian Court in the eighteenth century and the family has been close to Romanovs ever since; his mother is of aristocratic French and Austrian birth. Born in 1894, the year when Nicholas II succeeded his father, Andrei has been accustomed from childhood to meeting the Czar and his family and to hearing them discussed as private individuals as well as public figures. Much of what he hears as a child he does not understand. Perhaps he never understands, even as a man, the pity his mother feels for the Czarina, the reserved, jealously possessive princess from Hesse who has so little feeling for the Russian people: nor is Andrei old enough to assess the Czar's responsibility for the shocking accident of the day in 1905 known thereafter as Bloody Sunday; all that he knows is that he has seen his father fatally wounded by a bomb while acting as equerry to the Grand Duke Serge. With an inheritance, generations-old, of loyalty to the sovereign, Andrei becomes a military cadet and later, like his father, joins the Russian Imperial Guard. He takes part in the disastrous campaign in East Prussia in the First World War, sees the sinister influence of Rasputin on the Romanovs, is captured during the Revolution and finally takes part in the White Russian investigation into the death of the Romanovs.

As a character, Andrei Hamilton is at once an actor and a spectator. A convincing background has been invented for him. Grandfather, uncle, parents, servants, comrades in arms, lend him existence through the part they play in his life, while historical fact is skilfully interwoven with the fictional course of Andrei's life as child, youth and man. But we are not primarily concerned with Andrei's personality. Often the conversation of his grandfather, the epistolary style of his uncle, are more revealing than his own first-person narrative. This is because Andrei is a central point of reference, a sounding-board, a mouthpiece. In the course of two extremely concentrated novels he offers not so much a history of Russia from 1894 to 1918 as a view of it – oblique, partial but never partisan. With reminiscence, letters, conversations overheard, dialogue in which he takes part, gossip, official reports, first-hand descriptions, Andrei draws portraits of the Czar and his family which have a special validity because they are not historical analysis but historical impression.

Andrei is not a rigid White Russian, nor is his narrative polemical. He sees the mistakes in government which led to revolution, he recognizes the idealism as well as the inhuman violence in peasants, soldiers, intellectuals. He is, all the same, the product of a particular environment and upbringing, and because his character is so firmly established he can (or the author can, through him) give us an interpretation of Nicholas II and Alexandra, an insight into a family at whose head were two people who made irrevocable mistakes but with whom 'died gentleness, youth, innocence, devotion, and that simplicity whose chief offence is loyalty'.

Stephanie Plowman has said that the initial impulse for her two magnificent books was a description in the memoirs of Baroness Buxhoeveden of 'a small, bedraggled group of horsemen, parleying in front of the great closed gates' at Czarskoe. They 'had ridden from Novgorod through two days of bitter cold and deep snow' to see the Czar, not knowing that he had abdicated. The name of the officer commanding the squadron was not given. Andrei Hamilton is the author's answer to this anonymity. [Stephanie Plowman: *Three Lives for the Czar*, London 1969; *My Kingdom for a Grave*, 1970]

**ANDY HODDEL** lived in a run-down district of Sydney with his widowed mother, a dressmaker. In spite of brain-damage caused by illness, he still played with the boys of Appington Hill. They had known him all their lives and could remember when he was foremost in the gang for energy and enterprise; they accepted the fact that he went to a special school and were patient with his black moods and his fits of noisy laughter, but they found their favourite game difficult to explain. They would lay claim to various public buildings, vying with each other to think of the most spectacular imaginary ownerships – the Public Library, the Town Hall, the Harbour ferries – and would enjoy the extravagant bargaining that followed.

Andy finally saw something he really wanted – the racecourse at Beecham Park, ablaze in the dusk with moving, intertwining colour. Wandering beside this coveted fairyland, Andy met a tramp who promised to sell him the place for four dollars. It was hardly his fault that Andy took him literally and with much difficulty

Andy Hoddel

Andy Hoddel from *I Own the Racecourse*, illustrated by Margaret Horder.

found ways to earn the money and pay it over, or that the various people on the course should humour the boy in his fantasy for the sake of his disability. There was trouble in store for Andy, and anxiety for his friends, before a way was found to bring the dream to an end without destroying the happiness and the new confidence which it had brought to him.

Patricia Wrightson marks Andy's difference from the other boys with subtle indications of his behaviour, his facial expressions, his mode of speech. As with Martin the Martian (q.v.), she uses the reactions of other people to extend her character-drawing. When Andy seems to be endangering the boys by his bold entry into the racecourse and his pathetically practical attempts to 'improve' it to his satisfaction, his friends react very differently. Matt and Terry are inclined to be impatient; they like to take life at a run and cannot understand Andy's mental processes, and their blunt, direct arguments only upset him. Joe, who is accustomed to wait for clever Mike to come up with an answer to every problem, is certain that Andy must be made to understand 'what was real and what was not'. Mike is sensitive enough to realize that Andy's simple outlook has its own value, and he is ready to support Andy's dream and to accept him as he is. When by a kind and cunning scheme Andy is persuaded to 'sell' the racecourse back to the Company and (with typical waywardness) wonders if he has enough money to buy a model 'plane,

Mike puts his friends right once more. What does it matter if Andy gets a 'plane and breaks it? 'He's got to have things sometimes, even if he does bust them.' While the rest of the boys accept Andy for the residue of sense left in him, with pity and rough comradeship, it is Mike who sees something of the innocence which is Andy Hoddel's recompense; he sees that Andy does, in a way, really 'own' the racecourse through his vision of it. [Patricia Wrightson: *I Own the Racecourse*, London 1968]

**ANDY PANDY** the puppet, with his smiling pink and white face and his blue-striped suit and cap, was devised for the BBC 'Watch with Mother' television programme for pre-school children; as he sang little songs, capered on his hobby-horse or danced a little dance, small children were happy to imitate him. Andy Pandy and his two friends, Teddy and the rag doll Looby Loo, were often in difficulties – with splashed paint, spilt food, torn clothes – but these only made them more attractive to the very young. Then, too, there was a congenial note in the introduction of various animals as well as such nursery desiderata as a rocking horse and a pedal car.

The three characters in the television programmes and in the attractive miniature books that followed are not quite as simple as they may seem. They have a miniature hierarchy as characters. Andy Pandy is something of the older brother in his behaviour: Teddy (like most fictional teddy bears) is endearingly clumsy and not very bright; while Looby Loo is recognized by these two as being 'only a rag doll', to be carried about propped up, occasionally lost, always looked after affectionately. Through tiny adventures, well within the experience of small children, a gentle continuous exercise in observation, a subtle encouragement to purposive play, has been offered to children by way of three puppet-toys who, in the estimation of thousands of viewers and readers, are genuinely alive. [Maria Bird, ill Marvyn Wright: *Andy Pandy and His Hobby Horse*, Leicester 1954; *Andy Pandy and the Ducklings*, 1954 and many other titles]

**ANGELA D'ASOLA**, red-haired niece of the famous printer-publisher Aldus Manutius of Venice, is one of the most attractive of the many girls who share the endeavours of youths in Geoffrey Trease's historical adventures. A hero and heroine who venture into danger together add piquancy and variety to many of his stories, each of them set in a period carefully chosen so that the association may be socially plausible. Angela's classical education has been as thorough as that of her companion and her home background a good deal more liberal. She makes a suitable travelling companion for Alan Drayton, a Yorkshire lad of seventeen who is sent by Erasmus to the house where the Aldine Press carries on its valuable work in reprinting classical texts. Alan is engaged to travel into Dalmatia to locate a rare manuscript reputed to be in the library of a remote monastery. He does his best to discourage Angela, who has followed him dressed as a boy, from

Alan Drayton and Angela d'Asola from *The Hills of Varna*, illustrated by Treyer Evans.

continuing a journey whose dangers – from pirates, shipwreck and the agents of a powerful Duke who covets the manuscript – are even greater than he had anticipated. Angela has endurance as well as tenacity on her side, and in spite of Alan's inborn belief in the superiority of his sex, he learns to respect a girl who might be one minute bewailing the effect of the sun on her fashionably white skin and, the next, laughing at her lacerated feet. The final view of Angela is of a demure miss accepting from a Florentine gentleman of mature years a proposal for which she has been manoeuvring for some time; a sweet little thing, just like a kitten, her betrothed mused. 'He had not yet learnt that kittens grow up into cats.' Zest, humour, suspense all enter the story by reason of the presence of Angela d'Asola. [Geoffrey Trease: *The Hills of Varna*, London 1948]

**ANNA MARIA** *see* GINGER AND PICKLES

**ANNE SHIRLEY** is adopted by Matthew Cuthbert and his sister Marilla when she is eleven, but she is not the orphan they had planned to take in. They wanted a boy whom Matthew, a bachelor farmer on Prince Edward Island, could train to help him now that at sixty he was beginning to feel his age. It is a shock to Matthew,

whose house at Green Gables is as isolated as he is shy, to find at the railway station not 'a smart, likely boy' but a girl with red hair and freckles, shabbily dressed, watching him with observant eyes 'that looked green in some lights and moods and grey in others'. Quite unaware of being a mistake, Anne captivates Matthew on the homeward journey by her vivacious and imaginative chatter and though brisk, practical Marilla is not so easily charmed, it is not only Matthew's unexpected firmness that gives Anne her chance of a genuine home, for her spontaneous affection soon conquers Marilla's reserve.

The long popularity of the eight stories of Anne and Avonlea owes much to the Pollyanna stories and *Rebecca of Sunnybrook Farm*, books which set a fashion for the orphan who becomes a ray of sunshine in dark lives. But there is nothing dark about Green Gables, nor has Anne the ineffable joyousness of Pollyanna. Her irruption into other people's lives is less dramatic and she is herself a more natural character than either of the earlier heroines. The atmosphere of the Avonlea books (at least of the first two, *Anne of Green Gables* and *Anne of Avonlea*) is good-humoured and light, with an outdoor feel about it, depending on episodes at home or in school in which Anne shows her bursting high spirits, her imagination (poetic and engagingly absurd in the manner of the early 'teens), her gift for friendship, her quick temper and equally quick affection.

A remark made about Anne by old Miss Barry may provide another key to the long life of this fictional character. 'That Anne girl improves all the time … [She] has as many shades as a rainbow and every shade is the prettiest while it lasts.' A heroine who is observant and genuinely interested in people is an asset to a novelist. Anne's creator was able to use her in later books as an excuse for anecdotes about local worthies, keeping Anne herself in the background to avoid repetition. The books concerning Anne's high school and college years, her marriage and growing family, are less entertaining than the first two in the series – to adolescents at least, for whom Anne's decorous romance with Gilbert Blythe must seem dull after the sprightly quarrels they indulged in as school-fellows. It is best to forget that the freckled, red-haired orphan ever grew up, for there is still much to enjoy in following her through the lively years between eleven and sixteen. [L. M. Montgomery: *Anne of Green Gables*, Boston 1908; *Anne of Avonlea*, 1909; *Chronicles of Avonlea*, 1912; *Anne of the Island*, 1915; *Anne's House of Dreams*, New York 1917; *Further Chronicles of Avonlea*, Boston 1920; *Anne of Windy Poplars*, New York 1936 (= *Anne of Windy Willows*, London 1936); *Anne of Ingleside*, Boston 1939]

**ANT** and **BEE** meet by accident. Ant's hat is too big for him, Bee's too small; both throw their hats away, then change their minds, go searching for them, and bump into one another. Still looking for the lost hats, they open numerous boxes, each marked with a different letter, and containing relevant objects. Their hats are found in a box labelled 'Funny Things' and when they have conveniently exchanged them, they are 'great friends'.

Ant and Bee and the ABC, which describes their first meeting, was not in fact the first book in which these two cheerful and useful insects were introduced to the pre-school world. The first story, Ant and Bee, is cleverly planned so that children can learn to read a few simple three-letter words; these are displayed singly and also fitted into the narrative, always being marked out by red type. The formula is repeated in three more books; later there are lively, painless introductions to counting, geography, colour, the days of the week, time, money, school and medical care, all with Ant and Bee in the centre. These two, with their amiable friend Kind Dog, are turned into tiny people by virtue of hats and accessories and neatly contrived faces which hardly alter their insect appearance. It is the idiosyncratic illustrations which have established them among the hotchpotch of human, animal and inanimate 'characters' cherished by the very young. [Angela Banner: Ant and Bee, London, 1951; More Ant and Bee, 1958; Around the World with Ant and Bee, 1960; More and More Ant and Bee, 1961; Ant and Bee and the Rainbow, 1962; Happy Birthday with Ant and Bee, 1964; Ant and Bee and the ABC, 1966; One Two Three with Ant and Bee, 1968; Ant and Bee and Kind Dog, 1968; Ant and Bee Time, 1969; Ant and Bee and the Secret, 1970; Ant and Bee Big Bag Buy, 1971; Ant and Bee and the Doctor, 1971; Ant and Bee Go Shopping, 1972]

**ANTHONY HENRYPOTTERY LUXULYAN PRETTYPIG** is made of china; he stands on the mantelpiece and watches the funnels of trains passing the window. Such is the china pig's obsession with trains that he succeeds in thinking himself into the middle of 'a Rather Curious Wood', the foliage 'consisting almost entirely of Third Class Excursion Tickets and little Station Lamps'. In this interesting place the finest locomotive is undoubtedly the noble and dignified Antimacassar, in which by courtesy of Mister Stuffingbox, Head-Chief-Driver of the Line, Anthony is permitted to travel.

The journey involves the interested pig with a Very Sorry Engine, the Permanent-highway-men and the

*Opposite.* An illustration by Nicole Claveloux from *Les Aventures d'Alice au Pays des Merveilles.*

Illustration from *More Ant and Bee,* written by Angela Banner, drawn by Bryan Ward.

The adventures of the china pig, Anthony, from *Anthony and Antimacassar* by Mary and Roland Emett.

Sulphate of Silicate Jam, dangerous Wood-choppers and industrious Foreshore Fishermen and a Pirate Chief with a suitable entourage. To return to his mantelpiece makes Anthony a little sad but a glance at the Byelaws on his Half-Ticket soon cheers him and inspires him to sing his little song, which had 'four hundred and twenty-six verses ... all exactly the same'.

It is hard to think of a happier setting for an Emett adventure. The artist's skill in line is demonstrated in the bizarre complexities of Antimacassar and a gentle, humorous affection can be deduced from his treatment of the pudgy little pig who accepts everything that happens to him in a spirit of affable curiosity; while few writers since Mary Emett have been as serenely ingenious with upper-case humour. [Mary and Rowland Emett: *Anthony and Antimacassar*, London 1943].

An illustration by Matvyn Wright from *Andy Pandy and the Willow Tree* by Maria Bird.

**ARABEL JONES** *see* MORTIMER

**ARCHIE** the boy detective, who enjoys enunciating his full name of Henry Archibald McGillicuddy, is not quite five foot two, with arms and legs like matchsticks and huge strong-lens spectacles. In his last two years or so at school he resolves to work towards a career as a crime photographer. His friends grow accustomed to being called upon for help by day or night when Archie has a case to solve. For his part, Archie learns to use his brain and to arrange 'all the facts until they make a pattern', so that he has made a good start by the time he is confronted with such problems as the theft of a ciné camera, sabotage in the clubhouse, the disappearance of the school bell and the substitution of damaged stamps for valuable ones in a private collection. Even on school trips to Spain and Italy there are mysteries for him to investigate.

Like all youthful detectives in fiction, Archie has luck on his side as well as intelligence, and plenty of cheek to balance his common sense. The crimes he investigates

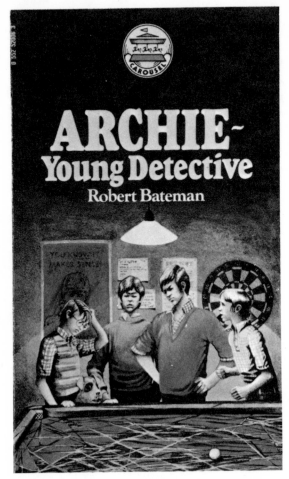

The jacket of *Archie – Young Detective* by Robert Bateman.

are amateurish and unsensational – an insurance fiddle, a land-grab, a bit of inter-school sabotage. They are primarily chosen as examples of Archie's acumen and the reader will probably be more aware of their serious nature than the young detective is, for although the boy's actions and background are true to life, they are described in a tone of energetic humour. Archie is sometimes overtaken by the police in the race to a solution; he often jumps to the wrong conclusions and occasionally gets himself and his friends into trouble; and he is hampered by the faithful Bonkers, 'a large, nondescript dog, a kind of cross between a sheep-dog and a small donkey', whose frying-pan feet impede most of the characters at one time or another and whose untimely and despondent cries echo hilariously through classrooms, streets and the peaceful sitting room of Archie's long-suffering parents. [Robert Bateman: *Archie – Young Detective*, London 1961; *Mystery for Archie*, 1963; *Archie Abroad*, 1964; *Archie and the Missing Stamps*, 1965; *Archie's Italian Adventure*, 1966; *Strange Case for Archie*, 1967]

**ARNOLD ALCOTT,** a working-class boy of fifteen, does not fit into the pattern of factory routine but has no paper qualifications to help him to move into a world that would satisfy his vague aspirations. While he is drifting towards a dead-end job he meets a grammar school boy and his sister Ruth. An intellectual girl hoping to be a teacher, Ruth willingly takes Arnold in hand, introducing him to classical music and to her current favourites among the poets. In this heady atmosphere the two of them progress timidly towards kisses and caresses, but no further, for Ruth is strongly conditioned by her background and frigid by temperament.

For his part Arnold is increasingly bewildered by the contradiction between his natural impulses and the demands of the intellectual world which he decides to explore now that he has a safe if minor office job. As his ambitions reach out from WEA classes to the possibility of a university place, he and Ruth grow away from one another, their relationship withered by differences in class and circumstance.

This is emphatically a story of class distinction and the effect of environment on character. Drawn in positive lines, the character of Arnold illustrates a problem existing in the past and especially noticeable today in the stresses that result from a move from one kind of life to another. But the analysis of Arnold's thoughts and feelings, running concurrently with the sequence of events during the years from fifteen to eighteen, is deep enough to mark the book as a novel and not a case-history. [Stanley Watts: *The Breaking of Arnold*, London 1971]

**ARNOLD HAITHWAITE** lives in the village of Skirlston and helps the official Sand Pilot to guide visitors over the expanse of beach, seamed with channels and dangerous with tides. Arnold has a home with old Ernest Haithwaite, whom he calls Dad. He never questions either the monotony of his life or his own background, until or day a stranger comes to Skirlston, a quiet-spoken and unnerving man who says *he* is Arnold Haithwaite and who begins imperceptibly but with a menacing determination to threaten Arnold's security. At first the lad pays little attention; to the low-toned remark, 'I like folk to listen to me ... I get cross when folk don't listen,' the lad merely replies 'Oh, give up ... and come along' and continues to help him across the sands, but when they stumble together into a channel, Arnold believes the man has been trying to drown him.

Sonny's invasion of Cottontree House is as steady as it is unobtrusive. He gains a hold over old Ernest and, as Arnold slowly begins to suspect, is actually the cause of the old man's physical collapse; nor is the odd relationship between Sonny and the slatternly woman he calls his fiancée encouraging, for Miss Binns seems in an evasive way to be warning the lad of danger. The man who at first seemed a joke becomes an ogre claiming Arnold's identity. There cannot be two Arnold Haithwaites, and though the boy does find out that he has a real right to his name, he can never know for certain whether Sonny had the same right in his generation. He can rest secure only because he knows that in their last struggle, which ends in Sonny's death by drowning, his enemy was the aggressor and Arnold had already conceded him the victory.

This magnificent story is narrated through Arnold's thoughts, through the comments of other people and in the increasingly terse, manic sentences which are as ugly as Sonny's fixed artificial eye and his harsh voice. The book has an intensely visual quality. There is little direct description but the words chosen to build a picture of the sands and the shabby village, of the people whose lethargic attitude to life makes them so vulnerable to the unruly actions of a psychopath, are placed unerringly so as to stir the imagination. This is a macabre contest between a lad who accepts his ambiguous background and a man who needs to steal his name to support a monstrous self-will and an equally monstrous inadequacy as a human being. Sonny comes as near to pure evil as any of the characters in children's fiction who have been drawn plainly and directly without the overtones of fantasy. [John Rowe Townsend: *The Intruder*, 1969]

**ARTHUR CLUCK** is a very young chicken with the unusual habit of riding on his mother's head – which habit is her only means of identifying him on the terrible day when he disappears and has to be sorted out by Ralph the owl from a crateful of identical chicks, all answering to the name of Arthur. Nathaniel Benchley's witty text and Arnold Lobel's equally witty pictures prove that character-drawing is not impossible in a perfectly simple 'I Can Read' story. [Nathaniel Benchley: *The Strange Disappearance of Arthur Cluck*, New York 1967]

**ARTHUR RAMSGILL** *see* DAVID HUGHES

**ASLAN** the lion plays a dual part in the chronicles of Narnia, being at once a talking animal and a symbol of Christ. When the friendly Beaver (in *The Lion, the Witch and the Wardrobe*) tells the four Pevensie children (q.v.): 'They say Aslan is on the move ... perhaps has already landed', each has a sudden inexplicable feeling. 'Edmund felt a sensation of mysterious horror. Peter felt suddenly brave and adventurous. Susan felt as if some delicious smell or some delightful strain of music had just floated by her. And Lucy got the feeling you have when you wake up in the morning and realize that it is the beginning of the holidays or the beginning of summer.' It is necessary for C. S. Lewis to strike a note of awe so that when Aslan offers himself to the White Witch as victim in place of Edmund, and is killed by her (in a scene all the more unpleasant because it is inexplicit), he will be recognized as Christ the redeemer, Christ crucified, just as his return, as a prancing, romping animal, represents the Resurrection.

The Christian symbolism in *The Magician's Nephew*

is less doctrinal and fits more easily the magic adventure in which Polly and Digory (q.v.) are concerned, for here Aslan is shown as the Creator in a Paradisal 'choosing of the animals' that is directly equated with the 'awakening' of Narnia and the elevation of Adam and Eve (the Cabby and his wife Nellie from Edwardian London) as the first King and Queen of the new kingdom.

In *The Horse and his Boy* Aslan is a Jehovah-figure, appearing as a real lion to Shasta and Aravis and their two horses. Readers might be forgiven for wondering why C. S. Lewis, having created in Bree a real animal personality, with traits such as snobbery, self-doubt and loyalty deftly accommodated to a horse's shape and behaviour, should have given him the second function of a kind of equine Doubting Thomas, as he explains to the mare Hwin that Aslan, 'the greatest deliverer of Narnia', cannot possibly be an actual lion. Continuing the Christian parallel, C. S. Lewis then (logically, but more sadistically than he can have realized) shows Aslan as the jealous god of the Hebrews. It is he who has wounded Aravis during the journey, and he explains to her that: 'The scratches on your back, tear for tear, throb for throb, blood for blood, were equal to the stripes laid on the back of your stepmother's slave because of the drugged sleep you cast upon her.' Aslan's dealings with Eustace Scrubb (q.v.) in *The Voyage of the 'Dawn Treader'* are just as coldly punitive.

The final manifestation of Aslan (in *The Last Battle*) is apocalyptic, and the relation between Christian belief and juvenile adventure here is still less easy to accept or explain. Narnia literally falls into chaos, while the children, with the good animals and creatures from sundry times and places, move through the Doorway into a world where Aslan 'no longer looked to them like a lion' and where he is given the capitalized 'He' of religious custom.

Among the multifarious characters in the Narnia stories, Aslan is the one most likely to be interpreted differently, and regarded differently, by adults and by children. Although C. S. Lewis regarded children's books as a proper branch of literature, he did all the same adopt in his fantasy cycle an avuncular manner which may have been acceptable to children as old as twelve in 1950, when the cycle began, but which in the climate of today has meant that the stories are read mainly by younger children. Perhaps at any date Aslan's true significance is less obvious to children than the author may have wished. Most children read the Narnia stories for action and excitement and they are likely to accept without Freudian doubts the sensual and sentimental aspect of Aslan's relations with the Pevensies (especially with Lucy). They need not notice, as adults must, the mawkishness and lack of cohesion in the way Aslan enters into the books; they need not worry about the sometimes ludicrous presentation of Aslan-as-lion which weakens the awe which the Pevensies felt when they first saw him, a presentation which could surely

Aslan among the creatures of Narnia from *The Lion, the Witch and the Wardrobe*, illustrated by Pauline Baynes.

only be possible in a work lacking in real humour (though with plenty of fun in it). Even if C. S. Lewis was sometimes thinking of the relation of godhead to dancing as the Middle Ages so often expressed it (and there is a marked debt to medieval allegory in all the stories), when he describes Aslan frolicking he shows us a creature more like Tigger than like Christ.

To many adults, whether they think of Christ as man, archetypal scapegoat or the Son of God, Aslan remains an inadequate and in some ways a distasteful character. He is, besides, a character who strikes at the very root of the adventure story. Virtue, in the Narnia books, is seen ultimately to lie in obedience and not in brave, hazardous free decision. Redemptive and authoritarian, the lion removes from the young heroes and heroines the true responsibility which, in the more finely-tempered works of Tolkien and Ursula Le Guin, the protagonists are permitted to hold to themselves. [C. S. Lewis: *The Lion, the Witch and the Wardrobe*, London, 1950; *Prince Caspian*, 1951; *The Voyage of the 'Dawn Treader'*, 1952; *The Silver Chair*, 1953; *The Horse and His Boy*, 1954; *The Magician's Nephew*, 1955; *The Last Battle*, 1956]

**ASLEIF SUMMERBIRD** seemed a mysterious figure to the young Norwegian prince Harald Hardrada when he heard a strange song about him. 'If you met him', said the Bonder, 'you would feel your eyes popping out of their lids, and you would fall to your knees before him, thinking he was Odin.' Not long afterwards Harald, held prisoner in a Finnish seashore village, was surprised to be addressed forcibly ('a weeping boy is neither use to God nor man') by an immensely tall, dark-faced man, whose hooked nose and sharp black eyes 'gave him the look of a bird of prey' but whose clothing was 'of so many and such fine colours, reds and yellows and greens, that there was no hawk and no eagle ever so gaily garbed'.

Asleif becomes protector and friend to Harald on a journey to the kingdom of the powerful Jomsvikings at Kiev and down the great river towards Miklagard. He changes his jester garb for deerskin clothes better suited to a hazardous boat journey and breaks his customary reticence to explain to Harald his Moorish origin, his childhood in North Africa, his life as a slave in Germany and his escape to the life of a wandering trader. Despite this account of his background, he remains mysterious to Harald as he directs this significant period of exile in the young prince's life.

As his name suggests, Asleif Summerbird is a wandering, almost a migratory figure. The tribes all over Europe and Asia look for him at certain times of the year. His standards of conduct, which sometimes seem to the chivalrous Harald lax and ruthless, depend on a shrewd assessment of people and a curious detachment from their emotional misjudgments. 'If men would only think a while before they rush into blood-feuds and vengeances, the world would be a better place

to do business in' he warns Harald. Yet in the end Asleif submits, or seems to submit to violence, for he saves the travellers from roving Patzinak warriors by giving himself up as a hostage.

Harald Hardrada recalls this strange companion of his youth as he girds himself for the battle of Stamford Bridge where, as omens have told him, his destiny awaits him. As he watches the enemy forces he is momentarily deceived by the sight of a soldier with a many-coloured coat, silver fox furs round his shoulders and a wolf's brush on his helmet. At the moment he realizes it is not Asleif, he realizes also that he has received his death wound. Interwoven with historical figures, and with historical fact memorably presented, the character of this strange Moorish trader and wanderer adds another dimension to the story, seeming almost like an elemental, visiting but not belonging to the world of the eleventh century [Henry Treece: *The Last of the Vikings*, Leicester 1964]

**ATLIN**, son of Nit-gass, chief of the Hotsath, has been trained in the ways of the Whale People from his earliest years but when he is twelve his father begins to educate

An illustration by Mary Weiler from *The Whale People*, a story describing the adolescence of an Indian boy in north-west Canada.

him more rigorously as his successor. The boy who has
always been a fine swimmer is now taught to endure
cold so as to face the dangers of a life adapted to the
Pacific Coast in north-west Canada. The boy who has
enjoyed fishing for salmon and herring now learns the
techniques needed to catch seal and sea-lion, until at
last he is pronounced ready to join in his first whaling
expedition.

The basis of Atlin's initiation is custom. His father
has inherited from his forebears the quasi-mythical intuition that makes him, as it were, a friend of the whales.
But prayers to them are not the sole reason for Nit-
gass's success as leader and whale-hunter. He also
explains to the boy in more immediate terms the duties
of a leader of men. Above all he communicates to the
boy his ambivalent attitude as a hunter. He believes he
catches whales not only because he keeps the rituals but
also because of his observation of tides and weathers
and of the behaviour of his intended prey. Atlin grows

up realizing that his father's skills are directly opposed
to those of his less successful rival, the jealous Eskowit,
whose people live in the next inlet. Eskowit, fiercely territorial, uses the magic of skulls and incantations to
ensure that dead whales will drift on the current into
his bay, where he may claim them. When Nit-gass is
killed and Atlin becomes chief, the youth's intelligence
helps him to make a lasting peace with Eskowit without
any loss of dignity for himself or the tribe.

In this notable reconstruction of the life of an Indian
tribe centuries ago, Roderick Haig-Brown has presented his hero historically but the emphasis on ritual
and on Atlin's spiritual growth endows him with the
dignity of myth. The several strands of ethnological
behaviour, mythical inheritance and human feeling
make Atlin a character richly endowed and entirely
credible. [Roderick Haig-Brown: *The Whale People*,
London 1962]

**AUNT PETTITOES** *see* GINGER AND PICKLES

**BABAR** the **ELEPHANT** escaped from the hunter who shot his mother and fled to a town, where he was befriended by a rich old lady who 'understood little elephants and knew at once that he was longing for a smart suit'. The new, mature, well-dressed Babar soon decided to return to his home land, promising never to forget his good friend. He found a country in confusion, for the old king had succumbed to eating a bad mushroom. Old Cornelius suggested Babar should be offered the crown, and after his marriage to his cousin Celeste the new monarchs set out by balloon for their honeymoon. They were wrecked on a cannibal island, escaped on the back of a friendly whale, and eventually reached land. Forced to perform in a circus, escaping again to safety with the old lady, they returned to Babar's kingdom to engage in war with invading rhinoceroses; and in the

An illustration from *The Story of Babar*, the first of many Babar books, written and illustrated by Jean de Brunhoff.

rehabilitation that followed the bloodless victory the old lady, a welcome guest, played a major part.

In subsequent books Jean de Brunhoff described the happy home life of Babar and Celeste and their three children, who were encouraged in mischief by Arthur, Celeste's little brother, and the monkey Zephir (q.v.). Babar takes the lead in the planning of the fine new town of Celesteville, bears bravely the responsibilities and

'Dodder begins his lonely journey up the Folly Brook' from *The Little Grey Men*, illustrated by D. J. Watkins-Pitchford.

anxieties of royalty and enjoys the trust and devotion of his subjects; having provided them with good houses, schools and festivities, he takes a chilly journey in search of Father Christmas, to beg him to extend his route to include the land of the elephants.

34

Jean de Brunhoff died in 1937 and after the war the first of many books was published in which his son Laurent continued the saga of Babar. While he has faithfully copied the style, characters and structure of his father's stories, the pictures show harder colour and a less imaginative handling of detail, and something of Babar's benevolent nature has been lost as he has become a kind of tourist whose travels (to Bird Island, to America and into Space) are described in a somewhat trite chronicle style. Then, too, the sly satire in the early books, the unobtrusive social nuances seen in Babar's conventional middle-class clothes and behaviour, the architectural style of Celesteville and so on, have been smoothed out as Babar has moved from the Great Forest into other spheres. His equable personality has triumphed over these changes, but is not so well pre-served in the miniature books in which the longer stories have been telescoped into texts whose curtness is scarcely supported by modifications of the original illustrations. Still less can we accept the crude television programmes in which a clumsy animated Babar lumbers through one trivial episode after another. Moreover, when we actually hear Babar speaking with a human voice the illusion that he is a real person is destroyed. However, Poulenc added a new and illumi-nating dimension to Babar when he composed a sequence of piano pieces that illustrated the first stories gracefully and expressively and subtly suggested Babar's pachydermatous moods and movements. [Jean de Brunhoff: *The Story of Babar the Little Elephant*, (1931 France) trans. Merle Haas, London 1934; *Babar's Travels*, 1935; *Babar the King*, 1936; *Babar's Friend Zephir*, 1937; *Babar's ABC*, 1937; *Babar at Home*, 1938; *Babar and Father Christmas*, 1940. Laurent de Brunhoff: *Babar and that Rascal Arthur* (1947 France) trans. Olive Jones, London 1948; *Picnic at Babar's*, 1950; *Babar's Visit to Bird Island*, 1952; and other titles]

**BADGER** *see* TOAD OF TOAD HALL

**BALDMONEY, DODDER** and **SNEEZEWORT** are the last gnomes left in Britain – or, not quite the last, for their brother Cloudberry left them some months before to find the source of the Folly Brook. Excited by the first signs of spring, the gnomes decide to go and look for him in their boat, the *Dragonfly*. After surviving an accident in the mill-race, they venture into the out-skirts of Crow Wood and hide in terror from Giant Grum, the gamekeeper. Further upstream they come to the Big Sea, a lake on an estate, where they are wrecked on an island from which there seems no escape; but Dodder finds a clockwork boat and discovers how to work it. The *Jeanie Deans* is a sturdy, well-stocked craft but it is now late autumn and the three travellers regret-fully decide to turn for home – where, to their delight, they find Cloudberry waiting for them.

His stories of an exciting journey to Spitzbergen and back with the wild geese are well received at first but after a while he becomes lazy and boastful; besides, the oak tree that shades their home is felled and there are signs of human interference everywhere. The gnomes decide to retreat to Ireland and travel a long way before their boat breaks up and Baldmoney sets to work to build a glider in which, towed by a friendly owl, they reach the country hospitable to their kind and find a safe home in a cave where a holy hermit once lived.

In his stories of the gnomes 'B.B.' is celebrating the English countryside, as he does in all his books. His gnomes are small, hairy beings 'but a very short step (for the normal imagination) from the wild woodland people'. Carefully equated in size with these, the gnomes differ from them only in their articulate enjoyment of the pleasures of fresh air, fishing, tobacco and good con-versation. Their companionable, tolerant, civilized atti-tude to life, their sense of fun and their response to the variety of the seasons give a wonderful atmosphere to the stories of their adventures. ['B.B.': *The Little Grey Men*, London 1942; *Down the Bright Stream*, 1948]

**BAMBI** the roe deer is born in a German forest into a life which at first is peaceful and secure with his mother's guidance. Gradually, as he grows older, he and his cousins Gobo and Faline begin to realize there is something called danger which they fear but cannot identify. It is, as he discovers one day, a thin, pale creature, giving out a heavy, acrid smell, from whose face comes a kind of dread, 'a cold terror', and who has, as Bambi sees with amazement, an extra leg high up near its face.

Into Felix Salten's moving study of the life of a forest deer, with its delicate balance of humanized words and natural animal behaviour, he works his philosophy of life and death, his love of nature and his hatred of violence – not the preying of one forest animal upon another but the inhuman menace of the hunter's gun.

A scene from Walt Disney's film version of *Bambi*, which did not succeed in reproducing the sensitivity and realism of Felix Salten's original story.

There is no false optimism in the book, however. Gobo, the fragile deer saved from death by Man, wears a halter which the other deer consider a badge of shame, while the sycophantic Dog who tries to explain his devotion to his master only fills them with horror and fear. Man's mercy, as we see through Bambi's reactions, is not to possess and tame but to succour and set free.

Like Sir John Fortescue in *The Story of a Red Deer*, Felix Salten gives his animals appropriate modes of speech – a rapid, wayward chatter to the squirrel, an affected idiom to the butterfly, a noisy and assertive one to the screech owl – but words do not affect the natural pattern of behaviour, and the verbal expression of feeling properly matches instinct. In a long history of falsifying, Walt Disney made no more drastic or mistaken change than when he showed Bambi as a cute, lisping celluloid puppet titupping through a rainbow-hued landscape. A child who came to the book after seeing Disney's cartoon would find it hard to believe that Salten's young deer was the same character. [Felix Salten (pseud. Sigmund Salzmann): *Bambi* (1926 Germany) trans. Whittacker Chambers, London 1928]

**BARNABY LITTLEMOUSE** lives in Toadstool Wood and enjoys suitable miniature adventures, always returning to a house in woodland-style architecture but furnished like a cosy suburban abode. Lightly humanized, the characters of Barnaby and his friends cannot really stand comparison with those of Beatrix Potter or Alison Uttley, but the stories about these engaging little animals were popular with small children two decades ago. [Racey Helps: *The Upside-Down Medicine*, London 1946; *Barnaby and the Scarecrow*; 1953; *Barnaby's Spring Clean*, 1956]

**BARTHOLOMEW CUBBINS** lives in a humble hut on the edge of a cranberry bog. From the doorway he can look up towards the balcony from which King Derwin surveys his kingdom, feeling as small as the monarch feels grand. One day the boy sets off to market wearing his only hat, 'the oldest and plainest hat in the whole kingdom of Didd'. Naturally he takes this off politely when the King passes in his carriage, but to his surprise he is arrested, for an identical hat, with its feather pointing upwards, still remains on his head and as he is led off to the palace, more hats keep blowing off his head.

Wise men, magicians, the Yeoman of the Bowmen, even that belligerent boy Duke Wilfred, all fail to stop another hat appearing on Bartholomew's head as soon as one is removed. The suggestion that the boy's head should be cut off is ruled out by the executioner, who insists it is against the rules for him to operate on anyone wearing a hat. Finally, when the unfortunate lad has been led up the turret stairs to his doom, the King accidentally finds a solution. The hats, swept off by the wind one by one, have become increasingly elaborate, and the monarch is tempted by the rubies and exotic plumes on the five-hundredth. He offers to buy it – and

immediately there is Bartholomew, bareheaded but with five hundred gold pieces to take home.

In this book, as in *And to Think that I Saw It on Mulberry Street*, fancy and reason are shown on a collision course. The two books, which took a surprisingly long time to reach England, are less zany than the later Seuss Beginner-Books, and one may be forgiven for preferring his chubby, ingenuous little boys to the nightmarish zoo animals which supplanted them. [Dr Seuss: *The Five Hundred Hats of Bartholomew Cubbins*, New York 1938]

**BASIL** is a mouse who, in the year 1885, designs the model town of Holmstead in the cellar of 221 Baker Street, a community of flats, shops, a town hall and other amenities, so that this super sleuth may live conveniently near to his (unwitting) mentor and model, Sherlock Holmes. Basil's close friend and associate, Dr David Q. Dawson, faithfully and admiringly records his cases, stressing Basil's international reputation and listening (not uncritically) as Basil plays his home-made violin. He reports many of his instant deductions too. ('He was once a sailor, he now follows the trade of carpenter, and he comes from the north-west of England. Near the coast, I'd say. Furthermore, his initials are H.H., and he traveled here by train.')

With his lean jaw and piercing eyes, his Norfolk cape and deerstalker (copied from Holmes's wardrobe by 'a clever little tailor'), Basil is a worthy disciple of the great detective, and his mouse-size cases are described by author and artist alike in a spirit of respectful parody, which never diminishes the personality or distorts the natural capacities of the brilliant, imperturbable mouse. [Eve Titus, ill. Paul Galdone: *Basil of Baker Street*, New York 1958; *Basil and the Lost Colony*, 1964; *Basil and the Pygmy Cats*, 1971]

**BASTABLES** (the) – Dora, Oswald, Dickie, Alice, Noel and H. O. – decide to be treasure-seekers because, as Oswald says when he puts forward the idea, '... it is always what you do to restore the fallen fortunes of your House'. The defalcation of their father's business partner has brought them to a semi-detached house in the Lewisham Road. The Bastables have an unmatched propensity for creating or getting into trouble, always from the best possible motives. Digging for treasure in the back garden, they succeed in burying Albert next door; their plans to rescue a benevolent old gentleman in distress, to publish Noel's poetry, to run a newspaper, to sell sherry on commission, all lead to retribution. In fact it is the only plan of theirs not designed to make money (entertaining a 'poor Indian' to dinner) that brings about a happy change in the family fortunes and a move to a fine house on the Heath. From here, and from the Moat House in Sussex where they spend one glorious summer, episodic adventures, all steered erratically by good though mistaken aims, make up the two later books about the Bastables.

The exploits of the family are described by Oswald,

The six Bastable children, drawn by Susan Einzig.

Dora, who is about fourteen when the adventures begin, feels very keenly her mother's last wish that she should 'take care of the others, and teach them to be good, and keep them out of trouble and make them happy.' The perceptive reader will see how hard it is for Dora, who still has plenty of the spirit of mischief in her, to have to 'talk like the good elder sister in books', as Oswald puts it. She is no coward but, like Susan in the 'Swallows and Amazons' stories, she suffers from being poised between the grown-ups and her siblings.

Alice at ten is a girl who (though emotional about animals) can be as tough as a boy in a crisis, quite unperturbed by torn clothes, insisting on having her hair cut short so that she can play boys' parts, and ready to defend the family honour with tooth and nail (literally in 'Over the water to China', in *The New Treasure Seekers*, when she does noble work in a fight with street boys, even if she does succumb afterwards to 'a sudden attack of crybabyishness').

Her twin Noel has a different kind of courage, the difficult courage of a child with fragile health and fluctuating energies. Though his brothers and sisters are protective when they need to be, knowing that he is afraid of dark tunnels and threats of police and that he is liable to faint in unpleasant moments, Noel never trades on this. He keeps his end up and provides his own encouragement by his imagination, which is nourished by wide reading (from which, also, he draws the phraseology he deems suitable for dramatic occasions). His habit of stopping to write poetry in the midst of action is not altogether popular with the rest but they never criticize either the habit or the poems, because it upsets him so much; his poetry tells us about his character and adds humour to a scene as well.

The youngest member of a family has a special position, and Edith Nesbit makes the most of this in characterizing H.O. In fact his character *is* to a large extent his position – that is, we both see and hear him *as* the youngest. There are times when he complains of being left out because of his age, and then family justice compels the others to include him: at other times he is just as ready to get his own way by insisting that he should be left out – of chores or punishment – because he is the youngest. His greatest moment is perhaps in 'The road to Rome' (in *The New Treasure Seekers*) when he hides in a dressing basket to get free transport to Rome, where he plans to become a clown and, as he says in his farewell note, 'When I am rich and reveared I will come back rolling'. The experience, which might be alarming to any child of eight, of being hurled about on the railway and dumped as lost luggage, gives H.O. only momentary qualms, and his anxious family find him enjoying an impromptu meal in the station office. It is clear that a name like Horace Octavius is totally inadequate for such an enterprising small boy.

The one Bastable who seems a little hazy in outline is Dicky, who stands between Oswald and the twins

but not in the first person. 'It is one of us that tells the story', the reader is warned at the outset, 'but I shall not tell you which: only at the very end perhaps I will.' Offhand but reverberant praise of Oswald ('... he knows it is through no merit of his own that he is much cleverer than some people'); sundry consistent opinions about girls' and dolls' tea-parties or about marriage; now and then a lapse into the first person – these are enough to reveal the truth. To use Oswald as narrator was a master stroke. It allowed Edith Nesbit to steer her narrative without seeming to do so and to add an ironic note to Oswald's artless comments on the adult point of view as it differs from that of a child.

Oswald does not only dominate the stories as narrator. He is also an organic character, growing and developing through the year or two covered by the three books. In *The Story of the Treasure Seekers* he is consistently puzzled by the unplanned results of his actions; his sense of what is honourable and what is not is a matter of upbringing rather than of understanding. But as time goes on simple adventures begin to pall – 'the worst of growing up is that you seem to want more and more to have a bit of the real thing in your games' – and with this illusion comes an increasing sympathy, reluctant though it may be, with Dora's view of life, a realization that 'Your feelings are a beastly nuisance, if once you begin to let yourself think about them.'

in age. At the beginning of *The Story of the Treasure Seekers*, Oswald comments: 'Dicky always wants everything settled exactly. Father calls him the Definite Article', and Dicky's words and actions are certainly consistent with this. For instance, in *The Wouldbegoods*, when he and Oswald decide that the girls' idea for the activities of their new Society must be carefully edited, Dicky suggests 'Let's begin by looking out for something useful to do – something like mending things or cleaning them, not just showing off'. But this seems to be the one point on which Dicky's character rests. Otherwise he is very much the second in command, occasionally asserting himself with Oswald but usually

giving him the backing he needs, his sensible manner making a useful contrast to the more flamboyant personality of his elder brother.

The Bastables, in their squabbles, and their united stand against the world, are recognizably a family. Edith Nesbit has skilfully manipulated the individuals she has created so as to make a family pattern which will allow her the greatest possible scope for variation on the theme of an intelligent, high-spirited group of children of seventy years ago. [Edith Nesbit: *The Story of the Treasure Seekers*, London 1899; *The Wouldbegoods*, 1901; *The New Treasure Seekers*, 1904]

**BEE-MAN OF ORN** is so called 'because his whole

An illustration by Maurice Sendak of the Bee-man in *The Bee-man of Orn*.

time was spent in the company of bees'. He may be 'ugly, untidy, shrivelled, and brown' but he is satisfied with his gently energetic, well-ordered existence; practical good sense is in evidence everywhere, especially in the neat arrangement by which he carries one swarm of bees 'in a pocket of his old leathern doublet', to provide him with food and company when he walks abroad.

Solitary by habit, the simple Bee-Man is hardly equipped to resist the mistaken opinion of a Junior Sorcerer who stops one day at his hut. Having studied for a long time 'exactly why the old Bee-Man did not happen to be something that he was not, and why he was what he happened to be', the Junior Sorcerer is convinced that the old man has been transformed and sets him on his wanderings to find out who he should really be.

In a cave watched over by a Very Imp, the Bee-Man, as it were in passing, rescues a baby from a dragon and is so strongly drawn to the little creature that he decides this must be what he is intended to be. Changed into a lusty infant by the delighted Junior Sorcerer, the Bee-Man is given into the care of the mother whose child he has rescued. Alas for cleverness! Years afterwards the Junior Sorcerer, now of Senior rank, passes through Orn again to find the Bee-Man has 'grown up into the same thing again!'

This wise little parable, told in limpid prose, presents one of the most pleasing portraits of a good ugly man to be found in junior fantasy, besides making, unobtrusively, an important psychological point. Maurice Sendak's illustrations for an American edition of 1964 celebrate especially well the warmth and wisdom of a storyteller beloved by children in the last century. [Frank Stockton: *The Bee-Man of Orn*, New York 1887. As picture-book, New York 1964]

**BEN BLEWITT** wakes on the morning of his birthday convinced that his one desire in life will be fulfilled, for his grandfather has as good as promised him a dog as a present. Slowly, reluctantly, he realizes that the parcel

Ben Blewitt with the spaniel Tilly's puppies, drawn by Antony Maitland for *A Dog So Small*.

from old Mr and Mrs Fitch can hardly be what he is expecting – yet in a literal sense it is, for it contains a needlework picture of a chihuahua, long cherished by his grandmother as the last gift of her sailor son. In a household as large and bustling as the Blewitts', emotional scenes are out of the question, but imagination finds a way to compensate for disappointment. Ben begins to believe that the tiny animal is a live dog, bold and responsive, so vividly can he see it behind his closed eyes. At last, rushing blindly over a crossing after the prancing Chiquitito, he is knocked down by a car. Recovering from his injuries, he visits his grandparents in Suffolk and there one of the spaniel Tilly's puppies becomes his special favourite and when the Blewitt family finds a new home near Hampstead Heath, Brown becomes in truth his own dog. But, as Granny Fitch remarks, 'People get their heart's desire . . . and then they have to begin to learn how to live with it.' When Ben goes to fetch Brown, who was once as small as his ideal dog, he finds a gangling mongrel, nervous instead of alert, clumsy instead of dainty. Angry and miserable, he takes the hated substitute-dog to the Heath and tries to drive it away – and, all at once, realizes that it *is* his wanted dog after all.

Because of the spare, selective simplicity of the prose, the weight of metaphor and emotion in the book is carried easily in the character of Ben. First, his position as the middle child of five is shown to be important; the practical outlook of his parents, the giggling chatter of his older sisters and the jostling and cheek of his younger brothers are reason enough for Ben's isolation and his quiet, dogged manner. Then his mood is indicated in phrases that describe, briefly but significantly, an exact gesture, attitude or movement. On Ben's birthday, while the family exclaim and speculate over the Fitches' present, he sits still and silent and his hands 'half-hidden by the wrapping-paper that his mother has picked up from the floor, clenched into angry fists'. His stance in the guard's van on the way back to London – 'he sat at a distance, on a crate of chickens, his face turned away from the dog' – is more telling than a direct statement of his feelings would have been. Rich in metaphor and feeling, *A Dog So Small* presents a character created in depth, endowed with individuality, whose problem may be translated into the experience of each and every reader. [Philippa Pearce: *A Dog So Small*, London 1962]

**BENJAMIN BUNNY** *see* PETER RABBIT

**BENJAMIN DICKINSON CARR** had a 'concentric twin'. That is, there was a little man inside him called George who spoke out now and then, in a deep and assured voice quite different from his own. Ben's mother had accepted George because 'Most creative children have imaginary playmates', but it suited Ben better as he grew older to keep George strictly inside him. This worked so long as George's admonitions were acceptable, but there came a time when he took such an opposite view from Ben's that life became difficult. Because of his exceptionally high I.Q., Ben at twelve found himself in a school for gifted children. He fell under the spell of William Hazlitt, whose nickname of Flash did not only express admiration. Ben was so flattered to be asked to help in William's chemistry project that he barely avoided an irrevocable quarrel with George, who insisted that William was a phoney and a danger to Ben.

Meanwhile Ben's father, who had re-married after a divorce, became concerned about the boy's behaviour and his wife, an ardent amateur psychologist, drew her own conclusions when she heard Ben talking in his sleep. Ben's sensible mother, though she found Marilyn's diagnosis of schizophrenia amusing, was obliged to send him to a psychiatrist, who realized that 'even the George part ... is in touch with reality'. That reality was, in fact, an ugly one. William and his girl friend were making LSD in the lab. and when Ben realized that George's estimate of William had been correct he took a desperate course to try to help the situation.

Elaine Konigsburg's very active metaphor of personality was indicated in the brackets round the original title of her book, but it proved so puzzling that it was subsequently changed to *Benjamin Dickinson Carr and His George*. The use of Ben's second self, his symbiotic friend and mentor, is part of the enigmatic, elliptical way in which she approaches the difficulties of growing up – which, to her, seems to mean growing together, for something young and undeveloped in Ben's emotional self has to catch up his precocious intellect. This is an exceptionally shrewd study of a gifted boy, in which humour and image combine in a rich texture. [E. L. Konigsburg: (*George*), New York 1970; first English edition 1971, new English edition *Benjamin Dickinson Carr and His (George)*, 1975]

**BENNY** is a little Jewish boy living in Fern Street, Manchester. Every spring for a week or so children come from all over the neighbourhood to play three nut games – cupky (a simple affair of skittling), another game built round the potholes in the flagstones, and (best of all) the game of skill which the proud possessor of a shoe-box is allowed to start with a loud 'Roll up! Roll up!' Where could Benny get a shoe-box? The ragman gave him an idea when Benny overheard him telling Evelyn, who was disappointed with the balloon he had given her in return for old clothes, 'You keep on giving, love. And one day you'll get the thing you want.' So, starting with his balloon, Benny embarked on a chain of giving, swapping and asking until one glorious day he got his box, for his dressmaker mother, who had not been willing to spare the one she used for her trimmings, was glad to exchange it for a more convenient biscuit tin, itself the end of a series of exchanges.

Within the neatly devised chain-story there emerges a rich, compassionate, warmly authentic picture of a working-class district complete with its own customs

One of Jillian Willet's illustrations for *A Box for Benny*.

and character, with which is twisted another chain, the chain-of-being of a small boy whose lively response to his own world changes as each encounter stirs new feeling and new understanding. [Leila Berg: *A Box for Benny*, Leicester 1958]

**BENNY,** known to generations of readers as 'Froggy's little brother', dies in a bare attic at the age of six, a child seemingly deprived of all the rights of childhood – food, parental care, fresh air, occupation. Yet Benny is one of the brightest, bravest, most resourceful small boys in the fiction of the last century. Secure in his brother's love and protection, he amuses himself with whatever comes to hand. He tries to harness the cat when he feels like playing horses and makes a real friend of a mouse, which gets a share of his meagre meals. His artless comments, his modest attempts at teasing, his vivid speech ('I wish we was like the cats, I does ... cos they're born with nice little fur trousers on their legs'), are the concomitants of a real personality. His death-bed dream of angels seems a natural fancy on the part of a small boy whose sensitive response to Froggy's stories has triumphed over the pains of his frail body. ['Brenda' (pseud. Mrs G. Castle Smith): *Froggy's Little Brother*, London 1875]

**BERIC,** son of Parta, chieftainess of a tribe of the Iceni, is sent as a boy to live in the household of Caius, commander of a Roman Legion. Though the boy accepts the education and manner of the Roman conquerors, he remains loyal to his race, so that when he is allowed to return briefly to the tribe he is ready to be persuaded that he might become the leader to rouse the Britons against the Romans. At the age of sixteen Beric is man enough to face a future of grave responsibility, realizing that 'our dissensions have been our ruin', but though he serves bravely in the forces led by Boadicea he is ultimately captured by Suetonius and taken to Rome. Eventually he accepts the post of librarian to Nero on condition that he need not take up any political stand. With such a change in allegiance it is inevitable that he should be exiled under suspicion of treachery and finally allowed to return to Britain to rule his people under Roman orders.

Hero only in title, Beric is a figure-head whose life illustrates various aspects of life in Britain and Rome in the second century A.D. The stilted manner of speech, though in part natural to Henty and his period, is dictated also by convenience; most of Beric's utterances are formal, designed to convey facts or attitudes to the reader. *Beric the Briton* is a fair example of Henty's method as an historical novelist. In his books, if any characters do come to life, they are minor figures who have no informative role in the story. [G. A. Henty: *Beric the Briton*, London 1893]

**BERKSHIRE PIGWIG** *see* GINGER AND PICKLES

**BERNARD** *see* MISS BIANCA

**BERTIE** is a pig of action; 'Deeds, not grunts', is his motto. At eleven o'clock one winter night, shortly before Christmas, he decides to go carol-singing. Hauling the sleepy rabbits, Peter and Benjie, out of their straw, he leads them through a tunnel in a chalk-pit and into a convenient lift operated by a mole. At that point the efficiency of the expedition declines. Mr Stone, first recipient of their attentions, does not appreciate their 'bewitching carols' and they have to leave hastily on account of the dogs. Undaunted, Bertie raids Mr Grahame's larder and provides a feast including cold chicken, trifle and champagne; the healths that are drunk put the animals into a deep sleep that puzzles the involuntary host next morning.

In this brief Christmas fancy Kenneth Grahame seems to foreshadow both Rat and Toad in the character of ebullient, dominant Bertie, while perhaps offering quiet homage by the way to Beatrix Potter. [Kenneth Grahame: *Bertie's Escapade*, London 1949, from a manuscript in the Bodleian Library entitled *First Whisper of the Wind in the Willows*]

**BETH ELLEN HANSEN,** who is twelve, is driven to school by a chauffeur, and Harriet Welsch (q.v.), despises her for her mousy ways and her habit of agreeing with everyone. Harriet's judgements are apt to be hasty but she does eventually realize that Beth Ellen is a more interesting person than she had thought. In *The Long Secret* she begins to visit the large house where Beth Ellen lives with her fierce, uncompromising grandmother, and begins to understand and sympathize with this reserved girl, whose mother is almost always away in Biarritz and whose sudden irruption into Beth's life with a new stepfather for her shows how much happier she is likely to be with her strict grandmother. The secret which the indefatigable Harriet discovers and partly understands is that Beth Ellen has been assuaging her doubts about life by sending anonymous letters telling

various people that 'Jesus hates you'. The feeling of power she derives from this helps her to find a voice of her own and to stand up to Harriet's teasing. Besides, if Harriet makes her feel protected at times, her constant assumption of superiority has been an important factor too in Beth Ellen's discovery of herself. This is an unusually subtle version of the 'poor little rich girl' character. [Louise Fitzhugh: *Harriet the Spy*, New York 1964; *The Long Secret*, 1965]

**BETSY** is nine when she has to leave the gentle, enclosed life in the city which she shared with Great-aunt Harriet and quiet Aunt Frances and go to her Putney cousins in Vermont. The idea frightens her, for she has gathered that they are 'a stiff-necked, cold-hearted, undemonstrative, and hard set of New Englanders'. Indeed, most things frighten Elizabeth Ann, who has been taught to think of herself as delicate and sensitive and has been used to having all her moods and fancies understood instantly by the conscientious ladies. When her Great-uncle Henry, who has made no tender enquiries about how she has stood the journey, hands over the reins of the wagon to her halfway to the farm, she is astonished to find that she can actually control the huge animals. It is the first of a great many surprises. One by one the little girl overcomes her fears – of the shaggy dog Shep, of Cousin Ann's abrupt manner, of the strong air of the country. She learns to laugh and to enjoy doing things for herself instead of waiting for other people to do them for her. Aunt Frances finds a changed child when she comes to Vermont to discuss Betsy's future and Betsy finds that the people she had dreaded not only understand her very well but also want her as a permanent member of the family. She remains one of the most endearing children in fiction, as the story remains a classic narrative of a protected child learning that happiness is not a passive state but an active one. [Dorothy Canfield: *Understood Betsy* (English title *Betsy*), New York 1916]

**BEVERLEY** children (the) – Edward, Humphrey, Alice and Edith – remained at Arnwood after their father was killed while fighting for the King, but when an old family servant, Jacob Armitage, by chance overheard a group of Roundhead troopers planning to search and set fire to all Royalist houses in the New Forest area he brought the children safely to his cottage in the forest, letting it be supposed that they had all perished in the fire and putting them into country clothes so that they might convincingly pose as his grandchildren.

The details of their forest housekeeping have made this story a favourite with children of many generations, especially as Marryat used a neutral style of dialogue so that the conversation sounds as natural as the various reactions of the Beverleys to farming and to housewifery. His picture of a Royalist family in the Civil War is an unusually balanced one. Though the Beverleys never forget their loyalty to the King and are rewarded

for it at the time of the Restoration, Edward falls in love with the daughter of a liberal-minded Parliamentarian, and their marriage is in keeping with the broad principles of industry and kindliness which provide a good foundation for the congenial course of the story. [Captain Marryat: *The Children of the New Forest*, London 1847]

**BEVIS** and his friend Mark enjoyed the freedom of the Wiltshire downs and farmland over a century ago. Their exploits – swimming, fitting a boat with sails, making rafts, catamarans, an efficient hut with a stockade and even a matchlock gun – are partly those remembered by Jefferies from his own country childhood; the book was written while he lay ill in a town late in his life.

This is no introspective self-portrait, but a direct, sincere presentation of a boy in his relation to a country environment. Bevis will shoot animals, not only for food but also to practise a useful skill. He is naturally aggressive, and his leadership of the local lads is not often challenged, although Mark rouses himself now and then to insist on some fair division of spoils or opportunity. ('You want everything your own way', he tells Bevis, and the reply comes at once, 'Of course I do. I'm captain'.) Bevis has another side to his character, in his sure response to the unexpected beauties and changes of nature and in his sensitive affection for his father, 'the governor' as he calls him.

Impatient, resourceful, energetic, full of an active imagination sustained by favourite books like *The Odyssey*, Bevis is one of the happiest creations in the stories which the young have claimed from adults as their own. In the evolution of the genre he looks back to the primal ancestor, Robinson Crusoe, and forward to innumerable descendants, foremost among them the brothers in B.B.'s *Brendon Chase* and Ransome's *Swallows and Amazons* [Richard Jefferies: *Bevis, the Story of a Boy*, London 1882]

**BIG TIGER** (Hu-ta) and Christian are two boys of twelve whose innocent and unplanned sortie from Peking initiates a long journey north of the Great Wall of China, across the Gobi Desert and through the provinces of Kanchu and Sinkiang as they were in 1922. Christian is the son of an English doctor, his life as closely organized by his ayah as his Chinese friend's is by the formal structure of his family. The two of them are accidentally carried off in a train full of soldiers mobilized in one of the revolutionary movements of the time. They become prisoners of war, but General Wu-Pe-Fu finds a use for them as messengers and on a journey that involves them with bandits, con-men and nomads, they take such part in dangerous adult activities as boys can reasonably do – lurking and overhearing, discussing and unravelling the significance of small incidents that perhaps only the young would notice.

Bevis and Mark build a hut; an illustration by E. H. Shepard from *Bevis, the Story of a Boy*.

In the magnificent geographical sweep of the book, against a strongly etched background of mountain and desert, the personalities of the boys unfold. Christian's impatience and drive usefully balance Big Tiger's constitutional tendency to accept every situation as unalterable. Christian writes on the last page of his notebook, at the end of their adventures, that Big Tiger's aged grandfather had patted their heads and 'said it was good thing for boys to start being brave and enterprising in their early years. Big Tiger and I think he's right there'. The casual adaptability of boys has seldom been more shrewdly, certainly never more originally, explored in fiction. [Fritz Mühlenweg: *Big Tiger and Christian* (1950 Germany) trans. Florence and Isobel McHugh, London 1954]

**BIGGLES** (James Bigglesworth) started as a pilot in the RFC and after the Second World War became a detective, serving with Interpol and ending at the head of the Air Section of the CID, responsible to Scotland Yard and supported by his long-standing associates – Ginger Hebblethwaite, Algy Lacey and Lord Bertie Lissie (who dropped his title but who reminded everyone of it by wearing a monacle and giving vent to such expressions as 'old boy' and 'by gad'). There have been at least eighty books about Biggles, during which time he and his comrades have chased crooks, found treasure, tracked down spies and survived every kind of danger in every part of the world.

Biggles was first created as the centre of stories in which Captain Johns could use his experience as a pilot in the First World War. A long series of this kind cannot afford much change in the circumstances or personality of its characters. Biggles and his comrades are very lightly distinguished from one another and in the later books they exhibit the cliché mannerisms and idioms which have become associated with the wartime RAF. Biggles exercises authority lightly, confident in his superior brains, acumen and knowledge of the world and showing a curiously matter of fact, detached attitude to his adventures (signalized by the frequent phrase 'he said cynically'). Besides being brave, practical and lucky, Biggles reads widely (it is hard to see when he has time to do this) and has a habit, better suited to books of information, of giving unsolicited lectures on relevant sidelines of geography or history, to which his colleagues listen gratefully. The contrast between these stiffly grammatical pieces of exposition and Biggles's normal clipped, outmoded slang might be more entertaining if it were not for the simplistic philosophy which has caused the books to be outlawed in some libraries in recent years. The title of one of the books, *Biggles defies the Swastika*, is typical of a certain us-and-them attitude which is being questioned more and more as a basis for junior adventure stories and which, with one or two exceptions, is the accepted attitude in the Biggles series – an attitude which belongs essentially to its early years. [Captain W.E. Johns: 'The White Fokker', in *Popular Flying* 1932; *The*

An illustration by Stead in *Biggles Breaks the Silence*.

*Camels are Coming*, London 1932 and several other collections of stories. 'Biggles' books: *Biggles of the Camel Squadron*, London 1934; *Biggles Flies Again*, 1934; *Biggles Learns to Fly*, 1935; *Biggles Flies East*, 1935; *Biggles and Co.*, 1936; and many other titles]

**BILBO BAGGINS,** when his great adventure with the dwarfs is some years behind him, sets to work on his memoirs, which he thinks of calling 'There and Back Again, a Hobbit's Holiday'. If the title has an ironical ring, in view of the terrors of Mirkwood, the rigours of the Lonely Mountain and the devastation left by the Five Armies, the irony does not come from Bilbo. He does not return from the adventure any less warm-hearted and ingenuous than he is when he sets out. He has changed, all the same. The strain of adventurousness he has inherited from his famous mother Belladonna Took has come to dominate the sober, cautious Baggins side of him, and the comment of the dwarfs that he is more of a grocer than a burglar proves untrue, for he has undoubtedly acted the burglar, and successfully.

When Gandalf the Wizard visits Bilbo's comfortable burrow-home at Hobbiton he fixes a notice on the door which indicates to the thirteen dwarfs that if they want to recover their long-lost treasure from Smaug the dragon, the hobbit is their man. The dwarfs annoy Bilbo from the start. They crowd into his house, command their favourite dishes for supper and breakfast, start on the journey without him and use him as a scapegoat for everything that goes wrong. All the same, as one danger after another (capture by trolls, near-suffocation by the hideous spiders of Mirkwood, imprisonment by elves, the blasting breath of Smaug) is escaped partly, if not wholly, because of the hobbit, they begin to realize that Gandalf was right in his assessment of this small, determined creature.

The scene of the exchange of riddles with Gollum by the underground lake is crucial to the story, for it is here that Bilbo picks up the little gold ring, Gollum's most precious possession, the ring that confers invisibility and thus gives Bilbo confidence and makes many of his later exploits possible. The confrontation with Gollum has a mystery and terror unlike anything else in the book. Whether or not Tolkien already had it in mind to develop this character further when he wrote *The Hobbit*, he chose a different way of describing him from the few but explicit classifying details with which he introduced the hobbit and the various beings he meets in the course of his adventures. Gollum is either described in negatives ('I don't know where he came from, nor who or what he was') or with phrases that stir imagination strongly (he has 'pale lamp-like eyes' and long fingers, he rows a boat on the cold lake where he lives on a 'slimy island of rock'). Then, too, as though evading identification, Gollum alludes to himself as a third person, 'my precious', a term he also uses for the ring of power which holds him in thrall to evil and with which he is associated so significantly in *The Lord of the Rings*.

The riddle contest he and Bilbo hold further deepens Gollum's character by linking him with one of the great languages of myth. Finally, the innocent, warm response of the hobbit towards life is evoked most of all by Gollum. Having defeated the creature by sheer luck and persistence, the hobbit suddenly has 'a glimpse of endless unmarked days without light or hope of betterment, hard stone, cold fish, sneaking and whispering'. The pity he feels adds a new, important element to the story, and it gives a final, sharp picture of Gollum, that unrealized and superbly real character.

Bilbo Baggins has no wish to be conventionally heroic; indeed, during the final, fierce battle of the Five Armies he uses the ring to help him, for if a magic ring is 'not a complete protection in a goblin charge ... it prevents your head from being specially chosen for a sweeping stroke by a goblin swordsman'. The deflationary remark is typical of the hobbit. Just so he counters the ceremonial farewell of Balin – 'If ever you visit us again, when our halls are made fair once more, then the feast shall indeed be splendid!' – with the characteristic answer 'If ever you are passing my way ... don't wait to knock. Tea is at four, but any of you are welcome at any time!' Moderate, too, but unmistakable, is the change in Bilbo's behaviour in Hobbiton after his return, but it is enough to isolate him somewhat from his neighbours. Because he is often visited by dwarfs and wizards, he is held to be 'queer', especially as he has taken to writing poetry. All the same, though his neighbours pity him, he 'remained very happy to the end of his days, and those were extraordinarily long'. If ever there was an autobiographical note in a book, this is surely one of the most endearing, in a story which Tolkien told by instalments to his children long before he put it into book form; there is surely a wry, urbane self-portrait in Bilbo Baggins.

Paul Kocher, in his book *Master of Middle-Earth*, rightly calls *The Hobbit* a quarry for *The Lord of the Rings* rather than the book for which the later epic was a true sequel. Certainly the humorous, intimate, relaxed tone of *The Hobbit* is entirely different from the orotund, concentrated magic of the saga of Frodo Baggins, who as hero bears a far heavier burden than Bilbo ever did. All the same, Mr Kocher hardly allows enough credit for the skill and the subtlety with which the character of the hobbit is drawn and the very mature attitude that lies behind his seemingly comic, even clownish behaviour in the story. The characters in the epic may stand taller, their words may carry further, but the hobbit is a personality as vivid and as recognizable. [J. R. R. Tolkien: *The Hobbit, or There and Back Again*, London 1937]

**BILL MELBURY,** a schoolboy of fifteen, is determined to be a writer but feels it safer to tell people that he means to teach. When his mother decides to move from the city to the wilds of Cumberland, he and his younger sister Sue find congenial friends in Penny Morchard, daughter of the scholarly bookseller in the nearest town, and Tim Darren, whose efforts at amateur detection help (or so he believes) to forward his ambition to enter the police force.

Geoffrey Trease has chosen his four characters well. Penny's energetic nature, the tenacity that compensates for her lameness, balance Sue's commonsense and her enthusiasm for country ways, while Bill's book-learning and Tim's flair for deduction stand them in good stead when they are involved with successive mysteries and activities – Sir Alfred Askew's sharp dealing over an archaeological discovery and a farm sequestered by the War Office (in *No Boats on Bannermere*), amateur theatricals in *Black Banner Players* and *Black Banner Abroad;* while in *The Gates of Bannerdale* Bill, now an Oxford undergraduate, helps to locate the college silver, lost for centuries. Just as Geoffrey Trease set himself to counteract the artificiality of the junior historical fiction of the '30s by more politically alert stories, so in the Bannerdale books he refreshed the tired holiday adventure

with its smugglers' caves and hidden treasure by showing boys and girls in everyday life, in the classroom and the kitchen, the local library and the café, and allowing them to entertain natural, gently indicated adolescent feelings for one another. His characters are not helped either by improbable good fortune or by exceptional advantages of mind and body. They are ordinary but individual boys and girls, maturing and changing over the five or six years covered by the books, drawn not in great depth (since this would be unsuitable for the genre) but with such details as are needed to ensure that the events of the stories properly relate to the actors in them.

Without suggesting that Bill Melbury is directly based on the author's self-when-young, it is permissible to point out how closely Bill's ambitions to be a writer and his deliberate gathering of experience parallel the experience of the young Geoffrey Trease. Trease himself has made it clear that he deliberately chooses for his historical novels civilized periods which will supply him with literate characters. No less in the Bannerdale books, books and theatre are a natural accompaniment to life. Then again, for first-person narrative it is necessary (though not all writers do this) to choose a suitable narrator. Because Bill Melbury wants to write he naturally takes charge of the stories and, in a kind of double bluff, sees the events he is engaged in as potential material for stories. We absorb his view of Penny Morchard, of old Kingsford the grammar school headmaster and Miss Florey, the redoubtable red-headed headmistress of the girls' secondary – a barely retrospective, one-sided, enquiring schoolboy's view. Youthful and instructable (but never naïve), Bill is a likeable, recognizable boy in terms of the '50s – recognizable, in fact, in the '70s as well, for all the supposedly greater sophistication and worldly knowledge of young readers of today. [Geoffrey Trease: *No Boats on Bannermere*, London 1949; *Under Black Banner*, 1951; *Black Banner Players*, 1952; *Black Banner Abroad*, 1954; *The Gates of Bannerdale*, 1956]

**BILL STARBRIGHT** *see* SUSAN BROOKS

**BILL THE MINDER** is employed as a surrogate nurse when his uncle, old Crispin the mushroom-gatherer, suddenly falls ill, and his wife Chloe, overburdened by ten children (of whom only one was good-tempered), decides she needs help. Bill reads all the books on the subject of Minding in the British Museum library and becomes 'as well known in the Reading Room of the Patent Museum at South Kensington as in his father's house'. Indeed, he becomes so skilled as a Minder that he wins the gold-mounted feeding bottle offered by the Duke at a Minding Tournament. When his job with Crispin's family comes to an end. Bill undertakes to look after the exiled King of Troy and restore him to his kingdom. and this aim he achieves after a long journey.

Bill becomes, in the later part of this wayward and

idiosyncratic book, little more than a compère for a series of strange characters who join his army on the slow march to Troy – characters like the Lost Grocer, the Wild Man and the Sicilian Charwoman, whose personalities are glimpsed in the stories which they tell and, more directly, in the superbly mad illustrations. [W. Heath Robinson: *Bill the Minder*, London 1912]

**BILLY BUNTER,** the Fat Owl of the Remove, began as a minor character in stories of Greyfriars School which centred round Harry Wharton, a headstrong youth sent to school for discipline rather than for education. Lively, candid Harry, one of a long line of schoolboy heroes, gathered round him a little group consisting of Bob Cherry, Frank Nugent, Johnny Bull and Hurree Jamset Ram Singh (whose wealth and position contrasted oddly with his astonishing Babu English). William George Bunter, at first just comic relief, soon swelled into monstrous prominence. A useful target for derision, abysmally stupid yet endowed with cunning, unashamed of his greed, cowardice and dishonesty and unaware of the absurdity of his excuses, with a personal idiom made up of animal grunts and screams, raucous laughter ('He he' instead of 'Ha ha') and the broken accents of temporary penitence, the fat boy soon dominated the pages of *The Magnet*, which adopted as a subtitle 'Billy Bunter's Own Paper'.

There are ways of enduring Bunter. One is to meet him as a magazine character, either in strip-stories or single anecdotes. In that form, the noisy slapstick episodes are totally unreal; there is no time to take the stylized characters seriously. When Bunter becomes the centre of long, properly constructed stories, it is not possible to avoid looking on him as a member of the human race and what one sees is shockingly displeasing. Bunter was conceived as a composite of four particular men known to the author: the combination of their mannerisms and appearance has resulted in a freak in a comic-fantasy world. [Frank Richards (pseud. Charles Hamilton): 'Billy Bunter' stories in *The Magnet Library*, 1908–29, *The Magnet* 1929–40; *Billy Bunter of Greyfriars School*, London 1947; and many other titles]

**BIRDIE BOYERS** comes with her family to a district in Florida settled by folk known in 1900 as 'Crackers', English families who had drifted there sixty years before and who still live a primitive kind of life. Lois Lenski uses Birdie as a way of describing a typical Cracker family, the Slaters. Birdie chooses a friend from the Slater family in spite of various unneighbourly acts on the part of the shiftless father. In fact she and twelve-year-old 'Shoe-string' Slater do their best to reconcile the two families and to help Mr Boyers to convince the local folk that strawberries could be established in the district as a paying crop. Birdie, we are told, looks like a little bird; she is given little beyond this one attribute. She is simply one of the many children through whom Lois Lenski reflected the old ways of life·surviving in many parts of the United States in the present century.

[Lois Lenski: *Strawberry Girl*, Philadelphia and New York 1945]

**BLACK BEAUTY** begins life as 'Darkie', running free on a farm, but his breeding is good. For this reason, and because the farmer who has bred him refuses to break or work him too soon, the horse has a strength and a sweetness of disposition which stands him in good stead in his long, eventful life. The various names he receives reflect his circumstances. When he goes to Birtwick Park as a riding and carriage horse, Squire Gordon's lady decides that 'Black Beauty' will suit the fine animal. The name is not grand enough, however, when Beauty goes to the stables of the Earl of S., there to be 'Black Auster'. With his knees ruined by a drunken groom, the horse descends in the social scale. After a depressing period in a livery stable he is bought by Jimmy Barker as a cab horse. Now 'Jack' is considered a suitable name, and as Jack he has a hard but happy life until the Barkers go to live in the country and Jack goes to the mean Nicholas Skinner, whose drivers bring the horse so low that the knacker seems inevitable. Just in time, lively Willie persuades his grandfather, Farmer Thoroughgood, to try the broken-down animal, and Willie's care of 'Old Crony' is so effective that Beauty is finally sold to two elderly sisters whose groom proves to be none other than little Joe Green, who tended Beauty in Squire Gordon's stable years before.

Like most of the mock-autobiographies of the nineteenth century, *Black Beauty* is planned to cover a variety of social settings; like most of them, it has a strong moral purpose. A note found after Anna Sewell's death stated that the special aim of her 'little book' was 'to induce kindness, sympathy, and an understanding treatment of horses', and although when the book first appeared it made little stir, it was not long before the RSPCA arranged to distribute it to children as propaganda. It is well known that the cruel fashion of using a bearing-rein on carriage horses came to an end partly because of this book. It took the invalid Anna Sewell seven years to write it, a few sentences at a time as her health allowed. Every sentence must have been weighed, every part of the plot thought over, every idea taken to its ·logical conclusion. There is not a word wasted anywhere in this short, mellifluous, quietly forceful tale. Above all, one imagines that as Anna Sewell wrote or dictated her sentences she thought of the years when she drove herself about the countryside and when she enjoyed the company of her brother Philip and his horse Bessie, so sagacious and so spirited.

Generations of girls have wept over the vicissitudes of Black Beauty and the sad death of Ginger, and yet it is not a sentimental book, nor an anthropomorphic one; the television series which masqueraded under the title *Black Beauty* shows what mawkishness can do to a good idea. In a way, Anna Sewell's book seems almost like a dialogue between horses and men. First, the horse's natural response to treatment by the expert, the

Black Beauty, drawn as a foal by Eric Tansley.

kindly, the ignorant and the vicious are extended (not distorted) by the use of carefully chosen words spoken by the animals, so that characters like Reuben Smith with his bouts of drunkenness, Alfred Smirk the humbug, the boy Joe Green and honest John Howard, the Squire's groom, are seen as nearly as possible as a horse would see them. Then, the words and thoughts of the humans reflect and confirm horse behaviour. When we read of the stormy night when the river bridge breaks, we first read of the horse's instinctive recoil and then hear the comments of the Squire and John on Beauty's cleverness.

The equine characters have clearly been chosen to illustrate the various ills against which Anna Sewell carried on her lifelong crusade with a Quaker's dignity and determination. The unfortunate chestnut mare Ginger, whose temper is spoiled early in life by bad treatment, and the astute, cocky old pony Merrylegs, add dark and light colour to a picture in which Black

Beauty is the central figure. [Anna Sewell: *Black Beauty*, Norfolk 1877]

**BLACKBIRD** finds the ideal territory in a suburban garden and realizes that he will have to fight Big-Bill Thrush for it. He puts Thrush to flight by hiding behind a leaf and moving it towards his rival. He proceeds to enjoy his garden with his mate and his two successive broods, notwithstanding anxious moments when it is invaded by a hawk, a rat and the next-door cat.

In this concise, lively story David Ross has set himself to describe typical blackbird behaviour with total accuracy and in some detail, keeping up at the same time a running commentary of thoughts and occasional comments from the bird. As he says in an afterword, 'Everything that Blackbird does in the stories he might do in real life, although whether he would think about it as Blackbird does nobody can tell.' Since nobody can tell, and since David Ross writes with such good humour, who will blame him for taking a most unusual

Blackbird confronts Big-Bill Thrush, from the book by David Ross, illustrated by Jennie Corbett.

line in the formation of an animal character, attributing a comically suitable personality to that ubiquitous, neat, black-coated garden bird? [David Ross: *Black-bird*, London 1968]

**BOBBSEY TWINS** (the) come in two sets. There are Bert and Nan, aged eight, who are dark and lively, and Freddie and Flossie, aged four, who are 'short and stout' with golden hair and blue eyes (Papa calls Flossie his 'Little Fat Fairy' and Freddie the 'Fat Fireman'). They live on a fashionable street in a lakeside town where their father owns a sawmill, and Dinah the cook and her husband Sam ensure perfect freedom for Mr and Mrs Bobbsey, who 'were both young themselves and always took part in their children's joys and sorrows'. The daily life of the children is organized on the whole-some and careful lines laid down in the improving stories of the previous century, though with none of the evangelical excesses of Mrs Sherwood or the ferocious punishments of Catherine Sinclair's Mrs Crabtree. Nan takes it for granted that she should now and then help to make clothes for the poor, while she and Bert help a farmer by picking his pears for market when he is ill. Charity does not rouse in them benevolent speeches, any more than a visit to Washington or even to London elicits from them any but the most demure comments.

The Bobbsey children offer a striking example of the way passive and uninteresting characters may enjoy a long life because of the veracity of their circumstances. To go through a long line of Bobbsey books (as count-less American children did, and perhaps still do) is to sit down daily before a nursery soap-opera, watching familiar scenes (sleigh rides, a fancy dress contest, fire-works, shopping, train journeys, a visit to a farm) in a world where accidents and disasters are innocuous and short-lived, and shortages, whether of money, friends or family affection, are unthinkable.

Laura Lee Hope writes in a preface to a new edition of the first Bobbsey Twins book, published in 1950, that she has brought the circumstances and environment of the twins up to date, but not their characters. Their lan-guage becomes more flexible and less pure (though not less grammatical). A garage for the family car replaces the stables, the married couple drop their darkie idiom, and Freddie plays football at school, but the twins remain the same ingenuous children first introduced at the beginning of the century. Perhaps their charm lies in their total lack of personality. There may be a special pleasure in reading of children whose lives are agreeably filled with safe excitements while their characters, like outline-pictures in a painting book, are ready to be given colours of the readers' own choosing. [Laura Lee Hope: *Bobbsey Twins: or, Merry days Indoors and Out*, New York 1904; *Bobbsey Twins in the Country*, 1904; and many other titles]

**BOBBY BAXTER**, known as Bax, is not sure that he really wants to move on to the Windsor Street Seniors in September, but when he and his mates – Jugears (called after his most obvious attribute) and shrewd, sar-donic Worm – find a derelict boat on the canal that runs through Millbridge, exploration fills the long summer holiday; and the first weeks at their new school pass almost unnoticed in the excitement of owning a puppy and the effort of earning the money to keep it.

Bax is the kind of boy who pursues the latest idea regardless of his own comfort and, sometimes, of other people's as well. Roger Collinson has drawn, easily and surely, the picture of a boy in an urban environment, a boy who one day feels almost grown up and, on another, is glad of his mother's consoling ways – in short, a boy with whom very many children have been able to identify. [Roger Collinson: *A Boat and Bax*, Edinburgh and London 1967; *Butch and Bax*, London 1970]

**BOBBY BREWSTER** is, it might seem, a perfectly ordinary small boy, but strange things happen to him. He holds conversations with an intelligent piece of chalk in the classroom, an athletic fly on the ceiling of his bed-room, an irascible sock on the washing line, his own dis-contented bicycle, a sad, redundant lift in a big store and a tinful of uncomfortably crowded sardines. A cat and a typewriter collaborate to help him with a school composition and a pair of unusual football boots enhances his reputation on the games field. Bobby is always pleased and interested by his odd experiences; his equable character is, in fact, dictated by the nature of the stories in which he has been the central figure for twenty years.

'And Bobby picked up a little plastic Father Christmas' from *Bobby Brewster's Wishbone,* drawn by Lilian Buchanan.

Bobby Brewster is just the kind of character to be accepted as one of themselves by the countless children to whom H. E. Todd has narrated the young hero's adventures, while the sensible values and stable home background of the stories make their own unobtrusive impression. These are essentially stories to be told, full of onomatopoeic words, lending themselves to simple mime and dramatic gesture, colloquial in humour and topical in domestic detail. For such stories Bobby – cheerful, eager, observant, opportunist – is an ideal and popular hero. [H. E. Todd: *Bobby Brewster*, Leicester 1954; *Bobby Brewster Bus Conductor*, 1955; *Bobby Brewster's Shadow*, 1956; *Bobby Brewster's Bicycle*, 1957; *Bobby Brewster's Camera*, 1959; *Bobby Brewster's Wallpaper*, 1961; *Bobby Brewster's Conker*, 1963; *Bobby Brewster Detective*, 1964; *Bobby Brewster's Potato*, 1965; *Bobby Brewster and the Ghost*, 1966; *Bobby Brewster's Kite*, 1967; *Bobby Brewster's Scarecrow*, 1968; *Bobby Brewster's Torch*, 1969; *Bobby Brewster's Balloon Race*, 1970; *Bobby Brewster's Typewriter*, 1971; *Bobby Brewster's Bee*, 1972; *Bobby Brewster's Wishbone*, 1974]

**BORKA,** one of six goslings hatched by Mrs Plumster, is different from the rest – she has no feathers. The doctor advises the distressed mother to knit some for her

The featherless gosling Borka is examined by the doctor; an illustration by John Burningham.

daughter, but the grey jersey makes swimming and flying equally difficult, and Borka is left behind when her family migrate in the autumn. However, she finds friends in the captain and crew of a coastal steamer and works her passage to London, where she finds a home at Kew among other unusual birds and a mate in handsome Ferdinand.

The Burningham goose, as familiar now as the Burningham dog, is seen in its oddest and most beguiling form in the person of Borka who, like other Burningham heroes and heroines (for instance, Trubloff, the mouse who wants to play the balalaika), suffers from being different and eventually reaps the rewards of integrity. [John Burningham: *Borka. The Adventures of a Goose with no Feathers*, London 1963]

**BOSTOCK** and **HARRIS,** two schoolboys in Regency Brighton, complement one another in an almost sinister way, Harris's powerful mind balancing Bostock's powerful limbs – or to put it in less flattering terms 'Harris was as weak as a kitten and Bostock was as thick as a post'. When Mr Brett describes to the class the custom in ancient Sparta of exposing unwanted infants, he notices with apprehension 'an unwholesome light in Harris's eyes'. His hope that it is a fever, not an idea, is unfounded. This curious custom, together with a memory of an earlier lesson on the founding of Rome, is turned over in Harris's mind, to emerge as a plan. Accordingly, with the admiring help of Bostock, he abstracts his youngest sister from her nursery and the two boys lay her tenderly in a dell on the Downs, secure in the belief that a vixen will conveniently appear to take the infant to rear as her own.

The baby is taken – but not by a vixen. Tizzy Alexander, pretty, feckless daughter of a retired major who teaches at Dr Bunnion's Academy, finds the baby while she is taking an unconventional walk with the Doctor's profligate son Ralph. Natural womanliness urges her to pick up the baby but hers are not the last arms that are to hold the placid Adelaide before she is restored at last to her distracted Mamma.

*Right.* Dorothy and her friends, illustrated by W. W. Denslow, from *The Wonderful Wizard of Oz.*

Bostock and Harris with the baby Adelaide, drawn by Fritz Wegner for *The Strange Affair of Adelaide Harris.*

*"You ought to be ashamed of yourself!"*

"Hmm," said the baker,
"ten dozen doughnuts is
quite a lot, but that's
what the note says.
We need an extra-big
bag for them."

Harris's enactment of classical practice, like a stone thrown into a pond, sends ever-widening ripples through the families of Bunnion and Harris and engages the attention of the seedy Raven, a private agent whose confused and neurotic investigations postpone a solution to the mystery of Adelaide's disappearance as surely as do the misguided efforts of the two boys to correct their disastrous mistake. Through a comically complex narrative, in which secret hostilities are revealed, secret longings confessed and secret vices exposed, the boys provide a rueful continuity as they follow the confused trail. As one clue after another proves useless, Harris becomes more and more despondent, while Bostock, with no defence other than his stolid stupidity, fearfully listens to his clever friend's doubts about God, truth and love. Still uncritical, he concludes that fate is against Harris, that 'there were still things in heaven and earth that even a genius might not overcome', while Harris himself, when all is sorted out and he recovers his self-confidence, kindly assures his friend 'I get the bellyache just like you do, Bosti, and the rain makes me just as wet'. He is not surprised, all the same, that Bostock refuses to accept that a friend who thinks 'high, like an eagle' could possibly be like his own stupid self. Meanwhile, their respective fathers, unaware of any distinction to be observed between their sons, apply the customary chastisement merely on suspicion – Captain Bostock 'with an old belaying pin he kept as a souvenir', while Dr Harris, 'a more cultivated man altogether', smites Harris 'with a volume of Harvey's *Circulation of the Blood'*. [Leon Garfield: *The Strange Affair of Adelaide Harris*, London 1971]

**BOTTERSNIKES** and Gumbles are creatures who live in the Australian bush. The Bottersnikes inhabit rubbish heaps, for as they are too lazy to make homes for themselves, they make do with tins of various sizes. Their constant ambition is to enslave the Gumbles so that they can be even lazier and the Gumbles, polite and obliging as they are, take a while to learn to protect themselves from their disagreeable neighbours.

The King of the Bottersnikes is more hideous than the rest. He has 'an ugly green face with slanted eyes, a nose like a cheese grater and a mean mouth with pointed teeth sticking out. The skin was wrinkly all over and little toadstools grew where the eyebrows should have been.' It is he who has the idea of putting the eminently squashable Gumbles into jam-jars so that they will be ready for work when needed. The Gumbles rely on Tinkergumble, the cleverest of them, to get them out of trouble, and in spite of Willigumble, accident-prone and always late, they manage between giggles to evade their lumpish enemies.

These amusing characters seem inevitable denizens

A page from *Curious George Learns the Alphabet* by H. A. Rey.

Desmond Digby's drawing of the Bottersnikes and Gumbles.

of the rubbish dumps and patches of bush beside Australian roads. Both in the turn of the words and in the descriptive lines of Desmond Digby's drawings, the book is in the tradition of that comic classic, *The Magic Pudding*. [S. A. Wakefield: *Bottersnikes and Gumbles*, Melbourne 1967]

**BRER RABBIT** the trickster can be matched with many other characters in beast fable – among them Anansi the Spider and the mouse-deer of Malayan folklore. Brer Rabbit has acquired a particular identity through Joel Chandler Harris, who collected and wrote down versions of plantation tales from Georgia, telling them through an imaginary narrator, old Uncle Remus, who gave to stories originally African the particular flavour of his personality. The old man tells the stories to the small son of the 'Miss Sally' who had been his audience in his younger days. He tells them just as they come into his mind. He may be reminded of a story by a particular dish on his supper tray, a storm of rain outside or a chance remark. He may be provoked when his listener has the temerity to express his own opinion about the relative merits of Brer Rabbit's quick wits and the tricks of his victims, Brer Terrapin, Brer Fox and the rest.

The old man's acceptance of his situation reflects a

way of life which is naturally unacceptable to the present day, nor is the dialect of the stories immediately accessible, though with patience and a little thought it can be understood easily enough. The particular value of using Uncle Remus as story-teller is that tales whose motifs and plots are familiar all over the world are given a special authenticity by him. Because the old man treats the world of Brer Rabbit as if it were real (and gives it a history of its own through his references to an earlier Golden Age when there was no dissension among the animals), it becomes totally real to the listener. No questions of scale or probability arise. It seems equally possible for Brer Rabbit to rob a vegetable garden or to think out the stratagem of the Tar Baby like a mischievous boy or to outdo Brer Fox in polite social amiabilities with Miss Meadows and the girls like a leisurely Southern gentleman. When these fables and folk tales are retold nowadays we receive them as beast fables full of amusing but representative characters; told by Uncle Remus, the characters are seen as individuals. [Joel Chandler Harris: *Uncle Remus: His Songs and Sayings*, New York 1880, dated 1881; (English edition under title *Uncle Remus and His Legends of the Old Plantation*, London 1881); *Nights with Uncle Remus*, Boston 1883; *Uncle Remus and His Friends*, Boston and New York 1892; *The Tar-Baby and other Rhymes of Uncle Remus*, New York 1904; *Told by Uncle Remus*, New York 1905; *Uncle Remus and Brer Rabbit*, New York 1907 (dated 1906); *Uncle Remus and the Little Boy*, Boston 1910; *Uncle Remus Returns*, Boston and New York 1918]

**BRETT** at eleven enjoys life in a New York apartment with her mother who is available, on equal and not oppressive terms, whenever Brett needs a listener. By now Brett has worked out for herself various sensible formulas to use when her schoolfellows ask where her father is. She is even prepared to deal with dogmatic Mary Jane who tells her 'Everybody has a mother and a father. That's how people get born.' Brett knows better: a father has never been part of their family. Independence and a flexible routine suit her very well and she prefers her mother's pony-tail and jeans to the elegance of Evelyn's mother, who is always going out on dates to look for a husband, as Evelyn casually puts it.

She is not embarrassed or anxious when the wolf-man with the beautiful wolf-hound comes into their lives; but when Grandma begins to criticize her daughter for allowing Theo to spend weekends in the apartment, and drops heavy hints about marriage, Brett is alarmed, especially as the suggestion of so radical a change in her life coincides with her sudden realization that she will soon be twelve and, as she tells the sympathetic Theo, 'The trouble with being twelve is you become an adolescent and you get mad at everyone all the time'. There is a wedding all the same, and the book ends with a question mark but, given Brett's character, with a good deal of hope for the future.

This kind of book can easily suffer from the wrong kind of comment. The picture of an unmarried mother who makes a virtue out of her situation could offend those who believe that books of this kind should always classify and computerize good and bad. It would be a pity if such a shrewd, perceptive study of individuals were outlawed or, conversely, if it were praised for a courageous stand against convention. In fact this is an expert example of first-person narrative, in which every detail and every conversation, reported or direct, is properly related to Brett, the speaker throughout. From her comments we can deduce a great deal about the smugly conventional Evelyn, who gets her ideas from *A Child's Guide to Divorce* and is so disastrously unprepared for life; about Grandma, who deplores her daughter's way of life, and Grandpa, who believes in freedom and courage; above all, we can guess at what Brett partly understands, her mother's approach to life. It is a relief to read a book written in a mood so far from the usual lugubrious, sickly or melodramatic tone of novels for the 'teens. Norma Klein's crisp, witty, intelligent style indicates that she is primarily interested in character – in the fascinating differences between one human being and another, the surprising effect they can have on one another. To do this through the words of a girl of eleven – brash, abrupt, unintrospective, sometimes naïve – is a real achievement. [Norma Klein: *Mom, the Wolf Man and Me*, New York 1972]

**BRIDGET WALKER** is called Vicky by her brother and sisters because her chubby face reminds them of the old Queen. When she first appears as a toddler in *Swallows and Amazons*, it is as a 'visiting native' with her mother that she tumbles about the camp where she longs to sleep. When at last she is included on a surveying expedition on the East Coast (in *Secret Water*) she ensures that she is not relegated to the role of 'the youngest' by making herself responsible for Sinbad the kitten. Her incidental remarks to and about Sinbad, especially in the critical moment when with Titty (q.v.) and Roger she is marooned on a causeway at high tide, show that she has learned from listening to her elders what kind of stoical behaviour is expected of her. Her cheerful chatter and her tentative queries throughout the *Secret Water* adventure demonstrate Arthur Ransome's talent for implying personality by modes of speech and behaviour. In particular, Bridget's huge enjoyment when she is made a 'human sacrifice' by the Eels, broken by momentary qualms in case it is not really a game, is exquisitely true both to her character, her age and her status in the family. Through Bridget, too, Ransome throws light on the other children; their attitude to the child, their often impatient but genuine affection and concern, tell us something important about all of them. [Arthur Ransome: *Swallows and Amazons*, London 1930; *Secret Water*, 1939]

**BROWNIES** (the), in Palmer Cox's version of them, made their first appearance in the magazine *St Nicholas*

Brownies in an orchard, drawn by Palmer Cox in *Another Brownie Book*.

the best part of a century ago. They are not at first sight obvious descendants of the traditional brownies of Scottish folk tale to whom the author had been introduced in his Canadian childhood. Certainly their mischievous, inquisitive natures belong to folk lore; they ride the farmer's mare by night, and in their role as helpers they harvest crops for a sick farmer and collect a winter's supply of wood for the parson. But their chief delight is to try out human sports and machines and to investigate the habits and imitate the customs of men. They learn to play lawn tennis and to ride bicycles (the penny-farthing type); they explore the White House and gaze at relics of the Revolution in the Old State House in Philadelphia. Their grotesque appearance, with bulbous heads and skinny limbs, is as much a part of the humour as their lively facial expressions as they rush from one scene to another in a jostling, chattering horde. [Palmer Cox: *The Brownies: their Book*, New York, 1887; *Another Brownie Book*, 1890; *The Brownies at Home*, 1893; and ten other titles]

**BUNKLE** is so-called because in the opinion of his older brother and sister he talked a lot of bunk when he was small – and still does. The Bunkle stories are mainly built round convincing wartime situations in which the children are involved with spies or with international crooks, in settings that vary from Orkney and the West Country to various European countries. Bunkle is given the kind of character that will usefully promote both exciting action and humour in a long series of competent and innocuous thrillers. A combination of cheek, devouring curiosity and a sharp, if undirected, intelligence, helped by a generous allowance of luck, establishes Bunkle as the catalyst in a series of situations which (allowing for social changes in the years since the books were first published) are still marginally plausible. Though time moves on in the long series, and the children grow older, Bunkle (who is about nine in the first book) has to remain somewhat childlike, since a lack of social aplomb and a certain innocence are essential for his part in the action. For this reason he is less believable as an individual in the

Bunyip Bluegum (*left*) with Bill Barnacle, Albert and Sam Sawnoff, drawn by Norman Lindsay for *The Magic Pudding*.

later books than in the first two or three. [M. Pardoe: *Four Plus Bunkle*, London 1939; *Bunkle Began It*, 1942; and many other books, ending with *Bunkle Brings It Off*, 1961]

**BUNTY WOOLCOT** has suffered more than his brothers and sisters from their mother's death. At six years old, when he is first introduced to the reader in *Seven Little Australians*, he is fat and lazy, usually grubby, with a most unattractive trait of cowardice which leads him to lie to get out of trouble with his choleric and unperceptive army father. It is clear that his faults, if they are basic to his nature, could have been corrected by affection and understanding but are only likely to be increased by the harsh words and floggings he earns from his father – who, like the conventional army officer he is, is far less concerned with the cause of Bunty's dishonesty than with the broken windows and stolen food which bring retribution on the unhappy child.

In the first book about the Woolcots, Bunty's difficulties are overshadowed by the trials of Judy (q.v.), who is virtually the central character. In *The Family at Misrule* Bunty moves into the foreground. Still graceless and sullen, he communicates only with Poppet, the sister nearest to him in age, who is shocked by his tale-bearing and lies but who never ceases to listen to and comfort him. Poppet's faith in him still holds when, falsely accused of stealing money at school, he runs away to a menial life in Sydney. 'I knew you were all sick of me and ashamed of me', he tells Poppet. 'I kept saying I'd get well and work hard and do something to make you respect me before I came back.' And since the real thief has been exposed, Bunty, helped by his father, becomes more open and amenable. These two books have the four-square reality of the stories of the Marches and the Carrs, and deserve to be better known. [Ethel Turner: *Seven Little Australians*, London 1894; *The Family at Misrule*, 1895]

**BUNYIP BLUEGUM** leaves a home that is hardly big enough for his Uncle Wattleberry's whiskers, and joins a strange trio consisting of Bill Barnacle, a hearty type dwarfed by a large hat, beard and feet, Sam Sawn-off, a penguin whose feet more or less have to be taken for granted, and Albert, a self-perpetuating pudding who can be 'Christmas, steak, and apple-dumpling Puddin' according to which way the basin is turned. After several painful encounters with a couple of dastardly pudding-thieves, who conceal their Possum and Wombat forms under various ingenious disguises, the champions appear in court after the Pudding has been arrested; they successfully baffle the 'legal ferrets' and retire to a tree-house with a market garden for Bill to run and a paddock where the Pudding can take exercise and 'shout rude remarks to the people passing by'. All the characters in this classic Australian tall story share an exuberant, slangy, rowdy, casual attitude to life which establishes its own characteristic humour [Norman Lindsay: *The Magic Pudding*, Sydney, 1903]

# C

**CADELLIN** the wizard is no more than a legend to the people who live in or near Alderley Edge in Cheshire, but to Colin and Susan, who meet him when they are staying at the Mossock's farm at Redmanhey, he is a friend. Cadellin is custodian of a cave where, deep underground, sleep the Knights, who will wake to save England at some future date. Because Susan has been given a beautiful crystal which is, in fact, the Weirdstone itself, she is both needed and protected by Cadellin when the stone is snatched by evil goblins working under orders from the witch Morrigan.

With Cadellin's counsel and power the Knights are protected and the stone recovered. But in the second adventure of the children the old magic is invoked, an essentially female power, outside the intellectual necromancy of Cadellin, and his role in *The Moon of Gomrath* is less active than it is in the first book. Tall, imposing, white-bearded, Cadellin belongs to a long line of wizards who from Merlin onwards have inhabited the lands of fantasy, but as a character he is less imposing and magic-seeming than the Merlin of Arthurian legend and less idiosyncratic than Tolkien's Gandalf. He is, in fact, like the other characters in Alan Garner's first books, mainly a vehicle for the author's informed and passionate recensions of the local legends of this part of Cheshire. [Alan Garner: *The Weirdstone of Brisingamen*, London 1960; *The Moon of Gomrath*, 1963]

**CAPTAIN FLINT** is the nickname given by the Walker children (in *Swallows and Amazons*) to the 'big fat man' they see on a houseboat, with a parrot by his side, and it is hardly surprising that they decide he must be a pirate. When they meet Nancy and Peggy Blackett (q.v.) and learn that he is their Uncle Jim, their view of him is not entirely altered – as can be seen in *Duck* and *Missee Lee* (q.v.), the two fantasies invented to liven up the winter. In those romantic tales of adventure, which are set on a Caribbean treasure-island and in a pirates' lair in the China Seas, Jim Turner is seen as a large, indomitable Englishman, capable of out-facing any enemy but (to suit the atmosphere of the stories) in a jocular and cheerful spirit.

It has sometimes been suggested that Uncle Jim is a self-portrait of Ransome, like him a traveller and a (would-be) writer; his book, whose fate we shall never know, is called '*Mixed Moss* by a Rolling Stone', a nice derisory touch from Arthur Ransome.

In fact Captain Flint is an essential part of the stories and his character may be said to depend on this. For the adventures of Swallows, Amazons and D's to be realistic they must be enterprising and yet essentially safe, and this means an adult must be in the offing – not a 'native' who will curtail plans of action but one who is game for anything (even walking the plank into the cold lake as an apology for misjudging the young) but with certain experiences and skills which may be called upon to save a difficult situation (for instance, to discomfit the persistent egg-stealer in *Great Northern?*). Because of his role in the stories, Captain Flint is not a wholly consistent character. Nancy's tart comment (in *Peter Duck*) that he has 'failed and failed again' and his occasional fits of irresponsible behaviour suggest that he is not the ideal companion in adventure that he might seem. Here is the case of a character conceived for a certain purpose who now and then threatens to escape from the bounds set by his creator, and so to upset the balance of the cycle of stories. [Arthur Ransome: *Swallows and Amazons*, London 1930; *Swallowdale*, 1931; *Peter Duck*, 1932; *Missee Lee*, 1941; *Great Northern?*, 1947]

**CAPTAIN PUGWASH** 'thought himself the bravest, most handsome pirate in the Seven Seas' but the truth is that the only person with initiative and sense on the *Black Pig* is Tom the cabin boy. While the gallant pirate captain trembles at the sound of the name of his deadly enemy Cut-throat Jake, Tom, with stratagem after stratagem, corrects his master's mistakes and helps him to escape retribution, contriving that the British Navy (under Admiral Sir Splycemeigh Mayne-brace) should arrest the wrong ship and the wrong crew, while Pugwash reclines on the beach on a heap of treasure.

Children have seen a good deal of Captain Pugwash since he made his début as a television character, a surprising number of years ago. As a character he is drawn in the simplest way, an entertaining if unsubtle descendant of Captain Hook. While it is convenient to be able to savour the verbal wit of the stories at leisure in their printed form, the visual slapstick and parody seem more amusing on the screen. [John Ryan: *Captain Pugwash*, London 1957; *Pugwash Aloft*, 1958; *Pugwash and the Ghost Ship*, 1962; *Pugwash in the Pacific*, 1973]

Captain Pugwash, drawn by John Ryan.

**CAREY FAMILY** (the), whose history has been traced sporadically in ten books so far, goes back to Norman times and has its centre in Wales, in the mansion and estate of Llanstephan in Carmarthenshire. The earliest Carey we read about bears the name of Daubigny, which in the early fifteenth century becomes the title of an earldom. Philip Daubigny does not see the family house, however, until after he grows up. He is the third generation of his branch of the family in Outremer, the English kingdom in the East which he helps to defend against Saladin during the Third Crusade. Thereafter, his descendants and collaterals serve their country and their name in time of war. Harry Carey defends his father's trading venture against the Spaniards just before the Armada (*The Hawk* and *The Galleon*); Neil and Denzil Carey support the King against Parliament in the seventeenth century (*For the King*); Charles Carey serves in France and the Low Countries with Marlborough (*Captain of Dragoons*) and his son Alan, in North America, is involved, as settler and soldier, in the war with France on the Canadian border (*Mohawk Valley*); Richard Carey takes on dangerous assignments in France during the Revolution (*Escape from France*) and later holds an exalted position in the army during the Peninsular War (*Captain of Foot*), where a young cousin, Christopher Carey, distinguishes himself; Christopher's nephew Nicholas fights in the Crimea (*Nicholas Carey*) and his grandson, John Carey,

serves in a new specialized unit in the First World War (*Tank Commander*).

The Careys are by family tradition and inclination involved in war and the sequence of books is in itself a kind of history of weapons, tactics, campaigns and plots. In most of the books a member of the family serves in at least one major military engagement – among them Hattin, Quebec, Sebastopol, Blenheim, Ypres and Edgehill; in all of them, hand-to-hand encounters ranging from formal duels to fist-fights with bandits, spies and anarchists, effectively illustrate changes in the techniques of aggression as well as demonstrating the characters of the Careys concerned. Escape, reconnaissance, imprisonment, disguise, the rewards of courage and the advantages of influence and money, the tedium of campaigning and the exhilaration of victory – it is such active aspects of warfare which engage the attention of the young heroes, though one or two are reluctant soldiers – the scholarly Neil Carey, for example, and fastidious Christopher, who dislikes the discomforts of the open field – none of the young men round whom the stories centre questions either the necessity for war or the righteousness of the cause. They accept without reservation that the Turks, the French, the Sioux nations, the Russians, the Germans, are enemies. Once or twice they find themselves opposed to other members of the family (for example, wild young Andrew Carey takes up the cause of Italian anarchists in the 1850s, and a Russian cousin brought up with Nicholas Carey appears against him in the Crimea); in such situations there is regret but no introspection.

The dangers and demands of war are most fully explored in the Carey books when more than one central figure is involved. Richard Carey and his cousins, wayward Jeffery Standish and Armand d'Assaily, all take part in the rescue of the head of the French family from prison during the French Revolution (*Escape from France*) and each one shows a different aspect of the action. During Marlborough's campaign (*Captain of Dragoons*) Charles Carey, an honest soldier and exceptional swordsman, supports his cousin John, who serves in the regiment, with money to back his gambling debts and, in a final confrontation, faces the effect of John's long jealousy of him in tragic circumstances. In the Crimea, (*Nicholas Carey*), the brothers Nicholas and John Carey, one a naval captain and the other an army major, conveniently illustrate the participation of the two services, while Nicholas's attempt to extricate his young cousin from dangerous involvement with Italian revolutionaries widens the field of international politics still further.

Although the numerous Careys, from the reigning head of the family at any period down to the youngest child playing with toy soldiers in the nursery, are properly differentiated, the young heroes are not drawn in depth and family likenesses are no more striking than the strong resemblance of their attitudes and exploits.

Three generations of the Carey family: Philip in
*Knight Crusader*; Neil in *For the King* (both drawn by
William Stobbs); and John in *Tank Commander,*
drawn by Victor Ambrus.

These active adventure stories are, in effect, complicated and fascinating battle-games. There is no room in them for intricate personal relationships. The Careys are drawn to suit a particular purpose and must be met with this in mind. [Ronald Welch: *Knight Crusader*, London 1954; *Captain of Dragoons*, 1956; *Mohawk Valley*, 1958; *Captain of Foot*, 1959; *Escape from France*, 1960; *For the King*, 1961; *Nicholas Carey*, 1963; *The Hawk*, 1967; *The Galleon*, 1971; *Tank Commander*, 1972]

**CAROLINE TEMPLETON**, a pigtailed thirteen-year-old, thinks of little but ponies and lives for the school holidays when she leaves England in 1940 for her home on the Channel island of Clerinel, to rejoin her pony Dinah, her journalist father and her brothers, Mick and young Thomas. But when fat, seven-year-old Thomas says, 'slowly and unctuously, "Ole Hitler's goin' to take this island"' she has to face facts. What will become of Dinah if they have to leave?

When by a series of accidents and misunderstandings she and Mick are separated from their family in the evacuation and left behind, her first reaction is one of relief. Now she will be able to look after Dinah. But their home has been commandeered by the Nazi General heading the invasion and the two refugees have to hide in the cave which had always seemed to Caroline such a romantic and exciting place for Club meetings.

In the subsequent adventure Caroline grows up a little. She conquers her habit of loquacity in difficult moments. She masters fear, dismay, and even her fury when she finds that Dinah is being ridden (incompetently) by fat Nannerl, the General's grand-daughter. She has to revise some of her superficial assumptions about people. She is surprised to find that she is sorry for the lonely, spoilt German child who longs above all to be a Pony Club member, and she has to revise her opinion of M. Beaumarchais, father of her friend Peter, who she had hastily decided was a Quisling.

The less imaginative, steadier Mick has an altogether

Caroline with her pony Dinah, drawn by Stuart Tresilian for *We Couldn't Leave Dinah*.

Faith Jaques's illustration of Carrie and Nick from
*Carrie's War*.
*Left*. Juliet Waley as Carrie with Andrew Tinney as her
brother Nick and Tim Coward as Albert in the
television serial *Carrie's War*, produced in 1973.

more responsible attitude to the dangerous situation
they are in, and he copes as one would expect a boy
of his calibre to do, frankly admitting he is afraid but
taking practical measures to protect his sister. Caroline
is really the central character of the book and events
are coloured by her responses and the changes that circumstances bring to her impetuous nature. In a sequel,
*The Polly Harris*, Caroline and Mick, staying in London to be coached for exams, are involved in another
adventure mixing danger and mystery, and Caroline
goes through much the same process of making immediate judgements on people and having to reconsider
them. But her character seems less emphatic and in a
way less important in this story. Besides, a revision a
few years ago, to bring the crime and social details in
line with the present, has meant that Caroline's
character, which belongs very much to the 1940s, seems
curiously limited and unconvincing in the new context.
[Mary Treadgold: *We Couldn't Leave Dinah*, London
1941; *The Polly Harris*, 1949]
**CARRIE** and **NICK WILLOW** are evacuated from
London to a Welsh village during the Second World

War and are billetted on Samuel Evans, who keeps a
grocer's shop. After the first homesick days they adapt
themselves to his fussy ways and religious bigotry and
even learn how long to stay away from the house when
he falls into one of his rages and rails at his sister, meek
Auntie Lou. When Christmas comes they are sent to
a farm which belongs to Mr Evans's older sister Dilys
to fetch a goose. Carrie learns about the quarrel long
ago, when Dilys married the owner of the pit in which
their miner father was killed, and she pieces together
more of the story from what Hepzibah Green, who
looks after frail Mrs Gotobed, tells her. Hepzibah is
so honest and so shrewd that Carrie trusts and loves
her as much as her young brother does. Indeed, Carrie
becomes so deeply involved with the feud between Mr
Evans and his sister that when Mrs Gotobed dies in-
testate and Hepzibah is told to leave the farm, she makes
a wild effort to put matters right which she can never
forget; as she and Nick leave the village to join their
mother, she sees from the train that the farm is burning
and is certain that disaster came because she threw the
skull away which was reputed to hold the luck of the
family.

Nina Bawden begins her story at the end, when
Carrie, recently widowed, comes to Wales with her

Caxton's printing press from *The Load of Unicorn*,
written and illustrated by Cynthia Harnett.

children and on impulse stops in the village and allows
herself to remember and recount the story of that
strange, isolated period in her life thirty years before.
As we go back into the past, the grown woman
remembering the past gives place to the girl in the
present observing and trying to understand what she
sees. Nina Bawden gives her characters reality not by
describing them but by letting us see what they think
of one another and how much they understand. We
learn about Nick by noticing from his remarks, to Mr
Evans particularly, that he has a shrewd, detached way
of knowing what people are like because he is not old
enough to be confused by their inconsistencies, whereas
Carrie, although she dislikes Mr Evans for his meanness
and his bullying manner and sympathizes with Auntie
Lou, can despise the one for her passive resistance and
can feel sorry for the other because he is tired and
despondent and over-worked. We learn what Albert
Sandwich, that erudite schoolboy, is like by the way he
teases Carrie for her romantic guesses about people and
their motives, and by the way Hepzibah teases him.
There is a continual shift of focus in the story as its complex plot is carried along by way of conversations and
unspoken words and thoughts; the book has an extraordinarily close texture and gives a remarkable illusion
of reality. [Nina Bawden: *Carrie's War*, London
1973]

**CAXTON** is described in *The Load of Unicorn* as
he might have been late in his life, a man of affairs,
once powerful at court as a mediator and in the concerns of the Merchant Venturers, now fascinated by the
craft of printing, which he has brought from the Conti-
nent to London. We look into the windows of his house
at the sign of the Red Pale, in the Almonry at West-
minster; we listen to his wise counsel and watch his
quick action as he instructs Bendy in his duty as
an apprentice. Above all we see him as a man who loves
youth and progress but who also delights in the chivalric past, feeling that much has been lost in the long,
confused years of the Wars of the Roses.

A younger Caxton is glimpsed briefly in *The Writing
on the Hearth*, when he is himself apprentice to the
mercer Robert Large, then Lord Mayor of London.
Large had himself been apprenticed to Dick Whitting-
ton and the two books are linked by this character with
*Ring Out Bow Bells*. To meet characters in this way, in
more than one story and in different contexts, helps to
give them authenticity and to accommodate the mixture
of fact and fiction essential to the drawing of their personalities. From another point of view, a character who
appears before us at more than one period of his life
takes on a special reality and this encourages our belief
in the documentation of his historical background.
[Cynthia Harnett: *The Load of Unicorn*, London 1959;
*The Writing on the Hearth*, 1971]

**CECILY JOLLAND** comes to Mantlemass in August
1485, a girl of sixteen who 'had never brushed her own

Cedric Errol

hair, or knotted a girdle'. Her nobly born mother died
when she was five and throughout her girlhood her
father, Sir Thomas Jolland, used her as the tool of his
ambition. Soon after her mother's death he made a marriage between her and Lewis Mallory, second son of a
powerful Lancastrian supporter; later Jolland changed
to the Yorkist side and disavowed the match. After the
death of Richard III Jolland flees to France, leaving his
helpless and hapless daughter, unwillingly, in the care
of his estranged sister, Dame Elizabeth FitzEdmund
(q.v.).

To Cecily the country folk of the Sussex forest are
like foreigners, with their strange dialect, and her aunt's
voice and appearance rough and distasteful. Not many
months later, when the girl has changed her trailing silk
gown for durable wool, her deerskin slippers for strong
shoes from the village cobbler, Cecily looks back at herself as 'a puppet – a dead thing – a bundle of sticks tied
with gold thread'.

In Sussex Cecily's life takes a happy course after she
encounters cheerful Lewis Mallory and nicknames him
Master Yaffle for his red cap. Touched by her timidity,
Lewis vows to help her to the kind of life she wants,
but their love for one another is threatened when
Cecily's father announces his own impending marriage
and his plans for his daughter. The girl who arrived at
Mantlemass seemingly with no will of her own now
shows her strength of character in resolving to have
Lewis against all opposition; her resolve and the secret
of her childhood marriage, now revealed, coincide
happily for the two lovers,.

The painful winning of independence is a recurrent
theme in Barbara Willard's Forest cycle; it is illustrated, with much psychological insight, in the lives of
Medley Plashet (q.v.) and Lilias Godman (q.v.). Barbara
Willard's close observation and knowledge of her
characters is evidenced when Cecily appears again (in
*The Sprig of Broom*) as mistress of Mantlemass after her
aunt's death, ruling a large household and bringing up
her sons Simon and Robin and her daughter Catherine
to face their own problems. [Barbara Willard: *The Lark
and the Laurel*, London 1970; *The Sprig of Broom*,
1971]

**CEDRIC ERROL** set himself to care for his mother
when his father died, and she for her part encouraged
his eager interest in people, which brought him so many
friends that he did not suffer from the quiet life they led
in New York. His democratic nature was somewhat
shaken when he learned that he was now heir to his
grandfather, the Earl of Dorincourt; his loving nature
was shocked when he heard about the family quarrel
which had followed his father's marriage and discovered
that his mother was not to go to the Castle with him,
but she explained matters carefully to him so that he
would meet the Earl without prejudice. He faced the
tyrannical and unbending old man with the courage of a
boy who had never had reason to dislike anybody; the

Reginald Birch's illustration for *Little Lord Fauntleroy*.

Mary Pickford as Cedric in the film of 1921.

charm and courtesy, the whole open honesty of the boy
won the lonely Earl's heart and brought the family
together in amity.

Little Lord Fauntleroy has become a synonym for an
effete, priggish, unboylike child. This distortion was the
result of the publicity that followed the publication of
the book and the production of the play made from it,
a publicity which associated for ever with young Cedric
the velvet suit which had been, after all, only a brief

fashion. The false idea of the boy's character came to be generally accepted even by people who had never read the book. It was supported to some extent by Frances Hodgson Burnett's asides about Cedric throughout the book, for they are almost always sentimental and they interfere with the impression of sturdy self-reliance and common sense which one gets from the boy's conversation and behaviour. Those who want to think him priggish and disingenuous find it easy to quote, out of context, remarks like his praise of his grandfather 'You are always thinking of other people, and making them happy, and – and I hope when I grow up I shall be just like you', ignoring the fact that Mrs Errol had kept from Cedric any suggestion that the old man was selfish and harsh, and forgetting the boy's

natural inclination to believe the best of everyone. In fact, in the manner of his period and not our own, Cedric Errol, Lord Fauntleroy, is a likable, believable small boy. [Frances Hodgson Burnett: *Little Lord Fauntleroy*, serialized in *St Nicholas* 1885; book form, New York 1886]

**CHARLEY** is really Rowan Weston but the paperboy's comment that she looks a 'proper Charley' when he sees her attitudinizing in the garden becomes current, even at school. Charley is, if anything, rather proud of the name but she sometimes feels she is less well regarded than Giles, her elder and Toby, her younger brother. The summer when Aunt Emm takes charge of the family in their parents' absence, it is settled that Charley goes alone to stay with her favourite Aunt

Charley runs away, drawn by Prudence Seward for the book *Charley*.

Louie in Norfolk. She is happy with the plan until she unfortunately reads a phrase in a torn letter from Aunt Louie to Aunt Emm. 'We don't want Charley' she reads; the next part of the sentence is missing. Too indignant to ask for an explanation, she decides to go into hiding when she reaches the village.

At first, running away is surprisingly easy. With a child's touchingly imitative housewifery, she finds the old hen-house which had been a hide-out in games with her brothers, and turns it into a home, with her cherished new paint-box on a handy shelf and flowers in a potted-meat jar on the box-table. But even with the comfort of her aunt's council house within view, she is not happy for long. Being alone, she has no outlet for her grievance against the aunts, and the excitement of thinking the police will be looking for her soon subsides into a sad apathy, for nobody seems to care where she is. Successive moods of bitterness and day-dreaming end in despair, with the last of her money lost and a feverish chill weakening her resolve. Before she finds a refuge and is reconciled with Aunt Emm, the unkind sentence in the letter fully explained away, she has learnt a measure of wisdom through very real suffering.

Charley is a superbly well-drawn character. She is revealed in her relations with the aunts; in the holiday task, 'a sort of fairy story and picture diary combined', which describes the good moments of her Robinson Crusoe week; in what other people say about her, in and out of her hearing; in what she, mistakenly or otherwise, thinks that they think of her; in the running commentary she makes on what she is doing, what she has done and what she is going to do, and in the less conscious ebb and flow of mood and thought, verbalized for the reader. The indisputable individuality, the all-of-a-piece variety of Charley is contained most of all in her utterances; it is surprising to find how little she actually says, for her voice seems to ring through the book, with her cheeky apostrophes to the scarecrow in the field ('Hallo, Aunt Emm … your hat's crooked. That I will *not* tolerate'), and her riposte to Miss Joyce, the Sunday School teacher, who nervously suggests that the plasticine figures she has made to illustrate a parable (Aunts Emm and Louie, Charley explains) could be a kind of front row of the crowd waiting to be fed by Jesus. 'On the contrary,' Charley replies. 'These will be in the back row. There won't be any loaves or fishes left by the time it gets to them, and they'll starve to death.' Whose voice *could* this be but Charley's? [Joan G. Robinson: *Charley*, London 1969]

**CHARLEY CHAFFINCH,** once a prize-fighter, works for Sampson's Circus. As he tells the two boys, Jo and Jack, after he has burst upon them in all his glory, 'there ain't nuffink I don't do, from cuttin' the elephants' toe-nails with the edging shears to sewing up the tents where the nice little boys 'ave slit 'em open to 'ave a squint for nix.' The strident Cockney voice is as astonishing to the boys as his costume – a cap checked

Charley Chaffinch and his boss on the jacket of *Sampson's Circus,* drawn by Charles Mozley.

black and white, a jersey striped in black and red, and trousers and shoes the colour of a lemon.

Useful though he is as a general factotum, Charley's ambitions – to juggle, to organize a human two-part donkey on roller skates – are frowned upon by Mr Sampson, though he is taken at his word when he offers to act as trainer to the tiger just bought for the show; brave, if noisy, Charley relies on veal cutlets to see him through the ordeal. His transformation into Professor Carlo Chappinski, 'our foremost authority on British bird life', complete with tail coat and oiled hair, is doomed to failure, for who could expect so highly coloured a personality to subdue itself to a scholarly gravity?

Charley's role is not only to provide comic relief in the story, though he does this superbly. He is the boys' chief protector in the adventure which takes them from a peaceful home near Bristol when Jack, Joe's adopted brother, is pursued by an enemy from his old life. The character of Charley Chaffinch, in short, shows what can happen when a novelist supreme in the creation of lively fictitious individuals turns his attention to children's stories. [Howard Spring: *Sampson's Circus*, London 1936]

**CHARLEY CORNETT,** aged almost five, lives in the Appalachian mountains, the youngest of ten and certainly not the least lively. When Miss Amburger calls on his mother to suggest he might attend the Little School to be held at Raccoon Hollow for six weeks that summer, Mrs Cornett warns her 'He's plumb full of curiosity'. Listening to his brothers and sisters talking about school, he is intrigued to learn that each day a boy or girl is chosen, for merit, to 'carry a flag and march at the head of the line to the bus'. Charley is certain that he will be the flag-carrier almost at once but each day when he alights from the bus he has to admit that he is still waiting for the honour. Curiosity leads him to experiment with the water tap and other pieces of equipment he has never met before; he takes more than his share of space and materials to make a Thing out of modelling clay; and when he comes to school in Uncle Hank's hat only one person really understands why he has to defy convention and keep it on even during dinner.

Then the day comes when Charley carries the flag – and with one hand, for tucked under his other arm is

Charlie Cornett, drawn by Nancy Crossman for
*Did you Carry the Flag Today Charlie?*

a book on snakes, a reward for helping to move books in the library, a tribute to his fresh imagination and a symbol of hope from the teacher, who is well aware of the struggle for literacy in hill settlements. This short book, symmetrically planned, provides a chart in words of Charley's environment, with the eager, gap-toothed little boy right in the centre, and with a sharp social point for those who will understand it. [Rebecca Caudill: *Did You Carry the Flag Today, Charley?*, New York 1966]

**CHARLIE BUCKET** lives with his father, mother and two sets of grandparents in 'a small wooden house on the edge of a great town'. Poor as they are, the grown-ups try to see that the boy at least has enough to eat but the thin, peaky child longs for chocolate, until one day an unexpected stroke of luck wins him one of the Golden Tickets which will make him one of a party of five children who will be shown round the huge Chocolate Factory run by the mysterious Willy Wonka. Roald Dahl's hyperbolic style of describing Willie Wonka, with his black goatee, his immaculate, formal clothes and his explosive mode of speech, is used also to introduce the other children who join Charlie and his quiet grandfather Joe Bucket on the strange tour. Augustus Gloop is repulsively greedy, Veruca Salt is odiously spoilt, Violet Beauregarde lives for chewing-gum as Mike Teevee lives for the small screen, and each one, in the course of inspecting Willie Wonka's astonishing machinery and his cunning variations on the theme of succulent sweetness, is appropriately and horrifically punished. Augustus is swept up a pipe in a stream of liquid chocolate and has the greed and the fat boiled out of him, Veruca is thrown down a rubbish chute as a bad nut by worker-squirrels, Violet turns purple after chewing experimental gum and Mike Teevee is radically changed by teleportation. Charlie is rewarded for his modest wishes with the gift of the factory.

The noisy, grotesque humour of the book belongs to the world of the cautionary tale, with Struwwelpeter, with Harry who chewed little bits of string and unfortunate Papa who was run over by a tram and mistaken for strawberry jam by his offspring. Charlie necessarily remains a passive character, his voice heard infrequently, and with difficulty against the strident notes of Willie Wonka and the greedy screams of the other children: caricature needs a point of rest and normality if it is to succeed. Two elements in the book, seem to stand somewhat outside the simple cautionary-tale style – the situation of the Oompa-Loompas, a race of pygmies brought from Africa to live virtually as slaves in the factory, and the treatment of the four geriatrics, which in the sequel, *Charlie and the Great Glass Elevator*, becomes singularly unpleasant as Mr Wonka's new invention, Vita-Wonk, changes Grandma Georgina first into an unborn minus-two-year-old and then into an aged three hundred and fifty-eight. There is a strong adult flavour in the political satire of the second book

which is far removed from the cautionary exaggerations of the first one, and quiet Charlie becomes merely a titular hero. [Roald Dahl: *Charlie and the Chocolate Factory*, New York 1964; *Charlie and the Great Glass Elevator*, 1973]

**CHARLOTTE** *see* GINGER, LITTLE TIM

**CHARLOTTE** the spider speaks to Wilbur the pig (q.v.) (as he lies sobbing in his pen, lamenting his lack of friends) in a small voice 'rather thin, but pleasant', announcing 'I'll be a friend to you. I've watched you all day and I like you.' Charlotte A. Cavatica – grey, 'about the size of a gum-drop' – is wise, inclined to be stately in her utterances, thoughtful as behoves a sedentary spider, and ready to put her skill at the disposal of Wilbur when his life is threatened. Charlotte spins into her web the words 'Some Pig', which convinces Mr Zuckerman that the pig is 'completely out of the ordinary'; Mrs Zuckerman's comment 'It seems to me we have no ordinary *spider*' goes unheeded. Nor does Charlotte ever get the credit for successive announcements that Wilbur is 'terrific', 'radiant' and 'humble'. The words fit Wilbur and his aspirations well enough and the astonishing happening is enough to ensure that the pig can look forward to a long life.

Charlotte is philosophical enough not to expect credit for her miracle, but in fact she has achieved something more than the saving of a pig from the bacon factory. She has somehow made Wilbur understand and accept the fact that she has to die but that she will live on in her children – a piece of mature knowledge which is part of the message in E. B. White's witty, humane, adept fable. 'A spider's life can't help being something of a mess, with all this trapping and eating flies. By helping you, perhaps I was trying to lift up my life a trifle. Heaven knows anyone's life can stand a little of that.' In a story in which every animal has an appropriate idiom – the insistent repetitive phrases of goose and gander, for example, and the blunt ruderies of Templeton the rat – Charlotte's voice is the most personal and

Willy Wonka leads a party of children and parents on a tour of his factory. Charlie and his grandfather bring up the rear. An illustration by Faith Jaques from *Charlie and the Chocolate Factory*.

Charlotte the spider and Wilbur the pig, drawn by Garth Williams.

the most touching of them all. [E. B. White: *Charlotte's Web*, New York 1952]

**CHARLOTTE** and **EMMA MAKEPEACE** live with their grandfather and his housekeeper at Aviary Hall. Independence is forced upon them, for old Elijah rarely communicates with them, and fat Miss Gozzling spends most of her time dozing. As a result, Charlotte has developed a sense of responsibility and her mischievous sister Emma often feels restricted by Charlotte's caution. In the adventure of *The Summer Birds*, Charlotte is the first to see the mysterious, slant-eyed boy who, when he follows her into school, seems invisible to the rest of the class, and it is Charlotte who has the first alarming but heady lesson in flying. When the boy chooses to lead Charlotte over the sea, she forces him to explain himself, to reveal that he is the last survivor of an ancient avian race which will die out unless he can persuade the children to follow him to his island home. Standing out against the romantic longings of the others, twelve-year-old Charlotte finds the strength of character to renounce the anarchic impulses of childhood.

The naughty, self-confident Emma of *The Summer Birds* grows in wisdom after a second strange adventure (in *Emma in Winter*). Two years have passed since the girl of ten launched herself into the sky. Now, at twelve, Emma lords it over her schoolfellows and leads them in teasing Bobby Fumpkins, who, though he is now accorded his proper name, is still thought of as Baby and still teased for being fat and spoilt. When Emma begins to dream of flying, she discovers to her surprise that her companion is no less than the despised Bobby. Awake, the two of them discuss the dreams they are sharing: dreaming, they fly back in time, past mammoth and dinosaur to the volcanoes and swamps of a newly formed world and finally to chaos itself, where they escape by the exercise of will and thought from a figure resembling their teacher, Miss Hallibutt – not the

lonely, ugly, warm-hearted woman of reality but the Gorgon figure of their surreptitious caricatures. Emma learns to be ashamed of her arrogant misjudgements as she faces her fear of losing her identity and admits that Bobby has stood up to the adventure better than she has.

Charlotte's sense of identity is achieved similarly in *Charlotte Sometimes*, by what amounts to a disintegration or division of personality. In her first term at boarding school she finds settling down in a new environment more complicated than even she had expected. In an inexplicable time-slip she finds herself back in the last year of the First World War in the person of Clare Moby, a schoolgirl of thirteen saddled with an ebullient ten-year-old sister Emily. An acute child, Emily soon senses that her sister has changed and she and Charlotte/Clare work out between them the pattern by which the girls regularly change places. Then news comes that Emily and Clare are to be moved into lodgings, leaving the dormitory where a particular bed seems to direct their movements in Time. Caught in the past, it is Charlotte and not Clare who goes with Emily to stay with the unfriendly Chisel-Browns and their lonely, effusive daughter Agnes. When ingenuity and good luck have restored the girls to their right times, they have not only discovered an unexpected link between them but they have somehow contributed to each other's emotional development.

With all the implications and intricacies of these three delicately pointed fantasies, Penelope Farmer never forgets the duty of a novelist to create believable character. In a sense both Charlotte and Emma stand for any girl who is at the stage of questioning and defining her own personality, yet they are never less than individuals. [Penelope Farmer: *The Summer Birds*, London 1962; *Emma in Winter*, 1966; *Charlotte Sometimes*, 1969]

**CHEE CHEE** *see* DOCTOR DOLITTLE

**CHRISTIAN** *see* BIG TIGER

**CHRISTIE** is a London waif who, because his mother had sung 'Home, sweet home' to him just before she died, likes to linger outside the attic in a poor lodging house to listen to the sounds of the barrel-organ as old Treffy plays it to console his loneliness. When Treffy is too old and frail to go out in the streets, Christie takes the organ to earn the few pence needed for their bare existence. It is in this way that he comes to know Mabel and Charlie, two children in a suburb who persuade him to visit the mission hall, where he begins to learn about the Home in Heaven for which he encourages the old man to hope as he lies dying.

The characters of Christie and the old man are drawn in outline, with a simplicity and directness that comes from the obviously sincere feeling in one of the most widely read of the evangelical stories of the last century. As with so many books of this kind, the mellifluous prose and the immediacy of the setting engage one's sympathy for a book whose message, insistent as it is, does not hide the natural lineaments and behaviour of the loving little boy. [Mrs O. F. Walton: *Christie's Old Organ*, London *c.* 1875]

**CHRISTINA PARSONS** drives up to her uncle's estate in a pony-trap at the very moment when her cousin Will is brought home, badly injured, from the hunting field. Her uncle's anxiety about the horse entirely overshadows any sympathy for Will and any but the most perfunctory interest in this twelve-year-old orphan, though Christina discovers his motives for inviting her pretty soon; he has an eye to the future and hopes that marriage with his elder son Mark will one day help to restore the debt-ridden estate to prosperity. Mr Russell, crippled, brutal in his attitude to his sons and insensitive to the feelings of other people, assumes that life must always be arranged to suit him. His selfish disposition has been inherited by the handsome, arrogant Mark, while Will, who hates and fears his father, with appalling courage walks on his broken leg so as to ensure that he will never have to hunt again.

Between 1908 and 1912 Christina grows up in this strange, uncivilized household. She is taught to ride by Dick, the stable boy; she learns to avoid quarrels with her uncle but is alternately attracted and repelled by Mark; she enlists Dick's help in saving an old horse from the knackers and so causes his dismissal; and after a final, irrevocable confrontation with Mark, she makes her decision between the brothers and elopes with Will.

In the ensuing years Christina learns that life with a penniless husband whose one idea is to build a new type of aeroplane can be as hard and as full of problems as life at Flambards, but she enjoys a precarious happiness until he is killed in the war. She returns to the only place she knows. Mark is missing on active service, Flambards is neglected, she is pregnant and still suffering from the shock of Will's death. She sets to work to farm the estate and though Mark returns to claim his property, the future is satisfactorily settled between them, with Christina sure that her love for Dick is more lasting than her uneasy, quarrelsome feeling for Mark. Christina is no conventional heroine of light romance. If she seems an admirable person in contrast to Mark, it is not because she is any less possessive but because her circumstances ensure that she works for what she wants, where Mark expects to have his desires instantly fulfilled. Dick and Will are drawn not as 'good' characters to illustrate a social or political point; they are simply not acquisitive people. Will wants to find out, not to have: Dick has a natural generosity which has been intensified because life has shown him that it is wise to want nothing, so that what you have seems all the more precious.

The Flambards stories are romantic and full of colour but they are not based on an artificial ballet of three men and a girl. They are smoothly but carefully argued studies of personality in which the effect of inherited traits is explored as thoroughly as the effect of environment and circumstance. Mark and Will do not develop – death takes Will while he is growing into a man, while Mark lacks the capacity to change. Christina is

The jacket of *Flambards,* written by K. M. Peyton and illustrated by Victor Ambrus.

*he was just in time to meet her train at Dover.*

An illustration from *Clever Bill* by William Nicholson.

changed by time and circumstance and she disciplines herself to her fortunes, but she survives because of a core of hard, single-minded determination which is all Russell and which is not subject to change. [K. M. Peyton: *Flambards*, London 1967; *The Edge of the Cloud*, 1969; *Flambards in Summer*, 1969]

**CINDERELLA,** most familiar of all fairy stories, has become the property of children for its magic transformations and the drama of the lost slipper as surely as it will always be the property of mankind in general for its basic wish-fulfilment theme. We would hardly expect children to be willing to exchange the pumpkin coach, lizard footmen and glass slipper of Perrault's version for the moral obliquities of the heroine of *La Gatta Cenerentola* or the primitive complexities of the story told in ancient China or indeed for any of the seven hundred versions of the story. Nor would we expect children to accept the fact that (in most of the versions except for Perrault's) Cinderella must be loved in her workaday state before she is revealed in splendour.

In spite of the attractive magic element Cinderella is, as we have had it from Perrault, an essentially domestic story, whose rags-to-riches plot is familiar to the point

of tedium in magazine stories and whose harsh demonstration of family jealousies can hardly seem merely comic to a reflective child. Quentin Bell in *The True Story of Cinderella* takes the courtly element still further, setting the story in 'the ancient town of Rosenburg' where Dr Hausfeld's two ugly daughters frantically seek husbands to the exclusion of their downtrodden half-sister until she is helped by her aunt in the guise of a court dressmaker. The eminently practical and satirical tone of this version can well dispense with the magical elements, while Beatrix Potter in her retelling almost obliterates the magic with profuse domestic detail and conversations that turn the fairy tale into a short novel. [Charles Perrault: *Histoires ou Contes du temps passé* (1697 France) trans. Robert Samber as *Histories or Tales of past Times*, London 1729. Quentin Bell: *The True Story of Cinderella*, London 1957. Beatrix Potter: *Cinderella* (unpublished, in Leslie Linden: *A History of the Writings of Beatrix Potter*, London 1971]

**CLEVER BILL,** a wooden soldier, is accidentally left out of Mary's suitcase when she packs for a visit to her aunt. After a brief but copious fit of weeping, the determined soldier follows the railway lines over hill and dale and 'ran so fast that he was just in time to meet her train at Dover' and to accept with a dignified bow the ceremonial bouquet (perhaps originally intended for Aunt) which Mary presents to him.

This classic picture-book set a standard for the composition and arranging of picture-book pages, in the integration of text and pictures and in the effective posing of scarlet-coated, busby-hatted Clever Bill to point up the qualities of loyalty and physical fitness which one naturally associates with a soldier, toy or otherwise. [William Nicholson: *Clever Bill*, London 1928]

**CLEVER POLLY** is alone in the house one day when a Wolf knocks at the door. Calmly Polly ushers him in and gives him such a generous slice of pie that he is too full to eat her, as he had intended, and as he ingenuously tells her. The next day she gives him chocolate cake and the third day she offers toffee, straight from the stove; the agonized wolf turns and flees, seemingly for good. It proved otherwise, however, for Catherine Storr later wrote two books prolonging the simple and effective joke of a wolf ferocious in intent but hampered by his slow wits, trying in vain to out-smart a quick-witted and unflappable little girl.

In vain the wolf turns to fairy-tale for help. When he instructs Polly in the order of events in *Little Red Riding Hood*, she manages to turn the tale against him point by point. Baffled and bamboozled by her confidently illogical logic, his disguises (as fox, Father Christmas, milkman and postman among others) quite failing to impress the child, the wolf suffers a final indignity when Polly's little sister Lucy, happily enjoying a romp with the animal, eats all his provisions and even has a good bite at him. -

Polly's mother-wit and Lucy's infant nihilism are too much for the wretched wolf. In the ambience of a middle-class intellectual family ('Where was this remarkable performance, Wolf?' Polly enquires, when he is describing the success of his invisibility), the stories are skilfully built round the simple contrast of brain and no-brain, and the characters of Polly and Lucy win credence by the mixture of real-life personality and nursery-tale tradition in which they are drawn. [Catherine Storr: *Clever Polly and Other Stories*, London 1952; *Clever Polly and the Stupid Wolf*, 1955; *The Adventures of Polly and the Wolf*, 1957; reissued in paperback as *Polly and the Wolf Again*, 1970]

**COLE HAWLINGS**, 'a little old man in a worn grey overcoat' with a big case on his back and an Irish terrier by his side, fascinates Kay Harker (q.v.). At first this old, wizened countryman seems to Kay the simple Punch and Judy man he professes to be, but when Cole entertains the boy and his cousins, the visions and splendours he conjures up convince them that he is something more.

Besides, someone – or something – seems to be after the old man. There are men enquiring for him, one with a 'gentle silky voice' that sounds unpleasantly familiar, and there are Alsatian dogs snuffing on his tracks. Cole quickly enlists Kay's help – first with his heavy case ('I do date from pagan times and age makes joints to creak') and then for help in concealing the magic Box which he has carried with him out of the Middle Ages. For Cole is in fact Raymond Lully, an alchemist who found the Elixir of Life and who is now seeking his contemporary Arnold of Todi, who had made the Box as a way of entering the far-distant past and had lost himself there. The dangers that encompass Cole are both realistic and magical. He escapes his enemies on one occasion by walking into a picture of a Swiss mountain and riding up it on a mule; he is kidnapped by Abner Brown's men in a taxi that turns into a kind of helicopter.

Probing still more deeply, one feels that Masefield is suggesting a still older identity for Cole Hawlings. With his power to call up the Phoenix and to manipulate natural growing things, he seems to be equated to some extent with the King Cole of Masefield's poem, as one of the oldest of British nature spirits. Through the old man Masefield adds a plangent note of mystery to the often absurd gyrations of Abner Brown and his dastardly gang in *The Box of Delights*. [John Masefield: *The Box of Delights*, London 1935]

**COLIN CRAVEN** has lived his ten years at Misselthwaite Manor as a virtual cripple in loneliness and misery of mind. When his mother died, his father could not endure to see the sickly baby, and, morbidly conscious of his own crooked shoulders, was convinced that the baby would grow into a hunchback if he survived at all. It is this miserable, ill-tempered, impatient, self-centred boy whom Mary Lennox (q.v.) hears weeping in the night and finally finds in a wing of the mansion where she has been forbidden to go. Mary quickly establishes a relationship with him which, precarious and quarrelsome though it may often be, is strong enough to help her to get Colin into the secret garden where she is sure he will grow well and straight.

Colin's unhappy situation, if it is read in period context, can be seen to parallel Mary's, and in a sense the characters of the two children are complementary. The book divides naturally into two parts, the first concerned with the way Mary changes from a cross little girl to an eager, responsive one, the second concerned with Colin's discovery that he is not an invalid and his struggle towards health. The dual pattern is not repetitive, for the characters of the children are carefully distinguished. Mary comes to life through a deep love of plants and natural things. Colin's strong will transfers easily from tantrums to commands. To help him walk Mary and Dickon (q.v.) must join him in a 'scientific experiment'; they will chant and invoke the Magic that is to make his back straight – in fact a version of the 'New Thought' current at the time when the story was written.

Childlike and yet precocious, Colin rationalizes to his

satisfaction the simple discovery that his cure depends on himself. Pride is always a virtue in Mrs Hodgson Burnett's eyes, a virtue connected with birth and breeding but one which Mary and Colin and Sara Crewe (q.v.) and Cedric Errol (q.v.) cultivate by themselves and justify by their efforts. [Frances Hodgson Burnett: *The Secret Garden*, New York 1911]

**CONSTANTINE PALAEOLOGOS**, last Emperor of the Eastern Roman Empire, is summoned to renounce his soldierly but simple role as Despot of the province of the Morea for the more onerous task of defending the city of Byzantium against the Turks. The author of *The Emperor's Winding Sheet* has built up a portrait of the Emperor in the terrible last year of his life by the use of a fictitious character, an English lad, Vrethicki, a victim of piracy, whose sudden appearance in the Morea is seized upon as the fulfilment of a prophecy; if he remains always by the Emperor's side, the City will not fall. Vrethicki (the Emperor's 'lucky find'), sees his master first through a mist of resentment, disgusted that his dark ringlets 'required the attentions of a barber with hot curling tongs every few days', marvelling at the simple life he chose to lead and his extreme attentiveness to religious observance.

Gradually 'the Emperor's most unwilling and resentful slave' learns to respect the man on whose shoulders rests the burden of the siege. He sees how the Emperor takes on himself the guilt of his people, regarding the Turkish oppression as a punishment sent by God; how he refuses to escape any of the hardships the citizens are enduring; how much he suffers from the palace intrigues and the rivalries of his allies. The contrast between the stiff, formal figure staggering under the weight of jewelled robes and the sallow, weary man in his nightgown is one that can plausibly be seen with increasing sympathy by the boy who is so near to him. If Vrethicki's admiration for the Genoese soldier Justinian prevents him at first from recognizing Constantine's gifts as a warrior and strategist, or his intuitive dealings with his men, in time he realizes the Emperor's courage and through the boy the reader comes to understand how a man who had plotted his way to the throne is purified of mortal desires and dies a noble death. It is a brilliant use of a fictional figure to reflect an interpretation of an historical character. [Jill Paton Walsh: *The Emperor's Winding Sheet*, London 1974]

**CORKY** (Cornelius Corcoran), a Cockney lad, is fond of building castles in the air but settles contentedly enough as the least important stable-lad in Mr Crater's delivery firm. He works hard and is soon allotted a pony of his own, the little mare Prim, but when his boon companion Ginger loses his job for chronic unpunctuality, Corky gives notice too. They tramp north and find jobs on a trawler, but 'the cold bleak draught of Reality' affects them, even though they get as far as Liverpool. The clouds of romantic fancy are dispersed from Corky's mind. 'We've lived and tried', he tells Ginger.

Corky and Ginger from *Pony Boy*, illustrated by Dick de Wilde.

'The world will allus be here – we can have another go at it.' Meanwhile back they go to London with no prospects but a warm feeling that they belong there.

Corky and Ginger have the characteristics commonly attributed to your true Cockney – the cheek, the ability to bounce back after disaster, the open sentiment. If their avocation of pony-boy has almost passed into history by now, they can still be matched as types in the streets of London. [Bill Naughton: *Pony Boy*, London 1946]

**CROOKLEG** is feared by the rest of the Dog Tribe because his life is not ruled by aggression but by a creative will which drives him to draw in clay or mud even though it is 'forbidden to make shapes'. When his village is destroyed by the Fox Folk, the lame boy takes refuge in the forest, where he finds Blackbird, a girl of the Fox tribe. When Blackbird is carried off by the brutish Shark, chief of the Fish people, Crookleg becomes for a time the protégé of Wander, head-woman of the River Folk; but they too are drawn into conflict with their neighbours, and Crookleg, obsessed with ideas about moulding and firing clay, leaves their huts and finds like-minded companions in the uncouth, friendly Red Men, to whose cave-drawings he is permitted to add his own pictures of running stags. Through them he finds Blackbird and the couple take custody of Wander's

baby after she is killed in a raid; after privation and hardship the three, knit into a family, reach a village, 'warm among the gentle hills', that promises 'a golden end to a black beginning indeed'.

In this spare, concentrated, poetically conceived story, the tribes which Crookleg encounters belong in a wide spread of time, from the late Stone Age to something resembling the Bronze Age. Their diversity emphasizes one of the principles which Crookleg works out for himself; he wishes 'that all people, the men and women and hares and owls and dogs, could agree to speak the same words ... Perhaps no one would fight then.' In his journey he discovers his own family pattern, which is not one of custom and blood-relationship but one of love and responsibility, and he finds justification for his compelling creative instinct. Within a magnificently taut, pictorial evocation of ancient worlds Crookleg takes his place as the seeker, who pushes ahead of his fellow men on the evolutionary journey – a journey not only towards better command of human relations and communication but also towards the difficult harnessing of reason and thought. Crookleg is learning to recognize his own personality, his own ideas, and to translate them into the words available to man at the beginning of time. [Henry Treece: *The Dreamtime*, Leicester 1967]

**CROW BOY** is not the only nickname he bears when he is young. When he first appears at the village school he is small and timid and the name Chibi, or Tiny Boy, seems to suit him well. Timidity is not an endearing trait and he is treated like the 'forlorn little tag-along' he seems to be. All the same, Chibi comes to school every day for five years, bringing his invariable lunch of 'a rice ball wrapped in a radish leaf' and consoling his loneliness by observing everything round him. Then a new teacher is wise enough to find out why Chibi is always alone. When at the talent show at the school year end the boy imitates the 'Voices of Crows' with such vigour and understanding that the whole audience can imagine the beauty and strangeness of his remote mountain home, he has truly earned the name Crow Boy which he bears thereafter.

There are many ways of making a psychological and social point. In a few direct, simple sentences the Japanese author-artist shows the quiet endurance and determination a child can display and has made a firm statement about tolerance. In his words and his impressionistic pictures he shows a small boy who is at once an individual belonging to a particular background and a boy of all times and all countries. [Taro Yashima (pseud. Jun Iwamatsu): *Crow Boy*, New York 1969]

**CULLY** the octopus first meets Timothy and Hugh Spens (q.v.) when they are drifting on a raft after their ship has been sunk by a German submarine. They are

Crookleg and Blackbird, drawn by Charles Keeping for *The Dream Time*.

only seven and five at the time and cannot remember much afterwards about the encounter except that Cully had a 'soft, warbling voice, rather like a flute' and was chiefly concerned that he should be introduced by his real name, which was Culliferdontofoscofolio Polydesteropont.

When the boys meet him again some years later, during an undersea campaign against the dastardly pirates Inky Poop and Dan Scumbril, he is still in company with Gunner Boles, who has trained him from babyhood but who has never managed to make him energetic. Cully, though fond of telling everyone how hard he works, is rarely seen in anything but a prone position. However, when the pirates succeed in cutting the knot at the intersection of the 59th Parallel of North Latitude and the 4th Parallel of West Longitude, Cully holds the ropes together till the sailors have time to splice them again. Thereafter he enjoys a luxurious convalescence with unlimited scones and blackberry jam, a sunshade to keep him cool, a medal from Davy Jones and a portrait of the beautiful Miss Dildery Doldero Casadiplasadimelody Stenkendorf Rustiverolico Silverysplash to contemplate; marriage with her seems no more than his due to the conceited creature, whose character has been drawn with the mixture of wild nonsense and circumstantial detail typical of Eric Linklater. [Eric Linklater: *The Pirates in the Deep Green Sea*, London 1949]

**CURDIE**, son of Peter the miner, has never been afraid of the malicious goblins who live deep underground, for he can always frighten them by loud singing; but one day he finds a way into their secret kingdom and learns that they are plotting to seize the little Princess Irene and marry her to the King's hideous son Harelip.

Little Irene, who has been sent from the city by her father for her health, has found her way to an attic in the castle where an old woman is spinning and has learned to love this strange great-great-grandmother of hers and to trust in her strange powers. Curdie and the Princess become good friends after he has led her past the goblins one dark night, and with his courage and the old woman's help he is able to save the Princess when the goblins finally divert a stream to flood the castle and seize her as their prey.

As time passes, with the princess now returned to the city of Gwyntystorm, Curdie grows careless and does wrong in 'never wanting or trying to be better', but when the mysterious old lady foresees more trouble she sends him to the city. Here, through the power she has given him, he is able to find out which of the King's subjects are plotting against him and to save him from the doctor's evil designs. The Kingdom is finally brought to prosperity and peace under the honest rule of Curdie and the Princess – until in after years people once more forget the good ways, and then, in a cataclysm, the city is destroyed and forgotten for ever.

In this strange and haunting tale of the conflict of Good and Evil, Curdie is a more active and interesting

Curdie with the beast Lina and Princess Irene with Lina from *The Princess and Curdie* by George Macdonald.

character than gentle Irene, for hers is an easy and natural education towards spiritual grace. But Curdie is a fallible lad; in spite of his hidden royal ancestry it is more difficult for him to believe in the old woman in the attic when he can see nothing but 'a heap of musty straw, and a withered apple, and a ray of sunlight coming through a hole in the middle of the roof ...' Where Irene has to receive and understand and wait, Curdie has to act, to summon up his courage and his loyalty and to develop the protective side of his nature. The stories are full of symbols – of fire and flowers, of the ugliness of sin and the beauty of repentance in the beast Lina, of life-giving bread and wine contrasted with secret poison – and the strange spinner in the attic may take many forms and have many meanings. But Irene and Curdie are very natural characters, with that peculiarly touching quality of youth which is one of the most striking sides of George Macdonald's work. He shared with Kingsley a loving respect for childhood which irradiates his stories. [George Macdonald: *The Princess and the Goblin*, serialized in *Good Words for the Young*, 1870–71, first pub. in book form, London 1872; *The Princess and Curdie*, serialized in *Good Words for the Young*, 1877, pub. in book form 1883]

**CURIOUS GEORGE** (called Zozo in Britain) is not curious in the English sense of 'peculiar' but in the sense found at the start of the first book about him – 'but he was always curious'. Easy as it is to give a human twist to a monkey countenance, easy as it is to think of a million and one comic situations into which an inquisitive nature might impel a monkey as easily as a human child, nobody would deny Margaret and H. A. Rey the credit for endless inventiveness and a sense of occasion as they involve George with stethoscopes and ink wells, wind and water, toy balloons and a space-ship, people and animals, in a series of minor accidents from which his friend the Man with the Yellow Hat is always able to rescue him. [H. A. Rey: *Curious George*, Boston 1951; *Curious George takes a job*, 1947; *Curious George gets a Medal*, 1957; *Curious George learns the Alphabet*, 1963; With text by Margaret E. Rey, ill. H. A. Rey: *Curious George flies a Kite*, Boston 1958; *Curious George goes to the Hospital*, 1966. English editions entitled *Zozo, Zozo takes a job*, etc.]

**CURLY FORK** wishes he belonged to little Danne, as Mr Fork does, and one day when his senior is late at the table (for he is enjoying a swim in the kitchen sink and unfortunately does not know how to tell the time), Curly Fork is delighted to deputize for him. Mrs Spoon marks a cake into twelve parts and with cake candles organizes an instructive and amusing clock game with the help of Knife and little Butter Knife.

This cheerful little book has a simpler approach to that landmark of the nursery years, telling the time, than the Ant and Bee (q.v.) book on the same subject. The personification of inanimate objects has seldom been more charming, direct and cheerfully comical than in

One of Bryan Ward's illustrations from *Mr Fork and Curly Fork*.

this brief tale, in which both dialogue and pictures contribute to the credibility of the inhabitants of the kitchen drawer. [Angela Banner: *Mr Fork and Curly Fork*, London 1956]

**CYRIL, ANTHEA, ROBERT** and **JANE** are digging in a gravel-pit in the hope of reaching Australia when they disturb a Psammead, a sand-fairy, who is bound, however grudgingly, to grant their wishes.

At first these wishes are hasty and ill-advised. To be as beautiful as the day is no consolation when Cook and Emma fail to recognize the children; the gold coins that appear in such magic profusion are not accepted as currency in the shops, and Robert, wishing to be large enough to beat the jeering baker's boy, finds himself billed as a circus freak. They all think better, in the end, of the desire to see a castle besieged and a band of Red Indians, but it is with mixed feelings that they finally agree to release the Psammead from his obligations and let him enjoy a prolonged sleep.

All the same, though they remember the disasters they are ready for more adventure when by strange chance a newly-hatched Phoenix and a magic carpet are added to their Camden Town nursery. 'They were not astonished', Edith Nesbit assures us, 'but they were very much interested'; and they remain interested through a journey to a Pacific island, the discovery of treasure and the disconcerting presence of 199 Persian cats in their house, all insistently proclaiming their hunger.

The adventures described in *Five Children and It* and *The Phoenix and the Carpet* belong to comic fantasy and depend on the incongruous association of medieval soldiery and angel-sized wings with domestic routine. It is essential to the balance of the stories that the children are never fantasized in any way but remain sturdily themselves, reacting within their own capacities. Like the Bastables (q.v.), they are a united and a diverse group. Anthea, conscientious and loving, is anxious for her mother's comfort and responsible towards their baby brother the Lamb, but still enjoys a youthful sense of wonder. Cyril, well aware of being the head of the family, accepts magic events with practical interest, and he and Robert, a boisterous and moody boy, insist on the prerogatives of their sex, whether they are navigating a flying carpet or avoiding the washing-up. Jane is very obviously the youngest of the quartet, sometimes afraid of the unexpected, sometimes resentful when Anthea or Cyril try to protect her, and occasionally displaying a quick intuition which helps them all out of difficulty. Like all Edith Nesbit's children, they are naturally enterprising and rightly scornful of anything pious or moral. The virtues they accept are those essential to family life – honesty, justice, kindness. The author's social conscience is expressed in asides to the reader, never through the children.

Their function is to reflect the bizarre, inconvenient, sometimes alarming course of magic, as the individuals they are. This is most obvious in *The Story of the Amulet*, in which they experience deeper and more urgent adventures with the Psammead, whom they rescue from a pet shop. Because of their earlier agreement the Psammead is unable to grant them any more wishes but, following his advice, they buy from a dingy little shop a curious blue stone. This proves to be half of an amulet and the word of power carved on it (and transliterated for the children by a learned gentleman lodging upstairs) takes them into the past to seek the other half, which will give them their heart's desire. The descriptions of Egypt (pre-historic and in Pharoah's time), of Babylon and Atlantis, Roman Britain and ancient Tyre, are carefully researched but it is not accuracy or even vividness of detail that gives the book its extraordinary force. It is the response of the children – always typical of them, always linking past with present, fantasy with reality. This is not the past of an historian but a past romanticized (if you will), coloured and irradiated by their imagination. [Edith Nesbit: *Five Children and It*, London 1902; *The Phoenix and the Carpet*, 1904; *The Story of the Amulet*, 1906]

# D

**DAB DAB** *see* DOCTOR DOLITTLE

**DAN** and **UNA,** who live in the Sussex Weald, have learned from old Hobden the woodman and other local folk how to follow the track of an otter and where to find the earliest wild flowers, but their knowledge of history is merely an accumulation of facts remembered from formal lessons and casual reading, until Puck (q.v.) brings people from the past to tell their stories. Dan and Una begin to feel that they are a part of history themselves just as much as the master mason and the shipbuilder, the French prisoner and the great Queen, the centurion and the Norman knight, all of whom seem so natural and at home with them in oast-house or hoppole wigwam or village church.

Unaffected, natural children, Dan and Una show their individual personalities in the way they listen to Puck and his friends. Dan is active and inquiring. He often interrupts with a question about ways and means – of warfare, of stone-carving, of travelling; Una is more interested in the speakers themselves. When the great Gloriana (who had once danced at a house nearby and left her worn shoes behind) tells of the two young men who would have fought one another for her favour, Una is repelled by the Queen's ruthless way with people.

Dan and Una are not the passive spectators of a grand march-past of characters in history; they are deeply interested, vocal listeners. Their interruptions and interpolations make the stories seem like extended conversations, in which one particular speaker predominates but in which there is, all the same, some interplay of character from the promptings, questions, comments and even criticisms of the others. Kipling's stories are not history lessons set in a dramatic frame. For any child who reads them they are emotional experiences, and for this Dan and Una are partly responsible. [Rudyard Kipling: *Puck of Pook's Hill*, London 1906; *Rewards and Fairies*, 1910]

**DANIEL BAR JAMIN** is apprenticed at thirteen to Amalek the blacksmith, in the village of Ketzah in Galilee, but five years later he runs away to join a band of rebels under the forceful leader Rosh. The rebels are dedicated to guerilla warfare against the Romans occupying Jerusalem, and their aims satisfy Daniel's vow of vengeance for the death of his father.

In this story of the lifetime of Christ, Daniel is seen as a youth looking for a satisfying way of life, confused by his responsibility for an aged grandmother and a sister whose mind has been unhinged by the shock of violence in infancy. Because the boy is not naturally violent, he is not always at ease with his leader's decisions. After he has spared the life of a miser on the road, because he looked like his dead grandfather, Rosh angrily comments, 'There's a flaw in you, boy, a soft streak. Like a bad streak in a piece of metal.'

When Daniel hears about Jesus the preacher from his friend Joel, he contrasts him with his own leader and affects to scorn his doctrines of peace and love, but subconsciously he is drawn more and more towards this man of warm and persuasive personality. As Daniel watches and talks to Jesus he slowly realizes that the power of love could in truth influence the world; his old heroes – Joshua, Saul, David and Judas Maccabeus – seem pale shadows of this quiet preacher and healer. The 'flaw' which Rosh saw in his character is proved to be the basis of a new and better life. Is the character of Daniel emphatic enough to sustain the weight of the moral message in the story? Each reader will decide this for himself. There seems to be enough substantial domestic detail, enough naturally evoked conversation, enough attention to the boy's personal motivation, to make Daniel considerably more than a mere vehicle for a sermon. [Elizabeth G. Speare: *The Bronze Bow*, Boston 1961]

**DANNY DUNN,** a lively red-haired boy of twelve or so, lives with his mother in Professor Bulfinch's house, where she acts as housekeeper and hostess for the impatient but kindly scientist. Danny's enquiring mind and pertinacious nature help him when he manages to get himself and his friends into awkward situations. It is his fault, for example, when because he accidentally presses a switch on the Professor's newly invented smallifying machine, the little group find themselves in a barn where a stone has become a mountain and a dragonfly a dangerous monster; but it is Danny's ingenuity that contrives a hot-air balloon from woven cobwebs so that he can rise to the level of Dr Grimes's ear when that friendly rival of the Professor's comes to look for him. It is Danny's idea to use the electrical impulses of a giant African catfish to put to flight snoopers who

Professor Bullfinch with Danny and his friends; an illustration by Ezra Jack Keats from *The Homework Machine*.

have been harassing the local tribesmen, and with the Professor's powerful laser he burns directions on the mountainside to guide a stranded tycoon (whom, incidentally, he has antagonized by a mischievous miscalculation just when the Professor is hoping for a grant for his next project).

Experimenting with a miniature computer, a mechanical probe and a time-machine, Danny displays equally the logic and the unreason in his nature. His friends Joe Pearson, a melancholy boy with a talent for instant rhyming, and Irene Miller, the lively daughter of an astronomer, make sure that Danny is reminded often enough of his failures to make it impossible for him to boast of his successes. This natural, independent and enterprising trio are excellent mouthpieces for the author. Because of their university environment, they are casual and knowledgeable about advanced science and technology, and through them many experimental concepts have been easily and clearly presented to young readers. But the Danny Dunn stories are not text-

books in disguise. If they emphasize that the sciences are an essential part of everybody's life, they do this with a blithe and alert humour for which Danny himself is largely responsible. [Jay Williams and Raymond Abrashkin: *Danny Dunn and the Anti-Gravity Paint*, New York 1956; *The Homework Machine*, 1958; *Danny Dunn and the Ocean Floor*, 1960; *Danny Dunn and the Heat Ray*, 1962; and other titles]

**DAVID** is puzzled by 'the man's' particular treatment of him and his instructions when he directs the boy's escape from the concentration camp which is the only home he has ever known. 'The man' is a guard and David does not trust him; during the whole of his journey from Eastern Europe by way of Italy, Switzerland and Germany to Denmark the boy is intermittently afraid that 'they' will try to get him back. All that he knows about the outside world is from prisoners talking in the camp; most of what he knows about people comes from the terrible scenes he has witnessed there. But one man, Johannes, before he died gave the boy a principle of conduct – if he remains true to himself, nobody can really hurt him. But David does not know who he is, where he comes from or what he is really like. His solitary journey gives him an answer.

He learns to be grateful, in a guarded and impersonal way, to the people who give him food or lifts or advice. He works out a story to explain why he is wandering through Europe alone. He learns, at last, how to smile, after he has been taken in by a warm-hearted Italian family, but he moves on before they can arrange a life for him. He learns that he has a place in the world when, by coincidence, he is given shelter by a woman who knew his mother, and at last, after a terrible winter in servitude to a brutal farmer on a lonely Swiss mountainside, he finds his true home.

As a character in a story, David is given very little external form. It is his being, his identity that we are concerned with, not what this dark-haired boy of twelve looks like. Because the story is also an allegory of love and tyranny, the central figure must be to some extent anonymous and representative. What we know of David is his essential self. We learn what he is like from the comments of other people, most of them deeply affected by the hurt, detached look in his eyes. He reveals himself as he considers his assets – the physical endurance developed in the camp, his knowledge of languages, his acuteness – 'He was familiar with treachery, and he knew what death looked like' he thinks to himself, – and we accept the implication of the fact that he considered that knowledge as an asset. The memory of Johannes, who gave him the only love he could remember, gradually merges with his concept of a just and powerful God with whom he makes bargains that touchingly show the bleakness of his past. Whether one reads the book as the story of a particular boy travelling a particular dangerous road, or as an allegory of Everyman's search for his soul, or as a political plea for peace and goodwill among men, the guarded, stoical figure of David stands strong and definite in it. [Anne Holm: *I Am David* (1963 Denmark), trans. L. W. Kingsland, New York and London 1965]

**DAVID HUGHES** has lived all his life at the shop with its old sign 'Carpenter and Joiner. Coffins made' which has stood for craftsmanship in Darnley Mills for three generations. His lame leg is taken for granted by his particular friends – Arthur Ramsgill, the sturdy, red-faced son of a local farmer and the Rector's son Peter Beckford – and David himself does his best not to hamper them in their various expeditions. But now, at ten years old, he is beginning to realize what his disability might mean in the future, and his lively imagination leads him into rousing dreams of an imaginary hero, a swashbuckling Tudor seaman called Sir Richard Hughes whose exploits he often recounts to amuse his friends.

In the course of four books the boys throw themselves energetically into various adventures, all the more successfully after an operation has put David's leg right. They solve the forty-year-old mystery of the colonel whose clock was left with David's grandfather for an unnecessary repair. They find congenial friends in a retired admiral and his servant and companion Guns, and with them restore a disused church, locate a lost statue of the Virgin, fire a cannon salvaged from a frigate of Nelson's fleet and construct a Roman-type ballista. In *Sea Peril* they build from scrap, with Peter's erratic but considerable engineering skill, a genuine 'bicycle-powered, paddle-driven punt'. Finally, in *War on the Darnel*, they carry out a campaign on the water against a local gang with whom they are competing in a money-making effort.

Philip Turner has marked out the characteristics of the three boys in outline so that together they can pro-

David Hughes with his friends Peter and Arthur, singing in the church choir; an illustration by William Papas from *The Grange at High Force*.

vide the necessary impetus for the crowded action of the books. Arthur is a natural athlete, more concerned with winning honours on the cricket field than doing his homework; but cheerful though he is, he is both knowledgeable and wise in the ways of farming, and his move from school to agricultural college is perfectly in character, as also is his scorn for a curriculum that teaches him about sugar beet, which is not a local crop, and assumes he knows nothing about hill sheep. Peter, a fine treble in the church choir, is apt to fall into incoherence when he is working on one of his inventions; that these often lead to damage and retribution never worries him.

David's personality is indicated more definitely – that is, we are often party to his thoughts and especially recognize his intuitive feeling for the past. However, the reality of the three boys comes far more from the depth and detail of the setting, the geographical exactness of the stories, than from analysis of their characters. In the sphere of Ransome (but with less spontaneity), in the manner of William Mayne (but with less wit), the books are notable for something rare in holiday adventure – for the moments, few and quickly described, when the boys are swept with sudden awareness of the beauty of a night sky, the complexity of people, the responsibility of the fortunate for the weak and oppressed. To mark such moments sincerely and unobtrusively is perhaps Philip Turner's chief contribution to the long, continuing line of domestic adventure stories. [Philip Turner: *Colonel Sheperton's Clock*, London 1964; *The Grange at High Force*, 1965; *Sea Peril*, 1966; *War on the Darnel*, 1969]

**DAVID MOSS** *see* ADAM CODLING

**DAVY CROCKETT** exists in history as a politician and as the hero of the Alamo: he exists in the imagination of generations of small boys as the hunter from Tennessee, with his coon-skin cap a type and a symbol in the enduring myth of the West. This many-sided hero also belongs to a unique minor branch of literature, the American tall story.

During most of the nineteenth century, almanacs carried a small amount of fact as an excuse for anecdotes about the man who weighed 'two hundred pounds, fourteen ounces' at birth and leapt so boldly out of his cradle that his uncle recommended that they 'plant him in the earth and water him with wild buffalo's milk, with boiled corncobs and tobacco leaves mixed in.' When the infant grows as high as the clouds and starts an avalanche miles away with his shouts, the family cuts him down to man size with axe, adze and whittling knife and sends him off to learn the hunter's craft.

Like Munchausen, Davy Crockett often kills several animals with a single bullet, and he once freezes a hostile bear with one look (only to thaw it out later and tame it for a pet). His meeting with Old Hickory (Andrew Jackson) and their various ploys are treated, in the almanacs, in the same airy fashion. They build up one of the strangest figures in New World mythology, part-clown, part-hero and still, distantly, a reminder of America's frontier past. [Erwin Shapiro: *Yankee Thunder*, New York 1944]

**DEE** (Dr John), variously seen as charlatan, sorcerer, scholar and traitor in historical fiction, is characterized by Cynthia Harnett in *Stars of Fortune* as a young scientist, feared and admired for his determined investigation of natural phenomena at a period when the Church deplored intellectual independence. Dr Dee acts as the confidant of the Princess Elizabeth, who is confined at Woodstock by order of her sister, Mary Tudor. The Doctor's lively sense of fun makes him popular with the large Washington family at Sulgrave Manor, while his experience and good sense enable him to help the older lads of the family when they engage in a dangerous attempt to free the Princess. In this ingenious mixture of fact and fiction, Cynthia Harnett has made good use of known facts about Dee and has built round his reputation as astronomer, mathematician and astrologer, a personality pleasant to read about and useful in forwarding the plot of her story. [Cynthia Harnett: *Stars of Fortune*, London 1956]

**DERRY LARKINS** works in Tom Jonas's coaching stable in the Devon town of Lynton. He understands why his mother has refused to let him take a job with the fishermen, for his father was drowned at sea, but all the same he envies his friend Billy Pritchard, who

Derry Larkins with the lifeboatmen, in *The Overland Launch*, written and illustrated by C. Walter Hodges.

is now old enough to take his place in the Lynmouth lifeboat. Derry's dormant feeling for the sea wakes when on a stormy night in January 1899 news comes that a ship is in trouble off Porlock. High seas make it impossible to launch the lifeboat from the harbour so she must be hauled over the steep hill to Porlock. Now every one of Tom Jonas's horses will be needed and Derry is included in the first stage of the journey. It is not altogether the adventure he has expected. He is soon cold, wet and weary, but pride and obstinacy keep him on his feet, and by one means or another he manages to stay till the end of the incredible overland journey.

The story of the overland launch is a true one and many of the characters described in the book really existed, but the author has chosen to view the events of that wild night mainly through the eyes of one fictitious character. If he had taken the panoramic view of an omniscient author, the narrative would not have been so concentrated. To have viewed the scene through the eyes of the horse-master or the anxious coxswain, or indeed any of the responsible adults, would have been to bring a touch of obvious fiction to a narrative which is almost painfully realistic. Derry, free from responsibility, quick of eye and responsive in mood, is the ideal person through whom to filter the action. His untutored remarks add a breath of humour to a taut story-line. [C. Walter Hodges: *The Overland Launch*, London 1969]

**DICK CALLUM**, bespectacled and outwardly vague, has inherited from his archaeologist parents a scientific bent which quickly earns him the respect of the Swallows and Amazons, although when they first meet him (in *Winter Holiday*) they class him with Titty (q.v.) (he is around the same age) as one of the little ones, and principally judge him and his sister Dorothea (q.v.) by their urban background. Dick's intellectual curiosity stands him in good stead. He does not resent being patronized by Nancy Blackett (q.v.) because he is eager to learn new skills – sledging (in *Winter Holiday*) or sailing (in *Coot Club*) for example. Because he is used to getting his information from books rather than by demonstration, his knowledge goes deeper than that of the Blacketts and even of the well-informed John Walker (q.v.).

Then again, Dick, although often absent-minded, is constructive. Where John is at his best using skills that he has learned from somebody else, Dick is capable of adapting his knowledge to unexpected challenges. It is he who contrives an electric bell to mark the return of pigeons to their cage (in *Pigeon Post*); with considerable courage he works out how to reach and rescue a cragfast sheep (in *Winter Holiday*) and in the Hebrides he comes into his own with his knowledge of ornithology (in *Great Northern?*). The Swallows and Amazons, with their essentially naval schemes, accept his capabilities and his intelligence with mild condescension. 'No one would have thought, to listen to Dick, that he was an able-seaman telling Captains and mates just what they ought to do.' The apotheosis of this quiet small boy is one of the shrewdest and most attractive aspects of Ransome's stories. Dick's strength is that he is not interested in himself, but is prepared to be actively interested in almost anything else. His personality offers convincing evidence that you do not have to be noisy or quick to excel; in this he is a perfect foil for the Blacketts. A comment made by his discerning sister seems to sum up his temperament. 'Sometimes,' she mused, 'in a queer way of his own, he seemed to hit on things that made stories and real life come closer together than usual.' [Arthur Ransome: *Winter Holiday*, London 1933; *Coot Club*, 1934; *The Big Six*, 1940; *Great Northern?*, 1947]

**DICK PLASHET** has a right, though it is not publicly acknowledged, to use the name Richard Plantagenet. In the year that Cecily Jolland (q.v.) goes to Mantlemass, Richard is a boy of sixteen living in the establishment of a certain Dr Woodlark, where he has been sent to receive a gentleman's education. Insecure and perplexed, with no surname of his own, the boy imagines himself 'a secret hero, a prince, a warrior – one to be discovered to his people only at a precise moment decreed by fate'. The day-dream is truer than he realizes. Woken suddenly one summer night, Dick is sent off on horseback with a young man who can tell him nothing of their errand. In a tent close to Bosworth Field Dick is presented to his father – the soldier king Richard III. He is promised that if the victory should go to York, he will be acknowledged as the King's son, but if Richard is defeated he must go into hiding, for he will either be killed or be used as a tool by ambitious dissidents.

After the death of Richard III on Bosworth Field, Dick goes into hiding. He works first as apprentice to a master-builder in London, later as a skilled handyman and guide in the forests of Sussex, where he calls himself Plashet after the hamlet where he lives. So that his unusual situation shall endanger nobody but himself, Dick Plashet does not marry the countrywoman Anis Bostel who bears him a son – for illegitimacy may make the oddly-named Medley (q.v.) safer from his father's enemies. Plashet is a desperately reserved man, educated far above a countryman's station, and never mixing with his fellow workers. He reads much in the books which he keeps safe from damp and dirt in a leather bag: he never seeks employment but waits for it to come to him – 'the favour must be on his side'. When plotters locate him he leaves his 'wife' and son hastily to draw danger away from them, and lives out his lonely existence in another part of the country. This quiet, dignified, mysterious character derives from a tradition that a son of Richard III did work in Sussex at the mason's trade, being buried at Eastwell in Kent in 1550 under the name of Richard Plantagenet. It is a remarkable feat of imagination and historical intuition that has presented a character so diverse. Dick Plashet is linked with those unhappy pretenders of the late fifteenth century and gains credibility by association with them; but where historians can only guess at the motives of Perkin Warbeck and Lambert Simnel, Barbara Willard has drawn her fictional character in depth, giving us clues from the beginning of his strange story to the man's strength and his weakness, his courage in protecting his family and his knowledge that he could be tempted by the promise of rank and fortune. [Barbara Willard: *The Sprig of Broom*, London 1971]

**DICK ULLATHORNE** lives in a mining village near Durham at the turn of the present century. Though he is clever at his lessons, he lacks his brother Kit's independent spirit and is content to join his father down the pit. But when Kit becomes a wage-earner, Dick no longer has a companion and he begins to visit his reclusive grandmother and to help out his formal education with her small library. Misfortune gives Dick the means to change the course of his life. Three days entombed in the pit leaves him with rheumatic fever and when he has recovered he realizes that though he has not been unhappy as a miner he wants something different for his future.

Simply and directly, against a firmly drawn background of a mining community some seventy years ago, Frederick Grice has drawn the portrait of a cheerful, lively, clever lad finding a way, and no easy way, to break away from the family pattern. [Frederick Grice: *The Bonnie Pit Laddie*, London 1960]

**DICKON**'s real name is Richard Sowerby but his nickname fits his blunt, cheerful character. The part he plays in the wonderful transformation of *The Secret Garden* is a very practical one. He understands the life in nature and knows exactly what to do not only to make things grow in the garden but also to help Mary Lennox (q.v.) and Colin Craven (q.v.), those twisted plants, to grow into health and happiness.

The home background of this engaging country lad shows how his happy temperament has been given scope to grow in the security of a cottage full to bursting with children, poor and humble but rich in affection and in the guidance of a wise mother. Dickon's background is important too in understanding his natural good manners. The head gardener says of him: 'He'd be at home in Buckingham Palace or at the bottom of a coal mine … And yet it's not impudence, either.'

As he is presented in the story, Dickon is an attractively real country boy, with red cheeks and blue eyes, his body 'as tough as a whitethorn knobstick'. It is also obvious that he is an example, as Cedric Errol (q.v.) is in a different way, of the author's preoccupation with class and environment. Reading the book in the light of modern social attitudes, it is easy to forget or to fail to notice that Dickon is not only a believable boy but also one of 'nature's gentlemen'. [Frances Hodgson Burnett: *The Secret Garden*, New York 1911]

**DIDO TWITE**, a brat of eight or nine with dirty, straw-coloured hair and sharp eyes, lives in London in a period specially rearranged by Joan Aiken, when the Stuart King James III is in the ascendant and the Hanoverians are trying to get their Pretender on the throne. Though the forceful Dido is far more interested in herself than in anyone else, she is drawn into the plots and intrigues of the House of Hanover, for her father has been storing arms for the conspirators in his cellar. Dido takes a light-hearted view of this until she grows attached to Simon, a protégé of the Royalist Duke of Battersea, who lodges with the Twites. She follows him when he is shanghaied and shipped off for Holland; her misguided efforts to free him result in a fire and the children take to the water. Simon is rescued and believes Dido has been drowned. However, she is picked up by a whaling ship and (in *Nightbirds on Nantucket*) plays a prominent part in frustrating a new Hanoverian conspiracy in which the sinister Miss Slighcarp and her associates plan to assassinate the King with a long-range gun fixed on a Nantucket headland.

Dido's genius for being in the right place at the right moment is demonstrated again when a year or so later (in *The Cuckoo Tree*) she is travelling by coach to London when she and her fellow passenger are involved in an accident and she is entrusted by the wounded Captain with an urgent dispatch. With her usual luck she finds friends as well as enemies along the way and it is largely because of her that St Paul's is not tilted into the Thames with the crowds come to see the new King Richard IV crowned.

Joan Aiken's Hanoverian stories are a unique blend of parody, satire, nonsense and logic, and Dido fits them perfectly. Her forceful slang, cleverly put together from the thieves' argot of the late eighteenth century, expresses her personality exactly. With splendid self-confidence she addresses everybody in the same blithe manner. When the King invites her to be one of his train-bearers in the coronation procession her reply is succinct: 'Thanks, Mister King, we'd be right pleased. If I can get back to Sussex directly arter, that is; I shan't feel easy till I see how my old Cap's a-getting on.' For Dido, in spite of her rough and ready ways, has a heart. [Joan Aiken: *Black Hearts in Battersea*, London 1965; *Night Birds on Nantucket*, 1966; *The Cuckoo Tree*, 1971]

**DIGORY KETTERLEY** *see* POLLY PLUMMER

**DIMSIE** (Dorothy Maitland) takes a strong line when she becomes a pupil at the Jane Willard Foundation. When at the age of eleven she reaches the Third Division she gathers a group of like-minded girls around her to found the Anti-Soppist Society, through which they hope to reform the slack, boring girls already in the form. No crushes, no kissing, plenty of effort on the games field – these bracing prescriptions are typical of the schoolgirl whose life is chronicled in a long run of stories, once very popular but now an obvious target for the mischievous comments of Arthur Marshall.

During the several books Dimsie learns to control

An illustration by Pat Marriott from *Night Birds on Nantucket,* one of the adventures of Dido Twite.

her quick temper, the 'wild, tempestuous little person, the ringleader in every sort of adventurous mischief' becomes a more perceptive girl. The stern line on sentiment which she promoted at the age of thirteen has, two years later, relaxed a little as she realizes that kindness can be as helpful as discipline.

When, as a young woman enduring a long engagement, Dimsie comes back to Jane's to teach for a term, she is asked to help the senior girls, since the head girl is a weak character and there is a bad spirit afoot. She sets about guiding a new Anti-Soppist Society, with its chief target the use of make-up, but with less confidence than she had in the Third Division. 'Right and wrong', she confesses to the Headmistress, 'don't seem quite so plainly right and wrong as they did when I was here as a schoolgirl; they waver about, and their edges get rather blurred, and it makes everything much harder.'

Dimsie is emphatically the central character in this set of school stories. Her personality comes over all the more strongly because none of the other characters in the stories is more than a two-dimensional figure. They provide a background for the study of a naughty girl gradually acquiring sense and wisdom. In the manner

of such stories, the first stage is considerably more lively than the second. Nor has the author been able to draw Dimsie as a convincing grown-up. She seems in idiom and outlook to be no more than a schoolgirl made over as an adult. [Dorita Fairlie Bruce: *Dimsie Moves Up,* London 1921; *Dimsie Moves Up Again,* 1922; *Dimsie Goes Back,* 1927]

**DOBRY**'s future seemed to his family to depend on the 'only poplar tree in the whole village'. His father, on a journey back from the mill with flour from newly harvested wheat, had broken a branch from a tree and pushed it into the soil of his courtyard, saying 'If this tree lives, grows, my son will live, grow big, grow very strong. He will be a great man. He will be a man with not just a spark of God in him but a whole fire!' The proud farmer was killed in the war, but Roda, his widow, and his robust old father, were mindful of his saying as Dobry grew in energy and imagination.

In this Bulgarian village, not long after the First World War, custom and belief were strong and simple. The boy grew by the pattern of the seasons, listening to his grandfather's store of stories, rejoicing in the first snow, watching for the coming of the gypsy with his tame bear. Then Dobry's intense, eager interest in the world round him began to show itself through his fingers. He drew, with charcoal – first a stork, to make into a kite for his playmate Neda, then the rooster in the yard, the family pigs, Maestro Kolu who made their fine stove; and though his mother was uneasy Grandfather taught her to be proud of her son's skill and convinced her that his destiny should lead him to a wider world than that of the family farm. 'If a boy is something', Grandfather assured her, 'it doesn't matter what kind of work he chooses ... Bring a boy up to use his hands and brain and heart, leave his guts in him and then let him alone.' The lesson did not have its effect all at once; but Roda was finally convinced when Dobry, with sudden inspiration, carved a Nativity scene from snow, deep in the night when everyone was asleep. So the boy grew and absorbed strength from the fields and woods he loved and from his fierce response to the natural world. Cheerfully and with no fear of the change, he set off as an untried youth to Sofia to study. secure in Neda's love and in his own determination. This quiet, firm picture of a boy growing up in the Balkans is notable for the interaction of place and people. [Monica Shannon (pseud. Atanas Katchamakoff): *Dobry*, New York 1934]

**DOC RACCOON** in a relaxed drawl explains why engineers are busy building a levée at Catfish Bend, first to a young raccoon who stops to greet him as he sits peacefully on the bank, then to a traveller who disembarks to stretch his legs while the *Tennessee Belle* takes on a load of cotton. The gift of a chocolate bar paves the way to a comfortable relationship which leads not only to the story of the great flood but, later, to the tale of how the animals were persecuted by an out-of-season hunter and how they finally hunted the hunters to distraction through the marshes. The third crisis which the raccoon describes concerns the infiltration of a rogue grey fox and a scabby urban rat who befuddle the innocent country animals into breaking a long-established truce and set up a reign of terror that was not easily broken.

The most insistent and obvious comparison that comes to mind when one reads these supremely easy, button-holing yarns is with Mark Twain. Like his great ancestor, Burman relates his characters consistently to their background, whether they are human or animal. Doc Raccoon, by virtue of his personality, is not only the obvious leader of the community but also the obvious link with a human reporter of events. Judge Black, an aphoristic, colubrine Abe Lincoln, has to concentrate hard on remaining a vegetarian. These two cronies have made common cause with a pessimistic frog who conducts the Indian Bayou Glee Club, J. C. Hunter the fox (a bit of a smart-aleck, his friends think) and a giggling rabbit given to unfinished rhymes. The five animals came together originally on a small mound of earth which saved them from flood and where the seemingly inevitable demise of one or two of their number was prevented by an agreement solemnly signed and eventually extended to the whole of Catfish Bend. With token clothing and individual idiom, the five associates plan like humans and act like animals. This gives the author opportunity on one hand for political allegory as sharp as Kästner's but somewhat more urbane, on the other for a strongly visualized riverside setting.

The humour in the books is many-faceted. There is the sardonic, straight-faced humour of incongruity. A blacksmith frog newly made a member of the Glee Club is eagerly imitated by the others 'so they could do something the old frog had always wanted, sing the *Anvil Chorus* from *Il Trovatore*'; J.C.'s typical reaction to this 'fancy piece' is to wish 'the frogs'd stick to *Sweet Adeline.*

Doc Raccoon and his friends sign a pact of non-aggression; an illustration by Alice Caddy in *Three from Catfish Bend*.

Adeline's a song you can roll around in your throat'. The role of the animals in reflecting humanity provides a humour that deepens from one story to another. The selfish attitude of New Orleans to the flood damage at Catfish Bend rouses in the reader only an amused exasperation. Conscience is pricked rather more seriously as we read how hunters disturb and devastate the pleasant sanctuary, but the ingenious campaign mounted by Doc Raccoon and his friends, told with throw-away detail, can still be enjoyed with a fairly easy mind. It is then we come to the third story, with its catalogue of woe as the infamous propaganda of fox and rat (about banks, tenement housing, dominant races and other 'advantages') brings the community into subjection, that we feel too close to similar events to smile quite so readily. But we believe the fantasy, whatever its effect on us. Doc Raccoon, that sensible, humane, intelligent animal, asked the author to 'switch a name or two' because 'He didn't want to get any animals into trouble'. Otherwise, Mr Burman assures us, 'I haven't changed a word'. [Ben Lucien Burman: *High Water at Catfish Bend*, New York 1952; *Seven Stars for Catfish Bend*, 1956; *The Owl Hoots Twice at Catfish Bend*, 1961; omnibus edition, London 1967; *Blow a Wild Bugle for Catfish Bend*, 1975]

**DOCTOR DOLITTLE** was invented, or grew, when Hugh Lofting wrote letters to his small son from the Front in the First World War. To comply with Colin's desire for pictures and his natural love of fun, the Doctor was conceived as a comic character: to alleviate the distress of a compassionate man caught up in destruction, he became a serious one. Hugh Lofting imagined an eccentric country physician in the stage-coach period, a man with a bent for natural history, who finally decides to give up his human practice to serve the animals he greatly prefers. The uniqueness of the doctor lies in one extra talent – he can communicate with animals.

The Doctor enters upon the new phase of his life almost by accident. His practice in Puddleby on the Marsh begins to decline as his patients retreat from the numerous animals he insists on keeping in his house. Finally his only remaining patient is Matthew Mugg, the cats-meat-man, who gives the Doctor the idea of earning a living as an animal-doctor (it is part of the wry humour of the books that the Doctor, by dealing directly with his patients rather than with their owners, puts payment, in money at least, out of the question). Matthew Mugg's proposal is warmly supported by Polynesia the parrot who, to the Doctor's excited surprise, offers to teach him animal languages, starting with the ABC of the birds.

The Doctor's character cannot be separated from his doings. Scientific curiosity and a bent for travel lead him to Africa, to South America, ultimately to the Moon. We learn incidentally that in an early, undescribed journey he reached the North Pole but was persuaded by

The doctor talks to Cheapside, the London sparrow, from *Dr Dolittle and the Secret Lake*.

Some of his animal friends from *Dr Dolittle's Circus*.

a deputation of polar bears to keep the fact a secret for fear that men should come to exploit the coal under the ice (the casual reference is one of many devices for compelling belief in the Doctor). Each of his expeditions is successful because of his particular gifts. When the ancient boats that are all he can afford founder beneath him, there are always helpful aquatic animals at hand. His medical knowledge is put at the disposal of a vixen with a flat-footed cub, a Moon Man with rheumatism, a Giant Sea Snail that has sprained its tail, and each of his patients, answering his eager questions, contributes to his store of unusual knowledge.

The practical side of his nature is seen in action when he establishes a post office in the African kingdom of Fantippo, with birds as postmen (each species being allotted appropriate routes and duties) and when he writes, casts and produces the Canary Opera and Puddleby Pantomime which takes London by storm. The initial premise of the stories, that the Doctor can communicate with animals, is at first stated simply and lightheartedly. *The Story of Doctor Dolittle* is short, understated and almost wholly comic, and the Doctor is to some extent led along by events. But as early as the second book (*The Voyages of Doctor Dolittle*) Hugh Lofting begins to deepen his hero's character. When the Doctor is offered a crown for his services to the warring Popsipetels and Bagjagderags, his sense of duty towards them is so strong that it needs all Polynesia's cunning to get him back to Puddleby. As the series proceeds, the compassionate side of the Doctor's nature is emphasized more and more, as he expresses (in lawless action as well as in pungent words) his hatred of hunting, zoos, badly run pet shops and any form of tyranny or aggression.

In order to integrate and strengthen the various facets of John Dolittle's character, to merge artistically and effectively the comic fantasy and the humane commonsense of the man, Hugh Lofting steps back as narrator, after the first book, giving place to Tommy Stubbins. This ingenuous youth, son of Jacob Stubbins the Puddleby cobbler, is nine years old when he first meets the doctor, by then famous throughout the West Country. Enthralled by the man and his ideas, Tommy eventually persuades the Doctor to teach him animal languages in return for any help he can give to the household. In time he becomes indispensable to the Doctor, and to the author, who uses him as a link between the books and speaks through his admiring and sympathetic comments on the Doctor's exploits.

Tommy – reliable, conscientious and keen – establishes a norm within the fantasy, placed as he is, firmly in the class and circumstance of the early nineteenth century. In a way his character helps to date the stories as much as such incidental details as stage coaches and sailing ships or references to Morland, Wilberforce and the Slave Trade or Rowland Hill's penny postage. The date when the Doctor and his friend Tommy are supposed to have lived matters as little as the date when they were first introduced to readers. The Doctor's views on the sadness of human error and the virtues of intellectual curiosity are as enduring as his total lack of self-consciousness. In one respect, however, Hugh Lofting's books cannot be accepted today without question. In the 1920s it was not universally considered derogatory to describe an African prince as a bumbling per-

sonage, who dreamed of a Sleeping Beauty who rejected him because of his black face and who appealed to the Doctor to make him white. The character of Bumpo, Prince of Jolliginki, as he appears more or less prominently in the first three Dolittle books, is offensive to present-day readers in spite of the context of fantasy, while the nicely judged details of the house-boat post office are coloured for us by the bluffly slapstick presentation of the uncivilized King of Fantippo. Like other books of their date, the Dolittle stories need to be presented as period pieces and to be read with some allowance for their date, if they are to continue, as they should, as nursery classics.

There are no such difficulties to be faced when we come to the animal characters in the books. Doctor Dolittle's original and permanent household consists of Polynesia the parrot, Chee Chee the monkey, Jip the dog, Dab Dab the duck, Too Too the owl and Gub Gub the pig. To these may be added later adoptions like the Pushmi-Pullyu, Whitey the white mouse, the circus dogs Swizzle and Toby, and the old horse Dobbin, together with visitors or outliers like Cheapside the London sparrow, Miranda the Purple Bird of Paradise, the canaries Pippinella and Twink, Sophie the seal, Speedy the Skimmer, Mudface the turtle and the strange moon-cat who is called Itty because Polynesia refuses to believe it is real. It is noteworthy that Itty is the only animal in the Dolittle books that has to be tamed and the only one which has no human traits added to its essential catness. For Doctor Dolittle, as for Lofting, perhaps the mystery of cats was impenetrable; certainly the species hardly fits the Puddleby ménage.

Hugh Lofting established his animal characters on several levels. First, they are never less than their natural selves: Jip's acute nose, Gub Gub's greed, Polynesia's loquacity. Chee Chee's nervous manner, are true to the facts of animal behaviour. Secondly, they operate, physically and mentally, in the world of humans – that is, they perform roles which seem natural because of our traditional beliefs about their animal natures. For example, since owls are traditionally wise. Too Too has a gift for figures and looks after the Doctor's financial affairs.

With Jip, the boisterous noise associated with dogs is translated into a jovial, hearty manner, expressed most often in teasing Gub Gub and in a useful lack of imagination, while the notorious faithfulness of the species is shown in his loyal, devoted attention to the Doctor's interests. With one of Hugh Lofting's sudden twists, the determinedly unromantic Jip is occasionally a vehicle for near-poetry, as he nostalgically analyses and separates the scents on the wind.

Polynesia the parrot claims to be 'either a hundred and eighty-three or a hundred and eighty-two' and remembers seeing King Charles hiding in the oak-tree when she first came over from Africa. As befits her great age, she shows a wisdom and common sense, and a dictatorial manner, which often help to check some extravagant plan of the Doctor's.

Chee Chee was rescued by the Doctor from his ignorant master, an Italian organ-grinder. The wistful expression in a monkey's eyes is deepened, in Chee Chee's case, into a permanent slight melancholy and a nervousness born of his experiences that sometimes becomes real fear. In one of the most affecting passages in the books (in *Doctor Dolittle in the Moon*) the monkey nerves himself to explore the fearful unknown jungles to find food when the party is in danger of starvation.

The character of Dab Dab the duck is the most distantly related to the animal species, for she is the Doctor's housekeeper and one has to imagine her lighting candles, scrubbing pots and making beds with beak and wings. Yet even here there are associations that make the humanization of the duck perfectly logical. A spotless, tidily organized linen-cupboard fits the lily-white image of a nursery-rhyme duck; a fussy house-wifely manner is suitable enough; while on one occasion when Dab Dab leaves her domestic role to become a ballerina in the Dolittle Pantomime, the actual shape of a duck is most persuasively translated into human terms, in Hugh Lofting's drawing as well as in his words.

The most strongly humanized of the animals, Gub Gub, is also the one most obviously based on a popular assumption – that pigs are greedy – and on appearances – for the pink rotundities of a young pig are extended to give Gub Gub a primal innocence in his role as *enfant terrible*. Much of our impression of him comes from the comments of the other animals, from Dab Dab's impatience at his queries about the next meal or Jip's caustic but good-hearted jokes at his expense or Polynesia's irritation when self-evident matters have to be explained to him. Gub Gub is ubiquitous in the stories and indeed has a whole book to his credit (*Gub Gub's Book*). Besides being a major outlet for Hugh Lofting's invention of comic situations, Gub Gub also provides endless opportunities for the verbal jokes, puns, malapropisms and nonsense which form an essential element in the humour of the books and which plausibly arise from the pig's given character. It is as acceptable that he should imagine (in the story of the Magic Cucumber which he tells in *Post Office*) special clothes-lines on which to hang the skin off cups of cocoa as that he should conceive of a 'History of Eating' that would include certain cases of Sherbet Scones, the Icebox Detective, and the Epicnic of King Guzzle the Second. *Gub Gub's Book* is a rollicking justification of greed and a confirmation of all the occasions when Gub Gub's contribution to a conversation is gastronomic. But he is not just the proverbial greedy pig. Hugh Lofting allows him a certain youthful charm, so that his companions are never ill-natured when they are laughing at him, and he suggests from time to time a strain of romantic yearning (for instance, in Gub Gub's

delight when he plays the part of Pantaloon in the pantomime) which is at once comic and serious.

If Gub Gub provides the main outlet for Hugh Lofting's love of verbal nonsense, the other animals are often a vehicle for the ideas which he passionately wants to convey to children. He uses animals not only because their behaviour seems to him so much more sensible and considerate than that of humans but also because their comments on human nature (caustic from Jip and Polynesia, resigned from Too Too and Dab Dab) are far more effective than they would have been if made directly by the author. There is something more than mere humanization here. [Hugh Lofting: *The Story of Doctor Dolittle*, New York 1920; *The Voyages of Doctor Dolittle*, 1922; *Doctor Dolittle's Post Office*, 1923; *Doctor Dolittle's Circus*, 1924; *Doctor Dolittle's Zoo*, 1925; *Doctor Dolittle's Caravan*, 1926; *Doctor Dolittle's Garden*, 1927; *Doctor Doolittle in the Moon*, 1928; *Gub Gub's Book*, 1932; *Doctor Dolittle's Return*, 1933; *Doctor Dolittle and the Secret Lake*, 1948; *Doctor Dolittle and the Green Canary*, 1950; *Doctor Dolittle's Puddleby Adventures*, 1952]

**DODDER** *see* BALDMONEY

**DOLOR**, Prince of Nomansland, is given this least happy of his many names by a little old woman dressed in grey who appears mysteriously at the christening and who seems to know a great deal more about him than anyone else – for instance, that the baby has been dropped by the state nursemaid and that his frail mother has just died at the palace. The injury to the Prince's legs makes it easy for his uncle the Crown Prince to assume power as Regent after the King's death. Plausibly defending his action, the Regent sends the little prince to the Blue Mountains 'for his health' and shortly gives it out that he has died on the journey.

Prince Dolor grows up in a high round tower, in the care of a woman whose own crimes, now pardoned, ensure that she will not reveal the plot. The little prince has hardly realized his loneliness before his strange godmother appears. Her words of affection and encouragement are as valuable to him as her gift of a travelling cloak. This shabby piece of green cloth carries him out of the tower to unimagined worlds and, though he always travels high in the air, the magic spectacles his godmother also provides bring the beauty of nature and the complexity of man clearly within his view.

As Dolor grows in courage and intelligence the woman who cares for him comes to love him as a person and finally, against orders, explains to him his own sad history. His anger at his uncle's treatment of him disappears when he is taken by a friendly magpie to peer into a room where he sees the Regent lying dead on his bed and witnesses in the city streets the terrible sight of a populace demanding a republic while unable to organize themselves.

Now indeed the boy's courage is needed to withstand

silence and fear when he returns to the tower to find his nurse gone. Finally won over by the way the boy has endured imprisonment, she has made her way to the city to tell the people they still have a king. So, after weary days alone, the lad is brought back to his rightful place by his repentant courtiers. Two secret blessings the fifteen-year-old king has in his new state – the cloak which helps him to learn the truth about his kingdom, and the secret friendship of his godmother. Guided by her, and by his strong character, he rules his people wisely and educates his oldest cousin as his heir so that he can one day renounce the crown and vanish on the travelling cloak.

The power of suffering to educate for good is expounded very directly, in a sweet, sober prose, in an allegory which bears every sign of having been told to a particular child. The attractive fairy-tale appurtenances and atmosphere of the story are beautifully equated with the sturdy moral attitude of the period in which it was written. [Dinah Maria Mulock (Mrs Craik): *The Little Lame Prince and his Travelling Cloak*, London 1874]

**DOMINIC,** a hound with a taste for action, one day packs his collection of hats, his piccolo and a few other goods in a bandanna, ties it over a stick and sets off to look for adventure. It is not long before he finds it. On the second day of his journey a witch-alligator advises him which of two forks in the road will lead to something interesting. Action follows soon enough when Dominic tangles with the Doomsday Gang (a band of weasels, cats, a fox, stoats and other animals traditionally associated with evil), nurses an ancient pig on his death bed and inherits his treasure, finances the wedding of the unfortunate pig Barney Swain (who has suffered from the dastardly gang), provides music for fairies (mice) to dance to at night, rescues a widow goose in distress and finally wins for himself a beautiful bride who has been patiently waiting for the coming of her prince.

Dominic sets off on an adventure, from the book written and illustrated by William Steig.

In this engaging piece of parody and pastiche, Dominic, the fortunate hero, never hesitates to help the unfortunate and indeed gives away most of his treasure, only to win a greater one in the beauteous Eleanor. His princely eye for the beauty of moonlight and dawn, his musical skill, are balanced by the efficacy of his nose and his sturdy handling of the spear he picks up, conveniently, on the way. Now he is all hound, now all fairy prince – now aggressive and cocky, now refined and reflective; his moods and roles change as he changes his hats (a point which William Steig emphasizes in the aptly satirical drawings that underline the story episode by episode). The dog is the perfect centre for a story whose humour is sly, swift and casual. 'Whenever there was trouble, his philosophy was to go right out and meet it at least halfway.' The qualifying 'at least' gives a clue to the author's blithe attitude to his theme, his subject and to the fairy-tale tradition in which Dominic has earned a private and special place. [William Steig: *Dominic*, New York 1972]

**DON MORGAN** comes from the United States to live in Canada with his Uncle Joe and Aunt Maud after his widower father is killed working in a mine. Don, at sixteen, is frustrated and restless, but determined (after a short season of trawl-fishing) to win the right somehow to work for himself in his own way. With his uncle's help the boy is given a licence to trap through one winter in Starbuck Valley on condition he can find a companion to share the rigours of the trip.

An expedition like this tests friendship as severely as it reveals character. Don has always trusted Tubby Miller and he is distressed when, in the woods, Tubby shows what he feels is cowardice; although the boys have been warned against Lee Jetson, a loner whose claim adjoins their own, and though at first Lee seems to be aggressive, Don refuses to believe he is dangerous. He is proved right when Tubby gashes his foot badly with an axe and has to be carried back to the township. At the end of a hard season Don admits, 'I learned something anyway, even I didn't make a killing.'

What Don has learned is that he does not really want to spend his life either hunting or fishing. His character illustrates very directly the difficulties of a lad who wants to be independent but who is not ready to measure either his ambitions or his capacities. What there is of individuality in the character comes from circumstances, from the setting of Don's adventures and from the author's open, straightforward statements, from time to time, of the way the boy's thoughts are tending. There is no introspection here but a natural, explicit alternation of moods which suits the open-air, active nature of the two books. [Roderick Haig-Brown: *Starbuck Valley Winter*, London 1944; *Saltwater Summer*, 1949]

**DONALD JACKSON** has been surrounded by authority for the whole of his fourteen years. His mother is a teacher at the school where he is a pupil ('she called him Jackson in school, and he called her Mrs Jackson, and of course the same thing very often at home'); his father is a strict Methodist and both parents weary him, and themselves, by measuring him against an invisible standard which does not satisfy him. His mainly silent rebellion is made more difficult because of the long, dragging unhappiness in the house since the accident which caused his sister's death, his father's paralysis and his own premature birth. Guilt and hatred build up in the boy; his only confidant, a sympathetic, unorthodox vicar, is soon to go to another parish; his father becomes seriously ill and is taken to hospital.

Donald's only escape from a monotonous misery lies in his own mind. He begins to move, in his involuntary thoughts, between the everyday world and a land of fantasy where a gigantic worm-creature, a macabre travesty of a legendary dragon, preys upon a village which Donald desperately wants to save. He becomes, first, servant to the lord who is trying to bring order to the shattered community, then squire to a visiting knight who, on seeing the gigantic track of the worm and smelling its noisome stench, disappears in the night. Finally Donald himself goes out against the monster when the lord, the father-figure, has been killed, but instead of facing certain death in the way chivalric honour prescribes, he runs away when he sees his weapons are useless. In the end, in visions which alternate more and more quickly with agonised visits to his father's bedside, the boy kills the worm by a trick and, guilty yet appeased of guilt, returns to his other self to face his father's death.

In this monstrous, coldly terrifying image William Mayne describes Donald's experience in fantasy terms as well as, elliptically and with detachment, in direct narrative of the everyday world. This is not the ordinary technique of character-drawing but a severely constrained, stark investigation of a particular situation and the state of mind it produces in a particular boy, a state of mind which, as Mayne implies, is at once an escape from grief and a way of admitting and suffering it. [William Mayne: *A Game of Dark*, London 1971]

**DONG WITH A LUMINOUS NOSE** (the) is Edward Lear's final, fantastical expression of his acute consciousness of his grotesque appearance; when he caricatured himself in letters to his friends, he gave himself successively smaller and neater features. The poem of the Dong was foreshadowed in one among several limericks he wrote about noses:

> There was an old man in a barge,
> Whose nose was exceedingly large;
> But in fishing by night,
> It supported a light,
> Which helped that old man in a barge.

That particular nose was a natural one: the Dong's nose was woven from the bark of the Twangum Tree, a container 'Of vast proportions and painted red. And tied with cords to the back of his head' and it protected a

Edward Gorey's illustration of *The Dong with the Luminous Nose.*

lamp to guide him through the dark as he searched sadly for the Jumbly Girl he had loved and lost.

The poem is the most haunting, comic and melancholy of all Lear's strange verses. It may hide a reference to Augusta Bethell, like the bizarre, painfully sad verses of *The Courtship of the Yonghy-Bonghy-Bo*; it may be that the great Gramboolian plain where the Dong roams represents a particular plain in Italy. Whether the poem *is* cryptic autobiography or a more generalized example of what George Orwell called 'a kind of poltergeist interference with common sense', it remains one of the most deeply affecting, crazily sad poems in the English language, as the Dong remains one of the most eccentric and searching portraits of a human being. [Edward Lear: *Nonsense Songs, Stories, Botany and Alphabets*, London 1871; *More Nonsense*, 1871; *Laughable Lyrics*, 1877]

**DOROTHEA CALLUM,** when she first sees an ice-yacht on the lake (in *Winter Holiday*), remarks 'It's very pretty'. The Swallows and Amazons are stunned. If Dorothea never wins the admiring respect the others soon learn to accord to her brother Dick (q.v.), it is perhaps because, while she has the kind of romantic outlook they are used to in Titty (q.v.), she lacks Titty's good sense and capability and she has besides an endearing but at times inconvenient silliness. As Dick's older sister Dorothea has a measure of maternal authority but she has no authority at all within the group of adventurers. It is in fact more natural for her to be alone, to think out and write stories. In her stories 'there were usually not more than two (children), or at most

four, and then perhaps a villain' and she is not happy, not at first anyhow, at being swept along in a crowd; she 'found it easy enough to make up stories in which everybody talked and talked' but she herself is not good at talking to strangers and tends to leave the initiative to the less self-conscious Dick.

Dorothea is essentially a follower, not a leader. Her one ambition is to be like the Swallows and Amazons. She dashes off with Dick to the 'North Pole' at the end of the lake (in *Winter Holiday*) because she is too eager to follow Nancy's (q.v.) instructions for this fairly stiff sledging expedition to check signals or even to wish the others were there too. Through blizzard and darkness she is buoyed up by the thought that she is doing what Nancy has ordered. After a day or two learning to sail with Tom Dudgeon (in *Coot Club*) she wishes Nancy could see her hands – 'They are so beautifully horny'. When she and Dick have to camp by themselves in a woodcutter's stone hut in the Beckfoot woods (in *The Picts and the Martyrs*), to conceal from fierce Aunt Maria that Nancy has invited visitors in her mother's absence, Dorothea tries to remember everything the other children do in camp. Comforting herself by treating the enterprise as a story ('Alone in the Forest' by Dorothea Callum), she forgets her fears of darkness and solitude as she learns how to get into a hammock, works out rations and wrestles with the ghastly job of making rabbit stew from scratch. In the end she 'felt about the eating of the first rabbit she had ever cooked much as if she were reading the proofs of her first book.'

This unexpected adventure in the woods not only

brings out an unsuspected vein of good sense in Dorothea. It also shows that she is truly a writer in the making because, derivative though her tales and titles may be, she is genuinely perceptive about people. As it becomes more and more difficult to keep Aunt Maria in ignorance of the presence of the D's, with postman, doctor and farmers all drawn into the conspiracy, she thinks to herself 'real life was like one of those tangles of string where if you found an end and pulled you only made things worse.'

Dorothea, author of 'The Outlaw of the Broads', shares with her brother Dick the pertinacity of a child brought up by parents who, one guesses, have always treated their offspring as adults. This pertinacity is exercised during the adventures which are alien to her nature and, far more, in the stories which she mumbles over to herself as she follows her more active friends, and uses as an unexpectedly useful guide line to life. It is her experience with fiction that first leads the Death and Glories to believe that they are being framed by nasty George Owdon (in *The Big Six*) and it is Dorothea who organizes the detective squad and marshals the evidence that is to save them from the law. It was perhaps with some inward amusement that Ransome developed the character of this demurely unbelligerent rival to warlike Nancy, who would certainly never have believed that she, the terror of the seas, was really the weaker one of the two. [Arthur Ransome: *Winter Holiday*, London 1933; *Coot Club*, 1934; *The Big Six*, 1940; *The Picts and the Martyrs*, 1943; *Great Northern?*, 1947]

**DOROTHY GALE** is blown by a cyclone from her Uncle Henry's farm in Kansas to the country of the Munchkins in the Land of Oz. Overjoyed because the farm-house has landed conveniently on the Wicked Witch of the East, the Munchkins give Dorothy her magic shoes but they cannot tell her how to get home and advise her to consult the Wizard in the City of Emerald. A scarecrow lamenting his lack of brains; Nick Chopper, turned into a tin woodman by the wicked Witch and left without a heart; a lion fierce of aspect but without courage – each of these odd creatures decides the Wizard might be able to help them too. After an adventurous journey the companions are admitted into the mysterious presence of the Wizard, whom each one sees differently; the Scarecrow sees 'a most lovely lady', the Tin Woodman a beast as large as an elephant, and the Lion a ball of fire. Only Dorothy sees nothing until her little dog Toto knocks over the screen which hides an insignificant 'old man with a bald head and a wrinkled face' who explains that he was blown to Oz from Omaha in a balloon and taken for a powerful king by the populace; shortly after he has granted the wishes of the travellers he repairs the balloon and flies off to Omaha, leaving the Scarecrow as ruler in Oz, with the Tin Woodman as King of the Winkies and the Cowardly Lion as ruler in the great forest.

Meanwhile Dorothy finds her way back to Kansas through the power of the silver shoes.

This forthright, practical little girl has been described as 'a sort of American tourist in Fairyland'. She enjoys numerous adventures in and around Oz (she appears in seven of the fourteen Oz books written by L. Frank Baum himself), always ready with a suitable form of address, whether it is for a queen, a dwarf, a hen or an enchantress. She follows her standard of conduct in any circumstance and is always ready with a kindly reproof for anyone who falls below it in courage or consideration; with the attitude and voice of a governess she roundly tells the Nome King 'It seems to me... that you are not as honest as you pretend to be', though she is afraid of his power. Her reaction to most of the surprising situations she meets is, in fact, more often one of interest than of fear. Indeed, the dangers that beset her in Oz are usually innocuous, for the author wrote of his first book, 'It aspires to being a modernized fairy tale, in which the wonderment and joy are retained and the heartaches and nightmares are left out.' The low-keyed tone of the books is possible, also, because so much of the magic is a question of elementary science and technology rather than of the true, testing supernatural. Dorothy remains throughout her adventures a simpleminded, honest, home-loving little girl, unchanged even after she is made an honorary princess and a permanent

An illustration from *The Wonderful Wizard of Oz*, drawn by 'Biro'.

*The Magic Roundabout* characters in *Dougal Round the World*, illustrated by David Barnett.

Florence, Dougal and Mr Rusty from the television series *The Magic Roundabout*, re-written and told by Eric Thompson.

resident in Oz, free from the tyranny of time. The characters in the Oz books are as simple and naïve as the situations; the magic has no overtones and enchantment has a purely physical effect on its victims. The wholesome, often sententious tone of the stories, and the feeling of confidence that good will always triumph over evil, comes most of all from Dorothy. [L. Frank Baum: *The Wonderful Wizard of Oz*, Chicago 1900; *Ozma of Oz*, 1906; *Dorothy and the Wizard in Oz*, 1908; *The Road to Oz*, 1909; *The Emerald City of Oz*, 1910; *Rinkitink in Oz*, 1916; *Glinda of Oz*, 1920]

**DOUGAL,** the fussy hero, or butt, of the television films of the *Magic Roundabout*, is so obviously characterized by his appearance and his way of moving that it might seem a risky business to transfer him to print. But Eric Thompson, who invented the names and extended the personalities of the toys created in Serge Danot's films, gave each of the characters a typical mode of speech, and even in some cases typical phrases. The tart, sarcastic words with which Dougal retreats from an embarrassing situation, and his love of mock-melodramatic exclamations; Zebedee the bee's incisive, domineering magic buzz; the melancholy haverings of Ermintrude the cow; Florence's naïve conceit; Dylan's pop-culture idiom – these confirm the characters in the many roles they play. So long as Dougal and his friends continue to express themselves with such a witty, sophisticated babble of nonsense, they will keep their position as cult figures in almost any age-group or walk of life. [Eric Thompson: *The Adventures of Dougal*, Leicester 1971; *Dougal's Scottish Holiday*, 1971; *The Misadventures of Dougal*, 1972; *Dougal Round the World*, 1972]

**DOWSABEL** the witch lives in a house on hen's legs on an island in a pond at the bottom of the Lindley's garden. The Lindley children freely enjoy Dowsabel's company, for though they have explained her to their parents, they are not believed, and somehow the embarrassing situations she involves them in are sorted out eventually without too much publicity. Dowsabel herself is apt to complain that her magic powers are not appreciated. Though she tries to educate the Lindleys, only Jane, the youngest, advances far enough to be able to vanish and to manage a broomstick. The four children get more fun out of meeting her friends Jemima and Beldame Maria (though they find the Irish exiles Belladonna Flanagan and Drear Malone a little too peculiar).

Dowsabel's eccentric appearance and happily casual attitude to life stem alike from a simple exaggeration of domestic cliché. Several degrees more odd than Mary Norton's Eglantine Price (q.v.), she obviously belongs to the class of spinster-gentlewoman. Her summer outfit bears this out – her 'chemise-type dress of perforated sacking' and her 'most original hat, an inverted waste-paper basket with ivy threaded through the holes'; so does the 'dampish-looking knitting' she carries about

Hag Dowsabel and Jane, drawn by Joan Kiddell-Monroe for *Rescue by Broomstick*.

with her. But her stilt house, her cat Sootylegs, her broomstick and her diet of flycake, baked spiders and cold bat are splendidly traditional. The constant shift between nonsense and modified sense in the story-cycle is caused by, and promoted by, this very original and comical version of the standard fictional witch. [Lorna Wood: *The People in the Garden*, London 1954; *Rescue by Broomstick*, 1956; *The Hag calls for Help*, 1957; *Holiday on Hot Bricks*, 1958; *Seven-League Ballet Shoes*, 1959; *Hags on Holiday*, 1960; *Hag in the Castle*, 1963; *Hags by Starlight*, 1970]

**DREM** belongs to a tribe living on the South Downs during the Bronze Age. One day he overhears his grandfather and mother talking and realizes that, because of his withered arm, they do not expect him to be able to win the right to be called warrior, when the time comes, by killing a wolf single-handed. Shocked and miserable, he runs from the village and is found in the forest by Talore the Hunter, who has himself learned to do without the hand he lost in battle. With Talore's encouragement Drem returns home and in due time serves the term of initiation with the rest, but through an unlucky accident he fails to kill his wolf and is forced to live and work with the shepherds, the Little Dark People con-

An illustration from *Warrior Scarlet*, drawn by Charles Keeping.

quered by the tribesmen. Learning their craft and absorbing some of their ancient wisdom, Drem comes to terms with his loneliness, the loss of his home and of his close friend Vortrix, the condition that marks him out from his fellows. Finally, in defending an old shepherd from the wolf pack, he faces and kills the huge brute that had escaped him in his first trial, and wins the scarlet robe of a warrior.

This direct, rich story, with its constant echoes of Kipling, has a theme which may be readily translated into the language and circumstances of any individual and any period and yet it is expressed through vivid and memorable historical details which establish Drem strongly and clearly in a particular time and a particular place. This is a story of growth, of fierce personal pride disciplined and controlled by loss and frustration, of the triumph of will over weakness, of determination over defeat. Cast in the form of a physical struggle, seen in terms of a world of almost three thousand years ago, the story has emotional overtones far beyond historical exposition. [Rosemary Sutcliff: *Warrior Scarlet*, London 1958]

**DUCHESS** *see* GINGER AND PICKLES

**DUCHESS** (the) belongs to the Carolingian era, judging from the names chosen for some of her children (Clothilde, Maude, Willibald, Guinevere and the baby Gunhilda), but her scatter-brained nature is dateless. Singing happily 'I'm going to make A lovely light luscious delectable cake', she stirs orthodox and odd in-

gredients together – 'Whatever she found she put into the batter, And what she left out didn't really much matter'. Light the cake certainly is. As the Duke remarks, when he sees her rising into the sky on the expanding dough, 'I fear an improper proportion of leaven Is taking my dear Duchess right up to Heaven'. Not all the King's commands nor the weapons of his soldiers can help. It is tiny Gunhilda who finds the solution when she wails 'I want something to eat'. So the Duchess eats downwards, the bystanders eat upwards, and all agree the cake *is* delectable. The Duchess is a splendid racy character, worthy of the gay doggerel and apt pictures that relate her bizarre story. [Virginia Kahl: *The Duchess Bakes a Cake*, New York 1955]

**DUDU,** the old lame raven, hobbles up and down the terrace of an old house in France. Because he is mysterious and solitary, little Jeanne is a little afraid of him. When orphan Hugh comes to live in the house, she lowers her voice when she speaks of Dudu; 'I think he's a sort of fairy', she tells her playfellow.

She and Hugh agree in most things, but the little girl does not entirely understand his delight in the tapestry in the room he is given for his own. Then Dudu takes

Dudu the raven perched on the head of Jeanne in a scene from *The Tapestry Room*, illustrated by Walter Crane.

SWAIN.SC

a hand. In and out of the dreams or night-visions of the children he moves. He leads Hugh into the castle guarded by peacocks which tower in the tapestry; he provides a team of frogs to pull the little boat in which the children, on another moonlight night, find themselves rowing on a stream; he sits on Jeanne's head 'as if he had always been intended to serve the purpose of a bonnet', when they rise above the castle on snow-white wings. Dudu has something of the acerbity and the heraldic status of E. Nesbit's Mouldiwarp (q.v.) and, like that strange creature, he is a repository of family history and fairy tale. He is the presiding spirit of a loosely-constructed, serenely-ordered sequence of dreams and incidental stories in which Mrs Molesworth matches magic and everyday in her unique way. The glow of loving-kindness shines over the book, expressed in the happy companionship of the very natural, imaginative children and in the reserved, mysterious, powerful character of the old raven. [Mrs Molesworth: *The Tapestry Room*, London 1879]

**DULCIE WINTLE** is the star of 'Mrs Wintle's Little Wonders', at least in her mother's eyes: the other children call her 'that awful Dulcie-Pulsie' or 'Little Show Off' and the staff refer to her as 'Mrs Wintle's Little Horror', but always in careful secrecy, for Mrs Wintle rules her dancing academy with ruthless vigilance. Since the child has talent, she has reached the age of ten without having to face serious competition, either in dancing or in the household, and she is upset that her mother has had to offer a home to the orphaned cousins Rachel and Hilary Lennox. 'She was the only child who was allowed to live in the house', she felt, and her behaviour to the two girls is as unpleasant as she dares to make it.

Hilary, whose mother was a fine dancer, *must* go the Royal Ballet School. This has been Rachel's credo as long as she can remember. Hilary is an easy-going, extrovert child. She gets on well with the Little Wonders and enjoys stage dancing, especially as she is a natural mimic, and in fact actually dares to enter a competition which Dulcie seems bound to win and gets the highest mark with a comic dance that is only too obviously a take-off of the spoilt child-star.

As time goes on, Rachel despairs of persuading Hilary to be serious about ballet. Her only happiness lies in lessons with Miss Storm, who encourages in her a love of good literature and a dramatic talent which, to Mrs Wintle's fury, leads to the very part in a film which Dulcie, with her usual conceit, has assumed would be hers. The story of the three girls, so entertainingly dissimilar, has an almost balletic symmetry in it, as Noel Streatfeild develops her young characters now in turn and now in relation to one another. [Noel Streatfeild: *Wintle's Wonders*, London 1957]

**DUNY,** born in a mountain village in the island of Gont, in the north-east of the great archipelago of Earthsea, was taken into his aunt's household when his mother died. He grew into 'a tall, quick boy, loud and proud and full of temper' and with a gift unsuspected until his aunt found him using one of her spells successfully. His power in raising a mist to ward off marauders from the Kargad lands was recognized by Ogion, a mage visiting Gont. It was Ogion who gave him his secret name of Ged, and took him to the great school for wizards at Roke, where as Sparrowhawk the boy served his apprenticeship. During this time the proud youth rashly accepted a challenge from a rival to raise a spirit from the dead; through a gap between the two worlds came a shadow from which he fled through the archipelago until, after learning humility in service to a poor village and in a confrontation with the dragons of Pendor, he learned that he could not escape the Shadow but must turn and face it. When the two stood together at last he found the Shadow bore his name; he accepted identity with it and became a whole person, with his capacity for good and ill equally his own responsibility.

During Ged's conflict with the Shadow he had been given part of an arm-ring, an ancient amulet of a dynasty once ruling in the centre of the archipelago and now dispossessed. In search of the other half of the ring, which could restore unity to a land torn with dissension, Ged penetrated the labyrinthine depths where Arha (Tenar) served as Priestess to the Nameless Ones. The dominant symbols of Ursula Le Guin's fantasy-myths, names and doorways, are prominent in this taut story, in which Ged joined the two parts of the ring and restored to the sad, lonely girl her true name and the blessing of light and air.

His last and greatest achievement came in his late middle age, when as Archmage of Roke he took on himself the task of finding the reason for the physical plagues and mental apathy spreading through the archipelago. With Arren, heir to the Principality of Morred, a brave, untried youth who had become his loyal disciple and friend, Ged travelled to the west and spent almost the last of his strength on the struggle with the enemy, a flawed mage who had denied his humanity by finding a way to become immortal. In this book Ged revealed his true strength, which was not only a matter of courage and learning, for it came also from something fundamental to his character as mage and person, 'a kind of lightheartedness ... a pure pleasure in his skill'. This is as important to the reader as it is consoling to Arren. For the Earthsea trilogy is not a moralistic piece of work. It has the impersonal, deep-searching, primitive pattern of myth; beyond ethics or religious belief, it leaves Man on his own.

Ged is drawn with the broad lines of myth. The pride that drives him to call up the dead and so to open a door to the shadow of evil, is the pride of all of us; his proclamation of the inevitability of death, when he enters the World of the Dead, is an affirmation we all try to make. It might seem at first that Ged's character is a matter of negatives. He is not subject to natural desires for food, violence or sex. He does not talk about himself but expresses a responsible philosophy of magic on behalf of all seekers after knowledge. Certainly the substantial, recognizable aspect of his character comes in part from the extraordinarily vivid, closely documented creation of the world of Earthsea. Ursula Le Guin's writing is so powerfully concrete that we come to feel we know Ged because he takes colour from scenes with a strong chivalric, Norse or primitive atmosphere. But Ged is a man who submits to the discipline of magic because of the gifts that lie in him. The difference between him and common humanity is the difference, perhaps, between a poet and other men. His reserve is not impenetrable. His grief and guilty fear after he has let the Shadow in is expressed in terms at once formalized and human. He refuses to enter into more than friendship with Tenar, (in *The Tombs of Atuan*) but with regret. Arren, his young companion on the journey to the Wall of Stones, sees his weariness as a human condition and Ged corrects himself after a speech in which he imagines the fame that he will earn from his enterprise with the humorous comment ('in the common tongue', as the author says, for he has been using the oratorical speech of a mage) 'A goatherd to set the heir of Morred on his throne! Will I never learn?' We do not identify with Ged – the character is too enigmatic and too remote for that; but we can match his changing attitudes and feeling with our understanding. [Ursula Le Guin: *A Wizard of Earthsea*, New York 1968; *The Tombs of Atuan*, 1971; *The Farthest Shore*, 1973]

**EDMUND** and **TERRY DOUBLE,** aged nine and ten respectively, are such good friends that 'they lived just as though they were one person', but Edmund is as much interested in food as Terry is indifferent to it: not unnaturally, Edmund is as fat as Terry is skinny. One Sunday they find their way into a strange world where, to their dismay, they are separated, for Edmund is unmistakably a Fattipuff and Terry a Thinifer, and the two nations are about to go to war over a neutral island claimed by both.

Edmund enjoys being secretary to Prince Vorapuff, especially because of the lavish meals, but Terry takes a little time to get used to President Rugifer, who is excessively critical. The boys find themselves facing one another over the conference table, as spokesmen for the fat and the skinny delegates. War and occupation follow, but the victorious Thinifers find themselves insensibly succumbing to the comfort-loving ways of their enemies and at last mutual tolerance and even intermarriage becomes possible, once the island, previously called Fattifer or Thinipuff according to conviction, is renamed Peachblossom.

In this pleasant parable of international politics the two lads enter and leave the underground country as

Edmund and Terry at a conference of Fattipuffs and Thinifers, drawn by Fritz Wegner.

easily as Alice entered and left Wonderland. Their father has been waiting impatiently for them for an hour, and it never occurs to the boys to wonder what they have learned, if anything, from their bizarre experience. [André Maurois: *Fattipuffs and Thinifers* (1930 France) trans. Norman Denny, London 1941]

**EDRED AND ELFRIDA ARDEN** *see* MOULDI-WARP

**EDWARD FROST** *see* MARTIN HASTINGS

**EDWINA BLACKADDER** is perhaps more a pretext for action than an active participant in it, but her soft heart and incisive speech are both totally individual and also typical of the kind of Cockney working-class gran who can exercise such a strong influence on her descendants. Fred has never got a straight answer to his questions about her age but he thinks 'she is probably pretty old as she's going bald and her legs are thin as sticks though the rest of her is quite fat. She wears corsets that poke up in front when she sits down.' Gran resists any effort to tidy her home up, though she does make an effort when she decides to take soft-spoken, soft-soaping Mr Gribble as a lodger. For all her strident comments to her grandson Fred and his friends, Gran is too sentimental to be the judge of character that she likes to think she is, and it is not hard for Mr Gribble to divert her attention and decamp with her money. Then the old lady shows her mettle, sturdily admitting her folly and facing the fact that her life's savings have gone. Naturally everyone rejoices when a picture long stowed away in her attic proves to be worth £350, and it is typical of Gran that she celebrates by giving the 'handful of thieves', the boys who have foiled the thief, a lavish meal. [Nina Bawden: *A Handful of Thieves*, London 1967]

**EEYORE** *see* WINNIE-THE-POOH

**EIGENWILLIG,** or 'Self-willed', is the unfortunate name bestowed upon the infant son of King Katzekopf and Queen Ninnilinda by the Lady Abracadabra, the Queen's great-aunt and 'a very powerful Fairy', who warns them that their son will be selfish by nature and must on no account be spoilt. Predictably, the prince grows into a spiteful child, a torment to the governesses of his youth, the Ladies Brigida, Rigida and Frigida, and, after a good beginning, an even worse playmate for the amiable Witikind, son of a neighbouring Count.

When the Hope of the Katzekopfs steals Abracadabra's wand and turns his playmate into a hare, her patience is exhausted. Recovering her magic emblem, she turns the prince in his turn into a ball and rolls him to Fairyland, whence after a stern seven years he returns to become Regent to his senile father and finally to be crowned King Katzekopf the Good.

The descriptive names of this improving tale clearly denote its nature. The author's admitted aim was to 'excite the sympathies of the young on behalf of others, and to set before them in its true colours the hideous sin of *selfishness*.' But the fanciful elements in the story come from another source altogether. Disliking the rational moralities of Mrs Edgeworth and others of the time, Francis Paget wanted to try on the present generation 'the grotesque nonsense, the palpable, fantastic absurdities, the utter impossibilities of a Tale of Enchantment'. In the first edition he hid his authorship behind the fiction that it had come from the pen of 'that William Churne, of whom Bishop Corbet writes, and who, two centuries since, seems to have been the great authority on all matters connected with Fairy-land'. Conceived in the dual spirit of Jacobean fairy lore and Early Victorian literary theory, the royal and supernatural characters of the story are the oddest mixture of the grave and the grotesque. [Francis Paget: *The Hope of the Katzekopfs*, London 1846]

**EILONWY,** Princess of the House of Llyr Half-Speech, the Sea King, is Lloyd Alexander's witty, possibly ironical version of the damsel in distress of chivalric legend. When Taran (q.v.) first sees her in the castle of the sinister Achren (q.v.), she seems to be an acquiescent pupil of the evil enchantress, though circumstances soon prove otherwise. Tall and slim, with a 'delicate, elfin' face with high cheekbones, Eilonwy is far from being a fragile girl in need of protection. Indeed her feminist attitude is often a danger to Taran, for she insists on taking part in his quests, even in the last dread battle against the forces of evil; her fury when he tries to protect her for her youth and sex is diverting but hardly to be taken seriously all the same.

A combative girl, Eilonwy keeps her offhand attitude to Taran and her scorn of the unpractical masculine concept of honour, though as the books proceed she grows less dogmatic, and by the end of the Prydain chronicles she has come to realize the value of having been brought up as a young lady and not the surrogate boy she likes to be. It is not in her to accept the state of womanhood as anyone else might. She has learnt, she says, that 'A lady doesn't insist on having her own way. Then, next thing you know, it all works out somehow, without one's even trying. I thought I'd never learn, though it's really quite easy once you get the knack.' Offhand, even when she finally gives up her chance of an eternally magic other-world life to be ordinary with Taran, Eilonwy is in many ways the most human and likable character in the cycle; with Taran, she promotes the contemporary flavour of speech and outlook which contrasts with the traditional aspect of the books and contributes to their particular elusive atmosphere. [Lloyd Alexander: *The Book of Three*, New York 1964; *The Black Cauldron*, 1965; *The Castle of Llyr*, 1966; *The High King*, 1968]

**ELIZABETH FITZEDMUND** is married off to a royal bastard by her ambitious brother Thomas Jolland, who hopes to gain advancement for himself during the Wars of the Roses. When her husband dies, the young widow leaves the manor at Sheen where she has endured a bitterly unhappy marriage and settles at the small

Elizabeth Small

Ellen Montgomery

Elizabeth with her five dolls; an illustration by Cecil Leslie from *Five Dolls and Their Friends*.

manor farm of Mantlemass in Sussex. Elizabeth sets herself up as a skinner, breeding coneys and selling skins 'for the trimming of mantles and caps' not only in London but in France, the Low Countries and Italy as well. She cherishes her independence and teaches her town-bred niece Cecily (q.v.) to do the same. It never troubles her that her ability to bake, brew, carve or shear sheep is not considered fitting for a gentlewoman, and in ruling her household she boasts that her hands can be 'silk or iron on a rein'.

With her practical, home-spun skirts above her ankles and her natural air of authority, Dame FitzEdmund, a woman earning her living in a man's world, is a particularly interesting character in the late fifteenth century. She can be matched by other characters later in the sequence of Mantlemass stories – for example, Lilias Rodman (q.v.) – and Barbara Willard has used them to illustrate certain economic and social truths as well as developing their several personalities. Dame Elizabeth remains important above all as the founder of the Mantlemass dynasty, which the author has followed to the middle of the seventeenth century. As the chronicle of a family it shows brilliantly the intricacies of marital lines and the continuance of certain inherited characteristics, both physical and psychological. [Barbara Willard: *The Lark and the Laurel*, London 1970]

**ELIZABETH SMALL** gives herself this surname after the day when she began to visit, as landlady, the gabled dolls' house where her five little dolls live. She has always preferred the house when the front door is shut because 'when the dolls were shut in and nobody stared, they did all kinds of things' and not just what she 'made happen herself'. All the same, when one day she looks

in at the windows and sees how untidy everything is, she decides it is time she spring-cleaned the dolls' house. 'If you had the sense you was born with, you'd know how to get small, 'stead of only knowing how to get big', remarks the rude monkey who lives on the roof. It seems natural that he should speak to her, for Elizabeth often talks to him, and she is scarcely more surprised to find that she can walk in through the front door (though rather more so when Vanessa mistakes her for the new charlady and only belatedly recognizes her as their landlady).

Once Elizabeth has fulfilled all the requests pressed on her by the dolls – for blankets, a new battery for the lights, real food instead of plaster dishes – she enters with delight into the life of her tenants. Their activities are as familiar and as fragmentary as if they have somehow been snipped off her own life. There are picnics and tea parties, a wedding and a funeral (with Elizabeth as the vicar each time), a train journey through the nursery, an outbreak of measles and an operation, spring cleaning and decorating for Christmas. New scenes develop from the presents her godmother gives her for the dolls' house – a telephone, a parrot in a cage, a baby in a cradle; but most of all Elizabeth enjoys the clashes of temperament inevitable in a household that includes bossy Vanessa (who boasts that she is the daughter of the Duke of Cranberry), giggly Amanda who carries on a reprehensible flirtation with the monkey, and the paying guest, Jacqueline, who never seems to learn any English. Together with Lupin, the youngest doll, who wears nothing but a vest, and the gentle Jane, who writes poetry, the dolls lead a varied life, enlivened now and then by the monkey's interruptions down the chimney or his occasional appearances in disguise (as a sweep and a visiting Duchess, for example). The dolls alternate amusingly between correct behaviour and a total disregard for time and consistency, sharing in the glorious liberty which Elizabeth's imagination has allowed them. [Helen Clare (pseud. Pauline Clarke): *Five Dolls in a House*, London 1953; *Five Dolls and the Monkey*, 1956; *Five Dolls in the Snow*, 1957; *Five Dolls and their Friends*, 1959; *Five Dolls and the Duke*, 1963]

**ELLEN MONTGOMERY,** a little girl of nine living in New York over a century ago, had to leave everything she loved in life when she was sent to live on a farm in the backwoods of New York State with her father's half-sister, Miss Fortune Emerson. To the refined, sensitive child everything was strange and a great deal was upsetting. Her aunt's tart comments on Ellen's gentle manners and her lack of domestic skills seemed to reflect on her mother and to cut her off from her as surely as the miles that lay between them. But Ellen did not lack friends. The rough farmer Abraham Van Brunt, who at first seemed to her a frightening giant of a man, found ways of diverting the worst of Aunt Fortune's tirades. Then there was Alice Humphreys, whose affection was as welcome to Ellen as her kindly direction in book learning (which Miss Fortune affected to despise) and in Christian principle (to which Miss Fortune seemed to pay little heed). Many other people helped her to bear the news of her mother's death and her father's loss at sea. Though for a time she was obliged to go to her mother's family in Scotland, Ellen's heart was always with her American friends.

There have been too many changes in theories of child psychology for it to be possible to think back to a time when it was considered perfectly reasonable to expect Ellen to forgive Aunt Fortune for withholding her mother's letters and, later, the news of her death. Christian humility and obedience are constantly demanded of Ellen at moments when any right-minded child would feel entirely justified in an outburst of anger.

The other stumbling-block in the way of understanding *The Wide, Wide World* is the matter of Aunt Fortune's character. It must have been as impossible for the children of 1850 as it is for those of today not to take Ellen's part and cordially fear and dislike the unbending woman whose ruling passions were thrift and good housewifery. But there are plenty of indications in the story that Fortune Emerson has a softer side which she hates to show and that she envies people who find it easy to make themselves liked and to enjoy popularity. The undercurrent of mature emotion in the domestic stories of the last century more than compensates for their didacticism, and that didacticism does not hide the veracity of Ellen's story. Generations of young readers have skipped Alice's sermons to enjoy reading about the dyeing of the white stockings or the pork-cutting bee or Ellen's brush with nasty Mr Saunders or the afternoon when the tormenting Nancy Vawse rummaged through the child's tidy drawers while she lay helpless in bed. In spite of everything Ellen is truly a child and one whose feelings, by whatever strange rule they are kept in order, are understandable at any period. [Elizabeth Wetherell: *The Wide, Wide World*, New York 1850]

**ELMER ELEVATOR** lives in Nevergreen City near Evergreen Park on the coast of Popsicornia – or so we are told by his son, who relates a series of nonsense-adventures, each attributed to 'my father'. It seems that Elmer's life takes an interesting turn when he learns from an alley cat about a dragon, trained to carry passengers marooned on Wild Island, who is being exploited by jungle animals. Pacifying tigers, lion, gorilla and rhino with items from his luggage (such as toothpaste, brush and comb and chewing gum), the resourceful Elmer flies off with the rainbow-hued dragon and after an interlude on Feather Island (in *Elmer and the Dragon*) where the resident canaries present him with three bags of gold from a buried treasure, he reaches home to lavish gifts on his mildly anxious parents. In a third story Elmer rescues a family of dragons trapped by hunters in a cave beyond the Awful Desert.

When his parents repeat certain local rumours about him, he only replies: 'Why Father, you don't mean you really believe all that nonsense, do you?' It is impossible to resist this inverted appeal by the author that we should believe in his nonsense. [Ruth Stiles Gannett: *My Father's Dragon*, New York 1948; *Elmer and the Dragon*, 1950; *The Dragons of Blueland*, 1951]

**EMIL TISCHBEIN** lives in Neustadt with his widowed mother, a hairdresser in humble circumstances. Because of his widowed mother, Emil has long ago resolved to be a model boy but, as his creator insists, 'his resolution was not always easy to keep.' Certainly it is not his fault that on his way to Berlin by train, he is robbed of his money while he is asleep. He has woken quickly enough to see that the oddly friendly Herr Grundeis is getting off at the Zoological Gardens station and it takes no time to decide to follow the thief and get back the money entrusted to him. Pursuit is not easy but help is at hand. Gustav-with-the-horn, a forthright boy, is quick to sympathize with his problem and mobilizes a gang of Berlin boys who play their various parts so effectively that Grundeis is caught and handed over to the police, who are delighted to get their hands on a man they have long wanted.

The glory of this pioneer cops-and-robbers story lies in its characters – Gustav, the born general, with a kind if hearty manner; the Professor, whose father is a judge and whose plan of campaign is masterly; little Tuesday, very conscious of being the youngest of the 'detectives',

Emil and the thief Herr Grundeis, drawn by Walter Trier.

and all the more determined to be supremely efficient at the telephone; Pony Hütchen, Emil's cousin, pert and dictatorial, well aware of the advantages of being one girl among many boys.

Above all, there is Emil – sometimes afraid, always concerned for his mother, enjoying the speed of the chase and the excitement of talking to reporters and the police, a totally convincing mixture of sense and sensitiveness on one hand, impetuous innocence on the other – a proper boy equally in the context of Germany in the '30s and the world of boyhood at any time.

It seems a pity that Kästner was tempted to write a sequel, involving Emil and his friends with a seaside entertainer. In the two years that have passed since the Grundeis adventure Emil has grown dangerously like a prig, and the decision he has to make concerning his mother's plans for a second marriage introduces an element that makes *Emil and the Three Twins* a totally different kind of book from the much imitated and well established classic. [Erich Kästner: *Emil and the Detectives* (1929 Germany) trans. Eileen Hall, London 1931; *Emil and the Three Twins*, trans. Cyrus Brooks, 1935]

**ERIC WILLIAMS** longs above all things to go to school but when he becomes a day-boy at Roslyn, when he is twelve, the handsome, high-spirited lad draws upon himself the attentions of Barker, a hulking bully who hates him at first sight because of 'the new boy's striking contrast with his own imperfections'. Barker makes Eric's first term miserable until the warm-hearted Russell stands up for him; then the bully, afraid to continue his physical attacks, contrives to throw suspicion on Eric of using a crib in a Latin lesson. Barker's torments do permanent damage to Eric by provoking his strong tendency to pride and defiance, and his good opinion of himself is further encouraged by a senior boy, Upton, whose patronage tends to divide Eric from his contemporaries, his good friends, honest Russell, the lively extrovert Duncan, scholarly Owen and chivalrous Montagu.

When after a year Eric becomes a boarder in Dr Rowland's house, he has it in his power to become an instrument of good in the school. Circumstances, and the flaws in his own character, conspire to set his feet on the downward path. Intoxicated by popularity, the boy fails to stand out against the corrupt influence of Brigson, in the classroom and the dormitories. Gradually he becomes hardened to foul language, to perversions (merely suggested by the author), to cribbing and brutal horseplay. He woos an attractive junior, Wildney, who is already an accomplished malefactor, and through him Eric courts disaster by drinking, smoking and neglecting his school work. The lingering death of Russell, whom Eric bravely rescues from drowning, halts his degradation for a time; the remonstrances of Montagu and of Mr Rose, a perceptive master, only increase his reckless, defiant behaviour. His final sin of arriving drunk and

incapable to evening prayers condemns him to expulsion, but the pleas of his friends and his own penitent tears persuade the headmaster that he may still make good, and indeed he does, although for a time it seems otherwise. Wrongly suspected of having stolen money, blackmailed by the publican who has played a considerable part in his downfall, the unhappy boy runs away and endures a terrible voyage as a cabin boy on a merchant ship, which ultimately brings him to a repentant deathbed.

The change from innocence to degradation in Eric is described in terms that seem today strained and over-emotional. Farrar was writing to expose the brutalities and moral dangers of public school life as he knew it, with a reforming zeal as strong as that of Dr Arnold and as strong a belief in the discipline of Christian life. Thus although his 'moral cliffhanger' (as John Rowe Townsend has called it) has, as a story, tremendous force and variety of action, the characters are conceived entirely for a purpose. In particular Eric's behaviour, logically motivated by the events of the story, is seen to rise from one fault, which he shares with many Luciferian heroes in nineteenth-century fiction – the sin of pride. This choice of a besetting sin sometimes makes it hard for us to accept Eric's motivation as the author intends it. For example, the boy's rage at being caned is intended to show the bad side of his character; to read a modern attitude into the episode is to falsify it. The author's purpose makes it essential for him to see Eric as an extreme example of innocence corrupted and repentant, a totally black and white figure. This almost hysterically over-drawn portrait inspired many more – among them Tom Brown (q.v.) and Talbot Baines Reed's Loman (q.v.) and Oliver Greenfield (q.v.); but those later portraits were drawn with greater moderation and are easier to understand today than the picture of Eric Williams. [Frederic W. Farrar: *Eric, or Little by Little*, Edinburgh 1858]

**EUSTACE CLARENCE SCRUBB** calls his parents Harold and Alberta, for they are 'very up-to-date and advanced people'; his upbringing has not made him particularly intelligent, however, and he is heartily disliked by his cousins the Pevensies (q.v.) because 'deep down inside him he liked bossing and bullying'. Edmund and Lucy, sent to stay at Eustace's home for the summer holidays (in *The Voyage of the 'Dawn Treader'*), spend a good deal of time talking about Narnia to cheer themselves up. One day they are looking at the picture of a sailing ship when Eustace bursts in and begins to torment them. Suddenly the three children find themselves precipitated into the sea and then hauled up on to the ship, where Edmund and Lucy are overjoyed to see their old friend Prince Caspian (q.v.), now King of Narnia, sailing in search of his father's loyal lords who have been banished by the usurper Miraz.

The journey is long and varied but Eustace, seasick

Eustace Scrubb and his cousins are precipitated into the adventurous voyage of the 'Dawn Treader' in the world of Narnia; a drawing by Pauline Baynes.

and resentful, persists in treating the affair as an unpleasant joke, complaining of the food and tormenting
the valiant mouse Reepicheep (q.v.), whom he looks on
as a performing animal. He shows a still worse side of his
nature when, on a certain island, he witnesses the death
of an aged dragon and finds its treasure in a cave; for
his selfishness and greed he becomes a dragon himself
with a dragon's skin and instincts but still with a human
power of thought. The slow, painful access of conscience
is paralleled by the physical pain he endures when Aslan
(q.v.) strips off his skin to turn him into a boy again.

The regenerated Eustace is himself the central character in another adventure (*The Silver Chair*), when he and
Jill Pole, a fellow pupil, are transported into ancient
lands and given a set of rules by Aslan through which
they must conduct the search for Prince Rilian (q.v.),
son of the now aged King Caspian. Eustace plays as
much of a hero's part as he is allowed, but he and Jill,
though they work hard at arms drill and try to conquer
their fear of the enchantress and her allies, are really
manipulated by Aslan through the rules he has given
them. Since the other children in the Narnia stories are
'good' (Edmund's lapse being single and brief), Eustace
and to a lesser degree Jill, as they argue and squabble
their way through the land of the giants, seem superfici-
ally to be more interesting as characters; but in fact they
have only a limited freedom of action in the grand design over which Aslan presides. [C. S. Lewis: *The Voyage
of the 'Dawn Treader'*, London 1952; *The Silver Chair*,
1953; *The Last Battle*, 1956]

**FAIRY BLACKSTICK,** as rational as she is mysterious, after two or three thousand years of performing the duties of a fairy godmother, begins to think her contrivances have done more harm than good. And so, keeping her ebony wand mainly as 'a cane to walk about with', she declines to offer the expected magic gifts when a son is born to the King and Queen of Paflagonia and a daughter to the King and Queen of Crim Tartary. She merely wishes to the infants Giglio (q.v.) and Rosalba (q.v.) 'a little misfortune', as the best gift she can offer.

All the same, two more conventional gifts bestowed at the christenings of the preceding generation, an enchanted rose and ring, come by chance into the babies' hands and bring a measure of help in the misfortunes that naturally follow Fairy Blackstick's wishes. Her decision to act by reason rather than by magic is amply justified. Giglio and Rosalba develop characters of their own and learn to love one another without the aid of spells.

Fairy Blackstick is at once a pointed satire on the familiar godmothers of fairy tales and a sly mouthpiece of nursery morality, in which at least a few grains of serious powder are mixed with the jam of Thackeray's happy 'fireside pantomime'. [William Makepeace Thackeray: *The Rose and the Ring*, London 1855]

**FAMOUS FIVE** (the) consists of Dick, Julian and Anne and their cousin Georgina Kirrin, who always wanted to be a boy and who flies into a rage if she is called anything but George. The fifth member of the group, Timmy the dog, is addressed like a person and the children insist that he understands every word they say. Like Enid Blyton's other groups of children, the Secret Seven and the Find-Outers, the Famous Five exist for adventure and plunge into it without fear or thought. Thieves, kidnappers, spies, smugglers, are all powerless against their superior luck and their considerable skill in lurking and eavesdropping. Fear and perception are equally alien to these imperturbable adventure-seekers. When they are imprisoned on the Owl's Hill Estate they decide that to be held prisoner 'made life exciting, of course – but it did spoil a cycling tour'. Their voices sound precisely the same when they are recognizing an enemy and when they are asking Anne, the party's caterer, for another sandwich.

Anne's capabilities as a cook (largely demonstrated

The Famous Five, drawn by Eileen Soper for *Five Go to Demon's Rocks.*

with a tin-opener) and her tendency to scream at sudden noises constitute her claim to personality. Dick and Julian can only be distinguished by the fact that Julian is older and takes the lead, unless George dominates the situation, as she easily can and often does, for her temper, inherited from her father, is to be respected. This aspect of her character is carefully explained in every few chapters and in every book in case it may be overlooked, while Uncle Quentin's trait ('...such a truly brilliant scientist...has the finest brain I know...and yet loses some valuable paper or other almost every week') provides the impetus for those adventures which concern foreign powers and secret formulas.

Perhaps the most respectable reason for the popularity of the Famous Five stories lies in the variety

and thorough-going improbability of the plots. In a rare moment of fatigue Anne muses that it might 'be much nicer to read about adventures than to have them. But then probably the ones who only read about them simply longed to have the adventures themselves. It was all very difficult.' To sustain a long series of predictably improbable and routinely exciting adventures it is necessary to draw characters impervious to emotion of any but the most superficial kind. This Enid Blyton has done most efficiently. Whether she drew her characters in outline deliberately so that children could more readily identify with them or whether she was simply not interested in character is a matter of opinion. [Enid Blyton: *Five on a Treasure Island*, London 1942; and many other titles]

**FATHER CHRISTMAS** has escaped from the stereotyped image of pre-Christmas shopping days through the sympathetic treatment of artists like Jean de Brunhoff, but Raymond Briggs has finally given him personality in his shrewd, hilarious account, in strip-pictures, of his busiest day. From the early morning scenes, when the red-nosed, tonsured old gentleman wakes with the first of many exclamations of 'Blooming Christmas here again', through the halt for sandwiches and a banana on a roof-top (with a transistor handy for the weather forecast) to his last scheduled visit to the Palace ('Good! The flag's flying. They're in'), every detail is joyously logical, and the sight of this pillar of Christmas cheer, opening his presents with tart comments, relaxing with travel brochures and preparing for bed, is as witty and telling as the last close-up of a face crimson with irritation and fatigue, from whose mouth comes the final ironic greeting 'Happy blooming Christmas to you, too!' After this revelation, who will be able to return to the standardized figure again? [Raymond Briggs: *Father Christmas*, London 1973]

**FERDINAND THE BULL** has been from birth dreamy and poetic in temperament. He 'liked to sit just quietly and smell the flowers'. He sits peacefully under his favourite cork tree, happy to think that he will never be chosen to go to the great bull ring in Madrid. But an unfortunate encounter with a bee sets him 'puffing and snorting, butting and pawing the ground as if he were mad' just when five men come to select bulls for the coming season. Mistaking Ferdinand's pained antics for ferocity, they take him to Madrid, where his size strikes terror into the hearts of picadors, banderilleros and even the famous matador. Alas, the flowers in the hair of the ladies in the audience have a predictable effect. After an embarrassing scene he is taken back to spend the rest of his days in peaceful contemplation.

The wry, sly little fable has by now passed into current usage. It has enough ambiguity in it to enable it to be applied variously to the pacific, the gay, the poetic, while

Raymond Briggs's version of the irascible Father Christmas.

The poetic bull Ferdinand dreams beneath his cork tree: an illustration by Munro Leaf.

it is of course permissible simply to enjoy the joke. [Munro Leaf: *The Story of Ferdinand*, New York 1937]

**FERN ARABLE,** aged eight, is the daughter of a farmer, but she does not share a farmer's point of view – at least, not when it comes to ending the life of a runt pig. Her pleas are so heartfelt that Farmer Arable gives her the animal to rear. The piglet, adorned with Fern's currently favourite name of Wilbur (q.v.), flourishes exceedingly and the child sits for hours beside his pen, silent but listening with the ready ears of her years to the talk of the animals. It is in this way that she hears the old sheep informing Wilbur that the generous provision of food has only one end in view, 'smoked bacon and ham'; and hears Charlotte the spider (q.v.) promising to save her friend.

As a character, Fern performs more than one function in the fantasy of *Charlotte's Web*. Her reports of farmyard conversations and her defence of their authenticity are, in effect, the author's defence of his fancy, and perhaps his way of saying that fable is only truth in disguise. Through Fern, too, whose absorbed silence is far more eloquent than speech, a sense of wonder enters the story and illuminates it. Finally, no small girl or boy who loves animals and longs for them to speak could fail to identify, with envious delight, with the privileged little American girl, the first, though not the only, saviour of the 'terrific', 'radiant', 'humble' Wilbur. [E. B. White: *Charlotte's Web*, New York 1952]

An illustration by Hans Deininger from *Fingerling at the Zoo*.

**FINGERLING** is a finger-sized man, 'so old that he doesn't even remember himself just how old he is'. He lives in a comfortable home which he shares with a family of five mice in a mousehole behind the sideboard in a big house. Fingerling is able to talk to animals and is so well known to them that no matter what difficulty he may get into, there is bound to be a bird at hand to give him a lift or a spider to spin him a timely rope.

Fingerling's particular characteristics have been carefully chosen so that he can survive successfully in a long series. A gay, resourceful manikin, Fingerling has a kind heart, an enquiring mind and a conscientious attitude to society, all of which make him an ideal medium through which Dick Laan has been able to offer simple explanations of various aspects of life and to propound certain simple lessons in behaviour. [Dick Laan: *The Adventures of Fingerling*, London 1960; *Fingerling and his Friends*, 1960; *The Travels of Fingerling*, 1960; *Fingerling at the Zoo*, 1960; and other titles]

**FINN DOVE** is an orphan who has been placed in the custody of stout Uncle Toby, a man whose jolly public manner is belied by his vindictive treatment of the boy in private. Finn's mother married the lodger after her husband's death to gain security for Finn and his small sister Derval and her death means a loveless life for the children. But Finn feels that his sister Derval will suffer from the lack of love and understanding which he has hardened himself to bear; one day, stiffened into courage by undeserved blows, he decides to run away.

Finn knows that his grandmother O'Flaherty lives in the west of Ireland but he does not know the name of her village and he has no money to pay for the boat journey. By slipping on and off the boat in the crowd, snatching lifts, plodding across country, always a step ahead of the police and his uncle, Finn takes Derval safely to his grandmother's cottage, where she successfully upholds her own claim to the children against their legal guardian.

Finn denies that he had much to do with the miracle of his successful flight. There are so many who helped him – Moses the tinker boy, thieving Mickser with his junk cart, Michael the policeman, the Judge who forces plausible Toby to admit that he wants the children not from affection but because of an unexpected legacy whose interest he hopes to enjoy, if not, in a more sinister way, the principal.

Innumerable are the stories about children running away and there are many young heroes as brave and a few as perceptive as Finn. This particular story stands out for the offhand, brilliant power with which minor and major characters are established. The good and the bad stand very clearly on two sides in the book, their motives and their actions measured against the standard of Finn's integrity. [Walter Macken: *The Flight of the Doves*, London 1968]

**FIRETOP AND FIREFLY**, red-headed twins eight years old, steal after their father Hawkeye when he sets off to explore beyond the tribe's usual hunting ground. Their parents accept their presence cheerfully, tie them into a tree at night for safety and dry them when they fall into a river. In describing the small adventures of two children of the Stone Age, Lucy Fitch Perkins is able to draw a simple picture of what life might have been like in the Isle of Wight centuries ago. She links her characters with the present day by describing how they hit on the idea of keeping rabbits to breed for food; this emphasizes her point about the ladder of invention reaching from one era to another. [Lucy Fitch Perkins: *The Cave Twins*, Boston 1917]

**FISH** needs a nickname, because there is already another Jimmy in Llanwern and Jimmy Barnes is not so popular that anyone would want to be mistaken for him. All the same, because Jimmy Price goes home the same way from school, he gets used to Fish tagging along; he is sorry for the boy, who seems to be scared of his father and neglected by his step-mother. One day a stray dog attaches itself to Fish, and Jimmy unwillingly agrees to support him in a devious story so that his father will be forced to let him keep the animal. Floss becomes the centre of Fish's life and when she is suspected of sheep-running, he runs away to hide her. It is deep winter, but though Fish is afraid of the nights he spends alone, cold and hungry, in the remote barn, his resolution does not weaken. In the end it is the dog's intelligence that leads the searchers to the two Jimmies, to find them (in defiance of story-book sensationalism) tucked up in the hay and laughing over a comic.

Jimmy Price, who tells the story of the adventure, never goes beyond his own experience. We can read between the lines of Fish's artless tale of his childhood and see how much his background has contributed to his irritating bouts of whimsy or aggression. Jimmy is surprised when he overhears a conversation between the oily Mr Barnes and his mother and realizes that even an unnatural father may have his own point of view. He is puzzled, too, by Fish's obstinacy in regard to Floss, not realizing how much the boy needs something to love and care for. Besides, as a farmer's son, he knows how much trouble Fish's obstinacy could cause in the community. In this very circumstantial story, in which the characters truly belong to the land they live and work in, the two Jimmies by the interaction of their words and actions add the final touch of reality. [Alison Morgan: *Fish*, London 1971]

**FIVER** *see* HAZEL

**FLASHMAN** *see* TOM BROWN

**FLOPSY BUNNIES** *see* PETER RABBIT

**FORTUNE EMERSON** *see* ELLEN MONTGOMERY

**FRANCES**, a badger, suffers the small trials and apprehensions of childhood in a beguiling sequence of

"Hello," called Frances from the dining room. "I am calling on the telephone. Hello, hello, this is me. Is that you?"

Lillian Hoban's drawing of the badger Frances in *A Baby Sister for Frances.*

picture-books. She makes excuses for not going to sleep, she runs away (a few feet away under the table) in protest when her baby sister Gloria seems to be getting all the attention, and she learns to deal with some of the awkwardnesses that accompany a small child's move from the security of home into a wider world. The precise and affectionate documentation of Frances's suburban environment in the illustrations helps to smooth the path for a humanization that is unusually tactful. [Russell Hoban, ill. Lillian Hoban: *Bedtime for Frances*, New York 1960; *A Baby Sister for Frances*, 1964; *Bread and Jam for Frances*, 1964; *Best Friends for Frances*, 1969; *A Bargain for Frances*, 1970]

**FRANCIS COPPLESTONE** is a curate of remarkable height and conceit. The Smith boys, for whom he is engaged as temporary tutor, dub him the Streak. Mr Copplestone's teaching methods are unorthodox, and, unfortunately for the Smiths and for timid Maria (q.v.), decidedly inconsistent. Hardly have they got used to his demonstration of a bull fight than he hands out highly unsuitable subjects for essays; when James (q.v.) complains that he is only eight and has never heard of Machiavelli, 'the luck of the draw' is his only consolation.

Mr Copplestone represents that alarming type, the adult *enfant terrible* – alarming and painful at least to children. His total disregard for etiquette leads to scenes which are amusing but with an edge of unease. Such a scene occurs (in *Trespassers at Charlecote*) when he falls on his knees before the Prime Minister, Sir John Squerrye, begging leave to present a humble petition that a bodyguard of ordinaries, or penny-farthing bicycles, be formed 'to attend upon Her Majesty upon all state occasions, to minister to her safety, to enrich her dignity, to enhance her prestige'. The rolling periods, which would not have amused Queen Victoria, are typical of the man. So is his passion for penny-farthings – and indeed, the shape of his machine, which he never succeeds in mastering, is almost a grotesque image of himself.

Mr Copplestone is ubiquitous. After the mishaps at Jerusalem House (in *The Warden's Niece*) he announces that he is going to Ecuador. 'To one or two I have e'en promised a llama' he tells the Hardings, but he misses the boat (or so he says) and so unfortunately is available to make the summer as odd as the spring had been for the Smiths and Maria. Even the Bishop's tactful offer to arrange a living in a diocese of Natal (in *Trespassers at Charlecote*) does not remove the tiresome man from Oxford and its environs for long. His eccentric, entertaining and unlikable character offers endless opportunities for farcical and sardonic humour. With James Smith, that notable nuisance, Francis Copplestone gives Gillian Avery the chance to echo and parody the peculiarly rough, anarchic note of hullabaloo that resounds through certain domestic tales of the last century. [Gillian Avery: *The Warden's Niece*, London

1957; *Trespassers at Charlecote*, 1958; *To Tame a Sister*, 1961; *The Peacock House*, 1963]

**FREDERICK FRENCH,** son of a County Court judge, accompanies his father to court one day in a spirit of mild intellectual curiosity. In the middle of a tenancy case the plaintiff is shot dead, and the boy, whose idly observant eye has registered one or two interesting details, pursues his own determined, if amateurish, investigations.

Stories about young people in this kind of situation are two a penny: few are as thoughtful or as neatly turned as this one. The plot, concerning counterfeiters, is not unusual, but what matters most is the effect of events on the boy himself. Frederick is something of an intellectual snob as well as a social one, confident and knowledgeable but with only a superficial idea of what people are really like. His incautious enquiries educate him, abruptly and brutally. Through his own account of the affair we are allowed to glimpse, now and then, a far younger person, afraid, distressed and out of his depth. His 'little eye' is observant enough; his courage is never in question; his theories that the hunt for a murderer 'satisfies a moral longing' have some sense in them; it is his experience that is shown, subtly and surely, to be unequal to the task he has set himself. [Roy Fuller: *With My Little Eye*, London 1948]

**FROG** and **TOAD** garden, go for walks, drink tea, swim, mend their clothes, tell stories to one another and, in short, lead lives of comfort and mild eventfulness in a world that relates without fuss jackets and teapots, a cycle and a writing desk with the natural form and some of the natural avocations of a frog and a toad in nature. Glass-paned windows and bullrushes, an umbrella and a clover-head combine just as easily in the precise, exquisite water-colour illustrations, with their gradations of green and brown, and their skilful suggestion of personality and animal form.

With Frog as the responsible, somewhat dictatorial brain of the duo and Toad as the emotional, nervous, wayward one, the two animals are endearing, comical and perhaps a shade touching in their leafy lives. There can have been few writers since Beatrix Potter who use snatches of talk so subtly to indicate the human type within a true animal and few artists who so wittily, meticulously and sympathetically suggest personality through the entirely natural movements of animals. [Arnold Lobel: *Frog and Toad are Friends*, New York 1970; *Frog and Toad Together*, 1972]

**FROGGY,** a little street arab in late Victorian London, was really named Tommy, but the nick-name his father gave him 'because he was so often cold, and croaked sometimes when he had a cough', was generally adopted in Shoreditch, where he lived with his family in a comfortless attic. Poor though his parents were, they had brought up Froggy and his little brother Benny (q.v.) to be honest and God-fearing and had given them love instead of luxury. This stood Froggy in good stead when his mother died and his father was killed in an accident. Manfully taking on the responsibility of six-year-old Benny, this hungry child of eleven swept crossings for such pence as might come his way and resisted the temptation to better his finances by joining Mac and Dandy after he realized they were picking pockets.

Innocent yet wise beyond his years, touchingly brave and independent, Froggy was obviously meant to touch the hearts of readers unaware of the plight of the hundreds of slum children in the London of the 1870s. Yet if the story is a tear-jerker in modern eyes, there is nothing mawkish about Froggy, nor is he sentimentalized (not even in the scene where he writes to the Queen, ties the envelope with string and posts it to the Palace).

He loves the excitement of a crowd and has a gift for making the most of small things – a carrot, a ha'penny, a kind word. Above all, his love for Benny, his devoted care of the little boy, are shown to be an integral part of his nature as well as a legacy from his loving parents. After Benny's death, when Froggy has been taken to a Children's Home, he eagerly offers to take care of the pathetic waif Billy. No matter if we no longer feel in sympathy with the overt evangelizing of this book. It is none the less about real flesh and blood children, not just about a cause. ['Brenda' (Mrs G. Castle Smith): *Froggy's Little Brother*, London 1875]

An illustration from *Frog and Toad Are Friends*, written and illustrated by Arnold Lobel.

**G**

**GALLDORA** is 'just a home-made rag doll, with shoe-button eyes and a sewn-on mouth and black wool hair'. In her humility she believes that, being home-made, she is inferior to the rest of Marybell's toys, but she has an intelligent philosophy of life. As she is apt to say to herself consolingly as she floats down river, lies forgotten on a rooftop or is snatched by a passing dog, 'a doll's got to have something, and if she hasn't good looks education is useful.'

The formula of the Galldora stories is simple: the rag doll is perpetually being lost in circumstances that would destroy most other toys. Her resilient, cheerful nature allows her to enjoy everything that happens to her because she knows that even if Marybell is forgetful, and even if her own intrinsic value is small, she is truly loved and will always be found in the end. For the small children who enjoyed the stories when they were first broadcast and continue to enjoy them in print, the message is as valuable as it is lightly and humorously conveyed through Galldora's own words. [Modwena Sedgwick: *The Adventures of Galldora*, London 1960; *The New Adventures of Galldora*, 1961; *A Rag Doll Called Galldora*, 1971; *The Galldora Omnibus* (*with nine new stories*), 1973]

**GAMMON** *see* GINGER AND PICKLES

**GARGOYLE** the cat lives in the Rectory at Ramsley in Kent, where he is considered 'a surly, lazy cat'. Nobody sees the change that comes over him at night. It is while he is on one of his hunting expeditions that he makes the startling discovery that water has somehow replaced the familiar railway lines, and eventually he succeeds in alerting the Vicar to the fact that Ramsley, built on reclaimed marshland, has now broken from the mainland and is drifting south.

This unusual situation is given credence and shape through the character of Gargoyle. In his capacity as a mildly scornful observer he watches Captain Voice-pipe adapt to the situation and organize navigation as best he can. He sees various inhabitants leave Ramsley for more interesting scenes in France, Tarboosh, Equatorial Africa, a South Sea island and the west coast of Australia, going on shore himself each time to inspect the terrain but resisting any attempt to detain him.

His loyalty to Ramsley is defeated not by danger but by the cold in the church steeple where he has taken up residence when the town finally stops moving. With his usual self-confidence, he strolls into a tent in the Antarctic, quieting the dog team with 'a frozen green stare', and enquires jauntily 'Hallo.... You've been a long time coming to take me away. Got any milk?' The conclusion rounds off a neatly planned tall story in which the cat, personalized with a few swift adverbial or adjectival phrases, is the only character who is not caricatured. [Clive King: *The Town That Went South*, New York 1959]

**GED** *see* DUNY

**GENERAL WOUNDWORT** *see* HAZEL

**GEOFFREY** is the weathermonger in Weymouth, one of a few people who have power over the seasons and use it to serve their community. For England has undergone inexplicable Changes. Almost everyone has suffered a revulsion against technology and the country has reverted to a medieval agricultural way of life and, with it, to a superstitious horror which leads people to turn on anyone who has dealings with the evil machines. The people of Weymouth try to kill Geoffrey when he is found oiling the key to his uncle's motor boat. He and his sister Sally escape to France, but because they seem to be immune from the power of the Changes, they are asked to return to try to find their cause. Rumours and meteorological signs lead them to the Welsh mountains, where Merlin has been woken from his eternal sleep and is being kept in subjection by drugs given to him by the man who found him. Though Mr Furbelow believes he is acting for the good of mankind – for Merlin's power will perhaps end disease or war – the result of his action has been disastrous for England, for Merlin has in the anguish of awakening fulfilled the ancient prophecy and disturbed the balance of the world, turning it backwards to defeat the machines which he distrusts. His nobility is strong enough for him to resist the addiction he has developed, and in a natural cataclysm he is shut once more into the mountain, and England returns to its normal state.

The first story in Peter Dickinson's impressive trilogy is a fantasy-adventure in which the final complicated explanation of the Changes does not really match the spirit of youthful gallantry in which the plot moves forward. Returning to the subject in a second book set at an earlier date, *Heartsease*, Peter Dickinson describes the efforts of two young people to save the life of an

Reintje Venema's illustration of the rag doll Galldora.

American who has come secretly to England to find out why the country has cut itself off from the rest of the world. The village where he is captured is ruled by Davie Gordon, whose sadistic deeds are disguised as righteous witch-hunts. He incites the villagers to stone Otto, who has been found using a tape-recorder, but the children nurse him and eventually take him on an old tug down the canal to the sea. Though this book too has the movement and tension of adventure, character plays a greater part in it. The farmer's son Jonathan and his cousin Margaret are generous young people and their hatred of superstition and intolerance makes a strong point in the story.

The third book, *The Devil's Children*, takes a further step in exploring the Changes as they affect people rather than events. It opens with a scene in London when the Changes, in the early stages, have caused accidents, destruction and panic. Nicky Gore has been separated from her parents in the rush to escape from plague in the city. Desperate and afraid, she travels with a band of Sikhs into Surrey; they are not affected by the Changes but must avoid machines if they are not to be persecuted by their fellow men, and Nicky is able to warn them of danger, for she is strongly affected by the proximity of machinery. The Sikhs settle down to work a neglected farm and though the intolerant head of the village is hostile at first, the two communities come together in opposing a band of looters. Nicky has won a precarious comfort and peace with the Sikhs but the wise old grandmother realizes that the girl has shut herself away from human feeling as a protection, and persuades her at last to go to France and find her parents.

The three stories, originally published singly, were later issued in a single volume, with their order reversed, so that the Changes could be seen as a continuous process from beginning to end. The effect of this was to show up very plainly the different nature of the character-drawing in the three books. With the penetrating analysis of Nicky's feelings put first, followed by the moving contrast between the liberal attitude of Jonathan and Margaret and Davie's bigotry, the characters of Geoffrey the weathermonger and his sister, lightly drawn, seem unequal to the emotional implications of the Changes now that their story is placed as a climax to the whole.

A television adaptation of the three books, made by Ann Home of *Jackanory* in consultation with the author, has partly resolved this difficulty. To make a serial of ten episodes it has been necessary to have one central character throughout. Nicky Gore is seen first as the lonely, lost girl in the Sikh community, then as the 'witch' hounded by Davie Gordon and finally she goes with Jonathan to look for the cause of the Changes. The awakened Merlin, who is described more as an emanation than a person, is shown to be reacting powerfully against Man's misuse of his environment, but the

explanation for the Changes is ultimately left to suggestion, a challenge to thought and imagination. The new ending knits the three stories together in a neat and convincing way. However, it is obvious that a theme as demanding as this is best studied, ultimately, at reading pace, and the omnibus volume seems the best way to see how Peter Dickinson has related an exceptionally provocative and topical idea to a close examination of the behaviour of individuals under exceptional stress. [Peter Dickinson: *The Weathermonger*, London 1969; *Heartsease*, 1969; *The Devil's Children*, 1970; *The Changes*, omnibus volume with linking notes, 1975]

**(GEORGE)** *see* BENJAMIN DICKINSON CARR

**GEORGE H. RABBIT** appears at Mrs Weaver's bedroom door when she is nursing a bad headache. Perhaps because she is feeling ill, she is less surprised at the appearance of a rabbit wearing spectacles and speaking like a human being than her children are when George scolds them for squabbling as they come in for lunch.

George proves extremely useful to the Weavers. A born teacher, he has a bracing effect on the children's homework, and he is able to give Mrs Weaver a few hints about their manners, which she accepts gratefully – though, as she says, 'I'm never sure whether I'm talking to myself or to you!' The only person who is not even allowed a glimpse of George is Mr Weaver, for the rabbit feels it hardly proper to appear before someone who does not believe in him.

With his glasses and his pedantic love of long words, George is a wholly believable character to the reader. Nor is he in any way sentimentalized. It is perhaps largely because of the bitter-sweet ending, when Mr Weaver, indomitably rational, forbids the children to discuss taking the rabbit on their holiday in Canada, that George remains a four-square, enchanting enigma. [Agnes Sligh Turnbull: *George*, New York 1965]

**GEORGE REYNOLDS** *see* JOHN WALTERS

**GEORGIE**, the youthful hero of *Rabbit Hill* and *The Tough Winter*, is not a talkative rabbit and this is not altogether surprising, for his father, a Southern gentleman from Kentucky, has a flow of stately language which 'always continued until something stopped him' and his mother, a born worrier, talks loquaciously and endlessly of domestic matters (with no punctuation). Georgie is a rabbit to be reckoned with. Popular with the other animals on Rabbit Hill, he has a natural curiosity that stands him in good stead when he is hurt by a car and the Folks in the Big House bandage him and keep him indoors till he has recovered. Always active, always optimistic, Georgie prances through the summer and fights his way through the long winter that follows. The characters in these two books are sometimes eccentric (like Uncle Analdas, q.v.), sometimes typecast; Georgie is perhaps the most smoothly humanized of them all, the pattern of a nice, wholesome, ordinary, small boy.

These two animal fantasies can be read in several

Little Georgie in flight; an illustration from Robert Lawson's *Rabbit Hill*.

ways. It is tempting to see *Rabbit Hill*, written during the war years, as an allegory suggesting that man might learn to live and share with his fellow man just as the Folks, by their trust and generous provision of food, induce the Little Animals to leave the vegetable garden unplundered. Again, one might regard the stories as the pipe-dreams of a gardener who knows very well that good crops and a healthy animal community will never go together. But the books belong also to a long and honourable tradition in which animals are given personalities and certain domestic attributes while their specific natures are not distorted. Georgie's mother uses baskets to carry food to her burrow for the winter; Georgie learns from his father the 'checks and doublings' with which he can escape the local dogs. Each animal has his typical and appropriate character, from Porkey the stout and obstinate woodchuck and the dignified Red Buck (who condescends to the 'little fellows') to excitable, ubiquitous Willie Fieldmouse, Phewie the skunk (a connoisseur in garbage) and the Grey Squirrel, who has 'the *most* forgetful memory'. These animal characters need stir nobody's inhibitions about humanized animals; they are recognizably the affectionately delineated and rightful ecological tenants of a piece of Connecticut farmland. [Robert Lawson: *Rabbit Hill*, New York 1944; *The Tough Winter*, 1954]

**GERALDINE LE MARCHANT** and her brother Haddon are delighted whenever their mother calls at Mr Cranston's furniture shop, for then they can play with the two life-size wooden lions that crouch in the entry; while Haddon longs to ride them, Geraldine loves to imagine they are princes under a spell or that they come to life at night and roam where they please. When Geraldine is nine her father takes a post in South America and the children are sent to boarding school.

Geraldine runs away, drawn by L. Leslie Brooke in *The Carved Lions*.

Geraldine is eager for the new experience but at Miss Ledbury's establishment the principal governess is cold and unperceptive, and the girls seem rowdy and snobbish. The homesick child is comforted only by an under-teacher, kind Miss Fenmore, but when she leaves for another post there is nobody to notice that Geraldine's unhappiness has almost stupified her. Driven to desperation by her loneliness, Geraldine runs away, and in the dark, wet night she comes by chance to the furniture shop and falls asleep beside the lions. She is swept into a vivid, happy dream of finding her mother again, and the illness that follows her escapade seems almost like an extension of her dream, so kind and comforting are the Cranstons and so great the relief of being loved once more.

Geraldine's character is delineated quite simply in Mrs Molesworth's grave, measured prose. Though the girl tells the story herself, this imposes no limitation, for she is detached about her own faults and quick to see that her reserve and pride accounted for part of her unhappiness. Looking back as an adult to that miserable year of her childhood, Geraldine shows as plainly and simply in the description of her dream as she does in the account of her reactions to lessons, schoolfellows and the rigid discipline of school, how deeply a lonely child can suffer. [Mrs Molesworth: *The Carved Lions*, London 1855]

**GIGLIO** is destined through the christening gift of his godmother the Fairy Blackstick (q.v.) to suffer 'a little misfortune'. He becomes a poor relation at the court of Paflagonia and has no defence against the malice of the Prime Minister and the hostility roused against him at court. Besides, he has a more pressing reason for running away from his troubles, for in a foolish moment, deceived by the power of the magic ring, he has become enamoured of the hideous Countess Gruffanuff (q.v.), and has signed a promise of marriage.

Giglio's character stiffens, however, through the kind offices of his godmother. He becomes in exile the pride of the University of Bisforo and when he sets out to regain his rightful kingdom, he speaks blank verse 'as more becoming to his majestic station'. With a little more help from the Fairy Blackstick he finds happiness with Rosalba (q.v.). The rewards of virtue are nicely adjusted to this couple, who have found happiness through misfortune, while stout Prince Bulbo of Crim Tartary and the Princess Angelica, daughter of the usurper-king of Paflagonia, are bedevilled now and then by the enchanted rose but are seen to be little more than the natural victims of circumstance. Despite the wit and nonsense of this satire, Giglio and Rosalba are allowed a degree of natural humanity that is denied to the rest of the absurd characters. [William Makepeace Thackeray: *The Rose and the Ring*, London 1855]

**GINGER** is first cabin boy of the ss *Fidelity* when Little Tim (q.v.) comes aboard. His truculent tones ring out at once. 'Blimey... What's 'ere? A blooming passenger or is it the new third mate?' However, Ginger soon shows Tim the ropes and they become fast friends – all the more after Tim has rescued Ginger when he is washed overboard in a storm. The rescue is made easier because Ginger has secretly tried out the third mate's hair restorer and become the victim of Captain McFee's fury when his golden locks reach his waist and prove impervious to cutting.

Because Ginger is on his own in the world, Tim's parents willingly accept him as a member of the family. Tim often has to exercise a restraining influence on his impetuous friend – for instance, when he is caught under the cliffs by the tide when he goes shrimping. Consistently contrary and argumentative, Ginger contributes absurd names like Fishy and Seaweed to the discussion of what to call the unknown little girl the boys have fished out of the sea: but when Tim's schoolmates tease him about Charlotte, Ginger stands by him energetically in the playground fight that goes down in history as 'Tim's last stand'. The uncouth nose and insouciant expression of the gangling Ginger fit perfectly the sharp impression of his character that emerges from the many books. He makes a perfect foil for the steady, sensible little hero, and provides many moments of comedy (perhaps most of all in those remarks of his that have the peculiar authority of the verbal balloon). [Edward Ardizzone: *Tim to the Rescue*, London 1949; *Tim and Charlotte*, 1951; *Tim in Danger*, 1953; *Tim's Friend Towser*, 1962; *Tim and Ginger*, 1965; *Tim to the Lighthouse*, 1968; *Tim's Last Voyage*, 1972]

**GINGER AND PICKLES**, 'a yellow farm-cat and a terrier', keep a shop where they exercise great restraint in order to keep their mouse and rabbit customers. They give unlimited credit to compete with Tabitha Twitchit's rival establishment so that at last they are unable to pay the rates and have to shut up shop. Ginger finds employment in a rabbit warren and Pickles becomes a game-keeper, while their customers find they have to pay for their goods when the shop re-opens under the management of Sally Henny-Penny.

Ginger and Pickles' shop was in Sawrey, kept by John Taylor and his family, and Beatrix Potter dedicated the book to the old man because, as she remembered, 'he professed to be jealous because I had put his son John in a book as John Joiner'. There is a special piquancy in those of her stories which have Sawrey and Hill Top Farm as their setting, and not only because so many of the houses and lanes can be identified from her notes and letters. The genteel, Cranfordian behaviour of Mrs Ribby, when she entertains the Pomeranian, Duchess, to tea, her orderly house and her polite pretence of ignoring her guest's occasional inelegancies, make the comedy of the lost patty-pan all the sharper, and the same background of polite society, in *The Tale of Tom Kitten*, is as naturally and disarmingly contrived; Mrs Tabitha Twitchit's angry remonstrance to her children, free from their confining company-clothes, 'My friends

*Above and overleaf.* Some of the best-loved Beatrix
Potter characters : Jemima Puddleduck, Jeremy Fisher,
Little Pig Robinson, Mrs Tiggy-Winkle,
Samuel Whiskers, Tom Kitten and Mrs Tittlemouse.

will arrive in a minute, and you are not fit to be seen; I am affronted', seems entirely natural in the mouth of a cat, as the attitudes of Tom and his sisters, in the accompanying picture, are both childlike and catlike. Tom's later adventure, when he is rolled in dough by the old rat and his irritable wife, shows an exquisite balance between the human world, where the two matronly cats sit in their voluminous gowns by the stove, and the world behind the wainscot from which the rats make their raids on the dairy.

It is not necessary to think of these animals as being 'humanized', any more than it takes any effort to believe that Mrs Tiggy-Winkle is an excellent clear-starcher who carries on a thriving laundry business in a farm kitchen or that Jeremy Fisher, after narrowly escaping from a pike in the pond, entertains his friends, Alderman Ptolemy Tortoise and Sir Isaac Newton, to a meal of roasted grasshopper with ladybird sauce served on china dishes. Beatrix Potter relates the two worlds with such care and precision in words and pictures that the characters seem totally real as themselves while living in human settings.

There is perhaps a little difficulty when a human is placed in close relation with an animal, as Lucy is shown with Mrs Tiggy-Winkle. The device of suggesting that the whole story was a dream does not really solve the problem. We do not feel any such difficulty when Pigling Bland is offered a stool and a plateful of porridge by the deceitful Mr Piperson; scale is not distorted and the plight of a pig destined for market provides tension in the story just as well if we see Pigling and the pretty Berkshire Pigwig dressed up and articulate. Pigwig was a real pig reared by Beatrix Potter and the personality in her few shrill complaints and orders is entirely real.

*The Tale of Little Pig Robinson* is a curious mixture of fancy and reality. The little pig once seen on a ship in a Devon harbour had combined in Beatrix Potter's mind with Edward Lear's poem. Robinson's wanderings in a seaside town end with a voyage on a ship and a happy landing, like his illustrious namesake, on an island which is visited (eighteen months later, as the author states accurately) by the Owl and the Pussy Cat. The last part of the story is in sharp contrast to the richly described landscapes and the atmosphere of the little town, which lend reality to the innocent, inexperienced little pig.

Particular incidents in Beatrix Potter's life gave an added authenticity to stories like *Mrs Tiggy-Winkle* and *Jemima Puddleduck*, while the use of traditional tales and rhymes lent a special atmosphere to *The Tailor of Gloucester* and *Squirrel Nutkin*. Then, too, she was meticulous in selecting human attributes and accessories for her characters. When *The Tailor of Gloucester* was adapted as a play, she objected to one or two details; for example, she did not like the idea that Gammon and Spinach should be sent back to wash

their hands and tidy their hair. This was to make them children, she said, and she suggested sending them back for their thimbles, since the Tailor's were too big, and she added 'Besides mice have *fur*, not hair'.

Beatrix Potter was able to create animal characters which never jarred or invited false comparisons. She made them real by the settings and adventure which she created for them. Above all, she made them individuals through their voices. This is more apparent in her longer stories. The shorter tales like *Peter Rabbit* and *Mrs Tittlemouse* have characters established in a firm but general way, mainly by their behaviour and appearance. But Simpkin's angry exclamations, the sinister, nagging exchanges between Samuel Whiskers and Anna Maria, Aunt Pettitoes's parting advice and Alexander's cheeky, rebellious phrases, add one more dimension to these classic tales. [Beatrix Potter: *The Tale of Peter Rabbit*, privately printed 1900, 1st pub. edn with colour ills, London 1902; *The Tailor of Gloucester*, privately printed 1902, 1st pub. edn 1903; *The Tale of Squirrel Nutkin*, 1903; *The Pie and the Patty Pan*, 1905; *The Tale of Mrs Tiggy-Winkle*, 1905; *The Tale of Mr Jeremy Fisher*, 1906; *The Tale of Tom Kitten*, 1907; *The Roly-Poly Pudding*, 1908; (renamed *The Tale of Samuel Whiskers*, 1926); *The Tale of Jemima Puddleduck*, 1908; *Ginger and Pickles*,1909; *The Tale of Mrs Tittlemouse*, 1910; *The Tale of Pigling Bland*, 1913; *The Tale of Little Pig Robinson*, 1930]

**GLUCK** was the youngest of three brothers who farmed a secluded valley in Styria so fertile that it was known to everyone as the Treasure Valley. Though the land was enough to make the brothers rich by honest means, Schwartz and Hans richly deserved the nickname of the Black Brothers given to them by their neighbours. Gluck, who was only twelve years old, was quite the reverse, a fair, blue-eyed boy with a kindly nature, who was treated as a servant by his brothers.

One day in late autumn, when bad weather had spoiled the crops everywhere but in the Treasure Valley, and the Black Brothers were charging exorbitant prices for their corn, Gluck was minding the roast when a strange visitor knocked at the door. He was impressed by the odd little gentleman, with his round red cheeks and his huge black cloak, and let him in to dry himself by the fire. When his brothers returned and furiously ordered the guest out, they were both tossed into the corner and left gazing in astonishment at the little man, who promised to call again at midnight. His words were polite but ominous. At midnight he appeared as 'an enormous foam globe' in the room that had now been robbed of its roof. 'You'll find my card on the kitchen table' he called as he left, and next morning, viewing the desolation of the valley, they understood that they had been visited by 'South West Wind Esquire'.

The brothers now turned goldsmiths, regarding this as 'a good knave's trade', but they did not prosper and at last forced Gluck to sacrifice his treasured golden mug as a last resort. Out of the melting pot emerged a dwarf, the King of the Golden River, who explained to Gluck the properties of its waters. In the manner of fairy tale, the two wicked brothers were betrayed by their greed and became black stones, while Gluck, who gave up his chance of turning the river to gold by giving the holy water to those who needed it to save their lives, found gold enough in the rich soil which the river brought to the valley.

With its formalized characters and its symmetrical story line, this is one of the few literary fairy tales which fits satisfactorily into the tradition. Even the moral tone proper to its mid-Victorian date is appropriate, for Gluck and his brothers are recognizable as the three brothers so often used to show the value of generosity and compassion against greed and injustice. The dignified and rich style of the story and its remote setting add to its impressiveness. [John Ruskin: *King of the Golden River*, London 1850]

**GOGGLES GRIMSHAW** *see* JIM STARLING

**GOLLIWOGG** (the) originated as a picture-book character in a tattered old 'nigger doll' from America

Florence Upton's aunt lent to her. Almost annually between 1896 and 1909 Florence and her mother Bertha, who wrote the texts, offered to children picture-books narrating the adventures of the blackamoor and his friends the Dutch dolls. The Golliwogg soon became one of the most popular of all rag-dolls, with his ugly, friendly face and the strong primary colours of his jacket and trousers, until public opinion in our own time altered the trend; the original models for the stories are now preserved in a glass case at the British Prime Minister's home, Chequers.

The first book in the series set a pattern for the rest. The 'story' is told in a fluent, colloquial and infectious doggerel and the illustrations describe each situation in colour, with small footnote pictures in sepia added at the head or foot of the text-pages. In the first book Peggy Deutchland (sic) wakes in a shop at midnight on Christmas Eve and helps Sarah Jane out of her box; the two of them are dancing and playing leapfrog when 'The blackest gnome Stands there alone, They scatter in their fright.' Quickly the Golliwogg introduces himself and joins them in their frolic indoors and out, until he

The Golliwogg is carried home by his doll friends after a fall through the ice; an illustration by Florence K. Upton from *The Adventures of Two Dutch Dolls*.

falls through the ice while they are skating and has to be carried home and resuscitated.

Peggy, who remains in authority, and 'busy little Sarah Jane', together with Meg, Weg and the Midget, accompany the Golliwogg in enterprises which were in their time highly topical. They ride bicycles, engage bathing-huts at the seaside, join in a battle against red-coat soldiers and an expedition to the North Pole, and try for the Moon in a craft looking like a cross between a balloon and a zeppelin. They are arrested for 'scorching' in their auto-go-cart, a box on wheels run on a battery. In Holland, Midget is mislaid in a wooden shoe, and during a fox-hunt in England she walks boldly down an earth to drive out a reluctant fox. On safari in Africa they collect animals for the zoo, anticipating Regent's Park by many years with the 'rare okapi' they have captured.

Except for Midget, who provokes a special smile for her independence and her propensity for turning up in strange places, 'the girls' are well aware that their duty is to minister to the opposite sex. Sympathy, bandages and refreshments come from them as readily as gallantry and sturdy courage are shown by the Golli-wogg, who is hailed under the mistletoe at Christmas as 'This modest, gentle knight'. His large, bulbous countenance, more Polynesian than African, is always good-humoured, and it is easy to understand why the Golliwogg, with certain minor alterations, should have become a toy beloved by small children. It is just as easy to understand why the grotesque creature, together with the occasional lapses into Jim Crow idiom in the verses, should have made the books unacceptable in America at the present time. Social sanctions against books must sometimes be accepted when there is strong reason for them; but this need not alter the fact that the Golliwogg and his Dutch doll playmates, seen in their period context, have an ungainly charm that is uniquely their own. [Bertha and Florence Upton: *The Adventures of Two Dolls – and a Golliwogg*, 1895; *The Golliwogg's Bicycle Club*, 1896; *The Golliwogg at the Sea-Side*, 1898; *The Golliwogg in War!*, 1899; *The Golliwogg's Polar Adventures*, 1900; *The Golliwogg's Auto-Go-Cart*, 1901; *The Golliwogg's Air-Ship*, 1902; *The Golliwogg's Circus*, 1903; *The Golliwogg in Holland*, 1904; *The Golliwogg's Fox-Hunt*, 1905; *The Golliwogg's Desert-Island*, 1906; *The Golliwogg's Christmas*, 1907; *Golliwogg in the African Jungle*, 1909]

**GOLLUM** *see* BILBO BAGGINS

**GRAVELLA ROLLER** loves the sound of her own voice and thinks her name most unsuitable for one who longs to be an actress, but all the same she cannot help being excited when the King commands from Arthy's bakehouse a pie for two hundred people. Neither Arthy nor his brother Crispin, pie-maker in neighbouring Groby, has ever baked for the King before, and though Jem distrusts Crispin and advises her husband to use his own Standard Recipe, he

Gravella Roller, drawn by V. H. Drummond for *The Piemakers*.

borrows Crispin's special one for the occasion. Nobody can ever prove that it is Crispin's trick, and not Gravella's miscalculation over the seasonings, that makes the pie impossibly peppery; at any rate, Arthy's only recourse is secretly to set a fire to destroy bakehouse and pie together.

When he rouses himself from his depression and decides to enter a pie for two thousand for the King's Prize, everything has to be kept secret from Crispin; Gravella is enthralled by the contrivances (the con-version of Farmer Leary's barn into a bakehouse, the floating of the huge pie-dish down the river, disguised as a boat) which ultimately bring honour and fame to her father and to the village of Danby Dale.

Young Gravella provides the 'child's eye in the centre' of this beautifully judged fantasy, with its verisimilitude and its beguiling, half-historical half-nurseryland setting. Domestic logic accounts for much of the credibility of the story and it is authenticated also by the amusing device of family papers in the attic. Talented Arthy, with his professional attitude to his craft, and excitable Jem, living by the tenets of a grandmother who must surely have been a witch, illustrate between them the theme of the story, the pains and rewards of the creative temperament, while Gravella, with her eager approach to life, gives the book its particular zest and point. [Helen Cresswell: *The Piemakers*, London 1967]

**GREAT-AUNT AIREY** (who is really great-great-aunt to young John Bargate) has not visited her old home in Vendale for nearly fifty years; but when she arrives for her hundredth birthday there is a great deal that does not suit her and she does not hesitate to point out to John's mother that her cakes lack salt or to bully the mole-catcher to get his horse shod, and find a side-saddle for it. The horse is needed because Mrs Airey has determined to visit every chapel belonging to the Branchers, a small and seemingly heretical sect founded by her grandfather Abraham Bargate after a vision on the hills. The tenancy of the farm depends on her journeys, for if a certain stave, the Thumbstick, cannot be found by midnight on her hundredth birthday the lease will expire, and the farmhouse will by law become a chapel. Great-aunt Airey throws herself into the search, proving to be a formidable ally on any terms because of her total disregard of other people's views and her astonishing energy. Small and belligerent, defiantly dressed in red, madly independent, the terror of those men in the village who remember her of old, exhausting yet stimulating, Great-aunt Airey is one of Mayne's most vital characters. [William Mayne: *The Thumbstick*, London 1959]

**GREAT-AUNT DYMPHNA** is to the Gareth children 'more like a character in a book than a real person,' for all their lives they have been spellbound by stories of her escape from France in a coal-boat at the outset of the Second World War and by descriptions of her ramshackle old house in west Cork, where their father

Great Aunt Dymphna meets the Gareth children; an illustration by Edward Ardizzone from *The Growing Summer*.

*Opposite*. A scene from *Gumdrop on the Move*, written and illustrated by Val Biro.

spent his summer holidays as a child. When it is arranged that they should spend a year at Reenmore while their parents are in the Far East, they realize how little they really know about this mysterious relative.

Reality surpasses their most extreme speculations. Their first impression of Miss Gareth is 'that she was more like an enormous bird than a great-aunt; with her flapping black cape and the nose that stuck out of her thin wrinkled old face just like a very hooked beak'. Her clothes are as unexpected as her abrupt, uncompromising manner and her individual way of driving the old black Austin in which the bewildered, weary children are bumped along to Reenmore – not quite there, in fact, for the house has no drive and they have to finish the journey stumbling across a field in pitch dark, carrying their luggage.

With such a beginning, it is hardly surprising that the Gareths regard their great-aunt as an ogress. Her preparation for their well-being consists mainly of clearing a couple of bedrooms in the enormous, neglected house and showing them the kitchen where, she tells them,

they will find 'all they needed'. Since she never eats meat but subsists mainly on dubious concoctions from the hedgerows, the children would have had a still more uncomfortable time if they had not been helped out by Mrs O'Brien, who lives near by and comes to clean – and, as it turns out, to help them to develop a real respect and even affection for their eccentric hostess.

They begin to see the sense behind her refusal to cosset them and to learn a little, by watching and listening to her, about country matters and country lore.

Eccentricity is never allowed to become excessive in Noel Streatfeild's portrait of Miss Gareth. If the old woman changes the children radically, their visit has its effect on her too. It is clear to the perceptive reader that her abruptness hides a shy nature and her way of treating the children as rational equals is not only a compliment but also a reflection of the loneliness she never allows to overcome her spirit. [Noel Streatfeild: *The Growing Summer*, London 1966]

**GREY GOOSE OF KILNEVIN** (the) is still little more than a gosling but her pride is hurt when Jim

Sheila and the grey goose, from the jacket of *The Grey Goose of Kilnevin*.
*Left.* An illustration by Diana Ross from *The Story of the Little Red Engine*.

Three of Margaret Tempest's illustrations for the stories of Grey Rabbit, Hare, Squirrel and their friends.

Daley decides to leave her behind with the gander when he sets out one morning to market. And so, since the barn door has been left open by mistake, she takes leave of the farm and sets out down the road.

A short cut takes her to the Fair before Jim Daly but it also lands her in danger from Fat Maggie, who keeps the House of the Four Swans. Little Sheila, a foundling sorely exploited in the house, is soon in trouble for trying to hide the goose, whom she has christened Betsy and whom she treats at once as a friend; indeed, a mouthful of water from a certain stream gives the little girl the power to talk to the bird.

The gander at the farm ended a long list of warnings to the little grey goose with the most solemn one – 'If yez hear the wild geese flyin' overhead, don't look up'; but to travel with the wild geese is the grey goose's dearest wish. As she sets out with Sheila to fetch butter, the little goose dreams of flying, as Sheila dreams of finding friends and kindness. The companions on the journey too – the old Ballad Singer and his boy Fergus and the stout applewoman met at the Races – all cherish secret wishes, but they are united in their resolve to help the innocent little girl who so gallantly hides her weariness for the sake of the little goose sitting so confidingly in her basket. In the end all the travelling companions share in the new home and fortunes which reward the child for her endurance and for her trust in imagination. For this is a magic journey as well as an actual one, through a hard-hearted town, through race-going crowds, through a snow-bound wood, up in the sky with the geese and with the four Swan-children, and few writers know better than Patricia Lynch how to bring magic and everyday into harmony. Betsy the goose provides the link between the two elements. She collogues with the wild geese but 'leaped and tumbled through the air' when she tried to fly. She obligingly lays eggs for the wayfarers but later provides a fairy-tale feast for them from an empty basket. She shrinks in terror from the red-haired virago who wants her for the pot but she understands the divagations of their journey better than the humans do. Patricia Lynch gives her the last words of the story. The little goose, looking at the carving which Fergus has hung outside the magically rebuilt House of the Grey Goose, exclaims happily 'Ah! Am I that handsome? Ah! If the gander could only see me now!'. [Patricia Lynch: *The Grey Goose of Kilnevin*, London 1939]

**GREY RABBIT** lives with her friends Squirrel and Hare in a cottage complete with beds, saucepans and other adjuncts of a human's domestic life, but her herbal drinks and rush lights are not such as we would find today, for 'the country ways of Grey Rabbit were the country ways known to the author'. The animals have kept their simply outlined characters through forty-five years of stories about them. Grey Rabbit is a mother-figure, unselfish and industrious, sympathetic to anyone in distress.

Squirrel, vain and self-centred, yet appealing, plays a subordinate part in most of the stories, but Hare, with the natural characteristics of impetuosity and wildness and the added trait of conceit, gives the books another dimension, one of adventure. He is emphatically humanized, for instance in *Hare Goes Shopping* (1965), when he ventures to Little Poppleton on a 'bus, with a few pennies and a Roman gold coin in the pocket of his blue jacket'. The conductor takes him by the arm to help him off and the policeman tells him to go home after he has succeeded in explaining why he has tried to use an ancient coin in the supermarket. After the friends have enjoyed a pancake picnic, it is Hare who turns the frying pan into a banjo and assaults the ears of Owl and Fox, while his confident planning of one winter expedition (in *Little Grey Rabbit Goes to the North Pole*, 1970) leads the party in an exhausting circle through the snow.

However, Hare's excursions into the world of men are rare. In the main this very human-seeming life of birthday parties and washing days is led in secret parallel. Except for the fantasy fact that the three animals do live like country folk eighty years ago, there is little of what we could call magic in the stories, though the pegs which Grey Rabbit buys from a wandering gypsy rabbit do ring like bells when thieves are about, and in *Grey Rabbit Finds a Shoe* (1960) an elf allows the animals for a few seconds to glimpse the Little People whom their 'grandfathers' grandfathers' knew. The atmosphere of the stories is one of antiquity rather than of fairy tale. Grey Rabbit and her friends are repositories of country lore. They often sing snatches of rhymes and old songs and Grey Rabbit has a serenity that comes from observing domestic customs ages old. The traditional note in the stories puts out of the question any vulgarity or triviality in the humanization of the animals; they are the equals of humans, in these delicate, precise little tales, because they belong unmistakably to England's past. [Alison Uttley: *The Squirrel, the Hare and the Little Grey Rabbit*, London 1929; revised ed. 1968. (Many other books in the series)]

**GRIMES** *see* TOM

**GRUFFANUFF**, governess and lady-in-waiting to the Princess Angelica, has climbed to her position by toadying the royal family. Her husband is still porter at the palace gates when he unfortunately exercises his sense of power on a poor woman craving entrance. The disguised Fairy Blackstick (q.v.) turns him into a door-knocker, thus allowing Gruffanuff to benefit from a moment of enchantment when the magic ring is in her possession, by entangling Prince Giglio (q.v.) in a promise of marriage.

This grotesque character, a nice variant on the Ugly Sisters of fairy tale (and perhaps one of the ancestors of the stout contraltos of the Gilbert and Sullivan operas) is drawn satirically but still with a touch of the cruelty with which fiction, and the fiction of the last cen-

Gruffanuff, drawn by Michael Angelo Titmarsh
(Thackeray) in *The Rose and the Ring*.

tury in particular, has treated plain and unwanted
spinsters. [William Makepeace Thackeray: *The Rose
and the Ring*, London 1855]

**GUB GUB** *see* DOCTOR DOLITTLE

**GULLIVER**'s adventures have been adopted by
children because of the fantasy element which became
more prominent in the many chapbook versions, as
indeed it is also in the expurgated versions published
for children today. 'Gulliver's sojourn in Lilliput' has
always been the most widely known and liked of the
four sections. The flattering idea of being a giant among
pygmies has been used in countless children's stories,
most often in a fanciful spirit. A few authors have
stressed the responsibility of the large for the small;
Pauline Clarke, for example, describes in *The Twelve and
the Genii* the attitude of Max Morley (q.v.) to the lively
wooden soldiers he has discovered. The most direct and
the most interesting echo of Swift's satire, T. H. White's

*Mistress Masham's Repose*, is an adult book which has
rightly been made available to young readers. Maria
lives in a huge country house, her life governed by her
repulsive governess and the sadistic vicar, her only
friends the cook and an old professor living in the
rambling grounds of the estate. When one day Maria
finds that a colony of Lilliputians has been established
on the shore of a lake, her instinct is to treat them as
dolls; the professor not only explains their history to
her but also helps her to find her own independence
and freedom in respecting the claim of the Lilliputians
to the same human rights. The humanity and humour
of the story wholly justify its derivation.

Swift's second theme, of a pygmy among giants, is
also, perhaps understandably, treated most often in a
fanciful way for the young, although Mary Norton's
books about the Borrowers (q.v.) and Jane Curry's
*The Housenapper* and *The Lost Farm* suggest strongly
enough to an imaginative child the emotional fears
which go deeper than the actual dangers of such a situation. Erich Kästner in *The Little Man* and *The Little
Man and the Little Miss* hid his obvious concern so
deeply in slapstick and social satire that we end with
the impression that Maxie Pichelsteiner enjoyed most
of his life as a circus freak and at least suffered little
psychological harm from it. Thumbelina was Hans
Andersen's own creation; she owed nothing to folktale
and her story seems to reflect the author's own.
Although he describes in a very moving and specific way
the terror of a tiny creature adrift in a world of enemies
larger than herself, although he makes us feel with her
as she is seized first by the ugly Toad and then by the
Cock-Chafer, the anguish of being small seems less
strong than the fact that Thumbelina is alone, different
from everyone she meets and, ultimately, rejected by
them one by one for this reason. The joy she feels when
she finds the little King at the end of her wanderings
is the joy of finding someone her own size *and her own
kind*. Surely Hans Andersen has put into this character,
as in the Ugly Duckling and many others, something
of his own feeling as he tried to find a place for himself
in the world of men. Only E. B. White in *Stuart Little*
(q.v.) has tried to convey something of the horror and
disgust which fill Swift's description of Gulliver's life
in Brobdingnag. When the mouse-boy hides 'in a grove
of celery' in the dustbin to escape a dog, the author
comments 'It was a messy spot to be in. He had egg
on his trousers, butter on his cap, gravy on his shirt,
orange pulp in his ear, and banana peel wrapped around
his waist.' The cumulation of comic details, and Stuart's
habitual composure, do not hide the implications of the
scene. [Jonathan Swift: *Travels into Several Remote
Nations of the World*, by Lemuel Gulliver, London 1726.
T. H. White: *Mistress Masham's Repose*, London 1947.
Jane Curry: *The Housenapper*, New York 1970 (as
*Mindy's Mysterious Miniatures*); *The Lost Farm*, 1974.
Erich Kästner: *The Little Man* (1963 Germany) trans.

Illustrations by (right) Arthur Rackham, (below)
Arthur J. Gaskin and (bottom) Pauline Baynes for
Hans Andersen's classic story of Thumbelina.

James Kirkup, London 1966; *The Little Man and the Little Miss*, 1969; Hans Andersen: *Thumbelina* (1836 Denmark), London 1846]

**GUMBLES** *see* BOTTERSNIKES

**GUMDROP,** an Austin Clifton Heavy Twelve-Four, made in 1926 and the property of the artist Val Biro, has been celebrated by him in six picture-books. For the first of these he contrived an artful reason for describing the vintage car. It is stolen from its owner, a certain Mr Oldcastle, at a time when, reluctantly deciding to sell it, he has removed horn, speedometer, clock and other accessories to sell separately. The inefficient thieves crash the car in the town and Gumdrop loses more parts; headlamps are picked up in the ruins of the greengrocer's outside display, the engine and battery are appropriated to run a cement mixer, the wheels are commandeered by a gypsy for his caravan. The now derelict car, bought by an enthusiast, is furbished up and by patience and happy chance the lost parts are restored.

With theft as a recurring theme – for the car is usually being stolen or helping its owner to catch thieves – the books would be congenial to children even without the lively character lent to Gumdrop. Unusually, this does not depend on any fantasizing of the vintage car's shape (indeed, accuracy in every visual detail is an essential part of the success of the books); nor is Gumdrop given the power of speech or thought. Simply, the reader catches from those who meet Gumdrop, from Mr Oldcastle and Bill McArran to mayors, garage hands, children and crooks, the habit of apostrophizing the resourceful vehicle as 'him', and a personage he certainly is. [Val Biro: *Gumdrop: The Adventures of a Vintage Car*, Leicester 1966; *Gumdrop and the Farmer's Friend*, 1967; *Gumdrop on the Rally*, 1968; *Gumdrop on the Move*, 1969; *Gumdrop Goes to London*, 1971; *Gumdrop Finds a Friend*, 1973]

**GURGI,** one of several minor characters in the chronicles of Prydain, deserves the title of 'character' although when Taran (q.v.) first sees him he hardly knows whether the creature is animal or human. 'Its hair was so matted and covered with leaves that it looked like an owl's nest in need of housecleaning.' It has long, skinny, woolly arms, and a pair of feet as flexible and grimy as its hands. In appearance, and in his utterances, Gurgi is in some ways not unlike Tolkien's Gollum. He speaks of himself always in the third person in a tone of melancholy self-pity; his plaintive allusions to 'his poor tender head' often serve to lighten a sombre scene of danger or alarm. This trick of speech is coupled with a consistent use of assonantal or rhymed participles – 'Oh, joyous crunchings and munchings', for example, or, in happy self-praise, 'Oh, bards will sing of clever Gurgi with rantings and chantings'.

His part in the Prydain chronicles is that of finder. He locates Hen-Wen, he finds the Black Cauldron.

Always close to Taran, whom he treats almost as a god, he is a totally loyal and sleepless guard. It is clear that his habit of praising himself is an expression of his lack of self-confidence. Without either the wisdom of animals or the learning of men, he gains identity and value through service for others; it is not easy to convince him of this value. Taliesin the bard contradicts his humble disavowal of intelligence (in *The High King*) when he tells him 'Of wisdom there are as many patterns as a loom can weave. Yours is the wisdom of a good and kindly heart. Scarce it is, and its worth all the greater.' While Taran believes he is protecting this damp, shaggy servant of his, in fact he owes a great deal to his dogged faithfulness, and the richness of the Prydain chronicles owes much to the intricacies of this apparently simple comic character. [Lloyd Alexander: *The Book of Three*, New York 1964; *The Castle of Llyr*, 1966; *The Black Cauldron*, 1965; *Taran Wanderer*, 1967; *The High King*, 1968]

**GUS OLIVER** is the middle child of five. His father is fond of saying 'The jig-saw puzzle has been completed', which makes Gus think to himself that if he is a puzzle piece his outlines are 'awfully blurred'. Teased by his elders, outfaced by Serena's bossiness and the aggressive behaviour of four-year-old Simon, Gus has for so long cultivated a blank expression to signify indifference that it has become a habit. 'Pretty soon', he thinks to himself, 'he would have to start carrying around signs – signs that read: *laughter; scowling; puzzlement; curiosity; anger* – which he would have to hold up over his head, like the people in a parade who carried banners.'

*The Stone-faced Boy* is perhaps the most oblique and allusive of all Paula Fox's books for the young. Her central characters all have to come to terms with something – circumstances, other people or, most often, something in themselves. Gus is not freed by any sudden change in temperament. Rather, he is left at the end of the book with the power to escape from himself in his own hands. His great-aunt, who sees him more clearly than the rest of the family, gives him a geode with a crystal deep inside, a symbol, as it were, of his own condition. Then, he grudgingly goes out into the snowbound night, at Serena's behest, to rescue a trapped dog, and meets a surprising old couple. We are not directly told what effect these events have on Gus. Is it because Aunt Hattie, the old man, the jaunty old woman, are different from his family that they can give him an illusion of freedom? Is it because they have seen him as unique, not as the middle member of a group? It matters less to answer such questions than to feel the individuality of Gus, to realize that Paula Fox has successfully created him and challenged the reader to understand him from the clues she offers with her fictional framework. [Paula Fox: *The Stone-faced Boy*, New York 1968]

**GWYN** *see* ALISON

# H

**HAL** and **ROGER HUNT** capably assist their father, a hunter and animal collector, in assignments which take them all over the world; meanwhile, they remain seemingly the same age throughout. Hal is 'a steady nineteen-year-old, six feet tall, with the strength and brains of a man' and his brother Roger, six years younger, has enough courage to compensate for his frequent rashness. The characters are conveniently devised so that the widest age-range of readers will be able to identify with them; to make up for the absence of any development in the young heroes, the books are crammed with varied and melodramatic incident.

Among the human enemies Hal and Roger meet are the sinister S. K. Inkham, an old schoolfellow of theirs whose murderous weapons include a poisonous snake, a scorpion and a giant clam, and the plausible and cunning Revd Merlin Kaggs, who tries to sabotage their research in Undersea City, off the Great Barrier Reef, and who is finally devoured by a crocodile; to the long list of adversaries must also be added an infamous whaling captain and a jealous witch-doctor. Quick thinking and a generous allowance of luck also saves the boys from stampeding elephants, wounded whales, man-eating lions and various other animals, all bent solely on destroying the Hunts, while the brothers show an extraordinary capacity for absorbing instantly the scientific knowledge and techniques needed for seismological and ethnological research, underwater archaeology, pearl fishing, ballooning, marine biology and anthropology. Their wildly improbable adventures are chronicled in a series of tales of the kind once described by a critic as 'With-Harry-it-was-the-work-of-a-moment' books. [Willard Price: *Amazon Adventure*, London 1951; *Underwater Adventure*, 1955; *Volcano Adventure*, 1956; *Whale Adventure*, 1960; *African Adventure*, 1963; *Elephant Adventure*, 1964; *Safari Adventure*, 1966; *Lion Adventure*, 1967; *South Sea Adventure*, 1968; *Gorilla Adventure*, 1969; *Diving Adventure*, 1970; *Cannibal Adventure*, 1972]

**HANNO** *see* PING

**HAPPY LION** (the) has adapted contentedly to life in a well-kept zoo in a French town and enjoys the daily salutations of François, the keeper's son, the schoolmaster and Madame Pinson. The amiable animal thinks of them as his friends and he is upset when, finding the door of his house open one day, he strolls into the town to greet them and fails to find a welcome. Only François behaves like a true friend and sensibly escorts the puzzled lion back to the zoo.

Other difficulties are smoothed out just as readily. When the Happy Lion realizes he is the only animal without a mate, a lioness with 'soft, green sleepy eyes and a shiny yellow coat' is purchased for the zoo and there is soon a cub in the lion-house, christened François.

Entertaining as they are, the Happy Lion picture-story books contain surreptitious comments on human behaviour. At the end of the confrontation described in *The Happy Lion and the Bear*, our hero concludes 'As I see it now, one should not roar at people before one knows them better.' Not everyone is tolerant of the lion couple when François takes them to the seaside (in *The Happy Lion's Holiday*) but the Eskimos, ignorant of lions and therefore without prejudice, decide the great beast is 'nicer than a sea-lion' and make him welcome. In *The Happy Lion's Treasure* he comes to realize that the most valuable bequest he can make to his fellow animals is 'the secret of happiness'; 'To know how to love and to be loved, *that* is the treasure that makes you and those who know you so happy', he is assured by the wise raven.

The sententious side of the Happy Lion books has increased over the years, though it never spoils their buoyant tone. The lion is presented as a character, but in a realistic manner. He has no power to talk with humans and the tameness that allows excursions into town streets or on to the docks is more or less plausible. He is not clothed, and is humanized by certain modifications which Roger Duvoisin has made to a lion's head; the lips curve upwards in pleasure, downwards in melancholy and a straight, tight muzzle denotes deep thought preceding some oracular remark. The Happy Lion is still a lion, even if his behaviour does allow the author to glance obliquely and slyly at human beings. [Louise Fatio, ill. Roger Duvoisin: *The Happy Lion*, New York, 1954; *The Happy Lion in Africa*, 1955; *The Happy Lion Roars*, 1957; *The Three Happy Lions*, 1959; *The Happy Lion's Present*, 1961; *The Happy Lion and the Bear*, 1964; *The Happy Lion's Holiday*, 1967;

The Happy Lion with his family, drawn by Roger Duvoisin for *The Three Happy Lions*.

*The Happy Lion's Treasure*, 1970; *The Happy Lion's Rabbits*, 1974]

**HARDY BOYS** (the) Frank and Joe live at Bayport on the eastern seaboard of the United States, in 'an old stone house set in a large, tree-shaded lawn'. They have lived there for nearly half a century and are probably good for another fifty years, since their muscles and minds have remained fixed at the ages of seventeen and eighteen respectively. Fenton Hardy, their father, once a member of the New York Police Force and now running his own detective agency, has trained them in his methods (while being 'on as good terms with his boys as though he were an elder brother') and he calls on them for holding operations while he disappears on top secret work. The fact that these assignments involve his sons in danger has done nothing over the years to alter his behaviour. On the other hand, many external details

have altered in the cases which the Hardy Boys investigate; the 1959 edition of the first story, *The Tower Treasure*, has a note stating that the author has 'incorporated the most up-to-date methods used by police and private detectives' into the book. Transport for the young heroes has changed from flivvers and motorboats to helicopters and souped-up convertibles. Over the years they have been knocked out by every kind of blunt instrument, have escaped from fire and flood, suffocation, kidnapping, explosion, drugs, wild animals. They have accepted missions in every state from Alaska to Mexico. Year after year the cry has gone up from crooks (and critics) – 'We must get rid of the Hardy Boys'; they are still with us.

'Dark-haired Frank, eighteen, tall and keen-witted' and 'Joe, a year younger, with blond, wavy hair and an impetuous nature', are essentially formula characters.

Their names, traits, home circumstances and exploits were laid down by Edward Stratemeyer, originator of the series, in outlines handed to a long line of ghost writers all using the pseudonym F. W. Dixon; Leslie McFarlane was the first (and best) of these. Anything more than simple characteristics would have contradicted the unreality of the problems which Frank and Joe invariably solve. In company with their high-school chums, Chet Morton (whose addiction to food provides the opportunity for crude humour and endless local recipes) and Biff Hooper (a powerful boxer), the Hardy Boys pursue or are pursued by a succession of crooks, many of them employed by some tactfully anonymous 'foreign combine' and all of them provided with distinguishing marks (beards, protruding ears, scars, crooked noses or tattoos) which enable the boys to pick them out from people with open, pleasant, trustworthy faces who can be relied upon to assist them in their enquiries. Nor are their brains taxed by any search for clues; they merely follow their hunches, which always turn out to be right.

These have been the perfect puppets to manipulate in story after story of basically improbable and innocuous crime. The books have been rendered still

*"We must get to that courtyard!" Frank yelled*

The Hardy Boys in *The Mystery of the Aztec Warrior* by Franklin W. Dixon.

more innocuous and characterless since 1959, when the practice began of shortening them, cutting a good deal of incidental comedy and diluting what was, at least in McFarlane's day, reasonably interesting prose. So, with their days and nights far too full to do more than say hello and goodbye to their titular girl-friends, the Hardy Boys move confidently into the future, to continue in the exercise of their sole talent, that of making enough mistakes to lengthen the stories to the statutory twenty chapters. [Franklin W. Dixon: *The Tower Treasure, House on the Cliff, Secret of the Old Mill*, New York, 1927; and many other titles, ending with *The Mystery of the Spiral Bridge*, 1966]

**HARE** *see* GREY RABBIT

**HARRIET M. WELSCH,** aged eleven, is an exceptional child, although the bracing comments of her friend Simon Rocque (more usually called Sport) would keep her from realizing this if she were not already busy straining to become exceptional. Sport, who only wants to be a ball-player, and who is fully occupied in tending an absent-minded writer father, alternately admires and scorns Harriet's flights of fancy, while her tough school friend Janie Gibbs finds it hard to understand how she can be 'so curious about people' when they make such a mess of their lives.

It is Harriet's ambition, simply, to see and to know everything, to equip herself as a writer. To this end she goes out on a regular spy route, dressed in ancient blue-jeans and holed sneakers, wearing heavy black spectacles with no glass and on her belt the tools of her trade (flashlight, note-book and pens, canteen for water and scout knife). Looking through windows and skylights, perilously perched in the dumb-waiter of a private house, listening at doors or in cafés, Harriet accumulates facts – some puzzling, others almost alarming – about her victims. Something in her personality is satisfied by the particular activity of spying which her parents think of as a game and which she calls work; imagination, a sharp eye and an uncomfortable tendency to dislike people have contributed towards the energy with which she has filled more than fourteen notebooks since the age of eight.

When she follows her nurse, the formidable Ole Golly (q.v.), to find out whether she really has a man friend, she is struck suddenly with an important new idea: 'Is everybody a different person when they are with somebody else?' This interesting question helps her to command her behaviour when Ole Golly leaves to be married. Ole Golly, who has always encouraged Harriet to look straight at everything, has not been as successful in convincing her that she has also to learn to love people. This is evident when a group of her schoolfriends find her current note-book and read the far too shrewd and often malicious remarks which she has made even about her best friends. In mortified rage Harriet fights their carefully planned and cruel campaign of silence and snubs, and is soon in trouble at home and at school for

Harriet Welsch, drawn by Louise Fitzhugh for her book
*Harriet the Spy*.

hysterical and alarming behaviour. The solution arrived
at by her baffled mother and headmistress is to make her
editor of the Fifth Grade page in the school magazine.
Characteristically Harriet, in spite of her genuine penitence at having hurt so many people, cannot resist using
the pages for her own unique version of the truth.

An uncomfortable, prickly child, Harriet wins the
right to be herself in *Harriet the Spy* and keeps it in *The
Long Secret*, which is really Beth Ellen's story (q.v.). The
relentless realism with which Harriet's character is
drawn is seldom found even in the most stringent
analysis of mental disturbance. To present, sympathetically but honestly, a child who is at once clever and
malicious, beguiling and unattractive, is an unusual and
brilliant piece of character drawing. [Louise Fitzhugh:
*Harriet the Spy*, New York 1964; *The Long Secret*, 1965]

**HARRIS** *see* BOSTOCK
**HARRY THE DIRTY DOG,** a white terrier with
black spots, does not always see eye to eye with humans.
To run away when threatened with a bath seems to him
perfectly natural and, as a corollary, to get as mucky
as possible on the way. It is beyond him to be grateful
for the shaming rose-patterned sweater Grandma knits
especially for him, but an obliging bird unravels it. In
these and other episodes the lively little dog displays
the alert intelligence of a mongrel and a skill in evading
tiresome situations which children may well envy.
[Gene Zion: *Harry the Dirty Dog*, New York 1956; *No
Roses for Harry!*, 1958; *Harry by the Sea*, 1965]
**HATTIE BARTHOLOMEW** *see* TOM LONG
**HAZEL** and **FIVER** are brothers, the one as shrewd
and buoyant as the other is nervous and restless. Fiver
has a gift, or an affliction, which is not common to the
rabbit species; he suffers visions of the future, and at one
such moment he foresees great danger to the warren.
His frenzied warnings are largely ignored and it is only
a small group that sets out to find a new home – among
them the intelligent Blackberry, Dandelion the story-
teller, timid little Pipkin, tough, sensible Blackthorn, and
two rabbits of an older generation – Silver, who is a
nephew of Threarah, Chief Rabbit of the warren, and
Bigwig, a strong animal who belongs to the Owsla, or
élite, but feels he is not appreciated as he should be.

In their search for a safe home the rabbits are guided
by Fiver's vision of a high, dry hillside. Covering the
four or five miles that lie between their home field (which
soon after their departure is bulldozed for building) and
Watership Down, they suffer great hardship and danger
and by the time they reach a good site they have become
a compact and united group and have learned to be
flexible in their approach to changed conditions; even
Bigwig recovers from digging worms for the great bird
Kehaar whom they find lying wounded in a hollow on
the down and who proves invaluable to the rabbits as
a scout.

It is obvious that they must find females to share the
new warren. While Hazel tries to persuade the hutch-
bred does at Nuthanger Farm to join him, Holly leads
a deputation to a neighbouring warren to ask for
colonists. Efrafa is different from anything they have
known before. The warren is under the strict military
rule of a cold and efficient leader, General Woundwort.
They escape from being drafted into the system, but
after Hazel has been shot at the farm, and only one tame
doe has agreed to join them, they plan a second attempt
to win mates from Efrafa. This time the elaborate plan
worked out by Hazel and the great bird brings them their
females, but only after an alarming flight from the
General and a siege which ends in a terrible battle.
Woundwort, whose aggressive nature is outside rabbit
experience, vanishes undefeated, an enigma to the last,
while Hazel, who has held the group together by his
courage and his natural authority, finally achieves a

hero's death, being summoned to a new Owsla by Frith, the Creator of the rabbit world.

Rabbits might seem unlikely heroes and their adventures little suited to epic treatment. Richard Adams has proved otherwise. He has told their story in sober, dignified and compelling prose, with allusions to heroes of classical or romantic legend to colour it and with interspersed tales of El-Ahrairah (the Prince with a thousand enemies, who is to rabbits 'what Robin Hood is to the English') which, with references to the Creator, Frith, give them a history and a mythology. The characters are defined firmly at the beginning of the story and keep their characters unchanged to the end. They are personalized rather than humanized – that is, they do nothing that is physically impossible for rabbits, but they act according to well-defined personalities. As heroes of a story, rather than animals as subjects for research, they go beyond the norm. The new homes they make for themselves are burrows, not rabbit-sized cottages, but they do plan a large communal burrow where they can meet for company and story-telling; their weapons are claws and teeth, but they think and improvise as well as acting by instinct and habit; they keep to their ecological niche, but they can talk to other animals in a hedgerow argot (for example, to the mouse and the gull, and to the hostile cats at the farm); this of course adds to the dimension of comedy in the book. Occasional interpolations of scientific facts about rabbit behaviour balance their story-telling and conversation; the constant anxiety the travellers suffer on their hazardous journey is natural, not human, and their attitude to their females is equally the attitude of rabbits, though it has been analysed, apparently in all seriousness, as a reprehensible sexist attitude.

Richard Adams has disclaimed any moral purpose for his book and although there is very evident in it his love and concern for the particular small area in Berkshire in which events take place, his story has attained the status of a classic because it is an absorbing, superbly well-told story about individuals. The fact that they are individual rabbits makes it no less and no more compelling. [Richard Adams: *Watership Down*, London 1972]

**HEIDI** is five years old when her aunt Dete decides it is time the child's grandfather took his turn in caring for the orphan. The Alm-Uncle, with a wild and unhappy life behind him, has retreated to his mountain hut and cut himself off from the village below. Although he takes the child in grudgingly, Heidi's childish, affectionate ways thaw the old man's reserve, as they also win the friendship of Peter the goat boy and of his old blind grandmother. After two or three years Heidi's aunt Dete removes her from the mountain as summarily as she had left her there, for Clara Sesemann, daughter of a well-to-do widower in Frankfurt, needs a companion. Clara, a delicate child confined to a wheel-chair, is roused from her fretful lethargy by Heidi's lively chatter, but Heidi

herself is so homesick that although she comes to love Clara, she becomes ill and is sent back to the Alm hut. Here she happily resumes her old companionship with her grandfather and here Clara comes for a visit which helps her to throw off her weakness and lead a normal life.

The story of Heidi has always been popular even though the religious and moral message of the book is expressed more directly than present-day taste allows. Some modern editions in fact seek to spare children by cutting the long moral passages; this throws too much emphasis on the carefree aspect of Heidi's character and

Illustrations from two editions of *Heidi*: (*top*) by Vincent O. Cohen and (*bottom*) by Cecil Leslie.

life, and her time in Frankfurt comes to seem almost like a term of imprisonment. In fact the gaiety, freshness and vigour of the mountain scenes show us only one aspect of the child; her serious consideration for other people, her instinct for the good and true side of life, her innocent power to combat the dark moods of her elders, are just as important and need to be seen clearly in the context in which Johanna Spyri set them. Heidi is no less a real child because her story is used to illustrate certain matters of principle and to serve an educational purpose. However, the two sequels written by one translator of Heidi do not really succeed in extending her function into the grown-up world; it is as a child that this character is understood. [Johanna Spyri: *Heidi*, (1880 Switzerland) London 1884. Charles Tritten: *Heidi Grows Up*, New York 1938; *Heidi's Children*, London 1950]

**HELEN SCROPE,** the second of five children, tells the story of a landmark in their lives. All the Scrope children have well-marked characters. Patricia, the eldest, is inclined to be overbearing; Bobby argues his way through each day; Annis 'is as tiresome as tiresome can be with crying over everything' and Paul, with the obstinacy of a youngest child, has so often insisted on the truth of his fantasies that the others are inclined to disbelieve everything he says. Different as they are, the children are united in their affection for one another and in their efforts to endure the tyranny of Nurse, whom they consider 'a very cross person'.

The girls have something else in common – the stories started by Maria the nursery-maid, which they embroider for themselves, half scared and half delighted, about the Man-under-the-bed and about Bogy. Since they know in their hearts that these are only stories, it is hardly surprising that they do not believe Paul when he tells them he has seen Bogy. The small boy is punished by Nurse for telling untruths, but he *has* seen Bogy – or rather, has seen the distinguished naturalist who has come to live in seclusion next door after an accident which maimed and blinded him. As the children come to know and love him, they come to understand the real meaning of the term 'gentleman' and how they may achieve the 'gentle heritage'. The moral of the story does not obscure the lively humour of this picture of children who, in the strict discipline of a nursery of the 1890s, preserve the natural curiosity and resourcefulness of their years. [Frances Crompton: *The Gentle Heritage*, London 1893]

**HEN WEN** the oracular pig escapes from the dread realm of Arawn the Death King to the safety of Caer Dallben in the land of Prydain. Only Dallben the master enchanter knows how to interpret the ancient symbols carved on the ashwood letter-sticks when Hen Wen noses some out of a pile, but her everyday needs are supplied by Taran (q.v.), a youth of unknown parentage who bears the unromantic title of Assistant Pig-keeper. Alarmed by the Horned King, Hen Wen disappears, starting the first of Taran's many quests.

Hen Wen's last and most significant prophecy comes from her in spite of herself; her terror as she fumbles the sticks is one of many telling details by which the atmosphere of conflict and danger is built up in *The High King*. Hen Wen is presented as a real pig, her only utterance being the onomatopoeic words traditionally used to suggest pig-language, and when the prophecy has been fulfilled she loses her power to assist divination. It is left to the reader to decide whether this is symbolic or whether her alliance with a visiting boar and the subsequent birth of piglets have anything to do with the matter. Certainly Hen Wen may be classed with other characters in the books ( like Doli the Dwarf, for instance, and Fflewdur Fflan the incompetent bard) who are at once comic and serious. [Lloyd Alexander: *The Book of Three*, New York 1964; *The High King*, 1968]

**HENRIETTA THE FAITHFUL HEN** lives in style although her mistress, Mrs Fowler, is old and poor, for she has an old dolls' house for a nesting-box and a curtained cupboard under the sink for her dust-bath; but when Henrietta stops laying there is no food and no money for the rough-tongued rent collector. Poor Henrietta – she tries, but she has 'forgotten the trick'. However, she has listened intelligently to Mrs Fowler when she reads the newspaper aloud and she decides to dig for treasure. Happily a discovery which reduces her to tears of disappointment is identified as 'a most valuable Roman pot', and in due course a whole settlement is found under Mrs Fowler's garden. She and Henrietta plan their future homes (sunny and labour-saving for Mrs Fowler, castellated for the romantic bird), a film is made based on Henrietta's life, she marries her devoted admirer Mr Cox and sits down to write her autobiography.

Henrietta's second adventure (in *Henrietta's Magic Egg*), finds the entertaining bird as credulous and enthusiastic as ever, though this time the plot, centred

Henrietta on the shoulders of Mrs Fowler in *Henrietta's Magic Egg*, written and illustrated by Kathleen Hale.

on a tree with mysterious eyes and strange oracular powers, is more surrealist and less unaffectedly funny than that of the first book. In both, Kathleen Hale uses the skill in suggesting human expression in words and pictures which have made the Orlando books (q.v.) classics, but in the tales of Henrietta she adds one final stroke of wit. Mrs Fowler's dress, shawl and cap and her features suggest with casual confidence a totally acceptable resemblance between the joint heroines of the two picture-books. [Kathleen Hale: *Henrietta the Faithful Hen*, London 1943; *Henrietta's Magic Egg*, London 1973]

**HENRY HUGGINS** is one of those busy, conscientious, lively boys perhaps more readily found in fiction than in real life. Educated by sensible parents to be self-reliant, he realizes that it is up to him to make his wishes come true. At the age of eight he sells worms to fishermen to pay for a football; later, he delivers newspapers so as to buy materials to build a clubhouse. By the time Ramona the Pest (q.v.) goes to school, he is one of the official guards at the school crossing, which increases her embarrassingly obvious admiration for him.

Henry is no super-boy. When he gets permission from his mother to keep the stray dog he finds wandering in the town, he encounters difficulties when he smuggles it on a bus in parcel-wrappings. His corner in bubble-gum at school leaves him with an inexplicable deficit. In short, there is enough human inconsistency in Henry's nature and in his exploits to make him a personality of the humorous kind, as well as an acceptable focal point in several books. [Beverley Cleary: *Henry Huggins*, New York 1950; *Henry and Beezus*, 1952; *Henry and the Clubhouse*, 1962; *Henry and Ribsy*, 1964]

**HEREWARD THE WAKE**'s existence is attested in chronicles and ballads and from the eleventh century onwards legends have collected round his name. The novelist has one obvious starting point in regard to Hereward – his fight against William of Normandy. The epitaph which resounds on the last page of Kingsley's *Hereward the Wake*, 'Here lies the last of the English', is the climax of the study of a warrior conceived in a romantic style to suit Kingsley's own idea of a hero. Contemporary records have been used freely and sometimes with scant respect for historical probability. To give his hero status, Kingsley accepted the view that Hereward was one of the sons of Leofric of Mercia; noble blood was essential to satisfy current social ideas and to enlarge to tragic dimensions the character of a wild youth who does not even spare the Church from his irresponsible attacks. When he is exiled he asserts that he has been looking for an excuse to turn 'kempery-man – knight errant, as those Norman puppies call it ... and try what a man can do for himself in the world with nothing to help him in heaven or earth, with neither sword nor angel, friend nor counsellor, to see to him, save his wits and his good sword'. But the mercenary soldier soon returns to England, where William has been crowned King, as the champion of the English, and such exploits as the sacking of the Golden Borough are readily excused as part of Hereward's campaign against the Normans, although to modern eyes such actions may seem symptomatic of the manic nature of his earlier days. To soften and vary the pattern of bloodshed and death, Kingsley dwells on Hereward's love for Torfrida, who becomes his wife, and on his suppressed longing for Alftruda; these relationships are treated with an odd mixture of gentility and candour, so that Hereward's behaviour becomes, ludicrously, like that of an embarrassed and caddish Victorian husband.

In short, Kingsley's hero, largely of his own invention, behaves with a Tennysonian chivalry, lapsing occasionally into drunken violence which is Kingsley's version of the 'old days'. He becomes a hero in the real sense only in his defence of Ely against William when, suffering the hardships of his men, risking his life to spy on the enemy, he earns the comment from Sweyn of Denmark that 'if there had been three such men as Hereward in England, all would have gone well'. It is impossible to read Kingsley's novel now as his contemporaries would have read it but even they may have felt that the ill-digested conglomeration of truth, legend and fancy did not add up to a single individual so much as a multi-faceted picture based on certain fashions in looking at the past.

Henry Treece's picture of Hereward in *Man with a Sword* belongs as obviously to our own time, drawing on new interpretations of the sagas as well as on modern ideas of mental alienation. It is, nonetheless, a splendidly co-ordinated, skilfully constructed study in character, based on the established fact that Hereward was a warrior. Henry Treece sees him not romantically but with historical understanding. Adding to the few available facts a measure of novelist's intuition, he draws the picture of a man of cool courage and sudden furies (the berserk temperament which he depicts so often in his novels) who hired himself out as a swordsman and whose manic state was intensified after he was severely wounded by the Godwins. Hereward finally comes to England as an ally of the invader Sweyn of Denmark; he remains essentially a professional swordsman, admitting no personal loyalties, dominated only by a savage desire for revenge against the Godwins. In the last years of his life, when as a solitary, beleaguered figure in the Ely marshes he seeks William to make terms for his starving men, he seems a far more complex and dignified figure than Kingsley's pathetic automaton, and the description of the 'two old fighting-men', William and Hereward, wearied by the past, 'beating time with their wine-horns and carolling away at a ditty that the rest of the world had forgotten', shows more imagination than Kingsley's stiff, patriotic portrait does. Treece saw Hereward as a man always ready to assert his Englishness against the Normans but as an individual first and foremost, dominated by the ebb and flow of his berserk temperament. Edgar Atheling's words when Hereward finally relinquished his fierce hold on life – 'Hereward is the stuff of which the Gods make Kings, when it pleases them' – confirms him in history: Treece's magnificent novel also confirms him as a man. [Charles Kingsley: *Hereward the Wake*, 2 vols, London 1866. Henry Treece: *Man with a Sword*, London 1962]

**HITTY,** the heroine of Rachel Field's doll-autobiography, whose life reflects a century or more of American social life, was carved by an old pedlar out of mountain-ash wood in the state of Maine somewhere in the 1820s. In the 1930s, using a desk, paper and quill pen belonging to the proprietor of an antique shop, she writes her memoirs for posterity. Her first voyage with little Phoebe Preble on a whaling ship lands her on a Pacific island, where she is worshipped as an idol by the natives. Restored by happy accident to her young owner, she is taken to India, where she is lost and becomes the property of Little Thankful, a missionary's daughter. She goes to America, is lost once more and returns to the light of day to be adopted by quiet Clarissa, whose parents are Quakers. At the time of the Civil War she is packed away for safety, to be discovered years later by a dressmaker, who uses her as a fashion doll. Her exquisite outfits tempt rich little Isabella van Rensselaer,

Dorothy P. Lathrop's illustration of the wooden doll Hitty.

but she is stolen by street urchins and eventually becomes the companion of good little Katie, whose family works in a yarn mill in Rhode Island. Lost once more, in a hay loft, Hitty returns to life as a show piece, dressed for an exhibition by two old ladies, and after an unexpected flight down the Mississippi, she finds security at last in Miss Hunter's antique shop.

The mock-autobiography is a version of the domestic novel that goes back to the early nineteenth century in England. A certain piquancy is lent to a simple chronicle of domestic and social custom and event when it comes from a non-human narrator; a cat or a needle obviously see life in a refreshingly different way and it may be said that a doll character is particularly well suited to the form. The somewhat smug, enigmatic features of a wooden doll have inspired other writers before and since Rachel Field used the events of her heroine's life as the impetus for pictures of the world of merchants and seamen, city and country folk. Everything that happens is seen from the doll's rather caustic point of view. Among Rachel Field's many novels of America's past, graceful and authentic as they are, *Hitty* stands out as a literary triumph. [Rachel Field: *Hitty*, New York 1929]

**HOMER PRICE** lives in a tourist camp outside the town of Centerburg. His father looks after the filling station, his mother cooks for the lunch room, and Homer, in the intervals of washing car windows and sweeping out cabins, works on his hobby, building radios. Though he is presented to the reader as an ordinary boy, the scenes in which he figures show him to be somewhat unusual. For example, he tames a skunk which he christens Aroma and finds the animal useful when thieves visit the district. Because Homer is naturally inquisitive and also friendly, he receives confidences from various people and is often able to produce odd bits of information to help in solving problems. His character, lightly and easily developed, serves mainly as a centre for various mildly humorous or zany situations in which the American boy plays a more or less active part. [Robert McLoskey: *Homer Price*, New York 1943]

**HORATIO HEAVYSIDE DRAGON** is discovered by a small boy called Harold Heavyside Brown (but more usually known as Poo-Poo) when in an idle moment he wanders inside a fuchsia flower and emerges into a strange land. The adoption of Horatio is a certainty once he has proved to Poo-Poo's father how useful he can be as a cigarette lighter and to Poo-Poo's mother that his tail makes an excellent floor-polisher.

Dragons in myth, fairy tale and religious belief are serious symbols: in children's stories they are more often the source of humour fairly obviously deriving from their supposed flame-throwing attributes. A good many of Horatio's adventures are fiery – and useful. The sight of what happens to an ice-cream soda in his throat serves as a fine advertisement for Mr Quentin Fazackerley's soda fountain; he warms the lake for swimming;

he and his mate Ermyntrude use their breath as snow-clearers after a blizzard. A touch of mock-heroic in the narrative, a touch of the bashful small boy in Horatio, dispel any suspicion of disbelief at the time of reading. [C. S. Forester: *Poo-Poo and the Dragons*, London 1942]

**HUGH PROCTER** at eight years old is restless at home and takes so little interest in his lessons that his governess despairs of getting him in a fit state to follow his brother Phil to Crofton when he is ten. As things turn out, he goes to the school before he is nine, when neither Phil's advice nor his own nature have prepared him for the change he has so much desired. On the way to school in a coach he repeats to the man sitting next to him all that Phil has told him about Crofton. Unfortunately his travelling companion is a master at the school, who maliciously repeats the boy's ingenuous confidences. Hugh finds he has earned the nickname Prater the Second; not unnaturally his brother blames him for the fact that by schoolboy logic he becomes Prater the First. Miserable and homesick, Hugh resents the fact that Phil refuses to make things easier for him. Because he is worried about the possibility that his age, his long hair and his childish ways will lead the boys to call him a 'Betty', currently the worst school insult, he begins to walk in his sleep. After a time, however, helped by true friends, he gets hold of himself, though he remains self-absorbed and conceited.

Redemption comes, as so often in the improving stories of the time, through suffering. His foot is smashed in an accident and has to be amputated. His mother's encouragement helps him to determine not to trade on his infirmity when he returns to Crofton and though he occasionally lapses into his old state of resentful self-pity, he gradually turns into a sensible boy. Even with the shadow of stern morality that hangs over the story, first published in 1841, there is plenty of crisp detail in it, so that it deserves Mary Thwaite's opinion that it is: 'The first really natural story of school life'. [Harriet Martineau: *The Crofton Boys*, in *The Playfellow: A Series of Tales*, 4 pts, London 1841]

**HUGO** *see* JOSEPHINE

# I

**IRON MAN** (the), after a fall from a high cliff, is articulated through the chance agency of two inquisitive gulls and the accidental juxtaposition of an eye and a hand. Whole again, the giant stalks the countryside devouring tractors and chewing barbed wire fences like spaghetti, until Hogarth, a farmer's son, has the courage and sense to direct the monster to a rubbish dump. Now the Iron Man is accepted as a friend and when a gigantic space-being emerges from a distant star and sprawls over the whole of Australia, the world appeals for help to the giant it knows. Again Hogarth, the innocently-wise child, has a suggestion to offer. The Iron Man challenges the space-bat-angel-dragon to a duel, and twice the two of them stretch on a rack of fire – the Iron Man on a metal grid, the space-being on the Sun itself. Agonized and afraid, the Iron Man invites his adversary to a third round, but the creature surrenders, to serve the earth for ever by encircling it with the music of the spheres.

The antagonists in this extraordinary, concentrated narrative are symbols rather than characters, for each means something different to every reader. For some, the crux of the story is the fact that the space-creature's singing turns aggressive man towards the idea of peace. For others, there is significance in the theme of the enemy who is seen to be a friend. Others may interpret the idea of reconciliation intellectually (as the growth of wisdom, perhaps) or emotionally, as the balance of ego and id. The 'seasoning' of 'an inner personality by fantasies' is the core of Ted Hughes's work. The metaphor, as large as the Iron Man himself, suggests that we need to discover the wholeness in life, to accept as essential the duality of good and evil, and above all, to see as a guiding force the power of imagination. In Ted Hughes's personal myth, created for himself and for his own children, each reader must find his own myth. [Ted Hughes: *The Iron Man* (US title, *The Iron Giant*), London 1968]

**ISABELLA CLINTON,** called Sybille, is dismayed when at the age of fifteen she is commanded to the court of Richard II, to travel in his train to France and to bring back the seven-year-old Isabella, the princess who had been married by proxy to the English king after the death of his first queen, Anne of Bohemia. Richard's words, 'Keep my little Queen merry', and his sympathetic manner towards her ensure her loyalty in the un-

happy years that follow as surely as the child-queen, trying to grow up to her position and to learn to help the king, commands Sybille's devotion.

Isabella Clinton is that most debatable and difficult of characters, a fictitious personage given a place beside the great ones of history. Her background is well chosen. Noble by birth, adequately instructed in courtly manners, she can be accepted in the social and historical context as a proper companion for the child princess and as a witness to the tragic course of Richard II's reign. Her temperament – independent, strong-minded and capable of great devotion – makes her the mouthpiece Hilda Lewis needs for her interpretation of Richard as a man full of faults but much wronged. Lady Sandwich's remark on Richard's advisers – 'They should have handled him like a stallion ... but they whipped him on like a carthorse' – is but one of many remarks made to Sybille and stored up by her; together with her own account of such key events as the banishing of Bolingbroke and the fall of the king, they make a notably romantic and interesting picture of Richard and (in greater depth) of the 'gentle falcon', the child who loved him and whose only fault was that she was too young for her intelligence and honesty to influence him. The idea of viewing history through the eyes of a character implicated in it only peripherally is not a new one but Isabella Clinton is an outstanding example of its application. [Hilda Lewis: *The Gentle Falcon*, London 1952]

**ISLAND MACKENZIE** wins his name by reason of a desert island adventure which deprives him of eight of his nine lives. Mackenzie has accompanied Captain Jupiter Foster of the *Hollyhock* on many voyages and has always been popular with the passengers, but instinct tells him that it is no use trying to make friends with Miss Pettifer. When shipwreck not only robs the cat of his master but also throws him into the company of the tall, stern cat-hater, one of his 'lives' is sacrificed to Miss Pettifer's phobia, when in a fury at the cat's treatment of her knitting (the sweater on the needles has been started for the gallant captain) Miss Pettifer zips the animal she calls Em into her knitting-bag and tosses him into a pool.

Almost at once remorse makes her pull him out again. In other ways Mackenzie escapes the dangerous atten-

The Iron Man, illustrated by George Adamson.

Ivor the steam engine, drawn by Peter Firmin for *Ivor's Outing.*

tions of mermaids, crocodiles and cannibals, and when the captain appears in the nick of time to rescue Miss Pettifer from the cooking pot, the affectionate and opportunist little cat knows that he now has a double chance of a happy life to come.

A strong point of humour in the book comes from the contrast between the cat's interpretation of Miss Pettifer's actions, unreasonable and peculiar as they seem to him, and Miss Pettifer's equally bewildered reaction to cat behaviour. The gradual approach of two ill-assorted castaways towards each other is beautifully contrived. [Ursula Moray Williams: *The Nine Lives of Island Mackenzie*, London 1959]

**IVOR THE ENGINE** was the locomotive of the Merioneth and Llantisilly Rail Traction Company Limited, a small railway 'in the top left-hand corner of Wales'. With his driver, Jones the Steam, and their colleagues Owen the Signal and Dai Station, Ivor steamed along on his useful run, and was a happy engine, until he heard the Grumbly Choral Society practising and fell into a melancholy fit. His worried driver had him overhauled in vain; then he happened to catch sight of Ivor shedding 'a single dirty tear' as the voices of the choir drifted towards him, and he devised a method by which he and Ivor could discuss his secret wish. When Evans the Song told the disappointed Jones that he could only use the engine if he had 'a Good Bass note', Jones, nothing daunted, bought organ pipes from an old roundabout and welded them on to Ivor's boiler. Ivor went nervously to his first rehearsal, and was a sensation.

In a sequel, as a staunch member of the Choir, Ivor pulled the trainload to the Eisteddfod at Llanmad and helped to win the silver wreath. Once again desire outran capacity – for how could he swim with his fellow singers? Once again the resourceful Jones and a steam crane solved the problem.

Peter Firmin, infinitely perceptive of the unexpected beauty of inanimate objects, has allowed the shape of an old-fashioned steam engine to establish Ivor's personality without additions or distortions, while the crisp idiomatic speech and thoughts given to the engine casually and easily maintain his right to be considered as a character. [Oliver Postgate, ill. Peter Firmin: *Ivor the Engine*, London 1962; *Ivor's Outing*, 1967]

# J

**JACK**, the protector of the dainty heroine in *Mopsa the Fairy*, becomes wholly responsible for the pretty little being whom he has found in a nest because he kisses her and, as the old apple-woman explains, 'she cannot now take the same care of herself that others of her race are capable of.' As he and Mopsa (q.v.) sail down river in a magic boat and climb the purple mountains to enter Fairyland, he accepts the apple-woman whether she is behaving as a servant should or whether she berates the Fairy Queen as an equal. He notices but does not seem to fear the way Mopsa grows, first to one foot one inch, then into 'a sweet little girl of ten years', then into a beautiful young woman. But he does learn from his adventure that 'What you can do you may do'. His adventure has an allegorical, almost surrealist side to it which does not interfere with the pleasantly extrovert boy's initiative. [Jean Ingelow: *Mopsa the Fairy*, London 1869]

**JACK** and **MAGGIE** argue over Jack's new book on natural history, for he has suddenly become an ardent butterfly-collector and insists that this is entomology, not cruelty, and that Maggie would like insects better if she would agree to go through the book with him. Maggie wishes it were possible to get inside books 'and meet the people that are in them'. Almost at once the children find themselves miniaturized and wandering through the pages of Jack's book, where butterflies, caterpillars, spiders and locusts, all excessively opinionated and loquacious, set to work to explain the invertebrate world in scientific and in personal terms.

As a serious naturalist, Edmund Selous wanted to establish, in a way suitable to the young, certain scientific facts and principles, and to emphasize the superiority of field studies over collecting, of cameras and binoculars over guns and butterfly-nets. Jack and Maggie, with their fraternal bickering and their easy acceptance of marvels, are a useful medium for the lessons. They can understand cryptic colouration when it is explained by the Leaf Butterfly, even if he is testy about 'various inferior artists' who try his trick; they are amused when the Ant-Caterpillar claims that artistic necessity is his chief motive for impersonation; on another occasion the children defend the human race valiantly against the Katydid's comment that it is hardly normal 'To have ears in one's head instead of in the joints of one's legs'.

Jack and Maggie surrounded by locusts in an illustration by J. A. Shepherd from *Jack's Insects*.

The rolling, polysyllabic sentences, full of wit and of information, reveal animal personalities to the attentive and privileged audience of two cheerfully receptive children. [Edmund Selous: *Jack's Insects*, London 1910]

**JACK MARTIN** seems to Ralph Rover (q.v.), 'lionlike in his actions, but mild and quiet in disposition'. Obviously a natural leader, Jack makes many of the discoveries that make life comfortable for the castaways of *The Coral Island*, his good education helping him to identify and test fruit-bearing trees and to regulate his behaviour towards 'savages' or missionaries. When we meet Jack again in *The Gorilla Hunters* he is little changed. In seven years he has become a giant of a man with 'a beard like a grenadier's shako' but he is still good-natured and leisurely. Willingly joining the expedition to Africa, Jack, in the manner of his day and age, shoots animals and people with equal readiness. When they reckon up their bag of gorillas (thirty-seven), it is Jack who remarks 'Pity we didn't make up the forty'.

With his prowess at arms and his skill in making an effective army out of King Jambai's disorganized subjects, Jack is an obvious reflection of the imperialist of his day and, in the climate of our times, a not altogether pleasing example of a boy who has never really grown up. There is little chance of modern children forcing their way through the blood-stained thickets of Ballantyne's prose, or accepting his values in these books. [R. M. Ballantyne: *The Coral Island*, London 1858; *The Gorilla Hunters*, 1861]

**JACKANAPES** is unmistakably an ape but at the same time his character is seen in human terms, just as he consorts with men and women without causing comment. In one story a Recruiting Sergeant tricks him into taking the Queen's shilling and only Miss Pussy's (q.v.) generosity saves him from being sent to the wars. In *The Bran Tub*, four linked stories describe how he plots to win one of Miss Pussy's three heiress nieces for his bride. They outwit him neatly by posing successively as a profligate, an invalid and a prig, in scenes which are pure social comedy.

Like Miss Pussy, Jackanapes was originally drawn (in 'Miss Pussy and Old Jackanapes') as a simple folktale trickster, but he soon develops into a subtle villain, increasingly plausible, governed by vanity, with an ape's hatred of derision and a scoundrel's resourceful and unregenerate outlook. The setting for his impostures is constantly changing. At times the scene seems to be vaguely Regency; at others he inhabits a world of knights, unicorns and enchantment. Mock-historical details of costume and behaviour make a piquant contrast with magical circumstance. In this context the character of Jackanapes, though it seems definable enough, is always a little elusive. Do we take him to be a serious moral corrective or a kind of jester? We never quite know, and herein lies the secret of his unquenchable, fascinating vitality. [Diana Ross: *The Wild Cherry*, London 1943; *The Enormous Apple Pie*, 1951; *The Bran Tub*, 1954; *The Merry Go Round*, 1963]

**JAMES DOUGLAS** is a black American boy left in the care of his three great-aunts while his mother is in hospital. His sensitive, rather nervous attitude to life perhaps began to show after his father had walked out on the family and it is certainly intensified by his fears at his mother's absence. Because nobody has explained to him exactly what is the matter with his mother, he has comforted himself with the idea that she has gone to Africa – an idea that stems from some of Aunt Paula's bedtime stories. Her allusions to the days of slavery have crystallized in his mind into a picture of his chieftain ancestor; a ring with a red stone found in the street confirms his belief that he is a prince and that his mother is away seeking his rights.

The ring must surely be a sign left by his mother. He is certain he will find instructions in a certain empty house, but when he goes there he finds no messenger but, instead, three older boys who bully him into stealing dogs and claiming a reward for finding them.

Paula Fox weaves the apprehensions of young James together, suggesting his terror through sudden sharp verbal pictures of the faces of his tormentors or of the huge empty structures of out-of-season Coney Island. She has emphasized his need for reassurance and love by showing how his fear of dogs turns to affection for Gladys, the poodle he has 'taken to the park' for her owner. Paula Fox develops James's character with the allusive, elliptical technique of an adult novelist. The result is a character not sharply defined but with a pattern which is revealed to a diligent and responsive reader, slowly and surely. [Paula Fox: *How Many Miles to Babylon?*, New York 1967]

**JAMES SMITH** at eight years old is a formidable child, small, plump, red-haired and freckled. Though his older brothers – thirteen-year-old Thomas and well-mannered Joshua, who is eleven – perpetually strive to keep him in his place, it takes a great deal to disconcert James. 'The great thing is not to argue with him,' is Thomas's advice to Maria Henniker-Hadden (q.v.) when she is introduced to the next-door family. 'He always has the last word.' Maria's comment on him in her diary, after their first meeting, is 'He is OUTRAGEOUS. If he was my brother I should fight him all the time.' Harriet Jessop, who meets him (in *The Elephant War*) a few months before Maria does, finds him terrifying, with his scowls and shouts and sudden explosions of opinion.

An ebullient, mischievous boy can soon become as tiresome to the reader as to his fellow-characters, especially when the wake of embarrassment he leaves behind him is described in several books. The sheer variety of James's misdoings inspires admiration, especially when (in *James without Thomas*) he persuades Lord Banbury to re-open the private railway on his estate. Though he is now ten years old, James is still impervious to any distinction of class, age or circumstance when he is visited by one of his good ideas.

He has an endearing capacity for being amused and Gillian Avery often uses this trait to tone down a ludicrous situation – for instance, the unfortunate conjunction of Mr Francis Copplestone (q.v.) with a bull, a duckpond and angry villagers (in *The Warden's Niece*). Indeed, the capacity for mischief in James seems

to be deliberately contrasted with the eccentricities of Mr Copplestone; irresponsibility may be engaging in a child where it is merely distasteful in an adult. In the books in which James and his brothers appear, Gillian Avery has availed herself of the tough attitude to youthful peccadilloes that is typical of mid-Victorian children's stories; the gentle touch of parody makes her admiration for such stories all the more noticeable. [Gillian Avery: *The Warden's Niece*, London 1957; *Trespassers at Charlecote*, 1958; *James without Thomas*, 1959; *The Elephant War*, 1960]

**JAMIE MORTON**, an alert lad of fifteen, is one of the scores of boys organized by the old man known as the Cleek into the loose fellowship of the Edinburgh Caddies. Like the rest of them, Jamie guides strangers, and runs messages but longs to play a more direct part in the affairs that trouble the city in the year after the defeat of the Armada.

His chance comes when Roger Macey accepts him as a guide to the house of the fencing-master John Forbes and James's practice in lurking and roof-climbing stands him in good stead when Macey sets him to watch the conspirators against King James and Elizabeth of England in Huntly House. There is grave danger for the boy, and moments of pure terror, as well as moments of pride; it is one of his most deadly enemies who remarks 'You are strong and bold and quick in the workings of your mind. And I know also that you are lucky. You have all the attributes of an adventurer but that last is the most important of them all – luck!' And an adventurer Jamie is clearly destined to become, for, as the Cleek realizes, he is older and wiser for his involvement in great affairs. Mollie Hunter has used her fictional character to particularize historical fact and to localize it in the city. [Mollie Hunter: *The Spanish Letters*, London 1964]

**JAN** is a waif living precariously in Warsaw under German occupation, in the early years of the Second World War. He tangles with Joseph Balicki when the father of the family, escaped from a prison camp, is searching the ruins of his house for clues to the whereabouts of his wife and three children. Jan, clutching a wooden box and a bony grey kitten, begs for the paper knife, in the shape of a silver sword, which is the only Balicki possession Joseph has found in the ruins. Joseph bargains with Jan; he may have the silver sword if he tries to find Ruth, Edek and Bronia and tells them their father has gone to his wife's people in Switzerland. Jan does find the

*Above.* Elisabeth Grant's drawing of Jamie Morton in *The Spanish Letters*.

*Left.* James listens for an approaching train, drawn by John Verney for *James without Thomas*.

Jan meets the Balicki children; cover illustration by C. Walter Hodges for *The Silver Sword*.

Balicki children in the end, and they set out on a dangerous, eventful journey which ends in the happy reunion
of the family and the adoption of Jan.

In this sincere, humane story, which is founded on
fact, the characters of Ruth, responsible and conscientious, of Edek who is dogged by illness and of
young, artistic Bronia, stand as representatives of children everywhere whose lives have been disrupted by war.
Beside them, Jan stands out as a personality. Skilful
pickpocket, ingenious thief, the uncertainty under his
jaunty independence is shown by the way he clings to
the box of treasures which stands instead of a home;
its contents, which include a gold curtain ring, a silver
tea-spoon, a feather from the tale of his pet cock (a victim of the war) and three dead fleas caught on a chimpanzee, tell us much about his wayward character.
Above all we get to know Jan through the way he
changes. For most of the journey he seems exclusively
concerned with the fate of the animals he meets and
whom he seems mysteriously to understand – from
Jimpy his cock to old Jasper, the farmer's dog in East
Germany. He seems to be motivated mainly by hatred
of the Germans and suspicious of everyone else. But the
weeks of travelling with the Balickis teach him that
people can be honest and loyal and that there is a meaning in the family pattern. [Ian Serraillier: *The Silver
Sword*, London 1956]

**JAN LAKE** is brought to Miller Lake's one stormy
night by a strange, ill-assorted couple, and becomes to
all intents and purposes the child of the mill, but there
is always something different about him. When his
brother Abel draws out the letters of the alphabet for
the child, he copies them without hesitation; he draws
pictures on his slate endlessly; he makes designs from
leaves, sticks and crushed flowers for want of paints.
Nothing can divert his innate genius for long – not even
the need to help his father, when the Lake children all
succumb to a cholera epidemic and the poor mother
loses her wits, not the insistence of Master Swift, the
old schoolmaster, who believes the boy's gifts should be
developed through science and other subjects that will
be useful to him in the future.

Jan's happiness as a child of the mill is more precarious
than he realizes. The rascally Cheap Jack stumbles by
chance on part of the truth of Jan's hidden past; he and
his wife kidnap the boy and set him to work as a screever
in the London streets. Cheap Jack is jealous of Jan's
quiet air of good breeding and his endurance, and makes
life a misery for the boy until he manages to escape from
his cruel master. He is taken as apprentice by a painter
who recognizes his exceptional artistic gift, and through
a series of fortunate chances he is recognized and rein-
stated in his real family. However, he refuses to take the
position of heir from his half-brother. 'I hope to live well
by my art' is no proud comment, but a natural remark
from a young man whose childhood has allowed his
honest, generous temperament to develop.

Jan Lake, drawn by Mrs Allingham for *Jan of the
Windmill.*

The Victorian intricacies of Jan's story, with its
romantic plot and its clearly marked social pattern, made
the book a favourite in the last century. These popular
attributes are supported at a deeper level by the slow
revelation of Jan's character. In a way it is a study in the
dual powers of environment and inheritance, for Mrs
Ewing suggests how much Jan owed to the home he
considers his own, the quiet march of the seasons and
the discipline of hard, conscientious work, just as clearly
as she shows the persistence of a gift unusual in the
family of a miller in rural England more than a century
ago. [Mrs Ewing: *Jan of the Windmill*, London 1876]

**JAN NEWTON** lives in a market town, where his
father has a greengrocery stall. The ginger-haired,
bright-eyed small boy, always eager for new scenes and
experiences, makes a good focal point for anecdotes
both amusing and shrewd. We can believe in his delight
when he is at last allowed to help his parents and other

*Right.* An illustration by Marlenka Stupica from
*Rotkäppchen,* a German edition of Little Red Riding
Hood.

To the tiger in the zoo

Madeline just said, "Pooh-pooh,"

Jan Newton sells miniature teddy bears in the market; an illustration by Beetles in *Jan the Market Boy*.

stall-holders in the Saturday market. Sometimes he is really useful, as when he sells twenty-four miniature teddy bears in one go; on other occasions he relaxes his conscientious efficiency – for instance, when he and his school-friend Billy race two caterpillars out of a cabbage, on a plank course laid over two orange boxes.

Jan is one of many young characters placed by Mary Cockett in particular environments or engaged in particular trades. They are always lightly but clearly characterized in the context of their backgrounds, many of them (like Jan) outside the middle-class setting that was still dominating the children's book scene in the 1950s and early 1960s. [Mary Cockett: *Jan the Market Boy*, Leicester 1957; *Seven Days with Jan*, 1960]

**JANE PURDY** belongs to an average urban American family. In many ways she is an average girl but in one respect she does not feel ordinary – she has no boy friend, steady or otherwise, and she feels inferior in the company of her more dashing fifteen-year-old school friends. Then she meets Stan Crandall, who is a year older.

*Left*. Madeline visits the zoo, from *Madeline*, written and illustrated by Ludwig Bemelmans.

A first date, finding out about each other, doubts about parental approval (and parental behaviour), jealousy, worries about dress and deportment – all the agonies of a girl moving into a new phase of life are described in the social context of almost twenty years ago. All the same, the book is still read. Jane's feelings are still those of the 'teens, for all the assumed maturity of our times, just as her self-doubt and self-communings belong to any period. [Beverly Cleary: *Fifteen*, New York 1956]

**JANEY LARKIN** is an only child who has found an unusual way to come to terms with loneliness. Her mother is dead and Mr Larkin has lost his Texan farm in the Depression and is now a travelling share-cropper. Their nearest neighbours, the Mexican Romeros, have a daughter of Janey's age who commiserates with her for having no brothers or sisters. But Janey has an answer for Lupe. 'I have a willow plate . . . a willow plate is better than brothers or sisters or anything.' This precious possession, which had belonged to Janey's great-great-grandmother, has become 'the hub of her universe, a solid rock in the midst of shifting sands'.

One day, Janey is sure, she will find a piece of water, a bridge, a house, a willow tree to match the pattern on the plate. She has the consolation of books too, above all the stories of King Arthur. Bravery, her father tells her, can be found anywhere, and so it proves, for the child exposes the deceits of the estate rent collector and wins a permanent home where the willow plate can have a place on the mantle-shelf.

Doris Gates is never sentimental about Janey. In every word, every action, every flick of her pigtails, this is a natural child, expressing with direct, eager feeling her zest for life. She is such a four-square, endearing, believable child that the other characters seem to draw life from her and the book becomes far more than a mere tract for the times. [Doris Gates, *Blue Willow*, New York 1940]

**JEM RATCLIFFE** is a London street-arab whose thin body and sharp eyes add point to his nickname of the Rat. Though the boy is crippled, he has complete authority over the boys who push him through the streets on a home-made trolley. His father, a schoolmaster ruined by drink, has ensured that the Rat speaks properly and observes a gentlemanly code of honour, while the boy fulfils his passionate desire to be a soldier by putting his gang through drill learned by watching the men at the local barracks.

Into his life comes Marco Loristan, a silent, shabby but distinguished boy who has been taught by his father to dedicate his life to the service of the European kingdom of Samavia from which they have been exiled. The Rat's immediate impulse is to throw a stone at him, snarling that he won't have 'you swells dropping in to my club as if it was your own'. But the two boys quickly find a mutual interest in the fortunes of Samavia. Inspired by the legend of a lost prince who will one day come to unite the country, they build up an elaborate game of 'going to Samavia', taking an oath of allegiance and studying in careful detail the map of the country.

When the Rat's father dies Stefan Loristan takes him in, and from being 'a sort of young Cain, his hand against every man and every man's hand against him', he becomes a responsible youth and is chosen to go with Marco to Samavia to give the word for the rising to secret groups of loyalists. For a Prince of the true line has been found, and the Rat soon guesses that Marco himself is the Prince, and his father the rightful King in exile.

Marco is a typical, perhaps even a stereotyped character, fortunate in his upbringing, handsome, endowed with courage and trained to absolute loyalty. When Frances Hodgson Burnett coupled with Marco in the dangerous adventure of Samavia the city-bred, independent, defiant Rat, she saved the story from any suspicion of sentiment or false glamour, and, besides, expressed once more her conviction that gentle birth can never be hid. [Frances Hodgson Burnett: *The Lost Prince*, New York 1915]

**JENNIE** the Sealyham has everything she can desire in life – food, comfort, a loving master – but she complains 'I am discontented ... There must be more to life than having everything.' So, carrying her 'black leather bag with gold buckles', she ventures into the world to look for something she has not got already. An advertisement for a leading lady in the World Mother Goose Theatre offers, specifically, 'something different', but Jenny must have experience before she can apply, so she takes a post as the seventh nurse for a baby who refuses to eat, and is involved with a hungry lion. This is experience enough. She is accepted as leading lady in a rousing dramatization of the nursery jingle, 'Higglety Pigglety Pop', in which everyone she has met on her travels takes part.

This happy piece of surrealistic narrative is dedicated to Jennie, the author's own dog, whose rotund figure and cogent speech dominate the book. Sendak's particularly humane humour and his engravings, with their pointed detail, underline the happy nature of the story. However, in spite of his insistence that the book is just a celebration, a joke, a tribute to the real Jennie, there are plenty of people who prefer to read into its lucid sentences various metaphysical and psychological profundities. [Maurice Sendak: *Higglety Pigglety Pop!* or *There Must Be More to Life*, New York 1967]

**JENNINGS**, an 'eager, friendly boy...with untidy brown hair and a wide-awake look in his eyes', irrupted into the community of Linbury Court Preparatory School aged (he prompted Mr Carter precisely) 'Ten years two months and three days last Tuesday, Sir'. His appearance, age and personality have not changed since the first story about him was broadcast in 1948 in the BBC's Children's Hour, although his favourite exclamation of 'Gosh Fish-hooks' has received various topical variations and his enthusiasms have moved with the times. Car noises have given place to space rocket countdowns and the clicking of a computer, and the expenditure of shillings and, later, new pence, has satisfied his desire for articles ranging from butterfly nets and foreign stamps to a snorkel.

Like William (q.v.), Jennings never deliberately causes trouble. The accidents and disasters for which he is regularly punished result from misplaced enthusiasm and an inability to appreciate the workings of cause and effect. Of all the schoolboys who have ever got lost on cross-country runs, engaged in elaborate financial transactions, experimented with home-made explosive devices, mistaken a visiting plumber or electrician for a school inspector, or a parent for a visiting plumber or electrician, none but Jennings could have turned a simple happening into such a hilarious sequence. Slapstick and farce must have an inner stability if they are not to become wearisome. The stories of Jennings are carefully and formally structured, with two or three story-lines prolonged, developed and intertwined until a final reckoning brings them all together and halts Jennings's impetuous course. He is supported by a skilfully varied cast of subordinate characters. His boon companion Darbishire provides a perfect foil for him; he is a polite

One of Maurice Sendak's drawings of Jennie the Sealyham.

Illustrations from *Jennings Goes to School* and *Thanks to Jennings*.

child with a vicarage background, earnest and bespectacled, whose deliberate utterances sound as though they were in capital letters and who is helpless to escape from Jennings's forceful plans. The shrewd, imperturbable junior master Mr Carter is as important in Jennings's career as the testy Mr Wilkins, who is apt to make 'a noise like an inner tube exploding under pressure' when roused and who never learns wisdom from his numerous encounters with Jennings. The varying attitudes and tactics of the people swept into the orbit of Jennings satisfactorily distract our attention and prevent us from examining too closely the plausibility of this disarming and destructive schoolboy. [Anthony Buckeridge: *Jennings Goes to School*, London 1950; *According to Jennings*, 1954; *Our Friend Jennings*, 1955; and other titles]

**JEREMY FISHER** *see* GINGER AND PICKLES

**JESSICA,** a thin, ragged child, lingers wistfully near a coffee stall set up in the early mornings on one of London's railway bridges. Daniel, who runs the stall for the benefit of the poor on their way to work, is touched by the child's forlorn look and promises to give her coffee and bread on one morning each week. Encouraged by Daniel's cold but consistent charity, Jessica follows him to the chapel where he serves as usher, accepting his warning that it is only for 'ladies and gentlemen' but fascinated by the organ and by the two pretty little daughters of the minister.

Winnie and Jane are not inhibited by ideas of class distinction. Jessica is warmly welcomed in the chapel, learns the message of Jesus, and Daniel, whose charity has been designed to attract the attention of his betters, is converted to true Christianity by the innocent honesty of the little waif and her courage in desperate illness.

Probably the best-known of the tract-tales of the last century, *Jessica's Last Prayer* is entirely keyed to its purpose. None the less, Hesba Stretton's sure touch with background detail, her obvious sincerity, lend to the child a reality that survives the intensely emotional and instructive tone of the book. If Jessica is an instrument of morality, she is also a child real in human terms, pathetic in her lonely, untutored craving for a better life. [Hesba Stretton: *Jessica's Last Prayer*, London 1882]

**JIM HAWKINS** *see* LONG JOHN SILVER

**JIM STARLING** is a pupil at the Cement Street Secondary Modern School in Smogbury and acknowledged leader of the Last Apple Gang, the alliance of Jim, Goggles, Terry and Nip hastily sworn when Jim sets out to prove his innocence of the mac-slashing in the school cloakroom. The gang soon adopts the more dignified title of Agency in order to celebrate Terry's flair for detection and at one stage, when 3B joins in a money-making project for Social Studies, it becomes Jim Starling and Co. Ltd., successively plum merchants, amateur barbers, scrapbook manufacturers and junk collectors.

The four members of the Last Apple Gang, all in their

fourteenth year, in general terms fit their background, the working-class district of a North Country town, and their characters are neatly differentiated. Terry Todd, pale and prone to asthma, has learned to be self-reliant because his mother pays little attention to him; he uses native wit and observation, as well as techniques borrowed from television programmes, in his self-appointed role of special investigator. Goggles Grimshaw, one of a large family, has his spare time eroded by their demands, but even collecting food for his father's pigs occasionally brings him useful information. Nip Challons, whose father keeps a pub, is better dressed than his friends, and though they are often exasperated by his fussy ways and his know-all manner, they have to admit that sometimes his curious habit of reading, and remembering what he has read, does prove useful; besides, they respect his ferocious determination to keep his end up in spite of his diminutive size. With their several talents, the boys throw themselves with zest into enterprises which are comic and occasionally dangerous. In *Jim Starling* they pursue lead-thieves, with some ingenuity, and in *Jim Starling Goes to Town* they are conned by a ticket-tout on the way to a Cup Final and end by uncovering a more serious crime. Other enterprises are slyly educational. They learn something about local government when they are looking for old Mr Dodge's lost Dalmatian (in *Jim Starling and the Spotted Dog*) and increase their knowledge of Smogbury's past history when (in *Jim Starling and the Colonel*) Jim undertakes to emulate the outstanding exploits of a lad of seventy years before.

The authentically ungrammatical speech of the four boys as they argue, confer, plan and speculate, was criticized when the first Jim Starling stories were published; their style was as innovative as the plots and characters. Nowadays it does not seem as bold as it did in 1958 to take heroes and action from a working-class milieu and to present a picture as realistic as fictional techniques allow of an environment very different from the then almost obligatory middle-class or suburban setting of junior adventure stories. E.W. Hildick's tales of Jim Starling are compounded of the stock ingredients of the traditional school story – food, fights and friendships – and the accuracy of every detail of lessons, playground rivalries, incomes, clothes and so on is the accuracy not of a social philosopher but of a highly skilled novelist finding humour in everyday life.

These are stories for entertainment, not sermons. At the same time, they do carry a message of a kind. It may soon be a matter of history that there was a time when people believed that certain types belonged to Secondary Modern schools and certain other, superior, types to Grammar Schools. When Hildick began his stories of Jim Starling he drew on his experience of Secondary Moderns and, strictly within the terms of his fiction, he demonstrated that intelligence, resource, sensitivity and ingenuity are not the property of one class. Perhaps

The Last Apple Gang, drawn by Roger Payne for *Jim Starling's Holiday*.

because of this strong though unobtrusive theme, Jim Starling is in a way the least recognizable of the four boys. Where their characters are sharply defined, he is less easy to analyse. For most of the time he seems like the rest – more sensible than his friends, perhaps, certainly more sensitive, but coming from the same background and sharing a common attitude to life. But there are moments, as he watches the others, or interposes between them, or makes a comment on other people, when he seems almost to be deputizing for the author. [E.W. Hildick: *Jim Starling*, London 1958; *Jim Starling and the Agency*, 1958; *Jim Starling's Holiday*, 1960; *Jim Starling and the Colonel*, 1960; *Jim Starling Takes Over*, 1963; *Jim Starling and the Spotted Dog*, 1963; *Jim Starling Goes to Town*, 1964]

**JIMMY PRICE** *see* FISH

**JIP** *see* DOCTOR DOLITTLE

**JOAN** and **JOY SHIRLEY** are cousins of fifteen living in an old abbey, where Joan's mother is caretaker. Joy is an orphan, sensitive and talented, who accepts Joan's devoted admiration almost as her right. Cecily Hobart, a rich girl of seventeen at a nearby school, brings her country dancing club on an expedition. As Joan guides them round the beautiful building, Cecily discovers she is working alone for an examination, because her mother can no longer afford to pay school fees. The members of the Hamlet Club decide to award their private scholarship to Joan, and when the quiet girl asks that it should go to Joy instead, to help her to a career in music, the fund is stretched to include both of them. In an almost too fortunate ending Joy turns out to be the grand-daughter of the abbey's owner and on his death she inherits the Hall, while the abbey becomes Joan's property as a reward for her care of it.

This romantic tale is the first of many. The stories interlock, new characters come and go, but the atmosphere of the abbey and the lush, almost hectically emotional scenes of friendship, jealousy or ambition remain consistent. To anyone who read the books in girlhood the impression that remains is one of colour – in the descriptions of old stone and ancient grass and of elaborate embroidered robes of the Queens elected year after year by the Club, and in the brilliant red hair of the cousins who remain the most strongly drawn personalities in this long cycle of schooldays, representing in their different ways the eager, creative moods and aspirations of adolescence. [Elsie J. Oxenham, *The Abbey Girls*, London 1920, and many other titles]

**JOCK OF THE BUSHVELD** was first introduced by the author to 'certain Autocrats of the Nightgown' when he was enjoying an honourable retirement after long years in South Africa. The story of how the pup fought a table-leg under the impression that it was a deadly rival, led to more requests from the children and to the command: 'It must be *all true*! and don't leave out *anything*!'. The result was a collection of anecdotes about the author's early years working with a supply train of ox-wagons in the Transvaal, between the Zulu and the Boer Wars, skilfully built round the character of Jock. The book begins with the 'Boy's' choice of the ugliest pup in bull-terrier Jess's litter of cross-breeds, and ends with Jock's death, a tragic accident, happening when he has once more shown his courage and devotion in battling with a much larger dog raiding the hen-house.

The small, golden-brindle, tenacious Jock (who soon

The brave and faithful Jock, drawn by E. Caldwell for *Jock of the Bushveld*.

shows that such derisive names as 'The Rat', 'The Odd Puppy' and 'The Object' are unsuitable), might well have been a convenient peg on which to hang reminiscences of travel over the veldt, of stalking game, of new chums and malefactors and refractory porters and eccentric prospectors. But the author insisted that he was telling Jock's story, and his deeds and temperament dominate all others. It would be easy to put together from this book a brief but effective social history of the Transvaal from the British point of view at the period concerned. It would be just as easy to put together from its pages a manual on the training of an all-purpose dog. This is in fact a notable portrait, of an animal treated as a friend but an *animal* friend, punished for breaking the rules of his training, admired for a courage out of all proportion to his small size, enjoyed for his instant understanding and for the expressiveness of his tail and bark. It is one of the best canine portraits in literature, for adults or for the young. [Sir Percy Fitzpatrick: *Jock of the Bushveld*, London 1907]

**JOE DARLING** *see* MATTIE DOOLIN

**JOEY BETTANY** is one of the first nine pupils at the Chalet School when her sister opens it. Although she is often in trouble for being untidy, she is the moving spirit of school plays and entertainments, always ready to encourage those of her friends who have talents to develop or shyness to overcome. During an illness she writes a spanking imitation of the Elsie Dinsmore books, some of which the doctor has lent her; amused at her efforts, he urges her to write within her own experience, and after she has won a prize in a local competition she announces in her usual positive way 'This settles it ... I'm going to start in right now and be an AUTHORESS.'

It is some time before Jo realizes her ambition and becomes a famous author of school stories and historical novels. Her apprenticeship to letters is interrupted by responsibility as a Senior and finally as Head Girl – a post she accepts unwillingly because she hates the idea of becoming 'grave and responsible' like some girls she has known. But Jo has a sense of humour that keeps her from turning into a prig. Her warm heart and sympathetic manner help her to deal with her peers, and troubles in her own family help to deepen her perception of other people and their needs.

The Chalet School stories, published over a period of at least forty years, have introduced young readers to scores of girls, each with one dominant trait illustrated through suitable vicissitudes. The clever and the careless, the earnest and the mischievous, the lonely and the debonair – one after another the girls appear, make their mark on the stories, and vanish again. Jo alone is drawn in some depth and forms a link between many of the stories, even when she is glimpsed only in the reminiscences of other characters. As the young wife of a doctor and, later, as a mother of triplet daughters, she remains her impulsive self. 'I always run into adventures one way or another', she confesses, and insists 'I refuse to become a dowager type, even if I'm overwhelmed with grandchildren.' None of the readers who have grown up with the Chalet School stories could believe such a thing possible. Though the episodes and the idiom of the stories now seem laboured and out of date, the character of Jo can still claim attention. [Elinor Brent-Dyer: *Jo of the Chalet School*, London 1926, and many other titles, ending with *Althea Joins the Chalet School*, 1969]

**JOHN CLEMENT SUMNER** is a spastic boy of twelve living outside Melbourne. The particular form of his disability allows him to go to school but a great many activities are barred to him and the shaking and speech difficulty which affect him at times both embarrass and infuriate him. So does the attitude of his peers, who are either effusively kind or nervous and stand-offish. John's condition affects his home life no less. His father and mother argue about the degree of freedom which they can safely allow him, and he knows this.

It happens one day that his mother has to go out. Reluctantly, she leaves John alone for the day. He has been waiting for the chance to follow a piece of advice given to him by a man who passed him in the street. 'Don't let anything stop you being the boy you want to be. The answer's inside you. A balloon is not a balloon until you cut the string and let it go.' And so, nervous, aggressive, determined, bruised and exulting, John moves a heavy ladder, sets it against the huge gum tree in the garden and climbs it, bringing alarmed neighbours, the local policeman, agitated parents and – at last – the promise that he shall find his own way, unprotected.

Ivan Southall uses his particular form of the stream of consciousness, stringing out in a grammatical, continuous and formalized way a mixture of daydreams, imaginary conversations, aggressive posturing, expressions of fear, anger, pique, scorn, shame, coarseness or self-doubt, to give a surprisingly natural impression that we are overhearing what goes on in the boy's mind. The method is perfectly adapted to the study of a boy whose imagination will and are as strong as his body is weak and who proves that he is not 'a peculiar little object … who had to be handled carefully like a broken egg' but 'the red-blooded boy who lived inside the one that shook and jerked and smudged his pages.' His brazen shouts – 'Ahoy! I'm John Clement Sumner up a tree' – are cries of victory that truly shake the reader. [Ivan Southall: *Let the Balloon Go*, London 1968]

**JOHN WALKER** is such a sturdy, dependable, extrovert boy that one would be tempted to think that Arthur Ransome had meant him as a type, if it were not for the moments when his self-control breaks down – for example, when he is accused by the Blackett's uncle of breaking into his houseboat in his absence (in *Swallows and Amazons*); the idea that anyone should call him a liar reduces the boy to a miserably emotional silence.

John Walker approaches the houseboat of Captain Flint, from *Swallows and Amazons*, written and illustrated by Arthur Ransome.

His behaviour is motivated by his upbringing. His father, a naval captain, has taught him to sail and to be resourceful, to take the responsibility for the rest of the family in which he stands as head of the younger generation, to be scrupulously honest and above all to govern his doings with common sense.

The famous telegram sent by Captain Walker to Holly Howe, when the Walkers beg for permission to camp on an island in the lake – 'Better drowned than duffers. If not duffers, won't drown' – becomes rather specially John's motto, almost his guiding principle. To be thought a duffer by his father must at all costs be avoided. So he loses no chance to develop his skill in seamanship (typically, the books he chooses to take to the island are about sailing). When (in *We Didn't Mean to Go to Sea*) the four Walker children are carried into the North Sea on a small yacht, through no fault of their own, John concentrates on keeping the ship safe and afloat in a fog and then on navigating it to the nearest port (which proves to be in Holland). All through the gruelling journey John's feelings, thoughts and actions, his doubts and decisions, depend on one factor – what would his father think? It is not John's fault that his plan for survival is unnecessarily dangerous. He is young, though trying hard not to be, and because his sense of proportion is that of a boy of thirteen or so he takes literally Jim Brading's casual warnings about salvage sharks – so much so that he never once thinks of accepting a tow or appealing for help. Once anxiety is over, his natural interest in the external world re-asserts itself. 'Nobody had meant to go to sea, but here they were, and an unknown land ahead of them.' A natural opportunist, John learns from his mistakes. As Master of the 'Swallow', the boat the family has hired for their Lakeland holidays, he is ashamed that his bad seamanship has caused her to capsize, but he is quick to find a workable way to raise her, without asking for outside help. In all the adventures he is concerned with, John shows an increasing sense of responsibility and a practical good sense that saves him from appearing to the reader as a complete prig. [Arthur Ransome: *Swallows and Amazons*, London 1930, and many other titles]

**JOHN WALTERS,** on a visit to his aunt and uncle in the Severn district, is prodding the bracken aimlessly on the hillside near their house when he comes upon a tunnel that seems to lead deep into the hill. John has been initiated into a secret society, a group of four school-fellows who all happen to be staying at home for the summer holidays, and they must be given a part in the adventure. Alan Hobbs, George Reynolds, Cuthbert Saunders (called Meaty because of his father's work) and Harold Soames (usually called Lightning for his restlessness) join with John in collecting equipment for a proper expedition.

*Above.* John Walters and his friends exploring an underground cavern in *The Cave,* illustrated by Geoffrey Whittam. A very different style of illustration is used by Laurence Hervey (*below*) in the second John Walters adventure *Down River.*

Alan takes the lead 'on the assumption that nothing could possibly have been started before he arrived' – and at first he seems to know what he is doing. Gradually the situation changes. The exploration of the cave and its many galleries begins to be dangerous. The boys have to traverse a narrow path with a precipitous drop on one side and to lower themselves to the floor of a huge cavern where an underground river rushes towards the open. Now Alan's companions begin to realize that he is less sure of himself than he seems to be. In a tense moment his incautious gesture of panic loses them the expensive electric lamp he has boasted about; his frantic tears express more fear of his father than of the peril they all face. Even now Alan does not relinquish his authority easily, but in spite of his defiant murmurs and bids for attention, it is George Reynolds, the quiet, biddable George, who takes charge and eventually finds a way out of the cave complex.

In this fine adventure story character is supremely important; action arises from the clash of differing temperaments and from the way each boy reacts to a challenge. Meaty makes no bid for prominence but his stolid, matter-of-fact courage has its own value. George, unhappy from the strained atmosphere of his home, responds at once to an opportunity that shows his steadfast endurance. Lightning, dominated by a clutch of older sisters, has developed an impetuous, reckless manner for fear of being thought sissy. John, a calm, sensible boy, has taken the trouble to learn something about rock-climbing and potholing from his uncle and uses his head in an emergency. Every word Alan utters, whether he is pointing out the shortcomings of his companions or aggressively justifying himself or weeping in terror, reveals the unhappy state of a boy whose boasts hide his terror of his father's tyrannical rages. There is no word uttered by any of the boys that does not tell us something of his particular motives for action and his status in the group.

The second adventure (*Down River*), which takes place a year later, has a rather more hackneyed plot than that of *The Cave*; in place of natural accident the boys face the hostility of smugglers using the cave as a store. The plot is exciting and the boys successfully help local coastguards to catch crooks, but in this book, as in the first, it is the personal tensions that hold the attention. John has been joined by his younger brother Andrew, whose nickname of Tadpole suits his small restless body. With shrewd humour Richard Church describes the first meeting of Tadpole with Lightning, who greatly resents the addition of a newcomer who seems to threaten his coveted position as the indulged junior in the group. There has been a split in the society too, for Alan Hobbs, still mortified by the way he was deposed from his self-appointed leadership in the earlier adventure, has 'reconstituted' the Club, and is now determined that he and his new, unpleasantly aggressive friends shall have the advantage in the

search for Roman remains in the cave. Having persuaded himself that it was John's fault that their first society broke up, Alan sets himself to make matters as difficult for the others as he can, and once more an adventure that does not work out as he had planned exposes his basic weakness of character. The two books show the depth that can be added to familiar formulas of adventure when the effect of character upon action is properly and subtly demonstrated. [Richard Church: *The Cave*, London 1950; *Down River*, 1958]

**JOHNNY CROW** entertained a motley crowd of animals in his newly-made garden. A tactful and unobtrusive host, he summoned the ape to measure the bear who 'had nothing to wear', supplied an umbrella

Johnny Crow, drawn by L. Leslie Brooke for *Johnny Crow's Party*.

when the crane 'was caught in the rain', took broth to the beaver suffering from his throat, listened politely as the whale 'told a very long Tale', and released various gullible animals put in the stocks by, of course, the fox. In a sequel, having once more 'plied fork and hoe' to improve his garden, the hospitable bird summoned the animals again for a party over which he presided with quiet dignity. Small, unclothed, alert, Johnny Crow is placed as a point of balance in pictures which show animals behaving in comically unzoological style, their doings captured for all time in teasing polysyllabic rhyme. [Leslie Brook: *Johnny Crow's Garden*, London 1903; *Johnny Crow's Party*, 1907]

**JOHNNY TREMAIN,** at fourteen, lords it over his fellow-apprentices Dove and little Dusty Miller. Their master, Mr Lapham the silversmith, relies more and more on Johnny, who already shows skill as a craftsman. The arrogant lad never troubles to wonder what his fellow-workers feel about him till a malicious trick seriously damages his right hand and makes it impossible for him to work in silver any longer. The accident drives Johnny to more reckless behaviour than ever before. With his hat at a rakish angle and his right hand permanently hidden in his breeches pocket, he behaves too insolently for the sympathy of the Laphams to continue, and he is forced to seek employment outside the family.

A fortunate friendship with the taciturn youth Rab, who works in the offices of the *Boston Observer*, leads to a job as a horse-boy and messenger, and eventually Johnny becomes a valuable observer for the Whigs in the explosive years before the first shot of the American Revolution is fired.

As he becomes more deeply concerned in the councils of Paul Revere and his friends, Johnny slowly learns to forget himself and his personal grievances, and he describes himself justly at sixteen as 'A boy in time of peace and a man in time of war'. In due course he earns the right to use the name of Jonathan Lyte Tremain which has been hotly denied to him by the rich merchant Lyte, who only wants to forget his sister Lavinia, disgraced by a runaway marriage; but status is less important to Johnny than the love of Cilla Lapham and the recovery of his own self-respect through danger, suffering and determination.

Notable as the book is as a fictional study of the Boston Tea Party and the events leading up to it, it depends finally on the sure delineation of the character of an unusual lad, moulded by circumstances and by the force of a strong personality. [Esther Forbes: *Johnny Tremain*, Boston 1943]

**JONATHAN** *see* GEOFFREY

**JOSE MALDONADO,** a Mexican boy of twelve, crosses the frontier into California illegally to join his father, who has been obliged to seek work as a labourer. The relief of being with his father does not last long for José, for Maldonado is moved elsewhere and the boy, pestered by an unpleasant man whose attentions fill him with bewildered alarm, runs away. Frightened, hungry and with a torn arm, he takes refuge in the loft of a Catholic Church, where a broken floor extends over a statue of Christ crucified. The next day the suggestible Josefa Espinosa, seeing blood on the statue, cries 'Miracle' to all who will listen.

The township of San Ramon has gone downhill since a new highway diverted trade from it and the Mayor, among others, is only too ready to quieten his own scepticism for the sake of the benefits that could accrue, but Father Lebeon, a practical man and an honest one, tries to restrain his parishioners until the case has been properly investigated. While the supposed miracle reveals people's natures in a searching and often unpleasant way, José tries to summon up courage to explain what has happened. Though he is afraid of being arrested for illegal entry and disturbed by the hysterical scenes which he witnesses near the church,

something in the affair has clarified his thoughts. He decides to go back to Mexico and try to follow his mother's wishes and develop his artistic talents.

Like all Theodore Taylor's books, this one has a strong, overt message and the characters are chosen and developed to illustrate certain aspects of modern life. Nor does the laconic, almost brusque prose-style encourage any real probing into José's character. It is all the more remarkable that he does stand out as an individual. The boy who nerved himself to refuse to travel without his dog has the courage it takes to change the plans of a lifetime. Faced with the complexity, the makeshift consolations of the civilized world, he takes the hardest step and the one that he knows is best for him in the long run. [Theodore Taylor: *The Maldonado Miracle*, New York 1973]

**JOSEPH NATHANIEL BROWN** (Joe to his family and friends) makes daily life in Kingston, Jamaica, more interesting by lapsing into day-dreams in which he is the sheriff up against rustlers, a composite of all the Western films he and his gang have seen on Saturday mornings in the old flea-pit in Carib town. Radio warnings of an approaching hurricane make little impression on his youthful heedlessness. However, by the time he has eaten, slept and watched his way through the alarming noises and still more alarming central quiet of the hurricane, the dramatic attributes of Westerns have taken second place in his thoughts. After he and Papa have walked to the town, have seen hanging wires and devastated houses and have even visited their intended new home (now looking like a 'giant birdcage' with the holes and gashes in its exterior) he has taken a step away from childhood and a step nearer to the understanding father whose companionship he sees suddenly in a new light. Describing the natural cataclysm entirely through Joe's eyes, and with the help of his spontaneous, unsophisticated voice, Andrew Salkey has sketched a Jamaican boy who is at once an individual and the product of a particular time and environment. [Andrew Salkey: *Hurricane*, London 1964]

**JOSEPHINE**, eight-year-old daughter of a woodcutter, is delighted to find two young fairies in the forest, one dressed in green with a peacock feather in his cap, the other in 'a lovely white silk frock all shimmering with spangles, and three silver stars in her golden hair.' They have run away from fairyland to escape from the hard work demanded by the efficient Queen. Josephine's sympathy is so cheering that they decide to take her back to Fairyland with them. Her two successive adventures there – one in Giantland, the other with seven-league boots which help her to outwit the Witch Slogarithma – trouble her parents, who call in the doctor to explain her excitable state, but they delight the child so much that only loyalty to her home stops her from accepting the Queen's offer to make her a naturalized fairy.

Josephine and her adventures are enclosed in an

outer envelope, as it were, of whimsical chat between the author and his daughter Janet, for whom he is evidently spinning his story night after night at bedtime. The pastiche of fairy tale and myth, the jocular asides and interruptions, hark back to the earlier years of Milne and Joy Street and so does the family-joke aspect of a story in which the heroine's character is taken for granted as the property of the private and particular listener. [Geoffrey Mure: *Josephine. A Fairy Thriller*, London 1937; *The Boots and Josephine*, 1939]

**JOSEPHINE** is the daughter of the rector of a Swedish parish. Her name is really Anna Grå, but 'she feels too small for it' and has decided to call herself Josephine Joandersson instead; her family humour her but her class teacher needs rather more convincing that the change is a reasonable one, and some of the girls at school make fun of her. She is given unexpected support from Hugo, son of a charcoal-burner in the forest, who likes to take his own line in everything, from the colour of his braces to the amount of time he is prepared to spare for school from more serious matters like caring for his spiders. The two individualists, the one as romantic as the other is practical, find their own way of coming to terms with school.

The three books about Hugo and Josephine are outwardly extremely simple. Maria Gripe moves from one episode to another, sparing with description and making most of her effects by pointed dialogue which records very directly both the immediate and the half-secret feelings of the children. Josephine's brothers and sisters are all grown up and she thinks she is not wanted in the family and that all sorts of plans and events are being hidden from her. She longs to be accepted at school and to find a way into the play-ground cliques. Hugo sustains her with his genuine independence of mind and his charm and intelligence make him universally popular, so that his loyalty to Josephine is all the more consoling to her.

Maria Gripe has not simply drawn static characters of the children; she has also shown them in an active relationship with one another. Without realizing it, Hugo teaches Josephine not to accept ready-made interpretations of other people but to observe them for herself. She learns to disregard the gossip about his father, who is in prison, and to accept his right to mourn his mother in his own way. She learns not to be possessive, when he gives his friendship to reserved Miriam, and to distrust the flatteries of Granny Lyra, who has so cleverly bought her affection by encouraging her to feel sorry for herself. The remarkable boy, after giving Josephine a home-made kaleidoscope which seems to symbolize his own vision of life, says goodbye to the school, for he is off to find out something for himself. 'I'm going to look for a confluence ... it must be something, terrific, tremendous ... I've got to find out how it happens ...' Maria Gripe shows us in a unique way how these two children happen. [Maria Gripe: *Hugo and Josephine* (1962 Sweden) trans. Paul Britten Austin, New York 1969; *Josephine* 1970; *Hugo* 1970. Original Swedish series began with *Josef'in* 1961]

**JOSH PLOWMAN** was fourteen when he decided it was his turn to visit Aunt Clara at Ryan Creek. His cousins had all been to the old homestead which their great-grandfather had built and they were fond of telling him 'Until you see Aunt Clara, Josh, gee, you haven't lived'. He was all the more anxious to go because his mother seemed to doubt whether he would be able to stand up to his aunt. In five days he learned the reason for her doubts. From a quiet home in Melbourne, where his dreams and his poems were respected and taken for granted, he was precipitated into a harsh, bewildering world – a world dominated by an incisive woman who seemed to feel she had a right to pry into his thoughts and the book where he hid his poems – all this while showing a warmth of feeling, an eccentric sense of the ridiculous, which made him enjoy her company and want to please her. What he found most puzzling was the difference between her view of the boys and girls of Ryan Creek and his own. She did not seem able to believe that they really hated and tormented him and certainly their behaviour when she was present was properly cordial and friendly. Confused by so many undercurrents of feeling, exasperated by clinging Laura and trying to make an impression on tough Betsy, Josh blundered from one mistake and misunderstanding to another until finally he brought a cricket match to a standstill by refusing to play in the ludicrous clothes which the alarming Harry had found for him as one of his practical jokes.

Josh realized that, however well his robust cousins

Hugo and Josephine, drawn by Harald Gripe.

had fitted in to the atmosphere of Ryan Creek, he had no place there. He had learned to respect his formidable aunt and had even understood her view of Harry, whom she was helping through school. He realized that the whole group of young people depended on her and that it was jealousy that prompted their remorseless, larking persecution. But he was too tired to fight any longer for the right to be himself, too tired of being knocked about and derided; he could only remain himself by announcing that he was going back to Melbourne and that, because the period of his visit was not officially over, he proposed to hitch there instead of travelling by train.

This noisy, quick-moving, hard-hitting story is written in Ivan Southall's own version of the stream-of-consciousness. The book consists partly of dialogue – pungent, individual and full of overtones – and partly of short sentences, often with present participles as their only verb, which give a startling impression of a boy's thoughts moving along with his actions. The formidable figure of Aunt Clara emerges from a welter of words which suggest, as children's stories rarely do, that any one person's view of another is bound to be partial, imperfect and puzzling. [Ivan Southall: *Josh*, Sydney and London 1971]

**JUDY WOOLCOT** is twelve when we first meet her, a thin child with freckles, dark eyes and curly dark hair that is never tidy. Her real name of Helen is only used by her father, when he is reproving her for unusually bad behaviour. For Judy, who usually progresses 'by a series of jumps, bounds, and odd little skips', is always in trouble, not for any base defect of character but because she is too impetuous and full of ideas to stop and think of the consequences of her actions. Though Captain Woolcot is deeply fond of Judy, whom his dying wife had especially commended to his care, his army upbringing leaves him neither the time nor the wisdom to help her to learn self-command. His young second wife, bewildered by the five children she now has to rule as well as looking after her own baby, is equally unable to calm or to understand Judy.

When after a particularly flagrant piece of mischief Captain Woolcot packs his daughter off to boarding school, he believes the problem is solved. But Judy is desperately homesick. She runs away and in making her difficult way back home, mainly on foot, she injures her lungs and suffers a long illness which calls forth all her strength of character. In time she recovers her old energy. As the doctor remarks, 'She seems to be always in a perfect fever of living, and to possess a capacity for joy and unhappiness quite unknown to slower natures.'

Judy Woolcot rushes beneath a falling tree to save her baby brother; an illustration by A. J. Johnson from *Seven Little Australians*.

He believes Judy has it in her to become a fine woman, but this is not to be. On a picnic, while the family is staying on an outback station, she is killed by a falling tree, having made her last impetuous dash to save the beloved baby of the family, 'the General'.

The greater flexibility of Australian children's stories, so evident in our own time, is shown in this family story of eighty years ago, in riotous scenes and robust talk in which the characters of Judy and her family are revealed. The unashamed sentiment in the description of Judy's death certainly belongs to its period, but no writer of any period would need to be ashamed of having put into the frightened, courageous girl's mouth words so sincere, poignant and universally true to life. [Ethel Turner: *Seven Little Australians*, London 1894]

**KATY** 'was a beautiful red crawler tractor. She was very big and very strong and she could do a lot of things' – like hauling a snow plough or a bulldozer. She belongs to the Highway Department of the City of Geoppolis and when an outsize snow-storm takes the inhabitants by surprise, Katy's efforts get mail vans and trains, fire engines and ambulances going, clear runways, carry materials for mending telephone cables and, in short, save Geoppolis from total breakdown.

Many vehicles in picture-books have more described personality than Katy has. The vehicle comes to life simply through the firm, cumulative, rhythmic prose statements of her exploits and by the equally firm composition of pictures in which her busyness is contrasted visually with the stillness of trucks, cars and people. The simplicity and directness of Katy's story has made the book a prime favourite with more than one generation of children. [Virginia Lee Burton: *Katy and the Big Snow*, Boston 1943]

**KATY CARR** is the eldest of six children and, at the sensible age of twelve, might have been expected to exercise a good influence over the rest, but pretty Clover's demure manner suits their Aunt Izzie better than Katy's boisterous, hoydenish ways. Katy cherishes four-year-old Phil and agrees well enough with stout, greedy Dorrie and lively little Johnnie (whose boy's name suits her so much better than her real name of Joanna), but she is too heedless to notice how often she snubs eight-year-old Elsie, who longs only to share some of the secrets of Katy and Clover and their friend next door, Cecy Hall. Katy, in fact, does as she pleases. She enjoys telling endless fairy tales to the children and organizing imaginative games and is surprised to find how often her ideas result in domestic disorder and retribution.

An accident brings her heedless childhood to an end. Thrown from a defective swing which she had been forbidden to use, she injures her spine and has to spend the next four years in bed or wheelchair. In her sojourn in the 'School of Pain' (that seminary so familiar in the domestic stories of the last century) she learns how much suffering and determination lie behind the loving words and considerate manners of her much-loved Cousin Helen, whose wheel-chair life she has always taken for granted. By the time Katy can walk again,

Aunt Izzie watches Katy Carr running to school, from the jacket of *What Katy Did*.

she has become a wise and capable housekeeper, having taken over the direction of the household after Aunt Izzie's death; she has learned to understand her sisters and brothers better, and is ready to embark on new experiences, at boarding school and on an extended tour of Europe.

Of the three books about Katy, the first is the most didactic and yet, paradoxically, the most lively. In the second book Katy seems a figure-head compared with the strong delineation of her selfish, vain cousin Lily Page and the ebullient Rose Red, and the emphasis on her virtues (shown in her refusal to flirt through the window with the college boys and her kindness to the unattractive Miss Jane when she is ill) seems no more than an interruption of the girlish fun and chatter. The third book is a Cook's Tour in which Katy is once more held up as a model of patience and forbearance, as well as an example of the good American who goes to Europe to see antiquities, whereas the ineffable Lily is interested in Paris and Rome only as centres of fashion.

The Katy books are vigorous and entertaining and, to British children, full of fascinating and unfamiliar detail. Their heroine, however, is not as strongly alive for readers today as Jo March (q.v.) and her sisters are. Nothing could be more different from the humane, civilized, household of the Marches than the breezy, games-playing, unmistakably middle-class home of the Carrs. The Marches even in childhood are never less than little women; they enjoy childish pleasures and display childish attitudes but emotional experience is always deep for them. Katy Carr serves her sentence with pain and her character changes as a result – or so the author implies; but the two Katys, the hoyden and the high-principled young lady, hardly seem to be the same girl. Louisa Alcott's moral philosophy and psychology seem to go deeper than the more bracing didacticism of Susan Coolidge; and though Katy is an attractive and memorable individual, her experiences do not transcend the barriers of time and fashion in the way that those of Jo March undoubtedly do. [Susan Coolidge (Sarah Chauncey Woolsey): *What Katy Did*, Boston 1872; *What Katy Did at School*, 1873; *What Katy Did Next*, 1886]

**KAY HARKER,** an orphan of seven or eight, is lonely in the large house where he lives in the charge of his governess Sylvia Daisy (q.v.), but he has firm allies in the maids, Ellen and Jane, and he is a philosophical child who has learned to make the most of opportunities. Besides, he has much natural curiosity and enough imagination to throw himself joyously into midnight adventures when he learns bit by bit about the lost treasure once entrusted to his great-grandfather.

Pleasantly polite, at times a little puzzled, as ready to play hide and seek with mermaids near a coral reef as he is to ride past the weathercocks on a flying horse, Kay deems it 'exciting fun, piecing out the story' of the *Plunderer* and the treasure. But by the time his old toys the Guards come home with the hoard, snatched almost from under the noses of Abner Brown and his gang, Kay has begun to grow out of the strict nursery routine in which he is at first constricted.

*The Box of Delights* finds him a few years older, returning from boarding school for the winter holidays, his unpleasant witch-governess gone and the kindly Caroline Louisa in charge of the house. In the adventure he now enjoys, helping the strange old man Cole Hawlings (q.v.) to escape from Abner Brown, and to keep the Box hidden, Kay is called upon to be braver and more independent than in the first book. His abounding interest in everything, his love of change and excitement, are as strong, innocent and appealing as before. It is tempting to regard Kay as in part a picture of Masefield as a child; certainly in a quick appreciative attitude to nature and people, poet and child are very close to one another. [John Masefield: *The Midnight Folk*, London 1927; *The Box of Delights*, 1935]

**KEN McLAUGHLIN** is the despair of his parents. His school results are disastrous and on his father's ranch in Wyoming he is constantly in trouble for minor accidents and omissions. Though his brother Howard was given a colt to train when he was ten, Ken does not seem to deserve this privilege; but his mother believes that his only hope of overcoming his sullenness and frustration is to have a special responsibility, and his father at last agrees.

Perverse as always, Ken makes what seems a bad choice. The yearling filly, which he calls Flicka or 'Little girl', has good blood from her sire but her mother Rocket is one of a line of unstable, uncontrollable, loco horses. The boy's troubles are not over even when he has won his right to try to prove that Flicka is normal, for she injures herself while jumping a wire fence in the search for freedom. As he nurses her back to health, Ken establishes with her a close relationship which satisfies some lack in him and helps him to succeed in a daunting task. This is a classic story of a boy's emotional growth. Published as an adult novel, it has been adopted by the young for its congenial subject and its emotional force. [Mary O'Hara (pseud. Mrs Mary Sture-Vasa): *My Friend Flicka*, Philadelphia and New York 1943]

**KEVIN** and **SANDRA** are orphans who live with their uncle in the North Country town of Cobchester, in a street whose romantic name, Orchard Grove, belies its dirty, ramshackle reality. Walter Thompson is a weak, shiftless man and the fat, grumbling Doris who has come to live in the house is no better than he is at understanding the needs of his two small children, Harold and Jean, so that a heavy burden falls on thirteen-year-old Kevin and thin, determined Sandra. After one of the worst of the quarrels that the children have long taken for granted, Doris walks out and Walter follows her, leaving the children to fend for themselves. Since they distrust authority and hate interference, they shut the house and retreat to Gumble's Yard, where their friend and ally Dick has found an attic in which they contrive a makeshift home; but a gang using the warehouse for stolen goods threatens their safety and they are forced to seek help from the adult world. Their disorderly lives are put on a firm basis and Walter, who has contrived to escape recognition as one of the gang, promises to start afresh with the family. When (in *Widdershins Crescent*) his lack of honesty and sense involve him in the shady dealings of a respected local alderman and again threatens the security of the children and of their new home in a housing estate, Kevin and Sandra once more make allowances for their uncle's nature and play their part as amateur detectives and surrogate parents to the younger children.

Kevin and Sandra move to Gumble's Yard, drawn by
Dick Hart.

A precarious life and an early acquaintance with the
contrivances of poverty have not warped any of the
children, nor are the two stories about them drab or
morbid; the narrative is far too lively, the characters
too full of life and bounce for that. Kevin and
Sandra may be old for their age but they still respond
in a natural, excited way to the surprises of Gumble's
Yard and the curious behaviour of Alderman Widdow-
son. As for the younger cousins, Harold is totally
believable, a child with an exceptional brain who never
doubts that everyone will put their minds to finding the
means for him to take the offered place at the Grammar School, a child whose dreams of being the great
inventor Sir Harold Thompson are merged with a more
normal addiction to space-ship noises, while his sister,
obstinate little Jean, lavishing her affection on a
battered alley-cat, has her own way of compensating
for a life of uncertainty. There is no attempt to conceal
the lack of support and affection which the children
suffer but they learn to depend on the affection they

have for each other. In a story as alive and vivid as
this, this is no abstract conclusion. [John Rowe Townsend: *Gumble's Yard*, London 1961; *Widdershins
Crescent*, 1965]

**KING TIRIAN** *see* PRINCE CASPIAN

**KIT HAVERARD** is really Jane Kitson Haverard
but for her Professor father the name Jane will always
belong to the wife who died when the baby was born.
Kit and her three older brothers have been brought
up by the faithful housekeeper Martha and by Laura,
the Professor's niece, a woman of strong, even dogmatic opinions. Jealously protective towards the Professor, Laura resents the girl's interest in her mother's
old aunts, and after Kit has had two unforgettable conversations with reclusive Aunt Henrietta, she has a new
confidence which Laura can hardly help disliking.
Hardly realizing how possessive she is about the
Haverards, Laura expresses it most of all in her attitude to Kit's musical ambitions. A 'sweet little voice' for
drawing-room entertainment is far more to her taste
than Kit's uncontrolled, untapped resources, and she is
determined that Kit shall train as a secretary so as to
help her father with his work. All through her teens
at home, at school and working at Friends' House in
London, Kit cherishes her ambition; she follows the
guidance of the old music teacher Papa Andreas, takes
one or two false directions but in the end becomes a
fine singer through genius, hard work and dedication.

Kit stands in her generation between two other aspiring talents. Her great-aunt Henrietta, whom she met
only a short time before her death, had been debarred
by her class and period from training as a singer and
had lived an embittered, lonely life as a result. Three
generations later, one of Kit's nieces, Laura Haverard,
fights against family opposition to be allowed to train
as an actress. Inevitably Laura's story (told in *The
Spring of the Year* and *Flowering Spring*) seems like a
repetition of Kit's, especially as the members of the older
generation reappear and recall past disappointments
and triumphs. Perhaps it is not only repetition that
makes the younger Laura Haverard seem less of an
individual than the attractive Kit with her diffidence
and her passionate application to her art. The Kitsons
and Haverards are Quakers. The two books about Kit
(*The Lark in the Morn* and *The Lark on the Wing*)
have a particular authority because of the background
of Quaker belief and behaviour, and Elfrida Vipont
shows subtly how far Kit's character has been moulded
by her upbringing. The unity of the books, and the
very convincing picture of families in all their variety
and closeness, depends on the serene, consistent Quaker
light that shines through the books. The three later
stories have less of this atmosphere and this may be
why they seem less distinguished. Laura Haverard and
her friends and relatives, old and young, are interesting
merely in the way that scores of characters in other
domestic stories are interesting, while the young people

in *The Pavilion*, who set out to restore some of the old family buildings and activities of the Kitsons, make little impression as characters, though their doings are lively and entertaining. In this group of stories, with their intricate family pattern, Kit Haverard undoubtedly makes the strongest impression. [Elfrida Vipont: *The Lark in the Morn*, London 1948; *The Lark on the Wing*, 1950; *The Spring of the Year*, 1957; *Flowering Spring*, 1960; *The Pavilion*, 1969]

**KUNGO**, an Eskimo boy living in the Canadian Arctic, flees from his home when, because of an act of kindness to a man who has injured a nearby tribe of Indians, his community is attacked and his sister captured. The boy learns about an old man living on a distant island who is reputed to have unusual skill in archery. With revenge always in mind, Kungo reaches the island and is adopted by the old man and his wife. At last the time comes when he is strong enough to string and pull the old man's great horn bow and he sets out for the Indian village, only to learn from his long-lost sister that there are things more valuable than revenge.

Based on an Eskimo legend, the story of Kungo is told so vividly and lucidly that the young Eskimo becomes real to the reader, for the clear analysis of his feelings and for the particular setting and circumstances of his life. [James Houston: *The White Archer*, New York 1967]

Kungo, the Eskimo boy, from *The White Archer*, written and illustrated by James Houston.

**LAN-MAY** lives 'in a pretty green valley near the great Yangtse River, in Old China'. Because she is the youngest, and the only girl, the little eight-year-old is lonely, and tired of being ordered about by her brothers; but she cannot rebel because her mother insists that girls must be quiet so that 'they will grow up to be quiet women' and not bother men. One day, tending her father's net in the river, Lan-May pulls out a bronze dragon and almost at the same time she sees walking towards her on the river bank a 'foreign' girl with yellow hair and a pink complexion, who delightedly agrees they shall pretend they are sisters.

Fom her long residence in the China of nearly half a century ago, Pearl Buck has sketched two little girls, each troubled by brothers and longing for a sister. Through them she has included naturally in her story a point about international understanding. Little Lan-May and her American friend are no less charming now that new attitudes have made us look askance at certain parts of the story. [Pearl Buck: *The Dragon Fish*, New York 1944]

**LARRY THE LAMB** and **DENNIS THE DACHS-HUND** have been at the bottom of most of the accidents and disasters that have disturbed the wooden peace of Toytown for almost half a century and have brought upon themselves disciplinary action from the fat, irascible Mayor in countless tales. Although the inhabitants of Toytown were first introduced in print, their unmistakable personalities were established in the radio broadcasts which went out from the early thirties on the Children's Hour of the BBC. The angular, stylized figures of the Toytown folk and their Arkville neighbours are familiar enough from Hulme Beaman's pictures, but their characteristic, unchanging idiom has always been more important – Larry the Lamb's reiterated 'Oh sir, Oh Sir' and 'I'm only a *little* lamb', Dennis's contorted Germanic syntax, the Mayor's angry splutterings, Ernest the Policeman's 'I knows my duty'. Standardized plots – kidnapping, disguise, practical jokes – take on new life because of the forceful and entertaining personalities who may still be heard sometimes, protesting, plotting and pronouncing, in broadcast programmes. [S. G. Hulme Beaman: *Tales of Toytown*, London 1928; *Stories from Toytown*, 1938; and other titles]

**LAURA** and **HARRY GRAHAM** live in Edinburgh with their grandmamma, Lady Harriet Graham, and their Uncle David; their father, who has gone abroad, engages a certain Mrs Crabtree to look after them, hoping she will counteract the 'extreme indulgence' with which he expects his mother and brother to behave towards them. Harry and his sister are too young to have enjoyed the benefit of their mother's affectionate discipline, which has moulded their older brother Frank into a thoughtful, intelligent and well-mannered lad. As impulsive as they are energetic, the young brother and sister follow their own inclinations. Their mildest exploits result in broken ornaments and torn dresses while, at the other extreme, Harry on one occasion sets fire to the nursery while he is idly experimenting with a candle and the snuffers.

Lady Harriet's gentle, prosy sermons do little to check the children's high spirits, and their uncle finds himself vastly amused by their pranks, for he loves to laugh and hates to see children reduced to a torpor of obedience. He knows that Harry and Laura are honest, affectionate towards one another and incapable of malice or cruelty, and he is prepared to laugh off even the social disgrace when the unfortunate Laura, while staying at Lord Rockville's house, Holiday House, is twice discovered by the grand company of visitors in apparel torn and water-logged, having first hidden in a holly bush to watch them and then rashly chased a flock of geese towards the pond.

If the kindly sermons of their grandmother do very little to check the children, Mrs Crabtree's severity curbs it only temporarily. This nursery vixen, 'wearing always the same pink gown and scarlet shawl, which make her look like a large red flower-pot', firmly believes that the beatings she administers are for the children's good, and indeed they are less cruel than her more ingenious punishments – the worst of them being on the day of the Grand Feast, when she humiliates Harry and Laura by refusing to supply more than their nightly milk and two biscuits for the little friends they have invited to tea on their own initiative. Mrs Crabtree suddenly appears in a different light when she is given notice, and the children realize that they do not really want her to go.

All the same, it is not Mrs Crabtree who brings Harry

and Laura to a more sensible frame of mind, but two graver and more impersonal task-masters – Time and Death. Harry's courage and his care for Laura, Laura's affectionate good heart, are always evident behind their mischief, and as they grow older they find the rule of reason has become easier. More important, the shock of learning that their midshipman brother is dangerously ill, and of watching at his death-bed, make it impossible for them to think any longer of the world as 'one scene of frolicsome enjoyment and careless ease'.

The sentiment seems as far as it could be from the hilarious scenes in the early chapters of a book in which the author deliberately sets herself to draw the characters of 'noisy, frolicsome, mischievous children' of a kind which never appear in the improving stories of the early nineteenth century and which she humorously suggests were in her own day almost extinct. Though there are lively, playful moments in *The Fairchild Family* and realistic glimpses of childhood in the tales of Maria Edgeworth, free, vivacious behaviour such as Laura and Harry exhibit in *Holiday House* was certainly a new pleasure for the young readers of 1839; nor is there anything illogical about the way mischief turns to sense and laughter shades into sobriety. The book is consistent in its theme and the characters remain true to themselves throughout. To modern readers even the moral and religious sentiments and the long-drawn-out description of Frank's death may seem less alien than the extent of the depredations of Harry and Laura. The child of the Welfare State, its waywardness analysed and its days protected, may well find the sheer scope of the mischief of Harry and Laura as enviable as it is astonishing. [Catherine Sinclair: *Holiday House*, 1839]

**LAURA INGALLS** was only five years old when she left the log-house in Wisconsin. Charles Ingalls had an adventurous nature and he had begun to feel oppressed by the rapid growth of the frontier settlement, so he and the family set off on the first of many journeys in search of prosperity and freedom. On the Kansas prairie Laura saw her father build a strong log house and settled down happily with her older sister Mary and baby Carrie, though she was afraid when she first saw an Indian and she was anxious in case the blizzard would keep Santa Claus away. When the land was declared Indian territory the family moved on to a sod house on the banks of a river in Minnesota, where the two little girls had their first taste of school; but the year's crops were ruined by locusts and they moved on when Laura was twelve to Dakota, where her father kept a store in a railway camp and then took up land on the prairie.

When quiet Mary was left blind after scarlet fever, it seemed that her ambition to be a teacher must be set aside, but Laura worked in the town as a seamstress to earn money to help to send Mary to a college for

Laura's sister Mary, drawn by Garth Williams in *Little House in the Big Woods.*

the blind; at the same time she also worked for a teacher's qualification and soon began to teach in country schools. She grew to love her good friend Almanzo Wilder, who had helped the Ingalls family through one desperate hard winter on the prairie. When Laura was eighteen she and Almanzo were married and began their life together on a farm in Missouri, where the struggle to make a living did not discourage two people with the experience of hard work behind them.

Few stories taken from real life are as honest as the stories of the Ingalls family, which were written down by the author in her late middle age. The continuity of the books and their unity of feeling are not

The eighteen-year-old Laura marries Almanzo in *These Happy Golden Years,* also illustrated by Garth Williams.

due to memory alone, nor are they simple catalogues of events. They are essentially a record of *family* life. in which Laura's lively personality is defined in the way she reacts to the many homes she knows, the way she trusts and relies on her parents to make a true home wherever they go. The concrete details of life in the woods, by the river, on the prairie, hold an endless attraction for children because of their intriguing difference from the world of today, but just as important is the feeling of love and security that runs through the books. [Laura Ingalls Wilder: *Little House in the Big Woods*, New York 1932; *Farmer Boy*, 1933; *Little House on the Prairie*, 1935; *On the Banks of Plum Creek*, 1937; *By the Shores of Silver Lake*, 1939; *The Long Winter*, 1940; *Little Town on the Prairie*, 1941; *These Happy Golden Years*, 1943]

**LAURIE (THEODORE LAURENCE)** *see* MARCH GIRLS

**LENTIL** is a happy boy except for one thing; he wants to sing but somehow cannot manage it. The alternative is a harmonica, on which he becomes so expert that he saves the town of Alto, Ohio, from serious embarrassment. It is the day when Colonel Carter, its most prominent and generous citizen, is due home after a long absence. Everyone goes to meet the train except Old Swep, who was at school with the Colonel and is jealous of his popularity. The morose old man, by sucking a lemon audibly, paralyses the members of the town band, and the only music available to greet the Colonel comes from Lentil's spirited rendering of 'She'll be coming round the mountain', which pleases the Colonel so much that he promises to present the town with a new hospital.

The little tale, not altogether innocent of satire, has the very atmosphere of small-town life and custom in it, and into the setting the gangling, tow-haired, obstinate small boy fits as surely as the harmonica fits his capacious, grinning mouth. [Robert McCloskey: *Lentil*, New York 1940]

**LEONARD** at six is at variance with his parents, for the Master of the House and gentle Lady Jane dislike the proximity of Asholt Camp, newly set up near the 'few ancestral acres and a nice old place in one of the quietest, quaintest corners of Old England', as the forthright head of the household puts it. But if he, somewhat dramatically, describes the army as 'tribes of savages in war-paint', his small son finds the activities of the soldiers enthralling and quickly establishes, to their mutual satisfaction, a firm friendship with an orderly, Irish O'Reilly, who helps the child to what his father feels is a supererogatory knowledge of army protocol and custom.

Leonard becomes a firm favourite with officers and men alike, his own preference being, rather naturally, for spectacular review marches and the splendour and rousing sound of church parades. It is while he is watching a gallop past of the horse artillery, eagerly standing

Gordon Browne's illustration of Leonard in *The Story of a Short Life.*

up in an open carriage, that he falls and is crushed. There follow weeks and months of pain; helped by his mother's devotion and by a new friendship with a young officer, a VC who openly admires and encourages Leonard's resolve to be brave, the child throws off his spoilt ways and dies as good a soldier as any in the regiment.

Children's books are not much less moralistic today than they were a century ago, but since it is the fashion to disguise moral precepts as sociological advantage or intellectual growth, it is impossible to read this touching, sincere story as our great-great-grandparents would have read it. Even two generations ago the open emotionalism of Leonard's accident, his morbid collection of stories about 'Poor Things' and his lingering death, were more acceptable than they are today. There are, too, social themes and nuances which fitted the pattern of the Victorian family book which might today be considered more suitable for an adult novel – the most obvious being the significant distinction between the Master of the House and his brother-in-law, who is a non-commissioned soldier in command of the barracks at Asholt Camp. All the same, social change should not make it impossible to appreciate the sure, sensitive drawing of Leonard's character. Even if his longing to be good, and to realize to the full the implications of the family motto *Laetus sorte mea*, is presented in a way which seems sentimental now, there is a quiet veracity in this picture of a boy listening to his elders, half understanding their standards of conduct and trying to live up to his version of them, which belongs to childhood at any date. [Juliana Horatia Ewing: *The Story of a Short Life*, London 1885]

**LEXIE** lives on a Tasmanian sheep-station with her father and older brother Kent. She is a quiet, reserved little girl of eight years old who often wishes that there were still aborigines living in the hills, as there had been when her great-great-aunt Rita played with little brown Merrina and was given the shell-necklace now kept in the family treasure-box; of the darker side of the story – of Rita's decline and death soon afterwards, when bush-rangers on the run slaughtered the aboriginals on the property – Lexie knows nothing. But one day she glimpses a laughing brown face peering at her from a bush, and rides off to steep, haunted Blacks' Gully again, after she has on impulse put the shell-necklace round her neck.

The prancing, laughing brown girl says she is called Merrina and calls Lexie 'Weetah'. The two of them find that gestures and grimaces do as well as words as they dance and chase together; somehow Lexie is able to explain to the alarmed Merrina that when she unzips her shirt she is not tearing her skin and Merrina finds a way to warn her about the 'fathers', who must always be respected and obeyed, and about the dread Nammà, Spirit of the Night. It is a happy time, until the day when Lexie hears the noise of gun-shots as two men on the hill begin a ghastly slaughter, mercifully blotted out when the child loses consciousness.

After a long illness, during which nightmares of violence and weeping make no more sense to Lexie than to her elders, she remembers little about Merrina and her family until some years later she is wakeful and anxious one night while the nearby ranges are searched for her brother, lost during a camping trip. Then Merrina gives their old signal, and Lexie climbs into Blacks' Gully and finds the missing boy.

Nan Chauncy used the character of Lexie as a medium for her own feeling about the now extinct Tasmanian aboriginals and their fate at the hands of the white settlers of the last century. It is a subject she explored again later in the historical story *Mathinna's People*. *Tangara* is emotionally closer to the subject because the theme is explored through the feelings of a child who mysteriously enters into the experience of another like herself in the past. The two little girls are delightfully real as they dance together, but Lexie is just as believable as a schoolgirl. She is not in any sense a disturbed child but one whose solitary, imaginative temperament responds uniquely to the influence of the necklace and of the gully round which hung the shadows of old gaiety and old unhappiness. [Nan Chauncy: *Tangara*, London 1960]

**LILIAS GODMAN** is born Lilias Rowan, daughter of Ursula, second wife of a quiet, kindly lawyer with three sons by his first marriage. After John Rowan's death his eldest son Robert takes care of his step-mother. Then plague comes to Kent; Robert dies and Lilias loses her mother too – and her home, for Robert's wife offers to keep her merely as a servant. Lilias is fifteen when she runs away, stunned by Jane's cruel suggestion that John Rowan is not her father. The entry of her birth in the church register offers only one strange fact – the name Medley, imperfectly erased, which seems to have been intended as one of the baby's Christian names.

Lilias gives herself the name Forstal from her mother's property while she works as a stillroom maid at Penshurst; when a marriage is arranged by her mistress, Lady Mary Sidney, she goes to Froredean with her iron-master husband Godman. Here she helps him with his work and bears him a daughter, and when he dies she determines to be Master of the foundry. It is to advance her business that she moves to Shrives Minnis and so comes into contact with the family at Mantlemass, and at last discovers her hidden relationship to them. Indeed, at their first meeting, she and Richard Medley feel an instinctive kinship, for each has the crooked shoulder which is their inheritance from the Plantagenets; but it is his brother Piers who claims her as a daughter, discovering for the first time that the week's happiness he had enjoyed with Ursula years before has not ended as completely as he thought.

Lilias's character, suggested by the title *The Iron Lily*, is shown in her behaviour, her manner of speech and her appearance. She outfaces the protests of her work-people in the forest when she decides to hire foreign labour; from loyalty and good business sense, she uses as a symbol and trademark the delicate iron lily which her husband fashioned; she tries to rule the future of her headstrong daughter Ursula as she rules her life and her longings. In this notable portrait of a woman working for her living through the reigns of Mary and Elizabeth Tudor certain traits inherited both from her mother and from her true father, Piers Medley, are carefully and convincingly blended. [Barbara Willard: *The Iron Lily*, London 1973; 'Winter's Tale', in *Young Winter's Tales 4*, London 1973]

**LISA PALFREY** *see* LOTTTIE HORN

**LITTLE BEAR,** hero of many small domestic anecdotes, combines the charm of a young animal with the piquancy of human role-playing. He enters a child's world as he waits anxiously for the hoped-for birthday cake, 'flies to the moon' with the aid of a cardboard box and some wire, and turns for reassurance to his mother after all his small adventures. Within the limitations of

Cat sees Mother Bear at the door,

and says, "Wait, Little Bear.

Do not eat yet.

Shut your eyes, and say one, two, three."

Little Bear, drawn by Maurice Sendak.

an 'easy-to-read' series, Little Bear stands out as a personality, represented without distortion, so that an occasional garment or a hint of human expression on his face need not annoy the hypercritical. At the same time the artist has shown Little Bear's home background with such warm-hearted veracity that the little animal becomes by courtesy a recognizable human child. It is a very tender and touching combination of two worlds. [Else Holmelund Minarik, ill. Maurice Sendak: *Little Bear*, New York 1957, and many other titles]

**LITTLE BLACK SAMBO** began life in a small book written by Mrs Bannerman and bound by hand for her two daughters, to console them for being sent to the hills while she remained with her husband, a doctor in the Indian Medical Service. The story has the simplicity and shapeliness of a folk tale and it is far removed from everyday life in India or anywhere else. Various elements in the story commend it for reading aloud – the artfully easy repetition, the enumeration of the little boy's grand new clothes and the suspense as he loses them one by one till his own safety is put in doubt; while the grotesque, primary-coloured pictures, with their exaggeration of facial expression and posture, seem congenial to children in the same way as the crude dramatic style of *Struwwelpeter*. The

story has a clear literary form, the robbing of Sambo being balanced by the ending in which his enemies provide him with his favourite supper.

None of the books that followed has the stylistic inevitability of *Little Black Sambo*, though they have similar macabre and economically sensational plots. They have often been criticized for these elements but children continue to enjoy fantasy scenes of dismemberment and similar disasters.

A far more serious criticism of the stories, that they disseminate racist attitudes among children, has meant that they are banned in American libraries and in many schools, and the publication of a boxed edition of the stories in England in 1972 brought prolonged and bitter discussion of the whole question here. It is obvious that Helen Bannerman had no intention of drawing deliberately offensive stereotypes of black characters, verbal or visual; it is equally clear that she wrote from the point of view of her period and not ours. Children's books must necessarily be especially vulnerable to changes in social attitudes and the evaluation of books as literature cannot always be reconciled with the assessment of the ideas contained in them. Every generation brings to the books of the past its own attitudes and beliefs; but nobody has the right to read in to books attitudes and beliefs that are not there. Ideally one would hope that *Little Black Sambo* could always be read in the way it was originally written, as a comic and neatly planned cumulative tale whose characters belong to the world of fantasy and not to the world of the listener (whether an English child, an American, an Indian or a member of any race or colour). While the multi-racial societies of the world are still in the sensitive process of settling down, this seems an unsuitable book to read aloud to a class or to be presented in any way that will suggest its relevance to particular children. As a folk tale, it belongs in any case rather to the nursery, to be shared by mother and child in an atmosphere where, one could hope, misunderstanding and false impressions could be avoided, and where it could be enjoyed as a piece of comic fantasy. [Helen Bannerman: *The Story of Little Black Sambo*, London 1899; *Little Black Mingo*, 1901; *Little Black Quibba*, 1902; *Little Black Quasha*, 1908; *Little Black Bobtail*, 1909; *Sambo and the Twins*, 1937; *Little White Squibba*, 1965]

**LITTLE BLUE** and **LITTLE YELLOW** are best friends, living on opposite sides of the street and playing together when school is over. One day Mama Blue goes shopping and warns her son to stay at home, but he goes out to look for his friend and they hug each other so vigorously that they merge and become green. Anyone is welcome to interpret as he will this crisp little tale in which irregular coloured shapes are seen to be actual characters without ceasing to be coloured shapes. [Leo Lionni: *Little Blue and Little Yellow*, New York 1959]

Little Black Sambo watches the tigers dressed in his clothes, from the book written and illustrated by Helen Bannerman.

**LITTLE COLONEL** (the), Lloyd Sherman, is five years old when her mother takes her to Lloydstown in Kentucky, where, unknown to the child, her widower grandfather lives. The Old Colonel is saddened by the death of his son in the Civil War and by the loss of his daughter, whom he had disowned on her marriage with a Yankee. In the manner of such tales, it is the child who coaxes him back to happiness by her artless confidences. In successive books, carefully planned so as to cover the accepted stages of a young lady's life, Lloyd goes to school, entertains her friends in the Colonel's mansion, flirts agreeably with the local youths, and at last gives her heart to the one who had for years seemed merely an old family friend.

Lloyd is a personality only when she is young enough to comment artlessly on her own faults. 'Oh, I'm got such a vile tempah, an' I stamps my foot when I gets mad, an' gets all red in the face. An' I hollahs at folks, an' looks jus' zis way', she remarks, and her sullen pout looks 'as if a thunderstorm had passed over' her face. When she is old enough to want to 'ease the burden of the world' or to muse in girlish modesty about growing up, she loses any claim to join Jo March or Katy Carr in the memories of young readers. Surely a spice of mischief is needed if a heroine is to remain a favourite in a succession of books. [Annie Fellows Johnston: *The Little Colonel*, Boston 1895; *The Little Colonel's Christmas Vacation*, 1905; *The Little Colonel's Knight comes Riding*, 1907; and other titles]

**LITTLE DIAMOND** had been named after a horse and his bed was directly over old Diamond's stall 'because he was a quiet horse, and did not go to sleep standing, but lay down like a reasonable creature'. When the stock of hay was low the boarded loft was draughty and one night Diamond seemed to hear a voice addressing him from behind a knot-hole which his mother had blocked with paper – 'What do you mean, little boy, by closing up my window?' And so Diamond began his long, magical, mysterious acquaintance with the North Wind. He was not afraid of her – he was too young for that; but he learned to respect her, to fear her wild manifestations in sea-storm and crashing tiles and, above all, to love her.

Borne on her wings, he walked the edge of the clerestory in a great cathedral; he was blown north in a sailing ship; he walked over ice to the Back of the North Wind and brought back the knowledge that 'Nothing went wrong there' and yet 'Neither was anything quite right' and that one day he must return there. All this was when he was still a small boy and the North Wind was showing him her power.

Meanwhile life changed for the humble, hard-working family. The Colemans lost their money and the coachman decided to set up in London with a hansom cab and by chance he was able to buy Diamond. Little Diamond learned to drive the cab and when his father fell ill he took it out himself, winning help and praise

Two of Frank C. Pape's illustrations from *At the Back of the North Wind*: (*right*) Little Diamond is lifted off the horse Diamond by his mother; (*above*) Little Diamond is swept up in the arms of the North Wind.

even from his rivals for his innocent, honest manner. And while his busy life went on, as he tended the new baby and the old horse, the North Wind exercised a remote but strong influence on his life. Sometimes he saw her, or thought he saw her, in dreams; her guises were many, she might be old or young, beautiful or terrible, but in the end he always recognized her. He tried to describe his dreams to Nanny, a neglected little waif who swept crossings, but though she liked his company she thought he was soft in the head and called him God's baby. However, one of the cabbie's customers recognized something unusual in the boy and when Diamond was old enough he took him into his household as a page boy. Here Diamond received the Christian instruction whose basis he had already learned another way. He still longed to be with the North Wind in her own country and at last the weary child found his way there, through death to eternal happiness. There is more than religious meaning in this haunting fantasy, for it describes allegorically the universal lesson of sorrow and trial, the instinctive search for perfection. Reality and image, an intellectual message and an emotional one, are united in the

description of Diamond's strange experiences and his quaint, innocent capacity for joy and understanding. [George Macdonald: *At the Back of the North Wind*, London 1871]

**LITTLE DUKE,** (the), great-grandfather of William the Conqueror, becomes Duke of Normandy when he is scarcely nine years old, after his father has been murdered. The Baron de Centeville, in whose castle the boy has been nurtured, has instructed him well but Richard's devotion is given to the father he saw so much less often than he wished. He is too young to understand why Abbot Martin should warn him against 'that accursed spirit of hatred and vengeance' which some of his household think he should feel; and then, he is a boy of bold spirit, who longs to earn some such name as 'Richard of the Sharp Axe', and wishes 'there were serpents and dragons to slay' in Normandy as in the sagas he listens to in the great hall of the castle.

His dauntless energy never leaves him and no doubt it suits the age he lived in better than certain other virtues lent him by Charlotte Yonge. But she was not writing history so much as the study of a child learning self-control in a hard school, triumphing over intrigue by his very innocence and honesty. When King Louis, fearful of the power of Normandy, removes the child from his home and keeps him under what amounts to house arrest, young Richard suffers as any child would suffer. He is homesick, lonely, confused, sometimes afraid. He learns to curb his quick temper because the King's frail younger son admires and depends on him. He even learns to control his fury at the bullying of the older Lothaire, a mean-tempered and jealous youth, and to show magnanimity when the situation changes and Lothaire becomes his prisoner. The Norman child whom the King describes as 'a thorough little Norwegian bear – fierce and unruly as the rest' is seen in this story as a very natural, attractive small boy, and if certain elements in his nature and his training belong rather to the nineteenth than to the tenth century, his story was after all offered as an example of endurance and courage to the young of the last century. [Charlotte Mary Yonge: *The Little Duke*, London 1854]

**LITTLE HOUSE** (the) stands right in the country, watching through her window-eyes the procession of the seasons and wondering what the distant city is really like. One day she finds out, for development encircles her until she is hemmed in by high buildings. Lonely, empty and neglected, the Little House dreams of the country till the 'great-great-granddaughter of the man who built the Little House so well' recognizes her and has her transported into the country where once again she is lived in and cared for and can watch the seasons come and go.

A classic picture-book, awarded the Caldecott Medal in 1943, *The Little House* is a rare example of the successful personalization of a building; perhaps it is simple for an artist to represent a face on a house-front,

but to suggest real personality, in words and in line and in colour, is another matter altogether. [Virginia Lee Burton: *The Little House*, Boston 1943]

**LITTLE KNITTLE,** son of Knitted Dad and Knitted Mum, meets 'a very pretty sewn girl called Threadle' and asks her to marry him. She offends his parents' family pride by giving him a 'lovely sewn jacket', but they forgive her and give the couple a knitted house as a wedding present. Alas, when the baby Pearley is born the two sets of grandparents press their claims so strongly that there is an ugly scene punctuated by unseemly oaths ('you cable stitch ... you gingham rag ...') and Pearley is left alone in a heap of frayed stuff and unravelled wool, the sad victim of prejudice.

The brief but spirited story of the knitted family depends on Renate Meyer's clever use of texture and colour to present floppy, odd, beguiling characters, knitted or sewn, all with 'faces' full of expression. In a sequel, *Mr Knitted and the Family Tree*, she introduces the kind of relationships that puzzle small children – aunts, in-laws, great-grand-parents and so on – through characters whose names (Two-Ply, Sheerest, Cable) indicate their origin, while twists in their patterns lend them a kind of zany personality. [Renate Meyer: *The Story of Little Knittle and Threadle*, 1971; *Mr Knitted and the Family Tree*, 1972]

**LITTLE LORD FAUNTLEROY** see CEDRIC ERROL

**LITTLE PEAR** lives in the village of Shegu in old China. Full of mischief, this lively six-year-old is delighted when a new baby is born, for now everyone will know he is a big boy. Eager to prove this, Little Pear sets out on sundry enterprises; he is lost in a pile of leaves during one afternoon's work; he begs for money on the high road and wanders to the next village, where he buys himself tea and a hat and contrives a donkey ride home. Skating, watching fireworks, enjoying a fair, helping with th pigs, Little Pear with his old-style pigtail and chubby face shares the typical moods and wishes of his age with small boys all over the world. The gentle, sympathetic humour of the stories, the universality of the character, are most in evidence in *Little Pear and the Rabbits*, when he tries to find something familiar to take to school when he goes for the first time. He catches a small frog which he slips into his pocket and so off he goes to school, still a little apprehensive but comforted – for 'Nobody knew about the frog in Little Pear's pocket ... Nobody except Little Pear himself.' [E. F. Lattimore: *Little Pear*, New York 1931; *Little Pear and his Friends*, 1934; *Little Pear and the Rabbits*, 1956]

**LITTLE PETE,** who is four years old, is not lonely though he only has his shadow for company. Sticks and puddles, kittens and a ladybird all intrigue him, but most of all he likes to watch people doing things – a man driving a road-roller, another wielding a pneumatic drill, a lady in a mechanized wheel-chair, a window-cleaner, a bricklayer. Pete now and then investigates their activities too closely but, true to the nature of small children, it is he who is stamping-feet furious, when the road-roller squashes his plasticine and the earth-remover picks up his whistle.

These tiny stories were written for the BBC's 'Listen with Mother' programme. Their humour and rhythm and the natural, authentic picture of a tough little boy, made them firm favourites. [Leila Berg: *Little Pete Stories*, London 1952]

**LITTLE PIG ROBINSON** see GINGER AND PICKLES

**LITTLE RED ENGINE** (the) has not visibly changed in the thirty years since it first ran sadly on its branch line from Taddlecombe Junction and longed to follow the 'Pride o' the North' and the 'Beauty of the South' on to the main lines and into the city. It longs for a name, too, instead of the number 394 which alone distinguishes it. In the first book of a long sequence (*The Little Red Engine Gets a Name*) the engine gets its chance to carry the King and is promoted to be a Main Line Engine, with the name 'Royal Red' and the proud designation 'By Royal Appointment'. Its appearance was created by the artists Lewitt and Him in dashing colour and given a jaunty air, with very slightly fantasized funnels and headlamps ingeniously and expressively turned into eyes. The twist of personality was imitated, with a little more rotundity, a little less wildness perhaps, when Leslie Wood took over as illustrator for the second book, *The Story of the Little Red Engine*.

The hero of the dramatic journey with the King has now returned contentedly to the daily round trip from Taddlecombe by Dodge, Mazy, Callington Humble, Never Over, Soke, Seven Sisters, Dumble and home. The names of the stations ring like an incantation through subsequent books and the little engine chuffs serenely and reliably along, taking ducks, geese, colts and the gamekeeper's cat to market, carrying a crowd of village folk to Molehaven for a day-outing, collecting others for a carol-singing evening in Taddlecombe. Year after year the engine passes Mrs Ransome's cottage where little dog Hurry sits by his kennel, the pond full of frogs, the hill where the sheep watch its slow climb and the level crossing where impatient cars pile up. There are times when Royal Red goes further afield – to London for an exhibition, to India to satisfy the whim of a Maharajah's son, to the workshops at Swincaster to be overhauled after its travels; and it is distinctly more important than the great engines it had once envied when it takes along to Taddlecombe those of its regular passengers who have volunteered to assist in an experiment with a space rocket.

Always alert, composed and efficient, the Little Red Engine, though less articulate than Thomas the Tank Engine (q.v.) and his colleagues, and less eccentric than Emett's engines, is perhaps the most appealing of all

personalized locomotives in children's books. The rhythm and point of Diana Ross's text and the serene landscapes through which the little engine moves create an atmosphere in which it is completely at home. [Diana Ross, ill. Lewitt-Him: *The Little Red Engine Gets a Name*, London 1942; ill. Leslie Wood: *The Story of the Little Red Engine*, 1945; *The Little Red Engine Goes to Market*, 1946; *The Little Red Engine Goes to Town*, 1952; *The Little Red Engine Goes Travelling*, 1955; *The Little Red Engine and the Rocket*, 1956; *The Little Red Engine Goes Home*, 1958; *The Little Red Engine Goes to be Mended*, 1966; *The Little Red Engine and the Taddlecombe Outing*, 1968; *The Little Red Engine Goes Carolling*, 1971]

**LITTLE RED FOX,** in spite of being a homeless orphan, insists 'I take care of misself' when Mrs Badger finds him in Thorp Wood and takes him home with her. Although the mischievous animal leads her two docile children into mischief, his foster mother persuades him in the end to submit to family discipline. She listens to his breathless tale of the beautiful white rabbit who must surely be Cinderella and forgives him for borrowing her best hat to offer to the swan princess instead of her lost crown. Meanwhile her robust and sensible husband protects the little fox from his wicked uncle, who seems anxious to train him in nefarious deeds, and supplies the necessary pennies when the three small animals want to go to the Wakes. Most of the little fox's adventures have a fairy-tale connotation which adds a touch of mystery to this boisterous little animal. [Alison Uttley: *Little Red Fox and the Wicked Uncle*, London 1954; *Little Red Fox and Cinderella*, 1956; *Little Red Fox and the Magic Moon*, 1958; *Little Red Fox and the Unicorn*, 1962]

Little Red Fox is given a wash and brush-up by his foster mother; an illustration by Katherine Wigglesworth.

**LITTLE RED RIDING HOOD** (the) 'the prettiest little creature that ever was seen', has suffered from many extensions of this definition since she was introduced into England in the early eighteenth century in a translation from Perrault. At one extreme she has been sentimentalized in versions that dwell on her pretty ways; at the other extreme, psychology has done its utmost with the idea of an innocent child in bed with a wolf. Most versions read by children today have avoided the stark ending of Perrault's version – 'And upon saying these words, this wicked Wolfe fell upon *the little Red Riding-Hood*, and eat her up' – choosing from the many kinder alternative endings the one written down by the brothers Grimm, in which the wolf is found asleep by a passing huntsman and ripped up, whereupon the little girl and her grandmother emerge safely (in one modern version the grandmother 'sat herself down on the rocking chair and picked up her knitting just as if she had come in from a day's outing'). As for Freudian interpretations of the story, Tomi Ungerer (in *A Story Book from Tomi Ungerer*, 1974) tells how the little girl, on the way to visit an unpleasant grandmother, is accosted by a wolfduke who carries her off to a life of luxury, while Grandma turns into a Norway rat. [Charles Perrault: *Histoires ou Contes du temps passé* (1697 France) trans. Robert Samber as *Histories or Tales of past Times*, London 1729]

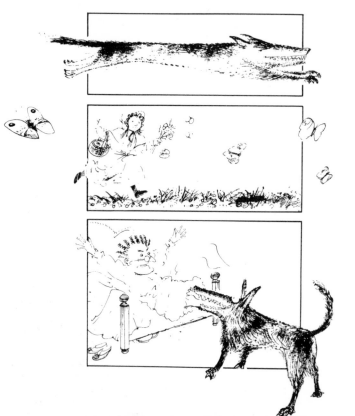

Illustrations from four versions of the story of Red Riding Hood: (*opposite above*) by Gustav Dore in *Perrault's Fairy Tales*; (*opposite below*) by Harriet Pincus in *Little Red Riding Hood*; (*above*) by Raymond Briggs in *The Fairy Tale Treasury*; and (*right*) by Edward Gorey in *Little Red Riding Hood*, retold in verse by Beatrice Schenk de Regniers.

**LITTLE STEAM ROLLER** (the), 'hero of this story', works with Bill Driver at London Airport. The policeman at the gate likes to tease Bill and enquire whether his 'fine car' is a Daimler, but Bill's reply 'Where were all your policemen the day the Little Steam Roller broke up the great Black Hand gang?' is final and crushing. The steam-roller in fact stops Mr King, who is smuggling gold nuggets disguised as children's bricks, because of a piece of paper which the villain drops by mistake and which the astute vehicle at once recognizes as a secret code. Acting instantly, without reference to his driver, he stops the getaway car and earns the Queen's Medal.

In similar books in the series, two more gallant vehicles, the Little Horse Bus and the Little Fire-engine, perform equally brave acts and prove that they are far from obsolete, while the Little Train finds running away from his branch line a chastening experience. While the texts allow all these vehicles gender, thought and speech, neither illustrator humanized them by twisting accessories to suggest features. Dorothy Craigie's pictures for the first editions are fanciful enough in style alone to suggest a measure of humanization, while Ardizzone, with a gentler and more naturalistic approach, has been content to allow gallantry and resource, adequately described in the texts, to be suggested in the action which he meticulously and beautifully depicts. [Grahame Greene, ill. Dorothy Craigie: *The Little Train*, London 1946; *The Little Fire Engine*, 1950; *The Little Horse Bus*, 1952; *The Little Steam Roller*, 1953. New editions ill. Edward Ardizzone: London 1973, 1974]

Illustration by Dorothy Craigie for (*right*) the Max Parrish edition of *The Little Steam Roller* (1953) and (*below*) Edward Ardizzone's illustration for the 1973 edition of the same book. *Opposite.* Dorothy Craigie's picture (*above*) and Edward Ardizzone's (*below*) for the *Little Fire Engine* (1950 and 1974).

He is known to everybody at London Airport as The Steamroller. The man at the wheel is called Bill Drive policeman at the gates sometimes laughs at Bill. "T fine car you drive," he says. "Is it a Daimler?"

— they had quite forgotten Tim. He was so small and frightened that nobody had noticed him.

Tim crept on to the bridge where he found the captain, who had refused to leave his ship.

One of Edward Ardizzone's illustrations of Little Tim on his first stormy voyage.

**LITTLE TIM** wants so much to be a sailor that he spends most of his time 'playing in and out of boats, or talking to his friend the old boatman.' Not surprisingly, Tim's parents tell him he will have to wait for years to satisfy his ambitions. But one day the old boatman takes him out to a steamer in the bay, and resourceful Tim stows away. At first he is miserable, for he is set to scrub the deck, but soon he becomes a favourite with the crew; when the ship is wrecked in a storm, and he and the Captain, last on board, are saved in the nick of time, he 'could not help feeling a bit of a hero', especially when the Captain asks his parents if he can come on his next voyage, as 'he felt that Tim had the makings of a very fine sailor.'

So seven-year-old Tim embarks on a series of seagoing adventures. On a voyage in the steam yacht *Evangeline*, chartered by Mr Grimes, he and Lucy (q.v.), together with the redoubtable Mrs Smawley, imprison a band of mutineers below decks. As ship's boy on the ss *Fidelity*, he stands up to the older, taller Ginger (q.v.) and rescues him when he goes overboard. With Ginger he pulls the drowning Charlotte out of the sea and fights the boys at school when they tease him about the little girl. A collision in fog, the strange disappearance of his parents, the hiding of the stray puppy Towser on the ss *Royal Fusilier*, the rescue of Ginger from a sea-swept rock, the affair of the wreckers at the lighthouse – in all these stirring events Tim is, as always, brave and sensible, and his observation of his seniors teaches him moderation, so that when he grows up and becomes the captain of a fine ship, he never beats his cabin boys 'with a rope's end.'

Little Tim was born, as Ardizzone has said himself, out of nostalgic memories of childhood days when he and his cousin Arthur roamed the docks at Ipswich, sometimes exploring the ships with members of the crew, at other times chased off when they took too many liberties. One may guess that the enquiring side of Tim's character, his gloriously confident, unselfconscious behaviour, are compounded of his creator's own character and his own wishes – the wishes of any small boy to grow up quickly and invade the adult world. Through matchless words and pictures, this much travelled small boy has become an enduring nursery favourite. [Edward Ardizzone: *Little Tim and the Brave Sea Captain*, London 1936; *Tim and Lucy Go to Sea*, 1938; *Tim to the Rescue*, 1949; *Tim and Charlotte*, 1951; *Tim in Danger*, 1953; *Tim All Alone*, 1956; *Tim's Friend Towser*, 1962; *Tim and Ginger*, 1965; *Tim to the Lighthouse*, 1968; *Tim's Last Voyage*, 1972]

**LITTLE TOOT,** 'the cutest, silliest little tugboat you ever saw', although (or perhaps because) he has the example of his father and grandfather before him, hates work and fears the open sea. His tricks earn him the rebuke of the huge tug *J. C. McGillicuddy*, whose path he impudently crosses, and the scorn of visiting liners, who all refuse his help, but after he has pulled a steamer off the rocks when waves and currents prevent larger tugs from going to the rescue, Little Toot suddenly becomes a useful and sensible worker. A later adventure takes him across the Atlantic and into the Thames, where he crosses the path of the boat race; he makes up for his mischief by pulling a wrecked barge out of the way of a procession of boats led by the Royal Barge. On another occasion he journeys up the Mississippi to find the steamboats described by his grandfather as 'horned monsters' which 'chewed fire and breathed smoke like dragons'.

The familiar formula of 'mischievous child makes good' is artlessly and comically extended here to a small tug which is lightly humanized by verbs of human behaviour and by pictures in which a face is contrived for Little Toot by a clever manipulation of bridge and bows. Just as cleverly Hardie Gramatky makes sly allusions to bygone social modes when he draws, for instance, the 'features' of a Southern Colonel whose whiskers and choleric expression derive convincingly from the front of a paddle-steamer. [Hardie Gramatky: *Little Toot*, New York 1939; *Little Toot on the Thames*, 1964; *Little Toot and the Grand Canal*, 1968; *Little Toot on the Mississippi*, 1973]

**LITTLE WITCH** (the) is only a hundred and twenty-seven years old and is not considered old enough to join

The Little Witch and her raven Abraxas, drawn by Winnie Gayler.

her elders on the Brocken mountain on Walpurgis Night. Her raven Abraxas is as critical of her ambitions as of her latest spell for rain, which brings a shower of buttermilk. Justifiably annoyed, the Little Witch flies off to the mountain after all, but is recognized by her aunt Rumpumpel and haled before the Head Witch, who decrees that if she is a 'good witch' for a whole year she may present herself for a test at the next Walpurgis meeting. Unfortunately both the Little Witch and her raven misinterpret the condition. When the Little Witch has performed various good deeds throughout the year she is aghast when she earns punishment, not reward, in spite of casting all the spells in the test correctly. She has the last word, however. Whether it is good or bad to burn all the broomsticks and spell books and reduce the witches to normality must be decided according to individual points of view.

This sequence of amusing episodes, which lightly parody traditional fairy-tale, is based on the nice paradox of what a 'good witch' may or may not signify. Acute readers may note that the Little Witch's good deeds (changing the mean forester's attitude to woodgatherers, saving a tired horse from a beating, rescuing a pet ox destined as a prize to be roasted, bringing about the reformation of a confirmed gambler) invariably mean pain or discomfort for somebody. Adult readers may also notice how cunningly this little fantasy (like the similar tales of a Little Water-Sprite and a Little Ghost) offer, in effect, pictures of childhood – of that happy period when mischief is charitably interpreted as enterprise and damage as the result of experiment. [Otfried Preussler: *The Little Witch* (1958 Germany) trans. Anthea Bell, London 1961]

**LITTLE WOODEN HORSE** (the) looks like all the other blue-striped, wheeled toys made by old Uncle Peder, but, unlike them, he has no ambition to see the world. All the same, when his master becomes poor and ill, the brave little horse sets out to earn money to help him. After weeks of toil for Farmer Max, he escapes from his harsh employer on a canal barge; he is taken across the sea on a trading ship, works in a coal mine, deputizes for one of the royal coach horses, acts in a circus, works for Black Jakey in a string of seaside donkeys and at last swims the ocean to make his way back to his master with the money he has so loyally guarded for him.

Wood is a frequent symbol of endurance in children's fantasy. Beside familiar characters like Hitty (q.v.) and Maria Poppet (q.v.), the Little Wooden Horse must take his place as one of those seemingly simple characters whose behaviour and exploits carry deeper meanings and touch unexpected depths of feeling in the reader. Staunch, loyal, unselfish, the Little Wooden Horse is all the more appealing because he is a reluctant hero. 'I am a quiet little horse', he says to himself as he sits by the fire with Uncle Peder, 'and for ever after I shall be rather a dull one ... But I shall always be the luckiest little horse in the world.' Affection and security are as important to

The Little Wooden Horse, drawn by Peggy Fortnum.

the character, and the story, as the variety and colour of the adventures which the little horse survives. [Ursula Moray Williams: *The Adventures of the Little Wooden Horse*, London 1938]

**LITTLENOSE,** a lively small boy with a nose 'no bigger than a berry', lives with his Neanderthal family in a cave where a huge fire burns continuously to ward off wild beasts and the chill of the Ice Age. One day,

Littlenose and his pet mammoth Two-Eyes, from *Littlenose Moves House*, written and illustrated by John Grant.

Littlenose uses a green pebble to buy a reject mammoth; too small to sell, complains the dealer, and 'who's going to buy this sort of animal', with its one red and one green eye. Littlenose has no doubts. Two-Eyes becomes his devoted mount and playmate and the odd couple blunder their way into numerous situations, in each one of which Littlenose, by luck or coincidence, enlarges his experience and often makes discoveries vital to civilization.

By accident he establishes the principles of boat-building, drawing, transplanting and irrigation; he invents a ladder and a toboggan; he finds a fossilized dinosaur in an ice cave and watches the hunting rituals of the much-feared neighbours, the Straightnoses. In a divertingly unusual setting, into which the author ingeniously introduces a good deal of anthropological material, a small boy exercises a natural curiosity which his elders, while enjoying its side-benefits, describe as mischief. [John Grant: *Littlenose*, London, 1968; *Littlenose Moves House*, 1969; *Littlenose the Hero*, 1971; *Littlenose the Hunter*, 1972; *Littlenose the Fisherman*, 1973]

**LIZZIE DRIPPING** is really Penelope Arbuckle. Her father works as a blacksmith and plumber in the Nottinghamshire village of Little Hemlock and her mother Patty 'had her feet as firmly planted on the ground as Lizzie had her head stuck in the air'. Here is the reason for the twelve-year-old girl's odd nickname – a local term affectionately used for 'the kind of girl who is dreamy and daring at the same time, and who turns things upside down and inside out wherever she goes and whatever she does'. Lizzie's temperament, and the name of the village, make it seem perfectly natural that a witch should appear in the churchyard, visible only to Lizzie (and then only when the crusty, cackling old woman chooses) and ready to give the girl a gentle push in the direction of sense by involving her in trouble.

The relationship that develops between the two is grudging and critical on the witch's part, delighted and apprehensive on Lizzie's. Lizzie is prepared to see a thrush turned into a toad but it takes her longer to trust the witch as a baby sitter or to accept her as a gate-crasher in a Fancy Dress contest, and she never quite forgives her for the way she evades the responsibility for the accidents and surprises which Lizzie is sure she causes. Subtly and with humour Helen Cresswell shows that the witch is an extension of Lizzie's inner self, that reason and unreason harmonize in the person of this imaginative girl. Lizzie Dripping's adventures were conceived first for television programmes; she and the other characters suit equally well the media of the printed word and the screen, as well as they fit – indeed, grow out of – the infinitely complex, agreeably simple pattern of English village life. [Helen Cresswell: *Lizzie Dripping*, London 1973; *Lizzie Dripping by the Sea*, 1974; *Lizzie Dripping and the Little Angel*, 1974; last two in hardback as *Lizzie Dripping Again*, 1974]

**LOIS SANGER** *see* MARLOWS

**LOMAN,** a boy of sixteen, has come to St Dominic's only eighteen months before. 'Clever, and good tempered, and inoffensive', he is not popular all the same, and there seems to be a faint suspicion of his honesty. When he is made a monitor and moves into the Sixth Form, he loses touch with his old class-mates and finds himself unpleasantly isolated. Looking for occupation, he gets into the clutches of Cripps, son of an old lock-keeper, whose public house is out of bounds but who provides welcome amusements for the young gentlemen of the school all the same. Loman is easily led to accept a fishing-rod (an exceptional and unrepeatable bargain) on approval. Unfortunately he accidentally damages it and his foolish attempts to return it without admitting this lead to more and more insistent blackmail. His attempt to win money by entering for the Nightingale Scholarship is doomed to failure when he steals one of the question papers and recklessly throws the blame on Oliver Greenfield (q.v.), and a bet placed on Cripps' advice gets rid of his last pounds. As he grows more afraid of the future, his position in the school deteriorates, and at last his only hope is to escape – as it turns out, to disgrace, illness and repentance.

The downward progress of Loman inevitably recalls that of F. W. Farrar's Eric (q.v.). A comparison between *The Fifth Form at St Dominic's* and *Eric, or Little by Little* shows very positively the change in social and religious attitudes in the years between their respective publication dates. The sexual innuendoes of *Eric* have disappeared and the evils of cribbing, theft and the demon drink are regarded as crimes rather than sins. In spite of the religious underpinning of Talbot Baines Reed's story, in spite of the occasional moral soliloquizing of the chief characters, there is all the difference between the coarsening of the unfortunate Loman, who fears punishment in this world, and the coarsening of Eric, over whom hangs the awful shadow of ineluctable damnation. It is not only because of their hearty humour that Talbot Baines Reed's books seem, for all the similarities of plot and character, to belong to a different world from that in which *Eric* first saw the light. Perfervid religious introspection about the next world has given way to more energetic Christian practice in this one. The sinner of the 1840s and the young delinquent of the 1880s would hardly recognize one another if they met. [Talbot Baines Reed: *The Fifth Form at St Dominic's*, London 1887]

**LONE PINERS** (the) are originally four, but they collect more members for their club along their adventure-strewn way. When David Morton and the younger twins, Dickie and Mary, are evacuated during the war, they find a home in a Shropshire village. Dickie's ingenuous remark to a neighbour, 'We've come to have a great adventure at Witchend' is prophetic; the diversity and unvarying success of the children in unravelling mysteries is only equalled by the Famous Five.

While the Mortons. with their new friend Petronella Stirling, are looking for a good place to camp, they find the perfect lookout beside a solitary pine. The Club suggested by Dickie is planned 'for exploring and watching birds and animals and tracking strangers', but almost at once the second part of the objective overshadows the first, for from their lookout they see curious behaviour at the isolated house of Appledore, and they soon find themselves in the middle of a spy-hunt which they bring to a successful conclusion.

The adventures which the Lone Piners engage in over the years are mainly directed towards foiling criminals (jewel thieves, industrial spies, kidnappers, picture-fakers or archaeological rivals) or outwitting enemies of the State, foreign powers aiming at sabotage, infiltration or the stealing of military secrets. Most of these adventures take place in Shropshire, though there are occasions when the Mortons find their knowledge of London useful. The stories are topographically authentic and improbable both in plot and characterization. The members of the club are chosen for particular attributes – David for his common sense, for instance, Peter for her sterling loyalty, Tom Inglis the farmer's son for his strength and his local knowledge, Harriet Sparrow for her experience with antiques; the twins usefully complicate the plots with their mischief and misunderstandings, and their beloved, long-suffering Scottie Macbeth has an 'uncanny instinct' for villainy which often proves invaluable. The personalities, realistic enough in themselves, are deliberately standardized so that they will fit the unexacting nature of the adventures and will exist in a vacuum of time. Each boy or girl is given a set description, repeated at the beginning of each story; they have been permitted to grow a year or two older through the years so that certain sentimental attachments may be introduced to vary the predictable scenes of tracking, overhearing and escaping, but it is essential to the nature of the stories that the children shall not be sufficiently individual to react in any but the most superficial way to danger. Revised editions of these extremely popular stories have brought technological and domestic details up to date, but the stereotyped system of character-drawing has not changed. In particular the dialogue is still characterized by a curious flabby profuseness which pads out the stories, as each character discusses or describes either what has happened or what may happen in the future. These mechanical exchanges are the main form of communication between characters whose relationships have only a minor importance in essentially active stories. [Malcolm Saville: *Mystery at Witchend*, London 1943; *Seven White Gates*, 1944; *The Gay Dolphin Adventure*, 1945; *The Secret of Grey Walls*, 1947; and other titles]

**LONG JOHN SILVER** is engaged as ship's cook

Robert Louis Stevenson (1850–94) photographed in Samoa near the end of his life.

by Squire Trelawney when he sails to find the island on Jim Hawkins's map where Captain Flint's treasure waits for the bold adventurer. The gullible Squire accepts without question the plausible old sailor's story that he is looking for a berth at sea for his health; he accepts with relief Silver's offer to find a crew, and it is not till they are at sea that the Squire and his friends realize that they have in fact provided a way for some of Flint's old associates to find the treasure for themselves. Jim Hawkins has been involved in the enterprise ever since the blind sailor came tapping up to his mother's inn; this quick-witted, observant lad helps the Squire and the Doctor to escape the mutineers and occupy a stockade on the island, and after various skirmishes, plots and counterplots, in which Jim is captured by the pirates, escapes and steals their ship, the pirates are defeated and the victorious party returns to Bristol, taking with them the pathetic castaway Ben Gunn, and Long John Silver, once more the 'bland, polite, obsequious seaman of the voyage out', who vanishes from the life of Jim Hawkins, leaving many questions behind him.

No better adventure story has ever been written than *Treasure Island*, none more richly exciting and absorbing and few more morally ambiguous. Because Jim Hawkins tells the greater part of the narrative himself, it has a boyish, headlong, unselfconscious quality in it.

Long John Silver, drawn by Robert Micklewright in *Treasure Island*.

Because Jim never questions that his side in the contest has a right to the treasure and that they are justified in using force to get it, we do not have to decide whether the good characters are not in fact thieves and pirates themselves. Jim's artless confessions of fear, his quick courage, make it possible to accept vigorous descriptions of violence and death in which sordidness and terror have no part.

Through Jim's eyes we see the characters in simple terms – the honest, impetuous Squire, with his benevolent air of authority, the steady, sensible Doctor Livesey, the half-demented castaway fumbling with words after years of silence. Only Long John Silver is undefined. Jim is outraged when he discovers the man's treachery, he resists his blandishments and fears his rage, but he never understands him – nor is he meant to. The one-legged man, with his parrot, has become the prototype of the piratical villain since Barrie parodied him in the character of Captain Hook, but he is not a simple character all the same. Stevenson said he based the character on 'an admired friend' whom he 'deprived of all his finer qualities and left with nothing but his courage, his strength and his magnificent geniality'. Stevenson may not have realized that his passionate love of action had made Silver a more obvious subject for admiration than the Squire or the Doctor or even the ingenuous boy Jim. Silver's enigmatic power over circumstance made it impossible for Stevenson to do anything but let him vanish at the end of the story, making it open-ended in spite of a careful tying up of loose ends. More than one writer in this century has boldly added to the chronicles of *Treasure Island* but nobody has so far had the temerity to follow Long John Silver along his unknown path. [Robert Louis Stevenson: *Treasure Island*, serialized in *Our Young Folks Weekly Budget*, 1 October 1881–28 January 1882; 1st pub. in book form, London 1883]

**LOTTIE HORN** from Munich and Lisa Palfrey from Vienna meet at the holiday home at Bohrlaken and discover that they are identical, except that Lisa has curls and Lottie has plaits. They discover that they are twins; when their parents were divorced, quiet, thoughtful Lottie went with her mother, while Lisa, living with a father who conducted an orchestra, has been indulged in her natural gaiety. No sooner have the girls worked out their relationship than they decide to bring their parents together, and to do this they agree to change places and try to impersonate one another.

Typically, Kästner's story is poised between fantasy and domestic realism. The characters of the girls are defined in simple terms to point the effect of Mr Palfrey's bewilderment at 'Lisa's' sensible remarks and his ex-wife's confusion when her quiet 'Lottie' bursts with giggles. The symmetry of the character-drawing was exaggerated in the film, *The Parent Trap*, made from the book, when Hayley Mills acted both girls, neatly differentiating between them. Behind the humour of the

impersonation there is a sober theme concerning the children of a broken home, expressed not in any comment of the author but through the artless remarks of Lottie and Lisa, who show a cheerful but real concern about their situation. [Erich Kästner: *Lottie and Lisa*, (1949 Germany) trans. Cyrus Brooks, London 1950]

**LOUIE** is head roundsman of the New Day Dairy Company; it is rumoured that he has been offered a directorship, even that he is the owner, which shows the reputation Louie has acquired in the neighbourhood. This enigmatic man is not only a super-efficient milk roundsman. To be trained by him, his one-time assistants say, 'was like a cross between going on an Outward Bound course and spending a year at Jesus College, Cambridge'. So fierce is the competition to work with him that Tim Shaw goes through agonies when with four other boys (the rest of the applicants having been shrewdly dismissed by Louie for good reasons) he faces the tests devised by this masterful, masterly judge of character.

Jumbled crates, abominably-written messages, a savage dog guarding a milk-bottle – these and other hazards are negotiated with reasonable success by Tim, who gets the job. Though Louie is never known to praise anyone, at least he has to look less loftily disapproving than usual when Tim not only finds the source of various mistakes and mishaps along the route, for which he has been blamed, but also helps Louie to ward off the attack of two thugs on one money-collecting Friday.

In fact Tim is accepted as a useful ally when Louie (in *Louie's S.O.S.*) becomes the victim of a far more serious campaign of rumour and sabotage, though the case is solved mainly with the help of three of Louie's old boys, who have won fame for themselves, largely owing to his early training, in the police force, at the Bar and on the stage. Tim and his friend Smitty are still Louie's boys one snowy Christmas Eve when to their amazement they see Louie's invincible stance disturbed, not by the appalling weather conditions and unexpected crises of the day but by American Pat, foisted on Louie for the day as observer-helper; her practical sense and self-confidence actually evoke respect from the imperturbable roundsman.

Louie is an influence, commanding respect for his specialist knowledge and his contempt for amateurs, his cunning and his probity. Is this the hero of a moral story? Far from it. The silent, forceful Louie is the centre of three of the most slangy, crackling, racy, verbally ingenious, parodic and hilarious stories of urban streets. If there *is* something of a moral hidden in the pages, some hint that it might be a good idea to aim at a high standard in a milk-round or anywhere else, Louie would be the last person to boast about it – or, indeed, to deny it. [E. W. Hildick: *Louie's Lot*, London 1965; *Louie's S.O.S.*, 1968; *Louie's Snowstorm*, New York and London, 1974]

Louie the milkman, illustrated by Iris Schweitzer in *Louie's S.O.S.*

**LUCINDA WYMAN**, much younger than the nearest of her four brothers, has never enjoyed her subordinate position in the family. When she is ten her parents go abroad for a year and she goes to live with Miss Peters, who teaches at the school Lucinda attends in New York. Miss Peters believes a child should be independent; her gentle sister Miss Nettie believes she should be happy; together they work out a way of caring for Lucinda without fettering her with rules or with the obligation of gratitude. From being a prickly child, subject to tantrums when she is thwarted, Lucinda becomes a joyful explorer of city streets – and city people. With the help of her friend M'Gonigal, the policeman on the beat, she helps Tony Coppini when vandals plunder his father's fruitbarrow; she decorates a Christmas tree for tiny Trinket, daughter of a desperately poor Polish couple, and mourns the little girl when she dies of fever. Up and down the streets on her roller skates Lucinda moves from one person to another, talkative, often tactless, always ruthlessly honest, enjoying their company

and giving them her trust. When the year is over Miss Nettie measures her and finds she has grown two inches: her character has grown far more than that.

The story of Lucinda's year of freedom is based on the author's own experience in a large family. In a second book (*Lucinda's year of Jubilo*) she describes the testing time for the family when Mr Wyman dies, leaving little money, and they move to the summer cottage in Maine. Here Lucinda makes an effort to subdue her own strong wishes and to control her antagonism to Carter, next to her in age and as ready to quarrel as she is.

Here, too, is a time of learning and growth, described with Lucinda in the centre but with perceptive glances also at the other members of the family, for whom a small house and straitened means have produced tensions. The book is harsher and more didactic than *Roller Skates* and perhaps even a little sentimental. Above all, the first book is likely to be preferred because it does something very rare in fiction – it describes, strongly and movingly, a child's experience of joy. [Ruth Sawyer: *Roller Skates*, New York 1936; *Lucinda's Year of Jubilo*, 1940]

**LUCY** *see* GINGER AND PICKLES

**LUCY**, **EMILY** and **HENRY FAIRCHILD** live in a modest but pleasant house in the country. It is a life of simple pleasures – a new doll or a new book, listening to stories, *alfrescò* meals; of steady occupation in lessons suited to their years; of social and religious duties – charitable visits to the poor, Sunday School. In the first part of the chronicles of the family Mrs Sherwood expressed through the words and deeds of Mrs Fairchild the evangelical view that every life must be spent in the expectation of judgement, that every misdemeanour, however small, must be accounted a sin, to be corrected by reference to God's laws as well as to the dictates of society. But Mr and Mrs Fairchild, though they have a moral injunction ready for every occasion, are loving as well as conscientious parents. Their exhortations are affectionately delivered and their punishments are free from tyranny or repressed cruelty. There is nothing of the majestic coldness of Rosamond's mother (q.v.) in Mrs Fairchild's rebukes when she gently explains, for instance, why Lucy must not envy Emily

for her beautiful new doll; and although, when she has finished speaking, Lucy is convinced, her behaviour when the doll arrives is as natural as any lover of childhood could desire. When Emily suggests that Lucy should pretend to be the doll's nurse and 'it shall sleep between us in our bed', Lucy replies, 'I don't want dolls in my bed ... don't tease me, Emily'.

Henry's position as the youngest in the family is just as naturally contrived within the stories. He is somewhat bumptious, always insists on the privileges of his sex, does not scruple to laugh at his sisters for their love of dolls, enjoys rough games; 'he was apt to be set up by any change, and when he was set up he was almost sure to get into a scrape, unless something could be thought of to settle him down quietly'.

The strong evangelical purpose of the book, at least in the first part, must be accepted as more immediately important to the author than characterization or storytelling. Even so, Mrs Sherwood obeyed her instinct as a novelist, as well as her aim as a moral teacher, when she wrote *The Fairchild Family*, and never more so than in her treatment of the character of heedless Bessie Goodriche. It is not only because she is so thorough-going in her mischief that she seems more alive than the little Fairchilds; it is also because Mrs Sherwood gave her a voice all her own. Idle, wasteful and ignorant in the extreme, as her great-aunt described her, always tearing her clothes, she 'talked incessantly, whether heeded or not, and seldom said anything to the purpose' but what she says gives a more than adequate indication of her personality, whether she is begging a pin from the 'dear girls' to pin up the latest tear in her dress or laughing when she spills tea down it. ('It is not hurt, aunt; it will all come out. I threw a cup of milk over it the other day, and no one could see the mark unless I stood quite opposite them and they looked quite hard at it.') One may be excused for finding Bessie a relief from the biddable Fairchilds, even if it does mean reading the book with hindsight; but it seems that the novelist in Mrs Sherwood found a special freedom in drawing her character. [Mrs Sherwood: *The History of the Fairchild Family*, 3 pts, London 1818, 1842 and 1847]

**LUCY BROWN**, a pretty, well-mannered little orphan, lives with a busy aunt and is very lonely. One day while she is playing in the Recreation Ground, ugly, rich old Mr Grimes, who is used to being jeered at by children, decides he must talk to gentle little Lucy. They become fast friends and when Mr Grimes falls ill, his resourceful housekeeper Mrs Smawley sends for Lucy to come and cheer him up. Predictably, Mr Grimes recovers, and adopts the child with her aunt's willing consent.

Lucy still has no young companion until one day, as

Title page and illustration from *The Fairchild Family*.

"Mr. and Mrs. Fairchild had three children, Lucy, Emily and Henry."—Page 1.

Now one day, as she was sitting on the garden wall, thinking and thinking, whom should she see trudging along the road but a small boy of about her own age? He was carrying a bundle and a stick.

The meeting between Lucy and Tim, drawn by Edward Ardizzone.

she sits on the garden wall of her country home, she sees 'a small boy of about her own age' trudging along the road with a bundle and a stick. It is Little Tim (q.v.), looking for a ship. Soon Lucy has persuaded Mr Grimes to charter a yacht and so the adventure begins (in *Tim and Lucy Go to Sea*) in which the children outwit mutineers.

Lucy Brown does not continue as Tim's friend, her place being filled later by the rather similar figure of Charlotte. In the years between 1937 and 1970, when a revised edition of *Lucy Brown and Mr Grimes* was published, public opinion had cast doubts on the casual way the little girl and the old man became friends. In the revised version Mr Grimes becomes 'an old family friend' to make Lucy's confiding behaviour acceptable. [Edward Ardizzone: *Lucy Brown and Mr Grimes*, London 1937; *Tim and Lucy Go to Sea*, 1938]

**LYLE** the crocodile is left with the Primm family by his circus owner, Hector Valenti. The family find Lyle useful domestically and lovable as a personality, and Lyle for his part becomes so fond of his hosts that he pines when his master returns to take him on tour, and finally becomes a permanent member of the Primm household, winning all hearts – even those of Mr Grumps, whom he rescues from a fire, and of jealous little Clover Sue Hipple, whom he saves (more appropriately, perhaps) from drowning.

The arrangement of a sofa-shaped crocodile on a sofa is essentially a visual joke. Lyle is a picture-book character. Colour and shape emphasize his central position in every picture, and a slight curving of his powerful jaw ensures that his toothy grin is seen to be amiable. The character-drawing in the Lyle books is as casually grotesque as their amusingly improbable plots and broad illustrative style. [Bernard Waber: *Welcome, Lyle*, New York 1962; *Lyle, Lyle, Crocodile*, 1965; *Lovable Lyle*, 1969]

# M

**MADELINE** is one of twelve little girls in a convent boarding school in Paris – the only one out of pattern. She is the only child who is not afraid of mice, the only one who even breaks out of the 'two straight lines' in which they walk out 'in rain or shine', the only one who has an appendix scar, the only one who falls in the river and is fished out by a dog – and the only one who knows best 'How to frighten Miss Clavel', their strict but devoted teacher. Ingenious rhymes and the endless inventiveness of a superb caricaturist have established for all time Pepito the Bad Hat, Genevieve the excessively fertile bitch adopted by the school, Miss Clavel (always seen either stiffly vertical or fully extended as she runs ever faster toward some anticipated disaster), and the demure individualist Madeline. [Ludwig Bemelmans: *Madeline*, New York 1939; *Madeline's Rescue*, 1953;

*Madeline and the Bad Hat*, 1957; *Madeline and the Gypsies*, 1959; *Madeline in London*, 1961]

**MANNY RAT** *see* MOUSE AND HIS CHILD

**MANXMOUSE** begins as a ceramic aberration; when what should have been the most beautiful china mouse in the world is drawn out of the oven it proves to be a blue creature, with 'a fat little body like an opossum, hind feet like those of a kangaroo, the front paws of a monkey' and long, transparent rabbit-ears. When the clock strikes thirteen in the night the Manxmouse, now animate, sets off to find his destiny – which, as he soon learns, is to be the prey of the Manx Cat.

Manxmouse is inspected by the Billibird, dived at by Captain Hawk, copied for Madame Tussaud's and sold by auction for a million pounds; finally, deciding to waste no more time before he faces his fate, the mouse

One of the pictures in *Manxmouse,* illustrated by Janet and Anne Grahame-Johnstone.

Meg, Jo, Beth and Amy, from a jacket for *Little Women*.

makes his way to the Isle of Man and there, by refusing to accept his Doom without a fight, finds that tradition allows him to reverse it.

Satire and parable account equally for this quaint, original character. The fantasy confirms one's impression that invented animals are often better able to carry a moral and show the wayward nature of mankind than real animals humanized. [Paul Gallico: *Manxmouse*, London 1968]

**MARCH GIRLS** (the) – Meg, Jo, Beth and Amy – live a frugal, useful life in a quiet Massachusetts town. Their mother gently guides them in Christian behaviour while their father is away serving as a chaplain in the Civil War. They make their own amusements, enjoy modest pleasures, befriend Laurie, the boy next door, who is as lonely as he is rich, and in the loving atmosphere of their home develop their several personalities. The chronicle which begins in their childhood follows their later fortunes in three more books which describe Meg's life as devoted wife of John Brooke; Jo's marriage to Professor Bhaer and the establishment of a school for homeless or deprived boys at Plumfield; Amy's marriage to Laurie and the death of gentle Beth, which saddens the family but leaves lasting, loving memories.

The story of the Marches is too familiar to need

repeating, and just as familiar is the fact that the first two books at least and some parts of the last two were based on Louisa Alcott's own family and experience. The turbulent, creative Jo, hiding in her attic where she can write melodramas and cry over her favourite books, owes as much to memory as the scene where Mother Bhaer, a famous writer for girls in her contented middle-age, hopes to escape autograph-hunters by pretending to be the maid. But transcription from real life does not necessarily result in a masterpiece. Obviously much of the social and domestic detail that has delighted readers for a century has a basis in fact; the affectionate, striving, liberal atmosphere of the March home is a reflection of the Alcott household, with the fears quietened which, in real life, Bronson Alcott's philosophy of life brought to the young Louisa, and with the moral standards of the family retained. But Louisa Alcott was a true novel-ist, with a technique both simple and adroit.

She established her characters by physical descrip-tion, sparing and usually dramatic; she focused on each one in a particular scene – Jo and Meg at the Moffat's ball, Beth at the piano in the Laurence mansion, Amy at school tossing the forbidden limes out of the window. She managed dialogue in a somewhat formal way. Most often the sisters speak antiphonally, each with one sen-tence at a time; Jo's first words – 'Christmas won't be Christmas without any presents' – start the first of many four-sided conversations in which no single voice can be mistaken for another. All the same, the characters are not developed in equal depth. The impression we get of Meg and Beth is a pleasant but rather general one. Amy, in *Little Women* and to some extent in *Good Wives*, looks like being an interestingly diverse person, but she retires into the background later as an attractive but remote figure, leaving the centre of the stage to Jo. Inevitably, Amy's marriage to Laurie seems a matter of statement and plot, whereas his friendship with Jo, which he had once hoped to turn into something more, is an active, developing relationship. He and Jo are the most alive and individual characters in the books and their conversations are always immediate and vital.

Jo March is the presiding spirit and spark of the four books. Louisa Alcott had a wonderful gift for creating recognizable individuals – from Aunt March with her parrot to that splendid, romping pack of boys at Plumfield – and one at least of these (flawed, enigmatic Dan) commands major attention. All the same, each one of them is seen intimately in relation to Mother Bhaer, and there is an almost formal structure in *Little Men* through which we learn about the problems of Jo's Boys as they confess them to her. Marmee's exhortations to the girls, too (so much more naturally maternal than critics are always willing to concede) seem to touch a deeper level when she is talking to Jo. This is not wholly due to the autobiographical element in Jo's character. The real and the fictional characters have been superbly integrated and grouped round one central character.

The wholesome simplicity, the ease and smoothness of the writing, should not be allowed to mask the fact that the stories of the March family are most skilfully written and planned as well as being among the most warmly human, entertaining and absorbing of all family stories. [Louisa M. Alcott: *Little Women or, Meg, Jo, Beth and Amy*, Boston 1868; *Good Wives* (as part two of above), 1869; *Little Men: Life at Plumfield with Jo's Boys*, 1871; *Jo's Boys and how they turned out*, 1886]

**MARCO** interprets his father's advice to 'keep your eyelids up and see what you can see' rather too broadly. When his walk to and from school yields no more inter-esting sight than 'a horse and wagon on Mulberry Street', the boy sets his imagination to work and piles a dizzy cumulation of fantastic scenes one on top of the other till he has a crowd of odd vehicles and odder people to describe. Alas, as he approaches his house, and his rational father, he hardly knows where to begin his astonishing report and ends by confessing with embarrassment that all he saw was 'A plain horse and wagon on Mulberry Street'. The present generation, deafened by the screams and blinded by the flashing brilliance of Dr Seuss's outrageously fantastic creatures, may find it refreshing to return to his first book, with its zany but intelligible version of the thoughts of a fanciful small boy. [Dr Seuss: *And to Think that I Saw it on Mulberry Street*, New York 1937]

**MARCHPANE** *see* TOTTIE PLANTAGENET

**MARGARET** *see* GEOFFREY

**MARGARET PARGETER** lives in the City of Lon-don with her father, a bookseller of dangerously liberal views. On her seventeenth birthday, in the year 1801, she makes her friends promise to use her full name rather than the childish Meg, and she is affronted because their medical student lodger, Robert Kerridge, refuses to treat her as an adult. When her father is arrested for writing and selling an inflammatory pam-phlet Margaret accepts help from Robert's father and goes to live in a Suffolk village near the prison. She hates her dependence on him; moreover, when the Kerridges discover that their son Robert wants to marry her they do their best to keep the young people apart. For the first time Margaret is forced to recognize the existence of class distinction, but pride and love sustain her until fortune turns in her favour. As Robert's wife she sees her chance to help the poor directly, while her father, free to establish a new shop, realizes that 'children's slates and reading books' can bring about reform as readily as, if more slowly than, revolutionary writings.

Hester Burton chooses well in placing her heroine, a girl of spirit, good sense and generosity of heart, in a position in society where these attributes could grow naturally. The affection and understanding between the girl and her father shed a glow over the dark days de-scribed in the book and balance with personal feeling and action the element of social comment in it. [Hester Burton: *Time of Trial*, London 1963]

## Margaret Thursday

**MARGARET THURSDAY** was given her surname by the Rector of Saltmarsh because it was on a Thursday, towards the end of the last century, that he found her 'on the steps of the church when I was a teeny-weeny baby. And with me in my basket there were three of everything, all of the very best quality'; a note, also in the basket, said: 'This is Margaret whom I entrust to your care. Each year fifty-two pounds will be sent for her keep and schooling.' Margaret is very proud of her story, but the full force of being a foundling is brought home to her when the money suddenly stops, after ten years, and she has to go to an orphanage.

The story of Margaret's adventures more than bears out the old saying that 'Thursday's child has far to go'. Her exploits are only too believable, even to climbing out of a top window in the orphanage and legging a narrow-boat through a canal tunnel. The rigours of the orphanage are less terrible than they might have been for her, since she has firmly allied herself with the three Beresford children, who enter the place at the same time. When Lavinia Beresford goes into service at the local Big House, Margaret takes the responsibility for her younger brothers – Peter, who like Margaret is nearly eleven, and charming six-year-old Horatio; and when she finds that Peter has borrowed books (a necessity for

Margaret Thursday, drawn by Peggy Fortnum.

A scene from the television serial *Thursday's Child* (1972), showing Susan Field as Ma Smith and Claire Walker as Margaret Thursday.

him) from a private library, she impetuously decides they must all run away; truly, as the friendly village schoolmistress admits, 'Margaret is a remarkable child but inclined to dramatize things'.

The adventures of the three children, working on a canal barge and in a travelling theatrical company, with the belated revelation of the true identity of the well-spoken Beresfords, make a rousing tale which owes its success less to its element of mystery, telling though that is, than to the character of Margaret. Margaret's behaviour is consistent throughout the story; her headlong mode of speech and her ingenuous self-confidence, her pride in the circumstances of her birth, make her so credible a heroine that it is no surprise when she declines to go to Ireland with the Beresfords to live with their newly-found grandfather Lord Delaware. 'I don't want to be anyone's daughter' is an unusual reaction but typical in her and, like the Earl, we can easily believe that she will, as she promises, make her name famous by her own efforts – 'it might be as an actress'. With her trenchant manner, her courage in adversity, her quick wits, Margaret is perhaps the most attractive and vital of all Noel Streatfeild's heroines. The author has said herself that the character is based at least partly on a girl who, on a Channel crossing, had told her the story of her own highly independent life. It seems no accident that Margaret Thursday should find her true vocation while playing Little Lord Fauntleroy on the boards; there is more than a touch of Frances Hodgson Burnett's heroes and heroines in this engaging, spirited foundling of eighty years ago. [Noel Streatfeild: *Margaret Thursday*, London 1970]

**MARGRET LECHOW** is fourteen when during the Second World War she comes with her mother to a billet in a west German town; her father is a prisoner in Russia and the family farm in Pomerania is lost. By chance Margret finds work which suits her exceptionally well at Mrs Almut's Great Dane kennels outside the town and makes a good friend into the bargain.

During the two years compassed by two stories we see Margret growing into a responsible young woman, with a happy courtship as the natural outcome of her development. There are other characters in the books as strongly drawn as Margret – her sister Andrea, for example, a born mimic with a generous allowance of charm; Mrs Almut herself who (as she says) holds a world championship for defeating bureaucracy; the young schoolmaster Christoph Huhnerbein, seriously disabled in the war, determined to teach his pupils to love and serve their fellow men; Mirri, the old 'bee-witch' who has never recovered from the death of her pacifist son. But because the deepest theme in the books is the healing power of nature and a natural, peaceful way of life, and also because the author's memories of her girlhood are expressed through Margret, it is she who is really the focal point of the action, as she is seen tending dogs, horses and sheep in the wonderful

moments of birth, working to the point of exhaustion but fulfilling herself in the satisfying way she has found. [Margot Benary: *The Ark*, New York 1954; *Rowan Farm*, 1955]

**MARIA** *see* GULLIVER

**MARIA HENNIKER-HADDEN**, orphaned when very young, enters upon a new and happier phase of her life in the summer of 1875 when, having run away from boarding school, she is given a home by her elderly bachelor great-uncle, Warden of Canterbury College in Oxford. The Warden supports her unladylike action, partly because he sees a chance to exercise his theories about a classical education for girls, and partly because he recognizes in Maria an unusual personality.

Her meeting with the three Smith boys from next door taxes her courage still more, for 'as far as she knew, she had never spoken to a boy in her life, except the ones she had had as partners at her dancing-classes at Bath'. Thomas writes in his diary, 'She is thin and brown and silent; but rather better than most girls', and Maria soon proves her right to be included in the various Smith enterprises, while pursuing an investigation of her own into the identity of the unknown boy in a drawing at Jerusalem House. Her discovery is praised by her uncle, though in somewhat sardonic tones – 'I should think few scholars have so many obstacles thrown in the way of their research'; but having to face embarrassment and opposition have done Maria a good deal of good.

She and her great-uncle, both essentially reflective people, are very happy together, and Maria is miserable when he dies early in 1877. She dislikes the plan that she should go to live with the Jessops, for she does not much like the emotional Harriet. Rescue comes just in time in the shape of Mr Burghclere, another elderly relative who arrives to transport the library he has inherited from the Warden to his home in Florence.

Maria is introduced to James, Joshua and Thomas Smith, a drawing by Dick Hart in *The Warden's Niece*.

Her sojourn in Italy (in *The Italian Spring*) is not one of unmixed pleasure, what with continuous rain in Venice, the boredom of illness and a friendship with Cordelia Squerrye which involves her in an alarming escapade. In the books in which Maria appears her character is shown in the process of evolution. She is never certain that she will be able to adapt herself to new relationships and her gradual acceptance of the diversity of people is interesting to watch. [Gillian Avery: *The Warden's Niece*, London 1957; *The Italian Spring*, 1964]

**MARIA JONES**, the youngest and by far the toughest of Kay Harker's (q.v.) cousins, once started the Bishop of Tadchester's car and drove it into a lamp-post and it is her proud boast that she has been expelled from three schools – 'the headmistresses still swoon when they hear my name breathed'. When Abner Brown, masquerading as Father Boddledale, is rash enough to kidnap her in the hope of getting nearer to old Cole Hawlings (q.v.) and his magic box, she is not at all frightened, not even when his wife Sylvia Daisy (q.v.) threatens to turn her into dog-biscuit if she refuses to co-operate. 'If ladies are pert to me,' she replies at once, 'I make them into cats' meat. Many a good caterwaul have I fed on meat like you, cold.'

Irrepressible, incisive of speech, 'little Maria' is one of the most notable characters who ever broke the orthodox pattern of juvenile fiction. Nobody could doubt her boast 'I shall shoot and I shall shock as long as my name's Maria'. [John Masefield: *The Midnight Folk*, London 1927; *The Box of Delights*, 1935]

**MARIA POPPET** was made by old Sprat, a dollmaker in Holborn, and was sold to cheerful Thomas Plummy as a present for his sister Ellen. The wooden doll went with her little mamma to Aunt Sharpshins, where Ellen learned the trade of milliner and where Maria was elegantly dressed in a lemon-coloured merino dress with a purple sash. The alert little creature did not stay for long in one place. She enjoyed a luxurious home in Hanover Square with Lady Flora and a kindly one with little Mary Hope; she watched the Lord Mayor's Show from a lofty perch with Brigitta, who danced in the streets to her brother Marco's organ; and she watched a pantomime from a box with Lydia and fell on to the stage, where pretty Columbine picked her up; and at last she found herself out of the city and comfortably settled at Ashbourn Hall, where Lucy, the last of her 'little mammas', lovingly cared for her.

Maria Poppet's character and fortunes have been skilfully worked out so that she can serve almost as a guide to various social scenes in the London of Dickens's time. Her comments on the grown-ups she meets in the rich West End, in prosperous Finsbury and in the alleys round St Paul's are as sharp as her descriptions of her various little mammas are affectionate. Her doll's dignity is never impaired and she is never afraid – not even when, burnt and bedraggled, she is carried off

Maria Poppet, heroine of *Memoirs of a London Doll*, illustrated by Richard Shirley Smith for a modern edition.

in the mouth of a large dog. Her tart, decisive personality is exactly what Richard Horne needed to express, with light but honest point, his feeling of compassion for the children who were exploited and ill-treated and his enjoyment of the natural gaiety of the more fortunate children whom he entertained with his drolleries. [Richard Henry Horne: *Memoirs of a London Doll*, London 1846]

**MARIANNE** falls ill on her tenth birthday and has to spend several months in bed. She is helped by brisk Miss Chesterfield who tells her about a boy she is also teaching who is making a slow recovery from polio. Marianne's imagination is stimulated by details of Mark's (q.v.) progress and by a stumpy pencil, which seems to her to have magic powers, found in her grandmother's workbox. She draws a house and a figure at the window and enters upon a series of dream

Marianne and Mark, drawn by Marjorie-Ann Watts for *Marianne Dreams*.

adventures in which she and Mark meet, eat picnic meals (a mixture of sausages, eggs and other objects easy to draw) and escape the power of the eyed stones which have taken on a sinister life of their own through Marianne's ill temper and which can only be defeated by the rays from the lighthouse on the horizon.

The alarming adventure is seen to rise out of Marianne's own nature. Into the story are projected images of her own anger, her desire for a companion in loneliness and perhaps also her fears of approaching adolescence. Catherine Storr draws Marianne from inside, creating a child who represents a certain difficult, shifting stage in development. This type of psychological characterization is still more evident in a sequel, *Marianne and Mark*, in which Marianne is on a visit to an aunt and uncle in Brighton. A psychiatrist and a probation worker respectively, her relations are determined to help her to grow out of her uncertain fifteen-year-old moods and their probing only makes her more lonely. The acquaintances she makes – two girls of her own age less well educated and living by a very differ-

ent social code – increase her adolescent unease and almost drive her into a false position. She tries to escape from her problems through consulting a local fortune-teller and indulging her belief that she can affect her destiny and that of others through dreams. From an unhealthy state of mind typical of her temperament and background she is rescued by Mark, who turns up in time to convince her that she is capable of a normal developing relationship with a member of the opposite sex. In the two stories, what she becomes is more important than what she actually is. [Catherine Storr: *Marianne Dreams*, London 1958; *Marianne and Mark*, 1960]

**MARK**, slowly recovering from polio, becomes in spite of himself an actor in the strange dream-adventure which Marianne (q.v.) apparently causes by drawing-magic. A clever boy, Mark has retreated into himself as a result of his illness and is therefore very vulnerable to Marianne's strong will when he meets her in the dreams they seem, mysteriously, to share. But though Mark usually follows where Marianne leads, he has a sturdy good sense and a courage that helps him to overcome the shame of his weakness and make himself fit enough to join her in the terrifying dash from the imprisoning house she has drawn to the healing lighthouse on the hill.

In *Marianne and Mark*, Mark repays Marianne's rather erratic affection in their earlier adventure by bringing fresh air (literally as well as figuratively) into the hothouse atmosphere of her day-dreaming existence. Mark is drawn in a more orthodox way than Marianne, as an average, likable, middle-class boy who can usefully help the reader to understand her. [Catherine Storr: *Marianne Dreams*, London 1958; *Marianne and Mark*, 1960]

**MARK APPERLEY** at fifteen is ready for active rebellion against his domineering grandmother, who has kept him cooped up on the Worcestershire estate under the tuition of the local curate, obsequious Mr Bilibin. Mark fancies that a letter to an imaginary girl, left unfinished where Mrs Apperley is bound to find it, will ensure that he is sent away to school, but instead, he is packed off, still in Mr Bilibin's charge, on a European tour – in 1849 a recognized form of education for the sons of gentry.

So begins a turbulent year in which the sheltered boy is first by chance and then by choice swept into the rising of Garibaldi, the siege of Rome and the rebel army's escape through the mountains. His frustrations are swept aside, his knowledge of the world increased, through his acquaintance with McWhirter, a journalist sending despatches and drawings back to London, with Tessa and Pietro Palma, two young and ardent rebels against French and Austrian domination in Italy, and briefly, the romantic leader himself. Mark returns to England an older and wiser boy after an escapade which proved to be a severe lesson in human relations.

Eleven years later (in *A Thousand for Sicily*), as a young journalist on the *Morning Herald*, Mark attaches himself once more to the rebel army, as an active observer in the sea journey and the capture of Palermo, this time accompanied for part of the time by Julietta Valdesi, half-English daughter of a Sicilian doctor. A predictable, gently romantic ending completes the adventures of a young Englishman who, with the attitudes and opinions of his time, remains understandable today.

In most of his historical novels Geoffrey Trease involves a young fictitious hero with an historical personage; in this way he can offer an interpretation rather than a closely considered portrait. Young readers today are more likely to understand the aims and ideals of Garibaldi if they are expressed through the dawning comprehension of a boy who can make the pattern of history seem relevant to our own times.

In the first book about Mark (*Follow My Black Plume*) he is shown to be ingenuous and inexperienced. He sees Garibaldi through a haze of hero-worship, only half realizing that intelligence is as necessary in a commander as the power of personality. Garibaldi, with his cowboy's poncho, red shirt and the black ostrich feathers in his wide hat, seems to Mark a man full of colour, a romantic hero indeed, 'a big man, barrel-chested, with a reddish-golden beard and a face like a lion's, broad-muzzled, tawny from sun and wind'. The young man of twenty-six sees Garibaldi as an old lion in his fifties, still savage, still capable of quick decisions and bold feats of arms, but saddened by his wife's tragic death and pained by rheumatism. Mark is older too, not at all sure that he wants to be a hero, knowing now the bleak realities and the compromises of war. Geoffrey Trease allows Mark in words, behaviour and verbalized thoughts to offer his own view of Garibaldi very directly. At the same time the way the boy talks with other characters – with the two ardent girls, Tessa and Julietta, with the absurd cleric Bilibin and the cynical McWhirter – tells us as much about him as it does about the minor characters who in their turn add reality to the books. [Geoffrey Trease: *Follow My Black Plume*, London 1963; *A Thousand for Sicily*, 1964]

**MARK AND WILL RUSSELL** *see* CHRISTINA PARSONS

**MARLOWS** (the) live in London and spend some of their holidays in Dorset, at Trennels, the house and farm which have belonged to Marlows for ten centuries. Giles, the eldest, is in the Navy like his father, and Peter is a cadet at Dartmouth, while the four eldest girls are at a boarding school to which the youngest Marlows, Nicola and Lawrie, go as new girls when the family chronicle begins. Nicola and Lawrie have always enjoyed the fun they can contrive from being identical twins, but they have other plans for their first term at school, for their sisters have all made their mark – Karen for her brains, Rowan in the games field, Ann as a pianist and Ginty for her charm and good looks – and they are determined to be just as successful. The first setback comes when they find their work is not up to standard and they have been placed in a lower form than they had expected. They feel the blow to the family reputation keenly and, being determined children, they try to assert themselves in other ways. To join the Guides seems a suitable way to make their mark, but their initiative on a trek gets them into trouble; they are used as scapegoats when Lois Sanger, who is in charge of the trek, makes a serious mistake in running it. However, the twins recover themselves in joining in a performance of *The Prince and the Pauper*, where Lawrie's talent for acting can hardly be overlooked.

The following Easter, while the family is staying at a seaside town, the four younger Marlows accidentally stumble on evidence that Lewis Foley, one of Peter's instructors at Dartmouth, is a spy, and they spend frightening days shut up with Foley in a lighthouse before naval police deal with the situation. Though this is a well-knit and exciting adventure story, it is also a

The Marlow children with the spy Foley, drawn by Doritie Kettlewell.

strong study in character, both in the appraisal of Foley's temperament and motives and also in the way each of the children reacts to the situation – Ginty with a dead-pan common sense that hides real fear, Nicola with a terrified courage that is partly romantic and Lawrie with her usual impetuous belief that she can save the situation. They return to school for the following term still determined to win a reputation worthy of the family but Lois Sanger continues to get them into trouble and Lawrie's hurt pride when she is not given the leading part in the Nativity Play leads her to play a trick of substitution which is held against her for a long time.

In the following summer the Marlows move to Trennels, which their parents have inherited on the death of their cousin, and Rowan bravely takes on the task of running the farm. She shares the central place in *Falconer's Lure* with Ginty, whose need to be liked has led her into a foolish friendship with a sentimental school friend. Lawrie's conceit inspires her to accost a famous old actress at a local Festival and to cherish her advice, while Nicola forms a pleasant friendship with Patrick Merrick through their mutual interest in hawking. The friendship suffers a decline later in the year, when they all become obsessed (in *Peter's Room*) with a romantic game based on the Brontë children's invented kingdoms of Gondal and Angria. Improvisation almost becomes reality, especially for Ginty and Patrick. Nicola is frightened at the feelings they have evoked and brings the game to an end.

In the brief February holiday of the next year they are again involved in danger (in *The Thuggery Affair*) when they chance upon clues that lead to the conviction of an unpleasant neighbour, Miss Culver, who has been pushing drugs with the help of city boys employed in her pigeon-breeding business. Here, once more, the reactions of the children, especially of Patrick and Lawrie, are of paramount importance. A month or so later Karen takes the centre of the stage when (in *The Ready-made Family*) she suddenly throws up her place at Oxford to marry a widower with three young children. The younger Marlows, especially Peter, rebel decisively and rudely against Edwin's pedantry and his bossy, condescending manner. This particular part of the Marlow story strikes deeply into the inconsistencies of human nature, and Nicola and Lawrie in particular are seen to be growing apart, for Lawrie, always disturbed when she is forced to notice other people's troubles, becomes tiresomely emotional and demanding, while Nicola understands something of the sad compromise of this ill-advised marriage.

In the latest instalment of the Marlow chronicle, *The Cricket Term*, the Marlows are back at school, again involved in a play and with Lawrie trying to get the coveted part of Caliban. Nicola has come to appreciate Edwin's scholarship and he has been finding out some Marlow family history of the Tudor period which unexpectedly includes her hero, Raleigh (the part played by Marlows and Catholic Merricks in Tudor politics is explored in two ancillary stories of great interest, *The Player's Boy* and *The Players and the Rebels*). In this book Lois Sanger, in her last term at the school, reveals the alarming extent of her dislike of the Marlows in some remarkably dishonest behaviour on the cricket field.

Boarding school stories provide a particularly fruitful setting for studies in character, since in a closed community small issues are apt to become large ones. The prolonged antagonism between the Marlows and Lois Sanger in particular is brilliantly described. Lois is a complex, flawed character whose actions and motives become more and more uncontrolled, while she almost cherishes the dislike of her contemporaries in indulging her jealousy of girls whose success seems to her to have come easily. Ambition and spite destroy her stability and the effect of her mania is felt everywhere in the school.

Antonia Forest develops her characters by choosing a particular sphere of action and looking at it from the point of view of one person after another. The greater part of her stories consists of dialogue, subtly and carefully used to suggest character; she rarely tells the reader what people are like, making clear by cross-reference the unconscious betrayal of concealed desires and antagonisms, jokes and gossip and argument. She keeps continuity in the sequence of stories partly by planning the plots clearly and integrating events skilfully, and partly by knowing her characters so well that she can show how they change as time goes on. Her time-scheme is not in fact entirely logical, for the first two books reflect the climate of the immediate post-war years, whereas *The Thuggery Affair* with its elaborate hippy jargon (so exact that it quickly dated) belongs to the late 60s. But the fictional time-scheme has its own more important logic and the definition and development of the characters is remarkably consistent and complete. This long, continuing chronicle of a family never stands still or gets caught up in its own complexity; it offers a satisfaction to the reader that comes of being able to make a deep acquaintance with the characters. [Antonia Forest: *Autumn Term*, London 1948; *The Marlows and the Traitor*, 1953; *Falconer's Lure*, 1957; *End of Term*, 1959; *Peter's Room*, 1961; *The Thuggery Affair*, 1965; *The Ready-made Family*, 1967; *The Player's Boy*, 1970; *The Players and the Rebels*, 1971; *The Cricket Term*, 1974]

**MARTA** the doll is made by Malkin, a powerful, envious toy-maker, as his entry for the King's Prize and as his final bid to defeat his rivals, Peter Toymaker and young Rudi. This is the first attractive toy the sinister Malkin has made, for as a rule his dolls are scowling and hideous. But Marta, despite her white skin, black hair and silky lashes, is not so different after all. After singing 'the angels' song in a voice that was sweeter than a nightingale,' the doll shows her true nature, screaming suddenly at the children who watch her, 'Pig face! ... Cowsfoot! Nutcracker! Your mother is a witch! Go and teach your grandmother to suck eggs!' Malkin cannot correct the bad strain in the doll and after she has displayed appalling bad manners at the prize-giving he forfeits the prize and goes into exile.

In the second book Marta has increased her stature (or seems to have done so) and queens it over the mountain fastness where Malkin is guarded by puppet soldiers whom his power has brought to life. She exercises her wiles on Rudi while her master is plotting to destroy the livelihood of his village, but evil is once more defeated. In the third book the doll-queen has been stirred by Rudi's honest goodness and by memories of his young brother Anders, who used to play with her. She runs away from Malkin and is found on the mountainside by Anders's two children, who take her home, believing she is a little girl. In the security of family life Marta learns to behave and, more significantly, she learns to love. In place of the key which animated her

Marta (*left*) with Anders and his children, whose
kindness helps the mechanical doll to become a
warmhearted little girl: an illustration by Shirley
Hughes in *The Toymaker's Daughter*.

as a doll, she has now earned a heart for herself and so has become in truth a child – and a good, generous one too, with the courage to return to Malkin to nurse him in his decrepit old age. The change is both believable and right in the context of a fanciful tale set in that remote folk-tale country from which the Little Wooden Horse (q.v.) also came. [Ursula Moray Williams: *The Three Toymakers*, London 1945; *Malkin's Mountain*, 1948; *The Toymaker's Daughter*, 1968]

**MARTIN HASTINGS** lives next door to Edward Frost on Barkham Street and his behaviour preys on Edward's mind to such an extent that he even enquires whether his father might not be happier working in Alaska. For Martin is a bully. Two years older than ten-year-old Edward, and considerably larger, he seldom sees his neighbour without addressing him derisively as Weird One before holding him down till he gives the word of submission – Uncle. Everything that goes amiss on Barkham Street, from ransacked nest-boxes to dogs running loose, is attributed to Martin; every disturbance in the classroom starts, somehow, with him.

In the first of two inter-related books Martin's outrageous behaviour is described from the point of view of Edward, a likable if bumptious boy whose obsession with the bully is only equalled by his passionate desire to own a dog. Indeed, when Uncle Josh, a confirmed wanderer, turns up, bringing with him a gentle, affectionate sheepdog, Edward is so far distracted from his fear of Martin that when the bully alludes to Uncle Josh as a bum, he hardly stops to think before launching himself into a fight which, oddly, leads to less rather than more aggression from next door, in spite of the fact that he is soundly defeated.

The various confrontations described in *A Dog on Barkham Street* are repeated in *The Bully of Barkham Street*, this time from Martin's point of view. We realize now that he is in a period of over-growth, that his position in a class of younger boys at school is partly due to the date of his birthday, and is not improved by his habit of escaping from his troubles into day-dreams. We realize how much the younger boy's taunts wound him and that bullying is the defence such a slow, lumbering, awkward boy would naturally adopt. We realize that his parents, both working away from home and neither of them very perceptive or affectionate, are responsible for much of his aggression, particularly because of the strong line they have taken in regard to Martin's neglected dog. 'How did a person get in a position where he didn't have any friends?' wonders Martin. Mary Stolz has answered his dismal question through the comments for and against him – comments from old Mr Eckman, who hardly enjoys being called Prune Face, from the schoolmaster Mr Foran, who is obliged to punish Martin but realizes something of his potential, from the neighbours who ironically suggest that his parents 'ought to lock him in an attic until he came of age'. The two books move easily on a wave of humour

and well-contrived incident, while they probe into some of the problems of a clash of personality. [Mary Stolz: *A Dog on Barkham Street*, New York 1960; *The Bully of Barkham Street*, 1963]

**MARTIN PIPPIN**, a wandering singer, comes to the village of Adversane in Sussex one April morning and meets a young man broadcasting seeds and weeping bitterly, for his lovely Gillian is locked with six keys into her father's well-house, with 'six young milkmaids, sworn virgins and man-haters all, to keep the keys'. Using stories and songs, riddles and games, Martin Pippin beguiles the maidens one by one and persuades each to give up her key. But in the end, strangely, it is Martin who wins the silent prisoner and not Robin Rue, lamenting outside the enclave.

Martin Pippin owed his inception to a holiday in Brittany in 1907 which filled Eleanor Farjeon with thoughts of troubadours and *aubades*. She moved the troubadour, a colourful, enigmatic and riddling fellow, into rural Sussex, for she planned *Martin Pippin in the Apple Orchard* partly for the consolation of an English soldier in France, and gave each story a setting which the exile would recognize.

As framework to the stories, which all reflect the *amour courtois* of the thirteenth century, she gives Martin long, provocative sallies with each of the six girls. The particular chaste boldness which belonged to the medieval Courts of Love seems to have spilled over into the Interludes, with their songs and dalliance, and there is a faintly enervating atmosphere in the book which recalls *Restharrow* and Mary Webb and Quilter's Merrie England tunes. Perhaps to those who met Martin when he first appeared he did seem debonair, witty and attractive: most young readers nowadays would probably think him prolix and facetious (at least in the apple-orchard, if not also in the daisy-field) and would dislike his attitude to women, whom he treats as queens and children in the same jaunty breath.

*Martin Pippin in the Apple Orchard* was probably not planned as a book for children, though its febrile emotionalism has given many adolescents the kind of pleasure they can derive also from the romantic novels of Georgette Heyer. *Martin Pippin in the Daisy Field*, a sequel written specifically for children, contains stories which are among the best of Eleanor Farjeon's offerings to the young. In this book Martin Pippin is, apparently, the father of a baby; he teases and plays with six small girls (Stella, Sally, Sophie, Selina, Sylvia and Sue) who enjoy the delightful illusion that it is they who are deceiving him and putting off their bedtime.

The teasing is light and free from the disagreeable overtones of the first book and Martin Pippin enjoys his adult jokes in an easy, acceptable way, but a surprise ending, in which we realize that he has in fact been dreaming on the day of his wedding to Gillian, abruptly turns him back into the troubadour. By introducing reality, of even such a relative kind, Eleanor Farjeon

Illustrations from *Martin Pippin in the Apple Orchard*, drawn by Richard Kennedy and from *Martin Pippin in the Daisy Field*, illustrated by Isobel and John Morton-Sale.

disturbs one with the feeling that she has packed into this ambiguous figure elements which do not truly harmonize. [Eleanor Farjeon: *Martin Pippin in the Apple Orchard*, London 1921; *Martin Pippin in the Daisy Field*, 1937]

**MARTIN THE MARTIAN** accepts the childish cognomen given to him by Cathy Brimble, for the children in the Sydney suburb to which he has descended from his distant planet can only understand him in terms familiar to them from comics and television. Martin has been sent on a short, controlled visit as part of his education and has assumed the form and speech of a human boy to make it easier for him to explore this new and interesting world.

George Adams and Cathy Brimble set themselves to make life easier for the boy, but they soon realize that Martin is no easy person to organize. His intense interest in life on Earth, his excitement over the colour and

Martin the Martian with his friends George Adams and Cathy Brimble, from the jacket of *Down to Earth*, illustrated by Margaret Horder.

pulsing activity of the city, bring him into danger. He attracts attention for his precocious language and anti-social behaviour; he is encircled by interested parties – a statistician, the Welfare workers in the district, a psychiatrist and George's inquisitive and sceptical friends, and there are many anxious moments before the alien is safely lifted away by a vessel which seems to the excited children like a blur of light.

Patricia Wrightson has followed up the possibilities of her premise skilfully. Martin has taken on something of the character of the boy he is supposed to be. He is inquisitive, cocky and as friendly as a puppy. Other traits mark his difference from the children he meets. The gentle, considerate way he treats Cathy, his occasionally patronizing manner with his new mates, his dislike of being treated as a child, all point to an intelligence developed outside our world as surely as the inconvenient fact that he glows with light when he is asleep. There are hints too, that his extra-terrestrial world is grey and inflexible; there is pathos in his excitement when he sees 'the wild, gay animals' in a child's picture lying in the old house where he shelters.

Patricia Wrightson convinces readers of Martin's identity, finally, by showing how each of the children react to him. George's hearty friendliness, Cathy's intuitive and practical attitude, Luke's insults ('A little green man! I've always wanted to see one of those!'), the inept remarks of the doctor and the platitudes of the psychiatrist – all these responses help us to believe that the boy has come from Space. His descent to Earth allows the author to make a political point; he is shocked that the children should think that his planet might want to conquer theirs. Far more important to the general theme of the book is its sad indirect comment on the inept, inconclusive way humans communicate one with another and the consolation that children do, against odds, make friends outside their own little worlds. As Martin says, George's friendship is 'one coal from the fire of Earth, to take back home with me.' The remark can be expanded to include everything from colour-prejudice to the wider thought that no man, and every man, is an island. [Patricia Wrightson: *Down to Earth*, London 1965]

**MARY ANNE** is a fine red steam shovel belonging to Mike Mulligan, whose pride in her capacities is unbounded. In the years that they have worked together on railway tracks, canals, highways and airfields they have never fallen below standard. It is sad indeed when more modern machinery makes Mary Anne redundant, but she redeems herself when she makes good Mike Mulligan's boast that she can dig the cellar for the new Town Hall at Popperville in a single day. But how are they to get out of the huge square when they have finished it?

The simple joke is greatly enhanced by Virginia Lee Burton's clever personalizing of Mary Anne in her illustrations. The addition of an eye and the suggestion of a mouth make the machine into such a real personality that it seems perfectly right that real tears should flow from it (or her) at the saddest point of the story. [Virginia Lee Burton: *Mike Mulligan and His Steam Shovel*, Boston 1939]

**MARY LENNOX** has 'a little thin face and a little thin body, thin light hair and a sour expression'. Both her bad temper and her yellow complexion are the result of a childhood in India. Her upbringing was injudicious, for her father's Government position took all his attention and her beautiful mother led a social life that left no time for a plain, cross-grained daughter. When Mary is nine her parents die in a cholera epidemic and the child is sent to live at Misselthwaite Manor in Yorkshire with her uncle. It seems as though life here will be as bleak as it has been in India. Mr Craven has shut himself up after his wife's death ten years before; though he provides for Mary's comfort, he does not want her company, and she is no more conciliatory with the servants than she has been with successive governesses in earlier years.

All the same there *is* comfort at hand for Mary. First, from Martha Sowerby, the country girl who teaches her to look after herself. Then there is Martha's young brother Dickon (q.v.), who fascinates Mary with his pipe and his tame animals, and the fretful invalid Colin (q.v.) whose temper, worse even than Mary's, makes her look critically at herself. The real cure for Mary's lonely, cantankerous nature, however, is not human. It is, simply, fresh air to promote health, and a secret to promote happiness.

There are many reasons why *The Secret Garden* is one of the best-loved of all stories for children. The garden itself, locked away for ten years, with bulbs and roses waiting to be released into life; the fresh simplicity and feeling of excitement running through the book; the two ruthless egotists in confrontation; the actual and subliminal change from dark to light, from stuffiness to fresh air, from misery to joy. Above all, here are three characters who are completely real and recognizable. Mary's tough, obstinate, wayward temperament has something basically good about it that only needs the right circumstances for it to bloom into energy and usefulness, as quickly as her sallow face freshens to a healthy pink. Frances Hodgson Burnett is surely remembering her own childhood when she describes the little gardens Mary contrived in India with a patch of mud and a handful of withered flowers and when she makes her heroine free of a garden as secret and dormant as the one she had found herself behind 'the little green door which was never unclosed' in Manchester. There are clues in the early chapters that make it per-

*Overleaf*. Two illustrations from *The Secret Garden*: the meeting between Mary and Colin and the two children with Dickon in the garden.

# The Secret Garden
## F. Hodgson-Burnett

Sarah Andrews as Mary Lennox, Andrew Harrison as Dickon and David Patterson as Colin in the BBC adaptation of *The Secret Garden*.
*Left.* The jacket of the 1951 Penguin edition of *The Secret Garden*.

fectly natural that Mary should climb out of the depths of gloom into the sunshine through her delight in weeding and sowing and freeing the old rose trees from tangled undergrowth. We can readily accept that a child like this should storm at Colin for his selfishness instead of being afraid of his hysterical fits, as the rest of the household are. We can appreciate that a child who has been both spoiled and neglected in childhood should actually have to *learn* to be interested in other people – and so forget herself. Nor will any young reader fail to see the absolute logic of Mary's remark to Dickon that he makes the fifth person that she likes. The others are his mother and Martha 'and the robin and Ben Weatherstaff'. This grouping seems no more odd to her than the fact that she has only liked five people in her life; it is one of many points through which the author shows that the change in her is subtly different from that in Colin, whose story runs parallel with hers. [Frances Hodgson Burnett: *The Secret Garden*, New York 1911]

**MARY-MARY** is so exasperated by the interfering behaviour of her elders that she announces 'When I'm a

A jacket illustration for *Mary-Mary*.

The original strip-pictures of Mary Mouse and one of Tony Linsell's illustrations for the latest edition.

lady ... I shall have lots and lots of children, but they'll all be exactly the same age. I won't have even one a little bit older than the others.' The remark is typical of her positive attitude to life: 'No, I shan't. I'll do it the other way' is the phrase most often heard on her lips – hence her nickname.

Mary-Mary is well able to make herself felt. If no-one else is at hand to support her, she will make do with her wind-up mouse Moppet; in fact he is the most satisfying person to reply to her complaints, her confidences and her self-congratulation. This small child levies on her brothers and sisters a constant emotional blackmail. It does them no good to tell her she is too young to join the New Year party, to be a guest at a wedding, to go on a visit; somehow this spiky little madam gets her own way every time. [Joan G. Robinson: *Mary-Mary*, London 1957; *More Mary-Mary*, 1958; *Madam Mary-Mary*, 1960]

**MARY MOUSE** annoys her untidy family so much by her constant sweeping and dusting that they send her away from home, but before she has time to become too miserable she spies an old dolls' house in the attic, empty and in need of a good clean. When the doll family return they are so delighted that Daddy Doll (a sailor) and small, pretty, tired Mummy Doll beg her to stay and help with the children. Even after she marries Whiskers the gardener and has six lively children she still works in the dolls' house.

Mary Mouse made her first appearance during the last war, in tiny books of strip-pictures printed on off-cuts. The miniature pictures, neat, two-coloured and unassuming, lent a certain charm to the character of Mary which was lost when the books were reprinted in an enlarged format with ostentatiously trendy illustrations. In the new presentation the thinness of narrative and characterization and the flatness of the prose became distressingly obvious, but it must be admitted that Mary had already lost some of her charm when the stories moved away from the dolls' house world and

introduced policemen, donkeys and even elephants with a bland indifference to any problem of scale. [Enid Blyton: *Mary Mouse and the Doll's House*, Leicester 1942, and many other titles]

**MARY PLAIN** lives in the bear pit at Berne in Switzerland; youngest of her generation, Mary is also the most enterprising, and her good opinion of herself grows faster than her sense. To start with she is greatly encouraged when she overhears a fur-coated lady comment 'Isn't Mary plain'; Mary promptly adopts Plain as a flattering addition. Her tricks may annoy selfish Munch and appal the aged, respectable Alpha and Lady Grizzle, but they attract attention from the Fur-Coat Lady and the Owl-Man, who sponsors Mary in the world of humans, answers her puzzled queries, patiently clears up after her various mishaps and thoroughly enjoys her company.

The basis of the numerous and popular tales about Mary Plain is, simply, the pleasure people derive from watching animals and comparing their behaviour with their own. The author confessed 'I know nothing whatsoever about the bears' real lives and habits; only through my many visits to them, they have become my friends, each with their own separate character.' She has added a discreet touch of fantasy to her descriptions of zoo animals who are well aware of being watched. Mary Plain learns to read and write; she speaks to people and is understood; she uses her paws sometimes like a bear and sometimes like a person, and there is no change needed in her physical shape when the author arranges for her to visit America, to experiment with a parachute, a rubber dinghy, a magnifying glass and so on. Droll, endearing, perfectly believable, Mary Plain is now enjoying herself as a new generation supplies an appreciative audience for her. [Gwynneth Rae: *Mostly Mary*, London 1930; *All Mary*, 1930; *Mary Plain on Holiday*, 1937; *Mary Plain in Trouble*, 1940; *Mary Plain's Big Adventure*, 1944; *Mary Plain to the Rescue*, 1950; *Mary Plain goes to America*, 1957; *Mary Plain's Whodunit*, 1965]

**MARY POPPINS** is blown through the door of Number Seventeen Cherry Tree Lane one windy evening, before Mrs Banks has even posted her advertisement for a Nannie to look after Jane and Michael and the twins, John and Barbara. Her somewhat critical manner surprises Mrs Banks, and her way of sliding 'gracefully *up* the banisters' intrigues the children. Her words are few; her suitcase, which looks empty, contains numerous necessities, including medicine which tastes differently to each child; and she promises the children, who beg her to stay for ever: 'I'll stay till the wind changes'.

Among the many positive statements with which Mary Poppins educates her charges is 'everybody's got a Fairyland of their own', but hers is exceptional, for it is, simply, the real world turned upside-down, irradiated, enlivened and revolutionized. In spite of her chronic sniff of disapproval, she has a carefully hidden sense of fun, and a sense of justice. She dispenses rewards for virtue as readily as punishments, and in both cases they are unusual and unexpected. Not that Mary

Mary Shepard's drawing of Mary Poppins and a scene from the film starring Julie Andrews.

Poppins is ever prepared to admit that anything un-usual has happened, even when her uncle's tea table rises to the ceiling with chairs round it ready for the visitors or when her compass takes the children on a lightning tour of the world. She is no vulgar waver of magic wands, even if her parrot-head umbrella seems to have unusual properties. Her inscrutable, conceited face keeps its secrets, though it does break into an occasional smile of pleasure and relax into something like affection when her charges show their need of her.

'Supposing you weren't Mary Poppins, who would you choose to be?' one of the children asks her; 'Mary Poppins' is the instant reply. It is unfortunate that film makers have decided that she should become somebody else – a conventionally pretty, whimsical young woman instead of an ageless personality looking like a Dutch doll, a stereotyped heroine as full of songs and synthetic charm as Mary Poppins is stiff and uncompromising.

Perhaps it is even out of place to suggest that Mary Poppins is an ironical composite of all the most charac-teristic attributes of that lost species, the old-fashioned Nannie. At least it would be true to say that she shares with the ideal Nannie the capacity for being always right, always having the last word and being, seemingly, immortal. [P. L. Travers: *Mary Poppins*, London 1934; *Mary Poppins Comes Back*, 1935; *Mary Poppins Opens the Door*, 1944; *Mary Poppins in the Park*, 1952]

**MATTIE** the hedgehog is born in a double hedge between two cottage gardens in a Devon village and spends her life foraging in the neighbourhood. Mating, hibernating, feeding young and pushing them into inde-pendence, she survives into her sixth year, her unusually long life being perhaps due to the man and woman who put out milk for her and put a splint on her leg when it is broken by a falling stone.

The story of Mattie is told without any trace of anthropomorphism. Her one distinguishing mark is a patch of short white bristles on one flank, due to pressure while her mother carried her to a new nest after being frightened by a cat; she is notably independent, but this is demonstrated simply in terms of her wander-ing habits. The direct, repetitive events of her six years are particularized by the descriptions of the gardens, lane and hedges in which she seeks food and shelter, by the introduction of people who observe her beha-viour and by the author's careful selection and arrange-ment of scenes. This is a moving and honest presenta-tion of an animal *as* animal. [G. D. Griffiths: *Mattie*, London 1967]

**MATTIE DOOLIN** at fifteen is broad-built and tall and dour with it; he is even silent with his friends Joe Darling and Willie Styles. The three of them are in their last term at school in South Shields and Joe and Willie are to go as apprentices to the local shipyards. Since Mattie's father, a docker, obstinately denies the value of an apprenticeship, Mattie knows it is useless to reveal his real ambition, to be a vet; besides, his school work has never been good enough. His parents refuse to take in the stray dog he rescues and to allow him to camp on the fells with Willie and Joe.

Then, sadly, the dog is run over on the very day when Mattie was taking it to be destroyed, and his remorseful parents find a camp-site for the boys on a farm in North-umberland. In little more than a week Mattie's life has taken on an entirely new direction. The more his two friends grumble at the silence of the country, the farmer's bossy manner, blistered heels, thunderstorms and the lack of shops and cinemas, the more Mattie real-izes that this is where he wants to work. After a day and a night of terror when he is lost in hill mist while

Mattie, drawn by Elsie Wrigley in *The Story of a Hedgehog*.

Margery Gill's illustration of Mattie Doolin.

searching for the farmer's young daughter, he is astonished to find himself offered a job as pupil by the man who seemed to prefer his more extrovert friends.

Among many stories about young people looking for a niche in life, *Mattie Doolin* stands out for the sturdy reality of the characters. It is a reality that comes partly from Catherine Cookson's knowledge of Tyneside, its people, streets and customs, and partly from her direct, simple way of presenting the reader with Mattie's thoughts and feelings and contrasting his reticent manner with Willie's self-conscious jokes and Joe's impetuous judgments. The same direct technique is used in a sequel, *Joe and the Gladiator*, which describes how Joe

Darling inherits a decrepit old horse and how he struggles to find the money to keep it from the knacker. The story, which ends with a surprising stroke of good fortune for Joe, completes the portraits which Catherine draws of the two lads in the first book, confirming Willie as one of those shallow practical jokers who will always somehow be excused by their mates, while Joe and Mattie in their differing ways show that traits which might seem to work against them (Mattie's inability to talk about things that matter to him, Joe's dislike of being small for his age) have really been decisive factors in making a good start in life. [Catherine Cookson: *Mattie Doolin*, London 1965; *Joe and the Gladiator*, 1968]

**MAX** wears his wolf suit one night because his mother has sent him to bed without his supper, calling him a Wild Thing. Max responds to the retributive power of the grown-up world by sailing away 'through night and day and in and out of weeks and almost over a year to where the Wild Things are'. Here his stern gaze cows the rampaging monsters; they call him 'the most wild thing of all' and make him their king. Proudly wearing his crown and brandishing his sceptre, Max joins in the wild rumpus till he suddenly 'wanted to be where someone loved him best of all'; so he sails back to his own room, 'where he found his supper waiting for him, and it was still hot'.

This classic delineation of a child's behaviour has caused more furious arguments than most picture-books. Teachers and librarians have expressed fears that the pictures, so stunning in the impact of their colour and humour, will alarm the small children to whom the book seems mainly to be directed. In fact, nobody has yet found a child who has been scared by the toothy, wistfully rampaging monsters who acknowledge the small boy as their superior. It would not be

Two illustrations by Maurice Sendak from *Where the Wild Things Are*.

difficult for any child to enjoy this reflection of his own impulses, even if he did not notice the drawing by Max at the foot of the stairs that gives the clue to the whole glorious adventure. [Maurice Sendak: *Where the Wild Things Are*, New York 1963]

**MAX MORLEY**, who is eight, finds the old house delightfully different from their former home in London and is determined to explore everything as quickly as possible. So it is that, finding a loose board near the window in the attic, he levers it up and finds twelve small, worn wooden soldiers. Hand-made, each 'carved

with his own face', the soldiers are joy enough to Max as they are; but one day, as he sets them in line and begins to beat a drum to complete the illusion, one of them suddenly comes to life and twirling energetically, 'he skipped along the ranks, punching some in the jaw, tweaking the noses of others, and tripping the feet of the most stolid'. It is the beginning of a time of joyous secrecy, of alarm and anxious planning.

Before long Max's parents, fascinated by the toys, begin to think that, with the house being so near to Haworth, they might be the very soldiers that Branwell

Max Morley's wooden soldiers make their way to the Haworth Museum, carrying their equipment on a roller skate; an illustration by Cecil Leslie.

Brontë was given when *he* was eight and round which he and his sisters wove their stories of the Twelves. Mr and Mrs Morley and the vicar, a Brontë fan, develop the theory from literary evidence: Max proves it by talking with the soldiers, and it is often difficult for him to explain the new and convincing facts that he repeats downstairs. In the roundabout way of such matters, a letter in the newspaper from an American professor, suggesting the value to literature if the soldiers could be found, coincides with local rumours about Max's find. His older brother Philip impetuously cables to America, reporters begin to sniff a news story, and the Twelve wisely decide to leave the attic. After an eventful and dangerous journey by road (on one of Max's roller-skates), by water (navigating a stream on a plank) and finally in triumphant drumbeat procession through the window of the Haworth Museum, the soldiers endowed with life by the Brontës and woken by Max find safety at last.

The characters of the Twelve are of course borrowed from *The History of the Young Men.* Butter Crashey the patriarch, with his dignified mode of speech; Stumps, often lost, with 'his round, turnipy head, and his stumpy,

rather bandy legs', who has a second identity as Frederick Guelph, Duke of York; the tall, dominating soldier, once a trumpeter, then honoured by Charlotte Brontë as Arthur Wellesley, Duke of Wellington; Gravey the doctor; Parry and Ross the intrepid explorers; the ambivalent Sneaky, 'ingenious, artful, deceitful and courageous' – Pauline Clarke has chosen scenes and episodes so that the personalities lent to the toys by the Brontë children can reveal themselves gradually in action and in speech.

Thus half the characters in her fantasy are derivative – brilliantly so. The other half illustrate an underlying theme, of respect for the individual. The attitude of the Morley children (and of their parents and neighbours) to the Twelve, tells us something about their natures. Max has the right kind of imagination to be chosen as a successor to the Genii; he believes in his games and in the animate lives of the Twelve. He realizes at once that they are people in their own right. He knows that he must not carry them down from the attic to the kitchen, but must give them the means (in this case, string tied along the banister rails) to find a way down for themselves. He never allows his sense of wonder to stop him from being tactful and respectful in his dealings with them. His sister Jane, who finds out by accident that the soldiers can come ́alive, is gentle and careful with them, and is admitted at once as one of the Genii, but Philip, who is old enough to be aware of the power of money, is accepted less readily. His remorse when he does find out who and what the soldiers are is what one would expect from this thoughtless but honest boy. In a sense the Twelve are a kind of testing point and the three children (as well as the vicar, who is allowed to see the soldiers marching to Haworth and accepts the marvel as a matter of faith) are each revealed in their true light by this magical and totally believable happening. [Pauline Clarke: *The Twelve and the Genii*, London 1962]

**MEDLEY PLASHET**'s unusual Christian name is chosen by his father, the solitary, mysterious Dick Plashet (q.v.), because 'his fortunes are a medley' and because when he is born he is wrapped in a coverlet of tawny-medley from the bed. As a boy Medley shares lessons with Roger Mallory, son of Lewis and Cecily (q.v.), together with the sons of the miller and an iron-founder in the neighbourhood. A small village has grown up round Mantlemass, the forest is slowly being cleared as iron eats up timber, but the Mallorys are still country folk. Medley is accepted almost as a member of the family, in spite of the difference in his breeding.

He is content with his life until his father leaves the family inexplicably and the superstitious villagers, always jealous of his mother's reserve, attack her as a witch and accidentally cause her death.

The lad is taken to live at Mantlemass and becomes secretary to Lewis Mallory. His old friendship with Roger deepens and so does the old teasing friendship with Catherine, whose nickname of Puss suits her cheerful, independent nature. Simon, the eldest Mallory, has been somewhat changed by a sojourn at court and tries to discourage the family's kindness to the boy, but Puss is firm that she will marry 'none but Melly' and her mother, mindful of her own unhappy childhood, determines that she shall marry for love. When Medley finds his father and learns of his birth and inheritance, all is happily settled and he becomes in due course master of Mantlemass. Here is another character who ensures the continuity of theme and plot in the Mantlemass books. Small, telling details constantly remind us of Medley's Plantagenet blood and his ambiguous status in the complex world of the late fifteenth century, and when he is finally seen as an old man (in *A Cold Wind Blowing*) there is no break in the reader's sure knowledge of him. [Barbara Willard: *The Sprig of Broom*, London 1971; *A Cold Wind Blowing*, 1972]

**MEG** the witch and her cat **MOG** form a traditional partnership but although Meg also possesses such necessary accessories as a broomstick and a cauldron, she is not very adept at casting spells. When she collects lizards, newts and frogs' legs to stir together for supper,

Meg the witch in the story *Meg's Eggs*, illustrated by Jan Pienkowski.

the result *is* eggs as she has planned but of unusual size and texture, and the dinosaurs that hatch out of them are somewhat troublesome until she finds a way to reduce them in size. Her spell to bring a wind when she and Mog go boating raises a storm that wrecks them on a lonely island and it is probably the ingredient Meg contributes to the Hallowe'en brew that turns her fellow witches into mice, which Mog tactlessly chases.

In these and other short, sharp adventures the caricature of a witch has been confirmed and extended by Jan Pienkowski, who has put aside his elegant linear magic for a strong, comic line which is dramatically descriptive of the absurdities of Meg and Mog. [Helen Nicoll: *Meg and Mog*, London 1972; *Meg's Eggs*, 1972; *Meg at Sea*, 1973; *Meg on the Moon*, 1973]

**MELENDYS** (the) – Mona, Rush, Randy (Miranda) and Oliver – who live in New York, decide to pool their weekly allowances and take it in turns to use the accumulated dollar and a half to pursue their particular interests on lesson-free Saturdays. Randy, who is ten, visits a picture-gallery and enjoys a luxurious tea with an old family friend whose reminiscences prove unexpectedly enthralling; Rush, a twelve-year-old with musical talents, goes to the opera and picks up a stray dog on the way home; Mona, who feels that plaits are childish when you are thirteen, nerves herself to have them cut off at an expensive Broadway establishment; while Oliver, indignant at being thought too young at six to enjoy an adventure by himself, quietly takes himself to the circus in Madison Square Gardens, and is

The Melendy children from *The Saturdays,* written and illustrated by Elizabeth Enright.

A scene from *In the Night Kitchen,* written and illustrated by Maurice Sendak.

brought home, bilious but rejoicing, on a police horse.

The Melendy children have individual voices and a communal voice as members of a united, if argumentative, family. When they move to the country to a house full of architectural aberrations, they quickly discover new possibilities for adventure. There is room in their lives (*Then There Were Five*) for Mark Herron, a schoolfellow whose miserable life with a miserly cousin is changed through their efficient interference, and when Mona and Rush go to boarding school (*Spiderweb for Two*) they arrange a treasure-hunt for their juniors which lasts from September to Christmas and leads to sundry accidents and discoveries.

Though the freedom of the countryside has been somewhat curtailed since the Melendys began their fictional lives, and a dollar and a half would finance little enough nowadays, the fresh, lively chatter of the books has not dated. Elizabeth Enright brings the Melendys to life through their appearance, their likes and dislikes and the way they change as they grow older, and has given them substance by a domestic background that does much to explain their warm-hearted, rackety, intelligent attitude to life. [Elizabeth Enright: *The Saturdays*, New York 1941; *The Four-Storey Mistake*, 1942; *Then There Were Five*, 1944; *Spiderweb for Two*, 1951]

**MICKEY**, waking in the night, 'fell through the dark, out of his clothes, past the moon and his Mama and Papa sleeping tight into the light of the Night Kitchen', where three identical bakers seize on him and mix him in their cake batter; but Mickey moulds the bread dough into a strange flying-machine on which he soars into the Milky Way to find the missing ingredient, so that the cake can be finished.

This artfully artless tale has been interpreted variously. The puritanical have raised eyebrows at what seems to them a masturbatory fantasy and have objected to the first full frontal nude child to appear in a picture-book. Many dislike the drabness of colour and the very unpretty treatment of the small hero, though few would deny the vigour of the expressions of amazement, sensuous joy, mischief and determination that sweep over Mickey's face. Sendak himself has pointed to the comics of his youth as one, perhaps the most important, source of the style and techniques he has used in the books, and the figures of the cooks, each with the unmistakable blob nose and sagging chins of Oliver

*Right above*. An illustration by Arnold Lobel from *The Strange Disappearance of Arthur Cluck*.
*Right Below*. Max confronts the monsters, illustrated by Maurice Sendak in *Where the Wild Things Are*.

Hardy, belong to the same period. [Maurice Sendak: *In the Night Kitchen*, New York 1970]

**MILLY-MOLLY-MANDY** had 'a Father, and a Mother, and a Grandpa, and a Grandma, and an Uncle, and an Aunty; and they all lived together in a nice white cottage with a thatched roof'. So begins the chronicle of the doings of Millicent Margaret Amanda, who, under the conveniently shortened version of her impressive name, became the model or secret playfellow of hundreds of children in the past that now seems almost as remote as history. But not quite. Small children still enjoy sewing with small bright pieces of material or making pastry men with currants for buttons or paddling in a stream or stamping in snow. Milly-Molly-Mandy's delightfully detailed domestic adventures outlast changes in fashion and coinage. [Joyce Lankester Brisley: *Milly-Molly-Mandy Stories*, London 1928; *More of Milly-Molly-Mandy*, 1929; *Further Doings of Milly-Molly-Mandy*, 1932; *Milly-Molly-Mandy Again*, 1948]

**MILO**, an American schoolboy, 'didn't know what to do with himself – not just sometimes, but always'. For lack of good teaching 'he regarded the process of seeking knowledge as the greatest waste of time of all'. A mysterious parcel changes all this. Inside is a tolbooth kit including traffic signs, coins for paying tolls, a map and a book of 'rules and traffic regulations, which may not be bent or broken'. In his pedal car Milo embarks on a journey that takes him to the kingdoms of Dictionopolis and Digitopolis and on a traditional venture to rescue the Princesses Rhyme and Reason, immured in the Mountains of Ignorance. Prominent among the sturdy, one-dimensional types in this witty allegory are Milo's travelling companions, Tock the watchdog and the Humbug, a beguiling beetle dressed in fashionable con-man dress, who is occasionally helpful.

Like Alice, Milo is the peripatetic centre of bizarre events, but he lacks the good sense and nursery logic of that Victorian paragon. The educational framework of the story, light-hearted though it is, demands that Milo should make mistakes in his vacillating drive towards learning. In the market-place of Dictionopolis he is tempted to purchase the words 'quagmire', 'flabbergast' and 'upholstery', expensive though they are: 'he had no idea what they meant, but they looked very grand and elegant'. However, good manners and determination bring him victory in the end. He becomes not a learned child but a child who wants to learn and admits that he need not regret the disappearance of the Tolbooth, for 'There's just so much to do here' that he will have no time for another trip. [Norton Juster: *The Phantom Tolbooth*, New York 1961]

**MISS BIANCA**, a very small mouse with a 'sleek, silvery-white coat' as soft and rich as ermine, lives in a porcelain pagoda. She belongs to an Ambassador's son and is accustomed to travel, mainly by air, in the Diplomatic Bag. Her life is excessively sheltered. She would be the last to credit that she would set out on an adventure by boat, cart, raft, wagon and other plebeian means of transport, in the company of Nils, a blunt Norwegian mouse, and of Bernard, secretary of the Mouse Prisoners' Aid Society, a 'short, sturdy young mouse' who works in the Embassy pantry and whose respect for the beautiful Miss Bianca makes him almost speechless. Yet so it is – for the Society has resolved to suspend its usual role of becoming the pets of prisoners to attempt an actual rescue, and since Miss Bianca's Boy is taken with his family to Norway, she becomes an essential part of the first attempt, to free a Norwegian poet from a Black Castle somewhere in the middle of Europe.

Miss Bianca and Bernard have somewhat different attitudes towards the adventure. Miss Bianca (after fainting, writing poetry and doubting her courage) packs 'a small hand-valise containing toilet-articles and a fan', while Bernard takes 'a stout cudgel and an iron ration of sealing-wax tied up in a large spotted handkerchief'. But although both Nils and Bernard are at pains to protect their refined companion, Miss Bianca's vanity gives her a self-confidence which can even at times be termed courage.

The adventure of the Black Castle, terrifying though it is, gives Miss Bianca a taste for action; she can no longer be content with a pampered existence at the Embassy, and in due course she plays a major part in the rescue of a small boy from a salt-mine, of another from an Indian palace where he is treated as a slave, and of a small girl who is cruelly exploited by a loathly Duchess in a Diamond Palace. On these adventures, and in dangerous journeys to the Antarctic and through the sewers of the Embassy, Bernard remains Miss Bianca's respectful and devoted admirer, and she gently but firmly keeps him in his place. The delightful contradictions in her character provide some of the wittiest moments in the stories. When she faces the bloodhounds Tyrant and Torment (in *Miss Bianca*) she feels no sense of fear: they are so obviously her social inferiors. When they offer her a seat that 'appeared to be a particularly well-scrubbed ivory bench', she tells herself, 'I must *not* look like the Colonel's wife visiting Married Quarters', and so she forces herself not to examine, till later, the 'very small shin-bone – gnawed', on which she has been invited to sit.

The satirical darts in these incomparable comic fantasies are skilfully aimed at human institutions and follies, but they would have less point without the beautifully sustained characters of the accomplished Chairwoman of the MPAS and the efficient secretary. The projects of the Society almost always start with a formal meeting, for, as the author remarks in parenthesis, 'Corporation rules and regulations, order and decorum, provide a solid foundation for individual

An illustration by David Gentleman for Kipling's *Jungle Book*.

A sorrowful Miss Bianca, drawn by Garth Williams for *The Turret*.

Miss Bianca presides over a meeting of the MPAS, drawn by Garth Williams for *Miss Bianca in the Salt Mines*.

heroism'. Just so, it must be allowed, order and decorum provide the literary foundation for the wit and humour, the sly incongruity of detail, in these stories. The quality of Margery Sharp's prose and the economy of her wit make her stories, and her characters, unique. So recognizable are the characters that they really need no illustrator, but one would hate to do without Garth Williams's view of Miss Bianca wiping a tear away gracefully with her tail (in *The Turret*) or climbing, still gracefully, the ivy of Mandrake's prison. Perhaps Garth Williams understood rather better than Judy Brook (who illustrated the first book in the sequence) or Erik Blegvad (who has illustrated the last three) the subtle mixture of naturalism and fancy which is needed if we are to see Miss Bianca and Bernard as their creator described and developed them in words. [Margery Sharp: *The Rescuers*, London 1959; *Miss Bianca*, 1962; *The Turret*, 1964; *Miss Bianca in the Salt Mines*, 1966; *Miss Bianca in the Orient*, 1970; *Miss Bianca in the Antarctic*, 1972; *Miss Bianca and the Bridesmaid*, 1972]

**MISS EGLANTINE PRICE** rides round her Bedfordshire village on her high bicycle visiting the sick, her grey coat and skirt and Liberty silk scarf, her pointed nose and skinny appearance, seeming to define her as a typical English spinster. But Miss Price is studying to be a witch. Carey and Charles find that their little brother Paul has woken in the middle of the night to see Miss Price riding her broomstick (wobbling a bit but with increasing confidence). When the three children get to know her and she calmly admits that she is leading a double life, they expect her to behave like a fairy-tale witch, but Miss Price's surprising skills have not changed her nature. Her work-room, with its glass jars and newt's eyes and hare's feet, her neatly labelled books of spells and incantations (*not* the same thing, she tells the children pedantically), her zodiac signs and skulls and stuffed alligator, have obviously been arranged by a careful housewife. Carey complains that it is 'very hygienic', to which she replies reprovingly 'Method and prophylactics have revolutionized modern witchcraft.' Nor does she alter her ingrained middle-class attitudes after she has contrived for Paul that one of the knobs on his bedstead shall take the children where they wish in the present or the past. When she joins them in an expedition to a South Sea island she is equipped with a string bag containing ginger-pop, hard-boiled eggs and sandwiches; she

Miss Eglantine Price as a demure spinster cyclist and in her other role (*overleaf*) as a witch who can travel back in time; drawings by Erik Blegvad in *Bedknob and Broomstick*.

carries also her umbrella and the mosquito-netted sun-helmet her father had in Poona in '99, and her demeanour when she competes with the cannibal witch-doctor is a masterpiece of class-conscious dignity.

When the children visit Miss Price again two years later, she cannot resist giving the bed-knob 'a little twist' to see if it still works. The children's trip to the London of 1666 decides her future once and for all. Compassion and hospitality alike oblige her to help Emelius Jones, a necromancer 'old before his time'. Miss Price quickly recognizes a kindred soul and transports herself to the seventeenth century as Mr Jones's wife and help-meet, leaving her possessions to be sold for the Red Cross and turning her back for ever on music lessons and benevolent visits. The touch of tart satire, not un-sympathetic towards that butt of fiction, the single English gentlewoman, adds something adult to the happy humour of these popular fantasy-adventures. [Mary Norton: *The Magic Bedknob*, London 1945; *Bonfires and Broomsticks*, 1947; revised in a single volume, *Bedknob and Broomstick*, 1957]

**MISS PUSSY** has seven brothers and sisters and as the only spinster aunt she is much in demand from numerous nephews and nieces. When the unpleasant joker Mr Jackanapes (q.v.) fills her enormous apple pie with frogs, having shared the inside with his boon companion Snatch, the frogs turn themselves into an orchestra and lead Miss Pussy and the kittens to a greensward where a magnificent feast is spread for them.

Miss Pussy has many of the attributes of a cat while walking on two feet and dressing like a lady. She begins as a typical folk-tale animal, humanized but with no particular traits of character. In 'Poor Pussy gets a Husband' (a story in *The Golden Hen*) she is jilted on the eve of her wedding to Old Tom Cat, and sits by the road-side lamenting till Reynard the fox offers her a number of suitors – dog, bull, cock, frog and the fox himself; she chooses Master Malkin from her own race and they are happily married. In later stories we find that in fact she has not married but has remained friendly with Old Tom Cat, whose bachelorhood she sustains now and then with a pie or a new shirt.

Indeed, her life might be almost soporific if it were not for the ubiquitous Jackanapes, who takes every means he can to disturb her calm – not by such simple tripartite tricks as he uses in the folk-tale-style 'Miss Pussy and Old Jackanapes'(a story in *The Wild Cherry*) but with elaborate stratagems worked out at great length and clearly showing the personalities of the two animals. Miss Pussy has infinite tolerance for Mr Jack-anapes. She is compassionate by nature and even when she suspects the ape's intentions she gives him the benefit of the doubt for, as she says, 'even in the heart of the basest and most trivial of creatures hidden springs of virtue may lie.'

Through the five collections of stories about Miss Pussy, Diana Ross, abetted by her illustrators, has made

The wedding of Miss Pussy, drawn by Gri for *The Golden Hen.*

A more humanized view of Miss Pussy by Shirley Hughes.

her increasingly human. She sews exquisitely, takes tea from Coalport dishes, sees her brother Tibert and his first wife through the first confinement and helps the Squire's lady with benevolent duties in the village. On her visits to the seaside town of Leamouth she enjoys a lobster tea 'to the strains of Offenbach' with her niece Selina.

The strain of sententiousness in Miss Pussy's character represents, I think, not satire but a gently whimsical look back at the moralistic trend in fantasy in the last century. In the last of the many confrontations between Miss Pussy and Jackanapes, the unscrupulous ape falls genuinely ill and Miss Pussy, returning home after nursing him back to his usual state of sly opportunism, realizes that she would not care to live without having him somewhere in her life; 'perhaps in the pattern of our lives we need the bad as much as the good.' In the evolution of the character of this charming cat, favoured by the fairies and accepted by everyone in the village, Diana Ross has tried an unusual experiment in fantasy, at once sophisticated, philosophical and coloured by magic. [Diana Ross: *The Golden Hen*, London 1942; *The Wild Cherry*, 1943; *The Enormous Apple Pie*, 1951; *The Bran Tub*, 1954; *The Merry Go Round*, 1963]

**MISSEE LEE** has succeeded her pirate father as ruler of three islands off the coast of China. The tiny Chinese woman has a personality which amply justifies her meed of a twenty-two gong salute, where her allies Tycoon Chang of Tiger Island and Tycoon Wu of Turtle Island rate only ten apiece. This inscrutable, indomitable lady has inherited from her mandarin grandfather a taste for learning fostered by a Western education in Hong Kong and England. To her sorrow, this had ended after only one year at Cambridge. When the Swallows and Amazons, with 'Captain Flint' (q.v.), are stranded on her coast she seizes on the English party as victims for her pent-up intellectual energy. No Chinese tortures here, but daily Latin lessons in which Missee Lee shows herself to be a remorselessly firm but excellent teacher.

This fascinating character, with her entourage, her new junk, her Cambridge breakfasts of ham and eggs and Oxford marmalade, is the composite creation of Walkers and Blacketts with their Uncle Jim. The story of Missee Lee was presumably told through a winter, perhaps the winter after their *Pigeon Post* adventure. Like *Peter Duck* it is fantasy developed from fiction, and it is amusing to speculate on the contribution made by each of Ransome's characters. Perhaps it is the sensitive Titty (q.v.) who realizes that Missee Lee would help them to escape not only because of her nostalgic feeling for England but also because she would naturally hide a womanly heart behind her pistol and her cold dominance of any situation. If at first (as Roger (q.v.) comments) 'she looked at us as if we were pet rabbits', she is later brought to admit the claims of that family solidarity which is the basis of all the Ransome stories and which would therefore be essential also to the stories which he allowed his characters to invent. [Arthur Ransome: *Missee Lee*, London 1941]

**MISTER** is the surrogate name which Samantha Morris gives to her black and white dog Radnor when it is endowed with the personality of a man. Sam, looking out of the classroom window, has noticed a man apparently walking *through* the door of the garage opposite. She and her friends Duncan and Kate Saumarez follow the man and discover him with a group of associates who have come from a thousand years in the future for refuge and are now building a time-machine so that they can return and overthrow the power of the Galas, or secret police, who rule their world. Because Justin, by being observed, has destroyed their secrecy, his intelligence is exchanged with that of the dog, as a punishment and as a guarantee that the children will not betray them.

Before long the children discover that some of the Galas have found their way to Earth. In the hiding, chasing and confrontations that follow, Mister the Dog-man plays an active part. The idea of a dog with a man's brain gives a certain piquancy to the story and dulls the edge of terror in certain scenes. It was perhaps for these reasons, and as an unusual twist, that Peter Dickinson built the idea of a man-dog switch into his BBC television screen-play. There is a real sense, in the book, of the discomfort and mental unease of the man, trapped as he is in an animal's body but with a man's recognition of danger. This experiment in psychology is far more than a mere gimmick in an adventure story. [Lois Lamplugh and Peter Dickinson: *Mandog*, London 1972]

**MOFFATTS** (the) – Sylvie, Joey, Jane and Rufus – live in the small New England town of Cranbury. In their daily doings from 1916 to 1918 they remain consistent in their given characters. Sylvie, always neat and self-assured, moves from piano practice and amateur theatricals at fifteen to become engaged when she is seventeen; her part in the stories, a minor one, is that of the responsible elder sister. Joey, too, as he moves from a noisy twelve to a more thoughtful fourteen, mainly appears as a foil to Jane, two years his junior.

Jane is a child of impulse and imagination, constantly making interesting discoveries; when she looks at places upside down from between her legs they seem clearer and brighter altogether; when she sits on the hitching post outside the house she can see both ends of their curving street; she is the only member of the family who is not introduced with a qualifying word – 'the oldest' or 'the youngest'. It is this last discovery that inspires Jane to call herself the Middle Moffatt and occasionally (owing to a misunderstanding on the part of the oldest inhabitant) the Mysterious Middle Moffatt. Jane's daydreams sometimes lead to trouble. She advertises a recital on the little parlour organ a neighbour has given her, forgetting in her enthusiasm that she has never learned to play; she plans to read all the books in the local

The Moffats, drawn by Louis Slobodkin.

library – in alphabetical order. Always hoping to surprise people – by learning how to read 'with expression', by becoming a champion basket-ball player – Jane lives every moment of life to the full.

Rufus fills out the years between five and seven pretty successfully too. He is one of those impatient small boys who keep up with their elders somehow, learning by imitation, an inner certainty consoling them for their mistakes. Rufus is astonished that his friend Hughie refuses to go to school; he has hardly known how to wait till he is old enough. He learns to write his name in a day when he finds that getting books out of the library is not as simple as he thought. Life has its disappointments for Rufus but he takes philosophically even the sad discovery that Mrs Saybolt's new piano has no invisible pianist but is merely a machine. He is content to play to himself when the others are occupied, especially as he has his 'cardboard boy', a grocer's advertisement, to chat to if he is lonely. His solo expedition to the local funfair with cardboard Jimmy and his apostrophes to him are among the most comical clues to his character.

The characters of the Moffatts, especially Jane and Rufus, are based on a selective cumulation of episodes familiar to any family. Innumerable small girls, in or out of fiction, have longed for real curls, or suffered the pangs and excitements of moving house; innumerable small boys have dug up seeds to see if they were growing or looked under a railway bridge in ecstatic terror. The Moffatts do all these things and more. They acquire

their solidity through the very natural snatches of talk among themselves and with their elders, and from the meticulously drawn background of their home, of Cranbury folk and Cranbury streets and Cranbury customs of half a century ago. [Eleanor Estes: *The Moffatts*, New York 1941; *The Middle Moffatt*, 1942; *Rufus M.*, 1943]

**MOLE** *see* TOAD OF TOAD HALL

**MOOMINS** (the) are an expandable family. To the basic unit of Moominpappa, Moominmamma and Moomintroll (with the Ancestor Troll who lives behind the stove and is never seen) must be added the disconcerting Little My, the Snork brother and sister (who are like Moomins except that they are not white) and the little rodent Sniff. Snufkin is a regular summer visitor and philosophical Too-ticky camps in the bath-house in winter. The hospitality of Moomin-valley comes partly from Moomintroll's gregarious nature and partly from the warmth and inner certainty that bring so many lost, lonely or confused individuals to seek reassurance from Moominmamma.

Fantastic and comic as these invented creatures are, they express certain basic ideas about human behaviour – people's responsibility to one another, the right to be private and so on. Behind the original, entrancing world of the Moomins one can also see the shadows of a Scandinavian landscape and folk lore. It seems that the Moomins have evolved from a race of trolls but now, instead of being hairy, nocturnal and hostile, they are tubby, benevolent, sunshine-loving animals, not unlike small hippopotamuses; they live in a house of conventional shape with conventional furniture, but they go into hibernation in November and sleep till spring. The friends and neighbours of the Moomins are as diverse and original as they are themselves. Fillyjonk looks like a demented dog on its hind legs; the Mymbles are bold little girls with their hair in topknots; and the Hemulens, who drift singly in and out of the stories, are as much like Moomins (though melancholy) as the Snorks, whose background is never explained. Agreeable mystery attaches to all the characters, but most of all to the Hattifatteners, who look like animated candles, without hearing or speech but able to recharge their energies during thunderstorms.

Moomintroll's eager curiosity initiates most of the action in the books. He sets out to find the observatory where he may find out about the comet which threatens danger to the valley; he is lost and found again in a flood which also introduces the Moomins to the astonishing world of the theatre; he experiments dangerously with the Hobgoblin's hat; he tries to make friends with the silent Groke, who freezes everything she touches. Meanwhile his father, an erratic and self-absorbed character, writes (and reads aloud) his Memoirs, and tries to find a new life on a lighthouse island where he has to face his own deficiencies. With grace, elegance and wit Tove Jansson carries us through her stories into odd corners

Characters from the Moomin series invented by Tove Jansson: Moominpappa, Moomintroll and Moominmamma, Moomintroll and the Groke.

Hemulen (*left*) and Snorkmaiden with Fillyjonk.

Snuffkin (*left*), Sniff (*below*) and Little My (*above*).

of life and makes pertinent comments on humanity. We have it on her own authority that the characters are based on her own family and friends; they are emphatically not human types. Fillyjonk is one particular obsessed housewife, with her wayward view of life; Little My is not just everybody's naughty little sister, but a unique, crabby, critical, deflatory child; the Hemulens are all bureaucratic and bossy, but each in different ways and with different degrees of melancholy; Snufkin is not 'the artist' but an individual whose music is made in solitude but nourished by his unpossessive friendships. Through these characters Tove Jansson has taken a wry, sympathetic and very straight look at the deepest and most personal philosophies of people in a community. [Tove Jansson: *Finn Family Moomintroll* (1948 Finland), London 1950; *Comet in Moominland*, 1951, both trans. Elizabeth Portch; *The Exploits of Moominpappa*, 1952, *Moomin, Mymble and Little My*, 1953, *Moominland Midwinter*, 1958, *Who will comfort Toffle?*, 1961, *Tales from Moominvalley*, 1963, *Moominpappa at Sea*, 1966, all trans. Thomas Warburton; *Moominvalley in November*, 1971, trans. Kingsley Hart. Language of originals is Swedish. First in series was *Kometjakten* (*Comet in Moominland*) 1946]

**MOONTA** is ashamed that he has reached the age of nine without being able to skate, for in the 'northernmost village in the northernmost province of the Neth-

Moonta, the Dutch boy, drawn by Nancy Grossman for *Far Out the Long Canal*.

erlands' it is always said that you skate before you walk. Though the boy's inadequacy is due to illness, because his parents are the village champions he sets himself determinedly to put matters right. False hopes as the ice forms and then melts again, rebukes that seem bitterly unjust ('Just because you were sick doesn't mean that a big kid like you can windmill around on these ditches and knock all the little kids black and blue'), hard falls, the ignominy of skating with a chair in front of everyone – Moonta doggedly accepts these and other setbacks and achieves a measure of stability. His father promises to take him to a mysterious distant goal he has heard people talk about – the New Church's Pipe; but Grandpa is set on doing the Eleven-Towns Tour of the province with his daughter and son-in-law. It will be a day and an evening gone, and tomorrow the ice may not hold. Angry and obstinate, Moonta strikes out alone to find the strangely-named landmark.

The story of Moonta has the feel of Dutch air and the sound of Dutch voices in it and, round and through and beneath everything, the sturdy figure of a boy fighting to equip himself for action and to catch up his peers. Here is a boy's voice persuading, complaining and enquiring; here are a boy's unspoken words to himself, setting himself a challenge and urging himself to rise to it; here is a boy's happiness, with parents who are proud of him and with the promise of pea soup for supper and

the forecast of ice on Monday. [Meindert de Jong: *Far Out the Long Canal*, New York 1964]

**MOORLAND MOUSIE**, a sturdy Exmoor pony, is caught with his cousin Tinker Bell in a drive and the two ponies are sold to the Coke family. Life at Wooten is organized and happy, for Patience and her brother Michael understand and love horses, and when three years have passed there is Old Jem to undertake the breaking-in. Unfortunately Mousie bolts at the end of a gallop and it is decided that he is too excitable to make a child's pony.

Sold for harness work, Mousie endures a period pulling first a butcher's, then a greengrocer's cart in the town, but he is rescued by Patience, whose care and good sense make him into a suitable mount for young Jack, who is inclined to be a nervous rider. The rest of Mousie's story, which he tells himself, consists of a series of treks, days in the hunting field and encounters with various horses and people.

The two stories of the Exmoor pony stand in an interesting position midway between *Black Beauty* and the latest gymkhana formula-story. The course of Mousie's life is varied by the autobiographies of other horses – including Lorna with her fat owner Flabbers, the pony Dawn whose temper was ruined by a stupid gardener's boy, the circus pony Midget and the chestnut mare cruelly rigged for racing.

As in *Black Beauty*, every episode in the Mousie books demonstrates some aspect of horsemanship or horse management. Mousie speaks from his point of view about the difference between Patience's deliberate, consistent style of riding and Michael's tougher treatment of Tinker Bell; he expresses a horse's view of road traffic, of changes from winter to summer feeding, of the etiquette of the hunting field. The autobiographical framework of the Mousie books was not imitated in the flood of pony stories which followed them, for the pony-mad readers of the '40s and '50s wanted to be able to identify with fortunate pony-owners, and horse-characters were now seen through the eyes of their riders. Inquisitive, dauntless, affectionate Mousie is a rare case of a genuine pony personality. ['Golden Gorse': *Moorland Mousie*, London 1929; *Older Mousie*, 1932]

**MOPSA THE FAIRY**, when Jack finds her in a bird's nest, is small enough to fit comfortably in his pocket: at the end of the journey they share she is a tall young woman, dressed superbly in a white satin gown with 'a little crown made of daisies', with a kingdom to rule and with a double of Jack to keep her company when he goes home to Earth again. But the essential Mopsa remains dependent on Jack, even when she is called upon to grow up and make decisions, and perhaps her affectionate, feminine character is needed in a story which, inside its fairy adventure, is really about a boy growing out of a heedless love of adventure through the need to protect someone weaker than himself. With her

graceful, submissive ways Mopsa, fairy though she may be, seems in fact an idealized picture of young womanhood, drawn for the delectation of the children of Victoria's time. [Jean Ingelow: *Mopsa the Fairy*, London 1869]

**MORTIMER** the raven is found in the street one stormy March night by 'a respectable taxi-driver named Mr Ebenezer Jones', who sees the bird hit by a motorcycle passing at reckless speed. Mr Jones takes the bird back to Number Six, Rainwater Crescent. It makes a bad start, eating its way through the contents of the refrigerator where he has shut it by mistake; but next morning his daughter Arabel seizes on it with delight, announcing: 'His name's Mortimer'. Although under school age, Arabel has a strong will and a good grasp of essentials. It seems to her perfectly reasonable that Mortimer should eat the bottom three stairs and the escalators at Rumbury Tube Station, or that he should be expensively obsessed by slot-machines, and one day prefer the breadbin to the coal-scuttle as a bed. She and Mortimer understand one another: those who do not (like her horrible cousins Cindy, Lindy and Mindy) get pecked.

The three five-part stories about Mortimer were first written for the BBC television programme *Jackanory*, and Bernard Cribbins, as narrator, should take part of the credit for Mortimer. Quentin Blake did wonders for the bird in his illustrations for the printed books, with the position of a feather or the direction of one of the bird's beady eyes. To Joan Aiken goes the credit for inventing two personalities as complementary as Arabel and Mortimer. Nonsense and verisimilitude, parody and deadpan statement, verbal wit and throwaway drama, a whole bag of literary tricks, have gone into her accounts of the disasters caused by the two small, determined allies, the doll-like, rock-like Arabel Jones and the hairy-beaked Mortimer, whose sepulchral croak and one word, 'Nevermore', (picked up from the postman) say all that needs to be said. [Joan Aiken: *Arabel's Raven*, London 1972; *The Escaped Black Mamba*, 1973; *The Bread Bin*, 1974; omnibus edition, *Tales of Arabel's Raven*, London 1974]

**MOULDIWARP** (the) appears to Edred and Elfrida Arden when they use an old spell to call up 'the Badge of Arden's house'. Edred, heir to old Lord Arden, and a proud boy, is tired of the restricted life they have had to lead since their father and their aunt's fiancé disappeared on an expedition in South America. His pride suffers more severely after the white mole which appears so unexpectedly fiercely complains of being obliged to 'make *him* brave and wise and show him the treasure'. The cantankerous little animal regards it as his personal duty to correct the boy's good opinion of himself.

Since the old spell has been correctly pronounced, the

Mouldiwarp must try to help the children to find a treasure, lost in the forgotten past, which could restore the Arden fortunes. Even while the children are talking to this strange representative of the family, Edred has succeeded to the title, for when they reach home they learn that old Lord Arden is dead. The brother and sister are sent into the past through the magic power of the Mouldiwarp, to become Arden children in the time of Henry VIII and of Queen Anne, in Regency England and at the time of Guy Fawkes. Sarcastic and grumbling, the Mouldiwarp protects them from danger, resolves their confusions, compounds their quarrels, and so far succeeds in influencing the self-centred Edred that in the end he is ready to admit what Elfrida joyously proclaims, that the return of their father is worth all the treasures in the world.

In their visit to the England of King James I, Edred and Elfrida become friendly with their cousin Richard, and in *Harding's Luck* Edith Nesbit uses a time-switch again to tell the story of Dickie Harding, a lame waif in Edwardian London whose disability is exploited by the shiftless tramp Beale. Dickie's only possessions, an old silver rattle and a cornelian seal, both bear the 'badge of Arden's house' and, like Edred and Elfrida, the boy happens by chance on a spell which takes him into the past, where he too seeks, and finds, the lost family treasure. Dickie meets the Mouldiwarp during his adventures and at one point is introduced to two counterparts – the Mouldierwarp, who is as gentle-

Jack and Mopsa talk to the applewoman, drawn by Dora Curtis.

A photograph of Edith Nesbit (1858–1924).

Edred and Elfrida Arden, whose meeting
with the Mouldiwarp leads to many
adventures; an illustration by
H. R. Miller from *The House of Arden*.

manly as the Mouldiwarp is rustic, and the Mouldiest-warp, a dignified and distant figure. These extensions of the Mouldiwarp may have been introduced to make it easier for the author to draw the fortunes of the three children together and to round off neatly the complexities of their respective positions in the family; but the wo superior white moles, heraldic though they are, have no personality, and might well have weakened the force of the Mouldiwarp, if that cross-grained, unassailable egotist of an animal had not been drawn with as enduring a personality as that of the Psammead (q.v.). [E. Nesbit: *House of Arden*, London 1908; *Harding's Luck*, 1923]

**MOUSE** and his **CHILD** (the), components of a clockwork toy, make two wind-up friends in the toyshop – a performing seal and an elephant; through long and dire adventures the child longs and hopes to see them again. The child, with his father, is sold to a family who bring the toy out each Christmas till it is accidentally broken and thrown on a rubbish-heap. Here a tramp picks it up; his rough repair restores the clockwork mechanism, but now instead of dancing the child up and down, the mouse lurches along, pushing it backwards in front of him. In this unsatisfactory state they are added to the slave gang of Manny Rat until they manage to escape. Pursued relentlessly by the rat (who is neurotically convinced that his fortunes are bound up with theirs for good or ill) and helped by a strangely invulnerable and prophetic Frog, the mouse and his child pursue their halting way, the child always hoping to find the elephant he thinks of as a possible mother,

both of them wanting to break their loving, irksome connection and their servitude to a key and to achieve the ideal condition of self-winding.

They encounter friends and enemies whose situation seems at times more hapless than their own – the shrews, murderous with territorial ambition; the crows, absorbed in an existentialist theatre and imprisoned in the concept of the Last Visible Dog; the musk-rat, eaten up with jealousy of the beavers, who deludes the mice with promises into long, wearisome labour. Friends and enemies come together in a final conflict in which the love-hate relationship between Manny Rat and his victims is finally resolved when Manny, reformed at least outwardly, finds the means to make the toys self-winding.

Literary allusion, satire, surrealist characters and situations, puns and conundrums, violence and pathos, enrich this brilliant, puzzling, disturbing fantasy. If it is legitimate to assume that it is an allegory of the human condition as well as a witty and exciting tale of adventure, there seems little profit in speculating on the exact meaning or intention of particular scenes or characters. This is a book that must be received into the reader's consciousness as a whole experience. The mouse and his child, if they are symbols, share a conjoined philosophy of life as they share the mechanical device that propels them. [Russell Hoban: *The Mouse and his Child*, New York 1967]

**MOWGLI**, the Frog, is given his name when he is adopted as an infant into a family of wolves, perhaps partly because of his soft hairlessness, certainly in part

The mouse and his child with Manny Rat, drawn by Lillian Hoban.

*Above and opposite.* Mowgli with Bagheera the panther and Baloo the bear, drawn by Stuart Tresilian.

because the wolves saved him from Shere Khan, the lame tiger whom they deride as frog-eater. Although Mowgli is accepted by the wolf pack and taught the Jungle Law, yet the time comes when old Akela loses his hold over the pack and in the leaderless days the young wolves turn against Mowgli, so that he has to leave the jungle for the village and use human strategies to put an end to Shere Khan.

It is not only on this occasion that Mowgli shows that he is a man and not an animal. He can always outstare his brother wolves and even the formidable panther Bagheera must drop his eyes before him. Moreover, though Mowgli respects the Law which has been knocked into him by Baloo, the bear, he has none the less a sense of fun and happiness, which his mentors cannot know. His reluctant days as a man are few, for the superstition of the villagers, roused by the jealous Brahmin Buldeo, drives him back to the jungle; but in the spring of his eighteenth year a melancholy which seems to him like a sickness drives him to accept, at last, that he needs human love and companionship.

It is significant that at the end of the poignant last story of Mowgli, *The Spring Running*, he once more

promises that he will never forget his jungle brothers and urges them not to cast him out completely. Mowgli is not Adam in the Garden of Eden, any more than he is the god that his foster-mother timidly calls him; he is not a totally fantastic creature nor the focal point of a satirical comment on human nature (though this is an important element in the stories). He is a human being growing painfully, and sometimes reluctantly, out of one world into another. His progress through the stories, with their emphasis on physical prowess, loyalty to comrades, obedience, has been likened to a boy's progress through the years of public school or his initiation into the discipline of army life. This last analogy has sometimes been carried to absurd lengths, with the various animals, from Colonel Bagheera downwards, being given army rank; but the intricate order of precedence and behaviour in a wolf-pack provides a simpler and more immediate source for the social organization of the jungle as Kipling describes it, and as he could have known it, if only in a very general way.

At a deeper level, Mowgli is a person who really belongs nowhere. Though he lives fully the life of the jungle (far more fully than he lives the life of man, if

we can judge by the isolated story, *In the Rukh*, which precedes the *Jungle Books*) yet he is not and never can be an animal, however thoroughly he assimilates their code and their idiom. His personality is a divided one. The sensuousness, the joyous activity, the colour and movement and the exotic, rhetorical speeches in the stories, are all subordinated, finally, to a pervading sadness. All his life Kipling had a passionate desire to belong – to a place, a group, a belief. We may speculate, but can never know for certain, how much of himself went to make the character of Mowgli. [Rudyard Kipling: *In the Rukh*, London 1890; *The Jungle Book*, 1894; *The Second Jungle Book*, 1895]

**MR BUMBLEMOOSE** is a Dutch schoolmaster of many moods and talents. Tall, stout, benevolent, he has moments when exertion is beyond him; in one such moment, he falls asleep in a park near an exhibition of sculpture and is labelled 'Vertical Sleeping Schoolmaster with Horizontal Sleeping Dog'. Sometimes he becomes obsessed by the need to invent something but usually regrets it – for example, when his electronic robot camera takes unflattering pictures of him and his animal household. He can work a spell now and then and deals competently with the hobgoblin found in the cellar of his old house.

Sometimes Mr Bumblemoose is in a mood to deplore

Mr Bumblemoose and his pets, drawn by Babs van Wely.

modern civilization, but he is usually forced to adapt himself to it. When his penny-farthing bicycle shows itself unable to cope with modern traffic, he is obliged to change to a more up to date model, and is eventually persuaded by his devoted pets to buy a car. There is something unique, however, in Mr Bumblemoose's dealings even with everyday life. His car, a rare make called Doremi, frequently stops and will only start when it has heard a song.

Mr Bumblemoose is vain – nicely, pleasantly so, but apt to launch into glowing accounts of his exploits as a mountaineer. His innocent pleasure in being well-known in the district is never allowed to become excessive – his pets see to that. There is Joachim the Learned Cat, who can make a tart comment when he feels like it. There is Yelper Heath-Overbank, a hound of distinguished but impoverished ancestry, whom Mr Bumblemoose found moping on a park bench and whose name pretty soon has to be changed from the Sad Dog to the Glad Dog. There is Rocket the Crow, who likes music-hall programmes and rude jokes. They love, respect and rule their kind master, who is a kind of quintessence of all philosophical, poetic, eccentric, conscientious schoolmasters, a comic character with constant unexpected depths to intrigue the reader and, no doubt, satisfy the author. [Hans Andreus: *Stories of Mr Bumblemoose* (1970 Holland) trans. Patricia Crampton, London 1971; and many other titles]

**MR McGREGOR** *see* PETER RABBIT

**MR PIPERSON** *see* GINGER AND PICKLES

**MR RUGGLES**, a dustman, and **MRS RUGGLES**, who takes in washing, live in the poor quarter of Otwell on the Ouse with seven children. A practical attitude to poverty, a sense of fun and plenty of affection enable the Ruggleses to enjoy life and to surmount their various problems, from finding ways to fit clever Kate out for grammar school to managing a day's outing to the sea. Some of the adventures that happen to the children are due to their temperaments – like Jim's abortive attempt to stow away on a cross-Channel barge and John's unexpected exploration of the middle-class world, that results from his passion for cars, while Kate's holidays were a matter of luck and of the Ruggles's gift for making the most of their opportunities.

The stories of the Ruggles family were written, as the author has said, as 'a shot in the battle against slums', in her indignation at the London she saw as a student. A deep interest in people and a strong sense of comedy dictated the form which that indignation took. After forty years it is easy to criticize the occasional whimsicality in the treatment of Mr and Mrs Ruggles, but it need not be forgotten that Eve Garnett's was among the first conscious attempts to go behind the cliché-portraits of 'the poor' found in many middle-class stories of the 1930s. Her portraits of the children are vital and universal. There is a shrewd understanding of childhood in the characters of stout, red-haired Lily Rose,

with her eldest-child's sense of responsibility and of spindly, intelligent Kate, with her inherited love of the country. There is a particularly natural and genial humour in the third book, *Holiday at the Dewdrop Inn.* The note of propaganda sounded occasionally in the earlier books has no chance of being heard against the cheerful tones of Kate, as she enters with enthusiasm into every village activity and makes friends with every inhabitant. This is not a class-oriented portrait but the picture of a real child. [Eve Garnett: *The Family from One End Street*, London 1937; *Further Adventures of the Family from One End Street*, 1956; *Holiday at the Dewdrop Inn*, 1962]

**MR TOOTLEOO**, a dashing sailor, is not discomposed by shipwreck, for he sits comfortably upon his hat; the friendly Cockolly Bird and her six chicks escort him to their own country 'where incense-laden breezes blow And feather-headed palm trees grow'. Here he eats so many of the goloptious fishes that he blows up like a balloon and is only brought down again because the Cockolly bird possesses a golden egg and understands the laws of gravity. Out of the egg hatches a gnome who officiously turns the bird into a crinolined lady and her chicks into 'Augustus, Araminta, Suke, Belinda, James and Marmaduke'. So ends, romantically, the first adventure of the pig-tailed sailor.

In subsequent tales, resourceful Mr Tootleoo provides a dragon-tutor for his unruly stepsons and takes an involuntary flight when the dragon snatches Mrs Cockolly Bird high in the sky. After further adventures as a ship's cook, marooned on a desert island, trying conclusions with a turtle, a tiger with toothache and an elephant, and enlisting the help of a king to collect the treasure he has discovered, the intrepid man journeys home on a magic carpet, to be re-united with his loving wife and to lead 'retired from the seas, A life of independent ease'. Nice touches of satirical wit help to establish the character of an unforgettable personality in words and pictures. [Bernard and Elinor Darwin: *The Tale of Mr Tootleoo*, London 1926; *Tootleoo Two*, 1927; *Mr Tootleoo and Co.*, 1935]

**MRS CRABTREE** *see* LAURA AND HARRY GRAHAM

**MRS EASTER** and her nephew Billy Gustie are rowing on the Serpentine with Mrs Easter's cat Pussy Purr when they see Billy's friend Julian with his Nannie and invite them to join them. Nannie decides to watch from the bank but she is hauled off by a cross ticket-collector when she discovers that Julian has her purse and she cannot pay for her seat. Meanwhile the boat party lands and Mrs Easter tries to console poor Julian by searching the nearby streets for the lost Nannie. There is more trouble to come. The sun comes out, Mrs Easter puts up her parasol and is blown high into the air, to land eventually on top of the Albert Memorial. A rescue is arranged, clever Pussy Purr is sent up with a note fastened to her collar, and all ends happily.

Mrs Easter is blown to the top of the Albert Memorial, from *Mrs Easter's Parasol*, written and illustrated by V. H. Drummond.

Mrs Easter, outwardly a respectable Kensington lady in a neat blue suit, rather enjoys her adventure. She is far too good a character to stay quietly in the pages of one book, and V.H. Drummond whisked her into the air again thirteen years later (in *Mrs Easter and the Storks*) when she and Billy Gustie take a holiday in Denmark. Once more her flight is caused by her parasol, but this time she transfers to the back of Sam the stork, in the search for his missing wife Sally, and she is soon involved with a spiky-faced, benevolent king, royally clad. The parasol initiates a further adventure with the King and his enemy Vilewort (in *Mrs Easter and the Golden Bounder*) and it takes her once more into the air from the snow-filled Park (in *Mrs Easter's Christmas Flight*), when she lands on Big Ben and is rescued by Farmer Christmas and his sledge.

Mrs Easter's first adventure is a real Londoner's frolic, and Hyde Park remains the most suitable and congenial setting for a lady who keeps her hat and her decorum through increasingly fantastic events. A lady of few words (and those words always polite and gracious) she has appeared for the delectation of children over a period of thirty years now, her dress and hair still immaculate and her purple and yellow parasol (and her character) still as fresh as ever. [V. H. Drummond: *Mrs Easter's Parasol*, London 1944; *Mrs Easter and the Storks*, 1957; *Mrs Easter and the Golden Bounder*, 1970; *Mrs Easter's Christmas Flight*, 1972]

**MRS FRISBY**, a fieldmouse, becomes the sole provider for her four children after the disappearance of her husband Jonathan. When spring ploughing becomes imminent, she prepares to move from their underground house in Farmer Fitzgibbon's vegetable field to a safe summer burrow near the river. Then the youngest child becomes seriously ill and the anxious mother, taking a dangerous journey past the farm to the home of the old white mouse, Mr Ages, is warned by him that Timothy must not be moved until the weather is warm.

It chances that Mrs Frisby, on her unhappy way home, has been able to free a crow from a tangle of silver foil just in time to save him from the dreaded farm cat. Jeremy Crow takes her to consult the owl and so she hears about the remarkably clever Rats of NIMH (q.v.) who by applying their acquired skill are able to move the concrete block in which Mrs Frisby made her winter home, and to re-locate it where the farmer will not reach it with a plough.

Mrs Frisby's home is an underground cavity, not a pretty mock-cottage, yet in her speech, her contacts with other animals, her methodical life, she seems to belong to the same world as Alison Uttley's Grey Rabbit. There is another aspect to this story of the American country-side. The fieldmouse, believable in her mouse-life, also earns by attraction a different kind of reality when she is involved with the science-fiction expertise of the rats. As far as the reader is concerned, Mrs Frisby is definitely in, though not of, the futuristic world of the Rats of NIMH. [Robert C. O'Brien: *Mrs Frisby and the Rats of NIMH*, New York 1971]

**MRS PEPPERPOT** is a pleasant, normal Norwegian housewife. But one morning she wakes to find herself shrunk to the size of a pepperpot, 'and old women don't usually do that'. Mrs Pepperpot is not the kind of person to lie in bed and brood over her dilemma. Instead, she cleverly persuades the mouse to clean the house ('or I'll tell the cat about you'), the cat to lick the dishes clean ('or I'll tell the dog about you') and the dog to air the bed, with a bone as reward. With similar threats and promises she induces the rain to wash the clothes, the wind to blow them on to the line and the sun to dry them, while with apt flattery she manages bowl, frying pan and pancake mixture so that Mr Pepperpot's supper is on the table when he comes home; and 'just as he opened the door, Mrs Pepperpot turned back to her usual size'.

Björn Berg's illustrations of Mrs Pepperpot.

This first story about the unusual Norwegian house-wife sets the pattern for many more, while Björn Berg, as illustrator, comically confirms the impression of sharp features and forthright personality which we receive from the text. A capable and experienced house-wife, Mrs Pepperpot knows how to improvise. She is fond of animals and her care of various foundlings, together with her friendly approach to wild creatures, amply repay her when she is in difficulties. Above all, her sense of humour and love of adventure ensure that she enjoys the most bizarre experiences – acting the Sleeping Beauty in a puppet show, playing horse and cart with a family of mice, carried by a crow to its nest. The ingenious detail in the stories, their meticulous attention to size and setting and their inventive fancy, culminate in the lively personality of the central charac-ter. Alf Prøysen and Björn Berg have together created an endearing and believable little woman who may claim to be included among the classic characters of nursery-rhyme and nursery tale. [Alf Prøysen, ill. Björn Berg: *Little Old Mrs Pepperpot*, (1957 Sweden) trans. Marianne Helweg, London 1959; *Mrs Pepperpot Again*, 1960; *Mrs Pepperpot to the Rescue*, 1963; *Mrs Pepper-pot in the Magic Wood*, 1968; *Mrs Pepperpot's Outing*, 1971; *Mrs Pepperpot's Year*, 1973]

**MRS PETERKIN** decides one day to take a drive, so the horse is harnessed and Mrs Peterkin, Elizabeth Eliza and the three little boys get ready for the journey; but when Elizabeth Eliza takes the reins the horse goes only a short distance before it stops. Whipping, lighten-ing the load, whipped cream snacks all fail to move it so the Peterkins consult the lady from Philadelphia, who observes the scene and suggests 'Why don't you unchain the horse from the horse-post?'

A similar incident in the author's experience is said to have given her the idea of drawing a family which applies strangely individual logic to everyday life. The Peterkins' ambitious educational plans – to share between them such useful languages as French, Russian and Sanskrit, to enjoy breakfasts with a bill of fare based on the alphabet – somehow miscarry not from want of sense but from an excess of it. Their placid acceptance of disaster is as invaluable as their conviction of being always in the right. Agamemnon, the eldest son, wonders why nobody will take up the patent for his new key of standard shape and size, while Solomon John thinks he might manage to be a doctor 'if he should not have to see his patients when they were sick'. Meanwhile the three little boys tumble about, chiefly preoccupied with their rubber boots. If Elizabeth Eliza deviates a little way into sense, this is not allowed to disturb the self-satisfaction of the rest of the egregious family. [Lucretia Hale: *The Peterkin Papers*, Boston 1886]

**MRS RIBBY** *see* GINGER AND PICKLES

**MRS TIGGYWINKLE** *see* GINGER AND PICKLES

**MUDDLE-HEADED WOMBAT**'s first friend, a Bush Mouse, encourages him in his scheme for making money by singing in the street; when they are taken to the police station they find a skinny tabby cat there already and the Mouse is so sorry for it that he decides to adopt it. After he has got over his jealousy the plump wombat accepts Tabby, even after the cat is heard to remark 'It's not everyone who has a friend like wonder-ful me!'

The three ill-assorted friends keep their firmly stated characters through a number of stories. Tabby remains exacting and conceited; Mouse is usually clever enough to get them out of difficulties; the Muddle-headed Wombat, true to his nature, asks unanswerable ques-tions and shows a happy incompetence whether he is riding his red bike, rowing a boat or acting the part of the Fairy Godmother in a pantomime which the friends give for the delectation of a family of impoverished ban-dicoots and other bush animals.

With their special Australian robustness, the absurd animals, each with his own personal and revealing idiom, provide endless humour by their efforts to extri-cate themselves from the ludicrous situations into which their temperaments inevitably lead them. [Ruth Park: *The Muddle-headed Wombat*, London and Sydney 1963; *The Muddle-headed Wombat on Holiday*, 1964; *The Muddle-headed Wombat in the Tree Tops*, 1965; *The Muddle-headed Wombat at School*, 1966; *The Muddle-headed Wombat in the Snow*, 1967; *The Muddle-headed Wombat on a Rainy Day*, 1970; *The Muddle-headed Wombat on the River*, 1971; *The Muddle-headed Wombat in the Springtime*, 1971]

**MURTAGH** and **WINNIE BLAIR** are sent from India for their health, to live with their reclusive uncle in the Ireland of the 1870s. Here they are joined by their older sister Rosie and the two little ones, Bobbo and Ellie. The children are allowed to run wild, dispensing with lessons and alarming their gentle cousin Adrienne who is barely grown-up and unable to control them. Rosie, at twelve rising thirteen, suffers from an in-convenient access of guilt at their unorthodox way of life but Murtagh and Winnie, as full of the pride of race as they are of misdirected energy, persist in leading the younger children on long forays into the country, con-tent to be dirty and ragged, admired by the village child-ren who follow their lead, and steadily more and more heedless of their elders.

In this robust tale, with its spirited dialogue and terse comment, Flora Shaw has drawn real children, recog-nizable as individuals, easily understood in their motives and far more than mere representative figures illustrating a social theme. In what amounts to a private parallel of Ireland's national troubles, the children smart under the unbending and hostile attempts of their uncle's agent Mr Plunkett to bring them to heel.

A scene from *Orlando Buys a Farm*, written and illustrated by Kathleen Hale.

Grace put on dungarees to protect herself from the prickly stubble. The Kittens dressed up as Red Indians. Blanche borrowed a Japanese doll and a saucepan from Mrs. Butterfield, and was the squaw. Tinkle and Pansy went scalp-hunting among the field-mice. Orlando snatched a well-earned snooze.

Flora Shaw has been fair to Mr Plunkett, through whom she shows something of the complexity of the Anglo-Irish hold in Ireland, but though the reader sees through Adrienne's troubled thoughts that his attitude is justifiable, and though Murtagh is intelligent enough to realize this too, it is likely that young readers will align themselves with the children – passionate, hardy, generous of heart, unruly and headlong in their determination to be themselves and to please themselves. Their mischief is, in the late Victorian manner, truly impressive. [Flora M. Shaw: *Castle Blair*, London 1878]

**MY NAUGHTY LITTLE SISTER** had 'brown eyes, and red hair, and a pinkish nose, she was very, very stubborn'. This description comes from a grown-up, reminiscing about the childhood days when she watched, with a mixture of envy and admiration, the exploits of her junior. Sometimes the naughty child is loquacious, chatting with her friends the milkman, the postman and the window-cleaner: sometimes she is quiet, and then her mother can be sure she is up to mischief – meddling with her sister's fairy doll or snip-

Henrietta Garland's drawing (*right*) of 'my naughty little sister' and Una J. Place's illustration (*below*) from the second book, *My Naughty Little Sister's Friends*.

*Left.* An illustration by Arthur Rackham for *Peter Pan in Kensington Gardens.*

ping everything with the embroidery scissors or sweeping her bedroom chimney with a feather duster.

With her boon companion Bad Harry, whose name speaks for itself, 'my naughty little sister' finds endless mischief at hand but she can be good if there is sufficient inducement – a privileged day at school for instance – and on one occasion her father was heard to remark that 'it was almost worth having her behave so badly when she could show afterwards what a good girl she really was'. The narrator's comment on this ('Our father was a very funny man') clinches the author's point of view that is easily perceived behind the artless descriptions which she has put in the mouth of someone remembering herself as a child.

Whether she is fidgeting or pretending to be shy or grumbling or hiding from retribution or paying a formal call on kind Mrs Cocoa Jones next door or going on a journey in the guard's van, this impetuous, determined small girl is always and unmistakably herself. [Dorothy Edwards: *My Naughty Little Sister*, London 1952; *My Naughty Little Sister and Bad Harry*, 1974; several more titles between these dates]

# N

**NANCY BLACKETT,** dressed in the 'comfortables' beloved by herself and sister Peggy (q.v.) ('red knitted caps, brown shirts, blue knickerbockers, and no stockings'), sails under a flag bearing the skull and crossbones and introduces herself to the Walkers as 'master and part owner of the Amazon, the terror of the seas'. Possibly Ransome wants to leave it doubtful whether the last phrase refers to the boat or to Nancy (whose hated real name, Ruth, is never allowed to be used). Even when she realizes that they can have more interesting adventures if the two families join, she proposes 'an alliance against old enemies – but we want the sort of alliance that will let us fight each other if we want to'. (The more intellectual Titty Walker corrects her – it is 'a treaty of offence and defence' that she means).

Nancy has always lived at Beckfoot by the lake with her family. To the understandably protective feeling of a local family in a beauty spot much frequented by tourists is added her natural belligerence and her need for action. Everything she does is quick, noisy and positive. She affects outlandish expressions – 'Barbecued billygoats' in Lakeland, the locally more suitable 'suffering lampreys' on the East Coast. Her vocabulary also includes a number of derogatory phrases which are freely doled out, particularly to Peggy, who is well accustomed to the word galoot with its various qualifying adjectives.

Because of the quieter, more controlled characters of John (q.v.) and Susan (q.v.) Walker, Nancy usually contrives to lead their expeditions. She is seen at a disadvantage when (in *Secret Water*) she finds that she is now the interloper in a land inhabited by 'savages', local children who already have their own well-organized ploys with boats and hide-outs. Eager for a 'war' in which she can once more be a leader, Nancy complains to Peggy that John and Susan are so determined to complete the survey their father has outlined for them that they have left no time for conflict. Their kidnapping of the only too willing Bridget (q.v.) elicits from her the explosive 'Bust those Eels'. Even when the children have decided on a joint corroboree, Nancy insists on a bit of a battle beforehand because 'It's a waste of good savages not to be attacked by them.'

But Nancy is not the boringly hearty extrovert she might well have seemed in the hands of a less accomplished writer. Her bluster hides a generous nature and she can, when she stops to think, appreciate points of view different from her own. When Dick and Dorothea Callum (q.v.) are expected for a visit in her mother's absence (in *The Picts and the Martyrs*), Nancy realizes that she will be expected to act properly as hostess. Though she 'feels a bit rum planning for nothing to happen instead of stirring things up', she adapts herself successfully not only to this situation but also to the far worse circumstance of Aunt Maria's unexpected arrival, for she realizes that unless she and Peggy put on a show of being polite, well-behaved girls in best frocks, it is her mother who will suffer retribution.

In short, in drawing Nancy Blackett, Ransome has shown that he can give his characters organic growth. The Nancy of *The Picts and the Martyrs* is very different from the Nancy of *Swallows and Amazons* and yet she *is* the same hasty, inventive, non-bookish girl all the time. [Arthur Ransome: *Swallows and Amazons*, London 1930, and many other titles]

**NANCY BRUCE** is essentially a city child and when at the age of nine she is sent to live in New Hampshire for a year with her grand-parents she is afraid she will find it hard to settle down in the country. As the seasons pass Nancy learns from her Swedish grandmother the meaning of the traditional festivals of her country and is warmly welcomed by her Carlson cousins, through whom she makes many new friends – some of them relatives, others neighbours, others again the family cats and horses with their various personalities.

Nancy is essentially a receiving rather than an active character. With her strong interest in people, she is to some extent used as a mirror to reflect the members of a small community of a quarter of a century ago and more, living in the spirit of old Sweden. The characters of Grandma and Grandpa Benson, of the Carlson girls, of the Polish farm-girl Wanda, of Alex Brown in his wheel-chair, are all as it were one-trait people (Grandmother with her sense of occasion, Grandpa with his dignified teasing, and so on); they depend for their reality on the way the eager, responsive Nancy sees them. [Jennie Linqvist: *The Golden Name Day*, New York 1955; *The Little Silver House*, 1959; *The Crystal Tree*, 1966]

**NANCY DREW**, the girl detective, starts with the considerable advantage of an enquiring and courageous disposition and a useful technical background, for her father Carson Drew was once a district attorney; Nancy always took an interest in his cases and indeed she 'had been present at a number of interviews with noted detectives'; and her father declares she has 'a natural talent for digging into interesting cases'. Her first case is undertaken to help family friends, but once she has found Josiah Crawley's missing will her reputation earns her as much work as she can deal with, while the enemies her father has made during his legal career have a habit of cropping up to menace him and to provide more work for Nancy.

Her methods are simple and invariably successful. Her second case (*The Hidden Staircase*) concerns old Nathan Gombet, who claims that Carson Drew has cheated him out of his rights; Nancy declares: 'I suspected he was a miser from his appearance'. Forty years later (in *The Whispering Statue*) she has only to look at Dr Keer's beard and intensely glistening black eyes to remark: 'He may be talented ... but I'll bet he's cruel and scheming.' She is right both times, of course. 'As a detective', her father comments, 'you have me backed completely off the map.'

There seems no reason why Nancy Drew should ever change, except for the outward modification, seen on dust-jackets, from the bobbed hair, flat chest and schoolgirlish expression of the 1930s to the young-lady face of the 1970s. A formula character for formula books, Nancy Drew (like the Hardy Boys (q.v.), Tom Swift and many others) was the invention of Edward Stratemeyer, who kept his syndicate of writers provided with outline characters and plots. In situations deemed suitable for a female detective – thefts of priceless antiques, documents hidden in old books, family skeletons, old houses with secret panels – Nancy Drew pursues her girlish way, her hair-style changing with the times but never disarranged. [Carolyn Keene: *The Hidden Staircase*, New York 1930; *The Bungalow Mystery*, 1930; *The Secret of the Old Clock*, 1930; and many other titles]

**NARGUN** (the) existed in a cave in the earliest days of the universe 'while stars exploded and planets wheeled and the earth settled'. Time wears down its rock-like shape; time – and man's activity – drive it on a centuries-long journey in search of peace and silence and bring it finally to a gully on the sheep run of Charles and Edie at Wongadilla. The brother and sister are delighted when their cousin Simon (q.v.), newly come to live with them, proves that he can see and converse with the sly, comical Potkoorok in the swamp and the Turongs lurking in the trees. But they do not know of the presence of the Nargun.

The other creatures wish the Nargun would go away from their land but dare not challenge its power, for its sad, angry cry at night frightens even the cheerful Potkoorok. As for the Nargun, driven frantic by the pulsing

of the bulldozer working on the hillside, dreaming of fire and of the stars, fierce without motive, it seems to desire revenge; yet when Simon and Charlie lure it into the depths of the mountain and a rock fall seals it there, the boy can only be sorry for its massive, voiceless loneliness.

The Nargun, a being evoked from a boulder, never humanized, allowed limited movement but the merest semblance of limb and eye, must be accounted one of the most remarkable myth-beings ever created – or recreated, if Patricia Wrightson found hints of it, as she did of the Potkoorok, the Bitarr and the Turongs, in aboriginal story. She offers as little description as possible, relying on effects of darkness or the surprise of sudden movement, on associative words (flank, muzzle, snout, lurch), to establish beyond any doubt the possibility that a boulder can have sentient being and, in a very primitive pattern, longings and desires that move it to dangerous activity. 'What is good?' the Potkoorok answers Simon's naïve question. 'It is the Nargun. It came from a long way south. It should go back'. Fittingly, the Nargun ends, or perhaps only rests for a century or two, deep in the rock where the Nyols bring it pieces of crystal and dead lizards and croon to it and where it feels once more 'the old, slow pulse, deep and enduring' of the earth's motion. [Patricia Wrightson: *The Nargun and the Stars*, London 1973]

**NIBBINS** is Kay Harker's (q.v.) favourite cat and certainly he is more trustworthy than the mysterious, seldom-seen Greymalkin or the deceitful Blackmalkin who purrs his way into the favour of Sylvia Daisy (q.v.) by spying on Kay. It is Nibbins in fact who starts the whole adventure of *The Midnight Folk*, waking Kay one night to lead him through wainscot passages and to explain to him that the house is in danger from enemies.

Not that Nibbins is a model character, by any means. Boon-companion of Rollicum Bitem Lightfoot the fox he is a notable robber of rabbit warrens and is not even averse to a little bat-hunting. But there are darker influences exercised on Nibbins, who was once a witch's acolyte, one of the little black cats who walk round the ring on meeting nights, dropping herbs on the magic fire. Even as he and Kay speed on stolen broomsticks to overhear the counsel of the witches, Nibbins thrills to the sound of a rousing moonlight-song, and Kay has to exercise all his authority to get him safely away. Nothing in Nibbins's fantasy-adventures affects the presentation of him as a real, affectionate, natural little housecat; he is one of the happiest of Masefield's animal characters. [John Masefield: *The Midnight Folk*, 1927; *The Box of Delights*, 1935]

**NICHOLAS FETTERLOCK** is brought up with Hal the shepherd's son as his foster-brother, in the shepherd's cot in the Cotswold hills. Nick's father, a merchant of the Wool Staple, keeps his own flock of sheep as well as buying and selling wool, and so it is natural

Nicholas Fetterlock faces the unpleasant Lombard who has struck his foster brother Hal: a scene from *The Woolpack*, written and illustrated by Cynthia Harnett.

enough that he should entertain at his house the agent of the great Medici banking house in Florence. But Nick has already seen the Lombard and his unpleasant servant at a disadvantage and, being a shrewd lad, he decides to watch for future visits from the pair; besides, he suspects his father's factor, a wool-packer who is building an unusually large barn for one whose Guild rules forbid him to trade in wool on his own account.

Though Nick's behaviour and background are carefully described to fit 1493, the year in which the story is set, his character could fit any period. His reaction to the news of his betrothal, by which his father hopes to seal an alliance with a prosperous Newbury clothier, is likely enough for any boy of twelve or so; it is by a boy's lurking and overhearing that he and his foster-brother (and his tomboy bride-to-be Cecily) find evidence against Leach and the Lombard, who are dealing illicitly in wool and seeking to discredit Fetterlock with the Guild. No very subtle character is needed for a practical historical adventure like this; an exciting story, plenty of information agreeably offered, and a likeable, outspoken, confident boy in the centre – these qualities, no doubt, won the book the Carnegie Medal in 1951. [Cynthia Harnett: *The Woolpack*, London 1951]

**NICKY GORE** *see* GEOFFREY

**NILS HOLGERSSON**, who lives on a small farm in Sweden, is at the age of fourteen still unmanageable, ill-tempered and lazy and, worse still, he 'teased and tormented the animals instead of caring for them'. One Sunday morning his parents set off to church, leaving him with a portion of the Bible to read. After a time. the lad falls asleep over his book and wakes to see an elf peering into his mother's best chest. What more natural than to catch the creature in a butterfly net. The little old man begs for his freedom but when Nils lets him go he boxes the boy's ears – and there is Nils, elf-size himself.

Now the boy is at the mercy of the farmyard animals whose lives he has made such a misery. To escape them he climbs on to a wall and is in time to see a young gander about to fly away with the wild geese. 'It would be a big loss to father and mother if he were gone when they came home from church' thinks the boy, forgetting his irresponsible ways; and he leaps on to the gander's back and is whirled into the air.

Off goes Nils on a long flight over Sweden – for the gander is determined to show the wild geese that he can do as well as they can, and Nils, for his part, does not want his parents to see him in such a sorry case.

Nils begins to realize how much he could do to help animals. Time and again he warns the geese – against sneaking Smirre Fox and other animals, against hunters and mischievous children. Often he is in danger himself; he survives a forest fire, and a plunge into the sea, lures the grey rats from Glimminge Castle with a wheaten pipe, is kidnapped by crows, helps an old horse to soften

One of Hans Baumhauer's illustrations from *The Further Adventures of Nils*.

his master's heart, and becomes on one alarming occasion a plaything for a family of bears. His experiences teach him to be self-reliant, and to respect the rights of animals, so that when he finds out he will be freed from enchantment if he takes the gander home to be killed for market, he refuses to accept the bargain – and finds that even so he has become a human boy again, safe at home.

The story of Nils was written in part to show Swedish school-children the beauties of their country. Every kind of landscape in every kind of season and weather is described as it might appear to a tiny boy riding high above on the back of a goose. The geographical aspect of the book is balanced by the theme of a naughty boy changed by experience. No book could better inculcate an intelligent love of animals than this tale of a natural, lively, noisy boy who converses with them in their own language and, while changing his attitude to life for the better, at the same time enjoys his multifarious adventures with engaging high spirits. [Selma Lagerlöf: *Nils Holgersson's Wonderful Travels round Sweden* (2 vols, 1906–7 Sweden) trans. Velma Swanston Howard as *The Wonderful Adventures of Nils*, New York 1907, and *The Further Adventures of Nils*, 1911]

**NIP CHALLONS** *see* JIM STARLING

**NODDY** is a 'kind little fellow' who lives in Toyland with his friend Mr Big Ears the dwarf and a great many other toys. He has a dear little 'House-for-One' and a green and red car which he runs as a taxi, but he has little business sense and is not always careful how he drives, so that he sometimes gets into trouble with Mr Plod the policeman. However, there is always someone ready to help him. The milkman will always give him free milk if Noddy lets him waggle his little wooden head so that the ball on his pixie hat rings. Noddy thinks it is fun to be him and hopes he will always have 'lots of adventures' but when they actually happen he is afraid and begs for protection from the nearest person larger and older than himself.

This monotonously infantile character, who is frequently heard to say that he doesn't like being sensible but would far rather be silly, seems to have been put together from the weakest and least desirable attributes of childhood. It is hard to explain the persistent popularity of these trivial, repetitive stories with their small, retarded, masochistic hero. [Enid Blyton: *Noddy and his Car*, London 1951; and many other titles]

**NOGGIN THE NOG** succeeds his father King Knut as king of 'that land of dark forest and snow which men call the land of Nog' in spite of the machinations of his wicked uncle Nogbad. The benevolent and chubby monarch made his début in a series of 'Starting to Read' books based on television programmes about the mock-Viking land where Noggin, his Queen Nooka and their son Knut live in a castle and their subjects in 'little houses with straw roofs and stone chimneys'.

In these simple tales and in the longer stories under the series-title 'The Saga of Noggin the Nog' (designed for children from five upwards), the two-dimensional characters are developed mainly in two directions. First, Nogbad the Bad makes various attempts on the serenity of his royal nephew, sometimes putting on unconvincing disguises (inside a clanking metal elephant, hidden in a giant presentation pie and so on), sometimes relying on the help of allies like his eavesdropping crows, the oily Emir Ahmed el Ahmed or the cultivated plants he calls Grundelstein's Greater Gripemat (but these prove to be of an 'obstinately kind and friendly disposition' and come down on Noggin's side after all).

Like most villains, Nogbad steals the show whenever he is on stage. As a positive character he can only be said to be challenged by Olaf the Lofty whose inventions more often than not make way for the second, and satirical direction of the stories. 'Today I will invent money', the gangling scientist decides, and that simple man of action, Thor Nogson, is soon dithering in a series of financial compromises. If Olaf's ingenious solution for the problem of the sooty storks (in *Nogbad and the Storks*), whose nests in warm chimneys are inconvenient,

is a useful piece of Heath-Robinsonism, his invention of the game of Hnafetafl (in *The Game*), which is played first with real people moving on chequered squares, then with carved figures, almost lands Noggin in Nogbad's clutches, and the 'greatest invention in the world', the Firecake, after blowing a hole in the castle wall, is still more dangerously exploited by Nogbad, till eventually Noggin remarks that Firecake is more dangerous than the Sword of Power because 'anybody could invent Firecake again if they are fool enough.'

Peter Firmin's illustrations, and animations, for the Noggin stories, with their Viking stage properties and saga devices, their engaging slapstick, confirm the simplistic characterization of these amusing books. They make their appeal very differently (and indeed will be read differently) by children and by adults. If for adults the pleasure is mainly the enjoyment of parody, perhaps for children it lies in the invitation to indulge vicariously in unashamed greed and sabotage with Nogbad or in benevolent bossiness with a king who is palpably a child like themselves. [Oliver Postgate, ill. Peter Firmin: *Noggin the King*, London 1965; *Noggin and the Whale*, 1965; *Noggin and the Dragon*, 1966; *Nogbad Comes Back*, 1966; *Noggin and the Moon Mouse*, 1967; *Nogbad and the Elephant*, 1967; *Noggin and the Storks*, 1973; *Noggin and the Money*, 1973. In the series, 'Starting to Read', with other titles, *King of the Nogs*, London 1968; *The Ice Dragon*, 1968; *The Flying Machine*, 1969; *The Omruds*, 1969; *The Firecake*, 1969; *The Island*, 1969; *The Pie*, 1971; *The Flowers*, 1971; *The Game*, 1972; *The Monster*, 1972. In the series, with other titles, 'The Saga of Noggin the Nog']

**NORAH OF BILLABONG** grows up on a cattle station in an outback district of Victoria. The first sight of her at fourteen – tall, slender, boyish, with untidy brown curls tied back with red tape, a freckled face with a square chin and honest, direct eyes – tells us all that we ever need to know of her, for she never changes. The title of the book in which she first appears, *Mates at Billabong*, is significant. Motherless since infancy, Norah has been brought up by the stout, devoted housekeeper, Mrs Brown, and by her father, David Linton, a man of strong, silent mien and high principles. She has always been a 'little mate' to the widower, to her big brother Jim and to his school friend and boon companion Wally Meadows who spends all his holidays at Billabong and is treated as one of the family.

When the first break from Billabong inevitably comes and Norah is sent to school in Melbourne to learn to be a young lady, Jim assures Wally 'they'd have to boil Norah before they made her prim' and indeed she is still 'up to all sorts of larks' even when she is Wally's wife, a mother and the settled mistress of her own home.

Norah's character is defined perhaps more by her position in the stories than by the simple statements the author makes about her or her mode of speech which is, rather monotonously, either teasing and slangy or womanly and sympathetic. She was the ideal heroine for the girl readers who eagerly waited for the latest Mary Grant Bruce in the 1920s and '30s. There was the excitement of finding out how Norah and the rest of the family would deal with various situations – confrontation with crooks and cattle rustlers, a grass fire, the discovery of a gold mine, accident, war. More than this, Norah appealed to the deep conviction that happiness lies in the freedom of the outback and not in the world of town and school. Hundreds of girls shed even more tears over the death of her first pony Bob than they shed over the sad parts of *Black Beauty*. Hundreds of girls, too, were quietly led into right ways of thinking for their time by noticing the chivalrous care for Norah which lay below the jocular teasing of Jim and Wally and by reading about all the lame ducks whom Norah, more than anybody, helped to a better life – from English Tommy Rainham, escaped to Australia from a cruel stepmother, to the little Chinese boy pursued by crooks for the sake of family jewels, the egregious Percival who after one visit learned sense and became 'Bill of Billabong', lonely Mrs Reilly whose daughter Norah cared for when her mother was ill – the list is endless. The compassionate, steadfast side of Norah, which sustains her through the anxious years of World War I, when Jim and Wally are at the Front, and which makes her universally beloved, contrasts with her tomboyish habits, her love of fun, of good horses and the open air. Her given character allows the author to conduct Norah (and her readers) up to and through her marriage with Wally with perfect propriety and with a sentimentality all the more marked because it is concealed under the inarticulate avowals which are so much a part of the Billabong books. Norah never really grows up; it is the illusion of experience that thrilled the girls of two generations ago. Perhaps this is the key to her character and to the books as a whole; she illustrates the concept of mateship which is in itself a somewhat immature idea. [Mary Grant Bruce: *Mates at Billabong*, London 1911; *Norah of Billabong*, 1912; *Back to Billabong*, London and Melbourne 1921; *Billabong's Daughter*, 1924; and other titles]

**NORMAN** and **HENRY BONES**, cousins living in the Norfolk village of Sedgewick, share an enthusiasm almost amounting to mania for amateur detection. Their adventures start when Norman is sixteen and Henry fourteen and last for an elastic fictional year or two. No spy in disguise, no jewel thief masquerading as a country gentleman (or gentleman's gentleman), no mysterious native or ghostly apparition is proof against Norman's powers of observation or Henry's wild but often successful hunches.

The stories were originally told by the author to the boys he taught at a prep. school, and became one of the most popular radio series on Children's Hour in the 1950s. The stories have a consistent pattern. Relatively simple but cunning plots are backed with stereotyped machinery – secluded old houses abounding in secret passages and forgotten tunnels, goodies and baddies who bear their characters in their faces (or, originally, in their voices). For such stories characterization must be simple and, in particular, the characters of the two boys must be consistent and instantly recognizable. It is all the more remarkable that though Norman and Henry are essentially types, reacting predictably to each and every challenge, yet something in their manner of speaking, in their particular habits of watching and listening, saves them from being as dull as most heroes of adventure-series. [Anthony Wilson: *Norman Bones, Detective*, London 1949; *Norman and Henry Bones, the Boy Detectives*, 1952; *Norman and Henry Bones Investigate*, 1953; *Norman and Henry Solve the Problem*, 1957; *Norman and Henry follow the Trail*, 1959; Also a paperback *Four Mysteries Solved by Norman and Henry Bones*, London 1957]

**NURSE MATILDA** arrives on the Browns' doorstep at the moment when the appalling reputation of their numerous children has spread so far that no domestic agency will deal with the household. The small, stout, black-clad figure, with her 'nose like two potatoes', her piercing black eyes and the one huge tooth 'sticking right out like a tombstone over her lower lip', dismays Mrs Brown. But Nurse Matilda deals as firmly with her doubts as she does with the children when she marches into the nursery and finds them engaged in drawing on the walls, executing the dolls, filling the inkwells with jam and carrying on other anti-social activities.

Nurse Matilda's methods are unexpectedly simple and effective. When she raps with her black stick, the children find they are quite unable to stop what they are doing. When they have been messily playing with porridge, putting their best clothes on the animals or running away over and over again to the point of exhaustion, they remember (or are reminded by the astute Baby) that they have only to say 'please' to be given the chance to behave properly. In this way Nurse Matilda teaches the unruly family the seven lessons of good behaviour; and, oddly, each time they beg for her help, and get it, her ferocious ugliness seems less noticeable, till the moment comes when they all realize they positively want this handsome person to stay.

This redoubtable character originated in a story which was passed down the generations in Christianna Brand's family and also in the family of Edward Ardizzone, her cousin, who shared with her the task of giving substance to Nurse Matilda, first in a short story in an anthology, *Naughty Children*, edited by Christianna Brand (London 1962) and later in three delectable books. Nurse Matilda owes her charm to the contrast between extreme physical ugliness and the beauty of affectionate discipline, the glow of goodness that communicates itself quite unfussily from the strange old woman to her charges. Mary Poppins (q.v.) performs something of the same function for the Banks family,

but unlike her, Nurse Matilda is not a magic person but a symbol, almost an embodiment, of that most awful of all nursery warnings, 'Stop making that face or the wind will change and you'll get stuck like it'. [Christianna Brand, ill. Edward Ardizzone: *Nurse Matilda*, Leicester 1964; *Nurse Matilda Goes to Town*, 1967; *Nurse Matilda Goes to Hospital*, 1974]

Nurse Matilda at her ugliest, among her unruly charges (*above*) and the comely woman she becomes (*right*), drawn by Edward Ardizzone.

'Collander Moll nearly dropped the basin in fright'; a drawing by Brian Robb from *Odd and the Great Bear*.

# O

ODD the bear and **ELSEWHERE** the clown are left behind in an empty house but they find a home with Hallelujah Jones, the gardener at next-door Fenton House, and his kindly, absent-minded daughter Collander Moll. Their own alliance is strengthened by the adventures they share, searching for Odd's arm (which is pulled off when they venture on the London Underground), acting as buskers for a theatre queue, pursuing thieves who have made off with Fenton House's valuable musical instruments. Odd and Elsewhere are not wholly toys (in spite of the many times they are stitched up by Collander Moll); they are not wholly human, though they mix on equal terms with people; they are not wholly children, in spite of their free, exuberant behaviour; nor are they magic in the most obvious sense of the word, though the stories about them are fantastic in character. These two attractive little creatures are drawn with Mozartian airiness and precision, like the music-filled settings for their adventures and the visual images so sympathetically lent to them in Brian Robb's drawings. They have their personal quests. Odd sets off alone into Wales to seek his ancestor the Great Bear, while Elsewhere, proud yet diffident, joins the great Gathering of Clowns to demonstrate his craft. Both quests, small though they are in scale, gain a substantial and teasing importance from the unique atmosphere of the story sequence, which happily is not yet completed. [James Roose-Evans, ill. Brian Robb: *The Adventures of Odd and Elsewhere*, London 1971; *The Secret of the Seven Bright Shiners*, 1972; *Odd and the Great Bear*, 1973; *Elsewhere and the Gathering of the Clowns*, 1974; *The Return of the Great Bear*, 1975]

OLE GOLLY, nurse to Harriet Welsch (q.v.), has a face that looks as if it was cut out of oak and dresses in 'yards and yards of tweed which enveloped her like a lot of discarded blankets ... and which she referred to as her Things'. Her trenchant manner hides her real affection for Harriet, whose ambitions she fosters by intelligent advice and discipline. As her sense of honour forbids her to look into the notebooks she has advised Harriet to keep, she can hardly realize how sharp some of Harriet's comments are but she does arrange matters so that Harriet shall understand something of the distinction between imagination and reality. Harriet's astonishment when she is taken to meet Ole Golly's hugely fat and simple-minded mother is nothing to her bewilderment when she hears her nurse being addressed respectfully and devotedly by a suitor and notices how different Miss Golly's submissive, high-pitched tones are from her usual bracing voice.

The casual unorthodoxy of Louise Fitzhugh's method of drawing character is closer to the technique of an adult novelist than to the simplistic methods of most writers for the young. [Louise Fitzhugh: *Harriet the Spy*, New York 1964]

OLGA LESLIE, daughter of a Scottish colonel stationed in India, runs away when she is thirteen from a school where, according to her, nobody likes her and the suet pudding has 'black-beetle's babies scattered through it, which you had to make believe were Smyrna currants'. Fortunately for Olga she finds the best possible person to help her – fifteen-year-old Clarice Clavering, who thinks life in the 1870s very dull and longs for the days when 'heroic deeds were the daily food of happy men and women.'

Olga seems fascinating at first but soon Clarice finds it was more comfortable to dream of hiding a king from his enemies than to keep the volatile Olga from discovery. Indeed, Olga's jokes and extravagant plans, her reckless masquerading as a ghost, make Clarice wonder whether she is quite right in the head. As the days go by there seems some reason to doubt Olga's account of herself and Clarice suffers from having to deceive her father and her kind governess as well as from trying to restrain Olga from further foolishness. The characters of the two girls, the natural affection they come to feel for one another, are shown with a freshness and flexibility and with a droll humour in striking contrast to the more sober tales usually associated with mid-Victorian fiction for the young. [Mrs Elizabeth Anne Hart: *The Runaway*, London 1872]

OLIVER GREENFIELD, a senior boy at St Dominic's, is eligible to enter for the Nightingale Scholarship, and is not likely to be seriously challenged except by his friend Horace Wraysford, the best 'all round' man in the Fifth. The two boys have moved up the school together and are enjoying their position, free from the monitorial responsibilities of the Sixth and acting as the amused patrons of the Juniors, who noisily congregate in rival packs known as Tadpoles and

Guinea-pigs. If Oliver, who is proud and reserved, is less popular than his best friend, this does not worry him until his sworn enemy and rival, Loman (q.v.), contrives to throw on him the suspicion of stealing one of the question papers before the scholarship examination. Oliver refuses to comment on the accusation, as he has previously refused to explain why he refused to fight a senior boy for insulting him. Oliver is neither cheat nor coward but circumstances suggest that he is; he is ostracized by the school and defended only by his ingenuous young brother Stephen.

Talbot Baines Reed makes it very clear that the ambiguous situation could not have arisen with any other member of the Fifth. The confident extrovert Wraysford or the sarcastic Anthony Pembury, for instance, would never have found themselves in such a situation. In the same way the author shows that the pride that leads to Oliver's disgrace also sustains him in his moral exile and makes it as impossible for him to seek revenge on his detractors as it is for him to go out of his way to prove his innocence.

There is none of the turgid evangelism or dramatic violence of earlier school stories like *Eric* (q.v.) or *Tom Brown* (q.v.) in *The Fifth Form at St Dominic's*. The serious parts of the story are constantly interrupted by farcical scenes involving the Tadpoles and Guinea-pigs, and by the refreshing drolleries of Anthony Pembury, a lame boy, son of a newspaper editor, whose promotion of a wall newspaper, *The Dominican*, provides one of the most lively interludes in the long line of English school stories. The characters are drawn not as examples to be marked and noted but as individuals, and none is more sharply or sympathetically drawn than the reticent, stoical Oliver Greenfield. [Talbot Baines Reed: *The Fifth Form at St Dominic's*, London 1881]

**OLLY TOOK** is station-master at Hartwarp, from which station a light railway runs in summer. There is also a branch line now only kept open so that Olly Took can communicate with his older brother the Gaffer, who still lives by the quarry though his job as a loader has now ceased. The brothers, argumentative as well as inseparable, talk to one another on a loud trumpet-telephone. As thin Olly and fat Gaffer share a propensity for sleep, they constantly complain of the interruption caused by the telephone, though they find frequent calls indispensable. Olly Took has his own interpretation of his duties. 'I don't hold with working at week-ends unless you can take a good rest during the week', he comments, ignoring the fact that his working week is pretty restful, too, since he has organized a team of willing helpers to keep the station in order and tend his bees, goats, rabbits, ducks and geese.

Prominent among his helpers are Jo, the Gaffer's cheerful daughter, and Charley and George, two lively village lads who encourage the eccentric station-master in various bizarre enterprises. They help to rescue several vintage cars and engines from the local dump and start a museum; watch with glee the effects of a self-raising powder he has discovered which can induce levitation; observe with some dismay the sight of Charley's father and aunts afloat on the village pond after an explosion due to chemical experiments by the Gaffer. In these and equally absurd adventures the children are drawn realistically to provide a measure of reason to counterbalance the wild behaviour of Olly Took and the Gaffer who (as is plain from Ferelyth Eccles Williams's pictures) belong to the world of fantasy. [John Pudney: *The Hartwarp Light Railway*, London 1962; *The Hartwarp Dump*, 1962; *The Hartwarp Circus*, 1963; *The Hartwarp Bakehouse*, 1964; *The Hartwarp Explosion*, 1965; *The Hartwarp Jets*, 1967]

**ONION JOHN**, six foot three in height and moustached, lives on Hessian Hill, outside the town of Serenity. John's central European name being unpronounceable, he has earned a nickname locally because of his productive vegetable plot. His house is built of piled-up stone and four bath tubs and is largely furnished from the town dump. The grown-ups laugh at his sympathetic magic – when, for instance, he ties rocks in a tree to shame the apples into growing faster – but they cannot convince the younger generation that it is not John's procession, the burning cedar branches and the hymn and John's immersion in the river, that bring the much-needed rain.

The boy most strongly convinced of Onion John's special powers is Andy Rusch, who from interest and affection has learned to understand some of John's language. Andy finds himself acting as interpreter when the town vote as their next goodwill project to build the strange man a proper house. The actual building fills the citizens with satisfaction; John for his part, though he tries to show his gratitude, is neither willing nor able to fit the pattern of Serenity. Eventually he moves away to a new, secret, unorthodox home, but not before he has shown Andy the way to achieve his own freedom.

Because this novel is about communication between human beings, the characters have to be to some extent enlarged and simplified, John being as completely innocent and country-wise as the people of Serenity are hidebound and proud of their conventionally benevolent impulses. Similarly Andy and his father are drawn as the ideal American father and son. Onion John's individuality has to be seen in the context of a particular kind of community which is forced to take a stern look at itself because of the stranger who refuses to be patronized. [Joseph Krumgold: *Onion John*, New York 1959]

**ORLANDO** the Marmalade Cat lives contentedly with his dear wife Grace and their kittens Pansy, Blanche and Tinkle, and independent though he is, he appreciates the attentions of their kind master, Mr Cattermole. However, there comes a time when the cats feel they need a holiday and although their master urges them to think 'of the mischief the mice will do if you

Kathleen Hale's illustration of Orlando, Grace and their kittens from *Orlando the Judge.*

go away', he finally gives in and orders a tent, while Orlando draws up a list of their requirements and the kittens impede the packing.

The first of many outings, expeditions and holidays enjoyed by the cats established a basic pattern. Life on a farm and by the sea, a journey to Persia on a flying carpet, a visit to aristocratic relatives in a French château and a rather more hazardous trip to the Moon, all give Orlando a chance to show how adaptable and imperturbable he is. He runs a zoo for a time and deputizes for Judge Wiggins in the Case of the Missing Cheese, when his astute offspring help to collect evidence in favour of the accused, Mr Gorgon and Mr Zola.

Orlando and Grace are well matched and lead a happy home life. Orlando, initiator of action and solver of problems, is never dressed up, whereas Grace wears such tasteful confections as the situation requires (a correct tweed coat and skirt when she takes the boisterous poodle for a walk, a capacious sailor-cum-bathing costume at the seaside, aprons and fur-coats and Turkish trousers as desired). The youngest of the kittens, Tinkle, has a special role as the indulged youngest, bumptious and rebellious, in and out of mischief, spinning little verses to assert his importance.

The humour of animals living as humans is expressed in puns and analogies; on the way to the Moon Orlando catches flying saucers full of milk in a shrimping net, and a thieving cat is sentenced to spend the rest of his life as Doorkeeper to the Home for Old Mice. The superb lithographic illustrations, crowded with comic, double-edged details, set new standards for picture-books when they first began to appear. Kathleen Hale used her own cat as a model for Orlando, and her skill as an artist is seen clearly in the way she relates real cats to a human world, in an outstandingly successful series of humanizations. [Kathleen Hale: *Orlando the Marmalade Cat: A Camping Holiday*, London 1938; *Orlando's Evening Out*, 1941; *Orlando's Home Life*, 1942; and many other titles]

**OSWALD TUBBS** is a music-hall artiste, a conjuror who makes up for being short and fat by considerable skill and an ebullient mode of speech which indicates that his life is a continuous performance. His nephew Dick Birkenshaw is astonished by his first sight of the strange figure in his check suit and yellow shoes but he soon learns to appreciate his uncle's accomplishments, and when Oswald presents him with the gold fox-head tie-pin that has fascinated the boy, it seems a notable and happy link with this peculiar man who has led him into some stimulating adventures.

Like so many of Howard Spring's characters, Oswald Tubbs hides under his oddity a great deal of wisdom and good sense. 'Self possession and decorum, please', he advises Dick, as they go together to the Lady Mayoress's ball in fancy dress. 'Never come to your public appearances in an agitated state of mind.'

His advice is as pertinent as that of quiet Uncle Henry Birkinshaw, which is based on his particular sphere of fish-keeping, and the two characters, dramatically contrasted, establish the humorous and stimulating atmosphere of the book. [Howard Spring: *Tumbledown Dick*, London 1939]

**OTTO**'s father, Baron Conrad, attacks and robs passing travellers from rockbound Castle Drachenhausen. The shock of the Baron's return, sorely wounded, from one such raid kills his gentle wife, and the baby Otto is sent to a neighbouring monastery, where his first twelve years are spent in godly learning. When his father claims him at last, the boy has barely begun to understand the new way of life and still suffers distress at its warlike basis, when in his father's absence he is stolen by a rival baron. A pawn in the struggle between the two families, Otto is rescued from imprisonment, but he has been mutilated by Baron Henry, and his father is killed in the escape. When Otto appeals to the emperor for help to recover his estate, he begs for mercy for Baron Henry's daughter, who has become his friend in captivity, and their marriage symbolizes the Emperor's determination to put an end to the wasteful feuds of the powerful barons.

Howard Pyle's own forceful illustrations, Düreresque and romantic, emphasize the contrast between the gentle, innocent boy and the turbulent, aggressive warriors who destroy his hand but not his spirit. The contrast is necessarily exaggerated to suit the particular view of the Dark Ages which Howard Pyle presents in a short tense story in which he merged his own highly pictorial idea of the past with the moral sentiments of his own time. [Howard Pyle: *Otto of the Silver Hand*, New York 1888]

**OWL AND THE PUSSYCAT, THE** *see* GINGER AND PICKLES

**OZMA OF OZ** *see* TIPPETARIUS

PADDINGTON, the animal personality first brought to life in *A Bear Called Paddington* (1958), is innocently enquiring, ineffably well-meaning but woefully clumsy and accident-prone. His wistfully self-satisfied look as he sits in a dark corner of the railway station (which later provides his name) enchants the reader as quickly as it charmed Mr and Mrs Brown, who caught sight of the bear as they were meeting their daughter Judy at the beginning of the school holidays. The Browns care for the animal with affection but they are bedevilled by his natural independence. Paddington is never dangerous but his curiosity, and the fact that he is living as humans do, cause endless comic accidents from the first day in the Brown's house, when he decides that the best way to eat pudding is to sit on the table and partly in the plate.

Michael Bond states once and for all the main premise of his stories: Paddington can talk to humans

*Above and overleaf*. Peggy Fortnum's drawings of Paddington Bear.

and they can talk to him. He is not a toy bear magically brought to life, but a honey-bear from South America with a passion for marmalade sandwiches; his Aunt Lucy, before she went into a home for retired bears in Peru, had advised him to stow away in a boat bound for England. His aplomb, his perfect English and his large hat cause mild surprise rather than incredulity in the station staff and in everyone who meets him. The central absurdity works simply because it is taken completely for granted. Though Paddington remains an animal in appearance and movement, he is more like another child in the family, whose peccadilloes are excused because he is different. Incongruity is the moving force of the stories; bears seldom paint pictures, enjoy theatrical performances, travel by underground. The humour of the stories might soon become commonplace if the central character were not an animal. The humanization of the bear is tactfully done. His disgracefully shabby old hat (it belonged to his uncle) is a trademark; otherwise, he occasionally wears a duffle coat or a yellow macintosh. Animal characteristics are never distorted and the social scene is within the understanding of most children, while the brisk narrative manner is equally approachable. Michael Bond's inventiveness never flags and although he has created other animal characters, like the mouse Thursday and Olga da Polga the guinea-pig, Paddington remains the favourite. All the books are illustrated by Peggy Fortnum who has helped to bring to life this original and delightful clown. [Michael Bond, ill. Peggy Fortnum: *A Bear Called Paddington*, London 1958; *More about Paddington*, 1958; *Paddington Helps Out*, 1960; *Paddington Abroad*, 1961; *Paddington at Large*, 1962; *Paddington Marches On*, 1964; *Paddington at Work*, 1966; *Paddington Goes to Town*, 1968; *Paddington takes the Air*, 1970; *Paddington on Top*, 1974]

**PADDLE-TO-THE-SEA** is a tiny model made by an Indian boy in the Canadian wilderness, to go in the canoe, one foot long, which he has carved from a piece of pine; along the bottom of the craft he has written 'Please put me back in water. I am Paddle-to-the-Sea'. For the boy has had a dream of the life of a great river born in the snow of the Nipigon country, flowing into the Great Lakes and at last into the ocean, and the little canoe and its paddler are to fulfil his dream. Each day he goes to look at the canoe on the hilltop and one morning he is just in time to see it slide into a brook made by melted snow. Paddle-to-the-sea is on his way.

Past a beaver dam, between great logs, the still, silent figure races in his craft till he is caught near a sawmill, but a French-Canadian lumberjack picks up the canoe, reads the message and acts upon it. He is the first of many people to help the little craft on its way; a fisherman and a coastguard on Lake Superior, a trapper, the mate of an ore boat, a girl on Lake Huron, a little old lady living near Montreal and many others rescue and

repair it and add their names to the inscription on the little craft. After four years, having survived ice, fire, storm and other dangers, the canoe reaches the sea and is picked up by a French boat off the Grand Banks; and when the story reaches the newspapers it is read by the young Indian who has started the whole affair.

Courage is always affecting in miniature, and the chronicle of this remarkable voyage, however useful and inspiring it may be as a geography lesson, is impressive most of all in its image of a tiny figure surviving in a world of huge perils. [Holling Clancy Holling: *Paddle-to-the-Sea*, Boston 1941]

**PAPA SMALL**, a white-American paterfamilias, sustains several roles as a vocational model before he is seen in a purely domestic context. The last book in the series is dedicated to 'all the children who asked, "Is there a Mama Small and Baby Small?"' The picture of his home life seems ahead of its time in one respect at least; Papa Small takes his share in the daily chores and even helps to cook the Sunday dinner.

In the earlier books, playing the parts of the 'Captain' of a sailing dinghy, a farmer, a cowboy, a fireman and so on, he copes with routine and with a few crises so that small children may acquire an outline knowledge (albeit idealized and old-fashioned) of the roles concerned. The educational aspect of the books is softened by the jaunty tone of the prose and by the pictures, which are cute and mannered and have a smooth simplicity that confirms that the Smalls live in a toy village. At the same time they show, unmistakably, that the chubby, smiling features of the hero are really those of a small boy assuming, and enjoying, the various disguises, one after another. [Lois Lenski: *The Little Sail Boat*, New York 1937; *The Little Farm*, 1942; *The Little Fire Engine*, 1946; *Cowboy Small*, 1949; *Papa Small*, 1951]

**PARGALES** (the) reckon they have worked in the chapter workshop from the very beginning of the cathedral and the boys now in the choir school know five generations of the family – old, old Mr Pargale and the new baby, both bald, neither actively working, enclosing from their respective ends the grandfather, father and son at present responsible for the wood and stone of the great structure. 'We've nussed her up from being no more than a chapel' is their view. 'We can see her breathe, and we don't reckon many can do that.' Unhurried and unflurried, they loom in the background of William Mayne's choir-school stories. Over the years (as it seems, over the centuries) they have adopted a deliberate way of moving; Eldest Pargale had once been heard to pronounce that working on a scaffold 'if you were quick there it was the same as being dead'. Work in high places has also led to a habit of antiphonal speaking, for it is important to know what everyone is going to do before he does it. Rooted in the past, confident in craftsmanship, amicably scornful of 'harchitecks', the Pargales see boys come and go, preserving a fatherly, relaxed manner towards them, ready to provide information about history or building techniques if asked.

Nothing disconcerts the Pargales. When mysterious noises in the Dark Entry (in *Words and Music*) give rise to tales of the Precinct Ghost, they bring the oldest Pargale to investigate in impressive procession, propelling him on a handcart, and he answers the questions he alone can deal with by nods and signs that are extremely expressive. Meanwhile the three middle Pargales descend the tunnel and deal with the defective drain which has caused the strange wailing, thus demonstrating the claim of the family that even if the Cathedral was made for services, 'They can't have them if it falls about their ears.' An entirely personal mode of speech and movement bring the Pargales unmistakably before us, carry-into the stories both humour and a welcome reflection of slow wisdom. [William Mayne: *A Swarm in May*, London 1955; *Chorister's Cake*, 1956; *Cathedral Wednesday*, 1960; *Words and Music*, 1963]

**PAUL BUNYAN** is a permanent part of American comic mythology and the creation and property of the lumber camp. His colossal size inevitably recalls such heroes as Finn McCool and his prowess as a hunter the feats of Baron Munchausen. He brushes his beard with a young pine tree pulled up by the roots and his measurements are calculated, hyperbolically, with axe-handles. This gigantic farmer and lumberman has a spouse as big as he is and a Great Blue Ox which helps him on one occasion to straighten a crooked road merely by pushing and pulling.

Some of Paul's adventures seem to belong to nature myth, others to be a natural extension of any hunter's tall stories, others again to be practical – Paul is credited with having invented the revolving grindstone, the grain elevator and the concrete mixer in spare moments. Probably the most significant item in his legendary dossier is the belief that he will not die until the last tree in the United States is cut down. [Wallace Wordsworth: *Paul Bunyan and His Great Blue Ox*, New York 1926]

**PAULINE, PETROVA AND POSY FOSSIL** The three 'fossils' of Noel Streatfeild's *Ballet Shoes* were 'collected' as babies by Professor Matthew Brown, almost as though they were part of his palaeontological studies, and brought up as sisters. Pauline had survived the wreck of a liner; Petrova was left alone in the world when her Russian parents died; Posy was born to a young dancer who could not make a living for her fatherless baby. In less than three years Sylvia, the absent-minded Professor's great-niece, was left to bring up three children when Great-Uncle Matthew vanished on yet another expedition. Because his financial calculations were inadequate, Sylvia Brown had to take in lodgers; in the manner of fairy tale, each of these contributed to the future of the girls. A benevolent rubber-planter tactfully put extra money in their way from time to time; two retired university women took care of their education; the dancing teacher on the ground floor found places for them in Madame Fidolia's stage school.

Having given her domestic tale the shape and something of the nature of a fairy tale, Noel Streatfeild then demonstrated her special talent for creating characters learning a professional skill. Pretty Pauline, whose dramatic talent is founded on a certain personal conceit, soon gets parts in pantomime; through her career we learn much about the by-laws governing children on the stage, as well as about production, rehearsals and so on. Petrova, a reserved and rather plain child, finds dancing a bore compared with the inside of a motor engine, but loyally accepts the training the other two girls enjoy. Posy is the first of several characters in which Noel Steatfeild illustrates the rare, complete dedication to an art; dancing, for Posy, is more important even than her affection for her 'sisters'. In spite of the fairy-tale ending of the story, in which each girl steps out in her chosen career, Noel Streatfeild is not at all starry-eyed about the stage. Her story reveals the tedium and physical weariness, the professional rivalries and disappointments of the theatre, always through the reactions of the three Fossils. *Ballet Shoes* was published at a time when tales of dancing schools and aspiring ballerinas were extremely popular; yet it is the only one of the scores of ballet tales which has survived, to be read today. [Noel Streatfeild: *Ballet Shoes*, London 1936]

**PEGGY BLACKETT** plays Mate to her elder sister Nancy's Captain in their continuous act of Amazon pirates. Of all the characters in Ransome's stories, she is the least recognizable as an individual. She is a born second-in-command, accustomed to being dominated by Nancy and often snubbed for talking too much – and indeed, she does rattle on. Domesticated, efficient as a camp organizer, she gets little credit for talents which impetuous Nancy takes for granted. Nor does Peggy expect credit. It is obvious that she admires her sister and when Nancy retires to bed with mumps (in *Winter Holiday*) she tries to adopt her mannerisms and her favourite oaths. 'Barbecued billygoats' comes uneasily from her lips, and she is relieved when Nancy is allowed to rejoin the party and she can relapse into her subsidiary role. Ransome uses her to throw into relief the sharper outline of the other children and also to establish the Blacketts as a unit alongside the more complex organism that is the Walker family. [Arthur Ransome: *Swallows and Amazons*, London 1930; *Swallowdale*, 1931; *Winter Holiday*, 1933; *Pigeon Post*, 1936; *Secret Water*. 1939; *The Picts and the Martyrs*, 1943]

**PENELOPE TABERNER CAMERON,** coming to Thackers in Derbyshire, does not know that her great-aunt Tissie's namesake, Cecily Taberner, had lived and worked in the kitchens three and a half centuries before, when the farmhouse was a small manor

Penelope Cameron with the Elizabethan boy Francis Babington from *A Traveller in Time* by Alison Uttley.

belonging to the Babington family. But while Penelope's older sister Alison seeks out local pleasures and her brother Ian learns to shoot, Penelope is absorbed in the history and atmosphere of the old house. Her love of legend and chivalry, of antique costume and custom, has grown during the solitude of repeated illness; besides, she has inherited second sight from her maternal great-grandmother.

At first Penelope is afraid when she looks into an upstairs room to see ladies in brocade gowns and lace caps playing a game with ivory counters, but her aunt accepts 'the people who once lived here' so naturally that she allows herself to be guided by her own sympathy for the Babingtons, whose life she enters intermittently. She becomes especially involved with the two sons – Francis, who becomes her playmate and friend, and Anthony, whose passionate devotion to the cause of the sad, imprisoned Mary of Scotland is echoed in her own heart. Penelope moves in and out of the past, unable to control the changes of time but accepted in the Tudor kitchens because she bears a name long used in the Taberner family and because, in the manner of dreams and visions, she fits easily into the way of life of Dame Cecily, the firm and kindly controller of the large household.

This is not to suggest that Penelope accepts the time-shift without question. If this were so, the book might have become stodgy, with her character merely used to outline a period in history for the young. *A Traveller in Time* is not an historical novel but a subtle study of extraordinary experience, the story of Penelope Taberner rather than of Anthony Babington. His tragic fate is mentioned obliquely, as something in the future. Alison Uttley's story is concerned solely with his plan to rescue the Queen from Wingfield, a mansion connected with Thackers by an old tunnel system. The one glimpse that Penelope has of the Queen is brief and affecting. It tells us more about the young girl than about the prisoner, for when she moves into the past Penelope remains herself, burdened with her knowledge that Mary of Scotland did in fact suffer execution. She cannot enjoy with her whole heart the insight into Tudor housewifery, madrigal singing or hawking, for she is constantly trying to decide whether she sees the past through dreams, whether Thackers was 'alive with the memory of things once seen and heard' or whether she has a double existence in fact. As the past strengthens its hold over her she is often desperately afraid in case a time will come when she is held there for ever. Her experiences take place on two separate visits. On the first she is a child and views the past as a child would. Two years later, she responds in a more mature way to the embodiment of past events, developing a closer relationship with the people and a more emotional responsibility for the events she sees. Her character is surely based on Alison Uttley's own feeling for the past as it is communicated by the old house which she knew

well as a child. This gives reality to a piece of characterization based not on a collection of traits but on a single line of emotional experience felt by an individual. [Alison Uttley: *A Traveller in Time*, London 1939]

**PERDITA** lives with Annie McLaren, in Mr Smith's large isolated house on the Western Scottish island of Skuaphort, where her foster-mother acts as housekeeper. Distance, and Mr Smith's reclusive ways, have kept the child from school; her abrupt, wild manners and outlandish, cut-down clothes, frighten the village children and drive them to persecute her. Stones and abuse and the rude nickname of 'the witch's daughter' have driven Perdita deeper into a shy, belligerent silence. In fact she is lonely and is given to haunting the quay to see the new people coming to the island, and at last she does find friends – Tim Hoggart and his blind nine-year-old sister Janey. Tim and Janey hardly believe Perdita's assertions that her mother was a witch, but when they are involved in Mr Smith's nefarious dealings they find they can rely on her flashes of intuition to help them in moments of danger.

Perdita's strange temperament makes its appeal to the other people in the story in various ways. Mr Smith's casual affection for 'his little witch, little changeling', as he calls her, leads him to take more risks than he might otherwise have done and this leads directly to his arrest. Tim learns to see through her affectations and recognize how lonely she is, while Janey's holiday has been enriched by her friendship. Perdita's life has been drastically changed too. She has lost Mr Smith, who had been a father-figure to her, and she has been exposed to feelings which she is too young to measure or to cope with, but Janey's serenity has helped her to face a changed future. As Janey's father puts it, the two girls have 'learned to see and hear things other people don't have time to, because they're always too busy just looking and playing'. The 'extra piece of ourselves that other people don't have', in Janey's phrase, is a sign of Perdita's individuality and explains a good deal of her behaviour. We can rely on Nina Bawden to draw her characters in such a way that they bring about events as well as being directed by them; this is particularly clear in the part Perdita plays in the events of *The Witch's Daughter*. [Nina Bawden: *The Witch's Daughter*, London 1966]

**PETER** is a black American boy who lives in New York and enjoys the freedom of the streets with his dachshund Willie and his boon companion Archie. We see him making the discoveries small children must make in any country – exploring his immediate environment, coming to terms with the new baby for whom his special furniture is appropriated, learning to whistle. He takes his first steps towards a wider community than that of his home when he invites a girl to his party; soon he is outfacing the big boys and entering Willie for a neighbourhood pet show.

There is an engaging simplicity in the way Peter's

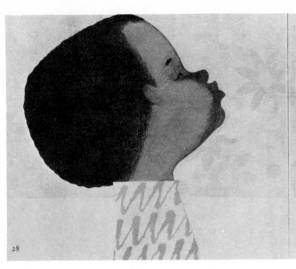

Peter ran home
to show his father and mother what he could do.
They loved Peter's whistling. So did Willie.

28                                                                                                  29

Two pages of *Whistle for Willie* by Ezra Jack Keats.

boyish energies are demonstrated in these picture-books. Ezra Jack Keats has used colour to denote mood and collage effects to suggest a small, enclosed world which to the child is full of gaiety and exciting possibilities. Like Kate Greenaway, he has conceived a particular locale in terms of childhood. [Ezra Jack Keats: *The Snowy Day*, New York 1962; *Whistle for Willie*, 1964; *Peter's Chair*, 1967; *A Letter to Amy*, 1968; *Goggles*, 1969; *Hi, Cat!*, 1970; *Pet Show!*, 1972]

**PETER BECKFORD** *see* DAVID HUGHES

**PETER CHURCHMOUSE** feels safe in Parson Pease-Porridge's church, with meals conveniently available in the rat-traps, until the unhappy day when he overhears the portly cleric, furious at the holes nibbled in the felt of the collection basket, resolving to get a cat. Certainly Gabriel, the friendly kitten who has been instructed to 'scare the rats away', is no danger to Peter, but where is he to find food now that the traps have been declared redundant? After several unsuccessful attempts to attract Parson Pease-Porridge's attention, Gabriel knocks over the inkpot in the vestry and Peter makes footprints on the blotter, besides biting a hole in next Sunday's sermon; the parson, donning a new and powerful pair of spectacles, at last realizes he has a church mouse dependent on him, and cheerfully provides a meal of cheese, after abandoning his ruined sermon for an extempore address on KINDNESS.

The absent-minded cleric, the resourceful church mouse and his engagingly literal kitten friend are later joined by the parson's spaniel pup, Trumpet Churchdog, whose miserable howls upset them till they discover he is cutting a tooth. Margot Austin humanizes these animals by giving them distinctive modes of speech (including Peter's habit of breaking into rhyme at intervals) and her monotone illustrations, whimsically comic in style, also suggest their several 'charac-

Peter Churchmouse with the friendly kitten Gabriel, drawn by Margot Austin.

ters'. [Margot Austin: *Peter Churchmouse*, New York 1941; *Gabriel Churchkitten*, 1942; *Trumpet Churchdog*, 1948; *Gabriel Churchkitten and the Moths*, 1948]

**PETER PAN** found the way to avoid growing up when he was a week old and flew away to Kensington Gardens, where he was accepted by the fairies as a Betwixt-and-Between. He sometimes went to look through the window of his old bedroom but he put off

*Left*. Arthur Rackham's illustration of the baby Peter in Kensington Gardens.
*Above*. The fight between Captain Hook and Peter Pan, drawn by Richard Kennedy.

going home for good until it was too late, for one night he found the window barred and saw another baby in his mother's arms.

The strange, brief fantasy, *The Little White Bird* (which afterwards became *Peter Pan in Kensington Gardens*) has echoes of myth in it, for the god Pan is present in more than Peter's name and Maimie's present to him of an imaginary goat; it has echoes of *Cinderella* and *The Snow Queen* in the sub-plot of the Duke of Christmas-Daisies and his inconvenient heart; it presents in an almost throw-away manner the central point of Peter's inadequate personality. To this fantasy many congenial additions were made when Barrie wrote the play of Peter Pan, which told how Peter coaxed the three Darling children – Wendy, John and Michael – to the Never-Never Land so that the Lost Boys should have a mother and how when they finally persuaded Peter to help them to return home, he resisted Mrs Darling's attempts to keep him and make him a real boy. The struggle in Peter between his moments of affection and his inhuman self-sufficiency, the reason for his eternal youth – these ideas are made less painful by a dramatic presentation. The crowded cast of characters allows Barrie's audiences to recall the most enjoyable figures of childhood – pirates, Redskins, mermaids, fairies, 'mothers and fathers'.

Peter Pan has many forms as a written story but ideally it should be seen first and then read. It contains ideas that are primitive, natural and essential and the humour and energy of the spoken word carries these ideas easily. Peter's remark 'To die will be an awfully big adventure' is easy to ridicule unless it is spoken and unless we see the boy marooned on a rock with the sea rising. Hook's 'Fetch me out that doodle-doo' and his last despairing 'Floreat Etona' as he is swallowed by the crocodile; Peter's malapropism, 'Dark and conister man, have at thee!'; the extraordinary mixture of emotion, terror and comedy needs to be heard, for, once heard, its complexity will remain in the mind of the reader. Similarly the characters, so simple and so subtle, live in action. Children will understand the full nastiness of Mr Darling's character if they have actually seen him pouring his medicine into the dog's dish, and a good actor can convey a great deal more of Peter's personality than psychological analysis can discover. [James Barrie: *The Little White Bird*, London 1902; *Peter Pan in Kensington Gardens*, 1906; *Peter and Wendy*, 1911]

275

Illustration from *The Tale of Peter Rabbit* and the writer and artist Beatrix Potter (1866–1943).

**PETER RABBITT** appeared first in a letter written by Beatrix Potter to little Noel Moore to amuse him when he was ill. Few stories can have been so perfectly calculated to entertain a child, with mischief a stage removed from a boy's world but still perfectly in keeping with it, and with a serene, well-ordered home waiting for the wandering Peter, with the logical outcome of his escapade, a dose of medicine for his upset stomach, and 'bread and milk and blackberries for supper' for his good little sisters. Miss Potter would never have made the mistake of introducing parental care and discipline into a story about, for instance, fish or frogs, but family relationships are perfectly suitable in stories about rabbits and they form a firm basis for the subsequent adventures of Peter's cousin, Benjamin Bunny, and the fortunes of his nephews and nieces, the Flopsy Bunnies, when they are captured by Mr McGregor and by Tommy Brock the badger. Flopsy's fury with old Mr Bouncer when his negligence puts her babies in danger, the behaviour of Peter's mother in the burrow, and the cousinly chatter of Peter and Benjamin, give the stories the special authority of natural truth and perfectly selected fancy. [Beatrix Potter: *The Tale of Peter Rabbit*, privately printed 1900, published edition with coloured illustrations, London 1902; *The Tale of Benjamin Bunny*, 1904; *The Tale of the Flopsy Bunnies*, 1909; *The Tale of Mr Tod*, 1912]

*Left.* Illustration from *The Tale of Benjamin Bunny*.

**PETER REGAN**, an Irish lad of fifteen who has just left school, does not like the idea of working on his uncongenial uncle's farm, so he takes himself off to Galway instead, walking forty miles or so, to look for a job. The job that in effect finds him is not altogether a pleasant one. Michael Joyce, having returned from Argentina, has bought from feckless Colman Donnelly a considerable piece of land. Here, from romantic sentiment mixed with good sense, Joyce has established a herd of deer. The local people are inexplicably hostile and before long a buck and three does are missing. Peter is offered the task of infiltrating the neighbourhood, as a holiday camper, to locate the missing animals.

Because Peter tells the story himself, we cannot look for subtlety of character, but the nature of the boy is clearly shown in his reaction to the unusual work. As he makes acquaintances in the village he comes to feel uncomfortable in accepting kindness under false pretences and as he comes to understand the country attitude to land ('Rights go deeper than buying and selling') he finds it hard to decide which side to take in an increasingly complicated state of affairs. In the end it is partly through his actions that the two opposed parties come to a reasonable solution. While the Irish love of genealogy helps to make peace, while the neighbours talk over Joyce's origins and his agricultural theories, Peter is contented with a future ahead of him and a good deal wiser about people than he was before. The enlightenment of youth has been described with humour and with a strong feeling for regional character. [Eilís Dillon: *A Herd of Deer*, London 1969]

**PETER WAYNE** loses his father, his Southern home and his cause in the American Civil War. Returning to his home in Georgia physically unhurt but shattered mentally by his experiences, he is astonished when the family lawyer tells him that 'Though you do not know it, you were very deeply wounded during the war.' He is unwilling to give up his hatred of Lincoln and his bitterness over the plight of the South; he cannot accept Mr Meadowbrook's assertion that he must 'realize that America comes before either North or South'. The wisdom of the old lawyer's words only comes home to him after many months of travelling to the West. The young man works in a gold mine and on the great Union Pacific railroad and learns to accept people for themselves and not only for their convictions. In part as a memorial to the memory of Professor Hauptmann, a Yankee who more than anyone else teaches him to hate bigotry, Peter Wayne returns home determined to help the South to become an effective part of the whole country. Peter Wayne is drawn not as an individual so much as a type who can illustrate the book's thesis; he moves effectively through varied scenes of action in various parts of the United States, but without really showing true individuality. [Leonard Wibberley: *The Wound of Peter Wayne*, London 1957]

**PETERKIN GRAY** – 'little, quick, funny, decidedly mischievous' – dances on to the scene in *The Coral Island* and crashes his way through *The Gorilla Hunters*, always the clown of the party, although in the course of the two adventures he does acquire a little stability and allows an innate sentimentality to show more plainly through his facetious remarks. To Ralph Rover (q.v.), meeting him again after seven years, he seems little changed, 'with the exception of a small scrap of whisker on each cheek, a scar over the right eye, and a certain air of manliness.' He still inspires protective feelings in his comrades, though he is now a famous hunter, and as such exercises some control over the expedition into the jungle to shoot gorillas (and any other animal that presents a worthy target).

In *The Coral Island* Ralph expresses what was presumably Ballantyne's aim in drawing the three heroes: 'We three, on this our island, although most unlike in many things, when united, made a trio so harmonious, that I question if there ever met before such an agreeable triumvirate.' Peterkin provides a certain comic relief for the weighty passages and the decidedly melodramatic moments of action that date the books. [R. M. Ballantyne, *The Coral Island*, London 1858; *The Gorilla Hunters*, 1861]

**PEVENSIE** children (the) – Susan, Peter, Edmund and Lucy – enter the land of Narnia, magically parallel with their own world, through a wardrobe in an old country house. It is Lucy, youngest in the family, who finds her way through the wardrobe first, and the others laugh at her story of Mr Tumnus the Faun. Being disbelieved upsets her, and she ventures into the wardrobe again, this time with Edmund, next to her in age. But he has been seen by the coldly beautiful White Witch (q.v.) and, bribed with a hot sweet drink and some Turkish Delight, he surrenders to her power and agrees to bring his sisters and brother to her. Though he betrays them, and the great lion Aslan, he redeems himself by his courage in the battle in which Good overcomes Evil, Spring puts Winter to flight, and the four children become rulers in Narnia.

One day time reverses itself and while hunting the White Stag they find themselves back in the old house, where time has stood still. They try in vain to return to Narnia until, a year or so later, they are transported there once more, to a wood near the sea where they find the ruins of their palace of Cair Paravel; and so they enter into the adventure of *Prince Caspian*, helping the young prince (q.v.) to defeat Miraz, regain his kingdom and restore the old happiness of Narnia. The adventure ends as abruptly as it began and Aslan warns Peter that he and Susan are too old to enter Narnia again. It is left to Edmund and Lucy, as a King and a Queen, to support Caspian (in *The Voyage of the 'Dawn Treader'*) in his quest through the Eastern Seas. Now they too are told that they must give up Narnia and learn to know Aslan in another way; they find out what this means (in *The Last Battle*) when Narnia gives place to an eternal kingdom.

The surname Pevensie is significant. Although the four children do not appear in every one of the Narnia stories they are constantly spoken of, not as children but as rulers. Even at the end of *The Lion, the Witch and the Wardrobe*, the simplest and most artless of the books, they are already using a chivalric language unlike their middle-class slang. As C. S. Lewis saw it, the aggressiveness they display from time to time is part of their role as champions of the Good; in all the stories, however, they show a hearty extrovert enjoyment of physical skill in battle, together with the dedication of sworn knights. To support the dual roles, of children enjoying encounters with talking animals, and monarchs of high responsibility, C. S. Lewis has had to draw their characters in simple terms. Edmund takes on an individuality in the first book of the cycle by virtue of his acts of malice, which are as much the acts of a resentful younger brother as of a Judas, whose part he assumes when the story is read as religious symbolism. Lucy has a certain attractive insouciance; she is more imaginative than her sister and is closer to Aslan, and more deeply affected by him, than any of the others. But on the whole the Pevensie children are less recognizable as individuals than many of the animal or fantastic characters – Puddleglum, for example, or the Sea Serpent who makes a brief but hilarious appearance in *The Voyage of the 'Dawn Treader'*, or the rascally ape Shift; nor is their chivalric dignity as convincing as that

Peter, Edmund, Lucy and Susan return through the wardrobe from the world of Narnia; an illustration by Pauline Baynes from *The Lion, the Witch and the Wardrobe*.

of the princes in the stories. The greatest check on one's belief in the Pevensies lies eventually in the fact that what they do depends on Aslan. Even when they seem to exercise their own judgment, they are demonstrably inspired by, or ordered by, the lion's great plan for Narnia and for them. They are part of a grand design, and though that design, ultimately a religious one, gives the books a seriousness and a poetic impulse beyond that of many other fantasy-adventures, in the long run it means that one vital element, of the active effect of personality on events, is missing from the cycle. [C. S. Lewis: *The Lion, the Witch and the Wardrobe*, London 1950; *Prince Caspian*, 1951; *The Voyage of the 'Dawn Treader'*, 1952; *The Last Battle*, 1956]

**PHILIPPA SEATON** lives with her widower father in a remote part of South America. As she says herself, she is at ten years old 'a somewhat old-fashioned child', her knowledge of the world gained from story books and make-believe, and she realizes that it is reasonable that her father should send her to school in England. At The Hollies Philippa learns to play hockey, writes poetry and acts in the school play and in a few years the little foreign plant has 'changed from a tropical blossom into an English rose.'

Philippa is drawn in a sentimental, generalized manner, more as an example than as an individual. This is the first of many school stories in which Angela Brazil develops the idea of a girl thrown into a strange environment, adapting to it and even, sometimes, changing it. The stiff, moralistic tone of this first book of hers, the stilted way the girl is described or placed centrally in scene after scene, was to change quickly to the more relaxed, jocose tone of the later school stories. [Angela Brazil: *The Fortunes of Philippa*, London 1907]

**PIED PIPER** (the) as Browning envisaged him is a robust, practical and resourceful version of the traditional jester of the Middle Ages, whose instant, angry revenge on the miserly Mayor and Corporation of Hamelin takes a little of the mystery away from the first description of the tall, sharp-eyed man and the seemingly benevolent power of his pipe, chiefly used 'On creatures that do people harm'. It is the mysterious, other-worldly aspect of the Piper which has been emphasized by illustrators, from Kate Greenaway's delicate-featured, graceful figure (which Ruskin thought was her finest work) to Alan Howard's conception of an archangelic figure who belongs completely to the tapestry-world of legendary apples, unicorn and phoenix

One of Gerald Rose's illustrations in *The Story of the Pied Piper*.

into which the Piper leads the dancing children.

Wit and swinging rhythm make this one of the most attractive of all narrative poems, as its plot is one of the saddest and most haunting. When Helen Cresswell let her imagination play on the theme, in *The Sea Piper*, she dedicated her story: 'In memory of the lost children of Aberfan 21st October 1966'. There is no incongruity in relating that tragedy to the light, fanciful story of Davy and Fancy Garter and their daughter Harriet, who begged the mysterious Sea Piper, brother to the Piper of Hamelin, to bring back the shrimps which were the livelihood of the village. The mysterious, mist-coloured figure who made a bargain with the mayor and the villagers so that he might have the gulls for company in his loneliness, is a powerful personal image, which plausibly relates to that of Browning. [Robert Browning: 'The Pied Piper of Hamelin', in *Dramatic Lyrics*, 1842; Helen Cresswell: *The Sea Piper*, London 1968]

**PIERS MEDLEY**, second son of Master Medley of Ghylls Hatch (*see* Medley Plashet) works with his father breeding horses, while his brother Harry, with the increasing demand for weapons since Henry VIII incurred the enmity of France by declaring himself the Head of the Church in England, has begun to investigate the iron-founding industry. Piers's life suffers a violent change when his uncle, Master of Novices at Pancras Priory, calls on his help to take a precious altar-piece to safety. In the course of a struggle with Thomas Cromwell's men, Piers saves a girl from attack and promises his dying uncle to protect her. Not till after Isabella has been nursed back to health and sanity and she and Piers have married does she confess that she is an outcast from a dispossessed convent, still a novice and bound by vows of chastity. Convinced of her essential innocence, Piers still fears she may be discovered by the spies of the Crown. They escape together into Kent, where Piers works for widowed Ursula Pilgrove and where Isabella bears a daughter. Still fearful of eternal damnation, the unhappy girl runs away and dies tragically.

When Piers returns to claim his daughter from Ursula a year later, they find solace and love together in a week of snowbound weather. The daughter Ursula bears is acknowledged by Piers many years later, when he is master of Mantlemass and of a thriving iron-foundry. His character illustrates particularly well the way Barbara Willard involves her characters in great national changes and upheavals. Piers is shown, in the course of three books, growing from a dirty, lanky schoolboy to a landowner in energetic middle age, and the appearance of his second, unknown daughter, Lilias Godman (q.v.) brings out fresh facets of his character. [Barbara Willard: *A Cold Wind Blowing*, London 1972; 'Winter's Tale', in *Young Winter's Tales*, London 1973; *The Iron Lily*, 1973]

**PIGLET** *see* WINNIE-THE-POOH

**PIGLING BLAND** *see* GINGER AND PICKLES

**PIGWIG** *see* GINGER AND PICKLES

**PING** 'lived with his mother and his father and two sisters and three brothers and eleven aunts and seven uncles and forty-two cousins. Their home was a boat

An illustration by Kurt Weise from *The Story About Ping.*

with two wise eyes on the Yantze River.' This obedient little duck has always been able to avoid punishment for being the last back at the boat at night; but one night Ping forgets the time and, afraid to go home, he hides in the reeds and next day is captured by a family who think he will make a pleasant addition to their meal.

The book is an outstanding example of the virtue of simplicity. The incantatory words of the text and the pure, appealing colours of Kurt Weise's illustrations say what they have to say with perfect tact and elegance. Ping is not presented as a person; the link between animal and human behaviour is forged in the total, sincere, simple tone of the story. [Marjorie Flack, ill. Kurt Weise: *The Story about Ping*, New York 1933]

**PING**, who is Chinese, escaped from his forest home near the Burmese border, during the war, and was brought up in a home for displaced children in England. When Dr Maud Biggin, an archaeologist, rents Green Knowe for the summer, she invites her great-niece Ida to stay, with Ping and Oskar (a Polish boy from the same Home) as companions for her. Ping says very little, but sometimes expresses himself in a birdlike trill of laughter, and the other two understand him very well. The children enjoy not only the everyday delights of boating and playing in water but also the stranger pleasures of early morning and moonlight, when they share a secret world with winged horses, a philosophical hermit, a laughter-loving giant. When Ping, one glimmering night, asks the river for a Word of Power, it answers with his own name HSU, and indeed he seems nearest to the summer's magic, while his gentle composure makes the unperceptive grown-ups seem all the more blundering and clumsy. Where Tolly (q.v.) responds to Green Knowe through the people who had once lived there, Ping understands it through the world of nature.

So it is Ping, and not Tolly, who is at the centre of the strangest, most haunting of all the Green Knowe adventures (in *A Stranger at Green Knowe*) when the gorilla Hanno breaks out of the London Zoo and finds a hiding place in the bamboo thicket at the end of Mrs Oldknow's garden. Ping had seen Hanno on a school outing to the Zoo and had shown his sympathy for the captive by giving him a peach. Then, the Head Keeper, who had reared Hanno from babyhood, assured him the gorilla would remember him: now, when Ping confirms his suspicion that Hanno is hiding at Green Knowe, he is nervous but not really afraid, for he and the gorilla have forest memories in common and Ping, who has learned through misfortune where to trust and where to stand aloof, feels sure that Hanno regards him as a friend. More than this, as the boy smuggles food into the thicket and watches Hanno, intuition tells him that he has been accepted as a little gorilla, and he holds to this some comfort after Hanno, who rushes out of hiding to defend him from a heat-maddened cow, has been shot by the local posse that finally tracks him down.

'Ping had the kind of imagination that never dismisses anything as ordinary' and the temperament to accept the extraordinary with a lively, unperturbed intelligence. The tragic note in this overwhelmingly powerful story, its immediate theme and its deeper implications, depend to a great extent on the subtle, unobtrusive interpretation of this attractive small boy and of the bond between him and 'that variable and incalculable whirlwind of muscle', the gorilla Hanno. [L. M. Boston: *The River at Green Knowe*, London 1959; *A Stranger at Green Knowe*, 1961; *An Enemy at Green Knowe*, 1964]

**PINKY PYE**, a skinny black kitten with 'one pure white paw and a white nose with a comical black spot just off centre', is found tangled in an old crab-net outside the door of the Pye family's holiday cottage. Pinky's chief claim to fame is that she learns to type – or so the doting Pyes insist, especially Mr Pye the ornithologist, whose machine she usurps for his experiments. Indeed, he allows her (or so it seems to the besotted children) to type the story of her life and adventures at The Eyrie, culminating in the extraordinary affair of the pygmy owl which blows into the attic and subsists on Uncle Benny's pet crickets.

Eleanor Estes brings Pinky to life by adding to the enumeration of her actions and appearance the loving comments of the Pyes as they watch her. Then, too, the author enters into Pinky's thoughts in a lightly whimsical manner that takes proper account of cat behaviour. Finally, she includes in the story extracts from the supposed autobiography written, in fact, by Mr Pye. By moving from one approach to another Eleanor Estes avoids sentimentality and gives the cat the kind of acquired personality which this particular species of domestic pet is apt to have. [Eleanor Estes: *Pinky Pye*, New York 1958]

**PINOCCHIO**'s mischievous tricks begin before old Gepetto has finished turning his new piece of wood into a puppet; a pair of eyes stare at him as soon as he has formed them, then the nose begins to lengthen by itself and the mouth to poke fun at him and when he has made legs and feet for the puppet, he gets a kick on the nose. As soon as the old man has taught Pinocchio to walk, he runs away and Gepetto is blamed for ill-treating him and thrown into prison. He is released in time to console the puppet whose feet have been burned off through his carelessness – and so, from one accident to another, their life continues. For Pinocchio has the heedless ways and affectionate heart of any boy. He is less disposed to listen to the wise counsel of the cricket (indeed, he flattens it with a hammer) than to the persuasion of the fox and cat whose glowing descriptions of the Field of Miracles induce him to risk his precious gold pieces; every time he promises the good fairy to obey her, to be good and go to school, he is led astray, until at last, playing truant in Playland, he is turned into a donkey. After more boisterous adventures he is swallowed by

Two illustrations by Gioia Fiammenghi from
*Pinocchio*; (*top*) Pinocchio is no sooner made than he
kicks old Gepetto on the nose; (*above*) his nose grows
longer with every lie he tells.

a giant shark and to his surprise finds another victim
inside – his dear Daddy, who has been searching for him
on land and sea. Pinocchio is at last convinced that he
loves Gepetto better than he loves idleness and mischief,
and with repentance comes the fulfilment of his dearest
wish – he becomes a real boy.

The wit and charm of the story of the puppet seems
as indestructable as his wooden body. There can be few
stories which survive so well the indignity of cutting or
re-writing. There is so much good humour and good
sense in the story and such pertinent, man-of-the-world
wisdom in the characterization of the fox and the cat,
the Showman Fire-eater, old Gepetto and the scape-
grace son, among others, that the most banal version
cannot destroy its vitality. Pinocchio is always himself.
In his utmost hunger he pettishly refuses to eat the skin
of the pears which Gepetto has sacrificed for him; in
direst poverty he still bargains for better payment from
the kind woman who offers to pay him for carrying her
water-bucket (like so many of his well-wishers, she is
the fairy giving him one more chance to redeem himself).

Although he does reform and becomes a contented,
good-looking boy, readers will note with some relief
that he does not change for the love of goodness but
for the love of people – a distinction which not all moral-
ists make when they write fantasy for children with a
concealed lesson in it. [Carlo Collodi (pseud. Carlo
Lorenzini): Story in *The Children's Journal*, Rome,
7 July 1881 and onwards; published in book form as
*The Adventures of Pinocchio* (1883 Italy) trans. M. A.
Murray, New York and London 1892]

**PIPPI LONGSTOCKING** – Pippilotta Provisionia
Gaberdina Dandeliona Ephraimsdaughter Longstocking – comes to live alone in Vilekulla Cottage
when her father is lost at sea. Confident that he will reappear, (perhaps after a period as king of a cannibal
island), this carrot-haired personality, with her odd
stocking, her pet monkey and the habit she has of picking up her horse bodily, leads a life of happy eccentricity
which Tommy and Annika find enviable. Sensible
Annika quietly resists being drawn into Pippi's most
outrageous exploits and learns when to take her seriously and when to wait till her mood becomes calmer.
It takes the school teacher a little longer, for Pippi plans
to be a pirate when she grows up and is not convinced
of the value of learning to be a Real Lady. Fortunately
for her, the only standards she ever has to conform to,
other than her own, are those of the Canny Canny
Islands, when she visits Captain Ephraim Longstocking, and even then Pippi has her own unorthodox way
of dealing with sharks and pearl thieves.

Pippi is admirably equipped to wage the secret
guerilla warfare in which most children are only too
easily defeated or disarmed by their elders. With her
great strength and athletic skill she is able to maroon
on the roof a couple of policemen who come to take
her to a children's home and to get the better of a
circus wrestler. All the same, Pippi is a girl, not a freak.

In spite of her apparent confidence in the pills which,
she assures Tommy and Annika, will mean they need
not grow up to 'a lot of dull work and stupid clothes
and corns and nincum tax', she shows that her future
lies in their world and not on a South Sea Island. Astrid
Lindgren gives enough clues to Pippi's carefully hidden
sympathy and generosity to give the stories about her
the humanity without which fantasy can become empty
fancy. [Astrid Lindgren: *Pippi Longstocking* (1945
Sweden) trans. Edna Hurup, London 1954; *Pippi Goes
Aboard*, 1956, *Pippi in the South Seas*, 1957, both trans.
Marianne Turner]

**POD, HOMILY** and **ARRIETTY** live under the
kitchen floor in a large country house. Safety-pins, postage stamps and other small articles are skilfully turned
into furniture, water is tapped from a convenient pipe,
light comes through a grating in the outside wall.
Homily, who is full of tales about the old days when
every room in the house was secretly inhabited by a
family of Borrowers, believes her family is now the last,

283

Two illustrations from the adventures of *The Borrowers,* drawn by Diana Stanley.

unless her brother Hendreary, who emigrated to a badger-sett across the fields, is still alive. She also believes that humans exist solely to provide the means of life for the Borrowers and that Great Aunt Sophy, bedridden upstairs, and her depleted staff (Mrs Driver the cook and Crampfurl the gardener) are the only humans in the world – except for the Boy who has come to Firbank while his parents are in India, and against whom Homily warns her daughter Arrietty – for Borrowers must never be seen by humans.

Arrietty is intrigued by the warning and does not share the dismay of her parents when one day Pod *is* seen by the boy, while he is trying to carry a dolls' house cup from the chimney-piece of a bedroom. When Arrietty meets the Boy herself they become firm friends, in spite of Homily's disapproval, and in fact it is the Boy who saves them when Mrs Driver discovers their presence and calls the rat-catcher in. Escaping through the grating, the Borrowers bravely venture into the fields, living for a time in an old boot in the hedge. They meet

Spiller, a borrower who has an enviably roving life trading on the stream in a knife-box boat, and with his help escape from Mild-Eye the gypsy and locate their relations in the keeper's cottage. ·

Here Arrietty finds a new friend to talk to, the cheerful boy Tom Goodenough, but after a time the cottage is shut up and the tiny family finds another home in a model village made by Mr Pott, whose friendship with the lonely, imaginative Miss Menzies helps him to believe in and secretly help the Borrowers. Unfortunately they are seen by his unpleasant neighbours and rivals, the Platters, who capture them in order to exhibit them to the public. After a dramatic escape from their attic prison in a gas balloon contrived by Pod, they return to Mr Pott's village, but although the house he and Miss Menzies have furnished for them is all that Homily ever dreamed of, she and Pod are nervous when they realize their presence is known and set out on a final journey to a disused mill. 'Stories never really end', as Mary Norton puts it. She leaves the Borrowers trying

to reconcile themselves to having Spiller one day as a son-in-law, rough though he is, for he and Arrietty share a taste for adventure.

In short, Mary Norton gives the Borrowers a future, as she has given them a past. These entrancing characters are believable not because they are magic (Arrietty is indignant that the Boy should assume they are fairies) but because they are complete in themselves, living fragmentarily (even their names are borrowed and scrappy) in their own adapted version of human life. Their appearance, their home, their domestic routine and their conversation, are described with minute, consistent detail; the author has explained that the stories come partly from the view of the outside world which short sight gave her in childhood. But it is not only brilliantly selected circumstantial detail that gives the Borrowers reality. Through Homily, with her reminiscences of the old days (of the Overmantels, a flighty family who lived in the morning room and smelt of cigars and brandy and Russian leather, and the Knife Machine boys who borrowed so boldly in the scullery, and the elegant Harpsichords in the drawing-room) we look briefly into a time when the race of Borrowers was extensive and well-established. Then, the story is authenticated by a second, enveloping narrative. Old Mrs May tells her young friend Kate what her brother had told her about his friendship with Arrietty; together they visit Firbank and the cottage, and Tom Goodenough, now an old man, tells Kate what he knows of the life of the family in the fields; the rest of their story comes partly from what Arrietty had written down in a tiny book that survived the passage of time and partly from what she told the quiet Miss Menzies. It is a brilliant, effective version of the old device of the family papers in the attic.

Finally, the Borrowers win credence as a family. As they make their alarming way from one hidden home to another their relationships to one another change and develop. Arrietty loves to listen to her mother's stories but already she is growing away from her parents. Her mutinous insistence that at twelve she is old enough to go out borrowing by herself is the first of many rebellious moments. Impetuous and fearless, she longs to escape from her confined, conventional home and to find freedom in the open air. The stories of the Borrowers may be read in part as parables of the human condition; we can hardly help thinking of them as refugees, for there is pathos as well as excitement in Mary Norton's account of their adventures. But ultimately these are stories about individuals and it is this that gives the books their vitality and satisfies imagination and feeling alike in the reader. [Mary Norton: *The Borrowers*, London 1952; *The Borrowers Afield*, 1955; *The Borrowers Afloat*, 1959; *The Borrowers Aloft*, 1961; *Poor Stainless*, 1971 (originally in *The Eleanor Farjeon Book*, 1966]

**POLLY** and **OLIVER** are cousins and perfect foils for one another. Polly Trott was born, as she is pleased to remind Oliver, on a troop ship in the West Indies, and she enjoys enlightening him on matters of army routine.

DAVID SCOTT DANIELL

Polly & Oliver

Besieged

ILLUSTRATED BY WILLIAM STOBBS

JONATHAN CAPE

Polly and Oliver, drawn by William Stobbs in *Polly and Oliver Besieged*.

For Oliver Crowe has not served for long in the army and is anxious to acquit himself well as drummer boy to a Regiment of Foot in its various sallies against England's enemies – in France, Spain, Sicily and India. The five stories about these two lively and resourceful youngsters of the Napoleonic period were originally written as radio plays for the BBC Children's Hour. The characters are necessarily simple, each having one or two traits which can be quickly recognized – like Polly's moments of confusion when adventures look like involving death, Oliver's pride in his country and his determination to help to defeat the enemy. These are not realistic stories but light-hearted adventures which call for the quick wits and hide-and-seek skill of children. Whether they are escorting a Rajah's treasure across India or guarding a Spanish princeling on the way to England, escaping from pirates or carrying secret despatches, Polly and Oliver, even if they are drawn in outline, are certainly no type-specimens. [David Scott Daniell: *Mission for Oliver*, London 1953; *Polly and Oliver*, 1954; *Polly and Oliver at Sea*, 1960; *Polly and Oliver Besieged*, 1963; *Polly and Oliver Pursued*, 1964]

**POLLY PLUMMER** and **DIGORY KETTER-LEY** live in London in the days 'when Mr Sherlock Holmes was still living in Baker Street and the Bastables were looking for treasure in the Lewisham Road'. The date and the allusions are important, for *The Magician's Nephew*, of all the Narnia stories, is the most strongly influenced by Edith Nesbit's domestic fantasies. Digory's uncle, an unpleasant student of magic, believes that he has 'a high and lonely destiny'; he has long been experimenting with the dust contained in an Atlantean box given to him by his godmother Mrs Lefay (the last fairy godmother in the world) and has at last succeeded in making certain coloured rings which he hopes can transport people to the Other World which he longs to explore. Lonely and unhappy in his uncle's house, where his mother lies seriously ill, Digory makes friends with Polly next door, and together through the rings they become involved in an adventure that takes place in three worlds – the world of Edwardian London, into which their rashness has introduced the powerful Queen Jadis (see the White Witch); the dead, empty city of Charn where she had long waited for release, and the new Paradise, the country of Narnia, which is created by Aslan (q.v.) from the ruins of the old, wicked land.

Digory and Polly are, like their counterparts the Pevensie children (q.v.), and Eustace (q.v.) and Jill, allowed freedom of action only under the direction of Aslan. In *The Magician's Nephew* the religious symbolism is particularly marked and it would not be surprising if the boy and girl seemed to be nonentities. It may be that they attract to themselves, by association, something of the liveliness of the Nesbit children; it may be that Pauline Baynes's especially apt use of period costume and lineaments, in her illustrations, adds life to them as well. At all events they are a couple of genuine

Polly and Digory fly across Narnia on Fledge, the flying horse, drawn by Pauline Baynes.

and likable children, who are never ossified by the formal speech and occasions that affect the behaviour of the Pevensies and who show none of the ecstatic or submissive reactions to Aslan which make the other children at times so disconcertingly priggish. [C. S. Lewis: *The Magician's Nephew*, London 1955]

**POLLYANNA WHITTIER** is possibly the most exasperating heroine in fiction. Fair and freckled, trusting and indomitably optimistic, she seems the epitome of everything that is priggish and sentimental in the fiction of half a century ago; yet it is impossible to dislike the 'glad girl' whose game reflects the courage of a truly unhappy child.

The 'Glad Game' begins for Pollyanna when her indigent clergyman father tries to console her because her gift from the missionary barrel turns out to be not the doll she hoped for but a pair of crutches: she should be glad, he says, that she does not need them. Certainly it is badly needed when Pollyanna is eleven, for within a fortnight of her father's sudden death she is packed off to her mother's sister, Miss Polly Harrington.

Proud and reserved, Miss Harrington's heart is hidden as thoroughly as her black curls are restrained in a bun; but Pollyanna uncovers the heart, and the curls, and Aunt Polly learns to live and love once more.

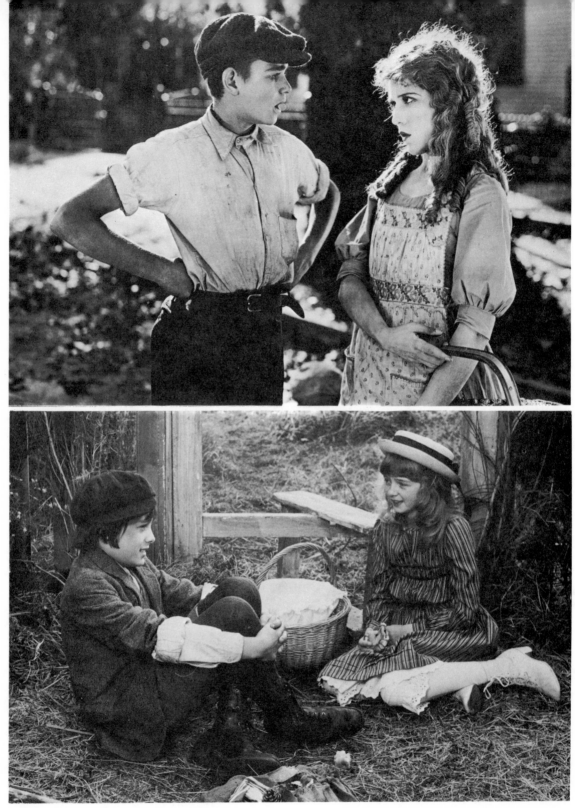

*Top.* Mary Pickford in the film *Pollyanna* in 1920.
*Above.* Elizabeth Archard as Pollyanna with Stephen Galloway as Jimmy Bean in the BBC serial *Pollyanna*, produced in 1973.

The inhabitants of Beldingsville learn the Glad Game after some initial perplexity. Because Pollyanna insists that there is always something to rejoice in, the dismal invalid Mrs Snow recovers her interest in life; reclusive John Pendleton overcomes his lifelong regret at not having won the heart of Pollyanna's mother and adopts the orphan Jimmy Bean, whom Pollyanna discovers sitting in the street, a fugitive from the local orphanage. So Pollyanna, reiterating at intervals her cry of 'I'm so glad, *glad*, GLAD,' transforms many lives, but her own is threatened when she is knocked over by a car. When she overhears the doctors say she may never walk again, she does for a moment lose her courage; but a book with such a heroine can only end happily. Dr Chilton, who is called in at Pollyanna's desire and who finds a specialist to cure her, proves to be Aunt Polly's former suitor, estranged from her for many years because he refused to bow to her arrogant ways.

In *Pollyanna Grows Up*, Pollyanna as a girl of thirteen takes a hand in the sad life of Mrs Carew, finds her long-lost son and sorts out the identity of Jimmy Bean. In the latter part of the book, as an eager, attractive young woman of twenty, she is still too good to be true but at least she has realized that the game 'wouldn't sound quite the same from me now, at twenty, as it did when I was ten. I realize that, of course. Folks don't like to be preached at, you know.' All the same, she does plenty of surreptitious preaching in the book, and a little quiet weeping as well, before the several couples in the story sort themselves out to the tinny sound of marriage bells. Perhaps Pollyanna should ideally be met only on the screen, where the sententious undercurrents of the books are necessarily subordinated to action and drama; at any rate, each generation has cherished its own film and television version of the Glad Girl. [Eleanor Porter: *Pollyanna*, Boston 1913; *Pollyanna Grows Up*, 1915]

**POLYNESIA** *see* DOCTOR DOLITTLE

**POOR CECCO** is a wooden dog, the cleverest toy in the nursery and the bravest. He is even brave enough to face Murrum, the ill-natured cat who loves to torment the toys and drops poor Tubby into a hollow tree, hoping they will never find her. Cecco sets out with the stuffed dog Bulka on a walk that takes them far into the country and involves them with adversaries more dangerous than Murrum. For on their way they meet Jensina, a wooden doll living on a rubbish dump, and when she joins them they are followed by a band of angry rats, anxious to recover from her their precious relic, the Tooth of Grimalkin. Resourceful and brave, Cecco is always in control, whether he is finding a way home for the tired travellers or organizing the rescue of Tubby or presiding over her marriage to Bulka or politely avoiding matrimony with forcible Jensina.

Poor Cecco and his friends were actual toys which belonged to the author or to her children; their personalities were developed from their appearance. Bulka,

a somewhat worn stuffed dog, is exactly the kind of accident-prone, hasty person who would have stitches constantly coming undone; the Harlequin doll can only strike attitudes and say 'Hey Presto!'; Anna the lamb is conventional and unenterprising, as befits a pull-along toy permanently fixed to a wooden meadow; Jensina, like Cecco, has the sturdy, enduring quality of wood. Each of the characters meets events in a particular way and has a particular mode of speech, from Tubby's sentimental repetitions and ramblings to the double-edged remarks which the snobbish nursery dolls, Gladys and Virginia May, direct at rustic Jensina. Affectionate memory, mature wisdom and humour and skilled writing brilliantly defined this nursery community. [Margery Williams Bianco: *Poor Cecco*, New York 1925]

**PRINCE CASPIAN**, heir to Miraz, King of Narnia, has been forbidden to speak of the old days when the White Witch was defeated and the benevolent influence of Aslan (q.v.) was felt in the kingdom. As the Prince grows older, however, his new tutor Dr Cornelius tells the Prince how his ancestors the Telmarines conquered Narnia and brought a race of men to live with the talking beasts; that Aslan really exists and that Narnia's ancient races have been killed or driven away by the conquerors. Caspian's resolution to bring back Narnia's glorious past is strengthened when he learns that Miraz murdered his father and seized the throne when Caspian was young. Cornelius advises him to seek help from the neighbouring ruler of Archenland. With the help of the Pevensie children (q.v.), Caspian succeeds in his task. As King of Narnia he sets out by ship (in *The Voyage of the 'Dawn Treader'*) to find the lords, exiled by Miraz, helped this time by Edmund and Lucy and their cousin Eustace (q.v.).

This journey is conducted, and described, in the spirit of one of those tests of knightly worth which abound in the work of Malory and Spenser. A certain dignity accrues to Caspian from the circumstances of his endeavours in battle and in the exploration of strange archipelagoes, but in another sense he is just a golden-headed youth, sharing adventures with the Pevensies, who speak and act like children even though they have been called back from the distant past of their reign in Cair Paravel. This ambiguity of age, stature and behaviour is found in all the Narnia books, with their mixture of chatter and formal speech, hoydenish romps and medieval combat, schoolroom feasts, high table ceremonies and the symbolic sharing of food. C. S. Lewis's firm hand on his plots and his simple, energetic narrative style reconcile the disparate elements in the stories. But we must accept that his characters – and in particular his princely heroes – cannot be drawn in depth but must be, as occasion warrants, regal figureheads or hearty lads.

Prince Rilian and King Tirian are really facets of the same character as Prince Caspian. Rilian (in *The*

*Silver Chair*), son of Caspian, as King, has to pay for his lack of self-control when, against the advice of wise courtiers, he rides from the court in search of a beautiful lady who is in fact the enchantress who killed his mother. His role in the book is largely passive, though he shows the courage of an untried youth, for he is freed from thraldom to the witch largely by the efforts of Jill and Eustace, who in their turn are guided by Aslan. The youthful behaviour of Rilian is necessary so that his behaviour can be matched with that of the children – for these are children's adventures, for all their chivalric overtones; but his words to the witch, in his moments of sanity, are lofty as well as brave, and when he returns to his father he bears on his face that look 'of all true kings of Narnia, who rule by the will of Aslan and sit at Cair Paravel on the throne of Peter the High King'.

King Tirian, last ruler of Narnia, is obviously more mature than either of the young princes, Caspian and Rilian. C. S. Lewis describes him as a man between twenty and twenty-five years old, with broad shoulders and muscular limbs and 'a fearless, honest face'. In his struggle against the Calormenes (in *The Last Battle*), Tirian is above all a warrior, a capable strategist and, after the first shock of surprise, well able to meet on equal terms the legendary Kings and Queens who have returned from the past to aid their kingdom. With the dignity of an Arthurian knight he trains Jill and Eustace to support him in battle and endures the chaos in which Narnia comes to an end and a beginning. The tone of *The Last Battle* is necessarily more sombre and more mature than that of the other books in the cycle. Yet Tirian is, like Rilian and Caspian, drawn to the same medieval pattern, and, like them, he is not a wholly active character, for his fortunes are directed by Aslan. In the three Narnian princes we must expect not personality but a representative regality and, at the same time, a playfulness that brings them within the understanding of young readers. [C. S. Lewis: *Prince Caspian*, London 1951; *The Voyage of the 'Dawn Treader'*, 1952; *The Silver Chair*, 1953; *The Last Battle*, 1956]

**PRINCE ELLIDYR** is one of many warriors who join Prince Gwydion in the attempt to seize the Black Cauldron, in which the evil Arawn is able to create an army of indestructible zombie fighters from the bodies of the dead. Like many of the minor characters in the Prydain chronicles, Ellidyr is recognized by certain fixed traits – envy, jealous pride, arrogance, in his case – which are seen as coming from some deep flaw or lack in his life; the cause of the 'black beast' which rides Ellidyr in fact remains a mystery. It is the function of this young warrior to show up by contrast the genuine humility of Taran (q.v.), central figure of the whole saga. Taran replies with quiet dignity to Ellidyr's insults on his unknown origin and when the ill-conditioned Prince demands the credit for finding the cauldron Taran accepts the incidental comment 'What is the honor of a pig-boy ... compared to the honor of a prince?', because the destruction of the cauldron is his immediate duty. Taran's uncritical patience and generosity finally impress Ellidyr. Grievously wounded, his pride assuaged by the thought that he has the power to destroy the cauldron, he leaps into it and dies as it bursts asunder; the mythical associations of the strange, foretold death add stature to the unhappy prince.

Ellidyr is an interesting example of a dual character. His threadbare attire and 'pale, arrogant face', his nervous, bad-tempered steed, his lofty manner, fit the derivative, chivalric element in *The Black Cauldron* and at the same time his character is seen in psychological terms, so that the human aspect, the universal lesson, of the Prydain chronicles is once more enforced. [Lloyd Alexander: *The Black Cauldron*, New York 1965]

**PRINCE GWYDION** *see* TARAN

**PRINCE PRIGIO**'s father (King of Pantouflia and grandson of Cinderella) is of traditional outlook, but his mother refuses to believe in fairies. At the prince's christening she has sundry magic gifts stowed away in a lumber-room; but she is not able to ignore the last present of all, for proof of its power is soon felt. 'The last fairy of all, a cross old thing' remarks 'My child, you shall be *too* clever.' The prince grows up learned, contumacious and conceited and makes himself unpopular in the kingdom, most of all when he declines (on most reasonable grounds) to go out first among the royal contestants against the dread Firedrake. However, it only needs the power of love to convince the prince that it is necessary for his future happiness to become a hero, and the various magic objects he has found in the lumber-room (useful gifts like seven-league boots and a wishing cap) help him to save the kingdom from destruction. Finally the Lady Rosalind suggests that if he makes a wish to be 'no cleverer than other people' he may be loved by his subjects as well as by her. He satisfies them both by wishing 'to *seem* no cleverer than other people.'

While it is less sparkling than Thackeray's *The Rose and the Ring*, a story which Andrew Lang admired above any other, Lang's book has the same parody, satire and fancy, held together by the character of Prince Prigio – so like a fairy-tale prince outwardly in his adventures, so unlike in his lack of humility and his casual refusal to behave like a hero.

The character, as originally conceived, is simple and amusing. Many years after the publication of *Prince Prigio* Andrew Lang added several anecdotes under the title *Tales of a Fairy Court*, which do fill a few gaps but which by elaborating Prigio's exploits rather blur the fine comic outlines of that attractively wayward youth. [Andrew Lang: *Prince Prigio*, London 1889; *Prince Ricardo of Pantouflia*, 1893; *Tales of a Fairy Court*, 1906]

**PRINCE RICARDO** of Pantouflia narrowly escapes

being handed over to a giant when he comes of age, but his clever father, King Prigio (q.v.), who is well versed in fairy lore, is able with perfect honesty to claim that his Eclipse colt, born ten minutes after the prince, is of greater importance. The King 'thought it best to bring Dick up on fairy books, that he might know what is right, and have no nonsense about him', but the effect is unfortunate. The young Prince Ricardo takes his reading so much to heart that he is 'always after a giant, or a dragon, or a magician' and his father is afraid he will fail his college exams.

The tales of Prince Ricardo play round the King's efforts to change his son's attitude by substituting ordinary objects for magic ones. This involves the Prince in some embarrassing situations (as, for instance, when he interferes in the affairs of James Stuart the Old Pretender, on one of his sallies into the past); however, the beautiful Jacqueline, who was once rescued by the Prince, is enough of an enchantress to save him from real danger.

The character of the Prince, drawn as simply as that of his father, is somewhat less amusing, possibly because the book about him is long drawn out and even facetious compared with the compact wit of *Prince Prigio*. [Andrew Lang: *Prince Ricardo of Pantouflia*, London 1893]

**PRINCE RILIAN** *see* PRINCE CASPIAN

**PRINCESS ALICIA**, daughter of King Watkins the First and his Queen, was the eldest of their nineteen children and took care of them all. One day, on his way to the office, the King was accosted by a belligerent old woman who gave him certain instructions, as a result of which Alicia came into possession of a fish-bone which, polished till it shone like mother of pearl, was to be kept by her until its magic power should be positively needed. The King, oppressed by financial cares and by the illness of the Queen, frequently suggested to Alicia that she might use the magic bone to solve their problems, but the prudent child preferred to use her own wit and skills to bandage the wounded in the riotous family and prepare meals when the cook decamped. She was only persuaded to obtain the King's overdue quarterly salary by magic when all else had failed. Whereupon the old woman, who was really the good Fairy Grandmarina, appeared to fit out the household in new luxury and to whip Alicia away in a peacock-drawn carriage in search of Prince Certainpersonio, a lively small boy who was happy to become Alicia's bridegroom. Since the fishbone had now done its work, the fairy threw it down the throat of the nasty pug-dog next door, which 'expired in convulsions'.

This engaging mock-fairy tale belongs with *The Rose and the Ring* and Andrew Lang's tales of Prince Prigio, but the comic details and whimsical tone of this picture of a London household could have come from none but Dickens (though he concealed his authorship of this Christmas story behind 'Miss Alice Rainbird aged

Princess Alicia, drawn by David Gentleman.

seven'). The character of Alicia, a superbly practical, imperturbable child, respectfully shrewd as regards her father, amusingly suggests at the same time a typical child's reflection of its own way of life and the engagingly warm-hearted humour of Dickens himself. [Charles Dickens: 'The Magic Fishbone', part of *Holiday Romance*, published in New York in *Our Young Folks*, January–May 1868, and in England in *All the Year Round*, January–March 1868; *Holiday Romance* first published in book form, London 1874]

**PRINCESS IRENE** *see* CURDIE

**PROFESSOR BRANESTAWM** made his debut on the radio but it was not long before the inaudible part of Norman Hunter's humour, his use of comic spelling, became apparent from the printed page. The time and word limits of a radio programme and the demands for a clear story-line, firmly stated characters and positive incident, fortunately coincided with Norman Hunter's illusionist talents. The skilled motions of a conjuror are as apparent in the Branestawm stories as they are when he performs on the stage; indeed, what is Branestawm if he is not an inspired conjuror, distracting attention from improbability but by entertaining clumsiness rather than by skill?

Norman Hunter has spoken the last word – a satirical but affectionate word – on the hackneyed subject of the

W. Heath Robinson's illustration of Professor Branestawm's invention for peeling potatoes.

absent-minded scientist. Professor Branestawm has simple tastes, several pairs of spectacles (usually mislaid and often worn all at once), the unconquerable optimism of an incompetent inventor and an erudite and incomprehensible mode of speech for everyone in the world except his one friend, Colonel Dedshott of the Catapult Cavaliers, 'a very brave gentleman who never missed a train, an enemy, or an opportunity of getting into trouble'.

Round these two friends (rather more Holmes and Watson than David and Jonathan) the stories are built on an unchanging formula. Indeed, what more could be needed than elaborate plans misfiring in every conceivable way, to the dismay of the Professor's patient, efficient housekeeper, Mrs Flittersnoop? The formula lends itself to endless variation and there seems little reason why the Professor should not continue indefinitely to invent mad machines like those which have made pancakes, caught burglars, stroked cats, found lost property or manipulated time since his career began.

The Professor's character has not changed over the years but the sphere of his operations has moved with the times. He has recently turned to an abstract form of inventing, in drawing up a dictionary (or 'fictionary', as he calls it) in which he offers the fruit of his researches into 'all those words that seem to have better meanings than the ones usually given to them'. This etymological frolic proves as conclusively that Norman Hunter is truly pungent (that is, 'a comedian who makes a play on words') as the stories of the Professor and his laconic military ally prove that he is a master of the art of fictional illusion. [Norman Hunter: *The incredible*

*adventures of Professor Branestawm*, London 1933; *Professor Branestawm's Treasure Hunt and other incredible adventures*, 1937; *The peculiar triumph of Professor Branestawm*, 1970; *Professor Branestawm up the Pole and other incredible adventures*, 1972; *Professor Branestawm's Dictionary*, 1973; *Professor Branestawm's Great Revolution*, 1974]

**PSAMMEAD** (the) is discovered by Anthea (q.v.) in a hole she is helping to dig in the gravel pit near the children's new home in Kent. It is a very strange creature indeed, with retractable eyes on long stalks, batlike ears, and a tubby body 'shaped like a spider's and covered with thick soft fur'. The Psammead ('in plain English . . . a Sand-fairy') is annoyed that the children do not recognize it. A good deal of flattery and cajolery is needed before it relaxes into a better humour and begins to reminisce about life several thousand years ago and its power to grant wishes.

The children soon realize that this is not such a blessing as they thought at first. Not only does the Psammead make endless difficulties, grumbling at having to blow itself up so often and insisting on various conditions to suit itself, but it refuses to advise the children, merely pointing out the folly of their desires, both before and after the event. In spite of its crabby nature, however, they become attached to the Psammead. It is largely through Anthea's good sense that matters are arranged so that after final wishes, necessary to redress the unfortunate embarrassment of Lady Chittenden's jewels, the Psammead is able to hibernate in comfortable darkness, safe from the water it dreads, and free from obligations.

The comedy of *Five Children and It*, as well as the

The Psammead, drawn by H. R. Millar.

fantasy, depends on the activities and personality of the Psammead. When the children find it again (in *The Story of the Amulet*), imprisoned in a cage in a petshop, dirty and despondent, it is still dictatorial but at least grateful to the children for rescuing it. It no longer brings about embarrassing situations but advises them, seriously and with authority, about the way they can use the power of the Amulet to go back into the distant past and eventually to win their dearest wishes. In conversation it is as trenchant as ever. 'You're still very ignorant and silly', it tells Anthea, while thanking her brusquely for saving its life, 'and I am worth a thousand of you any day of the week'. But it is only an intermediary in this second story, and although it accompanies the children on their time-journeys (in a woven bag the fish came in from Farringdon Market and later in a silk and towelling one lovingly sewed by Anthea and Jane) it keeps mainly in the background, for its function as a comic character cannot be allowed to interfere with the serious tenor of the adventure. [E. Nesbit: *Five Children and It*, London 1902; *The Story of the Amulet*, 1906]

**PUCK OF POOK'S HILL** does not care 'to be confused with that painty-winged, wand-waving, sugar-and-shake-your-head set of imposters', as he calls conventional fairies. When he steps into the ring of darkened grass Dan and Una (q.v.) see 'a small, brown, broad-shouldered, pointy-eared person with a snub nose, slanting blue eyes, and a grin that ran right across his freckled face'. As one of the old spirits, he is empowered to give them seizin, cutting a turf for each of them to symbolize their right to belong to a particular place, and he can promise them 'You shall see What you shall see and you shall hear What you shall hear, though It shall have happened three thousand year; and you shall know neither Doubt nor Fear.' So it is that the children meet the Norman knight Sir Richard Dalyngridge and Aquila, centurion of the Thirtieth Legion in Britain, Kadmiel, a Jewish physician from King John's time and Simon Cheyneys, a shipbuilder of Rye in the time of Queen Elizabeth; and through these and other people they learn to know the history of their corner of Sussex as well as they know its fields and thickets and streams.

The children can hardly understand Puck's great age ('my friends used to set my dish of cream for me o' nights when Stonehenge was new') but they see he is as natural a part of the countryside as old Hobden, woodman and hedger, whose family have lived in the district for centuries. Hobden's work with living, growing trees matches Puck's magic with the leaves of Oak, Ash and Thorn which ensures that Dan and Una will forget him and his marvels between-whiles.

Puck has many functions in Kipling's stories. Because he is ageless, he can act as an intermediary between the children and the visitants from the past; his ancestry is partly Shakespearean, and with wisps and echoes

Puck talks to Dan and Una, from *Puck of Pook's Hill*, illustrated by H. R. Millar.

from the comedies he adds literary decoration to the tales. He is the household brownie of folk lore, mischievous, intractable and elusive; he is also the elemental, the embodiment of old ways and old nature, who has outlasted many gods from over the sea. He shows Dan and Una their land and their heritage, and, through them, Kipling shows his England to children of all generations. [Rudyard Kipling: *Puck of Pook's Hill*, London 1906; *Rewards and Fairies*, 1910]

**PUDDLEGLUM** the Marsh-wiggle seems to Jill Pole, when he conducts her to shelter (in *The Silver Chair*), to be all legs and arms'. Their strange host, who becomes a trusty, if gloomy, companion in their enterprise on behalf of Prince Rilian (q.v.), is depicted as a human in Pauline Baynes's illustration of him, but greeny-grey, reed-like hair and webbed hands and feet, mark him as at least a mutant. As comic relief he seems

Puddleglum rides behind Jill Pole as they escape from the witch's kingdom; an illustration by Pauline Baynes from *The Silver Chair*.

more acceptable than many of C. S. Lewis's ancillary characters (Bree, for instance, or Reepicheep) because he is described with less of the self-conscious drollery which hangs intermittently on them.

Puddleglum's attitude of melancholy good cheer has a bracing effect on a book full of romantic echoes and high endeavour. He decides that 'a journey up north just as winter's beginning, looking for a Prince who probably isn't there, by way of a ruined city that no one has ever seen' – will be just the thing. 'If that doesn't steady a chap, I don't know what will.'

Whether Puddleglum is intended to be part-animal or just the humorous presentation of an East Anglian marsh-dweller, he is the obvious person to resist the wiles of the enchantress. Jill and Eustace and the brave Rilian are all seduced by her spells and believe that Narnia and the world above her dark kingdom are nothing but illusion, but Puddleglum is staunch in his memory of the sun. Perhaps he will never see it again, but he believes in it; and it is his large, flat, damp feet which stamp out the fire which is sending out mind-softening fumes; for all that they are 'cold-blooded like a duck's' they could be, and were, badly burnt. It is, because of its surprising rightness, one of the best moments in the book, as Puddleglum is one of C. S. Lewis's most impressive minor characters. [C. S. Lewis: *The Silver Chair*, London 1953; *The Last Battle*, 1956]

**PURRKIN** the cat is taught to speak by young Pete, who makes a particular friend of him, even persuading his father to make him a pair of boots so that he can emulate the fairy-tale hero. Delighted with his new accomplishment, Purrkin teaches Piggiwig and Ziggibock the goat to talk too. But in spite of their many adventures together, the cat wearies of the village and when by accident he breaks Grandmother's cream pot he sets out to earn money for a new one. After narrow escapes from gypsies and a flooded stream, Purrkin joins Klutsky's World Circus; he performs in the act of 'The Speaking Sack Snock-Snock' until he is so homesick that he returns home, laden with presents and with a fine new cream pot for delighted Grandmother.

Purrkin's personalized character, his lively spirit and enterprise, usefully promote numerous small adventures that reflect the mid-European peasant world of long ago, the 'comfortable, unchanging rural world of folk-tales which has become the common ground of fantasy everywhere'. [Josef Lada: *Purrkin the Talking Cat* (1935 Czechoslovakia) trans. R. Symons, London 1966]

**QUEENIE PEAVY** lives in a shabby home on a Georgia hillside. She enjoys a relaxed and happy relationship with her mother but outside her home she has to protect herself when her school-fellows tease her for having a gaol-bird father, and the only recourse the intelligent but undisciplined girl can find is to show off or to rage against them. The leaders of the small community, especially the schoolteacher and the town judge, try to help her by encouraging her desire to work in the infirmary. However, when she injures an unpleasant boy who has been her chief tormentor, the judge warns her not to be content to live 'in the shadow of the jail'. The words stay in her mind while she is trying to restrain her father from further crime. She comes to realize the uselessness of aggressive behaviour and to see that she is the sole arbiter of her destiny. 'She could reason that nobody expected much of her, and not make any effort to succeed in life. But who would she be hurting in the long run?' Self-control comes slowly and painfully to Queenie but the end of the story shows a happier future ahead for a girl whose character is revealed in her words and actions, in her relationships with other people and in the meticulously drawn background of her life. [Robert Burch: *Queenie Peavy*, New York 1966]

**RACHEL AND HILARY LENNOX** *see* DULCIE
WINTLE

**RAGGED DICK** was a bootblack whose cheerful
demeanour and business-like energy won him more customers in the streets of New York than most of his rivals
were able to attract. He was not at all ashamed of his
torn coat, which he liked to pretend had been worn all
through the Revolution by General Washington ('and
it got torn some, 'cause he fit so hard') and he thought
a day well spent if it earned him enough money to go
to a show at the Bowery or do a little gambling in the
evening. Honest and cheerful as he was, Dick was universally liked and he was not minded to change his state,
though he was illiterate and homeless, until one day he
chanced to meet a gentleman who asked him to take
his young nephew round the city.

While Dick introduced Frank to a world he had never
dreamed of, Frank stirred in Dick a vague ambition to
improve himself, pointing out that 'A good many distinguished men have once been poor boys'. Dick decided
to acquire an education. He began to save his money
instead of squandering it and when he befriended the
less successful lad Fosdick, an orphan with a good
education behind him, he acquired a 'private tutor' who
found Dick an apt pupil. Bearing in mind the assurance
that 'in this free country poverty in early life is no bar
to a man's advancement', Dick through hard work,
honesty and intelligence climbed high enough up the
ladder of society to be established in an office job with
good prospects.

Horatio Alger's enormously popular novels of New
York in the last century, and in particular his compassionate, moralistic tales about poor boys, were based
on his own knowledge of conditions in the city and on
his firm belief in endeavour as a certain way to prosperity. The purposive nature of Ragged Dick is, fortunately, not strong enough to hide the young hero's
robust behaviour or his droll turn of speech. All the
same, readers of today may regret that Dick's engaging
personal philosophy was modified by the search for
material security. Richard Hunter the trusted clerk is
less appealing than Dick sensibly changing his suit for
his 'Washington coat' to claim a letter addressed to
'Ragged Dick' or laying a trap for the man who stole
his bank-book or showing Frank the City Hall with the
remark, 'That's where the mayor's office is ... I once
blacked his boots by particular appointment. That's the
way I pay my city taxes.' [Horatio Alger: 'Ragged Dick'
and other stories in *Student and Schoolmate* from 1866;
pub. in book form as *Ragged Dick*, Boston 1867; and
many other titles]

**RAGGEDY ANN** has only one shoe-button eye when
Marcelle finds her in Grandma's attic. She is more than
fifty years old but she has such an adventurous spirit
that the rest of Marcelle's dolls find their lives considerably enlivened by her ideas. She is not afraid when she
is tied to a kite and flies into the air. She is not disconcerted even when she falls into the fork of a tree; she
makes the most of the experience and allows Mama
Robin to take some of her yarn hair for her nest. She

Raggedy Ann, drawn by author and illustrator Johnny
Gruell.

Ralph and his motorcycle, drawn by Louis Darling.

knows about dog-catchers and organizes a rescue just in time when Fido is lost and in danger. Battered, jam-stained, covered with paint, soaked in the river, Raggedy Ann comes up smiling. 'I was so happy I forgot to tell you', the little doll tells the tin soldier. When a kind lady, refurbishing her when she has been tossed in a bucket of paint, sews a candy heart inside her, 'It had printed upon it in nice blue letters, I LOVE YOU.' [Johnny Gruell: *Raggedy Ann Stories*, New York 1918]

**RALPH** the mouse lives with his family in a hole behind the skirting in Room 215 of the Mountain Dew Inn in California. Ralph finds his mother's timorousness irksome and his home limiting. He does not want 'to grow up to be a crumb-scrounging mouse' or 'to settle down in a nest of shredded Kleenex'; he wants freedom and adventure. Keith, his first human ally (in *The Mouse and the Motorcycle*) is so delighted with Ralph's enterprise in coasting on his miniature motor-bike that when Keith and his parents leave the inn the mouse becomes

the overjoyed owner of the toy. In the second story about him, *Runaway Ralph*, he takes off for 'a life of speed and danger and excitement', which he finds at the Happy Acres Camp. To be saved from the cat (who tells her kittens 'a live mouse is an interesting and instructive plaything') is small consolation when he is forced to live in a cage as the property of timid Garf; but he becomes as friendly with this boy as with Keith and even persuades the loner eventually to join in the life of the camp.

The humanizing of Ralph is carried out in a spirit of gay and practical fancy. The mouse is able to make the motorcycle move because he makes the right noises. The fact that the toy actually moves fast is established so calmly that it is equally easy to accept Ralph's use of it. He is established in the first book as a personality in human terms partly because of his obvious likeness to Keith. They are not surprised that they can communicate because 'Two creatures who shared a love for motorcycles naturally spoke the same language';

besides, they both want to grow up and are tired of being told to be patient. Ralph is somewhat more than a speed-maniac. For all his impetuous love of excitement, he is sympathetic enough to Keith's illness to face real danger to find him an aspirin, and in the second book he helps Garf partly for his own ends but partly because he is sorry for such a mixed-up boy. In fact he remains, engagingly, both mouse and boy. [Beverly Cleary: *The Mouse and the Motorcycle*, New York 1965; *Runaway Ralph*, 1970]

**RALPH ROVER,** the narrator of the adventures of *The Coral Island* and *The Gorilla Hunters*, has always wanted to sail to the South Seas, and when he is fifteen his chance comes. On the voyage he wins two friends – Jack Martin (q.v.) and the lively Peterkin Gray (q.v.). When the merchant ship they are serving in is wrecked on a coral reef, the three lads struggle to the shore and organize a Crusonian existence on the island, making their way home in a captured schooner after numerous encounters with pirates, cannibals and missionaries. Meeting again seven years later by chance, the three comrades travel to Africa, for Ralph, always deeply interested in the world of nature, has resolved to satisfy an over-riding ambition – 'I am determined to shoot a gorilla, or prove him to be a myth'.

Ralph is a contemplative character, given to sententious remarks about life and human nature. His good opinion of himself suggests a certain sardonic reserve on the part of the author. At least one suspects that when he allows Ralph to remark 'I have adopted . . . the habit of forcing my attention upon *all* things that go on around me, and of taking some degree of interest in them, whether I feel it naturally or not', he is not altogether in sympathy with his creation. All the same, through him Ballantyne is able to describe the natural history and social organization of South Sea islands or the African jungle and to promulgate current moral precepts. Ralph's comrades accept him cheerfully as he is – Peterkin greets him in *The Gorilla Hunters* as 'the same jolly, young, old wise-acre in whiskers and a long coat'. The reader of today, however, does not find it easy to appreciate this sententious character in his historical context. [R. M. Ballantyne: *The Coral Island*, London 1858; *The Gorilla Hunters*, 1861]

**RAMONA GERALDINE QUINBY** lives in an American town with her parents and her sister Beezus (Beatrice) who is five years older. If only she could be more like other people's sisters, Beezus muses: 'Just look at her – cooky crumbs sticking to the front of her overalls, her hands and face dirty, and those silly paper ears. She's just awful, that's what she is, perfectly awful – and she looks so cheerful.' It is true that Ramona is apt to look cheerful when she is perpetrating her worst misdeeds – accidentally wrecking two birthday cakes in one day, for instance, or inviting the whole of her class to tea on a wet day just as her mother has embarked on a family hair-wash; but she can throw a pretty tan-

trum too, and scowls are seen as often on her face as smiles.

Practical, down-to-earth Beezus finds it especially irritating that Ramona is praised for her imagination; when she pretends to be a clockwork toy and pesters everyone to wind her up, inexplicably the grown-ups seem to find it amusing. Ramona's exploits, spread through several books, are centred on a type-character in children's fiction, the lively, naughty child who enjoys the special dispensation of being the youngest. In some ways she could be considered the American counterpart of Dorothy Edwards's 'Naughty Little Sister'. If Ramona is not a type but an individual, this must be put to the credit of Beverly Cleary, who lightly but firmly sketches the child's relationships with other people and gives her a personal idiom and manner. Above all, she *develops* Ramona's character. In the last book about her, *Ramona the Pest*, Ramona, dressed as a witch for the school Hallowe'en procession, is suddenly visited by misgivings. Her mask is identical with several others and nobody seems to know who she is. 'What if everyone in the whole world forgot her.' The dawn of thought in a child of five or so has seldom been more comically or tellingly shown. [Beverly Cleary: *Henry and Beezus*, New York 1952; *Henry and Ribsy*, 1954; *Beezus and Ramona*, 1955; *Henry and the Club-house*, 1962; *Ramona the Pest*, 1968]

**RANDAL KER** lives in the Border country in the early sixteenth century, and in his childhood he hears as many tales of the Good Folk as of the battlefield. He is still very young when his noble father is killed on Flodden Field but after a reprisal raid into England the household retainers return laden with spoils from Hardriding Hall, and among them, hidden in hangings and carpets, a beautiful golden-haired child. Little Jean as she is called follows Randal wherever he chooses to go. Then one fatal day he is too bold and quick for her. She is afraid to go with him to the Wishing Well and sinks down in weary sleep. When she wakes the boy has vanished – for it is Midsummer Eve and his wish to see the fairies has been granted.

This is a picturesque version of the legend of Thomas the Rhymer, a legend which belongs particularly to the very Eildon Hills where the children wander. Randal, who mocked at superstitious fears of his old nurse and ignored the warnings of the Church, is held by the fairies for seven years, but at last, tasting water from a magic phial, he remembers the past and so Jean is able to claim him on Midsummer Eve through her faith and courage. Through the agency of the magic phial the ancient treasure buried in Roman times is found and used to raise the family to prosperity again; but the treasure of affection between Randal and Jean proves more precious and lasting to them.

No subtlety or depth is required of the two characters in this Victorian fairy tale. Randal and Jean are defined in part by Andrew Lang's faithful evocation of the hills and valleys and in part by the conviction with which he shows people guided by Christian principles but also dominated by a belief in ancient, local spirits. [Andrew Lang: *The Gold of Fairnilee*, London 1888]

**RAT** *see* TOAD OF TOAD HALL

**RAT,** the 'honest cellarman', has plenty of opportunities for spying at Seekings, a large house seamed with wainscot passages and underpinned with cellars, and in spite of his disreputable appearance and unhygienic habits, he is on the side of Kay Harker (q.v.). It is Rat's plain speaking, and his prying ways, that drive Kay to brave the dark cellar and free the friendly owl who has been caught by the witches while carrying important messages to him. Again, it is Rat who summons Kay to the river to help the cat Nibbins and Bitem the fox, trapped in a cave.

The seedy animal sees himself as a victim of persecution. 'I lives in a cellar, and I does a bit in the dustbin. But him as says I ducks and I chicks, he says what isn't it, because I never.' His greed allayed with sugar and raisins, he is soon complaining because Kay has no bacon rind to reward him – '...as for "tomorrow perhaps", that's when it's going to rain soup and the grass is going to grow spoons'. Rat is generously rewarded in the end, but he clears off to sea to collect a gang of pirates, the Wolves of the Gulf, who return to Seekings to lurk once more, in *The Box of Delights*.

Now an enemy of Kay's rather than an ally (he has heard that the boy is to be given a dog for Christmas), Rat acts as a spy for Abner Brown, helping him, not very efficiently, to track down old Cole Hawlings and his magic box. Little reward does he get from Abner. 'Up in the attic and down in the cellar, all weathers, all hours, for one who'd sell his mother, if he had one, for what she'd fetch as old bones.' Dirty, pungent in speech and uncouth in behaviour, varying in size as the fantasy dictates. Rat rolls through Masefield's two stories as one of his most enduring minor characters. [John Masefield: *The Midnight Folk*, London 1927; *The Box of Delights*, 1935]

**RATS OF NIMH** (the) live in a city where pickings are good and life agreeable till one day a number of them are netted and taken to a laboratory. The rats in Group A, who receive more powerful injections and more stringent tests, quickly begin to outstrip the other groups in intelligence, so much so that they learn to read and eventually escape. This group of rats now have intellectual reasoning as well as gregarious instinct to keep them together. They resolve to use their acquired knowledge to make a better life for themselves.

After several stages in their search for a home they come to the Fitzgibbon farm and there hollow for themselves a branching city lit by electricity (led from the farm supply), furnished with a library and other civilized adjuncts of life, and with a formidable educational programme for the younger generation and a stable democratic government.

Mrs Frisby (q.v.) is full of awe and admiration when Nicodemus and Justin finish telling her their story – but there is more to come. For the rats have read about something called the Rat Race and realize that they are in danger of becoming slaves to technology, and to devices which they have stolen from men. They must build a rat civilization of their own, dependent on nobody but themselves; their move to Thorn Valley with laboriously collected seed corn and other supplies brings about a firm, satisfactory climax to their efforts.

The Rats of NIMH are not humanized in the strict sense of the word. They are represented as a super-race, an evolutionary phenomenon resulting from man's interference with nature but capable of using intelligence independently of man. In this sense they belong to science fiction rather than to animal fantasy, to the worlds of Orwell and Andre Norton rather than of Kipling and Kenneth Grahame. Their connection with the human race does not lie in their actions (which are always strictly performed by paws, not hands) but in their philosophy, which in its far-reaching, honest model for a civilization throws, by implication, the searching light of criticism on the human world in general and the rat-race in particular. So, we have here a politico-social allegory, as well as an exciting story in the successful solving of Mrs Frisby's domestic problem. Those rats who are seen as individuals – the dignified Justin; Jenner, the erratic leader of a doomed splinter group; the schoolgirl Isabella, with her armful of books and her squeaky hero-worship of Justin – are characters as memorable as any in animal fantasy. [Robert C. O'Brien: *Mrs Frisby and the Rats of NIMH*, New York 1971]

**RAYMONDE ARMITAGE** at the age of fifteen is 'the most irresponsible creature in the world', with a smooth, guileless countenance and eyes that are 'capable of putting on a bewitching innocence of expression.' This does not always save the madcap from retribution, though she does not always deserve the punishment that exasperated members of the school staff visit on her, for as she is fond of boasting to her friends, 'I'm a kind of scapegoat for the school. Everybody's sins are stuck on me.' When Miss Beasley moves her school to Darly Grange Raymonde announces '...if you don't have a jinky term I'll consider myself a failure'.

She has already commandeered seven beds close together, to make planning easier. So here are Aveline, with a gift for stubborn silence in time of trouble; little Fauvette, clinging and cuddly; clever, variable Morvyth; Valentine and Ardiune, known as Salt and Pepper for their close and quarrelsome friendship; and demure Katherine, whose 'innocent grey eyes and doll-like complexion were the vineyards that hid the volcano.'

With this decorative wreath of names, this comprehensive set of temperaments, Angela Brazil skilfully sets her scene for a racy tale that takes place during the First World War – picnics and camping, a raft on the moat and the capture of a German spy, plus a ghost who proves to be as great a madcap as Raymonde, all in the space of one summer term. As in almost all school stories (with Talbot Baines Reed and Antonia Forest as honourable exceptions), education hardly seems to enter into the programme at all. Raymonde is typical of the characters Angela Brazil wove into her stories once she had evidently decided to concentrate on the charms of naughtiness. This excitable heroine initiates most of the action in the story and is the subject of jocular or admiring remarks from her friends on her energy, inventiveness and careless attitude to life; such remarks tell us all we need to know about her character and a good deal more about Angela Brazil's curiously idealistic yet shrewd pictures of school and schoolgirls. [Angela Brazil: *The Madcap of the School*, London 1917]

**REBECCA ROWENA RANDALL** is the second of seven children living on a small farm – Randall's Farm to the natives, but Sunnybrook Farm to Rebecca. Mr Jeremiah Cobb, who drives his own stagecoach, is the first person to receive Rebecca's artless confidences about her home and her dead father and the relief it is that there will be no more babies. He is not the last to remark on the remarkably clear, beautiful eyes that light up Rebecca's plain little face, eyes that 'had the effect of looking directly through the obvious to something beyond – in the object, in the landscape, in you.'

Rebecca's aunts had in fact offered to give a home to the eldest girl, Hannah, and they are not a little disconcerted to be faced with her irrepressible younger sister. The prim Sawyers seem the last people to appreciate a child who loves books and music, loves the challenge of the unexpected and never looks before she leaps. Many a clash of wills gives Rebecca's Aunt Miranda fears of irreversible wickedness, before the child's honest heart wins over her stiff aunt, with the help of Aunt Jane's timid sympathy.

Rebecca's character is delineated with humour. The child comes to life through her relations with other people – not only with her aunts but also with her slow but loyal friend Emma Jane; with 'Mr Aladdin', who succumbs completely to her naïve view of him as a fairy godfather; with the Cobbs, who can always be dazzled by Rebecca's 'merry conversation and quaint comments on life'; with Miss Maxwell, the schoolteacher, for whom Rebecca is an oasis in a desert of unimaginative pupils. Rebecca's impromptu sermon at the missionary meeting, her efforts on behalf of the feckless Simpsons, her notable success as assistant editor of the *Wareham School Pilot*, are landmarks through the years from eleven to seventeen, during which the girl fulfils the promise of that noticing child who rode in on the stage to Riverboro. When her promising future seems to be blocked by her mother's illness, Rebecca's strength of character is fully demonstrated. [Kate Douglas Wiggin:

*Rebecca of Sunnybrook Farm*, Boston 1903; *More about Rebecca*, 1907]

**REEPICHEEP** the Talking Mouse plays a part in the Narnia chronicles which at once emphasizes and contradicts his size. C. S. Lewis as a child had written stories in which some of his favourite characters were 'Courtly Mice'; Reepicheep has the manner and outlook of a true knight, as if mouse-size aspired as high as it possibly could. He makes his first appearance in *Prince Caspian*, 'a gay and martial mouse' who soon convinces the Prince by his courage and resource that he is an ally to be trusted. His grandiloquent manner of speech seems rather better suited to the Grail-quest of *The Voyage of the Dawn Treader*. Lucy knows she must not pick him up and cuddle him, as she longs to do, and the fact that Eustace (q.v.) takes the dauntless hero of the Second Battle of Beruna as a 'performing animal' is one of the many points scored against him on the journey which finally redeems him.

Reepicheep is the only one of the voyagers permitted to venture beyond 'the End of the World into Aslan's country'. Flinging his sword into the sea (the description seems deliberately to echo Malory), he steps into his coracle and paddles into the unknown. The various facets of Reepicheep's character – his loquacity, his insistence on due respect, his outsize courage and his chivalric manner, come together in *The Last Battle*, when Tirian sees the gates of the great citadel swing open to reveal 'a little, sleek, bright-eyed Talking Mouse with a red feather stuck in a circlet on its head and its left paw resting on a long sword'. To Reepicheep is given a central position in a scene that is impressive, grave and significant. [C. S. Lewis: *Prince Caspian*, London 1951; *The Voyage of the 'Dawn Treader'*, 1952; *The Last Battle*, 1956]

Reepicheep, drawn by Pauline Baynes in *The Last Battle*.

**RICHARD BIRKENSHAW** lives in Cheshire, a few miles from Manchester, and helps his father on their market garden. He enthusiastically runs a couple of roadside stalls selling flowers and lemonade, but his pride in his efficiency is affronted when a complete stranger, a small, gaudily dressed figure, makes nonsense of his wares with conjuring tricks; when he discovers it is his uncle Oswald Tubbs (q.v.), all is explained. From that moment life becomes varied and exciting for the lad. To have a conjuror for uncle seems to him joy enough; to have, as well, a second uncle who keeps a pet shop fits equally well with Dick's inclination. He is uncritically happy in Manchester, meeting the stout, kindly Mayoress, Gentleman George (masquerading as a busker to get material for a book) and the loquacious Alf Eckersley, who can balance a tower of baskets on his head, and many other colourful figures.

As the centre of an episodic junior novel Dick has just the right traits to act as involuntary showman for one of Howard Spring's most vivid collections of odd folk. The boy has a capacity for enjoying life, a confiding manner, good manners and a sense of fun, and he passes on his delight at the sights and sounds of Manchester in the '30s with no little gusto. [Howard Spring; *Tumbledown Dick*, London 1939]

**RIDIKLIS** is one of the Dutch dolls who survive the various misfortunes that beset the Dolls' House when Cynthia (a careless child and 'not a good housekeeper') inherits it from her Great Grandmother. The other survivors are Meg, Peg and Kilmanskeg, Gustibus and Peter Piper; their earlier more elegant names (Leontine, Charlotte, Amelia and Clotilda, Augustus and Charles Edward Stuart) have been altered to suit their battered appearance, just as their house becomes known as Racketty Packetty House when it is discarded in favour of Cynthia's new Tidy Castle. If Cynthia thinks of them as 'only a lot of old disreputable looking Dutch dolls', Queen Crosspatch (who tells their story) knows better. She knows how good-natured and high-spirited the dolls are and how fond of one another – so much so that the girls refuse proposals of marriage from two cocksparrows and a gentleman mouse just to stay with their adored Ridiklis. From their exile in the corner behind the door the dolls can see Tidy Castle; it is almost like being grand themselves, they say, to watch the Duchess reading in the 'sumptuous white and gold drawing-room' where Lady Gwendolen Vere de Vere plays 'haughtily upon the harp' and Lady Muriel coldly listens to her. True to their ebullient natures, the dolls of Racketty Packetty House get a lot of fun out of pretending that their dinner of turnips is eight elegant courses and accepting the mock titles conferred on them by Peter Piper. They even persuade themselves that it may be fun to be burnt, as the nurse threatens, for as ashes they can 'fly away into the air and see all sorts of things'; they do not have to prove this, however, for danger is averted by the fairies.

The lively Dutch dolls think they will never be noticed by the aristocrats – except for Lady Patsy, the only sensible member of the Tidyshire family, who finds them delightful and incurs the wrath of her family for visiting the old house to join in the fun. But kind hearts are more than coronets and when the Tidyshires are left by Cynthia in a lamentable state with scarlet fever, they come to realize the real worth of the ragged crew they have despised. Then a princess comes to visit Cynthia's nursery and lo, Racketty Packetty House comes into its own! But even after it has been moved to the Palace and the dolls have been mended and dressed in new clothes, they still dance and kick up their heels and laugh with the joy of living, and Ridiklis 'always remained the useful one'.

The rackety collection is said to have had its source in a large and amusing family whose liveliness Frances Hodgson Burnett much enjoyed. It is perhaps not surprising that when it was performed as a play in 1912 it was called 'a convincing argument against snobbery' and 'a very good lesson for the limousine children who scorn those of pedestrian parents', and perhaps not surprising either that at least one critic found Peter Piper, on the stage at least, far too vulgar and robust. It is amusing to notice, too, that even if the tiny fanciful story was intended as a rebuke to snobbery, the dolls' house was considered to be redeemed by the attentions of a princess. [Frances Hodgson Burnett: *Racketty Packetty House*, London 1907]

**ROBERTA, PETER AND PHYLLIS** had an exceptional mother. She 'did not spend all her time in paying dull calls to dull ladies, and sitting dully at home waiting for dull ladies to pay calls to her' but was always ready to play with them and to write special verses for their anniversaries. Because of the affection and freedom they had always enjoyed, they trusted their mother when she took them away from London to a small house in the country and told them their father had to be away for a time and they would be rather poor. They knew they must not ask questions, and indeed Roberta, a girl who was 'quite oddly anxious to make other people happy', was the only one who realized how serious matters were.

The children found amusement in the nearby railway station; they enjoyed the friendly chatter of Perks the porter and the dignified friendship of the Stationmaster, and they tried each day to be in time to wave to the old gentleman, who always travelled by the same train. Their efforts at helping family finances were energetic but sometimes unfortunate; Peter, for instance, had not realized that taking coal from the station stack was not coal mining. There was excitement in helping to solve the family problems of a sad Russian exile and a boy injured on a cross-country run, and a final surprise when the old gentleman, who had become their firm ally, set himself to right the wrong that had been done to their father.

Phyllis serves tea to the old gentleman, drawn by
C. E. Brock in *The Railway Children*.

Roberta waves her red flannel petticoat to warn an
approaching train of a landslide: a scene from the
MGM–EMI film *The Railway Children*.

*The Railway Children* was a popular story long before
it was filmed and televised. It is not, all the same, the
most notable in its characterization. The three children
are less sharply differentiated than those in the larger
families of the Bastables (q.v.) and the 'Five Children',
and an undercurrent of sentimentality over-rides the
humour in the book. This seems to emanate not only
from the romantically sad situation of the family but
also, in part, from the understanding mother. In spite
of her modest disclaimers and outgoing sympathy for
others, she seems in fact to be insisting all the time on
the reader's attention and admiration. Is it unfair to
suggest that there is too much of the author herself in
the character, that a curious secret conceit has interfered
with the free spirit of the story? [Edith Nesbit: *The Railway Children*, London 1906]

**ROBIN, DICKY, FLAPSY** and **PECKSY** absorb
from their avian parents principles much like those
which Mrs Benson seeks to instil in Harriet and Frederick as they feed the robins in the garden (not with
bread that might be given to the poor, but with crumbs
and scrapings). The robin offspring have some individuality to give savour to this very improving story. Robin,
who has a 'turbulent disposition', tries to claim half the
nest for himself, and thinks little of his mother's admonition that being the eldest does not give you a privilege
to domineer over your brother and sisters'. When the
day comes for the first flight, conceit brings a fall and
an injury that makes Robin permanently lame and
curbs his arrogance.

Dicky, whose plumage is unusually fine, is inclined
to be selfish and not as sensible as he might be. By the
time he is due for independence he and his sister Flapsy
begin to fly 'giddily about together' but they are trapped
and put in an aviary. Flapsy has an elegant shape and
a flighty character in contrast to her sister Pecksy,
whom the others jealously call 'the Favourite'. Sweet
and serene, though with no looks to speak of, Pecksy
on her first food-seeking excursion presents her mother
with a spider as 'the first tribute of gratitude which I
have ever been able to offer you.'

One hopes that the presence of some concrete detail
and even a touch of fun helped young readers of two
centuries ago to enjoy a book from which the author
hoped they would 'select the best for the own imitation,
and take warning by the rest.' [Mrs Trimmer: *The
History of the Robins*, originally *Fabulous Histories*,
London 1786]

**ROBIN, JOHN AND HAROLD HENSMAN,**
(aged fifteen, thirteen and twelve) live in the Dower
House at Cherry Walden; their parents are in India and
they are in charge of a maiden aunt whose 'petticoat
government' has over the years become very tedious.
Still more annoying, however, is the prospect of returning to boarding school when summer is on the way and
all the delights of country life are there for the taking.
It is Robin who has the idea of running away to Brendon

Illustrations by D. J. Watkins-Pitchford from *Brendon Chase*.

Chase; as he says, 'Why shouldn't we live in the forest like Robin Hood and his merry men?' The idea, at first shocking, begins to seem feasible. Then news comes that (as their parents put it) if they behave themselves they may come home on leave at the New Year. It seems only right to go back to school. Then Harold develops measles and his brothers are condemned to quarantine and the dismal prospect of lessons with the vicar. So, after all, it is off to the greenwood with hunting knives and porridge oats, matches and frying pan, and – at the last minute – the gun which the gardener keeps, in a neglected state, in his shed.

Brendon Chase is an ancient forest, eleven thousand acres in extent, with rabbits to be snared or shot, a secret pool in the middle for bathing and fishing, and no inhabitants except for old Smokoe, a charcoal burner whose deformed nose has given him a gnomelike appearance and a taste for solitude. In this fastness the two boys, joined later by the determined Harold, employ all their woodcraft so as to remain hidden and independent. Almost at once they find a huge hollow oak which makes a perfect home. Rabbits and fish and a strayed pig, unexpected victim of John's gun, with carefully husbanded oatmeal, provide a reasonable diet; a foray in the neighbouring village, when salt and oats run out, almost leads to discovery. Before life becomes too difficult the boys make the acquaintance of old Smokoe and they have reason to be grateful for his country lore – and his vegetable patch. Entertained by the efforts of Constable Bunting and others to find the boys, the old man keeps their secret. They might have been found when he has an accident with an axe and John has to fetch the doctor, but the boy contrives matters that time, or so he believes. They could be discovered when a bear escapes from a pantomime outfit; but still Smokoe keeps quiet. Indeed, the boys are almost ready to give themselves up when their father and the doctor, having worked out their probable whereabouts, appear at Smokoe's cabin, and three dirty, scarred, skin-clad boys emerge from under the bed.

'B.B.'s' epigraph expresses the theme of this incomparable Robinsonnade – 'The wonder of the world, the beauty and the power, the shapes of things, their colours, lights, and shades; these I saw. Look ye also while life lasts.' *Brendon Chase*, like the stories of the Little Grey Men and of Rufus the fox, celebrates a corner of Northamptonshire as the author knew it in his boyhood before the Second World War. Of the three boys who live their joyous, surreptitious life in the forest, from early summer to mid-winter, it is Robin who is characterized most deeply and who reflects most obviously the author's own feelings. It is he who responds most sensitively to the sights and sounds of the forest, though he takes as much pleasure as the others in hunting, in contriving tools and utensils and in outwitting the grown-ups. Beside him the responsible Big John and cheerful Harold, happy to be dubbed

Little John, are distinguished mainly by what they do rather than what they are. Through them we appreciate the humour and the excitement of the situation: through Robin we apprehend its emotional content. ['B.B.': *Brendon Chase*, London 1944]

**ROBIN HOOD** as a hero of ballad, romance and chapbook could derive at long distance from a Green Man, a primitive spirit of the woods. He could be based on an outlawed Earl of Huntingdon in the reign of King John or, as the Nottingham Robin Hood Society believes, a certain Robert de Keyne, disinherited son of a Lincolnshire knight, whose loyalty was not to Richard the Lionheart but to Richard of the Romans, brother of Henry III. Children have adopted the Merry Men in Lincoln Green as romantic and supremely imitable, and have standardized their characters as firmly as their bows and hunting horns and their philosophy of robbing the rich to help the poor. The language of popular versions of Robin Hood's exploits is usually affected and the style of the more dignified re-tellings of Howard Pyle, Rosemary Sutcliff, Ian Serraillier and Donald Suddaby still tend towards a formality that suits the conception of Robin as a legendary figure.

Geoffrey Trease's fictional interpretation of Robin Hood stands almost as a bridge between heroic-retellings and the search for historical evidence. *Bows against the Barons* was written in deliberate contrast to the one-sided social picture, the panache and glamorization, of the historical fiction offered to children in the 1930s. His Robin Hood lives in Sherwood Forest with Little John and Allan-a-Dale and other trusted men and carries on a guerilla warfare in an attempt to get justice for the poor, the inarticulate and the helpless. To Dickon, who has killed one of the King's deer to save his family from starvation, he is 'a man among men', who laughs at the legends of his noble birth. 'Aren't you satisfied with a common man as leader?' he demands of the people who flock to him, and he patiently tries to convince them that 'there are only two classes, masters and men, haves and have-nots'. If this simple interpretation does not seem as surprising now as it did forty years ago, it is partly because it has strongly influenced the course of historical fiction for the young since it was first published.

*Bows against the Barons* belongs to the political climate of the 1930s; the fears of the 70s lie behind another Robin Hood figure, John Christopher's Wild Jack. In the twenty-third century England, like the rest of the world, is ruled by a small élite who control a servant class recruited from people forced to live in the Outlands for lack of space in organized communities. Various tales are told about the man called Wild Jack who has become a leader and a legend in the forests of southwest England. A bogyman to children, a constant source

*Right and overleaf.* Two illustrations from *The Merry Adventures of Robin Hood*, written and illustrated by Howard Pyle.

The·Merry·Friar·carrieth·
Robin·across·the·Water:·

AZRAEL

Robin · ſhooteth · his · Laſt · Shaft :

H·P·

H.P.

of anxiety to the Councillors, he is a kind of Robin Hood, teaching those who flock to him that one day they will rise and fight for their rights. The tall man with his black beard and hooked nose saves the life and the reason of three boys who have escaped from one of the dread punishment islands; his intelligence, his simple forest weapons and customs, his strength and compassion are realized through them. His crusade against the Councillors and their evil domination suggests both Trease's Robin Hood and the romantic hero of legend. [John Christopher: *Wild Jack*, London 1974; Geoffrey Trease: *Bows against the Barons*, London 1934]

**ROBINSON CRUSOE,** the generalized figure of a castaway, fur-clad and practical, quickly became the property of children through chapbook simplifications of Defoe's story. It is the practical, adventure aspect of the story that has always attracted children, the well-documented, journalist's account of how a castaway builds a new, comfortable and well-organized life and even reconciles the alien Friday to it. Most of the many eighteenth- and nineteenth-century imitations and offshoots of *Robinson Crusoe* pursue the idea of the castaway either as a man finding God through suffering and solitude or as an allegory of the slow march of civiliza-

tion. The Robinsonnades written for children in the present century are very different. Whether they are set properly on a desert island or in some comparable geographical outpost, whether Crusoe is represented by a solitary figure or (most often) by a group, the emphasis is on the do-it-yourself adventure; a book like Ivan Southall's penetrating, stringent story *To the Wild Sky* is an exception.

Of the moral and educational Robinsonnades, *The Swiss Family Robinson* is the best known. The book grew out of conversations in the Wyss family in which the pastor forwarded his sons' education by encouraging them to imagine various possibilities in Crusoe's situation; the long sub-title of the edition of 1818, 'Being a practical illustration of the first principles of mechanics, natural philosophy, natural history, and all those branches of science which most immediately apply to the business of life', shows the educational object of the book. Robinson Crusoe experienced an access of religious feeling when he was in danger: the Swiss family from the first build their new life on the foundation of religion, starting each enterprise not with introspective appeals to God but with the natural, accustomed expressions of piety. This aspect of the story is con-

An illustration by Gay Galsworthy from *Swiss Family Robinson*.

veniently passed over by children of today in the headlong chase from one dramatic event to another.

Only one author has directly invited the young to think seriously about the psychological effect of solitude on a man's spirit. In *Friday and Robinson* (a junior version of his existential novel *Friday*) Michel Tournier drew a sardonic picture of an eighteenth-century merchant of conventional character who, after days of despair during which he descended to the behaviour of an animal, set himself (as Crusoe did in Defoe's story) to create as close an imitation as possible of the world he had lost, taming the island by taming its animals, growing crops and appointing himself Governor and drawing up a set of laws. This rigid way of life, with its elaborate time-table of duties, was extended to Friday, but though Friday accepted his role, his natural humour found secret outlets and at last his happy philosophy so far influenced his master that Friday became his instructor in the art of living; and when rescue came it was Friday who, lured by the promise of new enjoyment, left the island, Robinson who remained. It seems unlikely that this riddling, sophisticated version of the familiar story will ever make as much impression on the young as Defoe's story which they cherish, possibly because it suggests that there is always a way to tame adventure. [Daniel Defoe: *The Life and Strange Surprising Adventures of Robinson Crusoe of York, Mariner*, London 1719; *Further Adventures of Robinson Crusoe*, 1719; Johann Rudolf Wyss: *Der Schweizerische Robinson*, 2 pts, Zurich 1812 and 1813; as *The Family Robinson Crusoe*, probably trans. William Godwin, London 1814; as *The Swiss Family Robinson*, London 1818. Michel Tournier: *Vendredi ou La Vie Sauvage*, Paris 1971; as *Friday and Robinson*, trans. R. Manheim, London 1972]

**ROGER BRADLEY** *see* ALISON

**ROGER WALKER's** definition of civilization is 'Ices and all that sort of thing'. He is the youngest member on all but one of the Walkers' expeditions. Interestingly, Roger remains a typical 'youngest' even when his junior, Bridget (q.v.), is allowed to join them (in *Secret Water*). In *Swallows and Amazons*, Roger is about nine years old; by the time the party has gone to the Hebrides (in *Great Northern?*) he is eleven or so; but he is still making cheeky remarks with the air of a privileged clown, still apt to peel off from the main party in order to assert his independence. On one occasion he walks in his sleep and is heard remarking, typically, 'Of course I can.' Roger's outlook on life is modelled, one guesses, on his father and older brother John (q.v.). Like John, he sees his future in the Navy and, in his less irresponsible moments, he tries to act as a proper ship's boy, or able seaman, would do, although he develops early in the sequence a taste for engines which diverts his attention from the techniques of sailing. If in this more adult side of his character Roger seems to align himself with John, in the family pattern he is classed with Titty (q.v.) by

Roger Walker waves from the bows of the *Swallow* as the four children sail off to their island camp in *Swallows and Amazons*.

his elders and is always ready to share with her the habit of role-playing. Often, as they trot along behind the others, they tell scenes from their favourite stories or relive the Caribbean adventure (*Peter Duck*) which they helped to invent.

Roger changes very little as the books proceed. His importance is essentially that of a betwixt and between; in moments of danger he is all child, dependent on his elders and switching from apprehension to gaiety with childlike speed. As they drift across the North Sea (in *We Didn't Mean to Go to Sea*) he is soon diverted from the thought of danger when he is allowed to sound the fog-horn.

The way his personality is linked, unobtrusively, with father, brother and sisters helps to make this set of stories pre-eminent in its family relationships. There is never any doubt in our minds that the Walkers are not a collection of people chosen at random to suit a certain set of circumstances but a genuine family unit of diverse but related individuals. [Arthur Ransome: *Swallows and Amazons*, London 1930; *We Didn't Mean to Go to Sea*, 1937; *Great Northern?*, 1947]

**ROLLITT,** a pupil at Fellsgarth School, has no friends there even after he has worked his way up in three years to the Sixth Form. He hardly ever speaks and when he does he says 'either what was unexpected or disagreeable'. Visitors to his study are told to get out. He spends no money and is variously called mean or poverty-stricken. But Rollitt has become a celebrity in the school in spite of himself, partly because of his enormous strength (he has 'an arm like an oak branch, and a back as broad as the door') and partly for the sheer mystery of the boy. The end of his career at school makes up for its lonely beginning. He makes one friend at least – Fisher 2, a new boy, who interposes at a dangerous moment on the river when Rollitt is fishing. The friendship leads indirectly to a heroic rescue on the dangerous Hawk's Pike, an exploit which Rollitt shrugs off, embarrassed to let it be seen that he values little Fisher's comradeship. When he learns that he is suspected of stealing money, he disappears from the school.

Rollitt is solitary partly because he is conscious of being no gentleman. He goes to Fellsgarth at the behest of two ladies with a long-standing attachment to his mother. The situation of a boy from the working class unhappily enduring life in a public school is one that must be understood historically. Certain of Rollitt's reactions to his schoolfellows may seem laughable now, but the honesty of Talbot Baines Reed's interpretation of his character shows through the antiquated slang and outmoded taboos of the 1890s. *The Cock House at Fellsgarth* is worth reading if only for the unusual and touching portrait of this son of a builder, hiding out in a ruined tower with his Horace to work at and a supply of Abernethy biscuits, a hero to the little boys and a symbol of an unattainable life to his parents. [Talbot Baines Reed: *The Cock House at Fellsgarth*, London 1893]

**ROLLO HOLIDAY** belongs to an established, well-to-do American family of a century and a half ago; he drives out in the carriage, attends 'Miss May's' school in the village, crosses the Atlantic and sees some of the wonders of Britain and of Europe, either with his parents or his uncle George, whose sense of humour and ideas of education and discipline are more relaxed than usual at the time.

The many Rollo books, staple of American nurseries in the last century, were written principally for the delectation of the young but also to engage thought and reason, promote good reading and cultivate 'the amiable and gentle qualities of the heart'. Rollo's character and conduct are guaranteed to be worthy of imitation 'with the exception of some of the ordinary exhibitions of childish folly'. One might guess that even children accustomed to a didactic note in their literature would have sighed more then they smiled at such a hero.

Surprisingly, there are many moments in the stories when Rollo seems a perfectly admissible, even an engaging boy. Although he is almost always both the cause and the recipient of a reproof, an explanation or a moral discourse, there is a certain charm in his acquiescence, a naturalness in the manner of his questions, even

though it is obvious that they are designed to elicit some useful fact. There is plenty of fun in the earliest books, when Rollo and his cousin James, at the age of five or so, build a wigwam in the woods, scrape acquaintance with rough boys, squabble a little and grumble a little. As a pupil, Rollo works sensibly and with method and is eager to help Dovey, a rough girl from a poor home, to settle to school routine. One might have placed his characters and doings far later than the 1840s and '50s if it were not for the sternly rational nature of the punishments meted out by his parents, and for the severe standard of conduct expected of the boy (on one occasion, when he complains of bad weather stopping a projected expedition, he is told he is self-conceited, ungrateful, undutiful, unjust, selfish and impious, and is sent to the back garret to think over his misdoings).

Rollo's lively charm is less often evident in the later books, which were designed 'for the communication of useful knowledge'. But though we see Rollo learning to manage luggage and foreign money, how to comport himself in society, how to look after his adopted cousin Jane, how (in short) to be a proper gentleman, there are still moments when he is pure boy – as, for instance, when he begs for the journey to Paris to be by way of Newhaven because the boat starts from there at midnight, and he could then 'see all the people going on board by the light of lanterns and torches'. The literary tradition that reduces a fictional character to the role of listener is by no means dead and the Rollo books, pedantic though they often are, can stand comparison with some of the fact/fiction books of today. [Jacob Abbott: *Rollo at Work and Rollo at Play*, Boston 1834; *Rollo at School*, 1839; *Rollo on the Atlantic*, 1853; *Rollo in Paris*, 1854; and many other titles]

**ROSALBA** wanders from the palace when her father, King of Crim Tartary, is overthrown by the rebellious Duke Padella; but she is saved from starvation and exposure by the kind offices of a lioness and finds her way, a pert and amusing child, to the palace of Paflagonia. Here she catches the fancy of bored Princess Angelica, who makes her first a companion and then a lady's maid. Betsinda, as she is now called, suffers many reversals of fortune even after her true identity is discovered (in orthodox fashion, by the discovery of a shoe and a fragment of velvet which matches what remains of her original clothes). In so far as a character in a satirical play can be said to have individuality, Thackeray does allow Rosalba a certain quiet self-satisfaction which makes a comic point as against the attributes of the traditional waif of fairy tale.

*See also* Giglio, Gruffanuff, Fairy Blackstick. [W. M. Thackeray: *The Rose and the Ring*, 1855]

**ROSAMOND**, 'a little girl about seven years old, is walking with her mother in the streets of London', intrigued by all that she sees, and desiring her mother to buy this and that attractive object seen in a shop window, when she catches sight of a set of glass jars – blue, green, yellow and purple – in a chemist's shop. Rosamond's mother offers her the choice between the purple jar and new soles for her shoes (which are shockingly thin) and Rosamond, after canvassing in vain her mother's opinion, decides on the jar. When the jar is emptied so that fresh water may be put in it for flowers, it proves to be only plain glass after all, while Rosamond is obliged to limp on broken shoes for the agreed period, even missing a special outing with her father because 'no one must walk slip-shod with me.'

Poor Rosamond. Her remorselessly reasonable and well-regulated mamma takes every opportunity of making the child think for herself, for in this way she will learn good sense. Since the stories about the little girl – about lessons, hours of play, visits and visitors – are intended as examples of the educational theories which Maria Edgeworth had adapted from Rousseau, Rosamond might have turned out a very unconvincing fictional character, but in spite of her unpromising function in the story, she is a very real little girl.

The background of the comfortable house with its regular mealtimes and treats, has a domestic solidity that lends reality to the character. Then again, Rosamond's older brother Godfrey, who teases her, commandeers her for his games, advises her on her garden and has a protective eye for her comfort, adds a certain reflected actuality as well. We need a sense of proportion to interpret Rosamond's mother aright; to forgive her for warning the child, when she is looking forward to a 'party of pleasure', that too much eagerness may bring disappointment, for standing by calmly as the child decides whether to let her remove a thorn from her finger or escape anticipated pain ('The probable consequences are, my dear, that the finger will fester, or *gather*'). She speaks for her period, most of all when she decides to allow Rosamond, young as she is, to tour a cotton-mill 'because she was rather too fond of imaginary things, such as fairy tales, and stories of giants and enchanters; and it would be advantageous to give her a taste for truth and realities'. One would be more dubious about the effects of an education whose ultimate object was self-command if Rosamond did not give the reassuring impression that it would take more than her mamma to quench her spirit. [Maria Edgeworth: *Early Lessons*, 1801]

**ROSEMARY BROWN** utters precisely eighty-six words in the course of *A Parcel of Trees*, preferring to express herself with eyebrows, nods or flounces. It would be a mistake, though, to dismiss this formidable eight-year-old as a minor character, although she plays no part in the unravelling of the past history of the plot of land below the railway embankment which her sister covets as a refuge. The only reaction from Rosemary is the moment when she is shown one of the lawyer's model locomotives and at once wants to dress it as a doll. Her longest speech (thirty-nine words) is a dogmatic monologue about the regimen she is prescribing

for her own family of dolls. She is not shy but 'There was not much she wanted to say'. Yet every time she appears – silent, glowering and terrifyingly observant – there is no possible doubt about her presence. It would be possible to make out a case for Rosemary Brown as Mayne's most emphatically alive and brilliantly drawn character. [William Mayne, *A Parcel of Trees*, Harmondsworth 1963]

**ROSIE** hangs a sign on her door that reads: 'If you want to know a secret, knock three times.' The secret is that she has become Alinda, the lovely lady singer. Rosie organizes a backyard show and her eager audience respond well until Lenny arrives with his hose and fireman's hat and insists on doing his act. Subsequent roles as Alinda the lost girl (muffled in a blanket awaiting the coming of Magic Man) and, on the Fourth of July, a fire-cracker, display Rosie's versatility and demonstrate the power of her personality over her more stolid playmates. It is impossible to know whether one learns more about Rosie from her forceful words or from watching her expressive face and posture in each picture. [Maurice Sendak: *The Sign on Rosie's Door*, New York 1960]

**ROSIE** the hen goes for a walk; a fox follows her; she 'got back in time for dinner'. This is not truly an escape since Rosie is perfectly unaware of her enemy, or that she has foiled his evil designs by accident; it is hardly her doing that she steps on a rake that flies up and hits her pursuer, that she leads him into a pond and a haycock, catches the string that releases a bag of flour on to his head and takes a course that leads the unhappy animal under a row of beehives. Or is it by accident? The inexorable march of the hen, smug beak uptilted, is part of a sly joke brilliantly pursued in a one-sentence text and in pictures that display Pat Hutchins's penchant for brilliant combinations of crimson and yellow, for intricate effects applied to formalized farmyard and woodland figures. From beak to tail Rosie is a personality. [Pat Hutchins: *Rosie's Walk*, London 1968]

**ROSY VINCENT'S** 'nice little mouth' and 'two bright eyes' are often spoiled by pouting and frowning, for the little girl has been thoroughly spoilt during the years she spends with her aunt while her parents are abroad, and her mother finds it a weary task to turn her eight-year-old daughter into a sensible, well-mannered child. But Rosy has one compensating virtue – her honesty. It often gets her into trouble but it gives her mother hope that behind her tantrums and whining there is a sound character to build on. Rosy's dissatisfaction with life increases when Beata, a sweet-tempered child whom everybody likes, comes on a long visit while her parents are in India. Because Rosy finds it hard to dislike her she becomes even more surly towards the lonely, bewildered child.

The governess, Miss Pinkerton, is afraid she may lose her post if she checks Rosy, so the child's behaviour becomes worse, for she despises the governess for twist-

The cellar door opened and out came Alinda. She wore a hat with feathers sticking out, a lady's dress, and high-heeled shoes.

A page from *The Sign on Rosie's Door,* written and illustrated by Maurice Sendak.

past the mill

Rosie releases a bag of flour upon the pursuing fox, drawn by Pat Hutchins.

# RUPERT AND THE
# ENCHANTED PRINCESS

WHEN the little dame had driven off
    Rupert too on his way went
And soon a forest vast he reached,
    Doubtless the one she meant.

How in that forest could he find
    The lady whom he sought
He felt bewildered, there alone:
    "Oh, for some help!" he thought.

"Ha! Ha!" he heard a voice. "I know
    Whom you seek. I'll guide you there."
Rupert turned to see a little man
    Riding upon a Hare

A page from *Rupert and the Enchanted Princess* by Mary Tourtel.

ing facts to make Beata seem responsible for various acts of mischief or disobedience. Then Rosy's aunt arrives on a visit, accompanied by her maid-companion Nelson. Like Miss Pinkerton, Nelson is uncertain of her position and in consequence flatters Rosy so outrageously that she becomes spiteful towards Beata and even teases her beloved little brother Felix. But the discovery of the truth about a lost necklace vindicates Beata, who has been falsely accused by the spiteful Nelson, and helps Rosy to conquer her jealousy and let her natural frankness help her to a steadier view of life. The improving element in the story is absorbed satisfactorily in its shrewd psychology. Rosy's character is delineated with the certainty and point that distinguishes Mrs Molesworth's stories as a whole. [Mrs Molesworth: *Rosy*, London 1882]

**RUPERT BEAR** may not be the longest lived humanized animal in fiction (Tiger Tim probably has that distinction) but he may claim to have enjoyed a more continuous and extensive popularity than any other. He first appeared in 1920 in the *Daily Express* in a story called 'The Adventures of a Little Lost Bear', with Mary Tourtel's illustrations and with captions by her husband. More adventures followed, narrated day by day, always in one picture with an accompanying set of rhymes. Mary Tourtel wrote the stories and drew the pictures up to 1935; A. E. Bestall, who took over from her, continues Rupert's story today in newspaper series and in annuals. Many people regret the disappearance of the small square books that appeared before the Second World War, each containing a single Rupert story, but though a reprint of a few of these early stories a few years ago was quickly sold out, this was an isolated instance, and the post-war, suburban Rupert has ousted the amiable little bear who had one foot in Fairyland.

The character of Rupert was moulded to suit a basic narrative pattern, whose shape and psychological intention has not changed. The story of a child venturing from a safe home to a wider world and returning is fundamental in children's stories; the theme can be found in books as diverse as *The Hobbit*, *Finn's Folly* and *Where the Wild Things Are*. Rupert enjoys a safe, cosy home life, with a comfortably rotund mother and a pipe-smoking father who encourage him to help other people and are not more than mildly anxious when he is overdue from one of his expeditions. The obscene analysis of Rupert's relations with his parents in the journal *Oz* was directed at the post-war tales, obvious targets because, in them, action and detail are far closer to real life than the earlier stories were. Rupert's character has not changed in essentials. He is still an obedient and considerate son, a warm-hearted child-animal with a natural curiosity and an ingenuous manner that smooths the paths for him wherever he goes. But his position in the stories, and his circumstances, have changed.

The earlier stories were rooted in fairy tale, nursery rhyme and legend. Rupert's adventures took place either in a fairy-tale world of talking animals, magicians and monarchs crowned and robed, or in a world of chivalry, where knights rode noble steeds, Rupert was led by seneschals into banqueting halls, and Robin Hood and Wayland Smith were equally at home. In these early tales, imaginative details (a tiny coach drawn by mice, mischievous animated balloons, a magic umbrella) compensated for the plodding doggerel.

Sadly, the fairy-tale world has now given place to a more commonplace one. Rupert is now involved with smugglers, petty crooks and old salts with treasure maps, while the elves who appear occasionally are gauzy nonentities whose trivial tricks have no true magic in them. The change has taken much of Rupert's charm away. Now that he and his chums are involved as much with humans as with the denizens of Fairyland (with Girl Guides, a Chinese conjuror and his daughter, Sailor Sam and his lad Rollo, among others), he has changed from seeming a child fascinated by wonderful adventures to a pert and rather vulgar manikin disguised as a bear. The Rupert stories were originally a respectably lowbrow form of fairy tale; they gained a reflected colour from tradition. Now they are one-level, one-dimension frolics addressed to uncritical and inattentive readers. The journey from Fairyland to suburbia has been a sad one for Rupert Bear. [Mary Tourtel: 'The Adventures of a Little Lost Bear', daily picture-serial in *Daily Express*, London, 1920–35; pub. in book form, London 1921; Rupert Little Bear Library, 46 vols, London *c*. 1930–36; and many painting books and annuals]

**SAJO,** an Ojibway Indian, lives with her father and older brother Shapian in a log cabin in northern Canada. Her eleventh birthday brings an unusual gift of two beaver kittens which their father has found while on a hunting trip. The two children name them Chilawee and Chikanee, or Big Small and Little Small, and find them so tame and responsive that they seem to be friends rather than pets. Then, unhappily, their father is forced to sell Chikanee, the shyer of the two, to pay off a debt to the local trader. The children determine to go to the city and get the little beaver back. Taking their chance while their father is away, they journey down river by canoe, narrowly escape death in a forest fire and succeed in the end in uniting the two animals once more.

In the tradition of Thompson Seton, the story emphasizes those aspects of the two beavers which seem closest to humans, and Sajo's deep attachment to them is equally strongly described, the whole story working towards an emotional dénouement. The excuse for the sentimental tone of the book must be the author's desire to waken readers to the beauties of nature and animal life and to show that humans must be responsible for the world around them. [Grey Owl: *Sajo and her Beaver People*, London 1935]

**SALLY HENNY-PENNY** *see* GINGER AND PICKLES

**SALLY SMITH** lives near Boston, in the last quarter of the eighteenth century, with her uncles Joseph and Eben and her aunts Nannie, Deborah and Esther. She is excited when Uncle Joseph decides to move to Maine, where better farming land is available for those who are willing to leave civilized surroundings for a sparsely populated land. Only Aunt Nannie stands out against the enterprise, vowing 'I will never leave my own fire nor sleep in any but my own bed'; but Uncle Joseph finds a way to answer her objection and it is in a little wooden house drawn by a team of oxen that the delighted Sally travels through winter snow and spring thaw to her new home.

The little girl, with her black eyes and dark hair and her warm interest in people, grows into an attractive sixteen-year-old in the course of five books, but she never loses the generous spirit that is especially hers. Her fearless innocence (in *Five Bushel Farm*) impresses the Indians so that they willingly conclude an agreement with Uncle Joseph for the site of his house, their old burial ground. Her unselfconscious way with strangers smooths the path for Andrew Forrester, who is left destitute when his father's ship, the *Fair American*, is long overdue from a trading voyage. Her sympathy persuades Captain Forrester to help in rescuing Pierre, whose home and parents have suffered in the French Revolution, and her courage softens the heart of the moody Sultan (in *The White Horse of Morocco*) when the Captain and his party have been captured off the North African coast and sold as slaves. Finally, it is Sally's determination that helps her to save Uncle Joseph's farm from a fraudulent stranger who almost succeeds in seizing it.

'You are like a breeze from the north to us', the White Lalla, the Sultan's new wife, tells Sally when the child, making the best of her enforced sojourn in the harem, teaches the children American games and explores and makes friends wherever she can. Her eager, confiding manner does not entirely please Aunt Nannie, but it is not in Sally's power to behave like a young lady if it means she must 'learn to walk instead of running, and to speak more slowly, and not to laugh. Just smile, my dear'. The pleasing detail and exciting events of these stories of pioneer days would mean far less if it were not for the personality of Sally, which glows through their pages. [Elizabeth Coatsworth: *Away Goes Sally*, New York 1934; *Five Bushel Farm*, 1939; *The 'Fair American'*, 1940; *The White Horse* (later *The White Horse of Morocco*), 1942; *The Wonderful Day*, 1946]

**SAM,** or Samantha, the fisherman's daughter, 'had the reckless habit of lying'; her father calls her stories Moonshine; her cat Bangs (or so she fancies) uses the scornful word Flummadiddle; but little Thomas believes every word. It does no harm for him to hear that the 'ragged old rug on the doorstep was a chariot drawn by dragons', and perhaps only harms Sam herself, besides hurting her father, when she persists that her mother is not dead but has become a mermaid. It does harm Thomas, however, when in his hunt for Sam's imaginary baby kangaroo he is almost drowned near

Sally Smith, the endearing orphan of Elizabeth Coatsworth's series of books, here illustrated in *Away Goes Sally* by Caroline Sharpe.

Blue Rock in a storm. So Sam learns the hard way the difference between imagination and dangerous lies.

The brief text of this picture-story book outlines an important psychological point, probed more deeply in the pictures, which project the personality of a dreamy, self-centred child looking for ways to compensate for the death of her mother. [Evaline Ness: *Sam, Bangs and Moonshine*, London 1966]

**SAM GRIBLEY** is not happy living in New York. His father, who works on the docks, longs to go back to sea; his mother is a country girl. Sam decides, with his father's amused approval, to find the ruins of the old Gribley house in the Catskill Mountains and see if he can live off the land.

From May of one year to June of the next Sam works at his problem. He makes a house in a huge hollow tree, fishes and traps for food, and hides his existence from hunters and hikers. In fact, though he achieves a worthy independence he is not entirely alone. He takes a young hawk from its nest, tames and trains it, and so has someone to listen to a running commentary on his days. Besides, there are occasional visitors – a school-teacher looking for peace in nature, a boy from the village, his father who comes to check on his well-being.

The books reflects the back-to-nature feeling of urban folk. The character of Sam is indicated by what he does, by what he says, by the thoughts which are spoken or unspoken, by the records he keeps. In obvious descent from Thompson Seton's little savages, and perhaps also from Bevis, Sam is in his eager, outgoing, resourceful way a boy who possesses a certain individuality besides the life bestowed on him by setting and action. [Jean George: *My Side of the Mountain*, New York 1959]

**SAM PIG** lives in a thatched cottage with his brothers Tom and Bill and his sister Ann. While Tom cooks, Bill gardens and Ann mends, Sam 'got in everybody's way for he was young and simple'. But the wise Badger who acts as guardian and mentor to the four pigs defends him. 'You play the fiddle and keep us all merry. You are quite an important member of this household.' In his much-patched trousers Sam Pig keeps pieces of honeycomb, a bee or two, a frog, pebbles and snail shells, as well as Jemima the fieldmouse and her newborn children – all safely hidden between layers of patches; and though he is delighted with the new trousers which his long-suffering sister makes from sheep's wool in red and blue checks, these are soon in much the same state as the first pair.

Sam Pig might seem nothing more than a small boy in disguise if it were not for the echoes of folk-tale and fairy lore that add a special tone to his adventures. When he goes off to seek his fortune one day, he collects a cow, cat, dog and wren, and the travellers find a crock

Sam with her cat Bangs: one of Evaline Ness's psychologically pointed illustrations for her book *Sam, Bangs and Moonshine*.

The wise badger counselling Sam Pig and his brothers and sister in *Sam Pig Goes to Market*, illustrated by A. E. Kennedy.

of gold at the foot of the rainbow; when they try to take it home they are soundly belaboured by the hawthorn tree that guards the treasure. In another story Sam finds his comfortable seat on the hillside is a dragon which, waking to the sound of his fiddle, stays awake for a time to act as central heating for the pigs. Like Hare in the Grey Rabbit books, Sam Pig talks freely and confidently to humans and accepts lifts from friendly farmers when he wants to investigate the interesting world outside the wood. But in spite of the spirit of curiosity which is an important part of the character lent to him from humans, Sam Pig remains in many ways a natural and recognizable farmyard animal. [Alison Uttley: *Tales of the Four Pigs and Brock the Badger*, London 1939; *The Adventures of Sam Pig*, 1941; and many other titles]

**SAMUEL WHISKERS** *see* GINGER AND PICKLES

**SARA CREWE** has lived with her widower father in India until she is seven years old and neither knows how to bear separation when Sara, for the sake of her health, is placed in Miss Minchin's Select Seminary for Young Ladies in London. But Sara makes the best of her situation, helped by the company of her doll Emily who (she is sure) listens and sympathizes, and by the privileges accorded to her by sycophantic Miss Minchin because of her father's wealth and position.

For four years Sara is well looked after and if she dislikes Miss Minchin for her deceitful manner, she benefits from the lessons. Then tragedy strikes. Her father loses his money through the mismanagement of a friend and dies soon afterwards, a broken man. Miss

Minchin grudgingly but with typical opportunism keeps Sara to teach the younger children and serve as household drudge. Cold, lonely and hungry, relegated to a dingy attic, Sara endures the insults of Miss Minchin and the servants until the wheel of fortune turns in her favour once more. A reclusive gentleman next door, apprised of her sad life by his Indian servant, agrees to a plan that transforms the attic secretly into a bower of warmth and beauty. It comes out by chance that the benefactor is Captain Crewe's friend, who has regained the lost fortune and has been trying to trace the child, and the story ends with rewards for those who remained loyal to Sara in her decline and with discomfiture for cruel Miss Minchin.

This rags-to-riches story, for all its coincidences, depends wholly on character for its effect. The book needs, and gets, a strongly delineated heroine and one who can command interested sympathy, not sentimental acquiescence. Sara survives her trials because of her imagination, her courage and her intelligence. Intelligence shows her what Miss Minchin is really like and stiffens her pride so that she is able to outface the tyrannical woman. She is also helped by a lively imagination, nourished by books and deepened by misfortune. In the first years of separation 'pretending' has helped her to feel she is still close to her father. Later, in the cold attic, she assures slow, faithful Ermengarde, the only girl who has remained her friend, that she can bear her life 'if I pretend it is a place in a story' like the Chateau d'If or the Bastille. Becky, the little tweeny, whose devotion she had won in happier days, becomes 'the prisoner in the next cell', and Sara amuses herself by devising signals on the wall between them. Above all she keeps her courage up by deciding that if she had once seemed like a princess, with her rich clothes and expensive toys, now still more she must behave like one. It is a secret comfort, when Miss Minchin is 'in the midst of some harsh, domineering speech', to imagine that if she chose Sara could order her execution. 'I only spare you because I *am* a princess, and you are a poor, stupid, unkind, vulgar old thing, and don't know any better.'

If this particular manifestation of Sara's fancy seems more than a little snobbish nowadays, it must be remembered that she is drawn in the social context of nearly a century ago. The generosity and warmth of her relations with Becky are natural and childlike but it is equally a part of her character to feel and know herself different from the servant. It is not only in her gift for story-telling that Sara is manifestly in part a reflection of Frances Hodgson Burnett's own nature and attitudes. [Frances Hodgson Burnett: *Sara Crewe*, New York 1888; re-published as *A Little Princess*, London 1905]

**SCARECROW** *see* DOROTHY GALE

**SCRUFF RAFFERTY,** a mongrel 'mostly Scots collie', keeps watch over the railway goods depot in an Irish town. There are times when this 'happy tramp'

Scruff Rafferty, drawn by Alistair Grant.

worries about not having a pedigree. It is the reason, he is certain, why 'he wasn't being recognized for the great natural leader of dogs which he so obviously was'. When Ginger Rafferty at the depot decides to take him in the parade at the local show, Scruff is awarded a special prize for 'the best dog who represented a blend of six breeds or more' and he is heard to remark that 'he wouldn't be a thoroughbred if you paid him.'

The stories about Scruff and his associates were originally broadcast on Children's Hour in the BBC service from Northern Ireland. The narrator, an elderly Irish terrier, does full justice to the canine view of people as well as of other dogs. Each of the animals has a firmly and openly stated character, developed through appropriate action. Joe Louis McDaniel, a bull terrier, shakes 'the whole cat community' and after a period of disgrace on account of his aggressive habits, holds up a thief and becomes a police dog; François Villon Robinson, the pampered French poodle, complains of ill-treatment in his 'sharp niminy-piminy voice'; Towser Thompson becomes famous when his independently-moving ears are thought to make accurate weather predictions. There is Mandarin Metcalf, the pedigree Chow, an 'inscrutable Chinese dog who used to lie out in the middle of the town square and let the traffic drive round him';

there is Dai Bach Evans, the belligerent corgi and Archie Gault the noisy Scotch terrier and Fortunato Brown the circus dog. The canine guide round this superb gallery of comic portraits does his job with praiseworthy gravity and shrewdness and the author, by keeping in the background, disclaims responsibility for any whimsicality in the stories. [Roy Johnston: *The Scruff Rafferty Dog Stories*, London 1962]

**SEA PIPER,** (the), *see* PIED PIPER

**SEMOLINA SILKPAWS** brings her kittens to live at Mitten Row when they are still quite small and tells them they must 'walk sedately, paw in paw', for the neighbours will certainly be watching. 'We will walk with noses and tails in the air and be a real credit to you' reply the kittens, and the whole street sighs with relief to see that a genteel creature 'with really well-behaved, well-brought-up kittens' has come to live among them.

The short episodes in the four books about Semolina Silkpaws were shaped to fit the pages of the magazine *Good Housekeeping*, where they first appeared. They are based on a simple, workable formula. The cats live like humans. Mrs Silkpaws cooks on a stove, learns to drive a car, goes shopping, decorates the house for Christmas. The illustrator, Ronald Ferns, rarely shows the cats wearing clothes except for hats (top hats, a Mayoral bonnet, floral confections, sailor caps), which he uses to underline a particular theme or situation. Hats, in fact, constitute one of Mrs Silkpaws' few weaknesses, and when Frivol and Fluff offer thirteen hats for the price of twelve, to 'lady motorist cats able to carry home their own shopping', she cannot resist the temptation. These little stories, full of sly, satirical allusions to the world as we know it, owe their charm to the character of this maternal, elegant cat, who is always socially correct, always right and always entertaining. [Gladys Williams, ill. Ronald Ferns: *Semolina Silkpaws Comes to Catstown*, 1962; *Fireworks for Semolina Silkpaws*, 1964; *Semolina Silkpaws' Motor Car*, 1968; *Semolina Silkpaws Takes a Holiday Abroad*, 1972; omnibus edition, *All about Semolina Silkpaws*, 1972]

**SEPTIMUS QUINN** starts his career in the Navy of Nelson's day at fifteen when he is called up to serve on His Majesty's frigate *Althea*. His parson uncle, a hearty gentleman, hardly thinks Septimus has the qualities needed for a naval officer, however junior, in 1803. The boy is oddly fond of reading and always experimenting with chemical mixtures that make the Rectory uninhabitable. It is with some relief that the Rev. Theophilus sees his nephew off, little knowing that the first of numerous hilarious and unorthodox incidents is soon to occur. A fortuitous experiment enables Septimus to overpower a highwayman, and similar scientific efforts mark his progress up the ladder of naval fame.

Septimus distinguishes himself through several books (always in an unexpected and hardly correct manner) in sea battles and skirmishes, while a light romantic interest is supplied by his encounter with Denise de St Aulaye, an anti-Bonapartist spy who joins him in a daring escape after capture in France. Septimus Quinn could be called a junior Hornblower for the non-conformity that leads him into some ludicrous situations, but Showell Styles has designed his character to suit light adventure stories for the young and not ironical adult novels. Self-confident, apparently free from fear, youthfully chivalrous, incessantly curious about everything in the world (except his own personality), the spectacled young hero is entertaining enough in his own right to maintain his position in a series of books, anecdotal in construction, in which he plays the lead in a variety of scenes reflecting the naval history of the early nineteenth century. [Showell Styles: *Midshipman Quinn*, London 1956; *Quinn of the 'Fury'*, 1958; *The Flying Ensign*, 1960; *Midshipman Quinn Wins Through*, 1961; *Quinn at Trafalgar*, 1965]

**SEPTIMUS TRELOAR,** Rector of St Mary's Danedyke in the Lincolnshire Fens, was a policeman before he was ordained; he rose from being a bobby on the beat to the rank of a Chief Inspector in the CID. War service and some talent as a middle-weight boxer and rock-climber are also useful qualifications when it comes to solving two mysteries – one, the matter of a medieval gold chalice, the other a haunting (with a wholly convincing explanation) in the great Minster.

This 'large and elderly parson with the face like a bus smash' could have been a cliché character, an example of the muscular Christian, but Stephen Chance avoids this by cutting into his story a certain amount of obviously authentic parsonical routine and by indicating, simply but effectively, how Treloar relates to his superiors, his colleagues and his parishioners. The two sides of his life are splendidly convenient for the two thrillers, but the combination is not a gimmick. The character of Septimus Treloar is drawn in the round. There are enough clues to his integrity, his humane outlook on life, to motivate his action and give the book a steady but real core of feeling. [Stephen Chance: *Septimus and the Danedyke Mystery*, London 1971; *Septimus and the Minster Ghost*, 1972]

**SERAPHINA BROWN** goes to live with her Aunt Edna when she is thirteen, after her grandmother's death; her father died many years before and her actress mother has made earning a living the excuse for not looking after her. Aunt Edna, capably running her own hairdressing business, is sharp-tongued and unaffectionate and makes Seraphina feel she is not wanted. The girl comforts herself by inventing an interesting background to impress the girls at Medborough High School. She is soon entangled in her own deceit. It is one thing to say that her parents are exploring in Central Africa but quite another to prove it to sceptical Lydia, especially when a birthday present from them has to be surreptitiously bought and suitably wrapped. There is another problem – Aunt Edna is determined to

Seraphina and her friend Stephanie, illustrated by
Sheila Rose.

find Seraphina a place in her shop and discourage her
'highfalutin'' ideas about Oxbridge. Seraphina might
have drifted into self-pity if it had not been for her
friendship with Stephanie (q.v.), whose own troubles, as
she gradually learns, are a good deal more pressing than
her own. Realizing this, and learning from trenchant
Aunt Edna to face the truth about her mother's indifference, Seraphina shakes off her romantic fantasies.
First-person narration is brilliantly used in the book.
We are given the girl's thoughts and feelings but with
no sense of limitation since her account of other people
and their behaviour towards her is always clear-sighted
if at times mistaken. [Mary K. Harris: *Seraphina*, London 1960]

**SHANE MADDEN** is an orphan living on sufferance
with his Uncle Joseph in a village in County Cork. The
boy's dreary life is enlivened only by Uncle Tim, a red-
haired cattle drover who has promised that Shane shall
join him on the road when he has finished with school.
Too impatient to wait, and upset when his uncle's
present of *Gulliver's Travels* is accidentally spoiled,
Shane sets off to Dublin, where he believes his uncle has
gone. A stolen lift in a lorry gets him over the ground
more quickly than he had expected but he cannot find

his uncle and he gladly accepts the hospitality and
friendship of the O'Clearys, who keep a bookshop on
Ormond Quay.

The story of Shane's determined search for Tim, of
his work as shop-boy and of the dramatic return of his
uncle just in time to rescue little Bridget from a fire in
the shop, proceeds with all Patricia Lynch's warmth of
manner and ends, as her stories invariably do, in safe
domestic felicity. Shane has the dual nature of so many
of her heroes. He wants to win independence and yet
he finds the world outside his little corner not a little
intimidating. His character is drawn simply and affectionately and is illuminated by a brief moment of fantasy when one night he sees a stranger leaning on the
quay-side, sad and thoughtful. It is Jonathan Swift,
whose spirit has presided over Patricia Lynch's story,
as over the bookshop. 'I would protect ye,' cries the
man, 'as I tried to protect all the children of Dublin!'
It is with small surprises such as this that Patricia Lynch
so often lifts her characters momentarily out of the light
of common day and makes them mouth-pieces for
thoughts more far-reaching than their own. [Patricia
Lynch: *The Bookshop on the Quay*, London 1956]

**SHOESHOP BEARS** (the) – Boots, Slippers and
Socks – are described in Mr Shoehorn's stock-list as
'Three stuffed toy bears, large, medium, and small, for
the comfort, amusement, and edification of juvenile customers during the fitting of their footwear.' They chose
their names from boxes in the shop and have conveniently assembled themselves into a kind of family,
with Boots as 'father' and Slippers as an obvious
mother-figure, with her constant anxiety about damp
and moth, while mischievous, ginger-coloured Socks is
an obvious subject for quasi-parental care and discipline. After dark the bears enjoy the company of the
neighbourhood cats, who bring them the gossip of
Slumber Lightly, the cathedral town in which the shop
stands. It is through the cats that they learn that Mr
Shoehorn is retiring and that the shop has been sold
to a London firm. The new manager, a coldly efficient
man to whom they are merely 'Sundry soft toys,
juveniles, for the use of', leaves them in a dark corner,
unbrushed and in danger of moth. Paradoxically, it is
their dusty state that brings them to a happier future,
for Mr Wade advertises for an assistant and Polly Trinket, skinny, carrot-haired and determined, takes the job.
Unfortunately her enthusiasm in arranging the bears as
centre of a window-display displeases dignified Mr
Wade and the bears, after sundry disappointments, are
adopted by Polly.

The Shoeshop Bears are established firmly in the first
book and in the five books that follow they live happily,
first as beloved playthings for Polly's small brothers and
sisters, and later as child-comforters in Polly's own shoeshop. In the course of various adventures (on an outing
to a famous castle, by the sea, in a flooded rubbish
dump, for example), the bears make the acquaintance

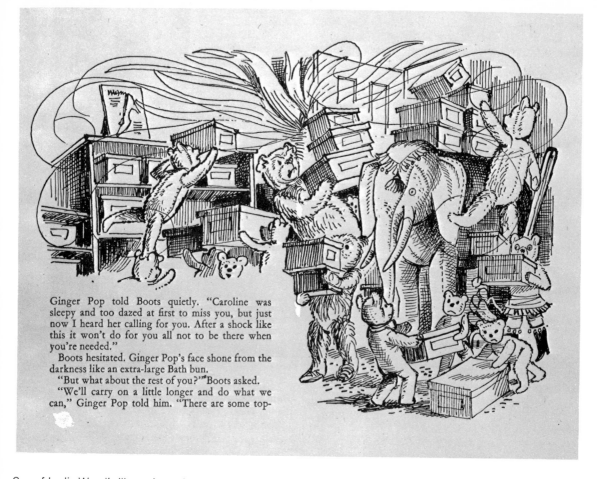

Ginger Pop told Boots quietly. "Caroline was sleepy and too dazed at first to miss you, but just now I heard her calling for you. After a shock like this it won't do for you all not to be there when you're needed."

Boots hesitated. Ginger Pop's face shone from the darkness like an extra-large Bath bun.

"But what about the rest of you?" Boots asked.

"We'll carry on a little longer and do what we can," Ginger Pop told him. "There are some top-

One of Leslie Wood's illustrations of the Shoeshop Bears and their numerous friends in *Boots and the Ginger Bears*.

of other toys, among them Hannibal the push-along elephant, Teabag the yellow plastic bear, Hi-Jinks, elegant in white nylon (an offer from a cereal packet), the ebullient bear Scottish Wagstaff and the bunch of twelve noisy ginger bears headed by Ginger Pop. Each of these characters adds to the fun of stories firmly rooted in familiar domestic scenes and situations. The touch of whimsy that is present in all Margaret J. Baker's books is kept under control partly by her invariably crisp and plausible detail and, above all, by her handling of her toy-characters. [Margaret J. Baker, ill. C. Walter Hodges: *The Shoeshop Bears*, London 1963; *Hannibal and the Bears*, 1965; ill. Daphne Rowles: *Bears Back in Business*, 1967; *Hi-Jinks Joins the Bears*, 1968; ill. Leslie Wood: *Teabag and the Bears*, 1970; *Boots and the Ginger Bears*, 1972]

**SIMPKIN** *see* GINGER AND PICKLES

**SIR TIMOTHY TIGER** lives on the chest of drawers in Roger's bedroom during the day, with his companion toys – a lion, a squirrel and a fox – but at night he comes

into his own. Roger's active imagination gives this small boy plenty of material to use in a heroic chronicle about the machinations of the Black Wizard who rules the Dark Wood. Little Priscilla, Roger's playmate, plays the part of the innocent victim, so that Roger and the intrepid Tiger can go to the rescue.

Robbers and a magic carpet, a palace ball and a man-eating giant are among the elements which bear witness to the author's devotion to the fantasies of E. Nesbit and traditional fairy tales. The book is nostalgic in spirit and Roger and his Tiger are convenient figures round whom suitably exotic and exciting scenes have been devised. [Roger Lancelyn Green: *The Land of the Lord High Tiger*, London 1958]

**SIR TOADY LION**, in reality Arthur George Picton Smith, acquired his nickname because it was the nearest he could get to pronouncing the name of his hero, Richard Coeur de Lion. As a child of five, with flaxen hair, 'burly contours and hale Jolly-Miller countenance', he 'enchants the women-folk', who cheerfully accept

323

behaviour that is in fact demanding and tiresome. Certainly Toady is a trial to his ten-year-old brother Hugh John. Both boys are soldier-mad, but in different ways. Hugh John organizes on conventional lines a campaign against the village lads, who claim rights in a certain ruined castle; Toady demands 'the Victowya Cross' before battle is even joined. Toady enjoys giving rein to his natural aggressiveness; 'ain't never nobody killed dead in the New Testament', he complains, when told he should love his neighbour. It is by stealth and determination, rather than by good planning, that he succeeds in rescuing the pet lamb stolen by the enemy, and the title of General of Commisariat is bestowed on him by his brother, who is himself at this stage General Napoleon Smith.

In a second book, *Sir Toady Crusoe*, the mischievous boy, no longer under the slightest control since his brother has gone to boarding school, engages in a dangerous adventure when he confidently leads the Australian boy Dinky to the seashore in search of Dinky's sister Sammy who has, Toady is certain, run away as a sailor. The child boldly questions everyone he meets, accepting tinkers, poachers and fishermen as he finds them, for as he says, 'Long as 'tis'nt money, you can trust most anyone. Lots o' people as looks bad – isn't.' For him, mankind is divided into 'My-People' who 'just does wot I likes' and 'Not-my-People', whom he disregards.

Though Toady is older in the second book, he is apt, when in trouble, to revert to 'all his coaxy-woaxy fetchingness of pronunciation'. Fetchingness is hardly the word we would use nowadays. It is not the excessive length of the two books which keeps them unread so much as the sentimental presentation of the hero through baby-talk and the fervent embraces and appreciative murmurs of all who come into contact with him. His code of life might well be accepted now by a typical bad-boy of fiction – 'Don't do anything *very* bad. Never get caught. Never tell, unless you get forgiven first'; his idiom is as unacceptable as his principles are natural. [S.R.Crockett: *The Surprising Adventures of Sir Toady Lion*, London 1897; *Sir Toady Crusoe*, 1905]

**SIRGA** is born to the lioness Owara on the same day as a baby, Ulé, is born to Tamani and her husband Moko Kamo, chief of the village of Porga. Something more than dates links the lion cub and the boy. The village witch-doctor had predicted that Tamani would bear twins and Owara would normally have borne two cubs. Surely the female cub and the male baby are brother and sister. This seems natural to Moko, a hunter whose skill and knowledge rests on the belief of his people that they are the subjects of Owara, lioness-queen of the land in which their village stands.

The link between Sirga and Ulé is a positive one too. When the cub is young her mother steals Ulé's milk for the cub; in the forest Ulé and Sirga meet, as infants, and form a lifelong bond in play and sleep. The bond is stretched but not broken when Ulé is carried away by raiders; he feigns lunacy when he is sold as a slave and his master sends him to a distant savannah to guard the herds of antelope which, again by tradition, are preserved for the lions, the true rulers of the land. Here boy and lioness find one another again and journey back to their own country to build a new life, separately but in eternal consciousness one of the other.

The story of Sirga, and the companion stories of Oworo the chimpanzee, Kpo the leopard and Sama the elephant, relate animals and man in a unique way. Though the lioness Owara is described, as queen and mother, in terms of human myth-making, she is not humanized. The bond between men and animals is nearer to a kind of totemism; it is the expression of a compact which, as the author explains, was made by men in the days when they first entered the district and sued to the animals for permission to hunt and to dwell in their land. Tribesmen and animals govern their habits by the same necessities. Elephants and nomads move at certain seasons: lion cub and youth alike endure a certain initiation. Through Sirga's story René Guillot expresses indirectly the deep, almost mystical experience of his sojourn in the Sudan, his feeling of kinship with the forest and its inhabitants. [René Guillot: *Sirga* (1951 France) trans. Gwen Marsh, London 1953]

**SMITH,** a 'sooty spirit' in the London of two centuries ago, 'quicker than a rat, sharper than a stoat, foxier than a fox', at twelve years old is an accomplished pickpocket, precociously acquainted with the seamy life in the alleys round St Paul's. Following a likely victim, Smith empties his pocket neatly and, minutes later, sees the old man stabbed by two men in brown whose rummaging makes it clear that something in that pocket was their aim. Smith, when he examines his prize, finds it is a document – and he cannot read.

Smith's illiteracy can be corrected, and in due course is corrected when the boy accepts the offer of the blind old judge Mr Mansfield, whom he has helped, to take him into his household as a servant. The judge's daughter, as always following her father's will with sweet compliance and inward rebellion, gives Smith the teaching he craves, but by the time he is equipped to read the document, the chance is lost; he has become deeply entangled in the affair of Mr Field's murder, has lost the trust of his employers and is committed to Newgate through the machinations of those whose interest in the document is far more sinister than his own. It is not until the complicated affair has been brought to a climax, the document explained, the villains identified and the coincidences accepted, that Smith comes to understand what his part in the imbroglio has meant to him.

Smith's well-concealed but strong sense of compassion is almost his downfall and certainly the cause of his suffering and redemption. If these seem large words,

Smith leads the blind old judge, Mr Mansfield, who takes the slum boy into his household; illustration by Antony Maitland.

the course of the book shows their relevance as it follows out the theme that appears in so many of Leon Garfield's novels, a young person's journey from innocence to experience. The mixture of humane sympathy and ironic exaggeration in the book is exemplified clearly in Smith's progress towards enlightenment. His hero, the boastful highwayman Lord Tom, is revealed as a coward, and the honesty which the boy has come to respect in the old judge is shown to be a matter of justice rather than of mercy. Smith himself, a culpable member of society, is seen in the end to be governed more by pity than by the tough attitude to life which he has been obliged to cultivate, and to be as much in need of protection from the real, emotional terrors and perils of life as the old blind judge is in need of the boy's guiding hand over the cobblestones of the city.

Like all Leon Garfield's novels, *Smith* is full of portraits of a Dickensian sharpness. His sisters, softhearted Miss Fanny and sardonic Miss Bridget, who foist their unusual standards of conduct on their little Smut; Lord Tom, who enjoys the hero-worship in the boy's eager questions about the High Toby; Judge Mansfield, whose inward eye sees more than most people, but not enough to fathom all Smith's depths – the boy lives in their speech as much as in his own words, as he coaxes, threatens, curses, ruminates, or laments the fact that he has to grow up. [Leon Garfield: *Smith*, London 1967]

**SMOKEY JOE** is born in a litter of five kittens in a rabbit burrow, his mother Fu the Ferocious preferring freedom to the enervating life of Indoors. Smokey Joe, following her against orders to see where she goes each evening, is persuaded by the saucer of milk at the farmhouse to become a house cat and to accept the human appellation of Smokey Joe as an alternative to the name of Ju the Jolly which was in line with ancient

cat tradition. His adventures combine the natural actions of a cat (chasing mice, fighting rivals, stealing food) with, in each book, a fortunate intervention in human affairs. On one occasion, for example, he alerts the Reid family to a fire in the stable and on another, when he goes with Ann as a temporary boarder at her school, he exposes the peculations of Mario the bad-tempered cook.

Laurence Meynell's method of converting the little cat into a character is strongly reminiscent of Kipling's *Thy Servant a Dog*. While avoiding Kipling's worst excesses of idiom and sentiment Meynell, like Kipling, makes use of facetious capital letters ('Fire is Best Friend and Worst Enemy') and allows his cat hero to comment freely on the behaviour of 'his' humans, though in a superior rather than a slavish spirit. Smokey Joe has a language, but it is composed of the ten sounds of Basic Cat Talk; thus his remarks to humans are offered with a running translation, a somewhat self-conscious device. All the same, Smokey Joe remains an independent and natural cat, as may be evidenced by one of his pronouncements: 'The four things that a cat likes doing most in the world are hunting, sleeping, washing and stretching.' [Laurence Meynell: *Smokey Joe*, London 1952; *Smokey Joe in Trouble*, 1953; *Smokey Joe Goes to School*, 1956; several more titles]

**SNEEZEWORT** *see* BALDMONEY

**SNIPPY** and **SNAPPY**, brother and sister fieldmice, are content to play in the hayfield until one day, inspired by their father's stories about the world, they decide to venture out in search of cheese. Following the unravelling thread from a ball of their mother's knitting wool, which a small girl has picked up, they reach a house and after commenting with surprise on items of furniture which they identify as giant plants or trees, they are about to investigate a mouse-trap when their father

Snippy and Snappy from the book illustrated and written by Wanda Gág.

opportunely arrives to stop them. The two little mice are given personality in Wanda Gág's pictures principally by very expressive gestures and attitudes which attractively suggest the movements of small children. The humour of incongruity is the most important ingredient in this charming picture-book. [Wanda Gág: *Snippy and Snappy*, New York 1931]

**SNUG AND SERENA** *see* TOAD OF TOAD'S CASTLE

**SONNY** *see* ARNOLD HAITHWAITE

**SPARROWHAWK** *see* DUNY

**SPECS McCANN** has a mermaid for a swimming instructress, climbs his own private beanstalk into the sky and chats on equal terms with a cuckoo inside a cuckoo-clock. The headmaster's son, who shares the adventures, accepts them with a matter-of-fact embarrassment that matches Specs's resourceful exploitation of them. After all, it is a pity to waste magic, even if you can never discover where it comes from. And so the two boys enjoy the grapes, figs and peaches they pick off a magic carpet, set about sensibly the training of Egbert, the dragon which hatches out of an egg Specs finds in a cave, and enliven three weeks at a seaside resort with the jar of Buck-U-Up-Oh pressed into Specs's hand by a mysterious (and Herculean) stranger on the train.

Specs McCann is one of Janet McNeill's most successful characters. He accepts that the things that happen usually end in the fulfilment of some perfectly normal ambition – to win a race, for example, to improve on a skinny body or to escape from the tedium of the form photograph – and his readers accept in the same spirit the entirely logical fantasy. After all, Specs *is* Irish. [Janet McNeill: *My Friend Specs McCann*, London 1955; *Specs Fortissimo*, 1958; *Various Specs*, 1961; *Best Specs* (selection), 1970]

**SPINACH** *see* GINGER AND PICKLES

**SPROUT,** whose real name was Rupert, was given his nickname by a nurse when he was only a day or two old; as he grew, the tuft of hair on top of his head dar-

Specs McCann, illustrated by Rowel Friers.

Sprout with one of his beloved elephants.

kened a little but it grew again after it had to be cut off as the result of an accident. From boyhood Sprout showed an extraordinary firmness of character. He cried more loudly and ate more than any other baby, and his first words were 'More in there' when his mother took his cup of baby-food away. By the time he was three, Sprout had added a second passion to his love of food – he began to collect elephants, with his usual single-mindedness. When he was four he set out alone to go to the Zoo, determined to match the boast of a boy at nursery school who had actually ridden on an elephant; the journey ended in the acquisition of Market, a red plaster elephant almost as big as Sprout. A little later he added to his collection Miss Crabbe, a lonely spinster whose bulk and wrinkles and protruding teeth were the best possible recommendation to his favour.

The adventures enjoyed by this square-shaped, determined child are entirely believable, given his character. His mother had learned that it was useless to try to deflect him from his purposes, and other people learn this too – the burglar, for instance, whom Sprout discovers by accident; the vicar who loses him on the carol-singing round because Sprout is engaged in looking after an enormous shaggy dog; and the seaside shopkeeper who finds that the innocent-looking small boy is not to be cheated out of the rubber dinghy which he has fairly won by his pertinacity. Silent except when roused by references to food or elephants, armed with the ruthlessness of childhood, Sprout might in any other hands have been tiresome: as Jenifer Wayne presents him, he is an active promoter of agreeable laughter. [Jenifer Wayne: *Sprout*, London 1970; *Sprout's Window-Cleaner*, 1971; *Sprout and the Dog-Sitter*, 1972; *Sprout and the Helicopter*, 1974]

**SQUIRREL** *see* GREY RABBIT

**SQUIRREL NUTKIN** *see* GINGER AND PICKLES

**STALKY, M'TURK** and **BEETLE** have come up the school together and in a five-year alliance have acquired their nicknames and a reputation for putting up a united front impervious to argument, force or public opinion. Though they do not minimize the importance of future careers, their paramount objectives in the present are two-fold – to enjoy as much freedom as possible and to take every chance of being 'stalky' and ingenious in their behaviour.

Stalky is constantly stating, in half-jocular tones, his claim to be a 'great man'. He is the planner of practical jokes, the executive brain of the trio. It is Stalky who contrives that the school sergeant and the rigidly orthodox housemaster, King, shall be taken for poachers by an angry landowner while the boys win the desirable freedom of his estate; it is Stalky who holds and distributes such funds as come their way and dictates the degree of impertinence, obstinacy or submission needed in a particular crisis. M'Turk, heir to an Irish estate, is the public relations man; his self-possession is never shattered and his capacity for silent scorn is equally

Kipling's schoolboy trio, Stalky, M'Turk and Beetle, illustrated by L. Raven-Hill.

valuable in attack or defence. It is Beetle, book-lover and poet, who provides ammunition for a skirmish which leads a visiting examiner to congratulate the master on his open-minded attitude to the possible Baconian authorship of Shakespeare; it is Beetle who supplies verses, war-cries and suitable quotations for their occasions.

Determinedly scorning such shaming phrases as 'the honour of the school', constantly invoking the more ludicrous scenes in *Eric*, studiously uncooperative and brilliantly ingenious, the triumvirate wage guerilla warfare against the bitter, misguided irony of King and the weak favouritism of Prout, while freely admitting how much the shrewd, honest dealings of the Head and the School Chaplain have influenced them.

The Stalky stories were based on Kipling's own school days at the crammers' college, Westward Ho!, and the character of Beetle is Kipling's derisive self-portrait, as those of M'Turk and Stalky are portraits, drawn in affection and admiration, of his two closest friends. In describing the life of an unusual school, he was in part trying to show the artificiality which he saw, perhaps read into, earlier school stories. This, he seems to suggest, is what boys are really like – blunt, idiosyncratic, unwilling to uncover their deepest feelings, hating hypocrisy, loving freedom. After nearly eighty years his school seems in some ways as distant from us as Tom Brown's, with its imperialist bias and its assumption that violent practical jokes, however painful to the recipient, are justified by their motives. But the characters – most of all, those of Stalky, M'Turk and Beetle – defy the passage of time. [Rudyard Kipling: *Stalky and Co.*, London 1899]

**STARR**, as the son of a Somerset dairy farmer, is rather more interested in making butter than in school work. David Rosley, taking a new bus route to school, likes this stoutish, flat-faced boy less well than Clipper, who is reputed to be clever but lazy, and black-haired Kitson who conducts their regular part-singing en route. Starr is inclined to grumble at David's inclusion, and he seems obsessed with keeping the rules the boys have put together on their journeys to and from the market town. But his gloomy stare proves to be something to do with his eyes and though he is apt to sulk when the others make jokes about his father's pedigree herd, he proves to be invaluable when the four boys set out to search the marsh for Iron Age remains before it is flooded. It is Starr who provides food for a memorable feast, cooking a chicken (which he had reared and fattened himself) with a lavish extravagance that speaks of experience and of an undoubted taste for food. His infrequent but usually relevant contributions to the idle or purposive chatter of the rest often throw a light on his own homeground, as a farmer's son in careful alliance with his neighbours. In this way William Mayne adds a new dimension to a story which is in the main concentrated on a few characters and a carefully restricted locale. He makes Starr known to the reader, with his occasional dry humour, his practical sense, his country serenity, his slow, self-protective appraisal of events, with notable economy and wit. [William Mayne: *The Member for the Marsh*, London 1956]

**STEPHANIE MARCIA AYRTON** ('World-famous contralto' as she styles herself on the covers of her exercise books) lives with her father in a quiet part of provincial Medborough. At the time when Seraphina (q.v.) is transferred to the High School, Stephanie is almost fifteen but has fallen back in school work because of pressure at home. Since her mother left the family when Stephanie was only three years old, she has been cared for by an excellent housekeeper, but after Miss Smith leaves to get married several bad successors confirm her father's belief that they will manage better by themselves. Because Stephanie is so full of energy and so forthright and eccentric in her behaviour, it is a long time before Seraphina realizes how difficult her life really is. Few of her schoolfellows have any idea, either, that Stephanie is upset by the barbed comments of their form-mistress, Miss Jason, who is understandably annoyed at what seems to her a wicked waste of Stephanie's good brain.

The girl's real gift for music and her instinctive response to colour and drama seem of little use at school,

but a fortunate chance starts her on the road to a promising future as a singer. This somewhat hackneyed contrivance in the book succeeds because of the quiet way the author has drawn this attractive, impetuous girl against a very real background of schooldays. The book captures with an unflurried authenticity the very tones and actions of a group of schoolgirls in their early teens. [Mary K. Harris: *Seraphina*, London 1960]

**STICKLY-PRICKLY HEDGEHOG** and **SLOW-SOLID TORTOISE** live 'on the banks of the turbid Amazon, eating green lettuces and things', but the Painted Jaguar who lives there too hopes to eat them. His mother has told him exactly how to catch these two animals but when he finds them, one rolled up and the other drawn into its shell, they confuse him with contradictory versions of her advice and easily escape from him. Fearing his mother, however, they set to work to learn each other's defensive mechanism and change their appearance so successfully that Mother Jaguar, who has to conceal her failure in order to preserve her authority, advises her son 'Everything has its proper name. I should call it "Armadillo" till I found out the real one. And I should leave it alone.'

This and other ingenious explanations for the appearance or behaviour of whale, camel, kangaroo, elephant, crab, cat, were offered by Kipling to his own small daughter, which accounts for the immediate, whimsical

Illustration by the author for the first edition of the *Just So Stories* in 1902.

"Excellent!" said Slow-and-Solid; and he held up Stickly-Prickly's chin, while Stickly-Prickly kicked in the waters of the turbid Amazon.

"You'll make a fine swimmer yet," said Slow-and-Solid. "Now, if you can unlace my back-plates a little, I'll see what I can do towards curling up. It may be useful."

Stickly-Prickly helped to unlace Tortoise's back-plates, so that by twisting and straining Slow-and-Solid actually managed to curl up a tiddy wee bit.

"Excellent!" said Stickly-Prickly; "but I shouldn't do any more just now. It's making you black in the face. Kindly lead me into the water once again and I'll practise that side-stroke which you say is so easy." And so Stickly-Prickly practised, and Slow-Solid swam alongside.

"Excellent!" said Slow-and-Solid. "A little more practise will make you a regular whale. Now, if I may trouble you to unlace my back and front plates two holes more, I'll try that fascinating bend that you say is so easy. Won't Painted Jaguar be surprised!"

*Above*. Stickly-Prickly Hedgehog and Slow-Solid Tortoise from Kipling's *Just So Stories*. Guilio Maestro's illustration from a 1970 edition.

tone of the stories. Two of them at least – 'The Cat that Walked by Itself' and 'The Butterfly that Stamped' – have a mature, philosophical idea concealed in them, and all of them evoke a distant world in which man and animals communicate naturally and obey the same natural laws. Of all the animal characters, probably the Elephant's Child is the most obviously and humorously humanized – so much so that his name has in countless families become synonymous with the kind of child who suffers from 'satiable curtiosity'. [Rudyard Kipling: *Just So Stories*, London 1902]

**STIG** lives at the bottom of a chalk pit in Kent, a pit into which the locals have tossed their refuse for years. Refuse to them, but not to Stig, who has turned some of it to good use, contriving a water-supply with a bicycle mudguard, a vacuum-cleaner tube and a tin that once contained weed-killer. Young Barney discovers Stig and comes to believe that his new friend is in truth

a cave-man who has lived in the dump since prehistoric times and he quickly appreciates the skills of this shaggy, black-eyed creature. Stig can shape effective flints from a chosen stone and though he has never struck a match and is ignorant of the uses of jam-jars, he learns quickly and helps Barney enthusiastically to improve his ramshackle home with a splendid window of piled jars and a chimney of flattened tins.

Stig's rough-hewn personality, his moments of sudden rage, his nose for a hunt, his whole life, free from convention and the demands of the grown-ups, represents a boy's dream of freedom – the freedom to be dirty, unpunctual, and untidy as he pleases and to enjoy solving a series of interesting and not too difficult practical problems. [Clive King: *Stig of the Dump*, Harmondsworth 1963]

**STRUWWELPETER**, whose name was finally chosen as title for Dr Hoffmann's collection of cau-

tionary verses, was originally drawn for the Doctor's three-year-old son, as an alternative to the 'long tales, stupid collections of pictures, moralizing stories' which were all he could find in the bookshops. Hoffmann knew that children did not 'reason abstractedly' (sic) and needed concrete, amusing, arresting examples to teach them good behaviour; these he set himself to produce. He used his drawings as well to soothe his small patients if they showed any fear of him. The starkly coloured pictures of disaster may not seem altogether suitable for the calming of nervous patients. But the tragedy that befell Harriet when she played with matches, Augustus when he refused to eat his soup and the huntsman when he was shot by the hare are all depicted with such comic symbolic details that it would need a very timorous child not to see their humour; and though the picture of Conrad without his thumbs is macabre indeed, critics and parents are unlikely ever to agree on its effect on

### 3. THE DREADFUL STORY ABOUT HARRIET AND THE MATCHES.

It almost makes me cry to tell
What foolish Harriet befell.
Mamma and Nurse went out one day
And left her all alone at play;
Now, on the table close at hand,
A box of matches chanc'd to stand;
And kind Mamma and Nurse had told her,
That, if she touch'd them, they should scold her.
But Harriet said: "O, what a pity!
For, when they burn, it is so pretty;
They crackle so, and spit, and flame;
Mamma, too, often does the same."

The pussy-cats heard this,
And they began to hiss,
And stretch their claws
And raise their paws;
"Me-ow," they said, "me-ow, me-o,
You'll burn to death, if you do so."

But Harriet would not take advice,
She lit a match, it was so nice!
It crackled so, it burn'd so clear, —
Exactly like the picture here.
She jump'd for joy and ran about
And was too pleas'd to put it out.

The pussy-cats saw this
And said: "Oh, naughty, naughty Miss!"
And stretch'd their claws
And rais'd their paws:
"'Tis very, very wrong, you know,
Me-ow, me-o, me-ow, me-o,
You will be burnt, if you do so".

(6)

One of the cautionary tales from *Struwwelpeter*, written and arrestingly illustrated by Heinrich Hoffmann.

And see! Oh! what a dreaful thing!
The fire has caught her apron-string;
Her apron burns, her arms, her hair;
She burns all over, everywhere.

Then how the pussy-cats did mew,
What else, poor pussies, could they do?
They scream'd for help, 'twas all in vain!
So then, they said: "we'll scream again;
Make haste, make haste, me-ow, me-o,
She'll burn to death, we told her so."

So she was burnt, with all her clothes,
And arms, and hands, and eyes, and nose;
Till she had nothing more to lose
Except her little scarlet shoes;
And nothing else but these was found
Among her ashes on the ground.

And when the good cats sat beside
The smoking ashes, how they cried!
"Me-ow, me-oo, me-ow, me-oo,
What will Mamma and Nursy do?"
Their tears ran down their cheeks so fast;
They made a little pond at last.

(7)

children. We can only conjecture whether children do in fact learn to behave any better after being exposed to this very positive, boisterous catalogue of crime and punishment. [Heinrich Hoffmann: *Struwwelpeter*, (1845 Germany) trans. as *The English Struwwelpeter*; or *Pretty Stories and Funny Pictures*, Leipzig 1848, distributed in England]

**STUART LITTLE**, second son of Mr and Mrs Frederick C. Little of New York, was only about two inches high when he was born but he could walk straight away and behaved like an adult. In short, Stuart was a mouse. He faced the immediate implications of this as calmly as his parents did and with more sense than his brother George. George quickly wearied of his ambitious inventions for Stuart's comfort, while the mouse just as quickly discovered that he could turn taps with a mallet made to measure and that he was more use on the end of a string than George's hairpin-hook when their mother's ring rolled down a grating. Resourceful and confident as he was, Stuart enjoyed life, in spite of minor accidents (like getting wound in the window-blind after swinging too hard on the cord), until he realized that his unusual condition brought emotional as well as physical problems.

When Mrs Little rescued a frozen wren, Stuart fell deeply in love with the little bird and when she flew away he set out in his miniature car to find her. On his adventurous journey north he was diverted for a time by Harriet Ames, a girl of his own size who accepted his invitation to row on the river; but the hired boat leaked and wounded pride made it impossible for Stuart to proceed with the acquaintance. He drove north again, with a lifetime to explore the world and with the feeling that 'he was headed in the right direction'.

E. B. White has faced the implications of his fantasy head on. His humour changes with each situation. The mood of his account of the model-boat race in Central Park is very different from his description of the terrible day when Stuart, hiding in a dustbin from an inquisitive dog, is taken away to the dump. The story that begins in cheerful if edgy fantasy darkens till it becomes distressingly poignant. Although Stuart has been accepted readily by bus conductors and strollers in the park, he can never belong either in the human or the animal world. It is not easy to read the book without a feeling of distaste at the idea of a mouse being born to a human mother. If this is to be overcome, it can only be by recognizing the sober meaning under the riddling humour of the book. [E. B. White: *Stuart Little*, New York 1945]

**SUE BARTON** leaves her comfortable home in New Hampshire at the age of eighteen to become a probationer at a large training school attached to a city hos-

Stuart Little, the mouse child of human parents, drawn by Garth Williams.

pital. Seven books pursue her career over a number of years, during which she changes from an ingenuous schoolgirl to a poised and contented married woman with four children. In her student year she learns to put the principles of nursing into practice; as a senior nurse she assists at operations and studies midwifery; she spends a year at the Henry Street Center in New York, working in poor districts; back in New Hampshire she is engaged by a local Farm Club as Rural Visiting Nurse; in a newly endowed hospital at Springdale she acts as Superintendent in the small nurses' training school; while her children are small she uses her experience to cope with emergencies at home; finally, back to nursing for a time, she works on the wards and realizes that this is her real *métier*.

Sue Barton's gradual progress up the ladder of training and experience is paralleled by her growing attachment to Dr William Barry. The pattern of their friendship, betrothal, estrangement and marriage is neatly related to her career as a nurse. She is so deeply absorbed in the Henry Street training that she defers her marriage and is in some danger of losing her Bill, while in the last book about her, when she has returned to ward nursing during his illness, she finds that being married to the head of the hospital has an effect on the way the other nurses regard her.

These are formula books, describing a certain career stage by stage. This imposes certain conditions: Sue Barton may not fail exams, no matter what her friends do, because there must be no break in the sequence; she must not have more than small faults of character, so that the image of a good nurse is kept; she must not be visited by serious doubts about her vocation.

Inevitably some of the minor characters in the books are more memorable than the central figures of Sue and Bill, since they are not invented to prove a point but, rather, to substantiate the fiction. The waif Marianna, whom Sue rescues while she is in New York; certain trenchant New England figures like Vaizey Ann and Ira Prouty; the impeccable nurse Lois Wilmount – these and others have more reality, in the literary sense, than either Sue Barton or her consort Dr Barry, who seems more like a knitting pattern model than a real man. However much one could wish that the author had been able to allow just one or two patients to dislike Sue's bedside manner, it is obvious that she could not have gone further than involving her in certain difficulties that rise from her impetuous nature. Sue Barton is not, even so, a 'perfect' nurse. She is not as good a judge of character as Bill is, nor as confident as her friend Kit; she is neither intellectually nor technically brilliant. Perfection would be as discouraging as too many blemishes in stories intended to persuade young readers to consider a certain career for themselves. Sue's chief attribute is her love of people and her warm, immediate, responsive sympathy for them, and it is on this gift of personality that the author bases her case. It is why Sue

Barton, in spite of the unconvincing blandness of her career and the syrupy atmosphere of her private life, is not as exasperating a character as she might have been. [Helen Dore Boylston: *Sue Barton, Student Nurse*, Boston 1936; *Sue Barton, Senior Nurse*, 1937; *Sue Barton, Visiting Nurse*, 1938; *Sue Barton, Rural Nurse*, 1939; *Sue Barton, Superintendent of Nurses*, 1940; *Sue Barton, Neighbourhood Nurse*, 1949; *Sue Barton, Staff Nurse*, 1952]

**SUSAN BROOKS** and **BILL STARBRIGHT** live next door to one another on a new housing estate. The two children aged nine and eleven make ideal foils for one another as they engage cheerfully in a series of adventures that are marginally serious and mildly mysterious. When Susan first meets Bill she is a little alarmed at the red-headed boy's boisterous manner; an only child, still recovering from a long illness, she is hardly prepared for so much energetic role-playing. But she soon learns how to recognize when Bill is being a Mountie, a cowboy or a detective, and proves to be just as good at following through an adventure.

The plots of the stories about Susan and Bill have been carefully chosen to fit the capacities of a serious little girl of nine and a bumptious boy of just eleven. They trespass on a local estate and win the heart of the crusty owner; on a seaside holiday they find a missing boy and frustrate a couple of (ineffectual) thieves. Secret drawers in a box, a secret door between two rooms, a smugglers' tunnel – these familiar appurtenances to adventure provide momentum for the books and a challenge for the children.

Eight adventures in less than a calendar year leave no time for Susan and Bill to change, or to reveal greater depths of character; a simple note on their appearance and personality is repeated in each book, to keep continuity. Though they are drawn to a fixed pattern (anything more would make the very elementary plots impossible), Susan and Bill do have a certain identity. They are not cardboard figures but they are drawn in outline so that it is easy for every reader to identify with one or other of them and enjoy the flattering illusion that life could be just as exciting in reality. [Malcolm Saville: *Susan, Bill and the Wolf-dog*, London 1954; *Susan, Bill and the Ivy-clad Oak*, 1954; *Susan, Bill and the Vanishing Boy*, 1955; *Susan, Bill and the Golden Clock*, 1955; *Susan, Bill and the Dark Stranger*, 1956; *Susan, Bill and the 'Saucy Kate'*, 1956; *Susan, Bill and the Bright Star Circus*, 1960; *Susan, Bill and the Pirates Bold*, 1961]

**SUSAN WALKER** shares responsibility for the younger children with her brother John but she is far nearer than he is to the world of the grown-ups. It is Susan who worries about damp clothes, makes sure (when she can) that the younger children get eight hours, sleep, sees that meals are properly spaced and balanced (Roger is not allowed to eat marmalade with corned beef, on one occasion) and, as John says, ... 'likes camp to look as if no one had ever eaten even a biscuit in it'. To most young readers her character is bound to seem less interesting than that of the others, but there is no doubt that Ransome intended her to serve as a kind of touchstone of reality; if anyone objects that no children could have been so consistently successful with their camping and exploring, the answer is that Susan's influence makes it possible. A bracketed note by 'N. Blackett, capt.' added to one chapter of the story the group makes up, *Missee Lee*, explains that Susan wanted to have inserted in the account of their imprisonment by Chinese pirates that their clothes were washed and returned to them, after they had suffered from fire and shipwreck. 'I told her it wasn't important, but Susan says it made all the difference.'

Susan's almost precocious sense of responsibility rests on firm principles. Her sufferings on the *Goblin* (in *We Didn't Mean to Go to Sea*) are partly due to seasickness but, far more, to acute distress at having broken, through no fault of her own, the promise she made to her mother. In Susan we see a girl who is well aware of the difference between the adult world and the world of children. Her attitude depends partly on the dates of the stories (1930 to 1947) and their middle-class background; it is necessary for the working of the familiar story convention by which parents are removed from any scene of adventure. Susan is uneasy when the Blacketts disobey the tyrannous orders of their great-aunt and steal away behind her back to meet the Walkers, whom Aunt Maria has decided are a bad influence (in *Swallowdale*). She is always afraid of upsetting her elders, because she knows this will involve her mother in awkward explanations and she is perceptive enough to realize that her mother's social standards differ from those of the easy-going Mrs Blackett. Throughout the stories she leans more and more to the side of 'the natives', until finally she is talking about her siblings as 'them' instead of 'we'. Not a popular character, perhaps, but a triumphantly real one. [Arthur Ransome: *Swallows and Amazons*, 1930; and other titles]

**SUSANNAH ELIZABETH FAIRFIELD WINSTON** is sent to spend the summer with her uncle in Regina, Saskatchewan. Her uncle, an officer in the Canadian Mounties, has some difficulty in persuading the Commissioner that the child will not interfere with his work. Six-year-old Susannah eagerly promises to behave, for she is completely under the spell of the uniforms and horses. 'I was wondering', she confesses to the Commissioner, 'how soon I could join the Force and when I'd get my red coat.' It seems unlikely that she will fulfil her ambition, especially as she is a self-willed child and some of her pranks cause considerable trouble. However, she does win a uniform and the proud title of Susannah of the Mounties, after her quick wits and observant eye have led to the detection of a criminal; and the first book about Susannah ends with a trip to London for Queen Victoria's Jubilee.

This lively child with her red-gold curls and her confident manner is introduced with a whimsicality which is out of tune with today's taste. In the later books about her she displays the same ingenuous way of approaching new experiences such as washing for gold in the Yukon (where even deep snow and dangerous ice-floes are greeted with her favourite epithet, 'Salubrious'); she stands up to the girls at Arundel Abbey, who scorn her outspoken ways and tomboyish manner, and she helps her cousins in the Quebec backwoods to outwit logging thieves. Her character, formally established in the first book and consistently developed in the second, begins to seem a little perfunctory by the third and the part she plays in *Susannah Rides Again* is hardly distinguishable from that of her cousins. The four books illustrate one of the chief dangers of a series; more often than not a character who seems at first sight real and appealing does not stand up to prolonged acquaintance. [Muriel Denison: *Susannah of the Mounties*, New York 1936; *Susannah of the Yukon*, 1936; *Susannah at Boarding School*, 1938; *Susannah Rides Again*, 1940]

**SWISS FAMILY ROBINSON,** (the), *see* ROBINSON CRUSOE

**SYLVESTER DUNCAN** 'lived with his mother and father at Acorn Road in Oatsdale'; the Duncans are a family of donkeys. Sylvester, clearly a romantic, is delighted when he finds an interesting red pebble to add to his collection and still more so when he discovers that it makes wishes come true. When, on the way home, Sylvester turns himself into a rock to escape a prowling lion, he realizes that he can no longer touch the pebble and may have to remain a stone for ever. Naturally there is a happy ending, brought about by a generous measure of coincidence and good luck.

The larger animals do not as a rule humanize well in visual terms but William Steig has overcome the inherent difficulties of depicting such an animal managing picnic food or seated in a comfortable house. With the help of suitably devised clothes, spectacles and facial expressions he has turned his donkeys, with kindly satire, into a recognizable suburban family. [William Steig: *Sylvester and the Magic Pebble*, New York 1969]

**SYLVIA DAISY POUNCER** is 'big, handsome, with something of a flaunting manner, which turned into a flounce when she was put out.' Her pupil, little Kay Harker (q.v.), thinks Sylvia Daisy is more like a rhododendron than a daisy and is afraid of her habit of hitting out unexpectedly while inspecting his slippers for damp. But he certainly does not suspect there is any connection between the overbearing governess and the Mrs Pouncer whom he glimpses at night, when strange things happen at Seekings, who has 'a hooky nose, a hooky chin, and bright black eyes, long dingle-dangle earrings which click, a poke-bonnet, a red cloak, a stick with a hooky handle, and pointing, black shiny shoes.' It is not until he searches his governess's room that he discovers she is in truth one of the witches seeking the lost Harker treasure.

Sylvia Daisy shares the fate of the coven leader, Abner Brown. She gets her just deserts, for as she spies on Kay, so she is spied upon in her turn, and in the end she and the gang leave the district. When they return a few years later, in *The Box of Delights*, they are once more in search of a treasure that is not their own, a magic Box brought into the present from the past. Sylvia Daisy has become the wife of Abner Brown, but their affected mode of address to one another ('my astuteness' she calls him, among other endearments) conceals on his side dislike, on hers a desire to dominate. 'May a weak woman make a suggestion, my Starlike Abner', she enquires, hardly concealing her scorn of his bungling efforts to locate the Box. The downfall of Sylvia Daisy is of great satisfaction to Kay and his friends, to the reader, and presumably also to Masefield, who is reputed to have based her character on vivid memories of two governesses who did not make his younger days very happy. [John Masefield: *The Midnight Folk*, London 1927; *The Box of Delights*, 1935]
**SYLVIE** and **BRUNO**, at once fairies and human children, move easily in and out of the two worlds manipulated by Lewis Carroll. One is the world of comic fairy tale in which an incipient palace revolution reflects, distantly, late Victorian social conditions. In this world Sylvie and Bruno are the children of the banished Warden and wander at will through the landscapes in the narrator's mind. In his day to day reality they appear now and then in an earl's gardens or drawing room to assuage the pangs of love suffered by Lady Muriel, with whom the narrator is involved as an elderly, much-loved friend – supposedly, Carroll himself.

Into this 'real' world the children carry characters already evident in the fairy world. Sylvie, a pretty little girl with curly brown hair and a loving disposition, is the typical elder sister who, in the absence of a mother, watches over Bruno with anxious responsibility. Bruno displays the characteristics of the typical small boy of nineteenth-century nursery fiction. 'Think of any pretty little boy you know, with rosy cheeks, large dark eyes, and tangled brown hair, and then fancy him small enough to go comfortably into a coffee-cup, and you'll have a very fair idea of him.' To twentieth-century eyes Bruno – spoilt, a little greedy, rebellious but loving in his better moments – is hardly an attractive character; perhaps the readers of the last century found it easier to accept the baby-talk which hardly seems to suit a fairy ('Can't oo make out *nuffin* wizout I 'splain it?'). It must also be conceded that Bruno's peculiarly childish logic, and Sylvie's gentle exasperation when confronted with it, are suited to their ages (presumably five and eight or thereabouts) at any period and in any society. There is more than a touch of Alice's robust good sense in Sylvie and of Looking-Glass logic in Bruno – enough to make it possible for adult readers to tackle this loose bundle of reflections on religion, society and personal relationships which has only the barest claim to be considered as a two-part book for children. [Lewis Carroll: *Sylvie and Bruno*, London 1889; *Sylvie and Bruno Concluded*, 1893]

# T

TABITHA TWITCHIT *see* GINGER AND PICKLES
TAILOR OF GLOUCESTER *see* GINGER AND PICKLES

**TAMZIN GREY**, who lives in the Romney Marsh village of Westling, exists for horses, like her friend Rissa Birnie, but the two girls, who are ten and eleven respectively, only manage to ride borrowed horses from time to time. Then Tamzin, with story-book good fortune, is given a white part-Arab, Cascade, by the owner, whose daughter has been crippled by a fall for which he unfairly blames the horse. Not long afterwards Rissa, whose father's timber business makes life easier for her (though not happier) than the circumstances of Tamzin's parson father, also gets her own mount, temperamental Nanti.

Stories like this were two a penny in the 1940s. Contrary to expectations, though, Tamzin and Rissa were not to be the centre of a series of hippomanic triumphs but, rather, the female element of a group of four for whom Westling, the neighbouring town of Dunsford, the marshes and seashore, were to provide a series of local adventures exciting and full of youthful gaiety. The two boys who complete the group, Meryon Fairbrass and Roger Lambert, add their own particular skills and attitudes to the stories. Roger, Rissa's cousin, is as practical and down to earth as she is, a nice, plain, good-tempered schoolboy, while Meryon, black-haired and dashing, boasts of his descent from a notorious local pirate and uses his year or more of seniority naturally and easily when the need arises.

The Romney Marsh children share some adventures with the Thorntons of Punchbowl Farm (q.v.). Tamzin meets the Thorntons while she is staying with an aunt in Hindhead (in *Punchbowl Midnight*) and becomes a friend of Lindsey, who is eleven years old like her at the time, and later visits are exchanged between the families. Inevitably the two sequences of stories invite comparison. Where the events in the Punchbowl stories rise directly out of their own farm, neighbours coming and going without making much impression on the close-knit group, Tamzin and her friends are shown as members of a fishing and farming community, with the Merrows at Castle Farm and rascally old Jim Decks the ferryman as sources for many incidents. As early as the second book in the sequence (*The Summer of the Great Secret*) smuggling is introduced as a theme, and the children, with the happy disregard for the law permitted in holiday adventure stories, eagerly lend Jim Decks a hand in augmenting his income illegally. In fact, the attempt to put Jim's life on a legal and peaceable footing supplies plots for several books, as the children run a news-sheet to help him to pay off damages he has caused by careless driving (in *Strangers to the Marsh*), organize a greengrocery business for him (in *No Going Back*) and make shocked comments on his conning of American tourists (in *The Hoodwinkers*).

Over a period of about five years Tamzin and the others deal with one or two crises in each book. Challenge may come from natural disasters (storm and flood in *Storm Ahead*, foot-and-mouth in *No Entry*) or from man's depredations (illicit traffic in horses for meat in *Cargo of Horses*, danger to a nesting hoopoe in *Strangers to the Marsh*, to seabirds from oil in *Operation Seabird*). The high incidence of adventure is made acceptable partly by the background of village life and village worthies and by the skilful dove-tailing of events and characters, but the Marsh books, even so, seem less sturdily attached to reality than the tales of *Punchbowl Farm*, with their less sensational, more indigenous plots.

Of the four chief characters in the Marsh stories (surrounded as they are by a host of firmly drawn minor ones), Tamzin is shown in the greatest depth. Romantic, conscientious, confident in the enjoyment of a liberal and loving family, responding eagerly to any request for help, she is almost always the initiator of action. Occasionally the more sensible Rissa puts out a restraining hand, but nothing can persuade Tamzin to leave Jim Decks to the course of justice. Romance enters the last four stories, gently but with a more definite point than in the Punchbowl Farm books. When the girls are in their fifteenth year and Meryon is seventeen, Rissa realizes that the close friendship between Meryon and Tamzin has become something more. She suffers a little, sensibly argues herself out of her heartache, but persuades Tamzin that it is a pity for the foursome to be broken up. Without too much fuss the four young people sort themselves out. Monica Edwards shows in the Punchbowl Farm stories how Roger and Rissa find their own partners in the Thornton family. She does not dwell too

Tamzin and Jim Decks the ferryman; illustration by Geoffrey Whittam for *The Nightbird*.

long on these relationships and indeed the gentle exchanges of words and hand-clasps between Tamzin and Meryon tell us nothing more about their characters than we know already. Only in the last book (*A Wind is Blowing*) is Tamzin shown coping with a crisis of emotion as well as of event. Meryon is blinded by ammonia while tackling a bank robber in Dunsford. In the first terrible days he refuses to see Tamzin, believing that he must leave her free to look for 'someone whole'. Tamzin is only fifteen but love and intelligence show her a way to reach Meryon with the simple tools of a tape-recorder and a lively collie which together they train as a guide dog. Meryon's dramatic recovery after an operation follows the convention of a happy ending, but the early days of suffering emphasize the staunch side of Tamzin's character which has been indicated quietly and clearly

in all the books. It is not easy to draw a genuinely good character and make her interesting rather than exasperating to readers; in Tamzin Grey, Monica Edwards has certainly succeeded. [Monica Edwards: *Wish for a Pony*, London and Glasgow 1947; *The Summer of the Great Secret*, London 1948; *The Midnight Horse*, 1949; *The White Riders*, 1950; *Cargo of Horses*, 1951; *Hidden in a Dream*, 1952; *Storm Ahead*, 1953; *No Entry*, 1954; *The Nightbird*, 1955; *Operation Seabird*, 1957; *Strangers to the Marsh*, 1957; *No Going Back*, 1960; *The Hoodwinkers*, 1962; *Dolphin Summer*, 1963; *A Wind is Blowing*, 1969]

**TARAN** might be best described as an apprentice-hero, whose metamorphosis from Assistant Pig-Keeper in Caer Dallben to High King of Prydain is sometimes reluctant, occasionally absurd, successful almost by accident and almost as much of a surprise to him as it is to the reader. Taran has been brought up by old Coll the farmer and Dallben the magician. If they know his parentage, they never reveal it to him, and as he grows towards manhood he begins to hope that he is of noble blood and to aspire to great deeds. In his very first quest, the search for Hen-Wen the oracular pig (q.v.), he begins to see how different life is from his dreams.

To begin with, the shaggy-haired, travel-stained stranger he meets by chance is not the Gwydion he has dreamed of, the 'great war leader'; he finds that being a warrior is not just a matter of getting a sword and using it. At the end of his first enterprise he is full of doubt about himself and believes 'What I mostly did was make mistakes.' In the quest of the Black Cauldron and the hunt for the kidnapped Princess Eilonwy (q.v.), Taran learns from his mistakes; he learns to value his comrades, however odd or inimical or ridiculous they may be; he learns to give due thought to his actions. Each decision brings him nearer to kingship. When he gives up a powerful brooch which could guide him in his difficulties to save Prydain, Gwydion tells him 'You chose to be a hero not through enchantment but through your own manhood'.

Later (in *The Castle of Llyr*) Taran is asked by King Rhuddlan to help the foolish Prince Rhun, and he humbles himself to do as he is asked. When he sets out to discover who he really is (in *Taran Wanderer*) he is often heard to give good advice to folk where in earlier books he would have been nervously seeking advice himself. He takes a large step forward in his development when he risks his life to save an old shepherd whom he believes to be his father, though he suffers an impulse to let the old man die because he is ashamed of finding (as he thinks) that he was born a churl and not a noble.

The character of Taran has less obvious individuality than many of the minor, part-comic characters. This is because he has to be a representative, of Good against Evil, of Man seeking his own identity, of Youth growing up. His inner growth is sometimes demonstrated in sharp particularized remarks; for example, as he prepares for the last great march against Arawn, Coll remarks 'I remember a day when an Assistant Pig-Keeper would have been all flash and fire to ride with Lord Gwydion. Now you look as glum as a frost-bitten turnip.' We do not know Taran as a person any better for such comments. We only know what other people think about him, and their thoughts always stress his steady progress towards maturity.

The underlying irony of Lloyd Alexander's story, indicated in Taran's role of Assistant Pig-Keeper and his humility as a result of it, successfully carries out his aim of writing a fantasy full of traditional overtones which will yet be a story of human beings, their frailties and their glory. Taran has to be at once a man and the anonymous, unidentified, cryptic prince of fairy tale. In the first of these roles he has some of the flexibility of human nature: in the second he is to some extent a ceremonial figure, and perhaps the latter role masks the former except in *Taran Wanderer*, where he most definitely shoulders the responsibility for himself. [Lloyd Alexander: *The Book of Three*, New York 1964; *The Black Cauldron*, 1965; *The Castle of Llyr*, 1966; *Taran Wanderer*, 1967; *The High King*, 1968]

**TARKA THE OTTER** is born in a holt in the bank of the Torridge River and ranges over an area in North Devon bounded by Marland Moor to the south and Lynmouth to the north; his story is brought full circle when he is hunted down the Torridge past his birthplace and escapes through the estuary to the sea. By instinct, imitation and experience he accumulates the knowledge of enemies or rivals, weather conditions, terrain, food supply, and Man, necessary for survival.

Tarka's name was invented by Henry Williamson, with the meaning 'wandering as water, or the little water wanderer'; he found out later that Ta, meaning water, probably indicated a Celtic origin in the placenames of North Devon. He gave the otter a name to identify him as an individual, but did not humanize him. Tarka feels fear or pain but we learn of his feelings only through his actions, as he evades hounds, tracks his mate, records impressions minute by minute through his senses. The author's intense, detailed observation of Tarka and his environment is that of a poet-novelist rather than that of a naturalist; that is, he is concerned with discovering an aesthetic pattern, not a scientific one, in nature. His literary approach transcends even his compassion for wild life; he is not writing an anti-blood-sports treatise and he accepts the suffering caused by otter-hunting, and the pleasure certain people derive from the sport, as part of the world he is describing.

The narrative form of his story is elegant and firmly designed. The repetitive and random nature of any animal's life sets a problem for the writer. One thread that runs through the story is the long, intermittent connection between Tarka and the great hound Deadlock, which ends in death for the antagonists. The progress of time and the seasons provides continuity and natural divisions in the story, and the recurring presence of other animals – old Nog the heron, for instance, Tarka's mate Whitetip, Kronk the raven – breaks the repetition of Tarka's days. Above all Henry Williamson gives us an intense vision of Tarka's life. We seem to see through the otter's eyes, looking as he does from under water at '...the huntsman's feet before him joined to the image of legs, and above the inverted image a flattened and uncertain head and shoulders'. Henry Williamson wrote 'Pity acts through the imagination ... and imagination arises from the world of things, as a rainbow from the sun.' The poetry and the pity of *Tarka the Otter* have imagination as their source. [Henry Williamson: *Tarka the Otter*, London 1927]

One of Barry Driscoll's drawings of Tarka the Otter.

*They hung up their stockings side by side*

Teddy Robinson and Deborah; one of the author's illustrations.

**TEDDY ROBINSON** is 'a nice, big, comfortable, friendly teddy bear'; he belongs to Deborah and 'wherever one of them went the other one usually went too'. A little worn by much loving, Teddy is dropped, lost and found, dressed for various roles or occasions; he is deposited in places (window-sills, shop-windows, on a bedside cupboard in a hospital ward, in the fields, even in a bird cage) from which he can see, observe and comment on the interesting and sometimes puzzling behaviour of people, trees, animals.

This endearing toy is an extension of his small owner. Whether his voice is gruff or squeaky, it depends on Deborah and expresses her own lively, affectionate nature. He reveals in his own ingenuous way Deborah's own night-fears and puts into words wishes that are partly hers and partly those she feels suitable to a tough little bear – to go to tea with the Man in the Moon, to ride a horse and drive a motor-car. As with his words, so with his actions. Teddy Robinson is entirely passive; he falls, lies prone, sits up as he is propped and is never allowed independent movement. Through the disciplined fancy of these small domestic scenes Teddy Robinson enjoys the vicarious, amusing and essentially safe adventures which a small girl might well invent for her favourite toy. [Joan G. Robinson: *Teddy Robinson*, London 1953; *More about Teddy Robinson*, 1954; *Teddy Robinson's Book*, 1955; *Dear Teddy Robinson*, 1956; *Teddy Robinson Himself*, 1957; *Keeping up with Teddy Robinson*, 1964]

**TELFORD** is, as he says, 'the h'end o' a line of railway men', for although his son Stroudley and his grandsons Stanier and Gresley follow the family calling, they have accepted modern engineering more easily than the old man, who still looks back wistfully to the great age of steam. He and his family, all named after famous Victorian railway designers and engineers, have come to live in the kitchen table drawer in the attic of an old house where Mark and his father, both model-railway enthusiasts, have laid out an extensive system of rails, points and stations.

Mark 'had never been a boy to believe in elves and goblins and such nonsense' until the moment when he sees 'a very tiny, little old man' with a battered peaked cap and moleskin trousers, poking the engine with his stick and mumbling about the past. Telford introduces the delighted Mark to his family and the boy becomes their devoted ally and protector. His mother worries about the hours he spends alone in the attic, especially when she hears him apparently talking to himself, but only two people are ever let into the secret – Peter from the village, and Zacharias Helmsworth, an old railway-man from America whose adventurous life has given him an open mind on most subjects.

Clever character-drawing is responsible for the continued freshness and vivacity of the stories, as clearly

Telford, drawn by Gareth Floyd.

as the variety of material provided by the handling of a model-railway layout. Telford is a splendid old man, cantankerous, opinionated and full of the wisdom and the prejudices of experience. His son Stroudley, sensible and silent, has been 'playing second fiddle to his father for so many years he just naturally let him have first say' but his grandsons – Stanier, who is clever and bookish, and the happy-go-lucky Gresley – are inclined to resent being treated as children, and Stanier comments laughingly on one occasion 'We'd better ship the old varmint off to China where he'll be treated with the respect he deserves.' Devoted to his elderly brother Brindley (whom he scorns, all the same, because he was a booking clerk), grudging with praise, brave in the face of danger, Telford can be outfaced only by his redoubtable spouse.

The meticulous detail and unconcerned handling of fantasy commend the books to any reader, but even model-railway enthusiasts cannot help but admit that it is the characters that make the books. The description of a derailment, the planning of a record-breaking run, the arrangement of a new branch line, might have seemed little more than a technical exercise without the activities, contradictions, advice and ingenious contrivances of Telford and his family, with their sturdy Victorian independence and their infectious belief in their own capabilities. [Ray Pope: *The Model-railway Men*, London 1970; *Telford and the American Visitor*, 1970; *The Model-railway Men Take Over*, 1971; *Telford's Holiday*, 1972; *Telford and the Festiniog Railway*, 1973; *Telford Saves the Line*, 1974]

**TERRY TODD** see JIM STARLING

**THOMAS KEMPE**'s tombstone, dated 1629, defines him as 'Apothecarie' but in fact he was a necromancer, or village wise man, as is evidenced by the fact that on two occasions his restless spirit, in the form of a poltergeist, returns to East End Cottage in the Oxfordshire village of Ledsham to seek an apprentice. When he first visits the cottage, in 1856, his eye is on ten-year-old Arnold Luckett, but Arnold's Aunt Fanny arranges for the vicar to perform an exorcism and Kempe's wandering spirit is imprisoned in a bottle, sealed up in the wall of an attic.

James Harrison, another ten-year-old of our own times, does not escape Kempe's mischief so easily. The sorcerer causes him embarrassment by leaving arbitrary notes conveying his dislike of the vicar, his recipe for finding lost articles, his conviction that old Mrs Verity should be investigated as a witch. Poor James, accused of sundry accidents in fact caused by Kempe, and arraigned roundly on the school blackboard ('James Harrison is my apprentice. He is idle and does not doe my bidding: I counsell thee to watche him'), is finally helped by Bert Ellison, plumber by trade, who has inherited a certain skill with the supernatural from his forebears, and the necromancer is finally put to rest in the crypt of the church.

The character of Thomas Kempe is a *tour de force*, for except for a touch of mist now and then, it is revealed wholly through what he writes – from the first jaunty advertisement ('Sorcerie Astrologie Geomancie Alchemie Recoverie of Goodes lost Physicke') to the sad confession left in James's private notebook ('I am wearie of this towne. There are people who practise strange thinges and I doe not understand their wayes') and his last poignant request ('Helpe me to goe. Finde my resting-place, and put there my pype and my spectacles'). The voice from the past rings out clearly and establishes the restless, mocking, conceited man as surely as though we had seen him. [Penelope Lively: *The Ghost of Thomas Kempe*, London 1973]

**THOMAS THE TANK ENGINE**, a 'fussy little engine', lives and works at a Big Station under the bureaucratic eye of a Fat Controller. It is Thomas's duty to prepare the coaches for outgoing trains and uncouple them after the return run 'so that the big engines could go and rest', but his energy is sometimes misapplied. He likes to whistle at engines dozing in a siding and make them jump and dignified Gordon, weary of juvenile horse-play, is delighted when the impatient Thomas dashes off one morning without his trucks. 'Look, there's Thomas, who wanted to pull a train, but forgot about the coaches!' the other engines jeer, and one or two similar accidents bring Thomas to his senses, so that he becomes a Very Useful Engine and is promoted to his own Branch Line.

The four stories in the book mainly concerned with Thomas are fair examples of the artless-artful technique which has kept the Railway Series in the best-seller lists for many years. Since 1945, when the Revd Awdry introduced his first engines, he has built up a whole topography of the island of Sodor and Man and has developed a railway system into which he has fitted a host of splendidly convincing characters. There is Duke, who is proud of being named after the Duke of Sodor and is frequently heard to observe 'That would never have suited His Grace'. There is Bud, a cocky American engine who 'doesn't care a dime for a few spills'. There is Oliver the Western Engine, who boasts 'What do I care for trouble. I just push it aside', but who is sorry for being conceited after his rebellious trucks have caused a crash.

As time went on the books included more specialized vehicles like coy Mavis the diesel engine at the quarry, Toad the loyal brakevan and Toby, the sturdy tram-engine with his cow-catcher and side-plates. There are carriages and trucks with personality like Henrietta, who complains that she has seen better days and finds a branch line demeaning. There is the belligerent red bus called Bulgy by the engines, who tells them: 'Come the Revolution, railways'll be ripped up. Cars 'nd coaches 'll trample their remains'; pride goes before a fall and Bulgy, taking a short cut to prove he can carry passengers faster than the trains, is jammed under a low

Thomas the Tank Engine, from the book by
Rev. W. Awdry.

bridge and ends his days in a poultry-field. The author himself makes an appearance now and then among the few human characters given a name, as an advisory and interested Thin Clergyman.

The humanizing of locomotives is no new thing in children's books and half the credit for the success of the engine stories must go to Gunvor Edwards, who has taken every chance to differentiate character by emphasizing the salient points of certain types of engine and coach, never altering shape or construction except by the subtle addition of 'features' at the front. To him also goes half the credit for the amusing and wholly believable presentation of the Fat Controller, the epitome of all self-important large frogs in small ponds.

But the Railway Series does not depend on visual effects alone. By ingeniously combining ordinary speech with onomatopoeic words (chuff, peep, agh, shooh and so on) and exact terminology, settings and action, this clever writer gives his engines 'voices' and behaviour which sharply denote personality. [Revd W. Awdry: *Thomas the Tank Engine*, London 1946; and many other titles]

**THORNTONS** (the) of Punchbowl Farm – Anthea, Lindsey, Dion and Peter – are, at their first appearance (in *No Mistaking Corker*), almost indistinguishable from the families in scores of pony-holiday stories. In this predictably fortunate holiday in a caravan, with its jocular chatter and horse-gossip, only one person really comes to life – Lindsey, whose determination to rescue the horses stolen by a routinely nasty local farmer overcomes her real fear of the dark; and Lindsey's character is a little too much coloured by her first-person narrative, inevitably precocious or naïve at times.

The second book, *Black Hunting Whip*, describes how the Thorntons move from Hampshire to Surrey, where Mrs Thornton has boldly invested in a farm and an ancient house, both derelict and neglected; the setting is now established in which the members of the family follow their several bents for three or four years. The reclaiming of overgrown farm land and the gradual building of a milking herd provide a continuous sequence of events in which the animals are invested with personalities by the children.

Dion is presented from the start as a born farmer; supported with money and encouragement by his father, a commercial artist, he reads up agricultural theory and works tirelessly after school and in the holidays. Through the stories he remains consistent, a character drawn simply and effectively from one point of view. The touches of fantasy (in *Black Hunting Whip* and *The Spirit of Punchbowl Farm*) when he and Lindsey follow up the past history of the farm, do not entirely suit his nature, though they make an appealing addition to the stories. Monica Edwards arbitrarily but conveniently switches Dion's position from third to second in the family in the middle of the saga, for Dion's prowess as a farmer was always a little unbelievable at the tender age of twelve. His rather static character is given a little more depth when he develops an unexpressed affection for the practical Rissa Birnie (*see* Tamzin Grey), who with her gift for handling animals is an obvious partner for the future.

Andrea develops from a rather bossy thirteen to an attractive and intelligent seventeen without changing over-much. She is always well aware of being not only the eldest but also the cleverest and most attractive of the four, but when her relations with her siblings are in danger of becoming strained she relapses into a more childish mode of behaviour, hoydenish or useful as the occasion demands. She comes nearest to becoming a recognizable individual in *The Outsider*, when the young people from Romney Marsh (Tamzin, Meryon, Rissa and Roger) come on a visit. Now a romantic sixteen, Andrea snubs her devoted local admirer and allows Meryon's gipsyish looks (and probably also his obvious attachment to Tamzin) to drive her into ostentatious gloom and self-conscious posturing. The basic good sense the author has always allowed her helps her through this adolescent dream and after a brief period of preferring the lure of the bright lights and the life of a model, she sensibly decides to try for a university place.

Lindsey's outlook on life is as consistent as that of Dion. Her conviction that freedom is vital for beast as for man directs her brave, childish actions in the early books no less than her more co-ordinated later efforts to protect a wild deer that has attached itself to the herd (in *The Outsider*), a pine marten caught and hidden because of rumours of a local squirrel shoot (in *Fire in the Punchbowl*) and the hungry puma cub hiding in the valley after its mother has been shot (in *The Wild One*). Lindsey's actions sometimes seem bizarre to the others

The Thorntons at Punchbowl Farm; illustration by Geoffrey Whittam for *Black Hunting Whip*.

but they seem logical enough to her, even when she decides that the newborn calf, whose fate in noisy lorries and at the slaughter-house she hates to contemplate, must be killed to save the life of the young puma. Her activities are never sentimental because of the sturdy practical side of her character and because everything she does ultimately stems from her love of the old ways, of farming and of the world in general. In the last books, when she and Roger realize how well they suit one another, their gentle friendship is perfectly gauged in terms of Lindsey's given character.

The stories of Punchbowl Farm are essentially family stories; they are substantial because in every crisis or unexpected event the characters react as individuals but also as a unit. Peter, the youngest child, plays a small enough part in the events of the books, and yet he has an importance as anchor-man in the family. Often it is in their comments on Peter, or their protection of him (as when Lindsey saves him from being gassed at a badger sett) that his brother and sisters seem most themselves. A long series of stories about a family depends for credibility on a nice balance of change and repetition. It was an advantage for Monica Edwards that she was able to base her books to some extent on the events, and certainly on the setting, of her own days in the Punchbowl, and this must have helped to ensure continuity. But the Punchbowl Farm stories are never transcripts from real life. They are properly organized pieces of fiction in which each character is by turn important in the narrative and each character gives and takes colour from the others. [Monica Edwards: *No Mistaking Corker*, London 1947; *Black Hunting Whip*, 1950; *Punchbowl Midnight*, 1951; *The Spirit of Punchbowl Farm*, 1952; *The Wanderer*, 1953; *Punchbowl Harvest*, 1954; *Frenchman's Secret*, 1956; *The Cownapper*, 1958; *The Outsider*, 1961; *Fire in the Punchbowl*, 1965; *The Wild One*, 1967]

**THUMBELINA** *see* GULLIVER

**THUMMA, THIMBULLA** and **UMMANODDA** are sons of Mutta-Matutta, a grey fruit-monkey, and Seelem, a Mulgar of the Blood Royal (brother to Assasimmon, Prince of the Valleys of Tishnar), who left the luxury of palaces and wandered to the forest where Mutta-Matutta lived. The names and ancestry of the three monkeys are as important as the incantatory prose and the echoes of folk lore which support their given characters. The pull of his ancestry impels Seelem to set off one day to 'seek after the Valleys of Tishnar'; his sons promise that if he has not returned in seven Munza years, they will follow him beyond 'forest and river, forest, swamp and river, the mountains of Arakkaboa – leagues, leagues away'. Their mother gives them weapons and food for the journey and, from a secret store, 'a red Oomgar's or White Man's Jacket with curved metal hooks' for Thumb and Thimble, and for Nod the 'little coat of mountain-sheep's wool, with its nine ivory buttons'. To Nod also she gives the Wonderstone, for this youngest monkey bears the secret signs of a Nizza Neela, a magic person.

Thumma, Thimbulla and Ummanodda, the three royal monkeys, making their way through the forest to seek the 'Valleys of Tishnar'; illustration by Mildred E. Eldridge.

Nod is, in a way, the Wise Fool of folk-tale. It is his carelessness that sets the hut on fire and precipitates their journey; in his youthful confidence he taunts hostile wild pigs and allows a beautiful water-maiden to beguile the Wonderstone from him. But it is Nod too who finds a way to escape the old Gunga, the fishing-monkey; in a strange interlude when he lives with a shipwrecked sailor he learns a few human words and a measure of capricious loyalty. Through a long journey, full of danger, the royal brothers pass through landscapes distantly African in atmosphere, helped in their greatest peril by the power of the Wonderstone which Nod carries, loses, finds, venerates.

Thumb and Thimble plod on their way, sometimes enjoying Nod's difference from themselves but always caring for him as the privileged child. Surviving the dangers of precipice, storm and lurking enemies, they stand aghast in Tishnar's orchard, where strange silver shapes seem to block the way, till they see them melt away at the power of the Wonderstone and see Nod himself momentarily transformed, 'silken-silvery, with every hair enlustered, his wrinkles gone'. At last they come to the end of their journey, with their father awaiting them and with 'a sudden weariness and loneliness' for Nod, now that danger and magic are past. In this mysterious, richly endowed story the inextricable mixture of good and evil, of beauty and terror, is communicated subliminally through the activities of the three monkeys, and most of all through Nod – Prince Ummanodda Nizzanares Eengeneela – who is at once pathetic and powerful, mischievous and dutiful, child and magician. [Walter de la Mare: *The Three Mulla-Mulgars* (later *The Three Royal Monkeys*), London 1910]

**TIEN PAO** tries calling his piglet Beauty-of-the-Republic when he finds himself carried down the roaring river at night, away from his parents and his baby sister; somehow to give the pig his sister's name is comforting. But he has to admit that name belongs to her, so the pig becomes Glory-of-the-Republic instead. Tien Pao is Chinese and the family has not long ago escaped from their village after a Japanese attack, but the Japanese are advancing and Tien Pao, who is very young, needs all his courage and resource to stay alive and safe.

Because he knows what a tasty meal Glory-of-the-Republic would make, he is reluctant to accept help but the long journey he has taken, his sense of loss and his deep fatigue at last weaken his independence and he submits to the rough, jocular kindness of the American soldiers who find and adopt him, the 'sixty fathers' who are convinced by the child's determination that there is a chance for him to find his parents again. And so he does, but this is no sentimental tale. Basing his fiction on a true incident of the Second World War in the Far East, Meindert de Jong has given full attention to the danger, privation and terror of the days during which

Tien Pao, drawn by Maurice Sendak.

Tien Pao acquits himself so well. The small Chinese boy is at once a symbol of brave childhood in danger and a very individual small boy, lively and even humorous by temperament, rising to an appallingly difficult situation in his own way. [Meindert de Jong: *The House of Sixty Fathers*, New York 1956]

**TIM PIPPIN** lives in a small village with his worthy mother and the pretty Primrose, whom she has brought up from infancy. Guided by a dream, the bold youth sets out for Giantland, carrying a sword found by his mother years before, determined to prove himself worthy of his well-loved Primrose and to bring home a fortune. Undaunted by the warnings of Death-Stroke, Gatekeeper to the Sleeping Giants, the nimble youth has soon choked and buried Giant Bigfeet and decapitated Giant Greeneyes and, exhorted by the beauteous Queen Mab, has taken as his motto 'Liberty, Justice, and Death to the Giants'. With a magic flower as a pledge of fairy support, and with renewed vows to Primrose, in spite of Queen Mab's promise that he shall marry a king's daughter, Tim pushes through the dread forest, evades the attentions of Uncle Two-Heads, slays a fiery dragon and manages to preserve the treasure he finds from Giant Greed and other claimants. His fame goes before him to the court of King Golden-Apple and the court is roused from its strange gloom when it is discovered that Primrose is the King's long-lost granddaughter. Crowned as his successor, Tim goes on to more exploits, when he faces and defeats Jennie Greenteeth the Water Witch, Black Rolf, the roaring bull of Giant Redbeard, and the base impostor Prince Dreadnought, while rescuing King Hubert and his Queen, parents of the modest and beautiful Primrose.

Tim Pippin rejoices in a very mixed ancestry. His humble birth, his courage and resource and the lofty language of his challenges belong to the English chap-

An illustration by 'Puck' of one of Tim Pippin's many heroic encounters with danger.

book tradition, and there are many episodes in the books that recall, in particular, the tales of Tom Thumb; but other incidents and details speak of a more distant and august source in mythology, while Tim's probity and moral sentiments, like the dulcet tones and appearance of Queen Mab, are evidence of the particular gloss which Victorian writers so often chose to add to the Elizabethan fairy world. Tim's conviction of being always in the right makes him as much of a cliché character as the aggressive, somewhat vulgar giants,

whose malformation is abused in these stories, as so often, in the name of tradition. ['Roland Quiz' (pseud. Richard Quittenton): *Giant-land; or The Wonderful Adventures of Tim Pippin*, London 1874; *Tim Pippin: His Further Adventures in Giant-land*, 1874; *King Pippin*, 1874. All previously published as serials in *Young Folks*.]

**TIMOTHY** and **HUGH SPENS**, who are eleven and nine respectively, live in a large dilapidated house on the island of Popinsay in the north-east of Scotland. The

Timothy and Hugh Spens with their friends Sam
Sturgeon and Gunner Boles in their undersea adventure,
*The Pirates in the Deep Green Sea*; illustration by
William Reeves.

behaviour of the boys when they are involved in a
strange undersea adventure is so germane to their
natures that it is hard not to feel that they are the real
creators of it, and that it is a story-within-a-story like
*Peter Duck or Missee Lee* (q.v.). Just as the typical reading background of their class would be likely to throw
up the glorious confusion of pirates and old salts,
friendly sea-beasts and fisticuffs, so their sea-lashed
home makes it natural that they should take part in the
fight to prevent the wicked pirate chiefs, thin, brainy
Inky Poops and thick, brawny Dan Scumbril, from cutting the ropes that tie all the junctions of latitude and
longitude and substituting ties of their own making.
Even the names of the villains are corruptions of their
father's favourite objurgations against scoundrels and
nincompoops, while the powder monkeys who are on
the side of the goodies rejoice in the beautifully childlike
names of William Button and Henry String.

Timothy and Hugh accept very naturally, though
with occasional moments of apprehension, the alterna-
tions of victory and defeat, the encounters with Gunner
Boles (who fought at Trafalgar) and their own ancestor
Aaron Spens (a reputed pirate), the lackadaisical octopus
Cully (q.v.) and the great Admiral, Davy Jones.

Eric Linklater has let youth have its way in most of
the story but it is punctuated by wry satirical comment
of his own. For instance, the revolutionary intentions
of the pirates, whose plan to take possession of Davy
Jones's wealth to 'buy new rope' and 'tie new knots all
over the world' seems to the boys a lot of nonsense,
are undoubtedly in the mood of a liberal-minded,
well-read and superbly humorous country gentleman
writing not long after the Second World War. [Eric
Linklater: *The Pirates in the Deep Green Sea*, London
1949]

**TIMOTHY REED INGRAM**, reluctant focus of his
parents' ambition, is recovering from glandular fever
when he finds in the chimney of his own room a bundle
of drawings. Crude and untaught as they are, the
pictures (of a girl, landscapes, a church, an old house)
impress Tim by their sincerity and, far more, because
the initials on one of them, with the date 17 February
1910, are the same as his own. He is still more interested
when he discovers from a tombstone that the unknown
artist had died the day after the dated drawing, not quite
sixteen and the same age as Tim is now.

While Tim is exploring the churchyard he meets an
extraordinary girl whose scathingly matter-of-fact
manner disturbs him. Rebecca, who proves to be the
daughter of the vicar, applies herself to the mystery of
Thomas Robert Inskip and his drawings in a way that
is as typical of her as Tim's manner of investigation is
of him. Knowledgeable in parish matters, she discovers
that Tom was a farm lad working with horses on an
estate nearby. Meanwhile Tim's state of mind is especially receptive because of his illness and his adolescent
confusion about his own future; he finds himself intermittently sensing, almost merging with, Tom's feelings
and attitudes, so that the search for information
becomes for Tim at least a serious personal quest.

The stories of Tom Inskip and Tim Ingram, neatly
and logically interwoven, are based on far more than
a clever formal idea. Rebecca's comment about Tom at
the end of the book – 'I think he brought you to life' –
shakes Tim by its closeness to the truth, for the illusions,
dreams or what you will, through which he seemed to
enter the world of the farm boy, have strengthened his
resolve to follow his own bent. Tim was already
rebelling against his father's values and was merely ac-
quiescing in the plan that he should enter the family
advertising business. Tom's drawings not only move
him to find out what they represent; they also enable
him to recognize that he wants to use his own artistic
talent for self-expression rather than in the world
of commerce. He decides to stay in the village alone
when his parents return to the city life that suits them,
and to work for the blacksmith, with the goal of decorative iron-work not too remote in the future.

An illustration by Arthur Rackham from *The Wind in
the Willows.*

The search for the truth about Tom and his tragic death has given Tim a sense of the past and of the continuity of life; he comes to feel that one generation shapes another and that there is a responsibility 'to follow through one's own potential because it had been built up from all that had happened earlier'. This is not the only truth of personality that emerges from K. M. Peyton's tightly organized narrative. Tim is changed, too, by the surprises and perceptions that come from his talks with Rebecca. Nor is the social aspect of the story neglected. The position of Tim in the village is subtly contrasted with the way Tom, no less honest but inhibited by his station in life, moves tentatively from a correctly polite to a more personal way of addressing May Bellinger and Nettie. Tom seems less fortunate than Tim Ingram in terms of material advantages, but it is clear that he is more fortunate in his cheerful acceptance of life. But even this is not a dogma of personality. Tom emerges from the story as a normal, sturdy village boy in the years before the First World War. He enjoys improving his drawing under May's tuition but he is not introspective about it, for his feelings for Nettie and his duties as the family breadwinner are more important to him. May's comment on him is that 'he demanded very little and accepted what he had with a perfect spiritual grace'. Tim and Rebecca, children of their time, are inclined to make fun of the phrase and Tim, going further, does not think that Tom was 'so dumb that he would have been perfectly happy labouring for Mr Pettigrew until he died of old age'. The interplay of character, the delineation of personality through the comments of one person upon another, shape an intricate and moving story. [K. M. Peyton: *A Pattern of Roses*, London 1972]

**TIN WOODMAN** *see* DOROTHY GALE

**TIPPETARIUS**, who lives in the Country of the Gillikins in the Land of Oz, runs away from the cruel witch Mombi with Jack Pumpkinhead, a personage he has made and brought to life with a magic powder stolen from the old woman. The companions also animate a saw-horse they find on the way, which serves as a steed and proves a staunch ally in trouble. Tip is received in friendly fashion in the City of Emerald, but a fierce young woman named Jinjur leads a rebellion of discontented housewives and proclaims herself ruler in Oz. The powerful sorceress Glinda forces Mombi to confess that Tip is really the lost Princess Ozma under a spell, and the Scarecrow willingly relinquishes the crown.

Young Tip is altogether a more vivacious and natural character than Dorothy (q.v.) and the first book of his adventures (*The Land of Oz*) is more varied and exciting than *The Wizard of Oz*, with such characters as the pompous Wiggle-Bug and the cheerful, brash Jack Pumpkinhead to add their quota of humour to the main plot.

An illustration by Mabel Lucy Attwell for *The Water Babies*.

Tippetarius transformed to the all-powerful Queen of Oz; drawing by John R. Neill.

Tip is reluctant at first to submit to transformation – 'if I don't like being a girl you must promise to change me into a boy again' he tells Glinda. It is unfortunate that once he has become Ozma, all-powerful Queen of Oz, the boisterous energy and cheery voice change to the sweet, measured tones of an irreproachable sovereign. When Ozma is stolen by Ugu the Shoemaker, she waits patiently while her subjects search for her; a serene and somewhat sententious manner characterizes her in all her adventures. While Frank Baum lavished his considerable powers of invention on innumerable peculiar creatures of masculine gender, he seemed to feel that embroidery and pleasant chat were more suitable occupations for the royal princess and her friend Dorothy. [L. Frank Baum: *The Land of Oz*, Chicago 1904; *Ozma of Oz*, 1906; *The Lost Princess of Oz*, 1917; *The Tin Woodman of Oz*, 1919]

**TITTY WALKER** (her real name, Elizabeth, is never used) is unmistakably a middle-of-the-family child – introspective, sensitive, intensely loyal to her family. In *Swallows and Amazons* Titty, who is nine or thereabouts, is classed by John and Susan (q.v.) as 'Able-Seaman'. As such, Titty takes orders and is not called upon to exercise initiative but when she is left alone she copes valiantly – for example, when she is marooned with

Roger (q.v.), Bridget (q.v.) and the kitten on a tide-encircled causeway (in *Secret Water*). The strain on her nerves is all the greater because she knows that her own carelessness has brought others into danger.

Titty finds books just as real, sometimes more real, than everyday life. Left as watchman when John and Susan set out to capture the *Amazon* at night, she remarks 'I shall watch by the campfire, shrouded in my cloak.' One guesses that Titty is responsible for the most colourful episodes in the story of *Peter Duck*, which is made up by the children and Uncle Jim when they live on a wherry in the Broads during a winter holiday.

Imagination is a pain as well as a pleasure for Titty. In the third summer adventure (*Pigeon Post*) it is discovered that she alone has the power to locate water by dowsing. Terrified by the strength of the twig in her hand, she runs away to be alone. Her struggle to force herself to try again in private (since the whole holiday plan depends on finding water on High Topps) is a key to her character. So is the moment (in *Swallowdale*) when she is afraid the wax figure she has devised of the dreaded Aunt Maria may really have the power to harm her. As Susan says, 'she gets so stirred up by things'. Because of this, her character acts as a kind of leaven in the stories, toning down their over-active element and reflecting some of the gentler and more sensitive aspects of the other members of the Walker family. [Arthur Ransome: *Swallows and Amazons*, London 1930; *Swallowdale*, 1931; *Pigeon Post*, 1936; *Secret Water*, 1939]

**TOAD OF TOAD HALL** has been thought of as the central character of *The Wind in the Willows* since A. A. Milne's dramatic version was first produced in 1929. In fact the comedy of his love-affair with motor-cars, his arrest and trial for stealing one, his escape from prison and the final battle to drive the gangsters from the Wild Wood out of the Hall, is only one facet of Kenneth Gra-

Two illustrations from *The Wind in the Willows*: (*above*) Ernest H. Shepard's drawing of Toad's escape from prison disguised as a washerwoman; (*right*) Mole, Rat and Toad gaze after the motorcar which has driven their caravan into the hedge, illustrated by Wyndham Payne.

hame's celebration of the beauty and variety of the English countryside. Balancing Toad's slapstick adventure, the account of how Mole meets the Water Rat and learns to love the river stirs the imagination in a completely different way; his sudden passionate desire for his underground home, the hypnotic effect on Rat of the Seafarer's romantic account of his roving life, Mole's terrifying night in the Wild Wood, the awesome vision of Pan on the river-bank at dawn – all these scenes are essential to the book, which is as broad and varied and life-giving as the river itself.

Kenneth Grahame began the story of a rat and a mole for his son Alistair on his fourth birthday and it was expanded over several years, partly as a bedtime story and partly in letters. It seems that a giraffe appeared in the early part of the chronicle but was soon discarded. Certainly there is a consistency of species, scale and behaviour among the characters in the story, for which Grahame's deepest motive for telling it must surely be responsible, the evocation of a particular stretch of the Thames. Most of the animals are humanized in a way that does not contradict their natural forms and habitats. It seems logical to see Rat in a rowing boat and no very long step after that to the creation of an alert, observant, friendly animal wearing a blazer. Mole's shyness and his reflective disposition arise naturally from the comfortable simplicity of his underground home, and the carefully documented background of Badger is equally consistent with the way the animals live in two worlds, the recognizable world of man and the secret one of nature.

Toad is the exception. There is nothing toadlike in his behaviour, he is equated somewhat doubtfully in size with Mole and Rat, and a neo-Tudor mansion is not a particularly appropriate home for him; his character is based simply on the stout, grotesque appearance of a toad and it has been extended thereafter with comic exaggeration. Toad provides the particular kind of humour congenial to children: other elements in the book – the satire, the melancholy and the philosophy – are there to satisfy Grahame himself. The combination of elements have made the book a classic.

If Kenneth Grahame was reliving, perhaps even escaping into his childhood as he wrote the book, he put into the character of the animals the social attitudes and details of his life as a man. Beatrix Potter, whose care in matters of humanization was scrupulous, criticized Grahame for allowing Toad to comb his hair. 'A mistake to fly in the face of nature – A frog may wear goloshes; but I don't hold with toads having beards or wigs! So I prefer Badger.' But Grahame's animals enter into the world of man as Beatrix Potter's never did. Toad walks into a pub, and he is tried in an ordinary magistrate's court. If the caricaturing of Toad is unique in the book, the rest of the characters are men in a man's world. There is an urbane, clubbable, relaxed humour in the way the badger, the mole and the rat are personi-

fied that enriches the book just as much as the natural correctness of their behaviour as animals. [Kenneth Grahame: *The Wind in the Willows*, London 1908]

**TOAD OF TOAD'S CASTLE** is an honoured guest at the Rose and Crown, an inn run by William and Maria Field-Mouse, and he moves with authority in and out of the daily lives of their children, Snug and Serena. This lively brother and sister, who enjoy minuscule adventures in a pleasant flowery world, treat Toad as children might treat a family friend; they respect his age and status and revel in the stories he loves to tell.

Like Badger in the Sam Pig stories, Toad adds to the attractive setting of the stories the continuity and weight of history. Among the treasures in his ancestral home, safe in the roots of a willow-tree, are a silver shilling given to an ancestor by Queen Elizabeth I when she was a Princess and a silver spoon which George II had presented to another of his forebears. It is true that when he undertakes to educate Snug and Serena he can only help them to count up to seven, but he *can* tell them the names of the stars and recount the legends about them. Through him, the stories acquire a sense of the past and a touch of fairy-tale grandeur. [Alison Uttley: *The Little Brown Mouse* series: *Snug and Serena Meet a Queen*, London 1950; *Snug and Serena Pick Cowslips*, 1950; *Going to the Fair*, 1951; *Toad's Castle*, 1951; *Christmas at the Rose and Crown*, 1952; *Mrs Mouse Spring-cleans*, 1952; *The Gypsy Hedgehogs*, 1953; *Snug and the Chimney-sweeper*, 1953; *The Flower Show*, 1955; *The Mouse Telegrams*, 1955; *Snug and the Silver Spoon*, 1957; *Mr Stoat Walks In*, 1957; *Snug and Serena Count 12*, 1959; *Snug and Serena Go to Town*, 1961]

**TOBY TOTTEL** lives 'on a nice verdant common where it was bright as a looking-glass all day long and warm as a new loaf. Unfortunately the common is disturbed by people beating their carpets and hanging out washing and Toby, who is poetic rather than practical, resolves to seek his fortune. His quest becomes more specific when Bridget next door asks him a curious question – 'Why do you have pink furniture in your house?' Not only does Toby deny this but he assures her that pink furniture 'is only allowed for gentlemen who have got noble natures'. After this, of course, the stupid fellow has to set off to find this rarity.

In so far as Toby has a character of his own, as opposed to a folk-tale role, it is a rather tiresome one. He snubs his devoted Bridget and is not a little snobbish. But in fact Toby is not a doer but a moving object which gathers accretions. He meets strange people – the Baldheaded Woman and her son the lanky Stinker, the forester Fellafungobbelus, the epitaph-seller in Hedgehog Market, the Prince of Purganda who loses his favourite blood alley, the toad at the racecourse who can do the three-card trick, the giant who engages Toby to make his nightly soup of ants' bones. The familiar pattern of a journey to enlightenment, with Alice and

Pinocchio, comes to mind as we read of Toby's travels, but far more strongly the whimsical philosophy, the dotty sense, of some of the author's countrymen, notably James Joyce and James Stephens. [A. E. Coppard: *Pink Furniture*, London 1930]

**TOBY TYLER** is what 'the fellers' call him; he has no idea of his real name or who his parents were or why he lives with Uncle Daniel. All he knows is that Uncle Daniel, a deacon with a strong sense of discipline, complains that the boy eats four times as much as he earns with his daily chores, and when the circus comes to town it does not take Toby long to decide to run away. His ingenuous appearance, his 'round head covered with short red hair', his face 'as speckled as any turkey's egg' with freckles, his 'thoroughly good-natured look', make no appeal to his new master, Job Lord, who proves to be far more strict than Uncle Daniel and far less generous with the food that is Toby's great pleasure in life.

Job is in fact a brutal man and Toby is one of a long line of boys, all of whom have run away from his beatings and bullying. Toby would have found it hard to escape, for Job finds him the most useful of his victims and watches him closely, but the boy has friends to help him. His confiding manner and childish looks appeal strongly to generous-hearted circus folk like Ben the driver, and Mr and Mrs Treat, the Fat Woman and her skeletal spouse. Then there are friends nearer in age (like Ella the child equestrienne, with whom he learns to perform in the ring) or in size (like the chimpanzee whom he calls Mr Stubbs after an acquaintance and whom he treats as a friend).

This small red-headed boy, courageous but softhearted, whose conscience tells him almost as soon as he has left Uncle Daniel that the old man deserved better treatment, belongs very much to the fiction of the last century. If Toby Tyler is not a pattern of perfect behaviour, he is a good example of the genus boy who comes to understand right and wrong better because he is good at heart.

*Toby Tyler* is in fact a moral tale like so many of its period. It is not, though, a dull one. The American James Otis Kaler had at one period of his varied life worked in a travelling circus. If he uses his young hero to explode the prevalent idea in the minds of the young that circuses are glamorous and romantic, he still brings to his story something of the heady smell of sawdust and the glitter of tinsel. Above all, he enlivens what is in any case a pretty light load of preaching by the lively chatter, the tenacity and the touch of mystery that belong to this one small boy who, like innumerable fictional characters after him, runs away to join a circus. [James Otis: (pseud. James Otis Kaler): *Toby Tyler*, New York, 1881]

**TOLLY** comes to Green Knowe for the first of several visits to his great-grandmother in a time of winter floods and snow. Among the treasures in the ancient house,

Tolly listens to his grandmother's tale of blind Susan and the lost treasure within the house; illustration by Peter Boston.

the little boy is attracted most of all by a picture of a family, in which the three children especially seem to be gazing at him. As Mrs Oldknow tells him about these forebears from three centuries back, he begins to wonder if they are not still in the house; distant voices, laughter, shadows, the flicker of a skirt, all tantalize him, until Alexander, Toby and Linnet allow themselves to become visible to him and the tales he has been told about them are all marvellously confirmed by what they tell him themselves.

The following Easter, sitting with Mrs Oldknow as she repairs patchwork quilts made at the end of the eighteenth century, Tolly listens to the story of blind Susan whose sensible father, a sea-captain, brought little Jacob from Africa to be her servant and her companion in and out of doors. For Tolly, his discovery of lost jewels and the consequent restoration of the old house, are no more exciting than the moments when he glimpses and even speaks to Susan.

In the next year trouble comes to the old house. Tolly and Ping (q.v.), a Chinese boy whom Mrs Oldknow has adopted, share her distrust of Dr Melanie Powers, whose questions about an old book, once used in the house by a scholar in his unlawful researches, become more and more insistent. When the disguised witch uses her wicked magic against the ancient peace of Green Knowe, the two children bravely and intelligently work out ways to stop the plagues she sends into the garden. They find the precious book of alchemy, and with its help Melanie is changed from an arrogant, evil woman to a pathetic creature deserted by her Master.

The author's seven-hundred-year-old house is the setting for the fantasy adventures of Green Knowe and to some extent she has designed the characters to fit the house – that is, Mrs. Oldknow, with her knowledge of the past is its custodian and interpreter, while Tolly, with his sense of wonder and his quick, happy imagination, is the perfect person to explore every corner of house and garden and listen to their echoes. There is perhaps a danger for readers that the importance of Green Knowe may be allowed to overshadow the characters a little. Certainly atmosphere, the evocation of the past, are of supreme importance in the stories, but if Green Knowe gives life to the characters, it also receives life from them. The natural affection that grows between Tolly and the small, plump figure of 'Granny Partridge', their comfortable interchange of news and wonders, and the joys and sorrows of the children who belong to the past, provide a second dimension of human feeling which is as valuable as the elusive element of fantasy. [L. M. Boston: *The Children of Green Knowe*, London 1954; *The Chimneys of Green Knowe*, 1958; *An Enemy at Green Knowe*, 1964]

**TOM** the chimney-sweep goes to Harthover Hall with Grimes, his master, and, losing his way in the branching chimneys, comes down into a clean white bedroom where he sees in a mirror 'a little ugly, black, ragged figure, with bleared eyes and grinning white teeth' and realizes for the first time with shame and anger that he is dirty. The little girl in the bed seems by contrast like an angel, but she is human enough and her screams bring her nurse running. Tom leaps from the window, runs from a crowd of pursuers and, after a perilous climb down Lewthwaite Crag and a brief respite at the village dame-school, he finds the water he has longed for, slips in to clean himself, and becomes a water-baby. He makes his way down to the sea and there goes to school for the first time in his life, with stern Mrs Bedonebyasyoudid and loving Mrs Doasyouwouldbedoneby as his teachers. After happy, playful days in the Blessed Isle of St Brendan, marred by a few backslidings, Tom is sent to a strange, cold world where he sees Grimes imprisoned in a chimney and begs to be allowed to help him. The powerful fairy who releases Grimes – teacher, protector and creator as she is – sends Tom back to the world with little Ellie from Harthover, who has flitted in and out of his adventures as an unattainable dream and a very determined little girl.

PLAY BY ME, BATHE IN ME, MOTHER AND CHILD.

*Left.* Tom narrowly escapes the clutches of Ellie's angry nurse after climbing down the wrong chimney into the little girl's bedroom; illustration by Warwick Gable for *The Water Babies.*

*Right.* W. Heath Robinson's illustration of Tom's water-baby world from a 1915 edition of the same book.

Kingsley wrote the allegorical story of little Tom for his youngest son, Greville, to communicate to him certain ideas of redemption through punishment and justice on one hand and love and compassion on the other, and to suggest that science and Christian faith were reconcilable in the great wholeness of Nature, symbolized by the immobile, powerful figure of Mother Carey. Into the book he put his own preoccupations – his passionate desire to help the oppressed poor, spiritually and physically, his belief that an age of scientific discovery demanded humility, his sometimes unorthodox ideas of education. It has been the fashion in the present century to tighten the structure of this fascinating, unwieldy, richly conglomerate story by taking out many of Kingsley's asides, his snatches of scientific argument, his verbal pyrotechnics and what we are pleased to call his 'moralizing'. This is to alter the voice that spoke so affectionately and so maturely to his son and to reduce the book to a simple fairy tale. This was not Kingsley's aim. The many-sided nature of the book helps to extend the first, fairy-tale simplicity of Tom's character as it is defined, with such touching fidelity and feeling, in the flawed world of men and the beautiful, complex world of nature. [Charles Kingsley: *The Water Babies. A Fairy Tale for a Land-Baby*, London 1863]

**TOM ASS** is the youngest and least useful of Farmer John's sons. One day he meets a mysterious lady who offers him a gift: 'Whatever work you begin at sunrise, shall be sufficient to the day – and the sooner you take your road the better'. It is not long before he takes the road, after he has discovered that offering to help his mother pick stones off the garden and mend a wall entails whole days of work. By and by he meets the strange lady again and begs to be allowed to return her inconvenient gift. Her reply is to offer another to the 'Great Fool'. 'Since you will plainly never make anything of yourself, you shall be whatever your future wife chooses to make of you.'

How he meets Jennifer minding sheep in her uncle's orchard and how her merry comment on his story – 'Why you great donkey' – turns him in very truth into an ass; how she finds a way to start them both in life by using his first gift wisely; how they make their way to London and enter the cloth trade, grow rich in competition with the Hanse merchants and are summoned to the very presence of the King – these curious and surprising events are duly described, culminating in the restoration of Tom to human shape.

Tom's character, as may be guessed from his adventures, is an amusing folk-tale derivative; the late medieval setting and period details add credence to the story but do not interfere with the anonymity and agelessness of his character. Tom *is* an ass, puffed up with his own pride; paradoxically, because he becomes an ass while retaining his own power of thought, he grows in wisdom, for he can listen to and learn from others without hindrance. Over the years he grows weary of

Jennifer starts in dismay after the idle boy, Tom Ass, is transformed, literally, into an ass; illustration by Ionicus.

his enchantment but comes to value his comrade's loyalty and patience and at last, unexpectedly, to realize that he would be happy if she did, indeed, as the elf-woman seemed to suggest, become his wife. The translation of Tom (which perhaps has a hint of Bottom in it) is described with exquisite simplicity and demure humour. [Ann Lawrence: *Tom Ass or The Second Gift*, London 1972]

**TOM BROWN** goes off to Rugby with his father's admonitions still in his ears, to be made into a 'brave, truth-telling English gentleman', and almost at once gets himself knocked out in a gladiatorial football match, earning a dignified commendation from Brooke, the house captain, 'Well, he is a plucky youngster, and will make a player.' He shows as much stoicism when, as a new boy, he is tossed in a blanket in the dormitory and when he is roasted by the bully Flashman for refusing to sell the ticket for the Derby favourite which he has drawn in a lottery (a scene which to modern ears seems amusingly ambiguous). He becomes popular for his prowess in the games field and for making a firm stand, with his jolly chum East, against Flashman's demands for their services as fags (though the notorious bully is finally brought low not by the courageous juniors but by the demon drink).

Tom's passage from normally idle and mischievous lad to responsible senior is achieved fairly smoothly, with the aid of the sensible and serious exhortations of the Doctor and the more emotional pleas of Arthur, a delicate younger boy whom Tom takes under his protection (a situation in fact contrived by the Doctor to steady Tom's wildness and into which the present day reader finds it impossible not to read sexual overtones). Arthur brings Tom back to the habit of nightly prayers and leads him to give up cribbing (though his reform in this respect is inconsistent and produces one of the few amusing scenes in the book). When Tom leaves school he can boast that he has earned 'the name of a fellow who never bullied a little boy, or turned his back on a big one'.

Such ideas sound more attainable and distinctly more healthy than the morbid aspirations and backslidings of Eric Williams (q.v.), just as Dr Arnold's particular version of muscular Christianity was a step forward in the evolution of that unique closed community, the British public school. Thomas Hughes wrote his story to warn his own son of the difficulties he was likely to encounter when he went to Rugby and to express his admiration for Dr Arnold, who had been his own head-master there. Tom's later exploits at Oxford are long-winded and spiritless; he has become little more than a figure-head illustrating the perils of university life.

Tom seems a somewhat uninteresting and lightly-defined individual when he is compared with Talbot Baines Reed's schoolboys and the scenes of brutality so vital to the author's argument are described with a cer-tain reticence (though modern film treatments have done their best to define Flashman's brutality more closely). *Tom Brown's Schooldays* is often called the first *real* school story but it was to be almost thirty years more before the authentic voices of Anthony Pembury and the Tadpoles and Guineapigs spoke up for the cause of humour and personality in fiction as against solemnity and sermons. [Thomas Hughes: *Tom Brown's Schooldays*, Cambridge 1857; *Tom Brown at Oxford*, 1861]

**TOM INSKIP** *see* TIMOTHY INGRAM

**TOM KITTEN** *see* GINGER AND PICKLES

**TOM LONG** is sent to stay with his aunt and uncle when his brother Peter develops measles. Their flat is on the first floor of a large old house; another family lives below, and on the top floor old Mrs Bartholomew, who keeps a watchful eye on her tenants. One night Tom hears the clock strike thirteen, wanders downstairs and opens the back door to let in the moonlight. Instead of the backyard and dustbins he has expected, he sees a large, rambling garden. On the first nights of his happy exploration he is content to be alone but he is still happier when the little girl he has seen occasionally tag-ging after her unkind cousins at last speaks to him and they become playmates. Tom sympathizes with Hatty's unenviable position as an orphaned poor relation; he argues with her about which of them is the ghost, teaches her to swarm up trees and notices after a time that Hattie is growing up, while he remains a boy in pyjamas. As old Mrs Bartholomew dreams upstairs and sees her life unfold through the remembered years, Tom is strangely caught into her dreams through his own longing for a companion and for space to play in. And when he is at last shut out of the garden – for Mrs Bartho-lomew has in her dreams grown up and left the house for married life, and Tom is due to return home – time has, miraculously, brought the two night friends

Nicholas Bridge as Tom Long in the BBC serial *Tom's Midnight Garden.*

together in daytime. Tom and old Mrs Bartholomew meet at last, and know one another.

Philippa Pearce has turned her back firmly on that cliché character of fantasy, the dreamy, poetically-minded loner. Tom is a very normal boy. The running account of his visits to the garden which he sends to Peter are clear and circumstantial rather than intro-spective. He is always anxious to find explanations for what is happening; his persistent questions about time exasperate his Uncle Alan; he sensibly hunts through books on costume to try to find Hatty's dates; even if he does not understand time, he works out a way of managing it so that Hatty's skates can be in two places at once and he can go skating with her. When Tom meets old Mrs Bartholomew and their dreams become an unexpected and logical reality, his excited interest in finding so many guesses confirmed, so many puzzles

Peter Farmer's cover illustration for *Tom's Midnight Garden.*

# Tom's Midnight Garden

A. PHILIPPA PEARCE

explained, is no less part of him than the impulse of spontaneous affection that makes him run back to Mrs Bartholomew, after their carefully restrained farewell, and his aunt notices 'he put his arms right round her and he hugged her goodbye as if she were a little girl'. Here, surely, is the real triumph of Time. [A. Philippa Pearce: *Tom's Midnight Garden*, London 1958]

**TOM SAWYER** tries his Aunt Polly sorely sometimes but she punishes him less than he deserves for 'he's my own dead sister's boy, poor thing, and I ain't got the heart to lash him somehow'. The village of St Petersburg on the Mississippi, Mark Twain's fictional counterpart of the home of his own boyhood in the 1840s, provides endless opportunities for adventures which seem sensational in comparison with those described in story books today, for encounters with thieves or kidnappers can hardly be compared with the experience of Tom and his friend Huck Finn when, lurking in the churchyard at night, they witness a murder and flee in terror. Tom's energetic, guileful, cheerful nature has been the inspiration for countless stories about naughty boys – the most directly derivative being perhaps J. D. Fitzgerald's tales of the Great Brain, another Tom who leads a turbulent life in Utah in the 1890s. None of Tom's fictional successors has ever been such a believable mixture of honesty and deviousness, romantic role-playing and earthy jokes, nor has any story-book hero ever been presented in such superbly casual, vividly dialectal, humanely comic prose.

Two influences have moulded Tom – the Bible-guided, sincere morality of Aunt Polly, which has gone deeper than he realizes, and the enviably independent outlook of Huckleberry Finn, son of the town drunkard, who sleeps rough where he chooses and successfully evades the claims of society. If Tom admires Huck for his freedom and his power of spitting, Huck admires Tom for the conviction with which he adopts the roles of Robin Hood or pirate chief; the humorous temper of the book makes it possible to accept the two freedoms – poverty and imagination – on equal terms.

If this is possible when reading *Tom Sawyer*, it is less easy when we come to *Huckleberry Finn*, which many do not consider to be a children's book. It takes up the story of the two boys after their help in the capture of Injun Joe has brought them each a substantial reward. When Huck's father hears of this he returns to try to get his son's money, and Huck, already weary of life with the Widow Douglas, who has undertaken to civilize him, runs away with black Jim, who mistakenly believes that Miss Watson is planning to 'sell him down the river'. Although during the boat journey down the Mis-

sissippi Huck Finn is introduced to some extremely unpleasant aspects of human nature (for which even life with his Pap has not prepared him) and though first-person narrative imposes a certain air of maturity on him, he is as much of a child as Tom Sawyer is. He is confused by finding he has no consistent opinion of the two confidence tricksters he is involved with, and no certain idea of how far his own responsibility for Jim goes. His grumbling criticism of Tom's absurdly elaborate plans for releasing Jim from captivity shows not the practical scorn of an adult but the incomprehension of a boy who has had no chance to live out of books.

Generations of readers have approached *Huckleberry Finn*, a seminal book in American literature, with their own interpretation of Mark Twain's facetious admonition at the beginning, 'persons attempting to find a motive in this narrative will be persecuted; persons attempting to find a moral in it will be banished ...' Read as an allegory of questing man, it is not a children's book: read as a funny, touching, rambling, shrewd and honest story of boyhood, it is. [Mark Twain (pseud. Samuel Langhorne Clemens): *The Adventures of Tom Sawyer*, Hartford, Chicago and Cincinnati, 1876, and under separate imprint San Francisco, 1876; *The Adventures of Huckleberry Finn*, London 1884 (first American edition 1885)]

**TOMMY BROCK** *see* PETER RABBIT
**TOMMY STUBBINS** *see* DOCTOR DOLITTLE
**TOO-TOO** *see* DOCTOR DOLITTLE

**TOPSY** and **TIM,** brother and sister, are two average children in an average nuclear family who lead average lives in an average urban home. They made their début in the 1960s in a book for each day of the week, each one describing an incident (the new baby next door, friends to tea, hair-washing) whose familiarity small listeners and readers could enjoy. The children are deliberately stereotyped in the five-to-seven age-range and traditionally divisive in sex behaviour. Over the years the characters of Topsy and Tim have not changed, though they have grown a little older, but the tenor of their life has altered as plainly as their clothes (from frilly frocks and tartan knicker suits to anoraks and striped T-shirts). From the simplest adventures, like dancing round a bonfire or getting lost in a fog, they have advanced to the more trendy pony-trekking and hill-walking; they have visited the zoo and a football match and have recently been to Belgium and Holland. This has not changed their totally predictable behaviour, or the socially instructive situations they find themselves in when they learn about road safety and the dangers of meddling with unlabelled bottles and stationary vehicles. The undemanding characters of the children and the chunky, doll-like style in which they are illustrated must satisfy some desire for conformity and safety in young readers, for the books are very popular with children even as old as seven or eight. [Jean and Gareth Adamson: *Topsy and Tim's Monday* (-*Sunday*)

Huckleberry Finn and Tom Sawyer with a dead cat, from *The Adventures of Tom Sawyer.*

Topsy and Tim began to feel lost. The map did not seem to make sense. The needle of the compass was too wobbly to be any help.

"Which way shall we go?" said Tim.

Topsy had no idea. Luckily, the sheepdog seemed to know. He trotted ahead, then paused to wait for them.

"We'll follow the sheepdog," said Topsy and Tim.

Topsy and Tim by Jean and Gareth Adamson.

*Book*, 7 pts, London and Glasgow 1960–62; *Topsy and Tim's Foggy Day*, 1962; *Topsy and Tim go Fishing, Topsy and Tim at the Football Match*, 1963; *Topsy and Tim's Bonfire Night. Topsy and Tim's Snowy Day*, 1964; *Topsy and Tim go on Holiday, Topsy and Tim at the Seaside*, 1965; and other titles]

**TORRIE** feels mature in deciding that her reserved, withdrawn school-teacher father and homely mother are not really fond of one another and that her father's idea of leaving St Louis and venturing in a covered wagon all the way to California in 1846 is ridiculous.

These and many more of Torrie's childish assumptions are shaken during the adventurous journey (which, as she discovers much later, is taken largely because of her own poor health). To her astonishment her father, who at the outset of the journey has to depend on his young son Cal to start the oxen, gradually by force of character takes command of the wagon train and sees it through considerable dangers. Then again, her hasty assessment of the two young men who impinge on her life – the uncommunicative youth hired as driver, who will give no other name than Jess, and dashing, selfish Luke Egan – proves to be utterly wrong. Most of all, perhaps, Torrie is brought to realize the shallowness of her opinions when she learns the truth

about Jess's illiterate home background and perceives the courage of his search for a wider life.

The authors of this lively story show how events change Torrie and how much she learns from the opinions of others – her father's words about Jess, Jess's praise of her father, Luke's casual remarks about his fellow-travellers. Against a background of pioneering days, which is realized so easily and with such imagination that all the covered wagon clichés take on new life, they have drawn in firm lines the character of a self-centred, unperceptive girl waking to new knowledge of herself and other people. [Annabel and Edgar Johnson: *Torrie*, New York 1960]

**TOTTIE PLANTAGENET** is a farthing doll more than a century old, whose painted face and hair and durably wooden body match her sturdy, simple character. She is inherited by Emily and Charlotte and is made a member of the Plantagenet family, which is headed by Mr Plantagenet, a boy doll who had been badly treated before he came to the little girls and who as a result is always a little nervous, and his wife Birdie, who came off a cracker and is as cheerful and light-headed as her celluloid body and fly-away hair. They have as their child a tiny plush doll called Apple who is universally beloved and as their guard a pipe-cleaner dog called Darner because of the needle that constitutes his backbone.

The Plantagenets live a crowded existence in a shoe-box until the old family doll's house is sent as a present. Alas, their happiness is brief. In Tottie's early days she was scorned and hated by the valuable, kid-and-china doll Marchpane and she is not pleased to find herself next to her old enemy at an exhibition, any more than Marchpane is pleased when the wooden doll catches the attention of the Queen. Marchpane finds a chance to exercise her malice, for when the exhibition is over she is sent to Emily and Charlotte to complete the dolls' house family.

Whatever evil power Marchpane possesses, it is felt by Emily who, fascinated by her, insists that the dolls' house is hers and turns Mr and Mrs Plantagenet into the butler and cook. Steadfast Tottie reassures them. 'One day Emily will find out she is wrong.' But it is chattering Birdie who defeats Marchpane in the end.

Marshalling her thoughts with difficulty (for usually they rattle round her head like the beads inside it), she knows what to do when she sees Apple perched danger-ously near a lighted candle, while Marchpane looks on, smiling and unmoved. Apple is saved, Birdie falls forward and flares up into nothing, and Emily sees Marchpane as she really is.

The chronicles of dolls, with their oblique satirical, sentimental or philosophical comments on human nature, are not often as poignant as the story of the Plantagenets. The scale of emotion is as scrupulously kept as the exquisitely exact scale of the dolls' furniture and clothes and their playfully irregular routine. Tiny as they are, the characters are real in a novelist's sense and as important in their microcosm as any group of human beings in whom the tensions and clashes of per-sonality are illustrated. [Rumer Godden: *The Dolls' House*, London 1947]

**TREVITHIC** is Head Boy and Head Chorister of the

Mr and Mrs Plantagenet with Apple and Tottie; illustration by Tasha Tudor from *The Doll's House*.

choir school from the Ascension Day date of *A Swarm in May*, through the Festival summer of *Words and Music*, the November excitements of *Chorister's Cake* and the New Year epidemics and disruptions of *Cathedral Wednesday*. It is obvious that he has it in him to fulfil his ambition to become a Doctor of Music. It is equally obvious that he is a natural leader. If he spoke to the youngest singing boys 'they felt like newly-made barons for the rest of the day' and his self-confidence is so totally without impertinence that he can tease with impunity soporific Mr Lewis or Dr Sunderland (or even, now and then, Mr Ardent the headmaster). Capable, clever, diplomatic, never apparently at a loss, Trevithic plays a small but important part in *A Swarm in May* and *Chorister's Cake* and retires into the background in the other two books, for a good reason – the adventures in them could hardly have happened if his sensible authority had been exercised on events.

Trevithic is that rare being in children's stories, a likable and believable good character. Perhaps it is the slight edge of his Cornishness, a touch of the alien about him, that keeps him from seeming priggish. His benevolent, firm, sensible rule over his juniors is seen through the eyes of his subjects to be an entirely benign one. [William Mayne: *A Swarm in May*, London 1955; *Choristers' Cake*, 1956; *Cathedral Wednesday*, 1960; *Words and Music*, 1963]

**TYLER, WILKIN** and **SKEE,** the three Coley boys, live in a country district in Georgia. Their father works in a sawmill and they share between them much of the care of the hens, Vivian the surly cow and the routine household chores. It is the time of the Depression and money is short. Fortunately these lively boys are well able to make their own amusements – especially Skee, who has inherited a gift for music from his mother and can find a song for any occasion. His older brothers sometimes find it necessary to put seven-year-old Skee in his place, but the resilient youngster can usually hold his own. Wilkin is spokesman for the trio; he is 'better at talking to people outside the family'. When he wins a prize in his grade at school he refuses to go forward in his worn dungarees and boldly commandeers a pair of trousers from Mr Grayson's scarecrow for the occasion.

Robert Burch spent his own childhood in just such a country community as the one he uses as a setting for his three cheerful young characters and their exploits. Their loyalty to one another, their self-sufficiency and their gift for taking life as it comes, are all clearly shown to be the product of their environment and of their upbringing in a house full of affection and cheerfully accepted discipline. As Robert Burch shows, in spite of the Depression (or perhaps partly because of it) the characters he has created make the most of their circumstances. [Robert Burch: *Tyler, Wilkin and Skee*, New York 1963]

**TYLTYL** and **MYTYL** are the children of a poor woodcutter and his wife who have created such a feeling of love and safety in their cottage that the brother and sister only recognize that they are, in fact, happy children after they have taken a long journey, in a dream, persuaded by the Fairy Berylune to seek the Blue Bird who alone can cure her little daughter's illness.

The journey takes Tyltyl and Mytyl to the past (to the land of Memory) and to the Kingdom of the Future, with intermediate stages in which experiences of Love, Temptation and Death are foreshadowed. The characters in this allegorical play are simple; for instance, the Dog and Cat who accompany the children are, respectively, boisterously loyal and ironically sycophantic. Any subtlety of character would be out of place in such a highly decorated piece, which makes its points through mood and colour rather than by any intellectual argument. So, Tyltyl is an ideally brave, endearing small boy, Mytyl an affectionate child content to depend on her brother for safety and initiative.

This very firm division of role between the sexes would be enough to keep the play out of favour at the present time if it were not already, because of its hectic, sentimental tone, very far from the taste of the day. Regularly performed and greatly loved for at least two decades after its first publication, *The Blue Bird* both as a spectacle and a moral allegory was then superseded by the more relaxed and cheerful (though just as improving) *Peter Pan*, which was later to yield place to the splendidly unimproving *Toad of Toad Hall*. [Maurice Maeterlinck: *The Blue Bird* (1909 France) trans. Alexander Teixeira de Mattos, London 1909]

# U

UGGUG, son of the Sub-Warden of Outland, is the apple of his mother's eye, but though she is conveniently able to ignore his appearance (demonstrably the result of childish greed) and his totally unattractive behaviour, his father does at least try to discipline the child. Unlike Sylvie and Bruno (q.v.), Uggug does not infiltrate the world of everyday but remains in the kingdom of the narrator's cumulative dream of a fairy country where he indulges in vicious practical jokes and acts of mali-cious cruelty. In the second book 'His Imperial Fatness' is, logically, turned into a Porcupine. This thoroughly nasty character is made up of certain elements of beha-viour (cruelty to animals, greed, spitefulness and stu-pidity) which are frequently found in the fiction of yes-terday and not unknown today. [Lewis Carroll, *Sylvie and Bruno*, London, 1889; *Sylvie and Bruno Concluded*, 1893]

UNCLE ANALDAS, an opinionated and irascible

One of Robert Lawson's illustrations of the self-important but lovable Uncle Analdas and friends from *The Tough Winter*.

old rabbit, is left alone when his youngest daughter Mildred marries, and Georgie's mother, another daughter, worries so much about him that she sends Georgie (q.v.) to bring him on an indefinite visit. Georgie is horrified at the flea-ridden state of his uncle's burrow, and perhaps some of his disapproval gets through, for on the way back to Rabbit Hill Analdas grudgingly takes a bath in Deadman's Brook because 'women folks is funny like and particular about some things and your maw is *extra* particular'.

In contrast to his son-in-law's educated speech, Analdas uses a rich local idiom and shows no respect for persons. His judgement of the caretakers who look after the Big House through the winter is pungent; the man is 'a pasty wizendy little thing' and his wife is 'a slop'. He is just as forthright about the Folks, a truly benevolent young couple who own the Big House. They may be 'planting Folks', but when it is reported that the missing Georgie is safe in their house, Uncle Analdas, who loves to prophesy doom, is certain that he is being held as a hostage and will be tortured the moment any of the animals touches the new vegetables. The large box that appears in the garden contains, according to the gloomy old rabbit, guns, traps and poison, nor is he at all repentant when it proves to contain a statue of St Francis which is to preside over feasts spread for the animals through summer and autumn.

Uncle Analdas is hardly a comfortable guest for the rabbit family. All the same, there is something admirable about the stupid, obstinate animal. When matters really become desperate in *The Tough Winter*, Uncle Analdas decides the Folks must be fetched home to help. No doubt long privation has made him a little light-headed, but he commands respect as he stumps off down the road, shrinking from car headlights and mumbling 'Too many dingblasted ramifications' as he tries to remember Father Rabbit's description of the blue-grass country. Vain, self-important, tetchy, Uncle Analdas is the most entertaining of a cast of very entertaining animal characters. [Robert Lawson: *Rabbit Hill*, New York 1944; *The Tough Winter*, 1954]

**UNCLE BEAZLEY** hatches out of a most unusual egg, laid by a hen belonging to the family of twelve-year-old Nate Twitchell, in the small town of Freedom in New Hampshire. Identified as a triceratops by a scientific friend, the huge, good-natured beast, named for Nate's great-uncle, quickly causes a sensation throughout America. Use his hide for suitcases, suggests one unimaginative telephoner; another wants the animal to advertise his petrol station; another brings a tape-recorder to Uncle Beazley – who, however, remains silent.

Meanwhile Nate is happy taking the family pet for walks until cold weather comes and it is decided that he should escort Uncle Beazley to the National Museum in Washington. Unfortunately there are some who object to public money being spent on a useless creature, and during a debate in the House one Senator points out that Uncle Beazley is unAmerican. The threat of death hangs over the animal until Nate, devoted and resourceful as ever, appeals on television for a Dinosaur Food Fund and eventually returns to school, leaving his pet comfortably housed in the Zoo with an adequate endowment for the future.

Emphatically stated nonsense has a charm of its own. The benign character and huge bulk of Uncle Beazley are established with a delicate wit in a story that is not without feeling – principally because it is the boy himself who tells it. This small gem of comic narrative enjoys a wide readership still. A large figure of Uncle Beazley, constructed for the film that was made from the book, was presented to the Smithsonian Institute and now stands on the Mall outside the Museum of Natural History in Washington, to the delight of visiting children. [Oliver Butterworth: *The Enormous Egg*, Boston 1956]

**UNCLE BENNY** becomes an uncle the moment he is born, being the youngest of a large family; his eldest sister, wife of Mr Pye, treats him like one of her own children, while Jerry and Rachel regard him with a mixture of casual affection and respect for his unusual status. Benny's unclehood in fact points up his own engaging small-boy behaviour. Like a good many three-year-olds, Benny sucks his thumb and fondles an old blanket known as Bubbah, whose absence causes him some concern, though he is also anxious to prove his maturity by giving it up; indeed, his efforts to bring about 'the revolution to stop sucking my thumb' on his fourth birthday provide much of the humour in *Pinky Pye*. Benny's vocabulary shows signs of his close companionship with Rachel and Jerry, respectively six and seven years older than he is. 'Not interested' is his substitute for 'Don't want to', more proper to his age.

It seems a natural extension of Benny's special position in the family that he should play a major part in the two books about the Pyes.

In *Ginger Pye* it is Benny who 'finds' Ginger; the dog has heard the squeaking of Benny's push-chair and has broken away from his captors. In *Pinky Pye* Benny's crickets serve to keep alive the pygmy owl shut in the attic which rouses such excitement in the cats. Saddened as he is by the disappearance of his crickets, Benny has worked out an explanation ('I thought they had a plan and was all gathering in a eave to sing, like a choir'); but he is comforted when Rachel explains that the crickets kept a rare bird alive and he decides 'They're dead and he's alive. That's fair, isn't it?' There can be few small boys in fiction whose personalities rise as fresh and emphatic from such small, subtle touches. [Eleanor Estes: *Ginger Pye*, New York 1951; *Pinky Pye*, 1958]

**UNCLE GEORGE,** with a secret career in the Second World War behind him, works as a research scientist and trouble-shooter at two establishments, Fort X, and High Standing in Ashdown Forest, which is conveniently adjacent to Sleepy Hollow, Uncle George's home. Though he is the titular hero of John Pudney's eleven adventure stories, he usually plays an active but blundering second fiddle to the two lively boys, supposedly in their early teens, known as 'Fred and I', who are indistinguishable except that 'I', never identified by name, tells the stories.

The boys are hard put to it to explain Uncle George's work to outsiders, since they hardly understand it themselves. They usually try to escape with some ambiguous phrase like 'Science and Security', while Uncle George himself says 'I'm just a hard-working type – with a touch of genius, of course'. This ebullient character, 'stout, short-tempered, and grey on top', has certain traits which are necessary if the stories are to work at all. Most of the plots concern the theft of top secret aircraft modifications, new-style fuel, experimental hovercraft, scarce minerals and other things of interest to 'foreign powers' from countries that sometimes rejoice in Ruritanian pseudonyms like Cragovinia or Poldavia. In order to forward plots like these Uncle George has to be at the same time a specialist knowledgeable in advanced engineering and physics, given to unexpected experiments with explosives or underwater equipment and, on the other hand, strangely unsuspicious of inquisitive strangers and careless of his own safety and

the security of the secret papers entrusted to him. This dual personality gives 'Fred and I' the chance to play typical boys' parts in the action. A talent for eavesdropping balanced with impetuosity, a respect for Uncle George's ability combined with a natural desire to go it alone – these contradictory traits contribute to the stories, while humour is added in the main by the fact that the boys purport to dislike girls in their adventures but accept them readily as allies when they discover, as they invariably do, the virtues of female common sense and intuition. Uncle George's cook-housekeeper Emily and his gardener-handyman Mr Mattock also supply comic relief in those adventures which take place in or around Sleepy Hollow. If there is an element of parody in these formula stories, it is kept well under control and not allowed to interfere with the course of predictable but intricate and excellently written tales into which the characters fit very plausibly and usefully. [John Pudney: *Saturday Adventure*, London 1950; *Sunday Adventure*, 1951; *Monday Adventure*, 1952; *Tuesday Adventure*, 1953; *Wednesday Adventure*, 1954; *Thursday Adventure*, 1955; *Friday Adventure*, 1956; *Spring Adventure*, 1961; *Summer Adventure*, 1962; *Autumn Adventure*, 1964; *Winter Adventure*, 1965]

**UNCLE REMUS** *see* BRER RABBIT

**VELVETEEN RABBIT** (the) is a fine toy to find in a Christmas stocking, with his real thread whiskers and spotted brown and white coat and his ears 'lined with pink sateen', but he is quickly forgotten by the Boy, and being shy and diffident, he is snubbed by other, superior toys. Only the Skin Horse is friendly enough to explain that for a toy to be Real does not mean it is elaborate but that it has been loved by a child for a long time. When the Boy suddenly begins to play with the rabbit again and is heard to insist 'He isn't a toy. He's REAL!', the toy feels proud in spite of being worn and old. He remains confident of his special value, until the terrible moment when he is thrown in a sack with other toys, to be burnt because of the Boy's infectious illness. But

The Velveteen Rabbit ; illustration by William Nicholson.

the fairy who takes care of 'all the playthings that children have loved' turns him into a real rabbit, and he has the best of both worlds, for now he can leap and run and he can watch the Boy, who 'never knew that it really was his own Bunny, come back to look at the child who had first helped him to be Real'.

If the Velveteen Rabbit has personality, it is due rather to William Nicholson's presentation of him in line and crayon than to the somewhat mawkish tone of his conversation with the Skin Horse and the Wild Rabbits. The overt moral of the story has in the past commended it to many adults (it has even been used as text for a sermon) but the subject of love, loyalty and friendship is more indirectly and successfully canvassed in that masterpiece of toy adventure, *Poor Cecco* (q.v.). [Margery Williams (afterwards Bianco): *The Velveteen Rabbit*, New York 1922]

**VICTORIA NORTH** goes away to boarding school when she is eight and is not at all sure that she likes it, but Martha Sherman changes her mind for her. Martha is as dark as Victoria is fair, as positive as Victoria is timid and unassertive. Their friendship is signalized by the secret words they invent (ankendosh for mean or disgusting; leebossa, a word of praise; ick-enspick, Martha's favourite way of decrying any trace of sentiment).

Martha's wild ideas and impetuous behaviour soon ease Victoria's home-sickness and Victoria, for her part, though she is often alarmed by the extent of Martha's mischief, falls in with most of her plans cheerfully. Although to their school-fellows it might seem that Martha is the dominant partner in the duo, in fact Victoria's more submissive and more sensible behaviour does have its effect on that prickly child Martha, who fends off emotion as surely as she needs it. The characters of the two little girls are planned so that the behaviour of each of them will throw light on the other as well as offering a perceptive example of how friendship works. [Ursula Nordstrom: *The Secret Language*, New York 1960]

**VIOLET, SLINGSBY, GUY** and **LIONEL**, like that 'very energetic and frisky old cove' Edward Lear, who created them, 'all thought they should like to see the world,' so off they set in a blue boat with green spots, taking 'a small Cat to steer and look after the boat,

Violet, Slingsby, Guy and Lionel return from seeing the world on an elderly rhinoceros; Arnold Lobel's illustration for Edward Lear's *The Story of the Four Little Children Who Went Round the World*.

besides an elderly Quangle-Wangle, who had to cook the dinner and make the tea; for which purposes they took a large kettle. Violet, as the only girl, and the eldest at that, is inclined to be bossy with her brothers, but she has a kind nature; at one stage of the journey she 'most amiably knitted a small woollen frock' for several of the fishes which they had not already eaten, and still more skilfully untangles the pink worsted with which certain Crabs and Crawfish are attempting to make Mittens, finally finishing the job beautifully for them. With equally good manners (though with no special

skill) Slingsby, Guy and Lionel converse elegantly with a commune of Happy Blue-Bottle Flies, observe the Co-operative Cauliflower and organize their return home (after their boat has been chewed up by an 'enormous Seeze Pyder') on an elderly Rhinoceros who happens to pass by. Travellers as well-educated, imperturbable and resourceful could only have come from the pen of a master-traveller. [Edward Lear: *The Story of the Four Little Children Who Went Round the World*, ill. S. Mark, New York and London 1970 (from *Nonsense Songs and Stories*, London 1871)]

**WAHB**, one of four cubs born at one time to a Silvertip grizzly bear in a wild district near the Yellowstone Park, begins his education in the normal way by attending to his mother's example. Then she and the other cubs are shot and Wahb, by instinct getting as far from the dread spot as he can, begins a long, lonely, friendless life. With no parent to imitate, he has to learn by experience, often painfully. He has always been 'a gloomy little Bear; and the string of misfortunes that come on him just as his mind is forming make him more than ever sullen and morose'. With no mate, his energy goes into defending a territory that grows ever wider as he ranges further in search of food. He learns to open traps, but not without damage to his feet; as he grows old he is plagued by rheumatism, till by chance he finds a pool of medicinal water that helps his pain. His last days are made miserable through a bitter irony. A small roach-back bear, intruding into the Meteetse valley, uses trickery to place his scratches so high on prominent trees that the old bear, dispirited by pain, believes he is being followed by a giant rival and retreats from the part of his range where he can find most comfort. Finally weariness overcomes him and he lies down to die in a gulch filled with deadly gases which seems to offer a peace which for once does not have to be won by fighting.

Perhaps no writer since Ernest Thompson Seton has

Wahb, the orphaned grizzly bear, illustrated by the author, Ernest Thompson Seton.

worked out such a satisfactory way to individualize an animal. The conclusions Wahb comes to are expressed naturally in human terms that do nothing to distort their animal origin. Wahb's philosophy is 'for everyone knows that a good nose is better than eyes and ears together'; the author's follows logically: 'man has sold the birthright of his nose for the privilege of living in towns'. It is because Ernest Thompson Seton is so scrupulous in attributing nothing to his hero that would be inconsistent with the behaviour of a grizzly bear that he earns the right to allow Wahb the personal pronoun rather than the neuter, to translate the whimpers of the solitary bear cub into human words ('"Mother! Mother! Oh, Mother, where are you?" for he was cold and hungry, and had such a pain in his foot'). Above all, he earns the right to conclude his story with an extended prose-poem in which, as the weary, sick old bear succumbs willingly to the relaxing gases of Death Gulch, all the author's admiration for wild life, all his knowledge and emotional commitment, are blended in a magnificent climax. [Ernest Thompson Seton: *The Biography of a Grizzly*, New York 1899]

**WALLYPUG OF WHY** (the) is 'a meek-looking little creature' whose royal clothes fit very ill and who is

Girlie assisting the inept Wallypug, the rejected ruler of the kingdom of Why; illustration by Harry Furniss.

treated with disrespect by his subjects, whom he is required to address as 'Your Majesty'. When Girlie finds her way to the kingdom of Why to ask what seems a simple question, her sympathy is engaged at once for the ill-used monarch and she rejoices when, returning with the Wallypug from a very odd sojourn by the sea, she sees him assert himself at last when he finds that his tyrannous Doctor-in-Law has taxed 'getting up' so severely that whole populations have taken to their beds.

The genuine rule of the Wallypug does not last long. He is soon dominated by a cantankerous sister-in-law and is told 'a King is merely an ornament to the State'; being forbidden to abdicate, he wanders off into a fog. He appears for the last time on the Moon where, bowing to the inevitable, he forms himself into a limited company with the Doctor-in-Law as Managing Director.

In spite of the author's fondness for 'the simple-natured, good-hearted little fellow', it is unlikely that the enormous popularity the Wallypug enjoyed seventy years ago could ever be revived. Present-day readers have little patience with the pathetic and inept, and the fashion for puns and nonsense that produced so many imitations of *Alice* (among which the Wallypug books were most highly regarded) has taken new directions. All things considered, it seems best to leave the Wallypug wandering wistfully westward in the fog, to be remembered only by critics in nostalgic mood. [G. E. Farrow: *The Wallypug of Why*, London 1895; *Adventures in Wallypug Land*, 1898; *The Wallypug in London*, 1898; *In Search of the Wallypug*, 1903; *The Wallypug in Fogland*, 1903; *The Wallypug in the Moon*, 1905]

**WALTER THE EARL** in his history, 'Glorious True Facts in the History of the Minnipins from the Beginning to the Year of Gammage 880', told how the Small Ones were led to the Land Between the Mountains by the Great Gammage, escaping their enemies the Mushrooms or Hairless Ones, to live for eight hundred peaceful years in the valley of the Watercress River. In the year 880 the Earl was still engaged in the search for documents to add to his history, in spite of his reputation as a 'dry old bore'. Certainly he had little status compared with the Periods, a family descended from Fooley the Balloonist, who was said to have ventured outside the valley and whose precious treasures included a family tree (identified as a painting) and a picture of a house and a tree (known as the Family Tree). There came a morning, however, when the traditional authority of the Periods was challenged.

Walter the Earl was not the only inhabitant of the village who was unusual. Curley Green made what she called 'pictures' and Gummy composed nonsense rhyme; Muggles was 'a candy maker, which was a good steady sort of thing to be,' but her house was untidy and she was an incorrigible hoarder. The villagers worried about the nonconformity of the four, and were

The Mushrooms or Hairless Ones, dreaded
enemies of the Minnipins; illustration by Erik
Blegvad.

*Below*. Lonely Crustabread, Glocken, Scumble,
Gam Lutie and Silkie setting out from their
flooded village; Imero Gobbato's illustration from
*The Whisper of Glocken*.

still more alarmed when Walter the Earl found in his garden a hoard of weapons, cloaks, swords and trumpets, all hidden in the year of Gammage 480 to protect them from the mayor of the time, who was not interested in 'the dead past'. It was a pity that the mayor of four hundred years later was not interested either, but was far more concerned to stop Curley Green and the others from painting their front doors in bright colours instead of in the regulation green. Sent into exile for fear they might influence others, the rebels were looked at in a different light when they detected the first signs of an invasion of Mushrooms and were foremost in the struggle to repel them.

Some time later, after a flood, the river changed course and four new heroes, from another village, left the valley to investigate and save its fertility. Lonely Crustabread, Glocken and Scumble were content to follow the orders of two more dominating figures – Gam Lutie, whose family had always been learned in medicine, and the domineering Silky. In spite of minor dissensions, and much danger in the Desert Outside, the new heroes brought peace to the valley and stability to the river.

Glocken had always hoped to be a great hero, and when he actually met the famous leaders of the battle against the Mushrooms he was almost disappointed to find them just folk like himself. Even Walter the Earl, who came, he thought, nearest to being a hero, was spoiled by his shabby cloak and his terrible conceit and 'his regal tones became comic when the talk ran on simple subjects'. In fact Glocken learned, as the rest of the Minnipins had learned, that people are all ordinary and all unique – a lesson that is communicated in these two whimsical, ironic fantasies through the comic, pungent, idiosyncratic speech of the inhabitants of a fascinating miniature world. [Carol Kendall: *The Minnipins*, New York 1959; *The Whisper of Glocken*, 1965]

**WHITE FANG** is given his name by Grey Beaver, a North Canadian Indian who is amused by the way the wolf-cub instinctively bares his teeth when one of the creatures whom he recognizes as enemies bends to touch him. In fact, the cub is not wholly wolf, for Grey Beaver recognizes his mother as his own Kiche, half-dog, half-wolf, who had joined the wolf pack in a time of famine. So the cub and his mother are taken to the

Indian camp and there White Fang learns to hold his own against rivals and to pull a sledge; but his obedience to his master is forced, his attachment a matter of discipline and habit, not of love.

Life in the Indian camp and on the trail is hard but there is worse in store for White Fang when the Indian, bamboozled by drink, sells him to Beauty Smith, a man whose brutality is remarkable even in the North-West in the lawless days of the Klondyke gold rushes. Reducing White Fang to submission with club and boots, Beauty soon has a raging fiend on his hands. He quickly turns this to his advantage by exhibiting White Fang as the Fighting Wolf and amassing money from bets as he defeats one after another the champion dogs pitted against him. Finally it seems that White Fang has met his match in a bulldog called Cherokee but at a crucial moment of the fight Weedon Scott, a mining expert, with his musher Matt, breaks up the fight and forces Beauty to sell the shockingly wounded White Fang to him. He has bought a savage animal: through patience, determination and affection he revives the instinct of a dog, so long dormant. Still indomitable, aloof and capable of savage behaviour, but loyal and obedient to the man who has saved him, White Fang ends his days as a beloved member of his master's Californian home.

*White Fang* remains a classic study of a human–animal relationship. Right from the start, in what is still one of the best descriptions of a new-born animal testing and developing its senses and instincts, White Fang is shown as an animal, not as a human in an animal skin. Jack London insists that the dog was not 'given to thinking'; his frequent use of the verb 'to urge' seems to anticipate the biological term 'drive'. The idea that White Fang regards men as gods and wonder-workers is meant to epitomize the obedience and submission on the one hand, the mental and physical control on the other, which are the basis equally of the bond between man and domestic dog, and between the leader and subordinates in a wolf-pack. In the same way the sheer enjoyment of his own ferocity which keeps White Fang alive in the months of his imprisonment with Beauty Smith is seen as the result of a cubhood cut short and a life without affection or trust. Even the very explicit description of the 'love-master's' mastery of White Fang and his surrender is disciplined by natural laws; White Fang is torn between the instinct of a wolf to avoid men and a dog's inborn desire for contact and affection. Loyal, dignified, indomitable, White Fang is one of the best known and the most impressive of all animal characters in fiction. [Jack London: *White Fang*, New York 1905]

**WHITE WITCH** (the) takes more than one form and plays more than one part in the stories of Narnia. The remark of a dwarf (in *The Silver Chair*) that 'those Northern Witches always mean the same thing, but in every age they have a different plan for getting it' may give us licence to suppose that C. S. Lewis means the White Witch, the enchantress of *The Silver Chair* and the tempestuous Queen Jadis in *The Magician's Nephew* to be three aspects of one truth.

Each manifestation of the witch is in fact derived from a different source. For the White Witch of *The Lion, the Witch and the Wardrobe*, Lewis perhaps drew on George Macdonald's *Phantastes*, on *The Snow Queen* and on *Sir Gawain and the Green Knight*; she is by far the most compelling of his evil creatures, for the association of cold with evil goes very deep in Western thought, and the assemblage of images, descriptive details and explicit statements in the book make it easy to believe that this woman could have captured the allegiance of Edmund Pevensie (q.v.), freezing his heart as Kay's is frozen in Hans Andersen's story and using him to help her to conquer Narnia by keeping the land winterbound for ever.

The White Witch is a figure born of tradition, ruler over 'the Ghouls, and the Boggles, the Ogres and the Minotaurs ... the Cruels, the Hags, the Spectres, and the people of the Toadstools'; it is not through religious belief but through acceptance of fairy tale convention that we realize that her lust for power is evil while Aslan's assumption of power is good. When in *Prince Caspian* the dwarf Nikabrik tries to defend her murder of Aslan and to assert that her rule had been beneficial for his race, he suffers death, and this is recognized to be inevitable.

The literary sources that help to establish the character of the enchantress in *The Silver Chair* seem mainly Spenserian. When Prince Rilian (q.v.) impetuously sets out to seek and slay the serpent which has killed his mother, he is ensnared by the Queen of Underland, a beautiful woman whom he treats with devotion as 'a nosegay of all virtues, as truth, mercy, constancy, gentleness, courage, and the rest'. Jill Pole and Eustace Scrubb (q.v.), have the courage to watch Rilian in his frenzy and to believe him when, momentarily sane, he explains how he has been enchanted. But the Witch's spell is powerful, depending on incantation and sweet smells, and her insistence that 'There is no Narnia, no Overworld, no sky, no sun, no Aslan' almost defeats the humans. Not Puddleglum (q.v.), however. That staunch realist makes the only answer that can defeat the power of evil persuasion. Her world is a poor one, he tells her; if they *have* only imagined Aslan's world, they will believe in it all the same. His oblique defence of the good has its effect. The Lady melts and changes into a huge green serpent that is susceptible of death.

With *The Magician's Nephew* we move to a story that surely harks back to Edith Nesbit, for Queen Jadis, who

Pooh and Piglet tracking a 'heffalump'; an illustration by E. H. Shepard for *Winnie the Pooh*.

"Now!" thought the cunning Zephir,
"one more little effort and the time will be ripe.
My plan is a good one.
Tomorrow we will be far away."
Picking up his violin,
he played polkas and waltzes without a stop.
Polomoche and the Gogottes,
carried away by the music,
jumped about, turning and pirouetting.

Edmund under the spell of
the beautiful and evil White
Witch; illustration by
Pauline Baynes in *The Lion,
the Witch and the Wardrobe*.

had brought about the destruction of her kingdom of Charn in order to defeat her sister and rival, is essentially a political witch. When Digory by striking the bell in the deserted hall brings the stone Jadis to life, and she makes her dramatic and alarming appearance in the comfortable London of gaslight and hansom cabs, her disregard for human dignity shows her totalitarian attitude to life. Like the other two witches, Jadis is associated with folk lore, myth, and religious belief. When Aslan sends Digory to pick an apple from a distant orchard the Witch tries to tempt Digory to eat the fruit and acquire eternal youth. He obeys Aslan's

An illustration from *Babar's Friend Zephir*, written and illustrated by Jean de Brunhoff.

orders (obedience being the paramount virtue of the stories) and the Witch has to flee 'into the North of the world', where she will grow 'stronger in dark Magic' but will be kept out of Narnia so long as the tree flourishes, 'for its smell, which is joy and life and health to you, is death and horror and despair to her'. This is solemn stuff, but her character is at its most powerful when she is challenging the human world and demanding total government of it.

In fact, the witches in the Narnia books, while logically the opposite of Aslan, never really fit into their Christian aspect. Paradise and the Tree of the Knowledge of Good and Evil, the Crucifixion and Resurrection, the Day of Judgement – all these are embodied in the story, imagistically or in narrative, not concealed by the decoration of literary allusion. The witches never in any sense attain the stature of Satan. They are figures from legend and fairy tale, taken almost at second hand from some of the writers who influenced C. S. Lewis most strongly. [C. S. Lewis: *The Lion, the Witch and the Wardrobe*, London 1950; *Prince Caspian*, 1951; *The Silver Chair*, 1953; *The Magician's Nephew*, 1955]

**WILBUR**, the smallest and weakest pig born on Mr Arable's farm one spring night, is given a reprieve when eight-year-old Fern (q.v.) pleads for him; although Fern visits him almost every day in his pen in her Uncle Zuckerman's big barn, there comes a time when life seems to the pig very dull. 'I'm less than two months old. I'm tired of living' he announces and, encouraged by the goose, he pushes past a loose board and enjoys a few hours of freedom in the yard.

The next lack the emotional Wilbur feels is for love – for a friend who will be near him in good and bad weather – and though neither the self-centred rat Templeton nor the self-sufficient gander is prepared to satisfy his needs, a friend does appear, high up in the doorway. Charlotte (q.v.) the grey spider is a friend indeed to Wilbur, for though at first he wonders how he can like anyone who is, on her own showing, so 'fierce, brutal, scheming, bloodthirsty', common sense shows him that she is only living according to her nature. He comes to value Charlotte's companionable, wise talk and finally to acknowledge a very large debt to her, for with her skill she is able to save him by spinning flattering adjectives about him into her web. And when the pig has to accept that her life has come to an end, he is able to serve her memory by bringing back to the barn, from the Country Fair, the egg-sac that was Charlotte's dying achievement; and so 'her children and grand-children and great-grand-children, year after year,' live in the doorway, dearly loved by Wilbur, though he never forgets his first friend.

It is a triumph to have given Wilbur a personality, speech, human aspirations and moods without being facetious or sentimental. His youthful bumptiousness, his naïveté, his amiable dependence on others, may be said to be deduced from the behaviour and the appearance of a piglet; Wilbur grown-up is not described but merely understood. His absurd attempt to prove he can emulate Charlotte by throwing himself off the manure heap with a rope attached to him (but not to anything else); his pathetic and affronted reaction to the news that he is destined to be killed; his efforts to justify the word 'radiant' used by Charlotte by blinking his long eyelashes and doing 'a back flip with a half twist' – these and other actions show Wilbur as truly 'terrific', 'radiant' and 'humble'. [E. B. White: *Charlotte's Web*, New York 1952]

**WILD JACK** *see* ROBIN HOOD

**WILLIAM BROWN** lives in a village which, without his continual presence, might have been very peaceful. His attitude to his family is not uncommon among small boys ('The sort of things I want to do they don't want me to do an' the sort of things I don't want to do they want me to do') but his capacity for producing chaos is as remarkable as the extent of his good intentions. Time and again William is surprised to find that his well-meaning efforts to assist his brother Robert in his latest infatuation, to give clear directions to a stranger, to find customers for a new shop or saleable goods for a jumble sale, end in embarrassment for everyone and retribution for him. His approach to life is suggested in the rules he draws up for one of his many secret societies – 'One adventure to be done each week. As dangerous as possible. Deadly weapons may be used but axshul murder not allowed.'

William made his first appearance in a short story, 'The Outlaws', published in 1917 in *Home Magazine*, together with his admiring associates impulsive Ginger, cheerful Douglas and bookish Henry. Their difficulties with a baby, kidnapped with the best motives and offered cold boiled potatoes to eat, set the future pattern. All the stories have a symmetrical structure, with a main plot stated and developed, supported by sub-plots and moving towards a climax in which William's interpretation of events is bound to differ from everyone else's. No attempt to change him has ever succeeded. The cover of a reprint of 1972 shows him without his striped cap and his short-pants suit, looking smooth, tidy and normal in jeans and an anorak, but this is not the real William, not the goggle-eyed, knowing hooligan who has only two facial expressions – a broad grin when things are going right and a 'look of wooden imbecility' in moments of crisis. It would never have done to change William – or, for that matter, the lisping, pushing damsel Violet Elizabeth Bott or stage-struck Ethel or amorous Robert. Richmal Crompton made certain concessions to time. William's idiom was brought up to date now and then and certain allusions gave some indicatin of changing society, though most of William's exploits seem, even in later years, to be more in the mood of *Holiday House* than of today. [Richmal Crompton: *Just William*, London 1922; *More William*, 1922; *William Again*, 1923; and many other titles, ending with *William the Lawless*, 1970]

**WILLIAM THE DRAGON** is found behind a hedge in the garden where Lady Wilmount is peacefully reading – or, rather, the 'enormous green speckled egg' is found, by Jemima the dairymaid, in the nest of Henrietta the hen. Her ladyship takes a risk in deciding to try to incubate the egg but the little dragon who hatches out proved to be an ideal pet, even if he does object to having his portrait painted in a specially tailored coat from Harrod's.

William is conceived, described and drawn by a girl of eleven whose words show more than a touch of the observant naïveté that made *The Young Visiters* so uniquely funny. The presence of a harmless but skittish dragon in a taxi, on the beach, in the Church Hall, provides

So she spent the whole day in her library looking at books on dragons.

She even read what Darwin said about dragons and evolution. But it was no good . . .

Lady Wilmount and her ideal pet, William the Dragon, illustrated by the eleven-year-old author, Polly Donnison.

exactly the right touch of fantasy in a book that gives a devastating and demure picture of a much maligned and much satirized corner of society. [Polly Donnison: *William the Dragon*, London 1972]

**WILLIAM WATERMAN SHERMAN**, who had been 'teaching arithmetic at a school for boys in San Francisco for forty years', suddenly decided on a change and took off in a well-provisioned balloon, only to be picked up in the Atlantic three weeks later, 'half starved and exhausted, clinging to the debris of twenty deflated balloons'. His explanation of this strange occurrence, was as exciting as the fact that calculations showed he had beaten Phineas Fogg's record circumnavigation of the world. Thrown upon the volcanic island of Krakatoa, the Professor had met an unknown colony of Americans, protected from the outside world by the dangerous movement of the island, enjoying a life of elegant luxury based on an inexhaustible diamond mine, a colony with its own intriguing history and its own ineffable scorn of the values of the outside world. He was interested to observe the inventive genius of the colonists and especially the ingenuity of their Giant Balloon–Life-Raft, which proved invaluable when the volcano finally destroyed the island and they made a communal escape.

The Professor, spare, suave and self-centred, easily holds together the various threads in this disarming tall story, with its parody, its satire on American institutions and attitudes and its fantasy world, conceived (like the Oz books) largely in terms of mechanical devices. With the calm certainty of a teacher and the confidence of wealth (for a pair of 'diamond cuff-links made simply of four diamonds the size of lima beans' provide assurance for the future), the Professor takes the reader all the way with him. [W. Pène du Bois: *The Twenty-One Balloons*, New York 1947]

**WILLIE**, who is four years old, is whole-hearted about everything he does. He practises standing on his head so often that he is able to hand out tickets at the circus tent while supporting himself on one hand. Just as efficiently he practises gestures which he associates with the police force, his new goal. He annoys his baby sister by treating her as traffic, but after he has shown initiative over a fire in the Corner Shop, he switches his ambitions again and practises fire-fighting with the garden hose and his father's ladder. The unexpected chance to do a real bit of fireman's rescue work for Miss Jones the school-teacher leads to his last and most unexpected ambition – to go to school and learn enough to qualify for one or other of his chosen roles in life.

Willie comes to life in three short, simple tales by virtue of Dorothy Clewes's humorous, telling details of his speech. He lives, too, through Ardizzone's sympathetic representation of a small boy who, like his own

One of Edward Ardizzone's delightful illustrations of Upside-down Willie handing out tickets at the circus.

Little Tim, can hardly wait to usurp the place of the grown-ups. [Dorothy Clewes, ill. Edward Ardizzone: *Upside-down Willie*, London 1968; *Special Branch Willie*, 1969; *Fire Brigade Willie*, 1970]

**WILLIE WONKA** *see* CHARLIE BUCKET

**WINNIE-THE-POOH** began as Edward Bear, a teddy bear belonging to A. A. Milne's small son Christopher which made an occasional appearance in the humorous domestic poems published in *Punch* from 1924 onwards. His was a bumbling, loving personality which owed as much to the child's imagination as to the father's invention. Of all the characters in the two

books of stories, Pooh's shows this dual origin most plainly. Piglet's diffidence, his tremulous courage, suggest a mainly adult personalization, and certainly Eeyore's alarmingly gloomy nature, bitterly self-deprecating comments and the embarrassingly incoherent orations he occasionally delivers are not characteristics that a child would claim for a toy, without some prompting.

The witty definitions of character offered in one of the mock-serious papers of *The Pooh Perplex* point obliquely to the careful definition of some of the characters – for instance, the equating of Rabbit with 'the

Four of Ernest Shepard's famous and much-loved illustrations of A. A. Milne's stories: (*below*) Christopher Robin, Winnie the Pooh and Piglet watching Eeyore enter his new house 'looking as comfy as anything'; (*bottom*) Christopher Robin, with Rabbit, Pooh, Piglet, Kanga, Roo and Owl setting out on their 'expotition' to the North Pole; (*overleaf left*) Pooh finds Eeyore's tail being used as 'Wol's' bell pull; (*overleaf right*) Tigger's rescue from his tree-climbing adventure.

PLEZ CNOKE
iF AN RNSR
IS NOT REQID

capitalist manager par excellence' – but this kind of satire will not do for Pooh. He can survive even being described (in another of the satirical pieces) as 'the Orphic deity with seasonal-sacrificial-redemptive crop-growing characteristics.'

It is significant that a book satirizing the more pedantic types of scholarly writing should use the Pooh books as a starting-point. Pooh and his friends are as well-known as the characters in *Alice* or *The Wind in the Willows*, and rightly, for they have been created in an affectionate partnership and presented with brilliant technical skill. Through Ernest Shepard's sympathetic drawings we can see what Pooh and Kanga and Tigger and the rest looked like; through their small adventures (planning to trap a Heffalump, looking for the North Pole, playing Poohsticks) we see how they dealt with their daily life; but in their conversations we discover

them most surely – in Roo's crushing maternal asides, in Eeyore's irony, in Piglet's anxious questioning and, above all, in the trustful exchanges between the boy and his bear. [A. A. Milne: *Winnie-the-Pooh*, London 1926; *The House at Pooh Corner*, 1928]

**WIZARD OF OZ** *see* DOROTHY GALE

**WOMBLES** (the) live in an extensive burrow on Wimbledon Common, where their lives are usefully spent in tidying up after the wasteful Londoners up above. As a by-product of their symbiotic existence, the bear-like creatures not only vary their vegetarian diet with picnic left-overs, but also enjoy many of the benefits of modern civilization, for Tobermory, a gifted engineer, directs the repair or conversion of all the broken umbrellas, rusty stoves and decaying mattresses salvaged by his fellow Wombles. The busy, orderly community is under the benevolent rule of Great-Uncle Bulgaria, who is apt to

The Wombles of Wimbledon Common: Tobermory and Great-Uncle Bulgaria, the puppets created by Ivor Wood, for the televised version of the book. *Above right.* Womble family outing, illustrated by Margaret Gordon.

ramble a bit (or so the young Wombles say) when he recalls his Victorian childhood, but whose shrewd old eyes, twinkling behind his spectacles, see more than is often realized.

Great-Uncle Bulgaria and Tobermory, with Madame Cholet the inspired cook and Miss Adelaide, who rules the Womblegarten, are the respected elders of the family, setting standards and encouraging talent among the younger ones. Among these, Bungo is in some ways the most prominent. We meet him when he is just old enough to start work and is privileged to choose his own name from the great Atlas kept by Great-Uncle Bulgaria (who does not scruple to point out to Bungo that his name, chosen at random rather than with discrimination, is somewhat ridiculous). Certainly Orinoco is a more dignified name, but the stout Womble who bears it thinks of little but food and the forty winks which settle his digestion and spare him the exertions of rubbish-collecting.

Meanwhile quieter Wombles contribute to the comfort of the burrow and the success of the Womble projects. The massive Tomsk, physically active and mentally slow, as Night-Watch Womble keeps the door and checks his comrades in and out of the burrow. Wellington, youngest of the working Wombles, is far more diffident than he needs to be: his scientific discoveries include a chemical mix that will dissolve plastic and a walkie-talkie made of tins. To these characters must be added some who enter the stories briefly but forcefully – Yellowstone Womble, for instance, with his transatlantic confidence; Cairngorm Womble, known throughout the Highlands as the MacWomble the Terrible; and comrade Omsk, whose conspiratorial behaviour puzzles the Wombles as much as their democratic organization puzzles him.

The light-hearted introduction of the Womble personalities and the pertinent details of their domestic economy have gradually given way to a more serious, even didactic note, but from the start the stories have always included a good deal of satirical comment on human activities. Litter preoccupies the Wombles exclusively in the first book; in *The Wandering Wombles*

container lorries thundering across the Common cause landslides in the burrow; established in Hyde Park (in *The Wombles at Work*) they energetically promote Womble Conservation Year by trying to purify the Serpentine and to remove the detritus of a Pop Festival; on this last occasion the suggestible Bungo has a fortunately brief interlude as a hippy, wearing beads and crooning. The lesson of the books is as plain as it is joyously funny in expression.

The Wombles are drawn firmly, each with a particular, undeviating character. This has helped to establish them as puppets in television films and on the stage in pantomime; but a good deal has been lost in the process. When dialogue is cut to fit a ten-minute episode or exaggerated to make the necessary impact on a theatre audience, there can be none of the gradual realization of character through speech and action which deepens the pleasure of reading. When the cult of the Wombles has given place to the cult of some new fantasy character, the rotund little creatures will perhaps be appreciated once more as subtle comic inventions. [Elisabeth Beresford. ill. Margaret Gordon: *The Wombles*, London 1968; ill. Margaret Gordon from Ivor Wood's puppets: *The Wandering Wombles*, 1970; *The Wombles at Work*, 1973; ill. Ivor Wood: *The Invisible Womble, and other stories*, 1973; *The Wombles in Danger*, 1973]

**WORZEL GUMMIDGE**, the Scarecrow of Scatterbrook, makes his rustling way into the sitting-room at the farm, to the astonishment of Susan, who is staying there with her brother John. They have already seen the scarecrow in Ten-acre Field, and Susan was certain then that she had seen it move, but they were so wet and miserable in the rain that John borrowed the umbrella that stuck out from the scarecrow's arm. It seems perfectly natural to her now that the scarecrow should come for his umbrella, and she is too much intrigued by the robin that flies out of his pocket (and, as the grinning Gummidge explains, is used as his handkerchief) to be at all alarmed at seeing a turnip-head take on something of the look of human features.

Susan and John soon become firm friends of Gummidge and in due course they are introduced to some of his friends – among them the melancholy Hannah Harrow, who suffers from mice in her straw; cheerful little Earthy Mangold, Gummidge's long-suffering wife; the sturdy, much-travelled ship's figurehead, Saucy Nancy; and Upsidaisy, who has an appetite for education.

Worzel Gummidge has an adventurous spirit and has no objection to being seen by humans, for he believes he is equal to any situation. His occasional attempts to act the handyman are more destructive than useful; when he is mistaken for Lady Piddingfold, who has consented to open a village fête, he determinedly closes it instead; his days as a circus performer and as proprietor of a restaurant are few but eventful. When he is suffering from wounded vanity he resorts to his particular talent –

WORZEL GUMMIDGE
Barbara Euphan Todd

ONE SHILLING AND SIXPENCE

A PUFFIN STORY BOOK

Jacket designed by Elizabeth Allridge for a 1941 edition of *Worzel Gummidge*.

the sulks; as easily as he swings his broom-handle legs into action and smooths the protuberances of his vegetable features, so, just as easily, he retreats into immobility until his detractors and victims have given up the search. Gummidge's chief butt is Mrs Bloomsbury-Barton, whose self-importance and stupidity are usefully shown up by his sub-malicious forays into her life.

The scarecrow and his friends are at their best in their natural surroundings; though circus and café provide new and amusing settings for Gummidge's anarchic behaviour, his character rises obviously out of the countryside, like his homely, dialectal speech. He is one of scores of fantasy-characters which obliquely correct human folly, besides giving children, in their over-organized lives, a chance to enjoy a vicarious freedom. [Barbara Euphan Todd: *Worzel Gummidge*, London 1936; *Worzel Gummidge Again*, 1937; *More about Worzel Gummidge*, 1938; *Worzel Gummidge and Saucy Nancy*, 1947; *Worzel Gummidge Takes a Holiday*, 1949; *Earthy Mangold and Worzel Gummidge*, 1954; *Worzel Gummidge and the Railway Scarecrows*, 1955; *Worzel Gummidge at the Circus*, 1956; *Worzel Gummidge and the Treasure Ship*, 1958; *Detective Worzel Gummidge*, 1963]

**ZEELY** helps her father Nathan Tayler with his hogs but eleven-year-old Elizabeth is sure she is a queen because of her immensely tall figure, her proud beautiful face and her colour, 'as deeply dark as a pole of Ceylon ebony'; besides, she has seen pictures in a magazine of Watusi women of royal blood, whom Zeely resembles closely. Elizabeth, who is on a visit to her uncle with her younger brother John, is a fanciful child who likes to add her own colour to everyday life. She feels cheated when she sees Zeely carrying heavy buckets of pig-swill or coping with a sow collapsed in the heat of the South.

Zeely with the eleven-year-old Elizabeth; illustration by Symeon Shimin.

Learning that the rumour of her royal birth is all round the village, Zeely explains to the child that her ancestry may be distinguished and ancient but that it is lost in the past and that she has learned, as Elizabeth must learn, to 'hold fast to reality' while keeping 'her fine way of dreaming'.

In this short, moving, subtle book Virginia Hamilton has drawn Zeely as an individual leading an ordinary life, tired of being conspicuous for her height and often lonely, since she does not 'have much time for friends'. There is nothing contradictory between this picture of Zeely and the fantasy built round her by Elizabeth. Zeely provides a way for the author to say something important about her social condition as well as about the innocent illusions and ardent affections of a child. [Virginia Hamilton: *Zeely*, New York 1967]

**ZEPHIR** the monkey is given by Babar, King of the Elephants (q.v.), to the Old Lady who befriended him in his youth and who tended the wounded after the war with the rhinoceroses. He goes to school with Babar's cousin Arthur and the three royal children and falls in and out of trouble – as, for instance, when (in *Babar the King*) he tries to taste the vanilla cream in the palace kitchen and is fished out by the tail by the furious head cook. But Zephir is as good-hearted as he is inquisitive. He watches anxiously by the Old Lady's bedside when she is seriously ill with snake-bite and his long arm comes in useful when little Flora swallows her rattle. He has his own private adventure when he joins the search for the missing Princess Isabel, who has been kidnapped by the monster Polomoche. Polomoche and his band are bored rather than wicked, and when Zephir has traced Isabel to her rocky prison, he amuses the monsters with tricks and stories and finally persuades them to dance, after which they fall exhausted into sleep and he and Isabel escape. In traditional fashion, General Huc promises Zephir Isabel's hand in marriage but, in the practical way of the Babar books, it is made clear that he will have to wait till he is older before he claims his bride. Meanwhile, the little monkey fulfils a useful function by supplying, with his agile form and cheerful expression, a comic contrast to the deliberate dignity of the elephants. [Jean de Brunhoff: *Babar's Friend Zephir* (1936 France), London 1937]

**ZOZO** *see* CURIOUS GEORGE

# ACKNOWLEDGEMENTS

*Photographs and illustrations are supplied by or reproduced by kind permission of the following:*

page
| | |
|---|---|
| 10 | Oxford University Press, Franklin Watts |
| 12 | G. Bell and Sons, C. Walter Hodges (ill.) |
| 13 | Mary Evans Picture Library |
| 14 | Macmillan |
| 15 | (*top*) William Heinemann |
| | (*bottom*) Dennis Dobson, Clarkson Potter |
| 16 | Albert Bonniers Förlag, Tove Jansson (ill.) |
| 17 | BBC copyright photograph |
| 19 | Collins |
| 20 | Bodley Head, McGraw Hill |
| 22 | Hutchinson Publishing Group |
| 23 | Macmillan |
| 24 | Kaye and Ward |
| 25 | Grasset & Fasquelle |
| 26 | Brockhampton Press |
| 27 | Faber & Faber |
| 28 | Transworld Publishers |
| 30 | Penguin Books, Pauline Baynes (ill.) |
| 31 | Collins |
| 33 | Methuen |
| 34 | Methuen |
| 35 | National Film Archive |
| 37 | Bodley Head |
| 38 | Bodley Head, Holt Rinehart & Winston |
| 39 | Kestrel Books |
| 40 | Brockhampton Press |
| 44 | Hodder & Stoughton |
| 47 | Beaverbrook Newspapers Ltd |
| 48 | Macmillan |
| 49 | (*top*) Brockhampton Press |
| | (*bottom*) Jonathan Cape, Random House |
| 50 | Penguin Books |
| 51 | Dover Publications |
| 52 | Chatto & Windus, Houghton Mifflin and H. A. Rey (ill.) |
| 53 | Collins |
| 55 | Dover Publications |
| 56 | Angus & Robertson |
| 59 | Bodley Head |
| 60 | Oxford University Press, Criterion Books |
| 61 | Jonathan Cape |
| 62 | (*top*) Gollancz, Faith Jaques (ill.) |
| | (*bottom*) BBC copyright photograph |
| 63 | Methuen |
| 64 | (*top*) Frederick Warne |
| | (*bottom*) Radio Times Hulton Picture Library |
| 65 | Collins and Coward McCann |
| 66 | Faber & Faber |
| 67 | Holt, Rinehart & Winston |
| 68–9 | Allen & Unwin, Faith Jaques (ill.) |
| 68 | (*bottom*) Hamish Hamilton, Harper & Row |
| 70 | Oxford University Press |
| 71 | Faber & Faber |
| 73 | George G. Harrap |
| 74 | Brockhampton Press |
| 76 | Blackie |
| 77 | Kaye and Ward |
| 80 | Brockhampton Press |
| 81 | Oxford University Press |
| 82 | G. Bell & Sons, C. Walter Hodges (ill.) |
| 85 | Jonathan Cape, Doubleday |
| 86 | George G. Harrap, Taplinger Publishing Co. |
| 87 | Jonathan Cape, Christopher Lofting |
| 90 | Farrar, Straus & Giroux |
| 92 | Chatto & Windus, W. P. Scott, Edward Gorey (ill.) |
| 93 | J. M. Dent & Sons |
| 94 | (*top*) Brockhampton Press |
| | (*bottom*) BBC copyright photograph |
| 95 | J. M. Dent & Sons |
| 96 | Oxford University Press, Henry Z. Walck |
| 97 | Tom Stacey |
| 100 | Bodley Head, Knopf |
| 102 | Bodley Head |
| 103 | Jonathan Cape |
| 105 | Penguin Books, Pauline Baynes (ill.) |
| 107 | Brockhampton Press |
| 108 | Hamish Hamilton, Coward McCann |
| 109 | Hamish Hamilton |
| 111 | Lutterworth Press, Unieboek B.V. |
| 112 | World's Work, Harper & Row |
| 115 | George G. Harrap |
| 117 | (*top*) Viking Press |
| | (*bottom*) Macmillan |
| 119–20 | Frederick Warne |
| 122 | Longmans |
| 123 | Faber & Faber, J. B. Lippincott |
| 124 | Collins, Random House |
| 125 | Brockhampton Press |
| 126 | Faber & Faber |
| 127 | Penguin Books |
| 128 | Collins |
| 130 | Macmillan |
| 131 | (*top to bottom*) George G. Harrap, Allen & Unwin, Collins |
| 134 | Bodley Head, McGraw Hill |
| 135 | Collins |

# Acknowledgements

*page*

136 Harper & Row
137 (*top*) J. M. Dent & Sons, E. P. Dutton
   (*bottom*) Penguin Books
138 Allen & Unwin
140 Routledge & Kegan Paul
143 Faber & Faber, Harper & Row
144 Abelard-Schuman
146 Methuen
148 Collins
149 (*left*) Evans Brothers
   (*right*) Penguin Books
150 G. Bell & Sons
151 Jugoslavanska Avtarska Agencija, Atlantis Zwergen-
   bucher
152 André Deutsch, Viking Press
153 Brockhampton Press
155 Bodley Head
156 Collins
157 William Heinemann
158 Longmans
159 Jonathan Cape
160 William Heinemann
161 Frederick Warne
163 Chatto & Windus, Seymour Lawrence, Harald Gripe
   (ill.)
164 Ward Lock
165 Blackie
167 Hutchinson Publishing Group
168 Longmans
170 Methuen
171 Lutterworth Press. Harper & Row
172 London Society for Promoting Christian Knowledge
174 World's Work
175 Chatto & Windus
176 Blackie
179 William Heinemann
180 (*top*) Dover Publications
   (*bottom*) Collins, Harcourt Brace Jovanovich
181 (*top*) Hamish Hamilton
   (*bottom*) Collins, Atheneum
182–3 (*top*) Max Parrish, David Highams Associates
   (*bottom*) Bodley Head, Doubleday
184 Bodley Head, Henry Z. Walck
185 Abelard-Schuman
186 (*top*) George G. Harrap
   (*bottom*) BBC Publications, John C. Grant (ill.)
188 Popperfoto
189 Bodley Head
191 Macmillan
192–3 Wells Gardner, Darton & Co
194 Oxford University Press, Henry Z. Walck, Edward
   Ardizzone (ill.)
196 William Heinemann
197 Blackie
199 (*top*) Collins, Random House
   (*bottom*) BBC copyright photograph
200 Collins
201 Joseph Cundall
202 Faber & Faber
204 Faber & Faber
206 Hamish Hamilton
208 Oxford University Press, Richard Kennedy (ill.)
209 Hamish Hamilton
210 Penguin Books
212, 213 William Heinemann, J. B. Lippincott
214 Penguin Books
215 (*top*) BBC copyright photograph
   (*bottom*) Collins

*page*

216 (*top*) Brockhampton Press
   (*bottom*) Hodder Causton
217 (*left*) Collins, Harcourt Brace Jovanovich
   (*right*) National Film Archive
218 World's Work
219 Macdonald & Jane's
220, 221 Bodley Head, Harper & Row
222 Faber & Faber, Coward McCann
223 William Heinemann, Atheneum
224 (*left*) William Heinemann, Holt Rinehart & Winston
   (*right*) Bodley Head, Harper & Row
225 Bodley Head, Harper & Row
226 Limited Editions Club, David Gentleman (ill.)
228 Collins, Little, Brown & Co
228 William Heinemann, Little, Brown & Co
229, 230–1* J. M. Dent & Sons, Harcourt Brace Jovanovich
232 (*top*) Faber & Faber
   (*bottom*) Lutterworth Press
234 Bodley Head, Harcourt Brace Jovanovich
236–8 Ernest Benn, Tove Jansson (ill.)
239 Lutterworth Press, Harper & Row
240 J. M. Dent & Sons, E. P. Dutton & Co Inc
241 Mary Evans Picture Library
242 Ernest Benn
243 Faber & Faber, Harper & Row
244–5 Reprint Society, Macmillan
246 Abelard-Schuman
247 Faber & Faber
249 Hutchinson Publishing Group
251 Hamlyn, Kathleen Hale (ill.)
252 Raphael Tuck
253 Methuen
257 Methuen
258 J. M. Dent & Sons, Random House
261 Brockhampton Press
262 André Deutsch
265 John Murray, Kathleen Hale (ill.)
267, 268 Collins, Houghton Mifflin
271 Faber & Faber, Putnam
273 (*top*) Bodley Head, Viking Press
   (*bottom*) World's Work
274 Brockhampton Press
275 Penguin Books
277 Mary Evans Picture Library
276–7 Frederick Warne
279 Penguin Books, Pauline Baynes (ill.)
280 Faber & Faber, A. S. Barnes
281 Bodley Head, Viking Press
283 Penguin Books
284–5 J. M. Dent & Sons
286 Jonathan Cape
287 Bodley Head, Macmillan
288 (*top*) National Film Archive
   (*bottom*) BBC copyright photograph
291 Bodley Head
292 Bodley Head
295 Macmillan
294 Penguin Books, Pauline Baynes (ill.)
298 Mulberry Press
299 Hamish Hamilton, William Morrow
302 Bodley Head, Macmillan
304 (*top*) Penguin Books
   (*bottom*) National Film Archive
306 Ernest Benn
307, 308 Dover Publications
309 Collins
310 Jonathan Cape
313 (*top*) Bodley Head, Harper & Row
   (*bottom*) Bodley Head, Macmillan

*page*

| | |
|---|---|
| 314 | Macdonald & Jane's |
| 316 | Blackie |
| 318 | Bodley Head, Holt Rinehart & Winston |
| 319 | Faber & Faber |
| 320 | Faber & Faber |
| 322 | Faber & Faber |
| 323 | George G. Harrap |
| 325 | Kestrel Books |
| 326 | Faber & Faber, Coward McCann |
| 327 | (*left*) Faber & Faber |
| | (*right*) William Heinemann |
| 328 | Macmillan |
| 329, 330 | Macmillan |
| 332 | Routledge & Kegan Paul |
| 334 | Hamish Hamilton, Harper & Row |
| 339 | Collins |
| 341 | Bodley Head |
| 342 | (*left*) George G. Harrap |
| | (*right*) Macdonald & Jane's |
| 345 | (*left*) Scottie Books |
| | (*right*) Faber & Faber, Knopf |
| 344 | Kaye & Ward |
| 346 | Lutterworth Press |
| 347 | Virtue & Co |
| 348 | Macmillan |
| 349 | Methuen |
| 350 | Raphael Tuck |
| 351 | Stellar Press |
| 352, 353 | Methuen |
| 355 | Faber & Faber, Harcourt Brace Jovanovich |
| 356 | (*left*) Macmillan |
| | (*right*) Constable |
| 357 | Macmillan |
| 358 | BBC copyright photograph |
| 359 | Oxford University Press |
| 360 | Virtue & Co |
| 362 | Blackie |
| 363 | Macmillan, Viking Press |
| 365 | Viking Press |
| 368 | William Heinemann, Doubleday |
| 369 | Macmillan |
| 370 | Hodder & Stoughton |
| 371 | Gollancz |
| 372 | J. M. Dent & Sons, Harcourt Brace Jovanovich |
| 372–3 | Bodley Head, Harcourt Brace Jovanovich |
| 375 | Methuen, E. P. Dutton |
| 376 | Methuen |
| 377 | Penguin Books, Pauline Baynes (ill.) |
| 379 | Sidgwick & Jackson |
| 380 | Hamish Hamilton |
| 381–3 | Methuen, E. P. Dutton |
| 384 | BBC copyright photograph |
| 385 | Ernest Benn |
| 386 | Penguin Books |
| 387 | Macmillan |

## Copyright notices

# Acknowledgements

372–3   Illustration by Eric Blegvad from *The Minnipins* (American title, *The Gammage Cup*) © 1959 by Carol Kendall, and illustration by Imero Gobbato from *The Whisper of Glocken*, © 1965 by Carol Kendall. Both reproduced by permission of Harcourt Brace Jovanovich, Inc.

375, 381*b*, 382 and endpaper. Line illustrations from *Winnie-the-Pooh* by Ernest H. Shepard copyright under the Berne Convention. Copyright, 1926, by E. P. Dutton & Co. Inc. Copyright Renewal, 1954, by A. A. Milne.
Colouring of the illustration on page 375 copyright © 1973 by Ernest H. Shepard and Methuen Children's Books Ltd.

381*t*, 383 and endpaper. Line illustrations from *The House at Pooh Corner* by Ernest H. Shepard copyright under the Berne Convention.
Copyright, 1928, by E. P. Dutton & Co. Inc. Copyright Renewal, 1956, by A. A. Milne.
*Winnie the Pooh* and *The House at Pooh Corner* are published throughout the British Commonwealth excluding Canada by Methuen Children's Books Ltd, in the United States of America by E. P. Dutton & Co. Inc. and in Canada by McClelland & Stewart, Ltd.

## Author's acknowledgements

I should like to thank the following people for generous help and advice: Miss Elizabeth Barrowcliffe and Mrs Brown and their colleagues in the Northamptonshire Libraries; The Superintendent and staff of the British Museum Reading Room; Miss Virginia Haviland, Head of the Children's Section of the Library of Congress in Washington, and her deputy, Miss Margaret Coughlan; Ms Zena Sutherland of the Bulletin of the Center for Children's Books at the University of Chicago Graduate Library School; Ms Carla Poesio of the Centro Didattico Nacionale in Florence; Ms Lisa-Christina Persson, formerly of the Lund Children's Library; M. Raoul Dubois and the French section of IBBY; The many publishers who allowed me access to their collections and filled gaps on my reference shelves; and my son Crispin, in whose company the picture research seemed like an efficient tour through hundreds of agreeable picture-galleries.

# INDEX OF AUTHORS

# Index of Authors

# INDEX OF TITLES

# Index of Titles

# Index of Titles